JOB

T0339641

'98

KATHRYN, ROSS, AND GEORGE PETRAS

A FIRESIDE BOOK
PUBLISHED BY SIMON & SCHUSTER

FIRESIDE
Rockefeller Center
1230 Avenue of the Americas
New York, New York 10020

FIRESIDE and colophon are registered trademarks
of Simon & Schuster Inc.

Designed by Irving Perkins Associates

Manufactured in the United States of America

10 9 8 7 6 5 4 3 2 1

Library of Congress Cataloging-in-Publication Data is available.

ISBN 0-684-81826-4

IMPORTANT NOTE:

This book draws together thousands of careers, companies, and associations from a wide range of sources. In all cases, we've tried to be accurate and up to date, but due to the timely nature of the material, inaccuracies may occur. Also, the inclusion of a company or career in this book does not constitute a recommendation; any recommendations of companies and careers we do make is our own opinion based on the data available to us. The reader must do further research on his or her own to determine if a career or company is the right choice.

CONTENTS

SECTION 1

CAREER OUTLOOKS 1998

SECTION 2

INDUSTRY FORECASTS 1998

SECTION 3

REGIONAL ROUNDUP 1998

INTRODUCTION

This is the 1998 edition of your guide to job hunting in the '90s—continuing our endeavor since 1990 to furnish the information that will make your job search productive.

New for this edition is an extensive section on using the Internet in your job hunt—complete with Internet job-hunting tips and helpful Web sites (see page 13).

WHAT'S IN THIS BOOK

▶ **Read this section, it will enable you to better get your money's worth from the enormous number of sources and material between these covers.**

At last count, by using this book you could access over 40 million jobs. That sounds ridiculously high—but using this book you can call virtually any government employment office at any agency, you can write or call virtually all of the *Fortune* 500, as well as many thousands of smaller companies, you can get a teaching job anywhere on the globe. But this book is most effectively used by those who read what follows.

▶ *Jobs '98* **is divided into three main sections: Career, Industry, and Regional—as well as some special sections devoted to minorities, women, and people with disabilities.**

These sections include major written portions. They describe what you need to know to consider and apply for a job in 1998—and in the near future. Basically, they cover:

- *Job and Industry Descriptions:* what the main jobs are in each area, what qualifications are needed, what you need to know about major career areas from advertising to utilities, what happened in the recent past.

- *Job and Industry Trends and Forecasts:* what the employment prospects are for 1998 and beyond, what is happening now and what will happen next.

- *Best Bets and Employment Spotlights:* which careers have the best long-term potential, seem interesting or unusual; which companies promise the best opportunities.

- *In Demand:* jobs in demand in various industries.

- *Average Salaries:* what to expect when you enter; as you advance.

- *National and Regional Employment Trends:* which parts of the country look good for employment; which areas are weak; predictions.

- *Regional Hotspots:* which cities or regions look particularly good for employment; what types of jobs are opening up, or why economy looks strong.

- *Assorted Top Ten Lists, etc.:* assorted charts, tables, etc., illustrating major employment ideas or trends.

▶ **The employers we list cover most major companies and organizations in the U.S.**

We include:

- *Top corporations in most major industries:* the top employers from advertising to utilities; with addresses and phone numbers.

- *Top companies in each state:* the top employers in each state; with addresses and phone numbers, from Alaska to Florida.

- *Major government employers:* the major government agencies, with addresses, phone numbers, and types of employees being sought.

- *Major international and nonprofit employers:* the major international organizations and nonprofits, including major employers of teachers overseas.

▶ **The sources we list help you actually contact the people who can get you a job.**

In general, we list several types of sources:

- *Career and industry associations:* useful to join or call to find out more; to meet potential employers; etc. Also: whether the association publishes directories, magazines that include classified ads for jobs, etc.

- *Career and industry directories:* useful directories that can be used in compiling a mailing list for a direct-mail job-hunting campaign.

- *Magazines:* and other periodicals that have job or career information, jobs listings, etc.

- *Other job or career sources:* computer databases, job hotlines, vocational programs, etc.

How To Use This Book

▶ **Now that we've described what's in this book, we'll describe how to use it.**

The textual portions are self-evident—they contain what you need to know to *begin* making a decision about targeting your job hunt. One key point: make certain you read *both* the career and the industry areas; for example, if you're interested in engineering, you should start with the Engineering section, but you should also read the industry areas that interest you, such as Computers and Electronics, Aerospace, and so on. And of course, check the Regional section as well.

▶ **What follows are some suggestions on how to use the source and employer lists in this book.**

These are listed in the approximate order you'll encounter them in the book. One key point: *Try to call these sources to verify addresses.* We live in a fast-moving economy. Names change, addresses change; associations and companies go out of business or merge, typos occur . . . your best bet is to check.

Associations

These are groups that represent major career or industry areas—from accountants to zoologists, from advertising to utilities.

How to use them in your job hunt:
Associations often publish magazines which contain information of use to a job hunter; sometimes they include job listings and, more importantly, by joining you can meet people in the field who can get you a job. The associations listed here are national associations, but be aware that most have local chapters, which you'll automatically join if you pay your dues to the national chapter.

In the Career section, we've listed hundreds of associations, and in most cases we've told you what particularly useful services they can offer you as a job hunter. Other services include placement or job referral services or career hotlines or electronic job listings. In the Industry section, we've listed the major industry associations—although many of these don't publish as much career information, they can be even more valuable as networking points.

How to contact associations: Call or write them. Be aware that often associations only help those who are members—so you may find it useful to join. Always investigate a little before paying anything to join. Although most associations listed here are large and reputable, you never know . . . And ask about any type of special membership—sometimes you can obtain substantial discounts.

Directories

These are listings of names of people within a functional career area or within an industry, or names of companies within an industry. Some directories, like those for international teachers, are more like listings of job opportunities.

How to use them in your job hunt:
Use them to compile a mailing list for use in a direct-mail campaign during a job hunt, or for a targeted mailing campaign. Note that many associations also publish directories, so when calling always ask if they do, and ask if they are available for purchase. Most sections of the book include directories which can be useful to your job hunt. We didn't list prices in most cases because by the time you read this, the prices will have changed. So call and check prices. But *be aware that directory prices are often very high.* They may not be high on a per-

listing basis, but many include thousands of listings and so cost in the hundreds of dollars.

Sometimes you may be pleasantly surprised; association directories, for example, are usually fairly inexpensive. One idea: ask for them at your library or at a nearby college library. And if you decide to buy one, be sure you know what you are getting. For example, some are compiled from telephone Yellow Pages and include little more than names, addresses, and main business—this is fine for some people, but others may want more details.

Magazines and Other Periodicals

We list two basic kinds of periodicals—those that are major journals in a field or an industry; and special job-hunting periodicals, which are basically compilations of job listings.

How to use them in your job hunt:

The major journals are an excellent way to get a "feel" for a career or a job—and decide if it's the right one for you. Just by reading a trade journal, you can get ideas on hiring, on what to say at an interview, on whom to write or cold-call for a job lead. In addition, many of these journals have job listings at the back. And the job-hunting periodicals are obviously useful if you want to answer job ads.

Before you subscribe: Call the magazine if you can; see if you can get a sample issue (if you can't find one on the newsstands or in the library).

Government Agency Listings

We've listed government employers in the Government section, some in the International section, some in the Technical, and some elsewhere. In most cases, we've included a personnel number, any job hotlines, personnel addresses, and other useful addresses and information. We've also told you how to contact local offices of agencies, so that if you live in Montana and want to stay in Montana, but are still interested in working for the federal government, you can easily find out your options.

How to use them in your job hunt:

You can call or write the personnel departments and the Office of Personnel Management (see page 75). But don't stop with personnel. We've listed government directories, etc., in an effort to encourage you to contact actual hiring or line officers at an agency—often, networking is the best way to get a government job.

International, Nonprofit, and UN Employers

We've listed, primarily in the International section, major employers in the public and nonprofit sector not affiliated with the U.S. government.

How to use them in your job hunt:

You can call or write them, as per instructions. In some cases, as with the UN, we explain your various options depending on what kind of UN job you're looking for.

Federal and State Employment Offices

These are the federal and state employment offices that usually have federal and state job information, as well as (in some states) other types of job help. They are listed in the Regional section, under each state.

How to use them in your job hunt:
Go to these offices to get postings of federal and state job openings, and the forms you need to apply. Some also offer recorded information.

Computer Databases

Resume databases are computer databases that generally include either resumes of job hunters, or, sometimes, information about companies *for* job hunters. We list the major resume and other databases related to careers.

How to use them in your job hunt:
Getting yourself listed can be a useful way of getting yourself a job—more and more recruiters are taking a look at these database services and calling people for interviews. Other services, such as job descriptions, which are sometimes on databases easily accessible by the public, can be useful to the job hunter as well.

Job Hotlines

Job hotlines are usually phone numbers which offer up-to-date, pre-recorded job information. Many are free; others charge a fee. We list job hotlines underneath the sponsoring organization—whether it is a government organization, a corporation, or an association.

How to use them in your job hunt:
Call them and get an up-to-date listing of *some* jobs that are available; but remember, the informal job market that you open up yourself through networking and so on is often more useful. Most hotlines are run by associations, and of course those run by the U.S. government are reputable. But be careful of disreputable hotlines, which advertise, promise hundreds of jobs (usually just ads from a newspaper), and can charge high fees.

Company Lists

We've listed thousands of the major corporations of the U.S. In each Industry section, we list the major companies of that industry. And in each Regional section, we include the major companies of each state.

How to use them in your job hunt:
Use the listings as a built-in mailing list for a targeted direct-mail campaign. Also, you may want to call the companies directly and ask for any employment material they may have. *A good idea*: if you're interested in a certain major company, call and ask for its *media kit*. Many major firms have these made up for journalists; they include clippings, annual reports, etc. They can be a great way of getting an inside idea of what the company feels about itself—and they give you an edge during an interview.

The Internet and Other Job Sources

New resources come online everyday that can help you find a job. Many of these are summarized in the Special Report (see page 12) in the next section.

In addition, we've also included names and addresses of special publishing programs for those who want training in publishing careers, information on leading vocational programs, how and where to get training in photojournalism, in desktop publishing, etc. These are explained in the text.

Once again, we hope this book is as useful for you as it has been for others, and that it aids you in making your job search quick—and effective.

SPECIAL REPORT: JOB HUNTING ON THE INTERNET

▶ **It's more than just hype.** The Internet—the huge electronic "highway" that connects your computer to thousands of databases, businesses, governments, and people—is being used by more and more job hunters, with increasingly successful results.

Using computer power in your job hunt can make a difference. The huge amount of information on the Internet can connect you with jobs you've never heard of. With a few clicks of your mouse, you can find thousands of job listings without leaving your home, you can list your resume and let it be perused by thousands of employers without going to the post office, you can learn much about your career area and get advice from people across the country and world. In particular, Internet job hunting can really make a difference if you're a job hunter in a remote area, or a job hunter looking for a technical or computer job. And every day, the Internet gets bigger, making it more advantageous to *non*-technical job seekers as well. And there's very good news for non-technical job hunters. Originally, Internet job listings were mainly technical; now over 60% of on-line listings are non-technical.

That said, there are drawbacks to Internet job hunting as well. The Internet is still "narrow"—there's still a lot outside its purview. Costs can add up, and even now, as the Internet has become more popular, it can still be clunky to use. From the job hunter's point of view, there's a lot of junk on the Internet. Because the Internet is open to all, the information you get can be false, redundant, outdated, amateurish, overly expensive, or even fraudulent.

Key point: the Internet is *one* way of getting the job you want—an electronic means of doing what you should be doing in *all* venues—networking to meet the people who can help you, searching all available listings of jobs, getting your resume out to people who do the hiring.

▶ **To summarize, there are several ways you can use the Internet and your computer in your job hunt.**

You can:

- *Search:* you can look for jobs electronically by finding database listings of job openings.

- *Post your resume:* and then let employers come to you.

- *Get information:* you can find up-to-date information on the career area or business you're interested in.

- *Get career help:* you can get career advice, have your resume written in the best format, even get a long-distance education.

Your best bet as a job hunter? Take a broad-based approach.

In the next few pages, we'll take a closer look at some of these job-hunting options on the Internet.

▶ The first step to Internet job hunting is to get connected.

If you don't have a computer or a modem, don't overlook your local library, or a nearby university library or career center. They may let you have access to the Internet for free or a small fee. Key advantage: a trained librarian can help you navigate the often confusing Net.

If you want to Net surf at home, you need a modem with your computer and a large computer service company or "gateway provider"—a computer service that gives you access to the Internet and lets you navigate the thousands of databases.

The large computer service companies offer access to the Internet in addition to their own special services, like "chat" groups or bulletin boards where you can talk via your computer with like-minded people. Usually, it's easier for first-time Internet users to use their services, although costs are often higher than with the more plain vanilla gateway providers. Even so, as of 1996 nearly half of all users of the Internet connect via one of the giants.

Below are the three major providers. They have many other services besides the ones we've mentioned here.

- *America Online* (800/827-6364): includes *Help-Wanted USA*, a job-opening database for managers, as well as *Career Board*, a computer bulletin board divided by function on careers and career topics, and *Online Career Center* (see next section).

- *CompuServe* (800/848-8990): includes *E-span* resume bank (see below, page 15) as well as many other services. About 80% of its subscribers are executives or professionals, and it includes discussion groups on a wide range of business and professional topics.

- *Prodigy* (800/776-3449): includes online resume bank; want ads from *USA Today* and *National Business Employment Weekly*.

Local gateway companies (check your local phone listings) offer cheaper ways of accessing the Net and the job banks and resume banks mentioned above. Like the giant computer services, usually they'll charge a flat monthly fee of $19.95 for unlimited use. But it can be cheaper. Recently, a local company in the New York area charged under $10 a month. Note: The economics of the flat rate concept is being debated, with some industry experts projecting a return to the old system of a flat rate for a specified number of hours—usually five—and a rate per hour thereafter. Others are suggesting that rates may be set up depending on degree of usage or when used.

▶ Search for a job using Internet job listings.

In the old days of the 1980s, job openings were pretty much listed in the classifieds of newspapers and magazines. No longer. The Internet includes thousands of current job listings—from corporations like Hewlett-Packard, to governments—like the state governments of New York, to job data banks like Career Path. Job hunters have a great opportunity here, and are increasingly using the Internet.

According to the Internet Business Network's "1997 Electronic Recruiting Index," in 1996 over 1.2 million jobs were offered via on-line services, over 1 million resumes were on-line, 3,500 employment Web sites were operating, and 5,800 firms were recruiting on-line. By the end of 1997, 3 million jobs and 2.5 million resumes were projected to be available on-line.

The job listings can be of several different types. One type is simply a newspaper classified. In this case, the databases have collected ads from newspapers and technical journals and you browse through them as you would any newspaper. Other types go into more detail.

One other type of listing is a job *home page* on the World Wide Web. The World Wide Web is the graphic part of the Internet, where companies and people post ads and information at a computer address called a "Web site." Job home pages are like ads only longer—usually a lot more detail about the job opening and companies is included. Some companies have their own Web sites that describe the company, and then offer special ways of accessing different types of job openings at them—click your mouse and you can find financial job openings or managerial job openings at the same company. Another click and you can e-mail your resume.

Getting to some of these job data banks and home pages can be tricky. Your best bet after you hook up with one of the computer services or gateway companies above is to start by checking out their listings, and then, by trial and error, find the areas that interest you. You can also find Internet addresses from the *Internet Yellow Pages* at your bookstore or posted on the Net, and for starters, you can use the addresses we've compiled at the end of this section.

Key point: more of these databases are compiled every day, others close down, so you'll probably want to go beyond this or any printed list. For example, via one database, we recently found specialized databases we'd never heard of before, like a specialized listing of San Francisco area jobs, or specialized technical jobs, or local government jobs.

Once you've found a job you're interested in, you can send your resume via the post office—or you can e-mail it to the company directly. Often, e-mailing is easier—but you should know the proper format for an electronic resume. See the section on page 17. One other point: on many of these sites you can post your own resume as well (see next section for details).

▶ **For the new or about-to-be graduate:** New graduates run into it regularly: How do I get a job without formal experience? Luck helps; diligence and persistence help more; and, of course, a good employment record helps even more. Four different routes to consider: If you're looking for:

1. *First (or entry-level) jobs:* Explore the resources of the major on-line providers or go directly to Web sites on the Internet noted below. In both cases, you will find a wide range of services from resume help to career-oriented information. Tip: Contact your college's Web site (if it has one) for employment information as well.

- **Jobtrak (www.jobtrak.com):** Good source for students/alumni of the 400 colleges/universities served by the site. Links to company pages and job fairs.

- **College Connection (www.careermosaic.com:80/cm/cc/cc1.html):** Features companies seeking new graduates. Job fair information. Links to universities. Resume help.

- **ROAR:** The Monster Board's (see below) specialized site for entry-level job listings and for recent college graduates.

- **JobWeb (www.jobweb.org)**

- **College Grad (www.alt.com/college/jobs/html)** or **(www.collegegrad.com)** or **(www.execpc.com/-insider/)**

- **Jobs Direct (www.jobsdirect.com):** For new and recent graduates. See their Student Zone for guide to creating a resume.

- **Black Collegian Home Page (www.black-collegian.com/):** Jobs and internships listings.

2. *Temporary jobs:* List with a temporary agency either directly or on a Web site. This can help you try out many different jobs, honing skills and getting experience while you search for a permanent job.

3. *Seasonal jobs:* The following sites are particularly good for those seeking seasonal jobs—students, teachers on summer breaks—or for retired or semi-retired people.

   - **CoolWorks (www.coolworks.com)**

   - **Peterson's Education Center (www.petersons.com/summerop/ssector.html)**

   - **Summer jobs/Internships/Field work (www.jobweb.org/catapult/jintern.html)**

4. *Internships:* A good way to get experience, paid or unpaid. Many companies provide information about internships on their Web sites.

   - **BrainBook Internship Index (www.reg.uci:80/ucl/sop/brainbook/internship.html)**

   - **Indiana University Internship Page (http://icpac.indiana.edu/interns.html)**

   - **The Princeton Review On-Line (www.review.com/career/internships_worth.html)**

▶ **Finding your specific job opportunity:** To find your specific job sources, use two techniques: 1) Go directly to corporate Web sites for their job openings, and 2) go to the general Web sites listing a wide range of jobs.

1. *Company Web sites*—Many companies list job opportunities on their Web sites. The sites also furnish company information useful to the job seeker.

2. *General Web site:* Although a general listing of such Web sites is not available, links to company pages may be found in such on-line business directories as Hoovers (www.hoovers.com), as well as ComFind (www.comfind.com).

Other sources include such indexes as Yahoo (www.yahoo.com), Alta Vista (www.altavista.digital.com) and Infoseek (www.infoseek.com).

For the general job-seeker, some major Web sites are listed below. They are only a sample of what is available.

* **The Monster Board (www.monster.com):** More than 50,000 listings. Entry level to senior executives. Focus: technical positions (60%) and East Coast. Links to company pages and job fairs.

* **America's Job Bank (www.ajb.dni.us):** Computerized links to 250,000 jobs from 1,800 state employment service offices. Service of U.S. Department of Labor and state employment agencies.

* **Newslink (www.newslink.org):** Comprehensive list of newspaper Web sites and their want ads on-line.

* **Commercial Sites Index (www.yahoo.com):** Lists over 14,000 company Web pages; in effect, a huge electronic address book.

* **CareerPath.com (www.careerpath.com):** Lists an average of 20,000 classified job ads of 21 major newspapers.

* **Career Magazine Database (www.careermag.com):** Mostly engineering and programming jobs.

* **Career City (www.careercity.com)**

* **Career Mosaic (www.careermosaic.com):** Technology focus; West Coast emphasis. Over 50,000 jobs listed. Has international gateway section listing jobs in Canada, Great Britain, and Asia.

* **E-Span (www.espan.com):** Much job search reference material, including salary information for various fields.

* **NationJob Network (www.nationjob.com):** Nationwide, with midwestern focus.

* **MedSearch USA (www.medsearch.com):** Lists about 2,000 medical/health-care positions.

* **Education Jobs (www.nationjob.com/education)**

* **Academe This Week (http://chronicle.merit.edu/.ads/.links.html):** For education (teaching and administrative) positions and academic-type jobs (museums, galleries, and social service organizations).

* **Legal positions (www.lawjobs.com)**

* **Online Career Center (www.occ.com):** Over 8,000 job listings from several hundred companies; resume posting service helps job applicants create their own home page resume.

* **Job Center Employment Service (www.jobcenter.com):** Matches resumes with available job lists. Matches are contacted via e-mail and resumes are sent directly to company.

- **ACS Job Bank (http://pub.acs.org)** and click job bank icon: Chemists, chemical engineers, biochemists, etc. For American Chemical Society members. Listings from *Chemical and Engineering News* and 40 newspapers nationwide.

- **Technical Employment News (www.peinews.com./pci):** Technical positions, primarily contract positions.

- **Insurance Career Connection (www.onramp.net/icc/):** Dedicated to insurance and managed care industry.

One quick tip: for a temporary job, list with a temporary agency either directly or on a Web site. You'll be trying out many jobs, honing skills, and getting experience until or while you search for that first, great job.

▶ **Post your resume on one of the Internet's Web sites.**

The idea here is to put your resume on the Internet and let employers come to you. This option usually works best for people with technical skills—since many of the employers doing the looking are high-tech companies, although this is changing.

An Internet resume is different from a hard-copy resume, although like a regular resume, it should be simple and direct.

We'll describe some of the differences. If by the end you're discouraged—don't be. Many of the services we've listed will help you create your own home page resume—for free or for a relatively modest fee. And there are also specialized resume services as well.

So what are the differences between a regular resume and a home-site resume?

First, your resume should be noun-heavy. Most companies use computerized key-word searching to find the resumes that interest them the most on the Internet. This means that they're looking for nouns that describe *functions*—not the action words most paper resumes emphasize. In other words, you're better off using the nouns that describe you (manager of technical services, MBA, Ph.D., physicist, bartender, etc.) than the verbs or adjectives that qualify you (dynamic, increased sales by 90%).

Second, your resume obviously has to be electronic—and that means you've got to create your resume in the correct electronic format so that it can be read by anyone else's computer. This means you must put it in proper ASCII text code. See your word processing manual for instructions. Tip: Test your resume. Call it up on-line to see how it looks.

Third, it should include certain special features. It should have an e-mail hyperlink—this lets prospective employers contact you directly by e-mail. If they're interested, you'll find an e-mail message on your computer.

Fourth, you normally should have "jumps" at the top of your resume. Underneath your name, you'll have certain key categories—like experience, education, etc. By clicking these categories, your prospective employer can quickly find out about you in further detail. But you don't want too many "bells and whistles." As with any resume, decide what's essential to your employer and proceed from there. For the bells and whistles and more details it is best to refer the employer to your home page, if you have one.

Security or safe sending is important. To be sure your resume is not being transmitted to your present employer or to selected other companies, check with the career site to determine if privacy measures are being used.

Most importantly, you should have a site on the Internet where you post your resume. You can create your own home site—many gateway providers let you do this for free, or you can go to a service. Here is your chance to use the verbs—to sell yourself—that may be missing from your electronic resume. Many of the addresses listed above will post your resume.

If all this sounds too complex to do yourself, consider doing your resume through a resume service or independent "Webmaster." Key advantage: they'll do the hard work for you by designing the proper resume. Some may also give you a site for your resume; others won't design your resume but will give you a site; and some will do so even if you don't have a computer.

Resume Help Services: In addition to the commercial on-line services listed above, specialized services create resumes suitable for Internet scanning.

- *Archeus: Guide to WWW Resume Writing Resources* (www.golden.net/~archeus/reswri.htm)

- *Internet Resume Database Registry* (amsquare.com/america/registry.html)

- *Resumix* (www.resumix.com/resume/resumeindex.html)

- *The Resume Doctor* (www1.mhv.net/acom/Acom.html)

- *Rockport: How to Write an Exceptional Resume* (www.his.com/~rockport/resumes.htm)

- *RPI—Preparing a Resume* (www.rpi.edu/dept/llc/writecenter/web/text/resume.html)

- *Skill Matrix* (www.agt.net/public/matrix/resumes.htm)

Some other resources:

- *The Riley Guide* (www.jobtrak.com/jobguide/index.html): Good directory of Internet job search services.

- *Be Your Own Headhunter Online*: (Pam Dixon and Sylvia Tiersten. New York: Random House, 1995)

- *Hook Up, Get Hired! The Internet Job Search Revolution*: (Joyce Lain Kennedy. New York: John Wiley & Sons, 1995) Both books are chock-full of detailed information for the Internet job hunter.

- *123 Resume Distribution Service* (www.webplaza.com/pages/Careers/123Careers/123Careers.html): free; gives resume information to employers.

- *JobTailor Employment Online Service* (www.jobtailor.com): free resume posting service.

- *Online Career Center* (www.occ.com): For about $40, job hunters get a home page in the OCC database for six months, with two links to other Web sites.

- *JobCenter Employment Services* (www.jobcenter.com)

- *Commercial Sites Index* (www.yahoo.com)

- Compuserve, Prodigy, and America Online all let you create your own Web site. See page 14 for telephone numbers.

There are many services that will write and post your resume for a fee. Rule of thumb: charges to create the resume home page should be under $100 and about $25 or so for a six month listing. Essential: check credentials, costs, and effectiveness *first*. Make sure the service follows the basic criteria listed above. Check the "counter" strategy—that is, if the service counts how many times your resume has been visited, and ask how they insure your resume is visited by the right types of employer.

▶ **Use many of the resources mentioned above to learn more about the company and the industry—and how to manage your job hunt.**

As you get to know the Internet, you can navigate among company home pages and learn more about the industry and big players in it.

Key point: many company home pages include information on the company itself—its key products, what it's doing, what benefits it offers employees, etc. This can be invaluable before your interview. Best bet: download company home pages and create your own personal career database. Some services collect information for you: *Career Magazine* has reprints of articles, includes excerpts from headhunter's book, etc; *Career Mosaic* (www.careermosaic.com) collects books and articles on jobs.

Some job hunters utilize user groups, "chat groups," or bulletin boards on the Internet to give them access to people and advice as well. One caution: you may never know whom you're *really* talking to.

Not qualified for the job you want? The Internet now even has home study courses. You may want to check:

- *The Internet University—College Courses by Computer* (Dan Corrigan, 1995, Cape Software Press, P.O. Box 800-5C, Harwich, MA 02645)

- *The Electronic University*: A Petersen's Guide (www.petersons.com)

- *Distance Learning on the Net* (www.homepage.interaccess.com/-ghoyle)

As always, check for any charges, accreditation, etc. *before* you put down any money or time. The *Distance Education and Training Council* (1601 18th St., Washington, DC 20009-2529) accredits home-study programs.

SECTION 1

CAREER OUTLOOKS 1998

ACCOUNTANTS, AUDITORS, BUDGET ANALYSTS, AND CREDIT SPECIALISTS

▶ **Accountants, auditors, budget analysts, and credit specialists prepare, analyze, and work with financial information for governments, businesses, and other organizations.**

As our society gets even more complex, the jobs of these specialists also become more complex and specialized. Here's a brief breakdown of the main job areas in accounting.

- *Public accountants:* work on their own or with public accounting firms. They perform a broad range of services for their clients including taxes, financial reporting, consulting, or auditing—preparing, analyzing, and checking the financial records to make certain all is in accordance with general accounting procedures.

- *Management accountants:* work in corporations, preparing budgets, maintaining financial records, and analyzing financial records for their corporations.

- *Internal auditors:* check the accuracy of financial reports within an organization; look for fraud and mismanagement. As financial reporting has become computerized, these auditors frequently come with computer backgrounds.

- *Government accountants and auditors:* either work preparing government records—or work in the IRS or local tax offices checking *your* records, making certain individuals and businesses are reporting and paying the proper amounts of taxes.

Within these huge areas, accountants often specialize. Public accountants may become experts in systems, or taxes, or auditing, or international accounting.

Like medicine or law, accounting is self-regulated by its own professional organizations—principally the American Institute of Certified Public Accountants (AICPA). The AICPA sets standards and writes tests that certify accountants in the business. Over 40% of the 1 million accountants and auditors are certified— most of them as Certified Public Accountants, or CPAs. To get a CPA you must take a grueling two day test in four parts—only about a quarter of those trying pass all four parts the first time. But a CPA opens up many accounting job opportunities.

Other certifications can also help accounting job seekers. The Institute of Management Accountants (IMA) gives the Certified Management Accountant (CMA), likewise, the Information Systems Audit and Control Association confers the Certified Information Systems Auditor (CISA) accreditation. See addresses at the end of this section.

▶ **Budget analysts develop, manage, and plan company or organization financial plans, while credit specialists focus on one of business's major concerns: Can our loan customers pay us back?**

Budget analysts work in private industry as well as government, with a large percentage in manufacturing, defense, and education. Because of the accounting responsibilities of this type of work, accountants are often employed as analysts; and at large corporations, a CPA is often a requirement.

Most budget analysts work with the annual budget cycle of large organizations. Basically, they accept input from line departments on their projected financial needs for the year, analyze these needs, and then formulate a financial plan to meet these needs. Budget analysts figure out if current projections are too high or low or at the right levels, then determine how to meet new costs, and submit their plans to senior management—or in the case of the federal government—ultimately to Congress. The budget cycle is usually annual, but after a budget is approved an analyst's work does not go away—he or she tracks spending and disbursements and checks to see that all is in accordance with budgetary projections. In addition, analysts may work on long-term budget plans.

While budget analysts are generally more concerned with funding *within* an organization, often a public organization, credit clerks, checkers, and authorizers more usually work for the private sector, at banks, retailers, wholesalers, credit card operators, and credit agencies—anywhere credit is granted and loans are made to those *outside* an organization or company. While senior officials decide on the ground rules of who should get credit, clerks and checkers do the actual work of verifying—they see that the people and companies getting their employers money are good credit risks—that they can pay it all back.

For more information on other financial jobs, see the Banking section, the Financial Services section, and the Managers section.

EMPLOYMENT OUTLOOK: Good over the long term; strong competition for the prestige jobs. Expect good prospects in the short term in: consulting, health care, financial services, technical-based companies, and information services.

▶ **Accountants should face a relatively strong job outlook.**

The U.S. Bureau of Labor Statistics projects that accountants and auditors should see the number of jobs growing about as fast as average for the next eight years—until 2005.

Two key advantages for employment: First, the complexity of financial transactions is increasing, and with this the need for properly trained accountants and auditors. Second, although *relative* turnover in the field is low (not too many accountants quit the profession altogether) there are so many in the field that there will be still large numbers of openings annually.

With this relatively bright forecast come some trends to consider:

• *Technical expertise:* will be more in demand. Key point: with increasing complexity comes the need for more specialized knowledge, particularly in computer systems.

• *Certification:* will also be more in demand. A CPA is becoming increasingly important. Many states are enacting stricter educational requirements for CPA candidates (applicants will have to have 150 semester hours of coursework before taking the CPA test); along with this, the CPA is becoming more in demand, along with other certifications, and advanced degrees; particularly an MBA.

• *Less job security:* will probably be the norm. In the old days accounting was dominated by eight large accounting partnerships called the Big Eight. In terms of employment, job tracks were predictable. Get a job in accounting, and you could pretty much predict where you'd be twenty years in the future. Then mergers and competition changed all this. The Big Eight became the Big Six, firms became more cost conscious, and more apt to fire employees, and . . . the old days were gone forever.

• *Changes in certain areas:* Remember the savings and loan crisis? Back in the '80s a large number of these financial institutions went bust—and angry shareholders blamed and sued public accounting firms for allegedly conducting substandard audits. (Actually, the rate of negligence was found to be less than 0.5%—about the same as in previous years.) Result: public accounting firms are now doing less traditional auditing work.

Hottest areas: cost accounting, accountants familiar with networks, accountants skilled in start-up situations who can help with the finances of new companies. See page 28.

▶ **Budget analysts: some good news and some bad news; credit specialists will find that recovery may increase demand for their services—although computerization will cut into job growth to a degree.**

The pool of applicants for budget jobs is increasing, according to the Bureau of Labor Statistics—and computers are replacing many human functions. But on the positive side, increasing complexity and a growing demand for sophisticated analysis point to the continuing need for well-trained, technically competent budget analysts. And analysts are more likely to keep their jobs in a bad economy. Except in the worst of circumstances, the budget cycle keeps on going and analysts are always needed. There are about 67,000 budget analysts today, and the government projects job growth at about the same rate as the economy.

Qualifications required for a good job are increasing. Although some applicants are still promoted out of payroll or accounting clerk positions, MAs or CPAs are preferred at major corporations, along with experience with relevant budgeting programs. Training is varied—most analysts find the best training is working on the job through the complete budget cycle, from reading projections to implementing procedures.

Employment for credit authorizers, checkers, loan clerks, etc., is expected to grow at the same moderate rate as that for budget analysts. In general, employment prospects tend to improve as interest rates go down—simply because more people tend to borrow; in addition, economic conditions play a strong role in borrowing and lending climate. One problem for employment: retail firms, credit unions, and banks increasingly are centralizing credit operations via more sophisticated computer technology. Where once a branch store made its own credit decisions, today it usually relies on a central credit operation covering an entire region.

The good news for loan and credit clerks, however, is that there is still a personal element in credit decisions—it's still hard to duplicate the intangibles of deciding who will repay a loan on a computer. For example, some small, conservative banks and S&Ls avoided the banking crisis by paying strict personalized attention to their customers and their businesses. That personal touch paid off—they're still in business. And they'll keep on hiring.

WHAT'S NEXT

▶ **More changes—even as the accounting profession digests all the changes of the recent past.**

Some major trends to look at:

Technology: The next step will be the use of expert systems and artificial intelligence to solve many complex accounting problems. One possibility, according to the American Institute of Certified Public Accountants (AICPA): the expense of such systems might make some firms specialize in narrow areas of expertise, and network or outsource for areas outside their specialties. Meanwhile, more sophisticated computers are already reducing the numbers of auditors and the time required to do a typical audit—and computer literacy will continue to be emphasized.

Competition: More and more of it, and a trend by firms to offer more nonaccounting and nonauditing services to beat the competition. In addition, greater differentiation and specialization by firms will result in CPA firms increasingly competing with other, non-CPA organizations for the same business. At the same time, look for alliances or associations between CPA and non-CPA firms to increase competitive advantages.

Specialization: Accountants will increasingly concentrate on expertise within certain industries—the rationale being that those who really understand the business will be able to perform better audits and other services. As *Fortune* magazine noted, it was significant that when Big Six firm Peat Marwick announced its new partners last year, it announced not only their functional areas (tax, auditing, or consulting), but also their areas of specific expertise, such as health care, banking, etc. More to the point: Firms will look for professionals with *systems expertise*—databases, networks, integrated financial packages, and the like. Also important: interpersonal and writing skills.

Standards: Look for even more rigorous hiring, training, and work standards, according to the AICPA. At the same time, the Institute is concerned that many of the "best and brightest" graduates are attracted to areas other than accounting.

▶ **Major changes in employment patterns.**

Until fairly recently, the employment outlook was not so bright, as major firms cut back on staff and streamlined their businesses. But depending on the continued relative strength of the economy, the outlook should continue to be relatively strong over the long term, despite the ups and downs of the economy. Entry- and mid-level employment trends were good in 1996 and early 1997. One major factor in hiring: much more emphasis on interpersonal skills. Key point: Accounting is now much more a team effort.

Major firms will continue to cut back on unproductive staff—including partners (who once had a pretty much guaranteed job). As elsewhere, the old days are over. The AICPA sees more major firm mergers on the horizon; and at the same time more small-firm start-ups, in a much more fluid industry. The job pyramid will flatten; with less higher-level employees, and more lower- and mid-level workers, including more para-professional accountants—people without CPAs who will work much like paralegals do in law firms.

Over the long term, the major areas that will show probable growth include:

Management consulting: As accounting firms continue to emphasize this specialty, demand will increase for accountants with business experience in areas such as marketing and computer systems.

International: As international trade increases, demand will increase for accountants with international specialties or expertise. This is a highly competitive area among major firms. Right now, accounting firms are moving into Eastern Europe and the new nations of the old Soviet Union. The next wave will be in the People's Republic of China and the rest of East Asia. Best bet: combine a CPA with language and area studies.

Investigative accounting: Also called "forensic accounting." Given the immense scope of fraud committed in recent years, accountants, preferably CPAs with experience in a firm's investigative unit (or with an enforment background) will be in greater demand. Particularly interesting is the newest area of this emerging specialty—Internet investigations.

Internal auditor: Internal auditing has been a normal entry-level position for newly qualified accountants who want to move into line corporate financial positions. But movement up and out of internal auditing positions has declined in recent years. Why? More corporate downsizings have prevented upward job movement. Also, recent corporate financial mismanagement problems have changed the focus of the jobs: Firms will be emphasizing record keeping and adequate tracking of money much more than in the past.

The good news is that the urgency of these problems has placed a premium on applicants with financial or computer experience in addition to traditional auditing skills. A $5,000–$6,000 salary premium for such additional experience is not unusual.

Environmental accounting: Environmental concerns are creating what looks like a new specialty—accountants who consult with outside corporations and write environmental compliance reports and help them avoid expensive lawsuits. Best bet: CPA with an engineering degree.

Senior citizens: At the other end of the spectrum, accountants with expertise in investment and estate planning for senior citizens will probably be in demand, as the number of elderly increases dramatically.

Cost accounting: Recently has seen a strong uptick in hiring demand, particularly for those with manufacturing backgrounds.

▶ **The outlook for women and minorities is improving.**

The good news for women: Recently, the *Journal of Accountancy* projected that 57% of new recruits were women in the past year. The problem, of course, is that women are underrepresented in the upper tiers; but even here, surveys show that women are gaining and moving upward in mainstream areas like auditing and consulting.

The bad news for minorities is that their underrepresentation in accounting continues. And while some minorities, including Hispanics and Asians, have increased their presence, black employment actually declined in percentage terms, although the number of black partners has increased. The AICPA has indicated concern over this problem, and has targeted efforts to increase black participation in the profession.

SALARIES

PUBLIC ACCOUNTING: A good rule of thumb: the larger the city and the larger the firm, the higher the salary. The average starting salary for accounting grads in the 1995 school year was about $27,900. Low- to mid-level salaries ranged from an average of $26,000 in small cities to about $30,000 in larger regional cities such as Atlanta. Upper mid-level salaries ranged from $30,000 in small towns to about $50,000 in major cities, and up to $75,000 or more in Los Angeles and New York. Higher salaries are found at Big Six firms. Partners at large firms earn from $100,000 on up; partners at the Big Six accounting firms earn over $220,000 on average. Best bet for high salaries: management consulting at the Big Six (or other majors). Key skills in addition to technical consulting skills required: strong sales ability; ability to manage corporate relationships.

CORPORATE ACCOUNTING: *Trend:* The best salaries and most offers tend to go to grads with a specialty. Best bet: budgeting, asset management, product costing. Beginning salaries averaged around $25,000; mid-level from $30,000 to $65,000 for the more experienced. Managers' salaries ranged from $40,000 to $80,000. Above these levels, major corporate financial officers and CEOs with accounting backgrounds received salaries far above $100,000. But the most recent figures for 1994 show a flat trend—some areas saw actual declines in income, overall, salaries rose less than 5%.

GOVERNMENT ACCOUNTANTS: Average salaries for accountants in 1993 were $46,300 and $48,200 for auditors. Starting salaries on average were $18,700 in

1995. Graduates with master's degrees or two years professional experience averaged beginning salaries of $27,800. However, this does not take into account the substantial benefits offered most government employees.

BUDGET ANALYSTS: Beginning salaries ranged from $23,000 to $29,000 recently; more senior analysts earned from $34,500 to $44,000. Managers earned from $41,000 to $62,000, depending on the size of the firm. Government analysts earned from about $18,300, with an average salary of about $35,000; supervisor and manager average starting salaries were $42,000.

INTERNAL AUDITORS: Beginning salaries in 1996 were in the $27,000 range. Senior auditor earnings were about $40,000, while managers earned over $45,000.

CREDIT WORKERS: Salaries vary widely, depending on experience and type of employment. Credit clerks average about $20,000; loan processors begin at about $19,000.

TOP ACCOUNTING FIRMS: The Big Six

Arthur Andersen and Co.
69 W. Washington St.
Chicago, IL 60602
312/580-0069
Known for its top-notch training program (most courses are offered at a special training facility in St. Charles, IL), and for its enormous consulting practice (particularly skilled in designing computerized management information systems). Almost merged with Price Waterhouse. It has many oil and gas clients.

Ernst & Young
787 7th Ave.
New York, NY 10019
212/773-3000
Formed from the merger of the old Big Eight firms of Ernst & Whinney and Arthur Young. Specialties include health care and financial services, banking.

Deloitte & Touche
PO Box 820
10 Westport Rd.
Wilton, CT 06897
203/761-3000
Formed from the merger of the old Big Eight firms of Deloitte, Haskins & Sells and Touche Ross; specialties include financial services, manufacturing (audits GM, Chrysler), and in particular, retailing. Clients include Sears, Macy's.

KPMG Peat Marwick
3 Chestnut Ridge Rd.
Montvale, NJ 07645
201/307-7000
Formed by the merger of the old Big Eight firm Peat Marwick with KMG Main Hurdman. Specialties include banking, insurance, and computers—strong in Silicon Valley.

Coopers & Lybrand
1301 Ave. of the Americas
New York, NY 10020
212/259-1000
Resisted merger mania in the eighties and early nineties; specialties include energy, utilities and particularly communications—its clients include AT&T, Bell-South, Nynex.

Price Waterhouse
1251 Ave. of the Americas
New York, NY 10020
212/819-5000
The oldest Big Six; known as the blue-chip firm, it long boasted more blue-chip clients and more *Fortune* 500 companies than its rivals. Serves multinationals like IBM, Kodak, and Exxon.

OTHER TOP FIRMS:

Altschuler Melvoin and Glasser
30 S. Wacker Dr.
Chicago, IL 60606
312/207-2800

Baird Kurtz & Dobson
P.O. Box 1190
Springfield, MO 65801
417/865-8701

Cherry Bekaert & Holland
227 W. Trade St.
Suite 301
Charlotte, NC 28202
704/377-3741

Crowe Chizek and Co.
P.O. Box 7
330 E. Jefferson
South Bend, IN 46624
219/232-3992

Richard A. Eisner and Co.
575 Madison Ave.
New York, NY 10022
212/355-1700

Goldstein Golub Kessler and Co. PC
1185 Ave. of the Americas
New York, NY 10036
212/372-1000

Grant Thornton
1 Prudential Plaza

130 E. Randolph Dr.
Chicago, IL 60601
312/856-0001

Clifton Gunderson and Co.
301 SW Adams St., Suite 800
Peoria, IL 61602
309/671-4560

Kenneth Leventhal
1211 Ave. of the Americas
New York, NY 10036
212/403-5200

McGladrey and Pullen
102 W. 2nd St.
Davenport, IA 52801
319/324-0447

Moss Adams and Co.
1001 4th Ave.
Seattle, WA 98154
206/223-1820

George S. Olive & Co.
201 N. Illinois St.
Indianapolis, IN 46204
317/383-4000

Pannell Kerr Forster
5847 San Felipe, Suite 2300
Houston, TX 77057
713/780-8007

Plante and Moran
P.O. Box 307
Southfield, MI 48037-0307
810/352-2500

WHERE TO GO FOR MORE INFORMATION

ACCOUNTING ASSOCIATIONS

American Accounting Association
5717 Bessie Dr.
Sarasota, FL 34223
941/921-7747
(Publishes *The Accounting Review*.)

American Institute of Certified Public Accountants
Harborside Financial Center
201 Plaza 3
Jersey City, NJ 07311-3881
201/938-3000
(Publishes journal with many listings—see following material.)

American Society of Tax Professionals
P.O. Box 1024
Sioux Falls, SD 57101
605/335-1185

American Society of Woman Accountants
1255 Lynnfield Rd.,
Suite 257
Memphis, TN 38119
901/680-0470
(Publishes career information, etc.)

American Women's Society of Certified Public Accountants
401 N. Michigan Ave.,
Suite 2200
Chicago, IL 60611
312/644-6610

Association of Government Accountants
2200 Mt. Vernon Ave.
Alexandria, VA 22301
703/684-6931
(Offers placement service for a fee via phone, publishes periodical with job listings, etc.)

Information Systems Audit and Control Association
3701 Algonquin Rd.,
Suite 1010
Rolling Meadows, IL 60008
708/253-1545

Government Finance Officers Association
180 N. Michigan Ave.,
Suite 800
Chicago, IL 60601
312/977-9700
(Publishes periodicals with job listings, etc.)

Institute of Internal Auditors
249 Maitland Ave.
Altamonte Springs, FL 32701-4201
407/830-7600

Institute of Management Accountants
P.O. Box 433
10 Paragon Dr.
Montvale, NJ 07645
201/573-9000
703/573-9000

National Association of Credit Management
8815 Centre Park Dr.
Columbia, MD 21045
410/740-5560
(Publishes monthly periodical, job referral service for members, etc.)

National Society of Public Accountants
1010 N. Fairfax St.
Alexandria, VA 22314
703/549-6400
(Publishes periodical with job listings, directory, etc.)

ACCOUNTING DIRECTORIES

Accountant's Directory
American Business Directories, Inc.
American Business Information, Inc.
5711 S. 86th Circle
P.O. Box 27347
Omaha, NE 68127
402/593-4600
(Broken into seven parts; cost of entire U.S. directory is $3,700; each part is less—for example, the Northeast directory of 23,000 addresses is $735, or about 3 cents per name.)

Firm on Firm Directory
American Institute of Certified Public Accountants

Harborside Financial Center
201 Plaza 3
Jersey City, NJ 07311-3881
201/938-3000
1-800/862-4272
(Lists thousands of firms. Phone for information—must be ordered via mail or fax.)

ACCOUNTING MAGAZINES

Accounting Today
425 Park Ave.
New York, NY 10022
212/756-5155
(Biweekly.)

*The American
Accounting Review*
5717 Bessie Dr.
Sarasota, FL 34223
941/921-7747

*The California CPA
Quarterly*
California Society of
CPAs
275 Shoreline Dr.
Redwood City, CA
94065
415/802-2600

CPA Journal
530 Fifth Ave.
5th Floor
New York, NY 10036
212/719-8300
(Monthly journal,
mainly New York–
oriented.)

CPA Letter
American Institute of

Certified Public
Accountants
Harborside Financial
Center
201 Plaza 3
Jersey City, NJ
07311-3881
201/938-3000

Florida CPA Today
Florida Institute of
CPAs
P.O. Box 5437
325 W. College Ave.
Tallahassee, FL 32314
904/224-2727

Internal Auditor
P.O. Box 140099
Orlando, FL
32889-0003
407/830-7600
(Bimonthly to
association members.)

*Journal of
Accountancy*
Harborside Financial
Center
201 Plaza 3
Jersey City, NJ

07311-3881
201/938-3000
(Monthly association
magazine; carries job
listings.)

*Management
Accounting*
Institute of
Management
Accountants
P.O. Box 433
10 Paragon Dr.
Montvale, NJ 07645
201/573-9000
(Monthly.)

*National Public
Accountant*
National Society of
Public Accountants
1010 N. Fairfax St.
Alexandria, VA 22314
703/549-6400

*The Practical
Accountant*
Faulkner & Gray
1 Penn Plaza
New York, NY 10001
212/971-5000

ADMINISTRATIVE ASSISTANTS, CLERICAL WORKERS, AND SECRETARIES

BRIEF BACKGROUND

Over 15 million people work as secretaries, administrative assistants, or in some sort of clerical job—and for the right kind of worker, the general outlook will be fairly bright.

Just as computers are taking away jobs for stenographers, data-entry workers, typists, and some clerks and secretaries, the increasing complexity of business will be creating jobs for others who can manage computers and people in what will be a much more complex organizational environment. And although the *rate* of growth in this area as a whole will be lower during the next ten years, the size of this job area is so large that there will be a large number of new job openings.

NOTE: This section is a general overview of secretarial and hotel jobs. For more information, also see the appropriate industry section.

EMPLOYMENT OUTLOOK: Good in general, especially for medical and legal secretaries, and those with strong computer skills.

▶ **As the economy grows, demand for skilled secretaries and clerical workers should grow.**

One reason for this improved outlook is simply numbers—there are so many people working in secretarial and clerical positions that openings will pop up simply as people retire or quit. Of the 9 million job openings projected by the year 2005, slightly over half will be due to replacement, and the rest will be new positions.

Another strong reason—there is a shortage of skilled secretaries, particularly at the top. In New York City, salaries of $50,000+ were not uncommon in 1997 for those with the right skills.

Best bet for secretaries: Be computer literate and be flexible, able to handle decision making. Know at *least* two or three major software programs, expect and prepare to be less of a typist and more of an executive assistant, helping schedule meetings, etc., and be able to work independently. In 1996, for example, according to the Dartnell Secretarial Want Ad Survey, over 73% of secretarial want ads requested such computer skills as word processing, spread sheets, or desktop publishing. You've got to present a *package* to your employer—jobs for typists, switchboard and computer operators, and word processors are expected to *decline* much faster than many other jobs. Increasingly today's—and tomorrow's—secretaries work more like information managers rather than like traditional secretaries. The work will go to those who are multi-faceted.

One problem: what about office automation? Will computers, voice mail, and a host of other gadgets reduce demand for secretaries in the future? To a certain degree, this is already happening. Many companies have replaced receptionists with voice-mail systems, some executives now prefer to type their own memos, and others prefer to share secretarial services now that computers have increased efficiency. *But,* even with all this innovation, demand should remain relatively strong as the economy improves. Many secretarial functions, such as scheduling, handling the public, etc., call for judgment that is far beyond the reach of computers. In addition, computers themselves need handling! To repeat: demand will be strongest for computer-literate, well-trained professionals. One group, Professional Secretaries International, offers certification for secretaries—the Certified Professional Secretary. In addition, the National Association of Legal Secretaries offers the PLS certification to qualified legal secretaries. These certifications can be useful for upper-level secretarial jobs.

In general: outlook good. The government projects the number of new jobs won't increase as fast as average on the whole—*but,* the job area is so huge that several hundred thousand new jobs will open up each year for new applicants as secretaries retire or quit. The better news: the number of jobs for legal and medical secretaries should increase in the next 10 years. More good news: employment outlook for highly skilled and experienced secretaries in most areas will be strong. Reason: companies foresee a continued shortage of high-level secretaries.

▶ **Outlook for clerical jobs: mixed.**

The bottom line? Many jobs are being computerized, leading to lower demand for clerks in many job areas. *But:* the absolute number of jobs is so huge that, as with secretaries, hundreds of thousands of new jobs will open up each year as clerical workers retire or quit. For example, there are over 3.7 million record clerks, who keep financial, payroll, personnel, of other records for corporations. Although experts predict the number of record clerks will decline in the next ten years, there are so many jobs that they also say this job area will remain one of the main providers of jobs in the next ten years. In addition, certain clerical areas will see job growth. Some areas that government projects will grow: adjustment clerks, medical information clerks, bill and account collectors. Key skill to have: computer; as clerical jobs become more computerized, better computer skills will be more and more essential—and a way to higher positions.

▶ **Clerical jobs in travel and hospitality: a good way to get your foot in the door.**

Taking a job as a reservation agent, ticket clerk, or passenger service agent is one of the best ways to break into the travel industry—although competition is tough. About 75% of these jobs are with airlines, others with cruise lines and other travel companies.

A brief description of key jobs: *Reservations agents* usually work on computer in centralized offices, booking reservations, answering customer questions. *Ticket clerks* actually sell the tickets at the airports, check baggage and visas, etc.; while *passenger service agents* usually help board passengers, check tickets, make announcements, etc. Sometimes the job duties overlap, but all require a pleasant attitude and an ability to work under pressure. Travel is a twenty-four-hour, fast-moving industry. It's also a growing industry with a strong outlook ahead, which makes this area a good bet for the future. However, this means that many people are interested in the field, so competition is tough.

Hotel work is another good way to break into the hospitality industry. Reason: Hotel work is perceived as glamorous, exciting. The reality? It can also be exhausting and stressful. But perks like free lodging and food make it worthwhile. And there's an added plus—a clerical entry-level job can be one of the best and fastest ways of making it up the corporate ladder at a major hotel or a chain. Hotels like to promote from within the industry. Best way: find a new hotel opening locally. Hotels like to hire people from the area—and new hotels will often hire inexperienced people. Once inside, many hotels have incentive programs for smart people eager to move up.

There are many job areas, including front office staff (handle reservations, telephones, etc., mostly in contact with guests), as well as food service staff, accounting, and sales and marketing. For more information on the different careers in hotels, write the American Hotel & Motel Association (AH&MA). The AH&MA also has a special educational program for entry-level people interested in the industry. For more information, contact: American Hotel & Motel Association.

NOTE: For information about other careers in the travel industry or hospitality industry, see the industry sections on page 479 and page 374.

WHAT'S NEXT

▶ **Job outlook brightest for legal and medical secretaries and clerks.**

The fastest-growing job machine in America is the local doctor's office. The government predicts that medical secretaries' jobs will skyrocket by 65% by the year 2005, assuming the economy grows moderately; legal secretaries will do almost as well, up 47%.

Why? Both these areas are part of the service economy, and as Americans as a population get older, more and more of us will be using medical and legal services. Other areas, such as medical records technicians, will also increase quickly, as will legal assistants (see page 37).

Legal secretaries should also find more job openings. They must be computer literate, and able to understand legal documents and work in a fast-paced, busy environment. Legal secretaries tend to be specialized, following the same specialized areas as their attorney-employers. Two growing areas: litigation and, especially, intellectual property law. For more information, contact the National Association of Legal Secretaries (page 38).

In all cases, there are uncertainties (health care reform may *reduce* paperloads, for example), but the odds are that secretaries in these professions will always be in demand.

One trend: When medical offices downsize, the need for medical assistants skilled at both routine clerical tasks as well as clinical tasks should see a strong demand for their services.

Hot trend: temping. More companies are coming to rely on temp secretarial services. Key: keep current with latest office software for best jobs.

SALARIES

SECRETARIAL: Salaries range widely on average, from $13,000 on up to over $80,000, depending on skill, experience, geographic location, and responsibilities. Average salary for all secretaries is $28,000, but high-level executive secretaries can earn $70,000 and executive assistants, $85,000. The average salary for an executive secretary/executive assistant is $35,000 to $36,000. At this level, however, the term executive assistant is more accurate; computer literacy is a must for advancement. Secretaries working for the federal government average $24,000, but receive generous government benefits.

MEDICAL ASSISTANTS: Starting salaries in 1994 averaged about $17,000; more experienced assistants averaged $21,000 to $22,000.

LEGAL SECRETARIES: In 1994, the median salary was about $28,000; less experienced employees averaged $17,000; more experienced legal secretaries averaged $37,000. One bonus: Many do some paralegal work—for extra pay.

CLERICAL: Office clerks' salaries vary widely, depending on industry, area, level of employment. The average is about $19,000; supervisory clerks earn much more.

TRAVEL: Reservations agents and ticket clerks make from about $13,000 to $15,000 starting, averaging about $26,000 mid-level. Hotel employees begin from the low; those who work (and study) their way up the ladder into hotel management can make $50,000 to $70,000.

BEST BETS

ADMINISTRATIVE SERVICE MANAGERS: This is a catch-all term for a wide variety of senior clerical jobs. Administrative service managers may be office managers, managing clerical staff and overseeing administrative functions. They may also supervise jobs such as procurement, property disposal, transportation, mail services, and inventory control. The job varies with the type of business and size—at small companies, a manager may supervise almost everything, at larger firms they're usually more specialized.

Job outlook: fairly good; new openings will increase about as fast as average; many more will open up as other managers retire or quit. Government experts predict that administrative service managers will be the clerical employees most likely to be kept by downsizing corporations; due to higher skills, usually longer job tenure. Salaries range from $16,000 up to $50,000 or more; most managers earned between $21,000 and $37,600.

WHERE TO GO FOR MORE INFORMATION

ADMINISTRATIVE ASSISTANTS, CLERICAL WORKERS, AND SECRETARIES ASSOCIATIONS

Air Line Employees Association
6520 S. Cicero Ave.
Bedford Park, IL 60638
708/563-9999

American Association of Medical Assistants
20 N. Wacker Dr.
Chicago, IL 60606
312/899-1500

American Hotel and Motel Association
1201 New York Ave., NW, Suite 600
Washington, DC 20005-3931
202/289-3100
(Publishes career brochures, runs special educational program for entry-level applicants.)

American Society of Corporate Secretaries
521 5th Ave.
New York, NY 10175
212/681-2000

Association for Work Process Improvement

185 Devonshire St.
Suite 770
Boston, MA 02110
617/426-1167

Executive Women International
515 South 700E
Suite 2E
Salt Lake City, UT 84102
801/355-2800
(Women who are in executive secretarial or administrative positions.)

National Association of Executive Secretaries
900 S. Washington St.
Suite G-13
Falls Church, VA 22046
703/237-8616

National Association of Legal Secretaries
2250 E. 73rd St.,
Suite 550
Tulsa, OK 74136
918/493-3540

National Association of Secretarial Services

3637 4th St., N.,
Suite 330
St. Petersburg, FL 33704
813/823-3646

9 to 5—National Association of Working Women
238 Wisconsin Ave.
Suite 700
Milwaukee, WI 53203
414/274-0925
(Although a general women's business association, does a lot of work and promotes legislation for secretaries and clerical workers.)

Professional Secretaries International
10502 NW
Ambassador Dr.
P.O. Box 20404
Kansas City, MO 64195
816/891-6600
(Publishes *The Secretary Magazine*, etc.)

ADMINISTRATIVE ASSISTANTS, CLERICAL WORKERS, AND SECRETARIES MAGAZINES

Administrative Assistant's Update
133 Richmond St., W.
Toronto, Ont.
Canada M5H 3M8
416/869-1177
(Designed specifically for Canadian secretaries.)

Secretary
2800 Shirlington Rd.
Arlington, VA 22206
703/998-2534
(Monthly association magazine for career secretaries.)

The Secretary Magazine
Professional Secretaries International
10502 NW
Ambassador Dr.
P.O. Box 20404
Kansas City, MO 64195
816/891-6600

ARTISTS AND DESIGNERS

[NOTE: For related information, see Advertising, page 217, and Fashion, page 322]

[NOTE: For related information, see Advertising, page 217, and Fashion, page 322]

BRIEF BACKGROUND

▶ **The role of design, the importance of visual marketing is now (finally) more appreciated; and ultimately, artists and designers will benefit.**

Despite the ups and downs of the economy, the long-term trend is clear. Art and design are moving into a more central spot in American society—and this means job opportunities.

The trend can be seen in corporate America. Companies are focusing more on product quality and design than in the past. More importantly, corporate America is beginning to appreciate the vital role of design in selling products in the world marketplace. Several MBA schools now offer design courses, the role of the creative staff in advertising is paramount, and job opportunities will return there as well. But . . . competition will still be very tough.

EMPLOYMENT OUTLOOK: The good news: According to federal government forecasts, employment opportunities should grow faster than average for artists and designers. The bad news: Competition, as always, will be hot.

A few optimistic numbers from the U.S. government: overall, artists and commercial artists are expected to see jobs increase by 32% to the year 2005—a relatively rapid growth rate; designers can expect a 24% rate, and interior designers a 34% rate—always assuming the economy grows at a moderate pace. These are reassuring numbers; but remember, the competition in the arts is almost always tough.

For example, each year, many more people graduate from the best arts and design schools like Art Center College of Design in Pasadena, California, than there are jobs available. Nearly 600,000 people are employed in arts and design as a whole—and about 40% of these people are self-employed.

Graphic Arts

▶ **Graphic arts will offer strong employment opportunities over the long term.**

As in arts and design on the whole, competition in graphic arts will be tough—particularly at the lower levels. However as the field gains in importance and new areas (such as computer graphics and Web site design and the like) emerge, opportunities should be growing.

Some areas to keep an eye on:

▶ **Magazine design: still attracting attention.**

Think of *Bazaar* and the facelifts at so many other magazines. These are examples of a trend affecting an entire industry. Expect more magazines to continue opting for eye-catching graphics and art direction to win over consumers. The result? Demand for skilled, creative magazine art staffs—and higher visibility for those already in the field.

For more information, contact: The Graphics Artists Guild (address on page 47). Also check with Graphic Arts Employers of America (listed under the Printing Industries of America).

▶ **One of the hottest—and fastest growing—areas: Web site designers and other Internet and computer-related graphics jobs.**

With the growth of the Internet and, more specifically, the World Wide Web, expect to see an increase in graphics and design opportunities linked to computers. The only problem: Because the Web is so new, the jury is out as to whether the opportunities will exist over the long term. In other words, the Web could turn out to be like CD-ROMs—which looked like they were going to catch on in a big way, but didn't, leading companies to scale back on production.

However, right now, the Web is still attracting interest—and creating job opportunities. Recently, Web site designers have become increasingly in demand, as more companies turn to the Web to advertise and market products and services. According to Yahoo, the largest Web cataloger, the number of home pages—Web sites for a specific company, product, etc.—has been growing from 10 to 15% each month; estimates as to the actual number of Web sites range from 90,000 to 250,000. The upshot? These companies need experts at Web page design to make their home page stand out and grab attention. This field is attracting a number of enterpreneurs who are setting up small design shops—which will continue to offer employment opportunities. Salaries typically range from entry-level pay at $25,000 to $35,000 with a college degree up to $85,000 for experienced designers.

▶ **Also headed for growth: *computer animators.***

With the success of such films as *Toy Story, Jurassic Park,* and *The Mask,* computerized special effects are becoming more and more widely used—not only in films, but in commercials, television shows, and video games as well. As a result, computer animators are seeing more job opportunities. Typically, to get into this field, one needs an animation background—even of the pen-and-ink variety. Salaries range from $45,000 to $100,000. Well-known companies such as Industrial Light & Magic have added staff; but most of the action is with smaller shops that have been opening recently. Downside? Smaller companies may offer employment opportunities, but can't necessarily offer stability.

▶ **Another job option: working with the design/marketing agencies.**

In many cases, design/marketing agencies are replacing ad agencies as visual positioning and marketing companies. Qualifications: talent, a good portfolio, and a good BFA gets your foot in the door. Another good way—internships with agencies. For job leads, check the *Design Firm Directory* (address on page 48), which lists hundreds of design firms, as well as listings of advertising agencies and book and magazine publishers. Lists and directories of these employers can be found in the industry sections on pages 219 and 423.

Increasingly important in the field: marketing professionals. As competition increases, it is no longer enough to know a few people and sell a few accounts. Many firms are turning to professionals to sell their services for them. According to employers, what is needed most is marketing expertise, a flair for selling, and a "feel" for arts and design. Actual artistic ability is not necessary, although for sales- and marketing-oriented artists, this can be a lucrative way of making a living.

▶ **A key skill to stay on the cutting edge in graphic arts and design: desktop publishing/computer graphics.**

More design and publishing companies are relying on desktop publishing and related computer uses. Key advantages: speed, savings on production and printing, ease in design. But some worry that the ease in changing layout and design may butt into employment—and companies could merge the positions of production artist and higher-paid designers. Question: Will the technology become too user-friendly and affect design employment?

Prediction: Probably not. In fact, the new programs often seem to require more training. Moreover, design is not just a technical skill, it is an art; no computer can mandate good taste. This is evident from some amateur desktop productions. The production values are high, but layout and typefaces may be very wrong.

Employment Prediction: In the next few years, as the dust settles, companies probably will have in-house desktop departments, with trained professionals running the programs. Key to a good job: a solid grounding in the technology (both operating system and the actual publishing software), production and typography, and, of course, design. *Getting in:* many universities and schools have now integrated desktop training into their commercial art curricula; on the publishing side, George Washington University in Washington, DC, has recently established a certification program, as has the National Technical Institute for the Deaf in Rochester, NY (716/475-6779).

Design

▶ **Industrial design should remain a strong area.**

Until recently, U.S. manufacturers for the most part essentially didn't manage design—this is evident just by looking at some products. That's not to say the U.S. is not producing top-rate designers; the problem is they've been underutilized. As the director of design from a major Dutch manufacturer stated: "I have 250 designers working for me in 20 countries and the Americans in that group stand tall. What is wrong is that U.S. companies don't understand the strategic value of design and relegate it to a second-rate position under engineering or marketing."

This is changing now. Industrial designers are focusing on creating tools, furniture, and toys that are truly *user friendly*—chairs that allow you to work without a backache, kitchen implements that can easily be used by the elderly, computer keyboards that don't promote tendonitis. Witness the interactive children's toys from Texas Instruments, the Narrow Aisle Reach Truck (design of the decade by the Industrial Designers Society), Good Grips big-handle utensils (designed by Smart Design, Inc.) and the Ford Taurus. Key: good designs are essential to international competitiveness—and U.S. business increasingly understands this. *Also*, the importance of design seems to be infiltrating into smaller U.S. firms, which often take greater risks. Best areas in U.S. design: medical, computer, information systems. Some corporate stars: Gillette, Black & Decker, Texas Instruments, Apple Computer.

Qualifications required: usually a BFA (Bachelor of Fine Arts) from an accredited school. Employees usually start at large manufacturing firms, but many are self-employed or, increasingly, work at design/marketing firms.

▶ **Another good area: package design.**

Over the past few years, packaging has become a far more important element in selling consumer items. (Watch for brighter colors, "neckers," "wobblers," shelf talkers, "snipes"—all trade terms, all describing designs intended to do the same thing: stand out from the competition.) According to some in the industry, package designers will reap the benefits.

For general career information in these fields, contact: Industrial Designers Society of America (address on page 47).

▶ **Interior design: will go through ups and downs along with the economy. Long-term outlook is positive.**

This is a very competitive field that felt the effects of the past recession heavily, as business and personal spending dried up. Long-term outlook good, however, with faster-than-average growth.

Entry into interior design is regulated in some states: Washington, DC, licenses interior designers; five other states regulate use of the title. The Foundation for Interior Design Education Research accredits interior design programs—currently there are about ninety accredited programs across the U.S. (For more information, write them at: 60 Monroe Center NW, Grand Rapids, MI 49503.) After three to four years of professional education and two years of experience, most top designers complete the National Council for Interior Design Exam and are certified as professional interior designers. In many design fields, professional education and certification are increasingly required for higher-level positions.

Fine Arts

▶ **Most fine artists, painters, sculptors, printmakers, and the like are self-employed, although many work as teachers in universities and schools.**

Outlook: Tough competition as always. One reason: there are few formal entry requirements and a lot of excellent artists. Also, the effects of the recession on the job market. Even with improvements, it takes time. The best way to success is the old way: Assemble a strong, varied portfolio that shows creativity and technical expertise, and then learn how to aggressively market your work to the right gallery owner. A BFA from a good school also helps—both for experience and learning as well as for contacts.

Another option: teaching. The only problem is that competition for teaching jobs is very tough, particularly as budget-strapped colleges and universities cut back on faculty, especially in the arts and humanities.

Best areas: 1) according to *The Chronicle of Higher Education,* any high-tech area; 2) "someone who does traditional printmaking and video would be a hot property," according to one expert.

Funding sources: For most of the arts, a significant source of money—and employment—comes in the form of foundation grants. To target the right foundation, check: *Foundation Grants to Individuals.* Also see the regional arts organizations listed at the end of this chapter. They award grants as well as provide assistance to artists. For more on how to pick and apply to foundations, see page 143.

The Visual Arts Information Hotline provides information on organizations at the national, regional, state, and local levels, including foundations and arts councils that support individual visual artists. The hotline is toll-free, provided as a program of the New York Foundation for the Arts in New York City, and operates in all fifty states, the District of Columbia, and the Virgin Islands. Individual fine artists in any of the visual arts—painting, sculpture, drawing, crafts, photography, mixed media, etc.—and in film/video may call, toll-free, 800/232-2789.

▶ **An offbeat art job: cartoonists.**

This type of drawing for a living is harder than most arts or design professions—most cartoonists do the gag writing as well. But there are bonuses: creative, recognized work, the attraction of reaching a large audience with your ideas and talent—and making them laugh or see things your way. There are very few full-time cartoonists: probably less than several hundred. Freelancers submit their work to magazines, which usually pay from $50 to $500 per cartoon.

According to one cartoonist interviewed in the *Occupational Outlook Quarterly,* a good cartoonist will sell about one out of every five cartoons drawn. Some may produce up to thirty a week, others less than five. Cartoonists aspiring to the comics have an even harder time. King Features, the main syndicator (a syndicator represents and sells the artist's work to newspapers around the country in return for a cut of the proceeds, usually 50%) receives thousands of strips each year. For those feeling lucky, contact the Cartoonists Guild (see listing at end of chapter); they offer a placement service. Or try submitting your work to a newspaper syndicator—addresses of syndicators can be found in directories listed on page 428.

Photography

▶ **As with other arts and design professions, photography will offer higher employment opportunities than the average—but competition will remain extremely tough.**

Photography is a very competitive field for a simple reason: there are more people who want to be photographers than there are jobs to employ them. Key to success: strong skills, good business ability, and in many cases, salesmanship or contacts. The good news, though: the government predicts employment of photographers to grow faster than the average for all occupations through the year 2005. This increased demand for photographers should develop as more companies, institutions, etc. rely more heavily on visual images to sell products and service or communicate to the public.

▶ **Employment spotlight: photojournalists.**

Technology is coming to the newsroom—and to the darkroom. Digital photography equipment, increased newspaper emphasis on graphics are transforming the role of the photojournalist—according to *presstime* magazine. The jobs: at some large dailies the photo department comprises a chief photo editor, forty-one photographers, fifteen technicians, a photo researcher, a photo equipment supervisor, three editorial assistants, and twelve photo editors.

Photo editors help plan and coordinate assignments, and understand both the technical aspects of photography and the editorial requirements of the paper. Job potential: problematic. Some see a reduction (usually by attrition) of production staff, and some even see problems for photographers themselves—since the electronic technology can make even the worst photos by an untrained reporter acceptable. Others say that demand for well-qualified pros will be good since composition and high-quality photos and layouts are essential competitive positioning advantages in the industry.

Prediction: good opportunities for photojournalists who are computer-literate in imaging technology, etc., *and* have experience. With both, demand exceeded supply in recent years. One caveat: Publishing is a *very* volatile industry—this year's hot job could be next year's dud. That's why anyone interested in competitive jobs like this should do their *own* research and talk to professionals about job opportunities.

Ideal candidate: besides computer literacy, a college degree with journalism training, technical knowledge of color printing, etc. Where to go for training: see list below; also the NPPA offers training (919/383-7246), as do the ANPA Technical Dept (703/648-1213), the Society of Newspaper Design (703/648-1308), the Center for Creative Imaging, Eastman Kodak Company (800/428-7400), Rochester Institute of Technology (716/465-5064), and the University of Missouri Electronic Photojournalism Laboratory (314/882-0348).

BEST COLLEGE TRAINING FOR PHOTOJOURNALISTS
(with combined graphics, journalism, and technical curricula, as recommended by veteran photographers; quoted in *presstime*, 1992)
  California Polytechnic State University (San Luis Obispo, CA)
  California State University (Long Beach, CA)

Ohio University (Athens, OH)
Rochester Institute of Technology (Rochester, NY)
San Jose State University (San Jose, CA)
Syracuse University (Syracuse, NY)
University of Missouri (Columbia, MO)
University of Texas (Austin, TX)
Western Kentucky University (Bowling Green, KY)

WHAT'S NEXT

▶ **Design will become more important and designers will reap the benefits.**

Newest trend: Universal design. The hottest aspect of industrial design. The Americans with Disabilities Act (ADA) of 1990 aims to guarantee the disabled the same access to jobs and transportation as the rest of us—and this means design challenges as designers try to come up with telephones and office equipment that can be used by the disabled, as well as the rest of the population. Key advantage: it usually works out that the new product is better used by *both* the disabled and nondisabled.

Another example of design's increasing role: The Corporate Design Foundation in Boston is giving grants to major business schools to provide for courses in design for managers. The result: design-oriented future managers who will emphasize creative talent—and pay for it.

Another trend: product designers are foregoing the traditional hourly wage rate and asking instead for performance bonuses of between 1 to 5% of sales. This has been the case with some toy and furniture designers in the past; it is finally coming to other product designers as well.

▶ **The future: the sky's the limit.**

Technology will revolutionize arts and design, creating entirely new creative categories, and new careers. Already the growth of the World Wide Web has generated new positions. Expect to see more Web-related jobs. In addition, as multimedia—a hybrid of computer, sound, video, even holographic imaging—grows in use, new arts and design jobs will be created.

Some designers are already working on interactive books; others are creating a new "computer aesthetic." At the same time, there is a return to classicism by other designers. In all the arts and design, there are cycles of fads, fashions, and major trends. One key aspect of technology: it will speed up these cycles—and at the same time increase their impact. Already, design firms are linking up into worldwide networks, just as advertising agencies are going international. Designers will impact much of the world, not just local regions.

Of course, as technology gives more power to the individual, there will be a countertrend: more designers and artists will be able to link up with their like-minded brethren—and manage to buck the major trends and keep their smaller visions alive.

SALARIES:

GRAPHIC ARTISTS AND DESIGNERS: Average salaries in the low $20s, median salaries around $30,000 to $40,000. Design shop owners, top freelancers, and top advertising creatives make considerably more. In general, the best average salaries go to designers working in art/design studios. Entry-level industrial designers recently averaged $26,000 at independent design firms and $33,600 in manufacturing companies. Average salaries for more experienced designers were in the mid $40s. At the director-of-industrial-design level, salaries may reach over $100,000; best salaries tend to go to those working in: business products, medical, automotive, and consumer products. In advertising, salaries range from $25,000 for low-level art directors in small agencies to $90,000 for more senior directors at large agencies. For the politically and artistically talented, there is room at the top for associate creative directors and creative directors, with significantly higher salaries.

COMPUTER GRAPHICS: Beginning from about $25,000 for assistant designers, increasing to an average of about $45,000 for designers, more for senior designers.

FINE ARTISTS, INTERIOR DESIGNERS, CRAFTSPEOPLE: A high number of self-employed, with widely variable incomes. Full-time workers earn median incomes of about $30,000—some much higher, others, particularly those on a part-time basis, much lower.

WHERE TO GO FOR MORE INFORMATION

ARTS AND DESIGN BOOKS

Design Careers
Heller, Steven, and Lita Talarico.
New York: Van Nostrand Reinhold, 1987.
(A complete compendium of career information, with excellent employment sections and advice.)

Graphic Design Career Guide
Craig, James. Watson Guptill Publications, 1983.

Selling Your Graphic Design and Illustration
Crawford, Tad, and Arie Kopelman. New York: St. Martin's Press, 1981.

Supporting Yourself as an Artist
Hoover, Deborah. New York: Oxford University Press, 1989.
(Everyone should have this book; excellent advice, material, and ideas on the practical side of artistic life.)

REGIONAL ARTS ORGANIZATIONS

Arts Midwest
528 Hennepin Ave.
Suite 310
Minneapolis, MN 55403
612/341-0755

Consortium for Pacific Arts and Cultures

2141C Atherton Rd.
Honolulu, HI 96822
808/946-7381

Mid-America Arts Alliance
912 Baltimore Ave.,
Suite 700
Kansas City, MO

64119
816/421-1388

Mid-Atlantic Arts Foundation
11 E. Chase St.,
Suite 2A
Baltimore, MD 21202
410/539-6656

New England
Foundation for the
Arts
330 Congress St.,
6th Floor
Boston, MA

02210-1216
617/951-0010

**Southern Arts
Federation**
181 14 St.
Suite 400

Atlanta, GA 30309
404/874-7244

**Western States Arts
Federation**
236 Montezuma Ave.
Sante Fe, NM 87501
505/988-1166

ARTS AND DESIGN ASSOCIATIONS

**American Center for
Design**
233 E. Ontario,
Suite 500
Chicago, IL 60611
312/787-2018

**American Craft
Council**
72 Spring St.
New York, NY 10012
212/274-0630

**American Institute
for the Conservation
of Historic and
Artistic Works**
1717 K St., NW
Suite 301
Washington, DC 20016
202/452-9545

**American Institute of
Graphic Arts**
164 5th Ave.
New York, NY 10010
212/807-1990

**American Society of
Furniture Designers**
P.O. Box 2688
2101 W. Green
High Point, NC 27261
910/884-4074
(Publishes magazine
with job openings,
referrals, directories,
etc.)

**American Society of
Interior Designers**

608 Massachusetts
Ave., NE
Washington, DC 20002
202/546-3480
(Publishes career
pamphlets, etc.)

**Americans for
the Arts**
1 East 53rd St.
New York, NY 10022
212/223-2787
(Publishes career
guide, etc.)

Graphic Artists Guild
11 W. 20th Street,
8th Fl.
New York, NY 10011
212/463-7730
(Publishes periodical,
etc.)

**Graphic
Communications
International**
1900 L St., NW
Washington, DC 20036
202/462-1400
(Major graphic arts
union; includes many
specialties; AFL-CIO-
affiliated.)

**Industrial Designers
Society of America**
1142 Walker Rd.,
Suite E
Great Falls, VA 22066
703/759-0100
(Placement service;

publishes magazine,
directory, etc.)

**Institute of Business
Designers**
341 Merchandise Mart
Chicago, IL 60654
312/467-1950
(Interior designers
involved in
nonresidential work;
Currently merging with
other association; call
for more information.)

**International
Association of
Clothing Designers**
475 Park Ave. S.
New York, NY 10016
212/685-6602
(Men's and boy's
clothing; directory,
placement service for
members.)

**National Endowment
for the Arts**
1100 Pennsylvania
Ave., NW
Washington, DC 20506
202/682-5400

**National Foundation
for Advancement in
the Arts**
800 Brickell Ave.
Suite 500
Miami, FL 33131
305/377-1140

New York Artist's Equity Association
498 Broome St.
New York, NY 10013
212/941-0130

New York Foundation for the Arts
155 Avenue of the Americas
New York, NY 10013
212/366-6900
(Provides grants and services to individuals and arts-related organizations in the United States. Operates the Visual Artists Information Hotline, a toll-free information line for visual artists in the United States (See p. 43.)

Printing Industries of America
100 Daingerfield Rd.
Alexandria, VA 22314
703/519-8100
(Maintains referral service for members; includes wide variety of jobs in design and printing.)

Professional Photographers of America, Inc.
57 Forsyth St.
Suite 1600
Atlanta, GA 30303
404/522-8600
(Publishes periodical with career information, etc.)

Women's Caucus for Art
Moore College of Art
1920 Race St.
Philadelphia, PA 19103
215/854-0922

ARTS AND DESIGN DIRECTORIES

American Art Directory
Reede Reference Publishing
121 Chanlon Rd.
New Providence, NJ 07974
1-800/521-8110
(Lists thousands of museums, libraries, schools, etc.)

Artist's Market
Writer's Digest Books
1507 Dana Ave.
Cincinnati, OH 45207
513/531-2222
(Lists hundreds of markets for art and design work—names, addresses, requirements, etc. For cartoonists, also publishes *Humor and Cartoon Market*.)

Design Firm Directory
Wefler & Associates
P.O. Box 1167
Evanston, IL 60204
708/475-1866
(Lists all types of design firms.)

Foundation Grants to Individuals; Foundation Directory; Corporate Foundation Profiles
Foundation Center
79 Fifth Ave.
New York, NY 10003-3076
212/620-4230
(The first directory is particularly valuable to artists seeking financial support from foundations.)

Graphic Artists Guild Directory
Graphic Artists Guild
11 W. 20th St., 8th Fl.
New York, NY 10011
212/463-7730

Graphic Arts Blue Book
A. F. Lewis and Co., Inc.
79 Madison Ave.
New York, NY 10016
212/679-0770

ARTS AND DESIGN PERIODICALS

AIGA Journal
American Institute of Graphic Arts
164 5th Ave.
New York, NY 10010
212/807-1990

American Artist
BPI Communications
1515 Broadway
New York, NY 10036
212/764-7300

ArtForum
65 Bleecker St.
New York, NY 10012
212/475-4000

Artweek
2149 Paragon Dr.
Suite 100
San Jose, CA
95131-1312
408/441-7065

*Communications
Arts*
410 Sherman Ave.
P.O. Box 10300
Palo Alto, CA 94303
415/326-6040

*Computer Graphics
World*
Penwell Directories
P.O. Box 21278
Tulsa, OK 74121
918/835-3161

Design News
Cahners Publishing
Company
275 Washington St.

Newton, MA 02158
617/964-3030

Graphic Arts Monthly
249 W. 17th St.
New York, NY 10011
212/463-6834
(editorial)
1-800/637-6089
(subscriptions)

Graphic Design: USA
Suite 405
1556 3rd Ave.
New York, NY 10128
212/534-5500
(Monthly magazine for
art directors, etc.)

Graphis
141 Lexington Ave.
New York, NY 10017
212/532-9387
800/351-0006

HOW
1507 Dana Ave.
Cincinnati, OH 45207
513/531-2222

(Bimonthly magazine
for graphic artists.)

Interior Design
249 W. 17th St.
New York, NY 10011
212/645-0067
1-800/542-8138
(subscriptions)
(Monthly for designers
and those in the
business of design.)

Print
3200 Tower Oaks Blvd.
Rockville, MD 20852
1-800/222-2654

*Professional
Photographer*
57 Forsyth St.
Suite 1600
Atlanta, GA 30303
404/522-8600
(Monthly for members
of Professional
Photographers of
America.)

ENGINEERING, COMPUTER, AND HIGH-TECH PROFESSIONALS

BRIEF BACKGROUND

▶ **This is a high-tech age—and as technology impacts our daily lives, the need for trained professionals will increase.**

The bottom line, of course, is to have the right specialty, as any worker in the defense industry can tell you. With cutbacks in defense, some defense engineers are having a difficult time transferring their skills to other areas. Despite the volatility in the computer industry, the outlook for the next few years is very good for most workers.

There is simply too much technological innovation for the job outlook to be anything but at least fairly strong in the long term—for most.

In general, the short term may be very rocky for many engineers, but the future looks brighter. There is simply too much to be done. From ceramic motors to solar technology to hazardous waste clean-up to giant infrastructure projects to moving the mountains of information generated by society, high-tech professionals will be needed. One important point: those who want jobs should keep abreast of the latest technologies.

EMPLOYMENT OUTLOOK: Overall, most areas look strong, particularly in the still dynamic computer industry.

▶ **General trend: positive times for engineering and computer professionals, despite cutbacks in certain engineering areas and continued volatility in the computer industry.**

On the whole, engineering, computer, and high-tech professionals face a positive climate. With technological breakthroughs continuing to impact on industry, with growth in the use of the Internet, with more attention being paid to staying on the cutting edge, both engineers and computer professionals are in demand.

Defense cutbacks will continue to result in layoffs of defense-related engineers, but the wholesale downsizing of the early '90s is for the most part over. Non-defense engineering areas look positive for the future. As for computer professionals, while the computer industry continues to be as volatile as ever, with start-up companies seizing attention and larger companies sometimes faltering, it continues to be one of the hottest areas in terms of employment.

The bottom line, then? This career area remains one of the best places to be for the rest of the '90s and beyond. Hottest areas in terms of employment: Software design, development and testing, digital/analog design, semiconductor design, and mechanical/robotics.

However there are some negatives: First, demand for older engineers has remained relatively weak in these post-massive-layoff times. Key problems: Fewer senior level positions and possibly age discrimination. One route out: contract work as a consultant. Second, laid-off defense workers are facing a very tough job outlook—with large numbers of people competing for few jobs. Some universities, such as the University of Southern California, have developed programs aimed at aiding defense engineers in career switching over to environmental engineering, which offers better long-term prospects. Finally, both engineers and computer specialists have been facing another employment threat: Many corporations are finding it cheaper and easier to hire foreign employees to do technical work—for lower wages.

The upshot: Overall, engineering, computer, and high tech jobs are looking good for the future, but competition will sometimes be tight. The key to staying ahead in the job hunting game: Staying on the cutting edge and targeting areas that show the strongest prospects.

▶ **First, a look at prospects for engineers—in general, the outlook is good.**

The past two years have been good ones for many engineers. Hiring in most areas is up—in some areas way up—and salaries have been increasing. According to some experts, pay is increasing at a rate not seen since the booming 1980s.

Of course, it's easy to talk about now. What about tomorrow? A lot depends on the economy—and what goes up may come down. But in general, the long-term outlook is good to excellent.

Some projections: Based on the latest Bureau of Labor Statistics projections for 2005, there will be a strong growth for computer engineers (computer engineering will exceed mechanical engineering to become America's largest engineering profession) and for consultants in most engineering specialties, and a moderately healthy growth for engineering managers and such specialties as biomedical engineers. Civil, mechanical, and chemical engineers may face a slower-growing market, but given the sheer numbers, job turnover alone will account for significant openings for job seekers.

Key trends: demand for software and computer engineers in early 1997 was "white hot"—expect the heat to stay on for the next several years—although an economic downturn may turn down the heat somewhat. Contract engineering was another big area, with one problem: Many employers wanted to hire their contract hires on a permanent basis but the contractees didn't want to give up the freedom and high pay.

One interesting development in early 1997: the beginnings of resurgence in hiring of some people with defense backgrounds, specifically with microwave, telecom, and voice-recognition systems experience. Nevertheless, defense-related engineering has been one of the weakest areas of the field.

In general: strong hiring. One major problem: hiring for older engineers—those with twenty or more years of experience—is much worse than for younger engineers.

Graduating engineers, in particular, continue to be in demand for jobs—often even as other engineers are being laid off. And, in general, the role of engineer is a crucial one in today's competitive industrial environment. Technological advances and competitive pressures continually require companies to rely on engineers to improve and update products and manufacturing processes, to help increase productivity, and more. Civil engineers will be needed to repair aging infrastructure; environmental engineers will be needed to develop, update and monitor pollution control systems. Following is a breakdown of the prospects in different engineering disciplines.

What are companies looking for: Skills combined with team orientation. Applicants are expected to work in team environments and possess strong interpersonal skills. In addition, employers expect engineers to continue their education throughout their careers and keep up with the latest technology.

A summary of major engineering areas:

ELECTRICAL AND ELECTRONIC ENGINEERING: This is the largest branch of engineering, accounting for roughly 350,000 jobs. Recent Outlook: strong. Best bets: electronics manufacturers, who will be relying on R&D to remain competitive; Internet service providers, who have been adding staff since early 1996. Also strong demand at telecommunications firms. In addition, more *low-tech* companies, such as wholesalers, retailers, finance companies, and health care providers, are adding EEs, as they automate services and processes. In general, EEs with computer-oriented skills, especially knowledge of programming languages such as C++, should find the most employment opportunities. The combination of electrical and computer engineering experience is one that many employers are seeking. An area to keep an eye on: Analog design. Even as the world goes increasingly digital, there is a demand for analog electronics—and a shortage of analog designers. Alternative job track: move into sales and marketing, explaining complex high-tech items to corporate customers. Best qualifications for this—at least five years experience, programming skills, technical knowledge of a company's equipment.

MECHANICAL ENGINEERING: accounts for almost one-fifth of all engineers; most engineers are in manufacturing. Even while overall employment in manufacturing is expected to decline, the picture is a good one for manufacturing engineers who can reduce costs and manage capital equipment projects; also more positions in construction. Similar increases expected in employment for *industrial engineers*, who design and implement production systems, now including robots, computers. Best areas: continued steady demand for manufacturing engineers and quality engineers with auto or consumer electronics backgrounds.

CIVIL ENGINEERING: Favorable employment outlook. Key reason: As our national infrastructure ages, civil engineers will be needed to repair and rebuild outdated bridges, highways, and tunnels. One problem: much of this improvement will be funded by government, which tends to fund projects slowly and is affected by budget cutbacks. However, the long-term picture remains positive.

AEROSPACE ENGINEERING: Hot competition—with more qualified candidates than there will be job openings. Problem: Defense cutbacks have already eliminated many jobs, and while R&D expenditures for new systems may remain stable, new jobs won't be added. On the nondefense side, opportunities aren't much better. In general, one of the weaker areas in engineering.

CHEMICAL ENGINEERING: Average employment growth expected through 2005. Best areas: specialty chemicals, pharmaceuticals, plastics materials, and in nontraditional fields such as electronics, food and consumer products manufacturing, and pulp and paper processing. Best opportunities? Look at smaller emerging industries such as advanced materials and similar high-tech areas. As with other engineering professions, downsizing has changed the chemical engineering job market, with many entry-level and midmanagement positions eliminated. In the absence of any staff rebuilding, such companies will employ outsourcing avenues, such as hiring consultants. Given this, expect job opportunities with engineering service companies—or temporary hires—and opportunities for sampling jobs and gaining a foot in the door.

Other engineering areas with generally positive outlooks and average employment growth expected: *safety engineers, process engineers, materials engineers* (as industry moves into ceramics, specialty plastics and other synthetics; this is a hot area and the U.S. is a leader), and finally to some degree *mechanical engineers*, reflecting a renewed emphasis on manufacturing, and the large numbers of replacements needed as engineers retire or move into management positions.

Prospects for *petroleum* and *mining*? Job growth is projected as low to nonexistent, but particularly with petroleum engineering, prospects could pick up if the economy shifts focus. Also: because fewer students are entering petroleum engineering, there will probably be a growing need for people to fill replacement positions.

INDUSTRIAL ENGINEERING: Low but steady demand for IEs in traditional standards-setting or plant-layout roles. Better yet, look for steadily increasing demand for IEs with business management skills/experience to function as management engineers. Improving product quality to stay ahead of competition is a major focus of the new industrial engineer. Computer skills are a decided plus.

ENVIRONMENTAL ENGINEERING: The industry—once forecasted as a growth area that was to clean up the environment—has been buffeted by: 1) a substantial government slowdown—spending for such efforts as the Superfund cleanup of the environment has fallen prey to budget deficits as well as to decreased regulations on private industry; and by 2) oversupply—ease of entry has created more small companies by laid-off engineers eager to capture a piece of the declining market. The tough business climate is forcing downsizing and mergers as companies attempt to create a large enough base to compete for the available government contracts, seek overseas markets alone or with partners, or seek specialized domestic niches.

There are currently between 25,000 to 50,000 environmental engineers. Job duties vary—monitoring pollution, setting standards, running Superfund projects, etc. Various specialties exist, ranging from noise abatement to solid waste management. Jobs can be with government (agencies such as the EPA), with consulting firms, industrial companies.

A barometer of the job market problems: In 1995, industry volume increased 5% but with a decline of 5% in the work force.

Bottom line: Long term growth looks gloomy.

An area of probable growth: environmental jobs abroad, as Eastern Europe and the old Soviet Union start clean-ups.

▶ **Architects and related positions—long-term outlook mixed.**

Expect stiff competition, particularly for prestige jobs in major cities. A coming area: environmental architecture. A stronger hiring trend: in elder housing; nursing home design; and other areas geared to this continuing growth market. Also, health care, "universal design" (architecture which takes into account people with disabilities), and correctional facilities' architecture.

Key skill: In a competitive environment, one of the best skills to have is CAD technology knowledge. More firms are relying on computer-aided drafting and design; as such, candidates with CAD ability have an edge.

For landscape architects: the long-term outlook may prove strong, as cities revamp parks and recreational areas, and in particular, as environmental concerns affect corporations and the public.

▶ **Outlook for the computer industry: changing and volatile, often marked by hot competition, but very strong employment opportunities.**

The computer industry will, of course, remain volatile. Because it is based on cutting-edge technology, layoffs and cutbacks are a way of life. But opportunities will continue to be very strong. A good example: Even as Microsoft laid off 120 workers in early 1996, they added another 2,500 new employees. So, in spite of periodic downturns and shakeouts, the computer and information-management industry will be a good place to be in the next ten years. According to figures from various experts, including the Bureau of Labor Statistics, job growth for computer programmers, systems analysts, and computer engineers will increase by over 80% by 2005; computer programmers will see slower growth, but should still face a positive employment picture. Of course, the news isn't all good—for computer operators jobs will decline. But the bottom line is simple—for the well-trained, technically up-to-date, experts see clear sailing ahead. Here's an encouraging factoid for the job hunter: Some experts estimate that almost 200,000 jobs are vacant today—because the industry can't find enough computer experts to fill them.

Of course, with new technologies and new companies always cropping up, more shakeouts are inevitable. The best advice for anyone in this industry, in the words of one seasoned veteran: "Be flexible."

▶ **Information systems: looking good.**

It's inevitable. As IS (information systems) enters the corporate mainstream, professionals are needed who can communicate effectively with nontech employees. Company recruiters are talking about the need for IS professionals with the social and business skills to implement the technical systems they design, and the people skills to supervise teams of employees—or at least get along with them. Again, this is especially important at the mid- to upper levels.

Job outlook in general: very good. Experts point to three different employment markets: companies with older mainframes and midranges that need IS people to keep them working; the client/server market; and networking.

Key qualifications: In general, companies are looking for people with a combination of computer and business skills. The specific computer skills an applicant needs vary according to the specific company and position. For example, hiring recently has been extremely strong for software professionals with C, C++, Java, and GUI (graphical user interface) backgrounds. But, in general, most areas are very strong.

A general requirement: staying on top of current and emerging technology. In addition, it's vital to be flexible. Today's IS field is fast moving and fast changing. What's hot today may not be tomorrow—so it's important to be flexible enough to move with the changing times.

As for the nontechnical skills required, these include project management ability, consulting skills, and so-called "people skills"—especially communications skills. As IS professionals increasingly interact with non-IS personnel, it's important to be able to get major ideas across in nontechnical language.

Industries that should offer good employment opportunities: health care, education, financial services, transportation, telecommunications, retail, entertainment. In addition, besides general corporate work, IS job hunters can consider independent consulting, working with a consulting firm, and work with software and hardware vendors.

The major job areas and outlooks:

SYSTEMS ANALYSTS, MANAGERS: going up. This is one of the fastest growing occupations, according to the federal government. There are currently over 800,000 systems analysts and computer scientists, who help computerize business or scientific tasks, or improve current computer operations. Constant training required, frequent development seminars, etc. Similar outlook and positions for operations research analysts, who primarily use quantitative methods (and computers) to study and streamline corporate or organizational operations.

COMPUTER PROGRAMMERS: Currently there are over 550,000 programmers. The job market for computer professionals has been surging. The major events accounting for this: 1) explosive growth of Internet-related companies and computer service companies; 2) development of computer system links by companies with their suppliers and customers (Intranet systems) permitting real-time monitoring of inventories and finances; 3) the year 2000 problem requiring intensive efforts to avoid computer crashes by reprogramming mainframe computers currently unable to deal with financial programs involving dates after 2000.

In addition, demand is increasing for experts to rewrite code in the now-antique COBOL language for aging, mainframe computers.

Demand will be strongest for experienced persons with college degrees in programming, with detailed knowledge of newest languages, computer networking, database management, and operating languages. Graduates of two-year programs? Far fewer opportunities. One recruiter's advice: "Go back to school and get a full degree." A potential development: computer jobs could be moving overseas. In order to take advantage of cheaper labor abroad, companies may rely more on overseas computer programmers in the future, according to the director of the Advanced Telecommunications Research Center at the University of Colorado. Given this, expect U.S. programmers to be responsible for more complex programming tasks—such as developing Internet-based applications, and multimedia software. Other good areas: Silicon Valley (of course), Boston, northern Virginia, North Carolina, Dallas, and Portland, Oregon.

▶ **Good bets for 1998 and beyond.**

CONSULTANT: A hot job prospect, especially as companies reorganize their business strategies in the postdownsizing period and employ outside experts for assistance on a project basis. Professionals with Internet experience and Windows NT are especially in demand. Despite their project status, many of these projects may not be short term in nature since, as they mature, ancillary and monitoring programs may be required. Six figure incomes for experienced computer professionals are not uncommon. Software architects who design complex systems average $85,000 to $90,000 incomes.

SOFTWARE ENGINEER: One of the hottest jobs for the rest of the decade. Jobs increased nearly 10% annually in the 1987—94 period and 12% in 1995 with forecasts of over 6% per year for the next 10 years. The only possible downside: more people are training to enter this field, which may mean tougher competition ahead. Entry level salaries run an average $30,000. Experienced software engineers typically earn from $40,000 to $60,000.

WEB SITE DESIGNER/WEBMASTER: One of the hottest new jobs currently, and one that seems headed for more explosive growth as more companies turn to the Web for marketing. For more information, see Best Bets, page 59.

COMPUTER HELP SERVICES/CUSTOMER SUPPORT: Not as technical a position as many others in the field, but one that continues to grow. In fact, many experts point to this as the fastest growing area of employment. One example: in 1989, 1/12 of all employees at a software company were in support positions. Now the number has doubled, to one of every six. Customer support staffers are the people who man a company's toll-free service line and answer the questions consumers have about their hardware or software. The need for technical skill varies according to the specific position. But most companies do require strong communications and "people" skills for this area. One interesting note: This is a particularly popular field for career switchers, possibly because it doesn't require a specific background. In fact, many companies consider ex-teachers ideal candidates. Salaries generally fall in the $20,000 to $29,000 range.

COMPUTER SECURITY EXPERTS: Electronic burglary is up, especially as more people use the Internet. As a result, network security in particular will be a major concern, and security experts will be the beneficiaries. Increasing numbers of firms outside of government and banks are hiring these experts, as thieves, hackers, and corporate spies threaten databases and the Internet. Typically, a degree in computer science, engineering, or telecommunications is required, and applicants must pass a security clearance. Salaries now range from $50,000 to $90,000.

Other jobs that look promising include: systems architects, database and tool developers, experienced project leaders, relational database experts.

▶ **What are companies looking for—especially in entry-level staffers?**

Good question—and one that many companies don't agree upon. Some want entry-level staffers to have a strong background in science—any science; others prefer liberal art backgrounds. Many say writing skills are a must, in addition to technical skills. But most companies *do* agree that grades aren't as important as enthusiasm.

WHAT'S NEXT

▶ **Continuing education: a must for most engineers, computer workers.**

Technological change will be rapid in the last years of the '90s. In response, engineers will have to stay current, or risk losing advancement potential or their jobs. One danger to engineers in specialized fields: in some cases, technology may make their specialty obsolete.

▶ **There will be continued volatility in the computer field, as new technologies spur new employment needs.**

After the micro revolution, the pico revolution with PCs on a chip? What further new technologies and software challenges with portable, palmtop, and handheld technologies, ever more powerful micros, new D-RAMs to best bottlenecks, AI, etc? The best way to weather the volatility is clear: Keep up with the new technologies through continuing education.

In all cases, college degrees and further education will also be in demand. For example, most newly hired programmers have college degrees or higher; a recent survey of PC designers found a shift from two-year technical degrees to four-year college degrees.

Key point: As virtually everyone is saying, the demand for computer professionals will continue to grow. But the days when an applicant with enthusiasm and one or two computer courses could expect an easy job hunt are over. Today, detailed knowledge of cutting-edge technologies is important, particularly since companies have restructured and merged and moved to client/server architecture. There are significantly fewer opportunities for applicants with traditional skills in mainframe or mid-range proprietary operating systems (although there is still demand—mainframes and minis haven't disappeared, and they still perform valuable functions). But the bottom line is clear: technology is evolving rapidly and the applicant who keeps current is ahead of the curve. One good bet: consulting, as outside firms are brought in to update corporate systems.

▶ **Women and minorities are few and far between in engineering and computers—but the percentages will change.**

Only 15% of high-tech professionals are women, they advance more slowly, and are far more likely to be unemployed. Even worse, after peaking in 1986, the number of women entering high-tech fields has leveled off. And some reports show more women are leaving the field, frustrated by sexism and lack of advancement. On the plus side: pay is roughly equal for equivalent experience, age. According to a Cooper Union survey, 70% of women surveyed said they were paid comparable wages for comparable work with men. Also, more women are beginning to appear in the top executive ranks, particularly at small companies.

Some bright spots for women: Currently about 21% of Hewlett-Packard engineers are women; automotive manufacturers are doing heavy recruitment on college campuses to attract women to their ranks.

The situation for minority engineers is similar. The shrinking labor pool is causing companies to step up recruitment of minorities. The problem? Minorities represent only a small percentage of engineering students, and a very small percentage of professional engineers and computer professionals. For example, only about 7% of all computer professionals are black. One way to combat this: watch for an increase in programs designed to attract minority students to the field. The National Action Council for Minorities in Engineering is already beginning a long-term push to increase minority involvement. And the Black Data Processing Association (215/843-4120) has now topped 3,000 members in 44 chapters nationwide.

The bottom line: Due to relative shortages of engineers in universities, expect more firms and schools to encourage minority and women's programs.

SALARIES

▶ **Key point: Engineering and computer science traditionally offer high starting salaries and, on average, relatively high pay throughout a career. But the big money comes from the management and supervisory side of engineering.**

ENGINEERING: higher starting salaries than most graduates, stable pay in midlevels. Starting salaries average about $35,000. Every year various surveys show the differentials among various specialties—usually the lowest beginning salaries are for civil and mining engineers by several thousand dollars; highest for chemical, environmental engineers. Engineers with master's degrees usually earn more, from the upper 30s to mid-40s. Mid-level salaries for most engineers range from $38,000 to $45,000, upper-level salaries average from about $60,000—$70,000 up to over $100,000.

According to the American Association of Engineering Societies, the median salary in 1994 for engineers in industry was $56,000; the federal government median salary was $55,800.

CHEMCIAL ENGINEERS: In 1996, median starting salary for graduates with BS degrees was $42,000, and almost $58,000 for Ph.D. graduates. Chemical engineers with ten-plus years experience had a median salary of $54,000.

ARCHITECTS: starting salaries average in the high 20s; those with experience average in the high 30s, up to $50,000 to $100,000 for principals or partners.

LANDSCAPE ARCHITECTS: salaries begin in the 20s for BAs; average from the 40s to the 50s for experienced architects.

COMPUTERS: Starting salary average in the $30,000+ range. Experienced systems analysts earn an average $44,000 to $55,000; programming analysts slightly more. Managers earn from $52,000 to $64,000; MIS directors $80,000 and CIOs, over $100,000.

ENVIRONMENTAL, HAZARDOUS WASTE: The need is there for specialists, but government funding is *not* there in a period of government deficits and elimination of controls on private industry. Limited opportunities may exist for solid waste engineers, process engineers, environmental engineers in wastewater, industrial waste, engineering geologists, geotechnical engineers. Background required: environmental engineering degree; BS or above.

The American Academy of Environmental Engineers offers short supplementary courses, provides listings of schools offering this environmental engineering. New trend: older engineers are taking courses, learning some aspect of this specialty. Salaries range from the 40s for BS on up to $50,000 for project managers, about $80,000–$100,000 for more senior management. Contact: American Academy of Environmental Engineers, 410/266-3311.

BEST BETS

INTERACTIVE MEDIA SPECIALIST: the job is still so new and rapidly changing that it's hard to predict just how rapidly it will grow or what the future will bring, but it looks to be red hot. These specialists work to pull together TVs and computers and bring information to viewers and users in compelling ways. To break in, your best bet is to get a degree in communications, computer science, and maintain a cutting edge technological base. Salaries range from $30,000 on up to the hundreds of thousands of dollars.

WEB SITE DESIGNER/WEBMASTER: One of the newer computer jobs—and one that has been growing explosively. The World Wide Web is the graphic-based portion of the Internet that contains graphic sites (consisting of one or more pages, actually screens, of pictures and information). Corporations have recently discovered the Web and are using it to either market their products or services, advertise, or post on-line versions of their magazines, newspapers, etc. Typically, designing a Web site requires knowledge of such tools as HTML (hypertext markup language), which is the Web's basic writing tool, as well as TCP/IP networking or the like. On the nontechnical side, writing skills and marketing expertise are a help. But most importantly, Web site designers need creativity. While learning the fundamental skills to design a page isn't all that tough, designing a page that attracts attention is. Web sites are often designed by teams—including graphic designers, writers, and HTML authors—as well as back-end programmers who enable the site to perform advanced tasks, such as automatic daily updates (for example, of stock prices), and a project manager who oversees the entire process. Entry level salary is about $50,000, average salary $80,000.

WHERE TO GO FOR MORE INFORMATION

[Note: Also see Aerospace, page 225; Computers and Electronics, page 288]

ENGINEERING, COMPUTER, AND HIGH-TECH PROFESSIONAL ASSOCIATIONS

(For many more computer sources, see "Computers and Electronics" in the "Industry section" on page 228.)

Air and Waste Management Association
1 Gateway Ctr.
3rd Floor
Pittsburgh, PA 15222
412/232-3444
(Publishes periodical with job openings, directory, etc.)

American Association of Cost Engineers
209 Prairie Ave.
Suite 100
Morgantown, WV 26505
304/296-8444
(Publishes periodical with some job openings, job referral service for members, etc.)

American Association of Engineering Societies
1111 19th St., NW,
Suite 608
Washington, DC 20036
202/296-2237
(An association of many other engineering associations; publishes salary surveys, etc.)

American Ceramic Society
735 Ceramic Pl.
Westerville, OH 43801
614/890-4700
(Publishes periodical, etc.)

American Chemical Society
1155 16th St., NW
Washington, DC 20036
1-800/227-5558
(Publishes various periodicals with job listings—see separate listing for *Chemical & Engineering News*; maintains job bank, listing service, counseling services, etc.)

American Consulting Engineers Council
1015 15th St., NW
Washington, DC 20005

202/347-7474
(Publishes various directories, etc.)

American Institute of Aeronautics and Astronautics
370 L'Enfant Promenade, SW
Washington, DC 20024
202/646-7400
(Newsletter with job listings; special newsletter for students with employment information, etc.)

American Institute of Architects
1735 New York Ave., NW
Washington, DC 20006
202/626-7300
(Publishes periodicals, directories, operates members' referral service.)

American Institute of Chemical Engineers
345 E. 47th St.
New York, NY 10017
212/705-7338
(Publishes periodical with job openings,

placement referral service, etc.)

American Society of Civil Engineers
345 E. 47th St.
New York, NY 10017
212/705-7496
or
1801 Alexander Bell Dr.
Reston, VA 20191
703/295-6000
(Publishes periodical with job openings, directories, job service for members, etc. See their resume link at 614/529-0429, which matches resumes against their employer job bank.)

American Society of Engineering Education
1818 N. St., NW
Suite 600
Washington, DC 20036
202/331-3500
(Publishes periodical with job openings, directories.)

American Society of Heating, Refrigerating, and Air-Conditioning Engineers
1791 Tullie Cir., NE
Atlanta, GA 30329
404/636-8400
(Publishes periodical, etc.)

American Society of Information Science
8720 Georgia Ave.,
Suite 501
Silver Spring, MD
20910-3602
301/495-0900

(Publishes monthly—sometimes bimonthly—newsletter devoted to careers and job openings.)

American Society of Landscape Architects
4401 Connecticut Ave., NW
Washington, DC 20008
202/686-2752

American Society of Mechanical Engineers (ASME)
345 E. 47th St.
New York, NY 10017
212/705-7722
800/843-2763
(Publishes periodical with job listings, etc.)

American Society of Safety Engineers
1800 E. Oakton St.
Des Plaines, IL 60018-2187
708/692-4121
(Publish periodicals with job openings, etc.)

American Welding Society
550 N.W. 42nd Ave.
Miami, FL 33126
305/443-9353
(Publishes periodical, job referral service, etc.)

Association of Energy Engineers
4025 Pleasantdale Rd.
Suite 420
Atlanta, GA 30340
770/447-5083

Association of Groundwater Scientists and Engineers

2600 Ground Water Way
Columbus, OH 43219
614/337-1949
(Publishes periodical with job listings, etc.)

Association of Old Crows
1000 N. Payne St.
Alexandria, VA 22314
703/549-1600
(Members are involved in defense, electrical engineering, etc.)

Association for International Practical Training
10400 Little Patuxent Pkwy.,
Suite 250
Columbia, MD
21044-3501
410/997-2200
(For students in engineering, sciences, or agriculture, arranges overseas exchanges with on-the-job training or research for up to a year.)

Association for Systems Management
P.O. Box 38370
Cleveland, OH 44138
216/243-6900

Environmental Careers Organization
286 Congress St.
Boston, MA 02210
617/426-4375
(Publishes special career publications; places students and recent graduates in short-term professional positions; career conferences, etc.)

IEEE Computer Society
1730 Massachusetts Ave., NW
Washington, DC 20036
202/371-0101
(Publishes members-only periodical with job openings, etc.)

Institute of Electrical and Electronics Engineers (IEEE)
345 E. 47th St.
New York, NY 10017
212/705-7900
(Publishers periodical with job openings; annual directory of members; career/employment guide, etc.)

Institute of Industrial Engineers
25 Technology Pk.
Norcross, GA 30092-2988
770/449-0460
(Publishes periodical with job openings.)

Institute of Transportation Engineers
525 School St., SW, Suite 410
Washington, DC 20024
202/554-8050
(Publishes periodical with some job listings.)

Instrument Society of America
P.O. Box 12277
67 Alexander Dr.
Research Triangle Park, NC 27709
919/549-8411
(Offers placement service, periodical with job openings, etc.)

International Society for Hybrid Microelectronics
1850 Centennial Park Dr., Suite 105
Reston, VA 22091
703/758-1060
(Offers members-only newsletter with job openings; publishes annual directory.)

National Action Council for Minorities in Engineering
3 W. 35th St.
New York, NY 10001
212/279-2626

National Society of Black Engineers
1454 Duke St.
Alexandria, VA 22314
703/549-2207

National Society of Professional Engineers
1420 King St.
Alexandria, VA 22314
703/684-2800
(Publishes directory, etc.)

National Solid Wastes Management and Environmental Industries Association
4301 Connecticut Ave., NW, Suite 300
Washington, DC 20008
202/659-4613

Operations Research Society of America
901 Elkridge Landing Rd., Suite 400
Linthicum, MD 21090-2909
410/850-0300
(Publishes journal with job listings, placement service.)

Robotics International of SME
P.O. Box 930
1 SME Dr.
Dearborn, MI 48121
313/271-1500

Society of American Military Engineers
607 Prince St.
P.O. Box 180
Alexandria, VA 22314-3117
703/549-3800
(Publishes directory of defense engineering organizations.)

Society of Automotive Engineers, Inc.
400 Commonwealth Dr.
Warrendale, PA 15096
412/776-4841

Society of Hispanic Professional Engineers
5400 E. Olympic Blvd., Suite 210
Los Angeles, CA 90022
213/725-3970
(Placement service, etc.)

Society of Logistics Engineers
8100 Professional Pl., Suite 211
Hyattsville, MD 20785
301/459-8446
(Publishes directory, etc.)

Society of Manufacturing Engineers (SME)
P.O. Box 930
1 SME Dr.
Dearborn, MI 48121
313/271-1500

(Publishes periodical with job openings.)

Society of Petroleum Engineers
222 Palisades Creek Dr.
Richardson, TX 75080
214/952-9393
(Publishes newsletter where members may advertise jobs, educational programs, etc.)

Society of Plastics Engineers
14 Fairfield Dr.
P.O. Box 0403
Brookfield, CT 06804
203/775-0471

Society of Women Engineers
120 Wall St.—
11th Floor
New York, NY
10005-3902
212/509-9577

(Resource center; publishes periodical with job openings; offers counseling to members.)

Water Environment Federation
601 Wythe St.
Alexandria, VA 22314
703/684-2400
(Publishes periodical with job openings.)

ENGINEERING, COMPUTER, AND HIGH-TECH PROFESSIONAL DIRECTORIES

(for more, check under associations)

Job Choices
National Association of Colleges & Employers
62 Highland Ave.
Bethlehem, PA 18017
610/868-1421
(Organizations, including government, with job opportunities.)

Directory of Chemical Engineering Consultants
American Institute of Chemical Engineers
345 E. 47th St.
New York, NY 10017
212/705-7338

Directory of Engineering Societies
American Association of Engineering Societies
1111 19th St., NW
Suite 608
Washington, DC 20036
202/296-2237

Directory of Engineers in Private Practice
National Society of Professional Engineers
1420 King St.
Alexandria, VA 22314
703/684-2882

Peterson's Job Opportunities for Engineering and Technology
Peterson's Guides, Inc.
P.O. Box 2123
Princeton, NJ 08543-2123
609/243-2121
800/338-3282
(Lists hundreds of corporations and government agencies that are hiring; includes detailed information.)

ENGINEERING, COMPUTER, AND HIGH-TECH PROFESSIONAL MAGAZINES

Architectural Record
1221 Avenue of the Americas

New York, NY 10020
212/512-4256
(Monthly professional

journal; valuable for inside look at industry; some job listings.)

*Chemical &
Engineering News*
McGraw-Hill, Inc.
P.O. Box 507
Princeton Rd.
Highstown, NJ 08526
609/426-7070
(Excellent industry
roundups are
particularly valuable as
overviews for entry-
level job hunters;
classifieds include
many job openings.)

*Chemical Engineering
Progress*
American Institute of
Chemical Engineers
345 E. 47th St.
New York, NY 10017
212/705-7338
(Monthly; many job
listings.)

Civil Engineering
345 E. 47th St.
New York, NY 10017
212/705-7514
(Monthly for American
Society of Civil
Engineers; many job
listings.)

*Engineering
News-Record*
1221 Avenue of the
Americas
New York, NY 10020
212/512-2000
(Good help-wanted
section; publishes top
companies' listings.)

Engineering Times
National Society of
Professional Engineers
1420 King St.
Alexandria, VA 22314
703/684-2800
(Association magazine

with some job openings
and employment
information as well as
other information.)

*Environmental
Management Today*
1483 Chain Bridge Rd.
Suite 202
McLean, VA 22101
703/448-0336
(Eight issues per year
for environmental
engineers, etc.)

*Environmental
Solutions*
312 W. Randolph
Suite 600
Chicago, IL 60606
312/538-8800
(Monthly for hazardous
waste specialists.)

Graduating Engineer
Peterson's Guides, Inc.
P.O. Box 2123
Princeton, NJ 08543-
2121
609/243-9111
800/338-3282
(Career advice; special
issues such as high-
tech careers, women
and minority hiring
trends, etc.)

*High Technology
Careers*
Westech Publishing
Company
4701 Patrick Henry
Dr., Suite 1901
Santa Clara, CA 95054
408/970-8800
(High-tech industry
tabloid with hundreds
of high-tech job
openings listed.)

IEEE Spectrum
345 E. 47th St.

New York, NY 10017
212/705-7560
(With over 500,000
circulation, has many
job listings; note that
this address is for the
magazine, association
address is given above.)

*Journal of Air/Waste
Management*
1 Gateway Ctr.
3rd Floor
Pittsburgh, PA 15222
412/232-3444

*Landscape
Architecture*
4401 Connecticut Ave.,
NW
Washington, DC 20008
202/686-2752
(Main trade journal;
eight issues a year.)

Machine Design
Penton Publishing
1100 Superior Ave.
Cleveland, OH 44114
216/696-7000

*Mechanical
Engineering*
345 E. 47th St.
New York, NY 10017
212/705-7786
(Monthly; carries many
job listings.)

Plant Engineering
1350 E. Touhy Ave.
Box 5080
Des Plaines, IL 60017-
5080
708/635-8800

Pollution Engineering
P.O. Box 5080
Des Plaines, IL 60017-
5080
708/635-8800
(Monthly.)

Product Design and Development
Chilton Way
Radnor, PA 19089
215/964-4355
(Monthly for design engineers.)

Technical Employment News
12416 Hymeadow Dr.
Austin, TX 78750

512/331-3918
1-800/678-9724
Fax: 512/331-3900
(Weekly magazine listing job openings in electronics, engineering, computers, etc.; subscribers can access BBS for on-line job listings.)

Water Environment/ Technology
601 Wythe St.
Alexandria, VA 22314
703/684-2400
(Monthly especially for consulting engineers and chemists in the field.)

OTHER JOB SOURCES

See federal job openings and organizations under "Government Employees," page 66. Also:

InternAmerica
Ford
Ford Careerworks
800/456-7335
(Bimonthly newsletter of intern positions listed by various corporations.)

Office of Personnel Management
215/597-7440
or
912/757-3000

Palace Acquire
AFCPMC/DCPR
Randolph AFB, TX 78150
800/847-0108
(Air Force intern program for engineers.)

Professional Development Center
Naval Facilities Engineering Command
200 Stovall St.
Alexandria, VA 22232-2300
703/325-0400
(Navy engineer intern program.)

GOVERNMENT EMPLOYEES

BRIEF BACKGROUND

▶ **Government employment is a catch-all term for the largest and perhaps the most diverse of employment categories.**

The federal government is the largest single employer in the U.S.—with well over 3 million civilian employees; add to these the millions of teachers, police, and administrators on state, county, or local payrolls. One can see that with such large numbers, despite cutbacks in spending, numerous jobs will open every day, in a wide variety of fields, in most areas of government—and in most areas of the country. Estimates are that the federal government hires more than 300,000 employees a year. And these federal jobs are located nationwide; 86 percent of all federal jobs are outside of Washington, DC.

▶ **Most government employees work for the executive branch, usually as part of the civil service.**

And a quick note for those who have forgotten high school history: the government is divided into three branches—executive, legislative, and judicial. Federal civil service jobs usually fall under the executive branch, although in some cases employees of the judicial and legislative branches are also civil service employees.

This section covers government employment in general, with the most emphasis on federal jobs—and a very comprehensive listing of major federal agencies and organizations. It also covers state and local government jobs, with an emphasis on administrative jobs. Teaching jobs, social work jobs, security jobs, etc., are covered under separate sections—although it's a good idea to read this section as well and to look at the sources at the end.

EMPLOYMENT OUTLOOK: Fair

While the bad news is that federal hiring is tight, the good news is that it is not eliminated.

▶ **Federal government employment levels will rise very slowly if at all; even so, opportunities will be there for the right people.**

The government projects that total federal employment will increase by only 200,000 in the next ten years. Considering it employs over 3 million people, that's a very small number. Hiring is definitely down. In a normal year, the federal government adds about 140,000 new employees to its rosters; in 1995 it added only around 45,000, which is still something.

But the job outlook for managers, scientists, and computer systems workers, lawyers, and other professionals will be brighter than those numbers suggest. Federal employment is already more managerial or professional than most other employers—nearly 80% of the government is made up of white-collar employees, compared with 25% of the national workforce.

It will be getting more so. Automation, computerization, and the shifting of blue-collar functions to private subcontractors will reduce jobs for drivers, machine operators, and most importantly, clerical staff. On the other hand, lower level government jobs tend to pay better than their equivalents in the private sector.

Bottom line: In general, upper level, more technical jobs offer the best prospects—procurement specialists, management analysts (except defense related), local environmental inspection officers, property management workers have all been mentioned as growth areas recently. On the downside: government priorities may shift rapidly; and so may job prospects. Best bet: focus on your own strengths, and get strong skills in your area.

▶ **Other positions will be opening up on the other side of government: Congress.**

Even when turnover isn't high among congressional jobs, staff jobs working for those in Congress have a very high turnover. One fairly recent study found that over 78% of people in staff jobs left during an eight-year period. One reason: staff jobs in Washington can be a good route to influential jobs elsewhere in government and outside as lobbyists, etc. One other reason: working conditions can be *very* grueling.

Best route to a job: know your congressperson. If you have the time or money, volunteering can be a good way of getting your foot in the door. Outside of working for a congressperson, staff jobs on various committees and subcommittees are sometimes open—and campaigns are another route. See addresses on page 90 on where to go for staff and campaign openings.

Other jobs can be found in various congressional offices, including the **General Accounting Office** (GAO), which is the legislative watchdog over the executive branch; **the Library of Congress, the Office of Technology Assessment** (OTA); and the **Congressional Budget Office.** (Addresses are listed on pages 82 and 90.)

See addresses on page 90 on where to go for staff and campaign openings.

SPECIAL SECTION: HOW TO APPLY FOR A FEDERAL JOB

First, we'll explain how the system is organized, so you'll be familiar with various terms and are able to target, find, and get the federal job you want.

How are jobs filled?

About 80% of government jobs are filled competitively—which means the openings are made public, applicants are evaluated by certain pre-set standards, and of course hiring is nondiscriminatory. Of course, this is the ideal, not necessarily the real. The standards and personnel practices are to a greater or lesser extent set by the Office of Personnel Management (OPM).

The other 20% of government jobs are called "excepted service jobs"—and are filled according to very specific criteria set by the individual agency. The Foreign Service of the State Department, the CIA, etc., are all excepted service jobs.

How do you find job vacancies?

There is no one central government listing of all jobs available—but there's a wealth of resources available to help you find the right job vacancy.
Here are some ways:

1. **Use the federal government's Employment Information Highway available at the Office of Personnel Management (OPM) or at the Federal Employment Information Centers at OPM area offices or at State Employment Service offices. This Highway includes a) Career America Connection and b) Federal Job Opportunities Board.**

   The Office of Personnel Management is the government personnel office. The OPM keeps a list of job openings at the federal level and helps applicants apply for many jobs. Recently they've been changing procedures to make job hunting more streamlined for applicants. One problem: as these changes are implemented, things could be confusing—and phone numbers or procedures may change.

   Your best bet: Call OPM's Career America Connection (automated telephone system) at 912/757-3000. The connection is open 24 hours a day, 7 days a week. Follow the menu-driven procedure to learn about worldwide federal job vacancies, salaries, benefits, recruitment messages, and other on-line information for job seekers, as well as to obtain job materials.

   Job seekers with access to a computer modem may also reach OPM's Job Opportunities Board, an electronic job bulletin board. This 24-hour-a-day, 7-day-a-week service offers job information similar to the Career America Connection. Or OPM may be reached through the Internet at: fjob.mail.opm.gov. (The address supports TELNET connections only.) Then, you'll be provided information, a number to call for more information, and you'll get or be sent application instructions.

   You can also find job vacancies at state offices (see individual address by state beginning on page 514). The Federal Employment Information Centers also have touch-screen computers describing federal job opportunities.

2. **Visit or call the agency or government office directly.**

   This can be the most productive, since you may hear of job openings before they get onto the OPM list, you may make contacts with hiring officials, you may learn what they're looking for in an employee and tailor yourself accordingly.

   Many agencies have special job hotlines or job postings, and so on. Have a good idea of the type of job you're interested in—but be open to other areas, and be aware that most administrative or professional positions with the federal government do not require a specific type of degree.

   How do you contact a federal agency?

   Most main offices of federal agencies and departments are listed beginning on page 75, with instructions on how to find local office numbers as well. Note that the personnel numbers are listed, along with job hotlines, but don't stop there. Try to get the specific numbers of the department heads or supervisors of areas you're interested in and speak with them directly. They, and not personnel, usually determine whom to hire. For more complete listing of offices and addresses and names of the major employees (there are thousands), check the *U.S. Government Manual.* It is in most libraries, or order direct from the Government Printing Office (address on page 82). Other government directories with names and addresses are on page 91.

3. **Buy or subscribe to any of a variety of private newsletters which list federal job openings.**

These can be excellent sources. In effect, instead of traveling to an OPM office/Federal Job Information Center, you have the job listings travel to you. The first two periodicals cited below list thousands of federal jobs by title, grade, location, and instructions on how to apply. The next two include job listings along with federal news, etc. Addresses and phone numbers are in the Periodicals section on page 92.

Federal Career Opportunities
Thousands of job listings, from secretarial to engineering

Federal Jobs Digest
(lists thousands of federal jobs, with contacts and addresses to which to apply, grades and salary levels; each issue has over 15,000 job openings)

Federal Employee's News Digest

Federal Times
(a periodical mainly for federal employees; includes many job listings in back)

4. **Call government job hotlines.**

The government now maintains job hotlines which can give you information on careers, jobs, and application information. These are listed under the appropriate agencies, if applicable.

5. **Go to a college placement office.**

Even if it's been years since you graduated, be aware that many college placement offices carry applications, and most importantly, the Federal Job Opportunity Listing—the computerized, updated federal job listing that's issued by the regional OPM offices.

6. **Networking**

An overused word, but with federal employment, it can't be used enough. Employees at the agency you want to work at can target opportunities for you, recommend you, tell you what to say and what not to say—in short, they can get you a job.

7. **Buy the *U.S. Government Manual* and *The Budget of the United States Government.***

This is a clever way to get a real headstart on everyone else. Every year the *Manual* is issued; every year it tells the policies and priorities of each federal agency or department. The *Budget* goes one better: it tells where the money is going. Often agencies with increased allocations will be hiring.

8. **If your experience and education warrants it, check on *mid-level opportunities*.**

A mid-level rating means a higher GS rating and more responsibility; moreover, many agencies have special programs for qualified applicants in certain areas.

9. **Find out about any special programs via the agency you wish to work for.**

Government agencies maintain special hiring programs for women, minorities, veterans, and persons with disabilities. Many have special programs for older job hunters, etc. Each of these can give you an edge.

Where do you apply for a federal job?

There are two basic places to which you send your material when applying for a federal job:

1. **The Office of Personnel Management (OPM) itself (or through Federal Job Information Centers at OPM area offices)**

The OPM is the central government personnel office—with its main office in Washington, DC, and regional offices and branches nationwide.

In some cases the OPM acts as a sort of job search firm, taking your application, evaluating or rating it, then placing your name on a list for referral to various government agencies—and all you do is wait for them to call you.

Now the system is changing. Your best bet is to call the OPM at 912-757-3000, find the jobs you're interested in via their menu-driven hotline, and then follow procedures from there.

The OPM used to administer civil service tests as well, but today only a few jobs, mostly for entry level jobs, require tests (although excepted service positions like that of the U.S. Foreign Service do require tests—see the International section on page 114).

Before 1994, after contacting the OPM, in many cases, you'd be given a Form 171 to fill out, which in effect was a government resume. This has been eliminated as an absolute requirement—now the federal government has moved toward accepting resumes—like the rest of the job market. But you may wind up completing the two-page Optional Application for Federal Employment, form OF-612. Check for specifics when you apply.

Read the requirements carefully and be sure your resume is complete and covers all the stated requirements; otherwise you may not be considered. Include:

- job announcement, title, grade
- your address, with day and evening phone numbers
- Social Security number
- country of citizenship
- veterans' preference, if any
- education, degree, with date
- jobs (civilian and federal) held

- company name(s) and address
- job titles, duties, and accomplishments. (Describing accomplishments is especially important. Although duties for equivalent jobs may be similar, your accomplishments will not be similar and may be your job advantage. Accomplishments tell more about you and can be reasons to hire.)

2. Better yet, apply directly at the federal agency, department, or office where you want to work.

You can do this for many jobs—and above all, for, those where the job is particular to one or a few agencies (air traffic controllers are particular to the FAA, for example), or where the job is one in which there is a critical shortage.

In general, this is the best way to get hired. There is one key advantage with going directly to a federal agency: they make the ultimate hiring decision, so if you don't have to, why go the extra step via OPM?

And by going to the agency, you can learn exactly what they're looking for, make contacts for future positions if you don't get the initial one, and get to understand the *informal* job market—in other words, get to network your way into a job.

If you've applied to an excepted agency: you'll learn their specific procedures for application when you apply. With some of these agencies, there may be a specific test (as with many jobs in the U.S. Foreign Service) to take, or very specific requirements. For jobs with some of these agencies—including the CIA, NSA, Foreign Service—see International Careers, page 109.

What types of federal jobs are there?

All types, of course. The government hires for virtually every position—from blue-collar to secretaries and clerks to high-level managerial and technical positions.

Virtually all federal civil service jobs are ranked according to a General Schedule (GS) rating. When you look at a job listing, you'll see a GS rating given. If you then look at a standard GS table (usually posted at a job center), you'll see the standard salary you get if hired at that GS level.

Ratings begin at GS-1; four years of college qualifies you for a GS-5 rating, nine months more of work along with college gives you a GS-7 rating, more experience rates more, on up through GS-18.

Each GS level includes ten "steps," ranging from 1 to 10. Salaries are determined by GS level and step number. Generally speaking, salary ranges can be extensive. Above GS-18 is another scale called Senior Executive Service.

Those are the levels of employment; what types of jobs are there? Recently, the Office of Personnel Management listed a broad breakdown of government job openings:

1. Entry-level administrative and professional jobs:

In many cases there are no specific educational requirements. These jobs are usually administered via the OPM; or, if you meet various criteria, you can apply directly to the agency in question.

In some cases, particularly at the lower levels, you may be required to take a test—but there no longer is a general "civil service" test. You'll find out details during the application process.

2. Specialized jobs:
These are jobs that require the completion of certain college-level courses. They include: accountants and auditors, biologists, engineers, foresters, mathematicians, and physical scientists.

In most cases, these jobs start at the GS-5 to GS-7 levels, but those with experience, advanced degrees, or both will naturally be hired at higher levels. In many cases, applicants with the skills in these areas are very much in demand.

Best way to contact employers? Contact the agency directly; or for college students and recent grads, try the job hotline for more information, or look for listings in one of the job newsletters.

3. Public safety jobs:
These include: air traffic controllers, Deputy U.S. Marshals, Treasury enforcement agents, U.S. Park Police Officers.

These jobs generally require some sort of bachelor's degree or the right experience, and the passing of a written test. The entry-level grades are between GS-5 and GS-7.

Best way to contact employers? Contact the agency directly, or look for openings in one of the newsletters.

4. Technical jobs:
These include a wide variety of support positions, from paralegals to lab technicians. Usually you should have at least two years of relevant experience, and/or a two-year degree or some combination of the two. In some cases, you'll have to take a written test. Technical jobs usually start at the GS-4 level.

Best way to contact employers? Contact the agency directly, or contact one of the area OPM/Federal Job Information Centers, or find openings in one of the newsletters.

5. Clerical and administrative support:
This is the largest category of government employment. Most start at the GS-2 level and require a high school diploma. These jobs are listed at OPM/Federal Job Centers and by the various newsletters.

Also consider:

6. Legislative staff positions:
These are *not* part of the normal federal civil service, but they're definitely where the action is, working either for a member of Congress or for one of its committees. Salaries average in the $37,000 range. Long hours are part of the job; turnover is high, with staff personnel averaging less than two years on the job. But the opportunities to learn—and to move up into other responsible government positions—is more than enticement enough for many people. For information on House of Representatives staff positions, don't call the OPM. Instead, call the House Resume and Referral Office at 202/226-6731. Call the Senate Placement Office at 202/224-9162. Resumes are kept on file for three months, but as with any job search, persistence and frequent followups are helpful.

IMPORTANT NOTE: After reading about the *formal* procedures for applying for a government job, remember that the *informal* routes are sometimes more important.

Just because a job is listed doesn't mean the hiring is open. Very often, section chiefs within the office already have someone in mind—by listing the job they are merely following OPM requirements.

Conclusion: the best way to get a government job is to network: target the organization where you want to work, get to know the people. Even though you will probably still go through formal procedures, you may have already been pre-selected. Final words from a person who has been in and out of government jobs—"Be persistent."

▶ **State and local government employment: growth tied to economy and rising privatization trend.**

The key is how far will privatization and economic cutbacks extend into the future—and how much if at all will defense spending cutbacks free up money for local projects. Also, in the wake of the L.A. riots look for some increase in targeted programs in the inner city.

Despite the cutbacks we're seeing now, federal labor statistics suggest that state and local government jobs will increase at an average rate—rising from about 15.5 million to around 18.3 million in 2005. Over half of those new jobs will be in public education (for more, see Teachers and Educators, page 180).

Where the other jobs will be:

First of all, don't forget the private sector for government jobs. In other words, as governments privatize—or transfer public functions to the private sector—remember that the jobs don't necessarily go away, they just go somewhere else. For example, Wackenhut Corporation, a giant Florida security company, manages prisons throughout the U.S., manages parking in Alaska, operates huge job-training programs—and expects government service jobs within the company to increase at an annual rate of over 10% per year for the next decade.

Few increases are expected in jobs at the very top (usually elected) levels of local city and town administrations. The reason is obvious: only a few new cities or towns will be incorporated in the next ten years. Principal means of employment: job turnover through elections. Average age of top city officials and council members is well over thirty; half are over fifty.

Good areas: social services (although low paying and despite cutbacks), budget and finance, law enforcement.

Another good way to go for a job: Many local governments offer *internships*. In 1992, *Public Management* magazine reported internships in cities and towns ranging from Angel Fire, NM, to Washington, DC. Salaries can range from zero to little above minimum wage to a solid, mainstream income. A good source of internships: *ICMA Newsletter* (address and phone number on page 190).

BEST BET

CITY MANAGER: professional contracted by city, town, or county council to run the local administration; has all the responsibility of a mayor except for being elected. Background: usually an MA in public administration, work as an analyst or assistant in a local government office. Salaries range from $28,000 in municipalities with populations of less than 25,000 to $104,890 in cities of between 500,000 and 1 million. Problem: these jobs can be tough to get. Best bet: new expanding communities in the Southwest. For information and jobs in this and related areas, check *ICMA Newsletter* (address and phone number on page 190).

▶ **As for state civil service, opportunities vary widely.**

State governments are organized in fifty different ways: some states fill many jobs primarily through patronage (knowing and supporting the right politician gets you the job); other states are well known for professional civil services.

Best way to go for a job: Check with local state employment office or state job center for information and job postings. Addresses for all fifty states are listed by state in the Regional section of this book, beginning on page 510. Also, as with the federal government, target informal ways of getting in. A few best bets in terms of quality administrations: state governments of Michigan, Minnesota, Pennsylvania, Wisconsin. Other jobs at the state level:

LEGISLATIVE STAFF: As state government increases in complexity, staff members have become more professional, far more important—and more numerous. Of course, downsizing has hit local and state governments, and has affected hiring in certain areas. Some advantages: easy access to jobs—usually few formal hiring requirements such as lengthy applications, background checks, etc. A good way to get an "in" on other state jobs. Best way to get in: Since there are often few formal hiring procedures, contact your legislators directly. On the downside: usually low paying, very high turnover. And then again, you can always run for the state legislature . . .

WHAT'S NEXT

▶ **Government will emphasize efficiency.**

The rest of the 1990s will be a period of frugality—emphasis will be on getting more per dollar. This trend will be found not only in the leaner and meaner corporations but in federal, state, and local governments as well. Look for efforts to streamline and maximize efficiency in government, look to efforts at bringing quality control, increased computerization, better and more efficient services.

SALARIES

CITY MANAGERS: Average salary about $60,000; varies according to region, size of city.

OTHER LOCAL GOVERNMENT JOBS: In 1988, the median annual salary of a city or town council member was $2,400; in cities with populations above 500,000, $40,000. According to the Bureau of Labor Statistics, mayors on average earned $8,239; in cities over 1 million the average was $87,751 in the late 1980s.

STATE GOVERNMENT: Legislators earned just expenses in eleven states; in the other thirty-nine states the average salary was $17,700 in 1987.

FEDERAL GOVERNMENT: Salaries ranged in 1991 from GS-1 step 1 (GS1/1) at $11,015, to GS-5/1 at $16,973, to GS-11 step 6 at $36,301, on to Senior Executive Service salaries at $70,000 and above. (With exceptions like $200,000 for the President of the U.S.) Mid-level salaries (GS-8 through 13) range from $23,284 to $57,650. As a rule of thumb, the federal government doesn't pay well on the top scales, but pays very well on the middle level.

WHERE TO GO FOR MORE INFORMATION

U.S. GOVERNMENT EMPLOYERS: EXECUTIVE BRANCH

NOTE: Government phone numbers and addresses for employment information are often changed—be certain to double-check all numbers and addresses. Furthermore, the government has been instituting a new telephone system called the Washington Interagency Telecommunications System, which has caused more changes than normal. Sometimes a recorded message will inform you of the new number. If not, remember you can call the government information number at 1-800/688-9889, regular information at 1-202/555-1212 for District of Columbia agencies, 1-703/555-1212 for Virginia agencies, and 1-301/555-1212 for Maryland agencies.

Office of Personnel Management (OPM)
215/597-7440
or
912/757-3000

(As mentioned in the text, OPM, in some cases fills the role of a government search firm; it also oversees the hiring practices of other agencies. *Offices of the regional OPMs/Federal Job Information Centers are listed in each region in the Regional sections. In general, contact the specific OPM nearest where you want to work.*)

Administrative Office of the U.S. Courts
1 Columbus Circle NE
Human Resources Division, Room G200
Washington, DC 20544
202/273-2777
(Provides administration services to federal courts; hires primarily acct., comp. sci., finance, and lawyers; some liberal arts backgrounds; for court positions you must refer to the individual court itself—see U.S. court directory in the Directory section for a listing of federal courts nationwide.)

Agriculture, U.S. Department of
Office of Personnel
Career Transition Resource Ctr.
SM-7
Washington, DC 20520-9660
202/720-2791
(A huge, and for hiring purposes very decentralized agency; hiring is usually done by individual USDA offices.)

Other USDA offices:

Agricultural Marketing Service
Field Servicing Office
Attn.: Animal and Plant Health
Inspection Service
Butler Sq. W., 5th Fl.
100 N. 6th St.
Minneapolis, MN 55403
612/370-2187 (job hotline and info)
(Most jobs in commodity grading and
market reporting; hires primarily ag.
backgrounds.)

Agriculture Research Service
Personnel Division
Bldg. 003, BARC-W.
Beltsville, MD 20705
301/344-1124
(Each year employs 100 scientists for
full-time research; also employs
technicians, etc.)

**Animal and Plant Health
Inspection Service**
Field Servicing Office
Human Resources Division
Butler Sq. W., 5th Fl.
100 N. 6th St.
Minneapolis, MN 55403
612/370-2227
612/370-2187 (jobline)
(Hires mostly agriculture, biology,
and lab technology.)

**Economic Management Staff—
ARS-HRD-MOB**
Recruitment Coordinator
Personnel Division
1400 Independence Ave. SW
Room 1423, S. Bldg.
Washington, DC 20250-0308
202/720-7657
(Hires ag. econ., econ., math.)

Farm Service Agency
14th and Independence Ave. SW
Washington, DC 20250
202/720-5237
(Hires acct., ag. business, admin.,
etc.)

Farmers Home Administration
Personnel Division
14th and Independence Ave., SW
Washington, DC 20250
202/245-5565
(Primarily hires ag. business, arch.,
and civil engin.)

Food and Consumer Service
Personnel Division
3101 Park Center Dr.
Alexandria, VA 22302
703/305-2351
(Above address is for DC area
positions; call for numbers of 7
regional offices; hires home ec.,
econ., business, and nutritionists.)

Food Safety and Inspection Service
Personnel Division
Room 3161, South Bldg.
14th and Independence Ave., SW
Washington, DC 20250
202/720-6617
(Hires chem, food tech. and vet.
backgrounds primarily.)

Forest Service
Washington Office
1621 N. Kent St.
Arlington, VA 22209
202/205-1760
(Call or write for the address of 9
regional offices and for positions
with one of the 8 research stations
and 2 labs; hires archaeologists,
engin., ed., forestry, and various bio.
specialties.)

**Office of Inspector General
(USDA)**
Office of Personnel
Personnel Operations
Room 31-W
14th and Independence Ave., SW
Washington, DC 20250
202/690-1622
(Employees with legal, comp., etc.,
skills; audit USDA operations.)

Rural Development–Rural Housing Service
14th and Independence Ave. SW
Washington, DC 20250
202/245-5565
(Primarily hires ag. business, arch., and civil engin.)

Rural Utilities Service
Personnel Management

Division
Stop 1532
14th and Independence Ave., SW
Washington, DC 20250
202/720-9560
(Primarily hires acct., bus. admin., and engin.)

Soil Conservation Service
Personnel Division

P.O. Box 2890
Washington, DC 20013
202/720-4264
(There are also local offices, listed in your local phone directory under "U.S. Government, Agriculture, Soil Conservation Service"; hires engin., soil conservation degrees, etc.)

Board of Governors of the Federal Reserve System
Division of Human Resources Management MS156
20th and C Ave., NW
Washington, DC 20551
202/452-3880
(Primarily hires econ. and attorneys in addition to administrative staff.)

U.S. Department of Commerce
Below we've listed major branches of the Commerce Department and the appropriate personnel addresses. Directly below are the main regional personnel offices. For information on regional Commerce Department jobs, call or write:

Personnel Officer
Central Administrative Support Center
U.S. Department of Commerce
601 E. 12th St.
Kansas City, MO 64106
816/426-7463

Personnel Officer
Eastern Administrative Support Center

U.S. Department of Commerce
200 World Trade Ctr.
Norfolk, VA 23510
757/441-6516

Personnel Officer
Western Administrative Support Center
U.S. Department of Commerce
7600 Sand Point Way, NE
BIN C 15700
Seattle, WA 98115
206/526-6053

Office of the Secretary
Office of Personnel Operations
U.S. Department of Commerce
14th and Constitution Ave., NW
Rm. 5877
Washington, DC 20230
202/482-0490

(Manage and direct Commerce Department policy, liaison-type jobs; hires business/lib. arts/law/comp. backgrounds.)

Bureau of the Census
Personnel Division
Room 1412, Bldg. Three
Washington, DC 20233
301/457-3371 (for college graduates)
301/457-4499 (vacancy listing)
(Hires stat., comp., and cartographers primarily.)

Bureau of Economic Analysis
Office of Personnel Operations
1444 L St. NW
Washington, DC 20230
202/606-5556

(Hires econ., stat., comp. sci., and acct. primarily.)

Bureau of Export Administration
14th St. & Constitution Ave., NW Room 1069
Washington, DC 20230
202/482-1900
(Licenses exports; hires tech., enforcement, engin., etc.)

Economic Affairs
(same address as above)
(Develops commercial policy; hires managers, economists.)

Economic Development Adminstration
(same address as Bureau of Export Administration)
202/482-5112
(Provides loans and aid to carry out economic development in the United States; hires managers, planners.)

Minority Business Development Agency
441 Fourth St. NW, Ste. 970N
Washington, DC 20001
202/724-1385
(Promotes minority business: call for the number and address of nearest local office.)

National Institute of Standards and Technology
Personnel Officer
Room A-123, Admin. Bldg.
Gaithersburg, MD 20899
301/975-3008
(Formerly the National Bureau of Standards; tests and studies new technology and materials; hires engin., comp. backgrounds, etc.)

National Marine Fishery Service
Personnel Division
1315 East West Hwy.
Silver Spring, MD 20910
301/713-0527
(An exciting agency that monitors the sea, sky, space, and sun. Hires scientists, econ., etc.)

National Technical Information Service
Office of Personnel
Operations
5285 Port Royal Rd.
Springfield, VA 22161
703/487-4680
(Sales-supported agency that markets technical reports, etc. Hires marketing majors, etc.)

Office of the Inspector General
Personnel Officer
Department of Commerce
14th and Constitution Ave. NW
Room 7713
Washington, DC 20230
202/482-4948
(Hires audit., law enforc. primarily.)

Patent and Trademark Office
Office of Personnel
Crystal Park 1, Rm. 707
Arlington, VA 22202
703/305-8231
Employment hot lines:
1/800/368-3064 (patent examiners)
703/305-4221 (24-hour job vacancies)
(Hires most backgrounds, partic. engin., sci.)

Commission on Civil Rights
Personnel Officer
624 9th St., NW
Washington, DC 20425
202/376-8364
(Hires econ., law, etc., backgrounds.)

Commodity Futures Trading Commission
Director of Personnel
3 Lafayette
1155 21 St. NW
Washington, DC 20581
202/418-5000
(Hires acct.,
investigators, law., comp. backgrounds primarily.)

Consumer Product Safety Commission
Chief of Operations
Division of Personnel
Management

4330 East West Hwy.
Bethesda, MD 20207
301/504-0100

(Works with industry
and the public; hires
engin., comp., health

sci., lib. arts
backgrounds.)

Department of the Army
Total Army Personnel
Command
Attn: TAPC-CPS-C
Pentagon
Room 1A909
Alexandria, VA 22332-0320
703/695-2589
(Contact for
information on army
employers not
mentioned below, and
for information on the
Army Materiel
Command, which
employs 100,000
military and civilians—
especially engin., acct.,
and librarians—across
the country.)

Army Corps of Engineers
Civilian Personnel
Division
Attn.: CEPE-CS
20 Massachusetts Ave.
NW, Rm. 4213
Washington, DC

20314-1000
202/761-0660
(Employs more than
40,000 civilians—hires
mostly engin., acct.,
and mgmt.
backgrounds.)

Army Finance and Accounting Center
Human Resources
Directorate
Attn: FINCU-DF,
8899 East 56th St.
Indianapolis, IN
46249-0301
317/546-9211
(Hires acct./fin./
admin./econ./comp.
sci., etc.)

Army Information Systems Command
Civilian Personnel
Office
Recruitment and
Placement
Army Garrison-FH
Fort Huachuca, AZ
85613-6000
602/533-2424
or

Army Information Systems Command
Civilian Personnel
Office
Recruitment and
Placement
Army Garrison-FR
Fort Ritchie, MD
21719-5010
301/733-7100
(Hires most college
majors to become
comm. spec., personnel
admin., systems
analysts, etc.)

Military Traffic Management Command
Career Program
Administrator
Attn.: MT-PEC
5611 Columbia Pike,
Room 735
Falls Church, VA
22041-5050
703/681-6892
(Hires engin.,
transport., lib. arts,
etc.)

Department of the Navy
Washington, DC
20350-1000
Hires people from most
backgrounds; for
civilian jobs, with any
of the following
commands: **Naval Air Systems, Naval Sea**

Systems, Space and Naval Warfare Systems, Medical, Naval Intelligence, Naval Security, Naval Military Personnel, Naval Supply Systems, Naval Facilities Engineering, Naval

Telecommunications, Naval Education, Military Sealift and **Chief of Naval Research**; for
personnel and Equal
Opportunity jobs
contact one of the
Regional Offices of Civilian Personnel

Management (OCPM)
listed below:

Staffing Division
Northeast Region
Office of Civilian
Personnel
Management
Bldg. 75-3, Naval Base
Philadelphia, PA
19112-5006
215/697-2000

Staffing Division
OCPM Capital Region
1921 Jefferson Davis
Hwy.
Crystal Mall No. 2
Rm. 417
Arlington, VA 22241
703/607-2297

Staffing Division
Pacific Region Human
Resources
Office of Civilian
Personnel Management

178 Main St., Bldg. 499
Pearl Harbor, HI 96818
808/471-0565

Staffing Division
Southeast Region
Office of Civilian
Personnel Management
5301 Robin Hood Rd.
Suite 130 A
Norfolk, VA 23513
757/444-1507

Office of Civilian
Human Resources
2730 McKean St.,
Ste. 1
San Diego, CA
92136-5294
619/556-4961

Administrator,
Logistics Career Intern
Program
Navy Career
Management Center
P.O. Box 2010

Mechanicsburg, PA
17055-0787
717/790-2000
(For civilian
internships, career
management
programs.)

Administrator,
Contracting Career
Intern Program
(same address as
above)

Comptroller
Navy Program
Management Office
153 Ellyson Ave.
Suite F
Pensacola, FL 32508-
5114
904/452-3783
(For financial
management career
intern program.)

**Department of the
Air Force**
hires from most back-
grounds, particularly
engin., acct., and comp.
sci.: for civilian jobs,
contact the Central
Civilian Personnel Of-
fice at your nearest Air

Force base; also check
ads, announcements
sent to nearby colleges,
and check the Air Force
Association magazine,
listed under Associa-
tions above.)

**Air Force Civilian
Personnel**

**Management
Center/DPCR**
Randolph AFB,
San Antonio, TX
78150-6421
210/652-6224
(For career intern
inquiries.)

**Defense Contract
Audit Agency**
CPO 8725 John J.
Kingman Rd. Ste. 2135
Ft. Velzoir, VA
22060-6219
703/767-2200
(Hires acct., etc., for
auditing jobs. Contact
this central office for

addresses of the six
regional offices.)

**Defense Information
Systems Agency**
Special Programs Unit
Civilian Personnel
Office
701 Courthouse Rd.
Bldg. Two, Room 210
Arlington, VA 22204

703/607-4000
(Employs comp., elec.
engin. backgrounds.)

**Defense Investigative
Service**
Resources Directorate
Personnel Operations
Divison
1340 Braddock Pl.
Alexandria, VA

22314-1651
703/325-1312
(Conducts security investigations, hires all majors for investigator and industrial/personnel security jobs; contact one of the 10 local personnel offices nearest you.)

Defense Logistics Agency
Civilian Personnel
380 Morrison Rd.
Columbus, OH 43213
1-800/458-7903
(Provides services— management of supplies and contract admin. for the military. Hires various backgrounds for many areas of management. Contact above for one of the 18 local offices near you.)

Defense Mapping Agency
Personnel Staffing Specialist
Aerospace Center
Attn.: POR
3200 S. Second St., Bldg. 37
St. Louis, MO 63118
314/263-4460
(Hires phys. sci., cart., geo., math., comp. sci. backgrounds.)

Department of Education
Office of Personnel
Department of Education
600 Independence Ave. SW
Washington, DC 20202

202/401-0559
(For DC-area jobs— call for numbers of 11 regional offices; hires ed., lib. arts, and poli. sci. backgrounds.)

Department of Energy
Headquarters
Operations Division
1000 Independence Ave., SW, Room 4E-090
Washington, DC 20585
202/586-8558
(Call for the numbers of the more than 17 local offices; hires acct., comp. sci., admin., eng., etc., backgrounds.)

Environmental Protection Agency
Recruitment Center
(PM-224)
401 M St, SW
Washington, DC 20460
202/260-2090
(The EPA also has regional offices with employment sections in 10 major cities; call above for addresses; hires most sci. backgrounds, as well as pub. admin., engin., and pol. sci.)

Equal Employment Opportunity Commission
Job Information Center
Equal Employment Opportunity Commission
1801 L St., NW
Washington, DC 20507
202/663-4337
(Hires primarily acct.,

bus., and law backgrounds.)

Executive Office of the President
Director of Personnel
Office of Administration
725 17th St., NW
Washington, DC 20503
202/395-1088
(Comprises 15 agencies that provide operational staff support to the president; includes the **Office of Management and Budget** and the **Office of Administration**; hires bus., econ., pub. admin., stat. backgrounds.)

Farm Credit Administration
Human Resources Division
1501 Farm Credit Dr.
McLean, VA 22102-5090
703/883-4000
(Banks and credit associations that lend to farmers; hires acct., agribusiness, bus., banking backgrounds.)

Federal Communications Commission
Associate Managing Director
Human Resources Management
1919 M St., NW, Room 212
Washington, DC 20554
202/418-0126
(Hires engin., law, econ., comp. spec.)

**Federal Deposit
Insurance Association**
Director of Personnel
550 17th St., NW
Washington, DC 20429
202/393-8400
(Hires all backgrounds,
including paralegals.)

**Federal Emergency
Management Agency**
Headquarters,
Operations Division
Office of Personnel,
Room 816
500 C St., SW
Washington, DC 20472
202/646-2500
202/646-3244 (job hot
line)
(Hires acct., bus.,
educ., pub. admin.,
comp. sci., law,
military backgrounds,
etc.)

**Federal Maritime
Commission**
Director of Personnel
800 N. Capitol St., NW
Washington, DC
20573-0001
202/523-5773
(Hires acct., bus. econ.,
law, etc.)

**Federal Retirement
Thrift Investment**

Board
Personnel Officer
1250 H St., NW
Suite 400
Washington, DC 20005
202/942-1600
(Hires acct., bus.,
comp. sci., law,
marketing, lib. arts.)

**Federal Trade
Commission**
Division of Personnel
Sixth and Pennsylvania
Ave. NW, Room 148
Washington, DC 20580
202/326-2020
(For DC-area jobs;
contact for addresses of
10 regional offices;
hires acct., bus.,
paralegals, sec., etc.)

**General Accounting
Office**
Office of Recruitment
441 G St., NW,
Room 4043-OD
Washington, DC 20548
202/512-5811
(Hires acct., bus.
admin., comp. sci.,
econ., fin., MIS, pol.
sci., soc. sci., etc.)

**General Services
Administration**
Office of Personnel

Central Office
18th and F Sts., NW
Washington, DC 20405
202/501-0398
(Contact for address of
field and regional
offices; hires arch.,
comp. sci., law, bus.
admin., etc.; note that
Kansas City regional
office has a job hot
line: 816/926-7804.)

**Government Printing
Office**
Chief, Employment
Branch
732 N. Capitol and H
Sts., NW
Washington, DC 20401
202/512-0000
(Hires acct., chem.,
comp. sci., engin.,
printing, mgmt., art and
design.)

**National Imagery
Mapping Agency**
Personnel Staffing
Specialist
Hydrographic &
Topographic Ctr.
4600 Sangamore Rd.
Bethesda, MD
20816-5003
301/227-3400

**Department of Health
and Human Services**
Division of Personnel
Operations
330 Independence Ave.,
SW, Room 1040
Washington, DC 20201
202/619-0146
(For HQ jobs—contact
for addresses of re-
gional offices; hires

acct., lawyers, most
other backgrounds.)

**Agency for Toxic
Substances and
Disease Registry**
Personnel Office
1600 Clifton Rd., NE
Atlanta, GA 30333
404/639-3311

(Hires sci. med.
backgrounds.)

**Alcohol, Drug Abuse,
and Mental Health
Administration**
Personnel Office
5600 Fishers Ln.,
Room 14c-14
Rockville, MD 20857
301/443-5407

(Hires med., psych., social workers, etc.)

Centers for Disease Control
Personnel Office
1600 Clifton Rd., NE
Atlanta, GA 30333
404/639-3311
(Hires sci. tech. and admin. primarily.)

Administration for Children and Family
Division of Management and Regional Operations
Department of Health and Human Services
901 D St., SW
Washington, DC 20447
202/401-9300
(Employees administer family programs; hires acct. and auditors.)

Food and Drug Administration
Division of Personnel Management
5600 Fishers Ln.,
Room 7B-43
Rockville, MD 20857
800/532-4440
(Hires med., sci., vet., and admin. primarily.)

Health Care Financing Administration
7500 Security Blvd.

Baltimore, MD 21244
410/786-3000
(For regional positions, contact HQ for addresses of regional personnel offices; hires acct., pub. admin., soc. sci., etc.)

Health Resources and Services Administration
Office of Personnel
5600 Fishers Ln.,
Room 14A-46
Rockville, MD 20857
301/443-5460
(Hires acct., admin. primarily; contact HQ for regional office addresses.)

Indian Health Service
Personnel Operations Branch
5600 Fishers Ln.,
Room 4B-44
Rockville, MD 20857
301/443-6520
(Hires dentists, hygienists, doctors, nurses, etc.)

National Institutes of Health
Division of Personnel Management
9000 Rockville Pike
Bldg. 31, Room B3C15

Bethesda, MD 20892
301/496-2403
(Hires dent., med., nursing, sci., tech., etc.)

Office of Human Development Services
(Same address as above; hires social service backgrounds for jobs that support state social services programs.)

Public Health Service
Personnel Office
OASH Personnel Operations Office
5600 Fishers Ln.,
Room 17A-08
Rockville, MD 20857
301/443-1986
(Hires health serv., sci., acct. backgrounds.)

Social Security Administration
Recruitment and Placement Branch
West High Rise Bldg.
6401 Security Blvd.,
Room G-120
Baltimore, MD 21235
410/965-4506
(Hires comp. sci. and a wide range of other backgrounds.)

Department of Housing and Urban Development
Chief, Staffing and Classification Branch
Office of Personnel and Training, APE
451 Seventh St., SW, Room 2258
Washington, DC 20410-3100
202/708-0408
(Contact for regional and field office addresses; hires acct., bus., eng., admin. backgrounds.)

**Department of the
Interior**
Personnel Office
Office of the Secretary
1849 C St., NW
Washington, DC 20240
202/208-3100

**Bureau of Indian
Affairs**
Division of Personnel
Management
Headquarters
1849 C St. NW
Washington, DC 20240
202/208-3711
(Hires sci., comp., lib.
arts, ed., social work
backgrounds.)

**Bureau of Land
Management**
Division of Personnel
18th and C Sts., NW
(MIB)
Washington, DC 20240
202/452-5120
(Contact for regional
offices; hires sci.,
animal sci., engin., lib.
arts backgrounds,
mechanics, etc.)

**Bureau of
Reclamation**

Headquarters
18th and C Sts., NW
Washington, DC 20240
202/208-4662
(Contact for regional
addresses; hires sci.,
engin., electronics,
econ. backgrounds
primarily.)

**Minerals
Management Service**
381 Elden St.
Herndon, VA 20170-
4817
703/787-1414
(Hires sci. and admin.)

National Park Service
Headquarters
Branch of Personnel
Operations
18th and C Sts., NW
P.O. Box 37127
Washington, DC 20013
202/208-4649
(Contact for regional
offices; hires
achaeologists, bus.
admin., hist., lib. arts,
foresters, etc.)

**Office of Surface
Mining Reclamation
and Enforcement**

Personnel Office
1951 Constitution Ave.,
NW—4451B
Washington, DC 20240
202/208-2953
(Hires accts., bio.,
engin. primarily.)

**U.S. Fish and Wildlife
Service**
Headquarters
440 N. Fairfax,
Rm. 308
Arlington, VA 22203
703/358-1743
(Contact for regional
offices; hires bio., lib.
arts, etc.)

**U.S. Geological
Survey**
USGS National Center
MS-215
12201 Sunrise
Valley Dr.
Reston, VA 20192
703/648-4000
(Contact for regional
offices; hires sci.,
engin. mainly; note that
USGS Central Regional
Office in Denver has a
job hot line:
303/236-5846.)

Department of Justice
Personnel Services
1200 Pennsylvania Ave.
Washington, DC 20530
202/514-6814
(Hires bus. admin.,
comp. sci., lib. arts
backgrounds,
paralegals, etc.; see
below for lawyers.)

Bureau of Prisons
Chief of Recruiting

Homeowners Loan
Corporation Bldg.
320 First St., NW,
Room 400
Washington, DC 20534
202/307-1304
(Hires criminal justice
backgrounds, accts.,
med., law enforcement,
soc. work, etc.;
increasingly prefers
college grads.)

**Drug Enforcement
Administration**
Office of Personnel
700 Army Navy Dr.
Arlington, VA 22202
202/307-4000
(Hires accts., chem.,
lib. arts, language
spec.; spec. agents with
acct., pilot/maritime,
language, tech., and
legal backgrounds in
demand.)

Executive Office for U.S. Attorneys
Security and Personnel
950 Pennsylvania Ave. NW
Washington, DC 20530-0001
202/514-2121
(gen. Treas. no.)
(Supports U.S. Attorneys' offices; hires wide variety of backgrounds for admin. and legal support positions.)

Federal Bureau of Investigation
Personnel Resources
935 Pennsylvania Ave. NW, Rm. PA750
Washington, DC 20535
202/324-4991
(Employment applications for special agents are usually initiated through the applicant coordinator at each of the 59 local FBI field offices— check your local phone book; for information and/or for most support positions as clerks, typists, etc., contact address above.)

Immigration and Naturalization Service
Central Office
Personnel Division
1425 I St., NW, Room 6032
Washington, DC 20536
202/514-2530
(Contact for regional employment offices; hires all academic backgrounds.)

Office of Attorney Personnel Management
Department of Justice
Main Bldg., Room 4311
10th St. and Constitution Ave., NW
Washington, DC 20530
202/514-6877
(Hires attorneys.)

U.S. Marshals Service
Personnel Management Division
600 Army-Navy Drive
Arlington, VA 22202
202/307-9600
(Hires all academic majors, accts., comp. sci., police admin.; dep. U.S. marshal positions require passing written test.)

Department of Labor
Office of Personnel Management Services
National Capital Service Center
Frances Perkins Bldg., Rm. S1002
200 Constitution Ave., NW
Washington, DC 20210
800/366-2753
(Hire most backgrounds.)

Bureau of Labor Statistics
College Recruitment/Special Programs
Department of Labor
2 Massachusetts Ave. NE
Washington, DC 20212
202/606-7828
(Hires most backgrounds, comp. programmers, econ., stats.)

Employment Standards Administration
Division of Staffing and Employee Relations
Frances Perkins Bldg., Room 53308
200 Constitution Ave., NW
Washington, DC 20210
202/219-6666
(Hires most academic backgrounds.)

Employment and Training Administration
Division of Staffing and Employee Relations
Frances Perkins Bldg., Rm. S5214
200 Constitution Ave., NW
Washington, DC 20210
202/219-5489
(Hires bud. analysts, econ., etc.)

Merit Systems Protection
Personnel Division, Room 850
1120 Vermont Ave., NW
Washington, DC 20419

202/653-5916
(Employees are
primarily attorneys and
support staff; hears and
decides federal
employment cases.)

**Mine Safety and
Health
Administration**
Human Resources
Division
Personnel Systems and
Services Branch
Department of Labor
4015 Wilson Blvd.
Ballston Tower #3,
Room 500

Arlington, VA 22203
703/235-1352
(Hires hygienists, all
backgrounds as safety
spec.)

**National Aeronautics
and Space
Administration
(NASA)**
NASA Headquarters
DP—Human
Resources
300 E St. SW
Washington, DC 20546
202/358-0100
(Employs primarily
engin., comp. sci.,
math., physicists, and

support staff; contact
for regional
employment and
addresses.)

**Occupational Safety
and Health
Administration**
Office of Personnel
Management
Department of Labor
Frances Perkins Bldg.,
Rm. N3308
200 Constitution Ave.,
NW
Washington, DC 20210
202/219-8148
(Hires all backgrounds
as mgmt. analysts, etc.)

**National Archives
and Records
Administration**
Maintains federal
records nationwide;
hires history, pol. sci.
backgrounds as well as
paper conservation
specialists. Key
employment addresses
below.

**Personnel Operations
Branch**
9700 Page Blvd.
St. Louis, MO 63132
314/263-3901
(General employment

information; contact
for addresses and
numbers of Federal
Records Centers
nationwide.)

**Office of the National
Archives**
Seventh St. and
Pennsylvania Ave., NW
Washington, DC 20408
202/501-5402
(Archivist or paper
conservator positions.)

Personnel Office
Office of Federal
Records Center

Civilian Personnel
Records
111 Winnebago St.
St. Louis, MO 63118-
4199
314/425-5761
(Archives specialists
positions.)

Personnel Office
Office of the *Federal
Register*
800 N. Capital St. NW,
Ste. 700
Washington, DC 20408
202/523-5240
(Writer-editors.)

**National Credit Union
Administration**
Personnel Management
Specialist
Personnel Office
National Credit Union
Administration

1775 Duke St.
Alexandria, VA
22314-3428
703/518-6300
(Hires nationwide,
principally credit
examiners.)

**National Endowment
for the Humanities**
Personnel Management
Specialist
Personnel Office
Rm. 416
1100 Pennsylvania

Ave., NW
Washington, DC 20506
202/606-8415
(Hires arts/hist./lit./
backgrounds as
program spec.)

**National Labor
Relations Board**
Personnel Operations
1099 14th St. NW
Washington, DC 20570
202/273-1991
(Investigates unfair
labor practices; hires
acct., bus. admin., law
backgrounds for field
examiner positions.)

**National Science
Foundation**
Staffing Assistant
Division of Personnel
and Management
4201 Wilson Blvd.
Arlington, VA 22230
703/306-1234
(Hires most majors,
pref. w/ acct., sci. to
serve as grants
specialists, etc.)

**Nuclear Regulatory
Commission**
College Recruitment
Coordinator
Mail Stop T-3A-2
Office of Personnel
Washington, DC 20555
301/415-7516 or
301/415-7530
(Hires engin., sci.
primarily.)

**Office of Personnel
Management**
Recruitment and

Special Employment
Programs Branch
1900 E St., NW, Room
1469
Washington, DC 20415
202/606-2700
(Hires HR
backgrounds, all
majors to serve in
various personnel
specialties.)

**Railroad Retirement
Board**
Bureau of Personnel
844 N. Rush St.
Chicago, IL 60611
312/751-4580
(Hires acct., audit., all
academic backgrounds
as well as crim. just.
for examiner position.)

**Securities and
Exchange
Commission**
Office of Personnel
450 Fifth St., NW
Washington, DC 20549
202/942-4150
(Regulates securities
markets; hires
accountants, finance,
comp. sci., attorneys,
economists, etc.)

**Selective Service
System**
Personnel Services
Director of the
Selective Service
System, Att. RMH
National Headquarters
1515 Wilson Blvd.
Arlington, VA 22209-
2425
703/235-2258

(Hires acct., comp. sci.,
bus., and pub. admin.
primarily.)

**Small Business
Administration**
Central Personnel
Office
409 3rd St., SW
Washington, DC 20416
202/205-6780
(Call or write for
regional office
addresses; hires acct.,
bank., credit, bus.
comp., sci., and pub.
admin., etc.)

**Smithsonian
Institution**
Chief, Staffing Services
Branch
Employment Office
995 L'Enfant Plaza SW
Suite 2100
Washington, DC 20560
202/287-3100
24-hr. Job Hotline:
202/287-3102
(Hires curators in
various fields, support
staff; turnover and
hence employment
opportunities are
limited; easiest for
secretaries, etc.)

**Tennessee Valley
Authority**
Employment Services,
ET 5C 50 P-K
400 W. Summit Hill Dr.
Knoxville, TN 37902
615/632-2101
(Hires engin., comp.
sci., etc.)

Department of Transportation
Central Employment Information Office
M-18
400 Seventh St., SW
Washington, DC 20590
202/366-4000
(Hires acct., bus. admin., lib. arts backgrounds.)

U.S. Coast Guard
Civilian Personnel Division
Transpoint Bldg., Room 4100
2100 Second St., SW
Washington, DC 20593
202/267-2229
(Civ. employment for accts., bus. admin., engin., etc.)

Federal Aviation Administration
Headquarters
400 Seventh St., SW
Washington, DC 20590
202/366-4000
(Hires elec. tech., engin., controllers, etc.; regional employment offices for all regional employment, including air traffic control specialists, are on page 255.)

Federal Highway Administration
Office of Personnel and Training
400 Seventh St., SW, Room 4334
Washington, DC 20590
202/366-0541
(Hires acct., bus., civ. engin., etc.)

Federal Railroad Administration
Office of Personnel
400 Seventh St., SW, Room 8232
Washington, DC 20590
202/366-0584
(Hires acct., econ., lawyers, etc.)

Maritime Administration
Office of Personnel
400 Seventh St., SW, Room 8101
Washington, DC 20590
202/366-4143
(Supports U.S. merchant marine, including training at the Merchant Marine Academy, etc.; hires acct., econ., mech/marine engin., etc.)

National Highway Traffic Safety Administration
Office of Personnel
400 Seventh St., SW, Room 5306
Washington, DC 20590
202/366-2602
(Hires engin., lawyers, math., lib. arts backgrounds.)

Research and Special Programs Administration
Personnel Office
Department of Transportation
400 Seventh St., SW, Room 8401
Washington, DC 20590
202/366-5608
(Analyzes hazardous material transport; hires engin. as well as lib. arts/bus. backgrounds.)

Urban Mass Transportation Administration
Office of Personnel
400 Seventh St., SW, Room 7101
Washington, DC 20590
202/366-2513
(Hires bus. admin., engin., etc.)

Department of the Treasury
1500 Pennsylvania Ave., NW
Washington, DC 20220
202/622-2000

Bureau for Alcohol, Tobacco, and

Firearms
Personnel Staffing Specialist
650 Massachusetts Ave. NW, Rm. 4170
Washington, DC 20226
202/927-8610
(The ATF hires all

majors; inspects, investigates, and enforces federal firearms, explosives, alcohol, violations—hires special agents, inspectors, bomb analysts, etc.)

Bureau of Engraving and Printing
Office of Industrial Relations
14th and C Sts., SW, Room 202-A
Washington, DC 20228
202/874-2778
(Hires applicants for printing and engineering positions as well as police and office work.)

Bureau of the Public Debt
200 3rd St.
Parkersburg, WV 26106-1328
304/480-7708
(Hires acct., comp. analysts, etc.)

Departmental Offices
Office of Personnel Resources
Employment Section, Room 1316
Department of the Treasury
15th St. and Pennsylvania Ave., NW
Washington, DC 20220
202/622-2000
(Hires economists, accts., etc.)

Federal Law Enforcement Training Center
Chief of Staffing
Glynco Facility
Glynco, GA 31524
912/267-2100
(Hires enforcement and investigative instructors.)

Financial Management Service
Recruitment
Coordinator
1500 Pennsylvania Ave., NW
Washington, DC 20220
202/622-2000
(Coordinates gov't. financial operations; hires mostly acct., comp. backgrounds.)

Internal Revenue Service
Personnel Office
Contact local IRS office

Office of the Comptroller of the Currency
250 E St., SW
Washington, DC 20219
202/874-5000
(Charged with upholding the safety of the U.S. banking system—hires accounting, business, banking, and econ. majors. There are six district offices nationwide. Below is the Central District address:

Office of the Comptroller of the Currency
1 Financial Pl., Suite 2700
440 S. LaSalle St.
Chicago, IL 60605
312/360-8800

Office of Thrift Supervision
Human Resources Division
1700 G St., NW, 2nd Fl.
Washington, DC 20552
202/906-6000

(Hires accts., bus. admin., etc., for S&L examiners, comp. prog., econ., lawyers, etc.)

Savings Bonds Division
200 3rd St.
Parkersburg, WV 26106
304/480-6112
(Hires managers, comm. spec., lib. arts backgrounds.)

Secret Service
Chief of Staffing
1800 G St., NW, Room 912
Washington, DC 20223
202/435-5800
(Four thousand employees with 65 field offices, hires primarily from corrections, criminology, or law enforcement backgrounds for special agent positions.)

U.S. Customs Service
OHR-Gelman Bldg.
1301 Constitution Ave., NW
Washington, DC 20229
202/634-5250
(Hires from virtually all disciplines for management, enforcement, and investigative positions.)

U.S. Mint
Chief of Staffing
633 Third St., NW, Suite 655
Washington, DC 20220
202/874-9300
(Hires bus./marketers.)

U.S. Postal Service
General Manager
Headquarters Personnel
Division
475 L'Enfant Plz., SW
Washington, DC
20260-4261
202/268-3646
(Also contact your
local post office.)

**Department of
Veterans Affairs**
Recruitment and
Examining Division
(054E)
810 Vermont Ave., NW
Washington, DC 20420
202/273-5400
(Employs applicants
from various

backgrounds, for
various departments;
medical personnel
check one of the 172
VA medical centers
located near you—
phone and address in
local phone directory
under "U.S.
Government.")

U.S. GOVERNMENT EMPLOYERS: JUDICIAL BRANCH

Personnel Office
U.S. Supreme Court
Bldg.
1 First St., NE
Washington, DC 20543
202/479-3404
(For all but

administrative office
and claims courts
inquiries.)

Personnel Division
Administrative Office
of the U.S. Courts,
Room L701

1 Columbus Circle NE
Washington, DC 20544
202/273-2777

Federal Claims Court
717 Madison Pl., NW
Washington, DC 20005
202/273-1270

U.S. GOVERNMENT EMPLOYERS: LEGISLATIVE BRANCH

U.S. Senate
Placement Office
Washington, DC 20510
202/224-9167

**U.S. House of
Representatives**
Office of Human
Resources
Cannon House Office
Bldg., Rm. 263
Washington, DC
20515-6610
Att: CAOKEF
202/226-6731

Library of Congress
Recruitment and
Placement Office,
Department E
The Library of Congress
101 Independence Ave.,
SE, LM 107
Washington, DC 20540
202/707-5627
(Hires librarians, bio.,
comp. sci., math., soc.
sci. backgrounds, wide
variety of tech. support
and mgmt. positions.)

**Office of Technology
Assessment**
600 Pennsylvania
Ave., SE
Washington, DC 20003
202/224-8996
(Evaluates technical
and scientific issues for
Congress.)

**US Congressional
Budget Office**
Room 410
Ford House Office Bldg.
Washington, DC 20515
202/226-2621

NATIONAL POLITICAL ORGANIZATIONS

**Democratic National
Committee**
430 S. Capitol St., SE
Washington, DC 20003
202/863-8000

(Clearinghouse for
applicants for work,
primarily voluntary, on
political campaigns.)

**Democratic
Congressional
Campaign Committee**
same address
202/863-8000

Democratic Senatorial Campaign Committee
same address
202/863-8000

Republican National Committee
310 First St., SE
Washington, DC 20003
202/863-8500

(As with the Democrats above, campaign work is one way of breaking into the Washington scene.)

National Republican Congressional Committee
320 First St., SE

Washington, DC 20003
202/479-7000

National Republican Senatorial Committee
425 Second St., NE
Washington, DC 20002
202/675-6000

GOVERNMENT ASSOCIATIONS

Air Force Association
1501 Lee Hwy.
Arlington, VA 22209-1198
703/247-5800
(Publishes periodical with directory, listings; check Almanac issue in May.)

American Society for Public Administration
1120 G St., NW,
Suite 700
Washington, DC 20005-3885
202/393-7878
(Publishes periodical with job listings, etc.)

Capitol Hill Women's Caucus
P.O. Box 599
Longworth House Office Building
Independence and New Jersey Aves.
Washington, DC 20515
202/986-0994
(Publishes list of jobs for members.)

Government Finance Officer Association
(Municipal Finance Officers Association of the United States and Canada)
180 N. Michigan Ave.
Suite 800
Chicago, IL 60601

312/977-9700
(Publishes periodical with job listings.)

International City Management Association
777 N. Capitol St., NE
Washington, DC 20002
202/289-4262
(Publishes directories, *ICMA Newsletter,* periodical with job listings, etc.; maintains internship program for undergrad. and grad. students—contact Joy Pierson, internship coordinator, at 202/962-3659.)

GOVERNMENT DIRECTORIES

Congressional Yellow Book
Leadership Directories, Inc.
104 Fifth Ave., 2nd Fl.
New York, NY 10011
212/627-4140
(Lists members of Congress, committees, etc.)

Federal Regional Yellow Book
Leadership Directories, Inc.
104 Fifth Ave.,
2nd Fl.
New York, NY 10011
212/627-4140
(Lists thousands of local federal offices nationwide—useful for

the non-DC federal job hunter.)

Federal Yellow Book
address same as above
(Lists thousands of major employees of Executive branch.)

FOCIS: The Federal Occupation and Career Information System
National Technical

Information Service (NTIS)
5285 Port Royal Rd.
Springfield, VA 22161-0001
703/487-4650
(PC-based interactive expert system that complements Federal Career Directory; guides user through hundreds of federal white-collar positions in hundreds of federal agencies, with descriptions of type of job, description of work, address,

qualifications, etc. Current version doesn't include job openings; future versions may. Cost at time of writing was $49.95; updated yearly.)

State and Regional Associations of the United States
Columbia Books
1212 New York Ave., NW, Ste. 330
Washington, DC 20005
202/898-0662
(Lists most associations state by

state and region by region; useful for the job hunter looking to contact local affiliates of major associations to use them to help in job hunt.)

U.S. Court Directory
Superintendent of Documents
U.S. Government Printing Office
Washington, DC 20402-9325
202/512-1800
(Lists federal courts nationwide.)

GOVERNMENT PERIODICALS

City & State
740 N. Rush St.
Chicago, IL 60611
312/649-5220
(Biweekly newspaper for state and local officials.)

Community Jobs
ACCESS
30 Irving Pl.
New York, NY 10003
212/475-1001
(Monthly; lists hundreds of jobs in the nonprofit sector.)

Federal Career Opportunities
P.O. Box 1059
Vienna, VA 22183-1059
703/281-0200
(Thousands of job listings.)

Federal Jobs Digest
325 Pennsylvania Ave., SE

Washington, DC 20003
800/824-5000
(Lists thousands of federal jobs, with contacts and addresses to which to apply; grades and salary levels.)

Federal Times
6883 Commercial Dr.
Springfield, VA 22159
703/750-8920
(Mainly for federal employees; includes many job listings in back.)

Government Executive
1501 M St., NW
Suite 300
Washington, DC 20005
202/739-8400
(Ten issues, mainly for federal executives.)

Public Sector Job Bulletin
(midwest/eastern

edition)
P.O. Box 1222
Newton, IA 50208-1222
515/791-9019
(Biweekly; lists many public-sector, mostly local-gov't. middle-management jobs.)

Jobs Available
(western edition)
P.O. Box 1040
Modesto, CA 95353
209/571-2120
(Lists job openings in public administration and research.)

Journal of State Government
The Council of State Governments
Iron Works Pike
P.O. Box 11910
Lexington, KY 40578-1910
606/244-8000

(Quarterly, professional journal for state legislators.)

The National Journal
1501 M St., NW
Suite 300
Washington, DC 20005
202/739-8400
800/424-2921
(subscription)
(Weekly gov't. magazine; note that the regular subscription price is almost eight times the faculty/student rate.)

Nation's Cities
1301 Pennsylvania Ave., NW
Ste. 550
Washington, DC 20004
202/626-3040
(Weekly tabloid.)

Public Employee
1625 L St., NW
Washington, DC 20036
202/429-1144
(Huge-circulation tabloid to members of American Federation of State, County, and Local Employees; useful in getting a feel for the major issues and problems of gov't. employment.)

State Legislatures
1560 Broadway
Denver, CO 80202
303/830-2200

HEALTH CARE AND MEDICAL SPECIALISTS

▶ **Despite all the uncertainties, health care hiring in many areas will be strong.**

You may have read about hospitals, health care companies, and pharmaceutical companies cutting back on jobs as they tried to lower costs. But don't despair—the bottom line is that employment in this field will grow. In fact, the U.S. government projects that health care will be the fastest growing sector of the economy, creating 4.2 *million* new jobs by 2005; accounting for 17.2% of total job growth. Why? Despite cost-cutting, new technology will allow doctors to treat previously untreatable diseases, allowing more people to survive—and increasing employment for those who diagnose, treat, and take care of them. Meanwhile, the U.S. population as a whole is getting older—this means more work as well, since older people are more apt to need and use medical services. However, there are increasing uncertainties in the entire health care industry over the long term. Some experts predict that layoffs will continue—and increase—over the next 20 years as competition between health care providers (such as hospitals and HMOs) heats up.

But many other experts are saying that scenario is much too rosy. They point out that managed care programs—which push patients into (cheaper) outpatient services more frequently, and cost-conscious insurance companies, are pushing back the rate of job growth—*and will continue to do so in the foreseeable future.* For example, the 5% annual job growth rate is now about half of that—and this lower growth rate will continue.

The bottom line, then? Short-term prospects look good in certain specific areas, but the long-term picture is mixed, in spite of the optimistic view of the federal government. The key, of course, is pinpointing areas of probable growth. More specifics on these growth areas follow.

EMPLOYMENT OUTLOOK: relatively strong, depending on the specialty.

First the bad news: The odds are that hospital employment will grow more slowly than before, since the new trends are to cut costs by going into managed care programs, and to treat patients as much as possible on an out-patient basis—outside the hospital. This means a decline in administrative and support jobs in hospitals. But on the other hand, it means *more* job opportunities for home health aides and home health care agency nurses (see below).

Other major employment trends: continued high demand for hospital technical specialists, and to take care of an aging and sports conscious population, more jobs for physical and occupational therapists. Some details below:

Some of the fastest-growing areas:

HOME HEALTH CARE WORKERS: In terms of percentage increase, this is the fastest growing job category in the U.S., with a 119% increase in jobs projected by 2005. The downside is that the work is hard and low paid. Home health care workers do the hard work of health care, taking care of patients at home; dressing, bathing, cooking, and cleaning for them. Some more specialized workers help the severely disabled or children. The entry requirements are not high; many states require training, after which a certificate is issued, but the pay is low, averaging somewhere around $6 to $10 an hour.

PHYSICAL THERAPISTS: excellent job outlook; as the average American gets older, sports and exercise become more mainstream—and all told, more physical injuries result. Also, improved medicine now can save the severely injured, again increasing the demand for therapists who can help rehabilitate them. Career advantages: autonomy (over 20% are in private practice; this trend will increase as hospitals continue to emphasize outpatient care), relatively high pay, personal satisfaction. Requirements: increasing as field becomes more technical. For entry level: degree or certificate in the field, and license. Some states require continuing education. Also in strong demand: **occupational therapists** (who work with all types of disabled), **physical therapist assistants and aides, recreational therapists.**

MEDICAL TECHNICIANS: many areas are fast growing and in high demand. Some of the fastest growing: EEG technicians (electroencephalograph or, in effect, electric brain scan operators), radiological technicians, medical records technicians (even with administrative cutbacks, the long-term trend in this record-keeping area is strong, particularly for those with extensive computer expertise). And although new technology may reduce some employment needs in medical labs, on the other hand, the new emphasis on prevention points to more physicals, more lab tests, and maybe more jobs for lab technicians as well—some experts project 25% job growth in the next few years. Best Bets for jobs: rural areas without many technicians, West Coast and Rocky Mountain states.

NUTRITIONISTS: Now finding employment outside of hospitals, schools, and nursing homes, as food manufacturers and restaurant chains attempt to meet the needs of an increasingly health-conscious public and stringent new federal requirements with food labeling, etc. In addition, jobs can be found with PR and consulting firms, sports medicine and corporate wellness centers. An expanding specialty: gerontological nutrition, planning meals for the growing elderly population.

PHARMACISTS: Now finding employment outside hospitals and businesses—more are employed by a wide variety of health care providers, as well as with powerful pharmaceutical manufacturers.

Other rapidly growing employment areas include: respiratory therapists, speech pathologists and audiologists, opticians, and podiatrists. Although not growing as rapidly as the professions above, there are many opportunities for lab technicians as well, particularly in the expanding (but volatile) biotech labs in San Francisco and other centers.

Also expect a rise in employment of physicians assistants (PAs). These are usually graduates of an AMA-approved school who train for two years, and are certified to take the place of physicians during routine tasks like taking medical histories or making preliminary diagnoses.

▶ **Registered nurses: more job hassles on the horizon—and some creative solutions.**

Some experts are optimistic about job growth in this field, projecting hundreds of thousands of *new* jobs on the horizon. But others are concerned. Why? Cost-conscious insurance firms and managed care programs are trimming budgets, and RNs are among the first to go. Instead, they're replaced by non-RN personnel as medical assistants, UAPs (unlicensed assistive personnel), and LPNs (licensed practical nurses)—see page 98. This is not only putting strains on hiring; many RNs are complaining that this makes their work harder at the hospitals as well.

So is there good news? Yes. As demand drops at hospitals, it is increasing in home care, outpatient centers, and neighborhood clinics. And demand is strong for RNs with advanced backgrounds. One cheering statistic: 67% of 522 nursing schools surveyed said that almost 100% of their graduates with master's degrees had jobs lined up for them when they left school.

Bottom line: Nursing is a growing—but changing—field where the best opportunities and working conditions go to those with advanced degrees.

Here's a quick breakdown by industry segment:

Hospitals: the largest employer of RNs—with roughly 2 out of over 3 RN jobs in hospitals. But, while there should continue to be a need for hospital RNs, other health care sectors will be *much* stronger in terms of employment growth. Many hospitals have cut back on their RN staffs, often while outsourcing many of their office, housekeeping, and medical records departments, as well as such sophisticated clinical services as radiology and orthopedic surgery. In fact, the University of California at San Francisco's Center for Health Professions predicts a cut of 200,000 to 300,000 hospital nursing jobs by 2000. Why are hospitals such a poor employment bet these days? Hospital cost-cutting, the growth of HMOs and other nonhospital health care providers, a cutback in length of patient stays, and an increase in outpatient care. Along these lines, expect the most rapid job growth in hospital's outpatient facilities, such as same-day surgery, rehabilitation, and chemotherapy. In addition, RNs with administrative skills will probably see increased demand as the role of a nurse changes to accommodate cost-cutting. Nurse practitioners, who in most states can prescribe medicine and, in effect, replace some functions of physicians, will generally see increased demand as well, as cost-cutters use them to replace more highly paid physicians.

Home health care: should see the fastest growth in employment for RNs. Reasons? The growing number of older people in the population who require some sort of in-home nursing care; the growing consumer preference for at-home care; and technological advances that enable more complex treatments to be given at home. Home health care RNs who are able to perform complex procedures will be especially in demand.

Nursing homes: also headed for faster than average growth. Again, this is due to the increase in older people—many of whom will require long-term nursing home care. In addition, as hospital cost-cutting results in shorter patient stays, there will be an increase in nursing home admissions. Finally, expect a growth in units offering specialized long-term rehabilitation for stroke and head injury patients, Alzheimer's treatment, and the like.

Outpatient services: including physicians' offices and clinics, HMOs, emergency medical centers, ambulatory surgicenters, will provide increased job opportunities. As health care expands and more complex procedures are offered outside of hospitals, these health care providers will be growing—and employing more RNs.

Managed care facilities/organizations: A growing employment area as managed care continues to overtake the health care industry. RNs—and nurse practitioners especially—are being utilized in a number of different ways by HMOs. For example, NPs may perform patient assessments, do home visits for older patients, and the like.

General employment trends: With the move toward more integrated health care networks, RNs may be rotating among different jobs and settings. As a result, RNs will have to be more flexible than in the past. In addition, expect an even greater emphasis on skills and experience.

Another trend: more nurses are getting more education. Most employers prefer a four year B.S. degree over a two year associate degree. Reason: the field is getting much more complex.

Nursing practice options: More than 100,000 advanced practice nurses in several specialties are carving out new roles in health care.

Nurse Practitioners (NP): A burgeoning career option, NPs are qualified to handle a wide range of basic health problems and can prescribe medicines in 39 states at a lower cost than physicians. They have a master's degree and training in such medical areas as pediatrics or adult or family health care, in addition to a four-year nursing education. Average salary in 1992: $43,600.

Under a 1997 agreement in the New York area between a major HMO (Oxford Health Plans) and a prominent hospital (Columbia-Presbyterian Medical Center), NPs are being assigned primary care status—instead of doctors—in managing the basic health needs of patients; and they will be paid at physician rates. The pilot project could be expanded if research shows results comparable to that of physician care; some early positive indications arose when another HMO followed suit with a similar program.

Clinical Nurse Specialists (CNS): RNs with advanced nursing degrees—master's or doctoral—who are experts in such specialized clinical practices as mental health, cancer care, or neonatal health. Salary range (1992): $30,000 to $80,000.

Certified Registered Nurse Anesthetist (CRNA): The oldest of the advanced nursing specialists, CRNAs complete 2–3 years additional studies beyond their bachelor's degrees. They administer more than 65% of all anesthetics given to patients. Average salary (1992): $77,000.

Other career options for nurses: nursing computer programmer, nursing legal consultant (who offers expert testimony in court cases), nursing scientist, medical equipment sales, and insurance expert. Expect nurses to find increasingly more lucrative employment in these specialties, and especially as nurse executives, who supervise nurses and nursing schedules, and earn executive-size salaries, often well into the six figures.

▶ **Licensed practical nurses: also facing good employment prospects through 2005.**

Employment of licensed practical nurses (LPNs), who work under the direction of RNs or physicians, also should be increasing over the next few years. As with RNs, employment at hospitals is the slowest area of job growth. Hottest spots? Nursing homes, home health care services, HMOs, and outpatient treatment centers such as physicians' offices, clinics, emergency medical centers, and ambulatory surgicenters.

▶ **Physicians: a changing marketplace. Expect hotter competition in some areas.**

There are already 600,000 physicians in the U.S.—and some are saying there are too many, with almost 280 doctors for every 100,000 people—up from only 160 per in 1970. This has led a panel of experts from the National Academy of Sciences to recommend that no new medical schools be opened; to restrict the supply of incoming physicians. That said, there is still good job growth, particularly for those with *generalist,* rather than specialist, skills. The reason? Too many specialists. With the rise in managed health care, demand has increased for primary care physicians—and decreased for specialists. As a result, generalists in fields such as family practice, internal medicine, and pediatrics should be facing stronger employment opportunities. And not all specialist fields are crowded. Otolaryngology, geriatrics, psychiatry, obstetrics and gynecology, and urology specialties all reported strong demand last year.

Although for the past two years over half the medical school graduates have opted for training in these generalist fields, it usually takes from 10 to 15 years for the supply and demand in health care to balance. As such, the demand for generalists should remain strong through the next decade. Thereafter, expect a shift to specialties again, especially as baby boomers enter their 60s. (One caveat to this scenario regarding the need for generalists: As a *Forbes* magazine article noted, computerized expert systems may reduce demand for generalists in the future. Reason: These computerized systems may do much of the diagnostics that general practitioners or family practice doctors do today.)

Over the long term, expect to see tighter competition in general for physicians' jobs. One reason: As hospitals merge and shrink under cost pressures from managed care, senior doctors—as well as senior nurses—can expect to be demoted or dismissed. As a *New York Times* report put it, "No institution needs two chiefs of cardiac surgery." Another reason: the changing face of the health care industry. HMOs often use fewer doctors per patient than traditional health care arrangements. For example, an HMO can use one doctor for every 800 subscribers, while the national average is one doctor to 415 people. If HMOs continue growing at their recent rapid pace, there could well be an oversupply of doctors by the year 2000—again, especially in the specialist category. Already moves are on to circumvent this oversupply. For example, to decrease the number of physicians in New York (which accounts for 15% of physicians trained in the U.S.), Medicare is paying hospitals to reduce their resident staffing 20%–25% within six years. Hospitals will receive Medicare payments starting at $100,000 in the first year for each resident no longer on staff, with payments declining to zero in six years. Another example: The Pew Health Professions Commission, a panel of health care experts, recommended that medical school admissions should be cut by 20 to 25% over the next decade—even as medical school applications have been surging, and that residency programs (doctor training programs) should also be cut back (primarily by limiting the admission of graduates of foreign medical schools). Whether or not this plan is actually followed through remains to be seen, but the bottom line is clear: The next ten years will be bringing about changes for physicians.

▶ **Potentially booming area for physicians and others: geriatric care.**

The nation as a whole is getting older—by 2030 over 20% of the population will be 65 or older—and this means more jobs for geriatric specialists, those who can medically treat elderly people. Current projections: the number of jobs will *double.* Best bet for entry into this field: an M.D. and a residency in family practice, osteopathic medicine, or psychiatry along with a geriatrics fellowship and a Certificate of Added Qualifications in geriatric medicine. Best employment areas: where there is a large elderly population—Florida, the Southwest states, New York. For those without M.D.s, the outlook is also bright for geriatric nurses, rehabilitation specialists, nursing and home health aides. Contact: The Gerontological Society of America (page 106).

▶ **Physician Assistants (PA): a growth area.**

This relatively new health-care-giver category has permitted physicians to improve their ability to handle or supervise treatment of more patients. PAs have a minimum of two years of college training and two years of specialized and accredited PA training, including basic medical sciences and clinical experience; they practice medicine under the supervision of licensed physicians, performing a range of services from basic primary care to higher technology procedures, including surgery.

▶ **Dentists: relatively stable.**

Spending on dental care has increased by over 4% a year, and because of that spending, Americans have excellent teeth; but enrollment in dental schools has been down—and because of that, Americans need more dentists. The ratio of dentists to the total population is going down from about 60 per 100,000 today to 44.8 in 2020—the lowest since World War I. Meanwhile, an aging population needs more dental care, and pediatric dentistry is also a booming specialty. Another hot spot: cosmetic dentistry for adults. And the outlook for dental hygienists is also bright: 42% growth by 2005.

▶ **Health care managers: opportunities available, but competition may increase.**

Health services have been expanding and diversifying—and health care providers have been emphasizing cost-cutting and greater efficiency. As such, the demand for health care managers, particularly those who can deliver, has been strong. However, while the government projects continued strong employment opportunities, other experts think otherwise. The reason? Health organizations have been merging and consolidating—and, as a result, one health services manager position exists where several once did. In fact, some predict a cut of 25%, even 50%, in health services management jobs over the next ten years. Even if this worst-case scenario doesn't bear out, the bottom line is clear: Over the long term, expect increased competition for HSM jobs, particularly in those areas that are weakest.

Strongest industry areas: HMOs, home health agencies, offices of other health practitioners, nursing homes, and personal care facilities. *Slower growth*: Hospitals. While still employing the most managers, hospitals will continue cost-cutting and streamlining. As such, expect hot competition. *Keep an eye on*: hospital management companies. These provide such services as emergency department assistance, information management systems, managed care contract negotiations, physician recruiting, even consulting services.

▶ **A new development: medical entrepreneurs.**

The changing face of the health care industry should result in a growth in medical entrepreneurs—people who create their own health care companies. These companies will probably focus on the growing, lucrative home health care market and offer mobile treatment vans staffed with paramedics and other medical personnel. Expect to see a rise in this area over the long term.

▶ **Veterinarians: employment picture good.**

It looks like a positive outlook for veterinarians over the next few years. Some of the reasons: As baby boomers age, there should be an increase in pet ownership, since people in the 34 to 59 year age group are more often pet owners. On the industrial side, demand for veterinarians should increase as livestock and poultry breeders and processors emphasize more scientific methods. Additionally, government attention to public health and disease control should also affect veterinary employment.

Best areas: specialty veterinary medicine—toxicology, pathology, academics. An interesting new specialty is wildlife veterinary medicine; traditionally, wildlife management has been the domain of ecologists. Two schools offering the program: the University of California, Davis, and the University of Wisconsin, Madison.

WHAT'S NEXT

▶ **New job categories as health care becomes more specialized.**

The first problem will be to separate some functions from nursing, letting nurses concentrate on the more intensive or technical aspects of patient care. One solution: a new job category, "registered care technician," to perform some of the "easier" tasks—like handling bedpans.

One way to ease the shortage of nurses might be to give nurses more autonomy on the job, make them partners to doctors. See, for example, the growth of the nurse practitioner (NP) as an adjunct to—and possibly in place of—physicians. However good this idea sounds, it probably won't happen in most cases very soon, at least according to one expert. Reason: physicians are too protective of their status, perks. Though increases in demand for PAs may permit physicians to increase their caseloads—and income.

▶ **Rise in outpatient facilities and services.**

Although hospitals currently employ the largest number of workers, the fastest-growing employment area will be in outpatient services. Between 1982 and 1988, the jobs in private hospitals rose by 10%, jobs in doctors' offices by 36%—and jobs in outpatient facilities by 81%. The Bureau of Labor Statistics expects this trend to continue, with growth rates of around 5% per year in the 1990s.

Another growth area: medical assistants. Key reason: as cost-cutting transforms medicine, these lower cost workers who often perform both administrative and medical support functions will be increasingly in demand. Problem: lower pay.

▶ **For those who like numbers, here's a summary of *some* of the fastest growing health care professions.**

Look at this as a quick guide to potential areas you may want to get training in for the future. The numbers are the latest numbers from the employment wing of the U.S. government: the U.S. Bureau of Labor Statistics. Projections are for percent growth to the year 2005—enough time to train and get a job. One caveat: Health care is a rapidly changing industry. What the government predicts, and what actually happens, may be very different.

Profession	Percent Growth:
High School diploma or less necessary to get a job:	
Home health aides	138
Home health care aides	130
Nursing aides, etc.	45
Some post-secondary training required:	
Physical therapists assistants, etc.	93
Occupational therapy assistant	78
Medical assistant	71
Radiological technicians, etc.	62
Medical records technicians	61
EEG technologists	54
Nuclear medicine technologists	50
Respiratory therapists	46
Medical secretaries	45
Dental hygienists	43
Surgical technologists	42
Pharmacy assistants	42
Licensed practical nurses	40
College degree required:	
Physical therapist	88
Occupational therapist	80
Podiatrist	37

SALARIES

MEDICAL ASSISTANTS: Hourly salary ranges from $7.51 to $10.20 an hour for those with less than 2 years experience; $9.60 to $13.12 for medical assistants over 5 years experience. Higher wages in the Northeast and West; lower in the Midwest and South.

PHYSICAL THERAPISTS: average starting salary about $26,500, rising to $47,000 with several years experience. Physical therapists in private practice may earn more than $100,000.
Other therapists make similar salaries.

NUTRITIONISTS AND DIETICIANS: starting salaries in the low $20,000s, mid-career salaries from $25,000 to $40,000 average.

MEDICAL TECHNICIANS: Salaries vary, beginning in the low $20s, mid-career in the mid-20s, supervisory in the low $30s. Highest salaries: nuclear medicine technologists.

REGISTERED NURSES: Salaries vary according to region, with highest average salaries in the Far West (including Hawaii and Alaska), New England coming in second place—and the mid-South coming in last. More generally, RNs make an average minimum salary of $28,531 and average maximum salary of $43,711 for staff RNs, as of October 1994. According to a University of Texas Medical Branch survey of hospitals and medical centers, the average median salary for a head nurse was $50,700; clinical nurse specialists, $47,674; professional nurse practitioner, $47,432, and the highest median pay, $73,444, for a certified registered nurse anesthetist.

The best and highest pay of all goes to *nurse executives*, who manage nursing care in hospitals. Recent surveys by Olney Associates, Witt Associates, and the American Organization of Nurse Executives reported salaries ranging from $42,000 to $170,000.

LICENSED PRACTICAL NURSES: Salary typically ranges from $300 to over $600 a week. According to the University of Texas Medical Branch survey, the average median salary for an LPN in late 1994 was about $24,000 a year.

PHYSICIANS: Highly paid, but medical school expenses can exceed $100,000—and residential salaries may be less than $10 an hour, taking in account the number of hours worked. The average income was about $189,000. Surgeons had the highest incomes, $230,000 in 1993 and general practitioners the lowest at $117,000. Health care reform will likely squeeze salaries in the next few years, with some exceptions.

Primary care physicians should see continued demand at least in the short term, as managed care increasingly is emphasized. Salaries in 1993 averaged $176,000, with a range from $110,000 to $190,000 depending on the specialty. One bet: salaries will continue to increase, as group practices, HMOs, and others seek to add more primary care physicians to their organizations.

PHYSICIAN ASSISTANTS: Median incomes in 1995 were $58,000, with $100,000 incomes not uncommon.

DENTISTS: Average gross is above $200,000, average *income* is about $90,000; higher for specialists such as orthodontists.

DENTAL ASSISTANTS: Starting salaries about $16,000. Salary rises to $20,000 after several years, according to the American Dental Assistants Association.

HEALTH CARE EXECUTIVES: Starting salaries in the mid-$30s, mid- to upper-level salaries in the $50s, $60s, and $70s. CEOs earn from $100,000 to $300,000—commensurate with top managers in other industries.

PHARMACISTS: Average salaries are about $54,000. Salaries are generally highest in the West; second highest in the East.

VETERINARIANS: Starting salaries average in the low $30s; mid-career vets in private practice average over $60,000.

PHYSICIAN ASSISTANTS: Earn $37,700 to $57,000 a year on average. Median income for first year graduates, $45,000.

BEST BETS

NURSE ANESTHETISTS: certified nurses trained in anesthesiology. CRNAs are in high demand, receive the highest average pay of all nurses (starting salary about $50,000, rising up to $70,000—the national average is over $63,000), and in effect perform the same work as anesthesiologists do prior to surgery. Requirements: BS in nursing or related discipline (more for teaching and management positions), RN license, one-year experience in acute care prior to entry into a CRNA program, which lasts two to three years. Must pass a certifying exam after graduation.

Contact: American Association of Nurse Anesthetists—address is on page 104.

OPTOMETRISTS: Vision declines with age—and our aging population is one reason why this will be a good area. Note: optometrists are not MDs, but hold a Doctor of Optometry degree (a four-year professional degree) and are licensed after passing a state board exam. Unlike opthamologists, optometrists do not do eye surgery—but they diagnose eye problems, prescribe glasses, contacts, and work on vision therapy. One problem: advances in technology mean that an optometrist can see more patients than before—somewhat reduces demand.

Advantages of the profession include reasonable hours, high pay (average salary over $60,000, those in established private practice more than $100,000), flexibility, and often personal autonomy—most are in private practice.

Contact: American Optometric Association—address is on page 105.

CHIROPRACTORS: Look for continued growth in this profession, particularly as our population ages—and as the corresponding number of skeletal, muscular, and neural physical problems increase. Chiropractors treat patients with these mechanical or structural problems, through a variety of techniques including manipulation of the spine, to realign spinal nerves and reduce pain and problems. Some specialize in various areas, including athletic injuries, neurology, and orthopedics. Education: Chiropractic is regulated by the states; in most cases chiropractors must complete at least two years of college (although four years and a BA or BS increasingly are the norm) as well as four years of course work from a chiropractic college, then they must pass a state board examination to receive a license to practice. Chiropractors hold a Doctor of Chiropractic (O.D.) degree, and may have additional certification in various specialties. Experts predict 36% growth between 1992 and 2005. Beginning income may be low (it takes time and money to set up a new practice), but the median income is $75,000, and salaries can reach $200,000 for the most successful.

Contact: American Chiropractice Association; address is 1701 Clarendon Blvd., Arlington, VA 22209; 703/276-8800.

WHERE TO GO FOR MORE INFORMATION

HEALTH CARE ASSOCIATIONS

American Academy of Physician Assistants
950 N. Washington St.
Alexandria, VA 22314
703/836-2272
(Publishes employment periodical with job listings, employment information, etc.)

American Association of Dental Assistants
203 N. La Salle St.
Suite 1320
Chicago, IL 60601-1225
312/541-1550

American Association of Homes for the Aging
901 E St., NW,
Suite 500
Washington, DC 20004
202/783-2242

(Publishes periodical for members with job listings.)

American Association of Medical Assistants
20 N. Wacker Dr., Suite 1575
Chicago, IL 60606
312/899-1500

American Association of Nurse Anesthetists
222 S. Prospect
Park Ridge, IL 60068-4001
708/692-7050

American Association of Occupational Health Nurses
50 Lenox Pt.
Atlanta, GA 30324
800/241-8014
(Publishes periodicals.)

American Association for Respiratory Care
11030 Ables Ln.
Dallas, TX 75229-4593
214/243-2272
(Publishes periodical with job listings.)

American Chiropractic Association
1701 Clarendon Blvd.
Arlington, VA 22209
703/276-8800
(Publishes directory, periodical with job listings, etc.)

American College of Healthcare Executives
1 N. Franklin
Suite 1700
Chicago, IL 60606
312/424-2800

(Publishes members-only journal with job listings, directory, etc.)

American College of Sports Medicine
P.O. Box 1440
Indianapolis, IN 46206
317/637-9200
(Publishes career periodical with job listings.)

American Dental Association
211 E. Chicago Ave.
Chicago, IL 60611
312/440-2736
(Publishes periodicals with job listings, career booklets, etc.)

American Dental Hygienists Association
444 N. Michigan Ave., Suite 3400
Chicago, IL 60611
312/440-8900
(Publishes monthly periodical, accredits hygienists, etc.)

American Dietetic Association
216 W. Jackson Blvd., Suite 800
Chicago, IL 60606
312/899-0040
(Publishes periodical, career and educational information, etc.)

American Health Care Association
1201 L St., NW
Washington, DC 20005
202/842-4444

American Health Information Management Association

919 N. Michigan Ave.
Suite 1400
Chicago, IL 60611
312/787-2672
(Publishes journal with job listings, directory, referral service, educational programs.)

American Hospital Association
1 N. Franklin
Suite 1700
Chicago, IL 60606
312/422-3000
(Primarily for administrators; publishes periodical with openings; publishes directory of thousands of hospitals.)

American Medical Association
515 N. State St.
Chicago, IL 60610
312/464-5000
(The premier U.S. medical association; many affiliations; numerous services, including job placement; publishes periodicals with job listings, etc.)

American Medical Technologists
710 Higgins Rd.
Park Ridge, IL 60068
708/823-5169
(For medical lab. technologists, medical assistants, etc.; offers placement services, various member services.)

American Nurses Association
600 Maryland Ave, SW

Suite 100W
Washington, DC 20024
202/554-4444
(Offers numerous services; operates placement service; publishes periodicals with job openings, etc.)

American Occupational Therapy Association
4720 Montgomery Lane
P.O. Box 31220
Baltimore, MD 20824-1220
301/652-2682
(Publishes journal, etc.)

American Optometric Association
243 N. Lindbergh Blvd.
St. Louis, MO 63141
314/991-4100
(Publishes journal with job listings, etc.)

American Osteopathic Association
142 E. Ontario St.
Chicago, IL 60611
312/280-5800
(Publishes directory, etc.)

American Pharmaceutical Association
2215 Constitution Ave., NW
Washington, DC 20037
202/628-4410
(Publishes periodicals with job openings, etc.)

American Physical Therapy Association
1111 N. Fairfax St.
Alexandria, VA 22314
703/684-2782
800/999-2782

(Publishes periodical with job listings, annual conference with placement services, career information.)

American Physiological Society
9650 Rockville Pike
Bethesda, MD 20814
301/530-7164
(Has career information.)

American Podiatric Medical Association
9312 Old Georgetown Rd.
Bethesda, MD 20814-1621
301/571-9200
(Publishes periodical with job listings, etc.)

American Public Health Association
1015 15th St., NW
Suite 300
Washington, DC 20005
202/789-5600
(The largest public health association in the world; publishes journal with job listings, maintains placement service, directory, etc.)

American Psychiatric Association
1400 K St., NW
Washington, DC 20005
202/682-6250
(Publishes periodicals with many job listings, including some for non-M.D.s)

American Registry of Diagnostic Medical Sonographers
2368 Victory Pkwy.,

Suite 510
Cincinnati, OH 45206
800/541-9754

American Registry of Radiologic Technologists
1255 Northland Dr.
St. Paul, MN 55120
612/687-0048
(Certification board.)

American School Health Association
7263 State Rt. 43
P.O. Box 708
Kent, OH 44240
216/678-1601
(For health workers in schools; placement service, etc.)

American Society of Cardiovascular Professionals/Society for Cardiovascular Management
120 Falcon Dr.—Unit 3
Fredericksburg, VA 22408
703/891-0079
(Publishes periodicals with job listings, placement services.)

American Society for Clinical Laboratory Science
7910 Woodmont Ave.
Suite 1301
Bethesda, MD 20814
301/657-2768
(For medical lab. technicians; has placement service, etc.)

American Society of Clinical Pathologists
2100 W. Harrison
Chicago, IL 60612

312/738-1336
(Publishes periodical with job listings, etc.)

American Society of Electroneurodiagnostic Technologists
204 West 7th
Carroll, IA 51401
712/792-2978

American Society of Hospital Pharmacists
7272 Wisconsin Ave.
Bethesda, MD 20814
301/657-3000
(Publishes periodical with job listings, etc.)

American Society of Radiologic Technologists
15000 Central Ave., SE
Albuquerque, NM 87123-3917
505/298-4500
(Publishes periodicals with job listings, etc.)

Association of Operating Room Nurses
2170 S. Parker Rd.
Denver, CO 80231
303/755-6300
(Publishes journal with job listings.)

Gerontological Society of America
1275 K St., NW,
Suite 350
Washington, DC 20005
202/842-1275
(Publishes periodical.)

Healthcare Financial Management Association
Two Westbrook
Corporate Ctr.

Suite 700
Westchester, IL 60154
708/531-9600
(Publishes periodical
with listings; maintains
job database for
members.)

**National Association
of Emergency Medical
Technicians**
102 Leake St.
Clinton, MS 39056
800/346-2368
(Offers placement
service, etc.)

**National Association
for Practical Nurse
Education and
Service**
1400 Spring St.
Suite 310
Silver Spring, MD
20910
301/588-2491

(Publishes periodical,
career directory, etc.)

**National Commission
on Certification of
Physician Assistants,
Inc.**
2845 Henderson Mill
Rd., NE
Atlanta, GA 30341
770/493-9100
(Certifying body.)

**National Federation
of Licensed Practical
Nurses, Inc.**
1418 Aversboro Rd.
Garner, NC 27529
919/779-0046

**National
Rehabilitation
Association**
633 S. Washington St.
Alexandria, VA 22314
703/836-0850
(Publishes periodical

with job listings;
placement service, etc.)

**National Rural Health
Association**
1 W. Armour Blvd.,
Suite 301
Kansas City, MO
64111
816/756-3140
(Publishes periodical
with job listings;
placement service, etc.)

**National Student
Nurses
Association**
555 W. 57th St.
New York, NY 10019
212/581-2211

**Society of Diagnostic
Medical
Sonographers**
12770 Coit Rd.
Suite 508
Dallas, TX 75251
214/239-7367

HEALTH CARE DIRECTORIES

Many of the associations listed above publish directories for various prices. Call
for details. Below, we've listed some nonassociation directories.

Hospital Phone Book
Reed Reference
Publishing
121 Chanlon Rd.
New Providence, RI
07974
800/521-8110
(Thousands of
numbers, etc., on
hospitals nationwide.)

*Nursing Career
Directory*
Springhouse Corp.
1111 Bethlehem Pike
Springhouse, PA 19477
215/646-8700

*Peterson's Job
Opportunities in
Health Care*
P.O. Box 2123
Princeton, NJ
08543-2121

609/243-9111
800/338-3282

U.S. Medical Directory
Reed Reference
Publishing
121 Chanlon Rd.
New Providence, RI
07974
800/521-8110
(Extensive listings of
health care facilities
and practitioners.)

HEALTH CARE PERIODICALS

American Journal of Hospital Pharmacy
7272 Wisconsin Ave.
Bethesda, MD 20814
301/657-3000
(Monthly; usually large number of job listings.)

American Journal of Nursing
555 W. 57th St.
New York, NY 10019
212/582-8820
(Monthly for members of the ANA.)

American Pharmacy
2215 Constitution Ave., NW
Washington, DC 20037
202/429-7519
(Monthly.)

AORN Journal
2170 S. Parker Rd.
Denver, CO 80231
303/755-6300
(Association magazine; many job listings for operating room nurses.)

Dental Assistant
213 N. LaSalle
Suite 1230
Chicago, IL 60601
312/541-1550
(Bimonthly to ADAA members.)

DVM: The Newsmagazine of Veterinary Medicine
131 W. First St.
Duluth, MN
55802-2065
800/346-0085
(Monthly; includes job listings.)

Emergency: The Journal of Emergency Services
6300 Yarrow Dr.
Carlsbad, CA 92009
619/438-2511
(Monthly journal for EMTs, paramedics, etc.)

Healthcare Financial Management
2 Westbrook Corp. Ctr.
Westchester, IL 60154
708/531-9600
(Monthly for managers and workers in hospital accounting, etc.)

Health Facilities Management
737 N. Michigan Ave.
Chicago, IL 60611
312/440-6800
(Monthly for health care center products managers, etc.)

Hospital Pharmacy
224 E. Washington Sq.
Philadelphia, PA 19106

215/947-1752
(Monthly.)

Hospitals & Health Networks
737 N. Michigan Ave.
Chicago, IL 60611
312/440-6800
(Semimonthly magazine for hospital administrators.)

Journal of the American Dental Association
211 E. Chicago Ave.
Chicago, IL 60611
312/440-2736
(Nine-issue/year periodical for members of the American Dental Association; carries job listings, etc.)

Journal of Dental Hygiene
444 N. Michigan Ave.
Chicago, IL 60611
312/440-8900

Nursing '97
1111 Bethlehem Pike
Springhouse, PA 19477
215/646-8700
(Monthly magazine.)

RN
5 Paragon Dr.
Montvale, NJ 07645
201/358-7200
(Monthly magazine for R.N.s.)

INTERNATIONAL CAREERS

BRIEF BACKGROUND

▶ **An international focus will be essential for the rest of the 1990s.**

Along with the increasing political and economic linkages in Europe, the other tremendous changes of the past few years—the collapse of the Soviet Union and the Warsaw Pact nations, the reunification of Germany, the economic revitalization of much of South America—are pointing to the urgent need for highly trained, internationally competent employees in government and business and with nonprofit groups.

These changes come at a time when exports have become an increasingly important segment of our GNP, up from 9% of the U.S. economy to 21% today. No longer can many companies casually slough off exports as an afterthought. Ironically, few realize that this "new" globalism is in some senses a return to the years before World War I, when levels of international trade and investment were similarly high. However, the one significant difference between then and now: this time, the odds look good that global interdependence will increase further. This is just the beginning . . .

With these economic and political changes has come a new realization that the world is indeed interconnected and interdependent—we must all learn how to get along. Unlike those years before World War I, one can see the gradual evolution of stronger political, cultural, and technological ties, and (one hopes) a new global sensibility.

So, for those applicants with the right mixture of skills and area expertise, the challenges are there, but the future looks bright.

▶ **"The successful managers of the future will probably be those who speak both Japanese and English, who have a strong base in Brussels and contacts in the Pacific Rim, and who know the cafés and bars of Singapore."**

For the late 1980s and early 1990s, this assessment of managers in the global marketplace by the Conference Board (an independent association of management executives) may have been accurate—but for 1997, there are a few changes.

Now, with the burgeoning of the Chinese markets and with the emerging Latin American economies, trilingual skills—Chinese, Spanish, and English—may well be the fundamental skill for a successful international manager. Or, with English so powerful, maybe the languages aren't as important as the intangible cultural skills of dealing with these powerful foreign markets.

But whatever the specifics, the bottom line is clear. Business is going international in a big way. At many corporations, large and small, international experience has gone from being a hindrance to being a necessity for top jobs.

Because the range of international jobs is tremendous, this section will cover only some of them—specifically, managerial teaching and government jobs abroad. For other positions, such as technical or medical positions, many of the same ideas apply. See those career sections for specifics.

EMPLOYMENT OUTLOOK: Strong in the long term, as the world economy becomes increasingly inter-connected.

▶ **Job seekers interested in international careers should remember one key bit of advice: The best way to get an international job is to already have a skill that can be used just as well at home.**

It's the same advice given year after year (in these pages as well), and it's worth repeating. Whatever you may read about looming shortages and job openings abroad, the best way to approach an international career is to develop a skill—from farming practices to health care management, from sales to economics—and *then* apply for international positions. The reason: most employers look for basics, not language skills, as the primary hiring prerequisite. Take a glance at any of the international job magazines (listed on page 126); you'll find most openings are technical- or business-oriented, with specific required skills listed. Of course, note also that language and cultural skills are often required; *both* are needed for a strong international resume.

▶ **Some good ways to get into a business career abroad: working for a large U.S. multinational, developing an international professional expertise, studying for an MBA abroad.**

Some of the largest international corporations are American—and many offer overseas assignments. *Fortune* magazine's listing of the world's biggest industrial corporations rates General Motors, Ford Motor Company, and Exxon as the three largest world firms—with General Electric as No. 6 and Mobil as No. 8. Yet don't stop there; much growth and employment during the rest of the nineties will be with smaller companies as well.

Most such international firms want their executives to have some overseas experience. A few examples: Merck has internationalized its training program, Dow Chemical wants future CEOs with experience running foreign operations. At least 80% of the top 300 executives at Xerox Corporation have had international experience. Key to applying to these firms: apply as a skilled expert *with* international expertise, not vice versa.

The bottom line: job applicants with overseas experience, knowledge of a key language, and strong management or technical skills faced excellent job prospects in 1997, and should see the same in 1998, even with regional downturns. Adventurous entrepreneurial types are setting up shop in Russia and other new states of the region; others see opportunities continuing in East and Southeast Asia.

Another key trend: Many U.S. firms are now rapidly expanding international operations—with new branches and manufacturing facilities overseas. Increasingly, young MBAs are put right to work overseas—a change from past practices for many corporations.

The key to many jobs: foreign trade.

But there are some hitches. Slower growth in Europe and Japan could mean the reduction of jobs in the U.S. at some major exporting corporations. Also there's the possibility of continued trade wars, which might hinder employment. And of course, growing competition for jobs will come from foreign nationals themselves, who have inside knowledge of their own nations that no American, no matter how well trained, can have. Nevertheless, the global economy is here to stay, and with it the long-term prospects for internationally oriented managers, marketers, trade finance experts, etc. will be strong. Second, the role of foreign language teachers and trainers will increase (see Teachers section, page 180, and below, page 117), particularly with corporations, as they recognize the importance of linguistic/cultural knowledge to business success. Third, the role of subsidiary international functions—such as U.S. international consulting, shipping brokers, and the like—will increase . . . along with hiring.

Another area of international jobs: various professions. The same rule of thumb applies—specialize in a professional or business area, along with an international area.

Some good bets:

INTERNATIONAL ACCOUNTING: Probably the best way to the top. According to the chief executive of Arthur Andersen, the next CEO would be "a person with experience outside the borders of the U.S. . . ." Fifty percent of Andersen's revenues were generated abroad recently.

INTERNATIONAL REAL ESTATE: According to a study by the major consulting firm Ferguson Partners, reported in *The New York Times,* the real estate firm of the rest of the nineties will be larger, possibly owned by foreign partners, and often with international branches. Needed: real estate execs with cultural and linguistic abilities to manage in this more international environment.

INTERNATIONAL MANAGEMENT: Increasingly, overseas experience is becoming essential to rise to the top of many large (and smaller) corporations. Best bet: learn a key language (Japanese, Chinese, etc.) *in addition* to strong business skills.

INTERNATIONAL FINANCE: Finance has gone international—better communications and less regulation have increased the flow of investment capital across borders. Problem: international banking has lost much of its luster since the loan problems of the eighties, but it looks like bankers are going to be more involved in major infrastructure loans once again. Lending to the Third World and Soviet bloc is more cautious. Best bet: concentrate on Asian financial services, international banking, merchant banking, currency trading. Key to this area: *most* finance is increasingly international, so no matter what area you specialize in, you will at some point be dealing in the international arena.

INTERNATIONAL LAW: Best route is to get a degree, join a top firm—and wait. Few jobs in international law right out of school. One way to utilize foreign language skills: immigration law. Currently an in-demand field. One problem: low prestige among some lawyers, law firms.

INFORMATION SYSTEMS: A potentially strong area—Europe. Particularly for U.S. managers with international experience, Europe will be a strong employer. One drawback: salaries and prestige are lower, but this is changing rapidly.

▶ **Some large multinationals hire Americans for international jobs straight out of business school—European business school, that is.**

Recruiting at various European business schools is up. One key advantage: getting the inside track in Europe. Recruiters in Europe like these grads because they know the European and world economies, are familiar with cross-cultural marketing; in short, they have firsthand experience in international management.

The competition is tough, partly because of fewer spaces. Only about 3,000 MBAs graduate from leading European schools each year (versus 70,000 in the U.S.). And prices are high. Some of the biggest names: INSEAD (Institut Européan d'Administration) Business School, IMD (International Institute for Management Development), IESE (Instituto de Estudios Superiores de la Empresa), ISA, the London Business School. Also check out U.S. schools: The American Graduate School of International Management (Thunderbird); Wharton, which offers much in international management; Babson (in Wellesley, MA), which sends students on internships abroad.

▶ **Where will the growth be in the new worldwide marketplace?**

Answer: Just look at your business magazines. China looks strong—in spite of the fact that some experts are predicting a slowdown in the next few years. Bottom line: China will have the world's largest GNP in the next century, and as its banking system and hinterland develop, opportunities will continue to increase. In fact, recruiters report that Chinese is one of the two top linguist skills in demand for managers.

Strong areas: Mexico and Latin America. Key points: Many strongly developing economics (and Mexico is turning around again), proximity to the United States. Spanish skills were also in strong demand last year.

Don't forget Southeast Asia, which, despite some short-term downturns, is still booming. And India, and Turkey—some experts are now predicting the Middle East could begin to take off, providing a peace agreement comes to fruition.

And Americans are thriving in Eastern Europe and in the former territories of the Soviet Union, where their business expertise is in high demand.

The bottom line is simple: Increased integration of the world economies is providing opportunities worldwide.

▶ **A global economy also has a significant downside for job hunters.**

There are many more highly qualified potential employees for American multinational corporations today than there were just a few years ago. The collapse of Communism opened an enormous job market to multinationals; so did the rise of telecommunications, which allows cheap and easy access to factories and employees overseas. Today, many U.S. firms farm out manufacturing and even service functions overseas; for example, an Irish branch of a major U.S. insurance firm handles U.S. insurance claims. This sort of outsourcing is perhaps inevitable—and it pays for *all* job hunters to be aware of the possibility that the job they're looking for in the U.S. may be sent overseas. *Key point:* keep up-to-date, flexible.

Employment spotlight: translators

Translators and interpreters (the first work with the written word, the second with the spoken) will be in demand throughout the next few years, as borders open and international trade increases. The main areas of employment are government and international organizations (the Department of State and other agencies, the UN and related organizations), and, increasingly, businesses that deal in the international arena. Banks are a major employer—and freelance work, usually arranged through an agency, is another option. Starting salaries range from the mid-$20s to the mid-$30s. One question: will new computer translation technologies hurt demand in the not so far-off future?

Requirements: in addition to language proficiency, a BA is helpful, writing or speaking ability a must, a specialized knowledge of business, science, or diplomacy is even more helpful, and accreditation from the American Translators Association (ATA) is helpful and commands respect because the pass rate is a low 35%, according to the New York *Daily News.* Best areas: Japanese, European languages. Biggest demand: translation of Japanese patent applications into English, according to ATA, but demand is increasing for most positions. The *Wall Street Journal* reports that translators are beginning to organize and lobby—perhaps pointing to better salaries and working conditions in the near future.

For more information, contact: American Translators Association. Address is on page 125.

▶ **Many government agencies, international organizations, and nonprofits offer specialized international career tracks.**

There are numerous options: working for U.S. agencies like the Department of State or Commerce, working for international governmental organizations, and working for foreign organizations. Some U.S. government options follow.

But first, one important note. As of the time of writing, the Congress has been considering merging several of these agencies or their functions into the Department of State. Call to check how these changes—if enacted—would affect your employment application.

DEPARTMENT OF STATE: Most workers are employed as U.S. Foreign Service Officers (FSOs), although some are employed as civil service employees. FSOs work at embassies abroad and in Washington at the department. The news of the past few years was the creation of a slew of new embassies—from Armenia to Uzbekistan. There are four principal specialties or functional areas: political (diplomats in the classic sense, who report on foreign political developments, meet with Foreign Ministry counterparts, negotiate agreements, and brief other officials), economic, administrative, and consular (issue visas, help U.S. citizens in distress).

If you're a successful applicant, you'll hear a lot about "needs of the service." This means that they, not you, have final say as to what functional and geographic area you'll go to—although you can (and should) learn how to politic well and acquire a good "corridor reputation," and get the postings you want.

Outlook for 1998: Normally, 25,000 people take the initial qualifying test, about 250 people eventually enter. In-demand language skills: Arabic, Chinese, Russian, Korean, Japanese, and now, most likely, some of the more exotic languages of Central Asia. Average age of applicants is thirty, but many older mid-career candidates are also entering. Civil Service jobs are also available.

Employment tip: Before applying for most positions, brush up on your U.S. and world history, economics, and culture. The Foreign Service likes to hire people with strong generalist backgrounds.

How to apply: The process is long and grueling; it may take well over a year to get a job. First, a written general knowledge test is given once in November or December across the U.S. Those passing are informed by mail, and invited to select a date for interview. A panel travels the country and you probably will interview when they appear in your area. Or you can travel to Washington, DC, for an interview there. The interviewing process is an all-day affair that includes personal interviews, group exercises, and a written administrative "in-basket" test. You are given a ranking in all the functional areas based on your performance. You also must obtain a medical and security clearance. If all goes well, and your ranking is high enough, you will get an offer. Write: the Foreign Service Recruitment Branch—address is at the end of the section. Note: The application deadline for the annual written test is usually in late summer or early fall; the 1998 initial qualifying test is tentatively scheduled for February 1998.

One employment problem: too many people. Currently the Foreign Service is overstaffed, particularly at senior positions. Efforts are being made to trim the workforce through attrition.

U.S. INFORMATION AGENCY: USIA officers serve in Washington and embassies abroad as press officers, cultural affairs officers, and administrative support staff with a mandate to upgrade the U.S. image abroad. USIA manages exchange programs like the Fulbright; it runs libraries overseas. Newest trends from the previous year: the agency is discussing launching a small business initiative, in effect, to show and promote the success of capitalism in areas such as the old Soviet Union where few positive models exist. The USIA employs about 8,800 people, half of whom work at U.S. embassies in 128 nations. How to apply: see addresses on page 121.

The Voice of America (VOA), which is the official U.S. overseas network, is also under the USIA. It employs over 2,000 people, mostly foreign language specialists and technicians. For most other USIA jobs, taking the Foreign Service test is the first step—see the above address and description. For VOA jobs, contact: Voice of America; address is at the end of this section.

U.S. AGENCY FOR INTERNATIONAL DEVELOPMENT (USAID): AID runs U.S. economic aid abroad—its employees work in the U.S. and in about seventy developing countries worldwide, often out of embassies or field offices. While in many cases other aid groups get the glamour, AID gets the job done, quietly helping to avert famine in various parts of Africa, working to improve agricultural marketing, and so on.

There are two main avenues of employment, via the civil service (usually more limited, often staff positions in computers, etc), or via the Foreign Service. Addresses for both avenues are listed on page 120. AID has recently revamped its internship program, called the IDI (International Development Intern) program. It will be a two-tier system, with one track (75%) for senior candidates with graduate degrees, work and overseas experience, and language ability, and a junior track for those with ability but limited experience. The internship itself will now involve one year in Washington (two for junior interns) and one year overseas.

AID has recently announced that it intends to recruit from a broader background rather than from predetermined areas, although those with accounting, agricultural, economics, health care, urban planning, and engineering degrees and experience are highly represented at AID.

Mid-level hiring of noninterns will continue, but at only about 20% of the year's new hires. Minority recruitment is a priority for the agency. Contact: addresses on page 119.

PEACE CORPS: The ads say it: "The toughest job you'll ever love." And it *is* tough—serving in some of the most undeveloped areas of the world, only basic expenses paid, and at the end, about $200 for every month served, possible college credits, and career help. But looking back, many say it was the best or most transforming part of their lives. Some other advantages: language training, travel, noncompetitive eligibility for government employment.

Some 6,800 Americans work as volunteers in 97 countries nationwide—age range from eighteen to over eighty; most are single and college grads, although neither is a requirement. Terms of service are two years spent abroad, plus a 10-to-12-week training course, generally in the country where you'll be serving. Preference is given to those who can speak host country languages, although the Corps offers training if you don't speak the language. Most volunteers work as teachers (38%); next come those who work in the environment (17%), health (15%), and economic development (14%). About 41% work in Africa, 23% in the Americas, 22% in Europe, Central Asia, and the Mediterranean; the rest work in Asia and the Pacific; 600 other Americans work as Peace Corps staff in Washington, 145 more at recruiting offices nationwide; another 200 or so Americans work as paid staff abroad. For staff positions, see address on page 120 and information on government employment on page 66, for volunteer positions see page 120.

In demand: volunteers with experience or degrees in agriculture, engineering, environment-oriented professions, fisheries, forestry, health, home economics, industrial arts, mathematics, nursing, most sciences, special education, technical (woodworking, metal, etc.), wildlife or resource management. Some 14,000 apply annually, 3,500 or so are chosen.

Employment tip: for those with liberal arts backgrounds, although you are eligible, you are not recruited actively. To enhance your chances—take courses in one of the degree areas above, get English as a second-language experience, learn Spanish, French, or Arabic, or show relevant experience.

DEPARTMENT OF COMMERCE: Overseas staffers include members of the Foreign Commercial Service. FCS officers serve in embassies and work to promote U.S. trade abroad and assist U.S. companies overseas. The application procedures are somewhat similar to those of the State Department.

Best bet: Jobs as commercial officers and counselors are excellent for midcareer business people who are bored, tired of the rat race, and want a change.

Other commerce jobs are in the International Trade Administration (ITA), the U.S. Travel and Tourism Administration (USTTA)—with offices abroad as well as in DC. See page 120.

Other U.S. government departments or agencies with international jobs include the Arms Control and Disarmament Agency (ACDA), the Central Intelligence Agency (CIA), the Defense Intelligence Agency (DIA), the Department of Agriculture (including the Foreign Agricultural Service [FAS]), the International Development Cooperation Agency (IDCA), the National Security Agency (NSA), and the Overseas Private Investment Corporation (OPIC).

Addresses are listed later in this chapter. For domestic agencies, see the Government section on page 75, and read the section on how to find and apply for specific civil service jobs.

Another option: working on congressional committee staffs in foreign affairs areas. The two key staffs are the **House Foreign Affairs Committee** and the **Senate Foreign Relations Committee** (see placement office addresses on page 90). Other staffs also include international orientation. *Requirements:* usually experience and degrees in international affairs, law, or economics. One of the best ways in is to have worked in a congressperson's office. Persons hired tend to be in their late twenties to early forties.

▶ **Outlook for other international jobs: fair, with much competition for the high-prestige areas.**

Rule of thumb: economists, technical specialists, and financial types do best—particularly when armed with an MBA or Ph.D. and significant experience.

Some international organizations:

THE UNITED NATIONS: Probably the toughest international organization to get into—political considerations make it even tougher, and budget tightening in the 1990s will make things harder. The UN offers high pay and perks, along with a large dose of politics.

Many UN jobs are filled through recommendations by the U.S. Department of State (for U.S. citizens). Specific UN agencies should be applied to directly. Addresses are listed at the end of the chapter.

THE WORLD BANK (officially the International Bank for Reconstruction and Development) and subsidiaries: charged with lending in developing countries, primarily infrastructure (dams, bridges, and roads) and agricultural lending, joint ventures, and investment settlement. Excellent pay and perks. *Best way to enter:* Young Professional Program. For experienced people usually in their late twenties, usually with MBA or Ph.D. and business, banking, or development experience. Training program rotates trainees through the Bank and its subsidiary arms; after about a year, trainees join a division. How to get in: applicants submit forms, transcripts, and recommendations, are interviewed several times, then selected. Very competitive.

Other international agency jobs—among many—include the International Monetary Fund (IMF), the General Agreement on Tariffs and Trade (GATT, an organization arising out of multilateral agreements to remove trade barriers), and the Organization of American States (OAS).

▶ **International teaching—for many, it's the only way to teach.**

It's not necessarily easy. Teaching posts can range from American schools in England or Germany to those in China or Central America; but some find it's an enjoyable option from the rigors of teaching in U.S. schools.

By far the largest employer of U.S. teachers is the Department of Defense, which runs the nation's ninth largest school system, with 270 schools in 20 countries with a staff of 13,000. Teachers who are hired work as members of the U.S. Government.

Another option: teaching at American overseas schools. Unlike the Defense schools, these are independent schools that depend on tuition payment—and they are often in more out-of-the-way places, usually in capital cities near U.S. embassies and other government and major corporate offices. The quality is generally high; students tend to be the children of U.S. diplomats. In both cases, salaries and benefits are usually very good, tuition for teacher's children is usually free, housing allowances are usually tax-free, the schools usually pay for storage of your U.S. household effects and/or the duty-free shipping of goods abroad.

Application instructions are on page 123.

▶ **Nonprofit sector: Some competition and often low pay make this a tough (although rewarding) area.**

The competition for jobs heated up particularly during the recession—but also due to the increasing desire of many very competent people to do something significant with their lives.

Key problem: With the exception of rich foundations like the Ford Foundation, which has generous salary levels and working conditions, many nonprofits pay lower wages, particularly at low- to mid-level positions. For example, Save the Children advertised a few years back for field director positions in various African countries at a (tax-free) salary of about $20,000. Upper-level positions sometimes pay considerably more.

The rewards should not be discounted, however. Amnesty International made the difference in the lives of many prisoners, many of whom would literally be dead without the organization's help. Save the Children, the Christian Children's Fund, and other organizations have had the same impact in many undeveloped nations.

Many nonprofits are a lot less lumbering and slow when it comes to action, and so they get things accomplished. There are some career advantages as well: firstly, nonprofits tend to be looser and more fun to work for—and at the same time may be very well run; secondly, they can be good places to get involved with and meet influential people; thirdly, the entire nonprofit area is just beginning to have a real impact now. Nonprofits are more than just secondary organizations—some of them have influence and power in their own right.

For some specific addresses, see the nonprofit organizations listed on page 121, and check ACCESS magazine, listed on page 126. This is an invaluable source of job listings for all types of nonprofit jobs.

WHAT'S NEXT

▶ International jobs will become more of the mainstream.

The reason is simple: the world is getting smaller. International concerns are everyone's concern—as is evident in the proliferation of individual U.S. state offices in Japan, the large number of foreign companies entering into joint ventures with U.S. companies, the rising levels of (and dependence on) business exports and imports overseas, the increasing interdependence of the world.

The inevitable outcome of this international focus: more jobs will have an international dimension—requiring one to three years in a foreign branch or subsidiary, or at least occasional overseas travel.

▶ Outlook for women: improving

Women make up only about 5% of those employed overseas. According to the Conference Board and a study by Moran, Stahl, & Boyer, these numbers should increase. An overwhelming majority of women working overseas were successful in their assignments, and even more conservative societies accepted their role as business managers.

The trend: increased overseas assignments. Most women are assigned to Europe (the U.K. has the highest percentage) or Canada, but hiring for jobs outside these areas should increase as well.

SALARIES

International salaries are impossible to categorize, as they vary widely according to industry or organization.

A few guidelines:

PRIVATE INDUSTRY: Check appropriate industry or career section.

DEPARTMENT OF STATE: Salaries are ranked similarly to the civil service, but by a Foreign Service rating. The entry-level salary is in the low $30,000 range, depending on qualifications.

PEACE CORPS: Monthly living stipend varies depending on where you're serving, but averages about $225 per month—with a $4,800 bonus given to those who complete their two years abroad successfully.

BEST BETS

INTERNATIONAL ACCOUNTING: Multinational business and foreign businesses and individuals in the U.S. have raised the demand for internationally trained accountants. Most of the work is handled by the top accounting firms, mostly the Big Six. Requirements: usually CPA and several years experience. Best languages: Japanese, French, Spanish, Portuguese.

INTERNATIONAL TELECOMMUNICATIONS: As many nations overseas strive to set up or modernize their telecom networks, U.S. telecom executives will be in strong demand. Key skills: technical ability with strong communications (human, not electronic) and personnel skills. Hiring is currently best in Eastern Europe, Pacific Rim.

UN GUIDE: For young people in their twenties. Guide jobs are easier to get than most UN jobs, are enjoyable, and can give a person at least a view of UN operations. Requirements: fluency in English and one other UN official language. Contact: see page 124.

WHERE TO GO FOR MORE INFORMATION

U.S. GOVERNMENT ORGANIZATIONS WITH AN INTERNATIONAL FOCUS

(*Important note:* See note on page 75 for important information on U.S. government agency phone numbers.)

Agency for International Development (AID)
Recruitment Division
M-HR-WPRS-R
Room 640-SA36
Washington, DC
20523-0036
703/302-4128
(Overseas development aid agency; above address is for Foreign Service positions; primarily hires accts., economists, development specialists, engineers, etc. Degree, two or more years' appropriate experience.)

Agency for International Development
Office of Personnel Management
Civil Service Personnel Division,
M-HR-POD-R
Room 627
Washington, DC
20523-0036
703/302-4036
(For civil service positions with AID; primarily hires acct., bus. admin., econ., and law background.)

Central Intelligence Agency
Personnel Division
Washington, DC 20505
703/482-1100
(Hires both operations personnel and analysts.)

Defense Intelligence Agency
Civilian Staffing
Operations Division
(RHR-2)
Recruitment Program

Department OP
Washington, DC
20340-5100
202/231-8228
(Hires computer,
science, foreign-area-
studies specialists, etc.)

Department of State
Recruitment Division
P.O. Box 9317
Rosslyn Station
Arlington, VA 22209
703/875-7242
(summer clerical)
703/875-7207
(student program
inquiries)
703/875-7490 (24-hr.
job hot line)
(For Foreign Service
employment.)

Department of State
Staffing Services
Division
Office of Civil Service
Personnel (PER/CSP),
2201 C St., NW
Room 2429
Washington, DC 20520
202/647-5810
703/875-7242 (student
program inquiries)
703/875-7496 (24-hr.
job hot line)
(Civil service jobs
include those for
applicants with
accounting, banking,
business admin.,
computer, finance,
management degrees,
etc.)

**Export-Import Bank
of the United States**
Personnel Director
811 Vermont Ave., NW
Washington, DC 20571
202/565-3946

(Employees, usually
with banking, finance,
accounting, or
computer backgrounds,
work in DC and
facilitate export
financing of U.S. goods
and services overseas.)

**Foreign Agricultural
Service**
AG Code 0593
Attn. Foreign Program
P.O. Box 2415
Washington, DC
20013-2415
202/254-8292
(Employees work as
attachés, etc., in U.S.
embassies abroad.)

**International Trade
Administration**
Personnel Officer
14th St. and
Constitution Ave., NW,
H4211
Washington, DC 20230
202/482-2000
(Promotes U.S.
exports, advises on
policy, hires primarily
economics/business/
marketing/finance
backgrounds.)

**International Trade
Commission**
Office of Personnel
500 E St., SW
Washington, DC 20436
202/205-2000

**National Security
Agency**
Office of Civilian
Personnel
Recruitment Branch
Attn: M322
Fort Meade, MD
20755-6000
1-800/255-8415

(Security agency
principally concerned
with signal
intelligence, codes,
computer security,
foreign intelligence.
Hires, linguists,
technicians, computer
experts, etc. Much
testing and
interviewing before
hiring.)

Peace Corps
Office of Personnel
1990 K St., NW,
Room 4100
Washington, DC 20526
202/606-3886
1-800/424-8580, ext.
225

Peace Corps
Office of Recruitment/
Public Response Unit
1990 K St., NW, 9th Fl.
Washington, DC 20526
202/606-3940
1/800/424-8580, ext. 93
(For volunteer positions.)

**Travel and Tourism
Administration**
Office of Personnel
Administration
14th St. and
Constitution Ave., NW,
H-1069
Washington, DC 20230
202/482-3811
(Encourages and
supports tourism *to* the
United States; hires
business/marketing/
statistical majors.)

**U.S. and Foreign
Commercial Service**
Office of Foreign
Service Personnel,
Room 3226
14th St. and

Constitution Ave., NW
Washington, DC 20230
202/482-2000
(Employees work in
United States and in
embassies abroad
promoting U.S. goods
and services.)

U.S. Information Agency
Office of Personnel
Special Services Branch

301 4th St., SW
Washington, DC 20547
202/619-4665
202/619-4539 (24-hr.
hot line)
(Employees work in DC
and in embassies abroad
promoting U.S. policies,
administering programs
such as the Fulbright
scholarships, etc.)

U.S. Mission to the United Nations

Personnel Office
799 United Nations, Plz.
New York, NY 10017
212/415-4000

Voice of America
Office of Personnel
330 Independence Ave.,
SW, Room 1543
Washington, DC 20547
202/619-3117
202/619-0909 (24-hr.
job hot line)

NONPROFIT ORGANIZATIONS: INTERNATIONAL AID-ORIENTED

ACCION International
120 Beacon St.
Summersville, MA
02143
617/492-4930
(Sponsors limited
capital small business
projects in South
America, workshops.)

American Friends Service Committee
1501 Cherry St.
Philadelphia, PA 19102
215/241-7000
(Primarily an overseas
development
organization.)

American Near East Refugee Aid
1522 K St., NW, No.
202
Washington, DC 20005
202/347-2558

American Organization for Rehabilitation Through Training
American ORT

Federation
817 Broadway
New York, NY 10003
212/353-5800
(Originally organized
to help Jews in Czarist
Russia; now the largest
nongovernment
vocational
organization.)

American Refugee Committee
Director, International
Programs
2344 Nicollet Ave.,
Suite 350
Minneapolis, MN
55404
612/872-7060
(Medical personnel;
primarily volunteers.)

Americares Foundation
161 Cherry St.
New Canaan, CT
06840
203/966-5195
(Organizes relief;
trains; and sends

medical supplies, etc.,
to Africa, Asia, etc.)

Amideast (American Friends of the Middle East)
American-Mideast
Educational and
Training Services
1730 M St, NW
Suite 1100
Washington, DC 20036
202/776-9600

Appropriate Technology International
International Director,
Finance and
Administration
1828 L St., NW
Suite 1000
Washington, DC 20036
202/293-4600
(Engineering,
economics, or business
background; Spanish or
French preferred for
applicants for this
"human-sized"
technology
development group.)

CARE, Inc.
660 First Ave.
New York, NY 10016
212/686-3110
(One of the largest
international/technical
assistance
organizations; hundreds
of employees;
experience in
developing countries
with appropriate degree
preferred.)

**Catholic Relief
Services**
209 W. Fayette St.
Baltimore, MD 21201
410/625-2220
(Large development
organization operating
worldwide.)

Childreach
155 Plan Way
P.O. Box 400
Warwick, RI 02887
401/738-5600
(Provides aid in Asia,
Africa, Latin America,
etc.)

**Christian Children's
Fund, Inc.**
P.O. Box 26484
Richmond, VA 23261
804/756-2700
(Supports children and
their communities in
undeveloped areas
abroad.)

Church World Service
475 Riverside Dr.

New York, NY
10115-0050
212/870-2061
(Sponsors community
development, relief
services.)

**Compassion
International**
P.O. Box 7000
3955 Craigwood Dr.
Colorado Springs, CO
80933-7000
719/594-9900
(Relief services
primarily for children
overseas.)

**Food for the Hungry
International**
7729 E. Greenway Rd.
Scottsdale, AZ 85260
602/951-5090
(Food relief and
development abroad.)

**Freedom from
Hunger Foundation**
1644 Da Vinci Ct.
P.O. Box 2000
Davis, CA 95617
916/758-6200

**Inter-American
Foundation**
901 N. Stuart St.
Arlington, VA 22203
703/841-3868
(Promotes development
in Latin America.)

**International Rescue
Committee**
122 E. 42nd St.

New York, NY 10017
212/551-3000
(Aids in counseling,
resettling refugees.)

Oxfam-America
26 West St.
Boston, MA 02111
617/482-1211
(Sponsors integrated
rural development,
food aid in poorest
parts of the world;
about fifty U.S.
employees, hundreds
abroad.)

**Pearl S. Buck
Foundation**
Greenhills Farm
P.O. Box 181
Perkasie, PA 18944
215/249-0100
(Aids Amerasian
children, etc.; about
200 emloyees.)

**Save the Children
Federation, Inc.**
54 Wilton Rd.
Westport, CT 06880
203/226-7271

**Winrock
International**
38 Winrock Rd.
Morriltown, AR 72110
501/727-5435
(Agricultural
development, technical
assistance; about a
hundred employees in
United States and
abroad.)

NONPROFIT ORGANIZATIONS: THINK TANKS, OTHER POLICY-ORIENTED, AND HUMAN RIGHTS

**Amnesty
International**
322 Eighth Ave.

New York, NY 10001
212/807-8400
(Premier human rights

organization
worldwide; fights for
political prisoners, etc.)

Asia Foundation
465 California St.
14th Floor
San Francisco, CA
94104
415/982-4640

Brookings Institution
1775 Massachusetts
Ave., NW
Washington, DC 20036
202/797-6000
(Premier research
organization; one
program is Foreign
Policy Studies, over
200 staff.)

**Carnegie Endowment
for International
Peace**
2400 N St., NW
Washington, DC 20037
202/862-7900
(Publishes *Foreign
Policy* magazine; about
a hundred employees.)

**Center for Strategic
and International
Studies**
Personnel Director
1800 K St., NW, Suite
400
Washington, DC 20006
202/887-0200

**Chicago Council on
Foreign Relations**
Vice President and
Program Director
116 S. Michigan Ave.
Chicago, IL 60623
312/726-3860

**Council on Foreign
Relations**
Personnel Manager
58 E. 68th St.
New York, NY 10021
212/734-0400
(Publishes *Foreign
Affairs;* about a
hundred employees,
mostly Ph.D.s, regional
committees.)

East/West Center
1777 East-West Rd.
Honolulu, HI 96848
808/944-7111
(More than 200
employees; founded by
Congress to promote
Asian-American
understanding.)

RAND
1700 Main St.
P.O. Box 2138
Santa Monica, CA
90407-2138
210/393-0411
(Premier research

institute; much national
security, public welfare
research; over 500
professionals
employed, mostly
Ph.D.s.)

SRI International
333 Ravenswood Ave.
Menlo Park, CA
94205-3493
415/326-6200
1611 N. Kent St.
Arlington, VA 22209
703/524-2053
(Consulting and
technical research on
contract for U.S. gov't.
and international
agencies; one of the
premier think tanks in
the world, with over
three thousand
employees, many
Ph.D.s.)

Tinker Foundation
55 E. 59th St.
New York, NY 10022
212/421-6858
(Promotes better
relations between
Hispanic and
Portuguese-speaking
nations and United
States.)

TEACHING ABROAD

**Fulbright Teacher
Exchange**
600 Maryland Ave.
Room 140
Washington, DC 20024
202/401-9418
1-800/726-0479
(Academic year and
shorter exchange

program for teachers,
grad. students, etc., in
various countries in
Europe, Asia, and
Africa. Deadline for
the next academic year
is usually in mid-
October; information
packet contains

application, host
countries, and full
details.)

**International School
Service, Inc.**
15 Rozel Rd.
Princeton, NJ 08540
609-452-0990
(This is a major

recruiter for non-Department of Defense U.S. overseas schools worldwide; they list positions worldwide, often in exotic areas such as Fiji.)

Office of Overseas Schools
Room 245, SA-29
U.S.Department of State
Washington, DC 20522-2902
(This is the Department of State office that handles overseas schools that the children of diplomatic and other personnel attend. These are *not*

official USG schools—there is no central "Foreign Service" of teachers at State, and unlike teachers with the Department of Defense schools, teachers are not USG employees.)

U.S. Department of Defense Dependents Schools
U.S. Department of Defense
Recruitment and Assignment Section
4040 N. Fairfax Dr.
Arlington, VA 22203
703/696-3068
(Annual listing and application for teaching and related jobs at

Department of Defense schools overseas.)

WorldTeach
Harvard Institute for International Development
1 Eliot St.
Cambridge, MA 02138
617/495-5527
(Primarily for volunteers; successful applicants teach or coach abroad for one year and receive housing and a small salary. Teaching experience and foreign language are not necessary.)

PUBLIC INTERNATIONAL ORGANIZATIONS

International Monetary Fund
Recruitment and Training Division
700 19th St., NW
Washington, DC 20431
202/623-7000

Pan American Sanitary Bureau
Pan American Health Organization
Regional Office of the World Health Organization
525 23rd St., NW
Washington, DC 20037
202/861-3200

United Nations
General Service Staffing Section
1 United Nations Plz.

New York, NY 10017
212/963-1234 (general employment information)
212/963-8876 (more specific information; call between 3 and 5 P.M.)
(For U.N. clerical, secretarial, U.N. guide jobs, etc. Call above numbers; or write with full details of background and job desired; or go to office Monday to Friday between 10 A.M. and noon.)

U.N. Children's Fund (UNICEF)
Division of Personnel
Recruitment and

Placement Section
3 United Nations Plz.
New York, NY 10017
212/326-7000

U.N. Development Program
Division of Personnel
1 United Nations Plz.
New York, NY 10017
212/906-5000

U.N. Population Fund
220 E. 42nd St.
New York, NY 10017
212/297-5000

U.N. Secretariat
Office of Personnel Services
Recruitment Programs Section
New York, NY 10017

World Bank, International Finance Corporation (IFC), and Multilateral	Guarantee Agency (MIGA) Vice President of Personnel	1818 H St., NW Washington, DC 20433 202/477-1234

OTHER JOB SOURCES FOR WORKING ABROAD: MOSTLY TEMPORARY, SHORT-TERM, OR VOLUNTEER

Association for International Practical Training
10400 Little Patuxent Pkwy.,
Suite 250
Columbia, MD 21044-3510
410/997-2200
(For students in engineering, sciences, etc.; arranges overseas exchanges with on-the-job training or research; for recent graduates also offers exchange programs in culinary, hospitality/tourism.)

CDS International Internship Program
330 Seventh Ave.
New York, NY 10001
212/760-1400
(For business, etc., college seniors; offers intensive German-language training, then five months internship with German firms.)

Exchange Division
The American-Scandinavian Foundation
725 Park Ave.
New York, NY 10021
212/879-9779
(For recent graduates twenty-one to thirty-five years old, with a few years' experience in agriculture, banking, etc.; provides six- to eighteen-month training internships in Scandinavian countries.
Note: Other foundations may offer similar exchange programs.)

International Christian Youth Exchange
134 W. 26th St.
New York, NY 10001
212/206-7307
(Offers scholarships; places volunteers abroad for a year in various positions—teacher, literacy, medical, environmental—and provides housing.)

Work, Study, Travel Abroad: The Whole World Handbook 1991—1993
St. Martin's Press, 1992; available at bookstores and libraries
(Describes over 1,200 study or work opportunities abroad, including many volunteer work and internships.)

INTERNATIONAL ASSOCIATIONS

American Translators Association
1800 Diagonal Rd.
Suite 220
Alexandria, VA 22314
703/683-6100
(Accredits translators; publishes periodical with listings; lists university translation courses; directory.)

International Studies Association
216 Herald Clark Bldg.
Brigham Young University
Provo, UT 84602
801/378-2695
(Publishes periodical with academic job listings.)

| National Foreign Trade Council | 1270 Ave. of the Americas | New York, NY 10020 212/399-7128 |

INTERNATIONAL DIRECTORIES

| *America's Corporate Families and International Affiliates; Principal International Business; The World Marketing Directory; Latin America's Top 25,000* Dun's Marketing Services | 3 Sylvan Way Parsippany, NJ 07054 1-800/526-0651 201/455-0900 *Directory of American Firms Operating in Foreign Countries* World Trade Academy Press 342 E. 52nd St. | New York, NY 10022 212/252-0329 *Encyclopedia of Geographic Information Sources* International Volume Gale Research, Inc. 835 Penobscot Bldg. Detroit, MI 48226-4094 800/877-4253 |

INTERNATIONAL PERIODICALS

| *Community Jobs* ACCESS 30 Irving Pl. 9th Floor New York, NY 10003 212/475-1001 (Hundreds of nonprofit jobs; career centers.) *Cross Border Monitor* 111 W. 57th St. New York, NY 10019 212/554-0600 *The Economist* 111 W. 57th St. New York, NY 10019 212/541-0500 (London-based internationally oriented general newsmagazine; carries some job listings.) *Euromoney* Euromoney Publications PLC Nestor House, Playhouse Yard | London EC4V 5EX England Fax 01-236-6970 (Major international finance magazine.) *Euroweek* Euromoney Publications PLC Nestor House, Playhouse Yard London EC4V 5EX England 071-779-8888 Fax 071-779-81617 *Far Eastern Economic Review* GPO Box 160 Hong Kong 852/508-4300 (Influential weekly business affairs magazine for the Pacific basin.) *Federal Career Opportunities* P.O. Box 1059 | Vienna, VA 22183-1059 703/281-0200 (Biweekly listing all types of U.S. government jobs, in United States and some overseas.) *Financial Times* 14 E. 60th St. New York, NY 10022 212/752-4500 *Foreign Affairs* 58 E. 68th St. New York, NY 10021 212/734-0400 (Influential policy journal.) *Foreign Policy* Carnegie Endowment for International Peace 2400 N St., NW #700 Washington, DC 20037 202/862-7940 |

*Foreign Service
Journal*
2101 E St., NW
Washington, DC 20037
202/338-4045
(Monthly; can be
useful background for
Foreign Service test.)

Global Finance
1221 Ave. of the
Americas
New York, NY 10020
212/337-5900
(Monthly magazine.)

*International
Business*
9 E. 40 St.
10th Floor
New York, NY 10016
212/683-2426
(Monthly; circulation
40,000.)

*The International
Educator*
P.O. Box 513
Commaquid, MA
02637
508/362-1414

*International
Employment Hotline*
P.O. Box 3030
Oakton, VA 22124
703/620-1972
(Job listings overseas—
wide range includes
corporations, U.S.
government, and
foreign organizations
and governments.)

*International
Employment Gazette*
220 N. Main St.
Suite 220
Greenville, SC 29601
800/882-9188

(Biweekly; contains
hundreds of listings;
many multinational
business jobs, heavy
emphasis for
engineering, education,
and business
backgrounds; some
gov't./U.N.-type jobs
as well; also offers
other services.)

*Overseas Employment
Services*
1255 Laird; Suite 208
Town of Mount Royal
Quebec, H3P 2T1
Canada
514/739-1108

Transitions Abroad
P.O. Box 1300
Amherst, MA 01004-
1300
800/293-0373

MANAGERS

▶ **How to succeed as a manager for the rest of the decade: be multilingual, a generalist with technical skills, computer literate, a doer, not a follower, a team player—or a team leader—a change agent.**

That's the ideal—the "new" manager who has emerged out of the downsizings and cutbacks of the past few years. Here's a brief summary of the changes that have occurred—and that face the job-hunting manager in 1998:

- **The "lean and mean" corporation is here to stay.** The middle levels of bureaucracy that were cut will stay cut, and more cuts at many firms are in the offing. Bottom line: the managers who are left won't push paper so much as lead people, or supervise technical projects.

- **The old days of comfortable hierarchies and guaranteed employment are over.** You'll be expected to think more as a freelancer—you'll have to compete *within* the corporation for employment on good projects, instead of just accepting an assignment. You'll deal directly with technical people—there won't be layers of managers between you and the factory floor, for example. Projects will be more team-oriented. Company organization charts will be flatter—more people will deal with each other as equals. And if you can't do the job well—you won't last long.

- **Competition will be fiercer, faster, and smarter.** Computer technology and the simple faster pace of things means that companies must be fast and flexible to survive.

- **Corporations will compete globally.** It's a cliché, but it bears repeating. Exports have been the engine of our economic growth; and like it or not, our corporations must sell abroad and face down foreign competitors at home to survive.

- **Corporations will be more involved with the public, with government, and with environmental concerns.** In some cases, corporations will take over government functions; in all cases, they must sensitize themselves to the growing diversity of our population, and our growing environmental concerns.

- **Finally and most importantly, the corporation of today and tomorrow will assume you have technical skills but emphasize "soft" skills—the ability to lead people, think creatively, understand the big picture and relate it to**

technical areas. Already, General Electric management training programs are emphasizing these soft skills, instead of the more technical, "hard" aspects of management traditionally taught in business schools.

This isn't to say the old ways are gone, or that the new ways will be achieved fully. But the consensus is that they will be the key to success in the competitive nineties.

Note: This section covers primarily general managers. For more specifics, see the appropriate section. For example, for managers in finance, see the Financial Services section, Accountants section, and Banking section. For trends and jobs in specific industries or areas, see the appropriate sections in the Industry section.

EMPLOYMENT OUTLOOK: Long-term outlook good for people with the right mix of technical skills and general background; in the short term, strong as companies continue to expand and the economy grows; expect a short-term downturn if the economy temporarily loses speed. Best for engineers with managerial skills, technically competent applicants with broad backgrounds; health-care professionals.

▶ **Management reorganization—from pyramid to pancake.**

This has been *the* organizational change of the past few years—and it looks like for much of U.S. business, it is here to stay. This is not to say that bureaucracies will cease to exist, but watch for continued change, continued "de-bureaucratization." The key reasons: *Speed.* Companies are emphasizing faster response time and product development, both of which are easier to achieve with fewer layers of managers to go through. *Cost.* Increased competition and the recession seven years ago prompted a continuing appreciation for the virtues of frugality, which includes keeping staff levels down.

▶ **Middle management: The changes of the past years are here to stay—meaning a whole new working environment.**

Most who work in middle management are well aware of the changes. Beginning during the mid-1980s—and extending well into the 1990s, and still going on—companies began cutting back layer after layer of middle management, in an effort to save money, focus on "core businesses," and make profits.

The bottom line: During this period well over one million management jobs were eliminated. And layoffs have continued.

But does this mean the outlook is bad now?

In most cases, the answer is a fairly strong "no." As one expert noted, for every massive layoff at AT&T there is a hiring surge at MCI; for every layoff at K-mart, there is a Wal-mart to step in and take up the slack.

And now there are changes in the wind. Key point: Companies are beginning to shift focus from a cost-cutting emphasis to a profit and growth emphasis—and that means, in general, that more managers will be hired. This doesn't mean that huge bureaucracies will re-form. At the same time, companies will continue to "trim the fat," and that means layoffs will continue as well, although probably on a lesser scale.

Regardless of trends, the days of layers of middle management bureaucracy are over. Outsourcing had eliminated many formerly "in-house" peripheral functions; most managers will be expected to contribute to the bottom line. This means less paper pushing, more team efforts, and more technical expertise required. And if you can't cut the job, there is far more likelihood that you'll be fired. There is less room for error. Key point: Most managers can expect at least four or five different jobs during their careers.

Outlook: Competition will probably increase as the economic expansion matures or temporarily slackens. But strong demand for managers in many areas is there.

Key point: As companies move from the cost-cutting strategies of the recent past to growth strategies to build or rebuild operations, this new focus will increase demand for experienced managers. The indicators: from mid-1993 to mid-1996, executive, administrative, and management occupations increased almost three times faster than overall employment—a 9% vs. 3% increase. While overall unemployment in mid-1996 was 5.4%, it was only 2.4% for management personnel. Lean-mean management meant few internal resources for promotion. Executive recruiter searches jumped 14% in the 1995–1996 period, with almost half of the searches for newly created positions.

Corporations will be looking for:

• **Broader responsibility:** Without many layers, managers must take direct responsibility for more projects.

• **More people to supervise:** On average, first-line managers will lead about 40 to 50 people, organized into various teams.

• **Tougher hiring practices:** Be prepared to defend what you can do, and why. Complacency is out.

• **At least lip service to the ideal manager concept of the 1990s:** A "people person," generalist with technical skills, etc.

• **Computer competence:** Forget programming languages, but remember how to use and understand the computer and various key programs. Computers will be an increasingly common communications, thinking, and decision-making tool—a "utility," in the word of one executive.

▶ **New changes may not all be for the better.**

One legacy of the past: For some, the new "lean and mean profit machine" is . . . mean.

Even though there's been a lot of good news—downsizings have decreased, and in 1996–1997 hiring for most managers was very strong—some miss the old days, when corporate loyalty was the norm and downsizings were rare.

And even with relatively strong hiring, the pace of executive life has quickened. Results are expected—or else.

And now some experts are questioning some downsizings, arguing that some corporations may have wielded the corporate knife a bit too heavily. Some companies, such as computer manufacturer Hewlett-Packard are cited as a good example of the ideal—it concentrated on offering early retirements and transfers instead of mass firings. Result: Good morale and a good bottom line.

▶ **So what's the future outlook for managerial jobs?**

As one would expect, management hiring will depend on the strength—or weakness—of the economy and, more specifically, the different industries. *Best tactic:* target specific companies that have restructured successfully and are strong enough to weather any economic downturns. More generally, experts say that the massive downsizing of corporations should be coming to an end—and companies will be adding managers. What are they looking for? "Change managers," to use the buzzword. In other words, the manager of 1998 and beyond must be flexible, growth-oriented, focused on innovation, and more generally, able to operate in a changing environment. Another trend: the hiring of outside managers. Companies will seek motivated leadership, whether from outside or within. Similarly, companies will out-source (go outside the company) with many aspects not considered a "core" business—this means that managers within these areas will have to find work outside their company.

▶ **Outlook for MBAs: good. For MBAs from top schools: even better—as long as the economy continues strong.**

As U.S. corporations restructure—or reengineer—themselves (to use the current buzzword), MBA demand will continue to sizzle. MBAs from top schools entering the booming consulting field can expect entering salaries that exceed $40,000 to $80,000 on average, and graduates from the second tier can also expect strong demand and high salaries. In 1995, students at one top school averaged three offers apiece; at another, over 85% were hired before the end of the summer.

▶ **A major trend: self-employment.**

By 2005, one-third of the increase in self-employed workers—*half a million jobs*—will occur among managers, administrators, and executives. Why? Partly from all those layoffs mentioned above. Many executives, realizing their relatively poor chances of matching their previous salaries/responsibilities, are taking their payouts and investing in their own businesses. Another reason: the baby-boom generation wants *control*.

▶ **Competition will be tough for many.**

First the good news, downsizing has taken its toll, but the massive restructuring of the past few years has slowed. According to the American Management Association, businesses are adding more jobs than they are cutting.

Now the bad news, at least for some. The older managers who were fired during the downsizing of the past few years, specifically the over-50 group, will probably face tougher than normal competition, particularly as underemployed members of the "Generation X" group (born after 1961) keep entering the job market. They tend to be well-trained, responsible (some reports indicate that they have unusually good savings habits, unusual with past generations of the 20-somethings) and more to the point—they're cheaper to hire. For the first time in recent years, the job outlook for these new entrants is good—college campuses are reporting increased hiring. Nevertheless, competition is still very tough, and many are working in jobs that are less than what they hoped for. One result: this is the most entrepreneurial generation ever, as younger graduates start companies—and create their own ideal jobs. Another trend: seeking—and getting—work in the more challenging areas of the world, including Eastern Europe, Central Asia, and the Pacific Rim.

▶ **Some career advice for younger managers in particular.**

Look at smaller companies. Many of the most successful managerial applicants found jobs with smaller corporations. The Small Business Administration found in a study that small businesses of less than 500 employees will create 70% of all new jobs; even if you discount these figures, you can see that opportunities are there.

▶ **Following is a breakdown of trends and outlooks for different managerial areas.**

First of all, a warning. After the slump in the early 1980s, very few people predicted that a boom was coming in financial services—and financial services employment. The predictions below are a reflection of what the experts are saying *now*; but unforeseen circumstances, particularly in these days, have a way of cropping up.

• **Management consulting:** Now that many companies have laid off employees, they're relying on outside help, and that's where consultants can come in. More important, in today's fast moving marketplace, a consultant may be called to quickly identify problems and solutions—there's often no time for long in-house problem solving. Companies call this "out-sourcing," consultants call it lucrative. Key point: with all the talk about "re-engineering the corporation" consultants will be needed to help do it. Best way to enter: usually an MBA or extensive experience within an industry. Key skills: technical or industry segment skills are essential, but also extremely important are sales skills. Consultants must be able to bring in new business and maintain current relationships.

• **Health care:** With an aging population increasing the demand for health care, and the expansion and diversification of the health care industry, this sector should offer decent employment prospects over the next few years, although some experts predict that layoffs and consolidation may affect this area. In 1996 and early 1997, this field was one of the hottest, according to executive recruiters. The bottom line? Competition may be fierce, depending on the industry sector—and some health-service managers may be facing the possibility of layoffs. Best skills to have? Clinical skills or patient-care experience; postgraduate degree. Best areas: HMOs, home health agencies, offices of the health practitioners, nursing homes, and personal care facilities. Slower growth: hospitals. Long-term hot spot: hospital management companies.

• **Supermarket chains:** according to industry sources, 680,000 new jobs will be opening in chains—with more challenging managerial and marketing jobs for skilled applicants.

• **Retail management:** Not the best of times overall, but hiring trends are relatively strong. 1996 was very good, as was early 1997. In terms of the industry, forecasts for the near future aren't so great. Why? Growing consumer debt (and a decline in consumer spending) and an overabundance of stores (America is "overstored" in the jargon of insiders). Both mean more competition among stores. Best guess for the short term: weaker outlook for jobs in general. But don't despair. Demand for good candidates will continue to be good. Why? Retail is very *unpopular* among MBAs—at the same time, with all the competition among stores, demand for talented executives will continue to be strong. Best bets? Strong companies like Wal-mart—in 1997 they were targeted to hire 1,000 college grads. Another plus in the industry: Despite lowish starting salaries, promotions are *fast*. Best bet: Target the best-performing retail categories. In general, though, expect hot competition.

• **Hotel management:** Mixed outlook. On one hand, increased business travel and foreign and domestic tourism will result in increased demand for hotels and motels—and so, managers. But much of the industry should be in economy hotels, which have fewer on-site managers than full-service hotels. Generally, these economy properties have a general manager, and the regional offices of the hotel management company employs department managers to oversee operations at several hotels. The good news: Trainee positions will remain good employment opportunities at the larger full-service hotels.

• **Computer management:** Hiring was red hot in 1996–1997, as technology companies expanded operations. Key point: With burgeoning technology applications, managers with program management skills to oversee projects will be in strong demand. In early 1997, high sign-on bonuses, and generous extra benefits were being offered to many job-changers in technology.

However, always remember this is usually a volatile area, and the years to come should be no different. In general, the trend is good to excellent. Although many expect a slowdown, the outlook in the software area—powered by a rapidly expanding Internet—is particularly good, as is overseas sales. Another good bet: marketing managers, as companies try to differentiate their products.

• **Restaurant management:** Long-term outlook bright, with the government projecting faster than average increases in employment. But the short-term outlook is more problematic, as industry experts predict that a gradual economic downturn will slow industry growth. Best opportunities for people with B.S. or A.S. degrees in restaurant and institutional food service management. Downside: highly volatile industry. A growing area: international. About seventy U.S. restaurant chains have international outlets, more expected. A related field that should offer job growth: *food service managers* in nursing homes, residential care facilities, and other health care institutions. In addition, supermarkets are stepping up their hiring of food service managers—as they add or expand prepared foods departments and such things as coffee bars and the like.

• **Financial management:** 1996 and early 1997 were good years for workers in the financial services industries—with record profits producing record bonuses. Executive search firms recorded the financial services industry as among the hottest area for managers. Demand was also especially strong for financial executives in technology-based companies. But with some projecting a downward or stable trend in the financial markets for the next few years, the best days are probably over for many professionals in this area. A strong trend: overseas employment.

- **Real estate and property management:** The long-term trend is good, particularly because housing, retail stores, etc., are increasingly situated in centralized developments—run by property, mall, apartment, or housing complex managers.

- **International management:** Overseas experience is increasingly the key to career development. As the economy goes global, the need is there for managers with international expertise. Many entrepreneurial managers have found jobs—and wealth—in the emerging states of Eastern Europe and Asia. Meanwhile, financial firms are aggressively expanding overseas, as are American computer firms. See International section on page 109.

- **Facilities management:** A long-term best bet. Facilities managers literally manage the physical structure and assets of a company or organization—from the real estate side to furniture to everyday maintenance. Reasons for growth: increasing cost-consciousness, need for effective cost control and planning. Only now is this area becoming a full-fledged specialty. According to *The New York Times*, training is scarce, confined to less than twenty-five colleges, including MIT, Iona, North Dakota State, and Brigham Young, among others. Best background: BA in facilities management, MBA. For more information: contact International Facility Management Association, page 139.

- **Human resources (HR):** Predicted to grow 32 percent by 2005, according to a moderate economic growth scenario by the government. Fastest-growing area: training. Entry-level jobs as employment interviewers (predicted growth much faster than average), job analyst. Good bets: HR generalists, followed by compensation and benefits specialists and organizational development specialists; labor relations staff, including arbitrators and mediators, international human resources managers, and information systems specialists. Also looking good: *personnel consulting*—particularly as businesses farm out various human resources functions. Best areas to the top management suites: strategic HR management, succession planning.

- **Buying and purchasing:** A weaker job outlook than many other managerial areas. The key reason: increased use of computers. With less paperwork involved in ordering and procuring, lower-level buyers who handled this work are being eliminated. In addition, companies are relying on long-term contracting and limited sourcing—which has cut down on the number of suppliers and the frequency of negotiations. The upshot? More competition for jobs—the best jobs tend to go to those with experience in such areas as product developing, sourcing, and overseas markets.

- **Best bet:** The retail industry has recently seen an uptick in hiring of merchandise planning and distribution specialists. The volume of merchandise retail chains are carrying is tremendous—and with store buyers' time more limited, distribution experts, who decide where merchandise should go when it is bought and who plan ahead for stores' needs, are in demand.

WHAT'S NEXT

▶ **The search for broad-based managers will widen.**

One interesting development: some manufacturing firms are shifting their entry-level hiring focus from the Ivy League to the Big Ten universities of the Midwest, according to *Industry Week* magazine. The reasoning seems to be that these people will be more like "typical" consumers, with a better competitive edge in manufacturing and marketing their products.

▶ **Service and quality—management focus of the rest of the 1990s.**

Even with manufacturing firms, product service will become key in selling manufactured goods. Manufacturers will concentrate on building strong dealer-distributor networks—and managers will face the complex task of making certain that lines of communication are strong between the plant, the dealer, and the customer.

U.S. business has accepted one aspect of Japanese business, attention to quality, and realized another current failing, lack of attention to service.

Companies that emphasize both will prosper—from low-end retailers like Wal-Mart to high-end computer giants like Hewlett-Packard. Managers who can motivate a good service attitude in employees will do well.

This is important. In the next ten years, there will be a shortage of educated or technically competent entry-level workers. Keeping and motivating good workers will be one of the most crucial functions of a manager. For example, according to Marriott Corporation's senior vice president of human relations, Marriott must sell itself to prospective workers, not vice versa.

▶ **Back-to-basics mood among U.S. MBAs.**

A good way to predict the future of U.S. business: look at what MBAs are studying now. Major trend on campus: away from investment banking; toward manufacturing, production, and, most of all, international.

SALARIES

According to a recent survey by the National Institute of Business Management, median managerial salaries for top executives at small to mid-sized companies were:

> **Chief executive officers and presidents:** $139,000
> **Marketing executives:** $90,000
> **Manufacturing executives:** $70,750
> **Sales executives:** $75,699
> **Data-processing executives:** $56,258
> **Financial executives:** $75,000
> **Human resources executives:** $55,000

Obviously, top executive salaries at large corporations are usually much higher. Below these levels, salaries vary widely.

HOTEL MANAGEMENT: depending on hotel size, assistant manager $32,000 to $53,000; for a manager, $45,000 to $100,000.

PURCHASING EXECUTIVES: average salary over $50,000 in 1995. Salaries range from a low of about $35,000 for buyers, up through the mid $40s for more senior buyers. Managers averaged in the mid $50s, materials directors in the mid $80s. Highest salaries in the Northeast/Mid-Atlantic states (average over $53,000).

GENERAL MANAGERS: wide variation. Rules of thumb: higher salaries in larger metro areas, in finance (until recently), large manufacturing and service firms. Median salaries around $45,000 to $50,000.

FINANCIAL MANAGERS: median salaries in the mid $40s to $50s. Salaries vary widely. Chief financial officers earned up to $80,000 in 1994 in small companies. In large companies, earnings can go over $200,000, including incentives and bonuses.

CONSULTANTS: entry-level salaries average about $30,000 to $40,000. Senior consultants/managers earn on average from $50,000 to $90,000.

HUMAN RESOURCES, PERSONNEL, TRAINING: median income for HR professionals was about $58,999 in 1993; more at larger firms or in larger cities. Top salaries exceed $250,000.

BEST BETS

"SMALL BIG CITIES": Smart job hunters can do well by checking the classifieds or targeting employment opportunities in some of the dynamic smaller cities of America, many of which are seeing much greater economic growth than their larger competitors. Some examples: *Memphis, Tennessee,* which has created over 100,000 jobs in the past ten years by emphasizing distribution businesses; in fact, it calls itself "America's Distribution Center." Nike, Square D, Disney stores, Williams-Sonoma all support such centers here. Also: *Charlotte, North Carolina,* with the 10th busiest airport in the world, and major divisions of headquarters of major corporations from Hearst to Microsoft. And *Cedar Rapids, Iowa,* which attracted hundreds of millions of dollars in factory investments. One word of caution: last year's "hot city" may not be hot this year, so you'll have to do some checking yourself.

SERVICE MANAGERS: Today's customer wants satisfaction—and service managers make certain he or she gets it. As technology makes it easier for customers to contact companies (via fax, e-mail, and telephone) companies are increasingly looking to service managers and staff to answer customers' questions and complaints, and offer technical and other forms of support. Increasingly, many firms rely on outside service centers, which are good areas for employment, as are small companies with emerging departments. Salaries for managers range from about $26,000 to $100,000 for national service managers.

HUMAN RESOURCES: Once on the second tier of American business, human resource managers are moving increasingly to the first. Principal reasons: a new shortage of qualified workers makes retaining employees more important; the rapid changes in our work force make human resource planning more important; the rise in two-income families has resulted in a rise in human resource programs (child care, spouse relocations, etc.); declining loyalty makes it easier for workers to quit; and finally, telecommunications and computers are making old management-employee structures obsolete—someone has to study, design, and help implement new systems.

Other duties: enhancing employee effectiveness, dealing with unions, enforcing government personnel regulations, developing benefits plans, supervising training. And some duties geared to the late 1990s: managing diversity programs, managing programs to help families within a corporate environment, international training, employee interaction programs. Requirements: usually a college degree, but not necessarily a specialized one, or advanced training (psychology, business, other liberal arts; sometimes an MBA).

In general, there are two tiers to the human resource function—at the top, the high-ranked generalist who supervises various specialists. At the lower levels, in addition to recruiters, demand will grow for compensation and benefits specialists. Also in demand: outplacement counselors and consultants. For the field as a whole, the Bureau of Labor Statistics predicts a high 32% growth rate through the balance of the 1990s.

Human resources is particularly important for women. Because they already occupy many top spots in the field, watch for women to move from high-level human resources positions into other more senior executive positions in the 1990s. Salaries range from $25,000 on up through mid-level and top-level salaries of $40,000–$80,000, to $120,000 at larger companies. Upper-level vice presidents at large corporations earn over $250,000.

WHERE TO GO FOR MORE INFORMATION

MANAGEMENT ASSOCIATIONS

American College of Physician Executives
4890 W. Kennedy Blvd., Suite 200
Tampa, FL 33609
813/287-2000

American Assembly of Collegiate Schools of Business
600 Emerson
Suite 300
St. Louis, MO 63141-6762
314/872-8481

American Chamber of Commerce Executives
4232 King St.
Alexandria, VA 22302
703/998-0072
(Publishes periodicals.)

American College of Health Care Administrators
325 S. Patrick St.
Alexandria, VA 22314
703/549-5822

American College of Health Care Executives
1 N. Franklin St.

Suite 1700
Chicago, IL 60606
312/424-2800

American Compensation Association
14040 Northsight Blvd.
Scottsdale, AZ 85260
602/951-9191
(For managers associated with compensation packages, etc.; publishes periodical with job listings; holds seminars.)

**American
Management
Association**
135 W. 50th St.
New York, NY 10020
212/586-8100
(The major association
for managers; offers
numerous programs,
has many offices in
United States and
worldwide, has
information service,
bookstore, etc.)

**American Planning
Association**
1225 S. Michigan
Suite 1600
Chicago, IL 60603
312/955-9100
(Publishes periodical
with job listings,
referral service, etc., all
for members only.)

**American Society of
Association
Executives**
1575 I St., NW
Washington, DC 20005
202/626-2711
(Publish periodical; job
referral service, etc.)

**American Society for
Public
Administration**
1120 G St., NW
Suite 700
Washington, DC 20005
202/393-7878

**American Society for
Training and
Development**
1640 King St.
Alexandria, VA 22313
703/683-8100
(Publishes human
resources journal.)

**Association for
International
Practical Training**
10400 Little Patuxent
Pkwy., Suite 250
Columbia, MD 21044
410/997-2200
(For recent graduates;
arranges
hospitality/tourism
overseas exchanges
with on-the-job
training or research.)

**Building Owners and
Managers Association
International**
1201 New York Ave.,
NW
Suite 300
Washington, DC 20005
202/408-2662

**Cable Television
Administration and
Marketing Society**
201 N. Union St.
Suite 440
Alexandria, VA 22314
703/549-4200

**Center for
Management
Development**
135 W. 50th St.
New York, NY 10020
212/586-8100
(Division of American
Management
Association; operates
extension institute, a
home study program,
etc.)

**Employment
Management
Association**
4101 Lake Boone Trail
Suite 201
Raleigh, NC 27607
919/787-6010

**Financial
Management
Association**
University of South
Florida
College of Business
Administration
Tampa, FL 33640-5500
813/974-2084
(Publishes periodical
with job listing.)

**Financial Managers
Society**
8 S. Michigan Ave.,
Suite 500
Chicago, IL 60603
312/578-1300

**Institute of
Management
Consultants**
230 Park Ave.
New York, NY 10176
212/697-9693

**Institute of Managing
Consultants**
521 Fifth Ave., 35th Fl.
New York, NY 10175
212/697-8262
(Professional group
that sponsors member
business referral.)

**Institute of Real
Estate Management**
430 N. Michigan Ave.,
7th Fl.
Chicago, IL 60611
312/661-1930
312/329-6000
(Placement service for
members; certifies
members, etc.)

**International
Association of
Assessing Officers**
130 E. Randolph
Chicago, IL 60601
312/819-6100

International Association of Business Communicators
1 Hallide Plz.
Suite 600
San Francisco, CA 94102
415/433-3400
(For managers in corporate communications and public relations.)

International Conference of Building Officials
5360 Workman Mill Rd.
Whittier, CA 90601
310/699-0541

International Facility Management Association
One East Greenway Plz., 11th Fl.
Houston, TX 77046
713/623-IFMA

International Food Service Manufacturers Association
180 N. Stetson
Chicago, IL 60601
312/540-4400

International Personnel Management Association
1617 Duke St.
Alexandria, VA 22314

703/549-7100
(Publishes periodical, directory, etc.)

National Management Association
2210 Arbor Blvd.
Dayton, OH 45439
513/294-0421

Society for Human Resource Management
606 N. Washington St.
Alexandria, VA 22314
703/548-3440
(Publishes periodical with job listings, directory; maintains HRM-net job databank of jobs listed in its periodical.)

MANAGEMENT DIRECTORIES

(For much more, see also "General Business Sources," page 503.)

AMA's Executive Employment Guide
Eileen Monahan, Editor
American Management Association
135 W. 50th St.
New York, NY 10020
212/586-8100
(Free to AMA members; lists search firms, job registries, etc.)

AMBA's MBA Employment Guide
Association of MBA Executives
227 Commerce St.
East Haven, CT 06512
203/315-5221
(For $10 each, sends a listing of corporations in three states of choice for one functional area.)

Dun & Bradstreet Million-Dollar Directory; Dun & Bradstreet Reference Book of Corporate Managements; Career Guide
Dun's Marketing Services
3 Sylvan Way
Parsippany, NJ 07054
800/526-0651
(Expensive but extensive listings of leading U.S. corporations.)

Directory of Corporate Affiliations

Reed Reference Publishing
P.O. Box 31
New Providence, NJ 07974
800/323-6772
(Expensive but good source for hard-to-find private firms.)

Peterson's Job Opportunities in Business
P.O. Box 2123
Princeton, NJ 08543
609/243-9111
800/338-3282
(Lists hundreds of corporations and organizations that are hiring; includes detailed information.)

Women Directors of the Top 1,000 Corporations
National Women's

Economic Alliance
Foundation
1440 New York
Ave, NW,

Suite 300
Washington, DC 20005
202/393-5257

MANAGEMENT PERIODICALS

(For *Forbes, Fortune,* etc., see also "General Business Sources," page 503.)

Across the Board
845 Third Ave.
New York, NY 10022
212/759-0900
(Monthly magazine published by the influential Conference Board.)

Facilities Design & Management
2 Penn Plaza
New York, NY 10019
212/714-1300
(Monthly for corporate facilities managers.)

FE/Financial Executive
P.O. Box 1938
Morristown, NJ 07962
201/898-4600
(Bimonthly magazine for finance executives.)

Forty Plus Newsletter
Forty Plus of New York
15 Park Row
New York, NY 10038
212/233-6086
(Four times a year; free to Forty Plus members, a group that helps over-forty managers find a job.)

Harvard Business Review
60 Harvard Way
Boston, MA 02163
617/495-6800

(Bimonthly; prestigious journal of business.)

HR Magazine
606 N. Washington St.
Alexandria, VA 22314
703/548-3440
(Monthly for human resources executives, particularly those in compensation, benefits, training.)

INC.
38 Commercial Wharf
Boston, MA 02110
617/248-8000
(Invaluable for targeting the fast-moving corporations that tend to do the most hiring.)

Industry Week
1100 Superior Ave.
Cleveland, OH 44114
216/696-7000
(Semimonthly; covers industrial management.)

Journal of Commerce
2 World Trade Center
New York, NY 10048
212/837-7000
(Daily business newspaper.)

Management Review
135 W. 50th St.

New York, NY 10020
212/903-8063
(Monthly for members of AMA.)

National Business Employment Weekly
P.O. Box 30
Princeton, NJ
08543-0300
800/323-6239

Personnel Journal
ACC Communications
245 Fischer Ave., B-2
Costa Mesa, CA 92626
714/751-1883
subscription address:
P.O. Box 50088
Boulder, CO 80321-0088
800/444-6485
(Monthly magazine for HR pros.)

Logistics Management
275 Washington St.
Newton, MA 02158
617/964-3030
(Monthly magazine.)

Training
50 S. 9th St.
Minneapolis, MN 55402
612/333-0471
(Monthly magazine for personnel in corporate and university training programs.)

PERFORMING ARTISTS

[NOTE: For more information and source material about film and television, see the appropriate industry sections.]

BRIEF BACKGROUND

▶ **For most performing arts professions, you need talent—and then you need luck. There are many more aspiring actors, dancers, and musicians than there are jobs.**

One example of the tight competition: According to the Screen Actor's Guild (SAG), over 80% of all performers who worked under a SAG contract a few years ago earned under $5,000—and less than 6% earned over $25,000.

But then again . . . As with any creative profession, *some* people make it. And to take another example from the acting profession, one actor a few years ago brought home $40 million as salary and bonus—with the added job satisfaction of being critically and popularly acclaimed. Some people have it all . . .

On the other side of the camera—or the lights—film and theatrical production careers will also remain competitive. (For more on film production careers, see Film and Entertainment on page 330.)

NOTE: This section only briefly highlights a few major trends and job reference material available. For further information, we recommend reading the books mentioned at the end of the chapter, and, most importantly, reading the appropriate magazines for up-to-the-minute employment information. Trends in creative careers change quickly—and hiring opportunities may not even last days, but hours.

EMPLOYMENT OUTLOOK: Poor for most, excellent for the few among performing artists, better for production people, administrative staff; but still intense competition.

Major Employment Areas

ACTORS AND ACTRESSES: Government experts predict that the number of jobs will increase—but then again, competition will continue to be extremely tough.

- **A widening field for actors.** Film, videocassettes, theater, cable shows, television commercials, new forms of advertising production, independent television shows, new regional theater (which can now sometimes support full-time actors).

• **More demand for acting talent.** Increasing use of videocassettes and increase in television/cable viewing (the average hours spent watching has gone up consistently) means yet more demand.

• **Increased theater productions.** Some experts are predicting that theater-going will increase in the next few years, leading to increased opportunities for actors. But (as it always seems with experts), others are saying just the opposite: the trend is down, particularly now that government arts funding is decreasing. One possible growth area: regional theater.

• **More regional power:** Acting is not just New York and LA. Florida in recent years had the third highest number of actors and screenwriters; Chicago, Florida, and Atlanta were all growing centers for television commercial production recently.

DANCERS: According to the U.S. Bureau of Labor Statistics, the job outlook for dancers in the long term is fairly good in terms of job growth. But that doesn't mean too much because jobs are so scarce—the number of dancers seeking work far exceeds openings. And more ominously, government funding declines seem to point to fewer openings in government-funded dance companies in the near future. On the bright side: there has been a renewed popular interest in dance in recent years.

Best areas: national dance companies, music video and TV, film production, universities, teaching dance.

One good source for jobs: The American Dance Guild maintains a placement service. Check address under association listings at the end of the chapter.

MUSICIANS: Music is a different profession—almost three out of five musicians employed recently worked part time; about one quarter were self-employed. On average about 260,000 people held a musical job in the past year.

Most musicians are concentrated in major cities where major orchestras and recording studios are located: Los Angeles, New York, Chicago, Nashville, and New Orleans. The cities themselves reflect the diversity of American music, from rock to classical to jazz to country and blues.

Government experts predict that employment growth for musical jobs will be faster than average—but on the other hand, because competition for jobs is so tough, most new musicians will find openings because other musicians have left the field. More to the point, it is difficult to be specific about musical jobs, because a lot depends on the *type* of musician, the area, the level of talent, etc. One key point: expect tough competition in virtually *any* area of music.

Some general employment notes:

• **In classical music and opera:** worries about a declining trend of audience attendance in the major market of New York. Problem for many orchestras and opera companies: finding—and keeping—audiences. For opera: decentralization out of New York points to more regional opportunities—but problems with reduced government, private funding.

• **In contemporary, rock, music:** competition is astronomically tough; job openings in bars expected to decline as bar attendance declines to the year 2000.

Highest dollar earners: country and urban music—but the bottom line is simple: do what you're best at.

Two general employment trends: multi-faceted musicians who can play more than one instrument or type of music may face better employment prospects. Many musicians can find jobs in peripheral areas—teaching, etc.

▶ **How to find a job in the arts: Be persistent.**

It is easy to say—harder to do. Many of the arts associations, such as the Dance Guild, maintain job banks. Check the associations listed at the end of the chapter.

▶ **Many aspiring artists of any type want to tap into product funding to advance their work. One obvious source is the foundations.**

Some people seem to win many more foundation grants than others. Very often the difference isn't talent, but finding the best foundation for your work. First, check to see if your type of artistic talent matches the type the foundation sponsors.

The best way—check: *Foundation Grants to Individuals* from the Foundation Center; address and information on page 146.

The same publisher also publishes *Foundation Directory* (listing thousands of national and local foundations) and *Corporate Foundation Profiles*. There are no standard application procedures; you'll have to write specific foundations and request instructions. In many cases, foundations only sponsor bona fide arts groups; in this case, the best procedure is to approach a local association or organization familiar with your work and have them apply on your behalf.

Key problem: declines in government art funding will continue.

SALARIES

ACTING: Most salaries are regulated by the unions; there are many variables, depending on the nature and venue of the work, residuals, and so on. Some representative *minimum* salaries in 1997: Broadway stage productions, $1,040 a week; off-Broadway $381 to $652 a week, depending on the theater's seating capacity. TV principal actors in a one-hour network soap opera could earn a minimum $683; a nonspeaking extra could earn $128 per hour. The median salary for Actors Equity members was $5,800 in 1995. Forty-six percent earned under $5,000 from acing. Obviously, many actors have to supplement their acting incomes with other work. Well-known actors, of course, earn much more, but they are in a very small minority. Only 1% earned over $100,000.

MUSICIANS, DANCERS, ETC.: Highly variable salaries, depending on specific art form, etc. Dancers' minimums in 1994 ranged around $600 per week. First-year dancers were paid a basic rate of $242 per performance and $71 per hour of rehearsal. Musicians' salaries ranged from $1,000 to $1,400 a week in major cities at top orchestras, with the season extending from 48 to 52 weeks. Earnings with regional orchestras were lower: $400 to $700 a week for a 25- to 38-week session.

BEST BETS

FILM EXTRA: A best bet more for the amateur, or the occasional actor and actress—although sometimes an extra does get noticed and does get a part. What extras do: Film extras form the "people background" to films and commercials. How to become one: In Hollywood, go to Central Casting, an agency that supplies extras to Hollywood films; it works with the Screen Extras' Guild, which extras must usually join in. In New York, contact a casting agency like Sylvia Fay (addresses can be found in *Backstage* magazine). Extras in New York are also usually union members, either with the Screen Actors Guild, Actors Equity, or AFTRA (addresses are listed at the end of the chapter). Outside of LA or NY, call the state film commission.

Competition: tough. In LA, a central list is maintained, and when shortages of a specific type occur, newcomers are added to the list. Outside of the major areas, opportunities are easier to find. Guild pay: For extras in a TV commercial in 1995, for example, $240 per day. For extras in a radio commercial: $185 per 90 minutes.

WHERE TO GO FOR MORE INFORMATION

PERFORMING ARTS ASSOCIATIONS

Actor's Equity Association Union
1560 Broadway
New York, NY 10036
212/869-8530
6430 Sunset Blvd.
Hollywood, CA 90028
213/462-2334
(Write or call for regional offices and phone numbers.)

American Conservatory Theater Foundation
450 Geary St.
San Francisco, CA 94102

415/834-3200
(Offers M.F.A. and holds auditions for entry; offers placement service, etc.)

American Council for the Arts
1 E. 53rd St.
New York, NY 10022
212/223-2787

American Dance Guild
31 W. 21st St.
New York, NY 10010
212/627-3790

American Federation of Musicians—East

1501 Broadway
New York, NY 10036
212/869-1330
(Publishes monthly tabloid with job listings.)

American Federation of Musicians—West
1777 N. Vine St.,
Suite 500
Hollywood, CA 90028
213/461-3441

American Federation of Television and Radio Artists
(AFTRA)
260 Madison Ave.

New York, NY 10016
212/532-0800
6922 Hollywood Blvd.,
Suite 900
Hollywood, CA 90028
1-800/367-7966

**American Film
Institute**
John F. Kennedy
Center for the
Performing Arts
Washington, DC 20566
202/828-4090
(Has internship
program; gives grants.)

**American Guild of
Musical Artists**
1727 Broadway
New York, NY 10019
212/265-3687

**American Guild of
Organists**
475 Riverside Dr.
New York, NY 10115
212/870-2310
(Publishes monthly
magazine, etc.)

**American Music
Center**
30 W. 26th St.
New York, NY 10010
212/366-5263

**American Society of
Composers, Authors
and Publishers**

1 Lincoln Plaza
New York, NY 10023
212/595-3050

**American Symphony
Orchestra League**
1156 15 St., NW
Suite 800
Washington, DC 20005
202/776-0212
(With hundreds of U.S.
orchestras as members,
a valuable contact point
for young conductors
selected by the league.)

**Association of
Independent Video
and Filmmakers**
304 Hudson St.
New York, NY 10012
212/804-1400

**Dance Theater
Workshop**
219 W. 19th St.
New York, NY 10011
212/691-6500

Dance USA
1156 15 St., NW
Suite 820
Washington, DC
20005-1704
202/833-1717

**International Society
of Performing Arts
Administrators**
2920 Fuller NE

Suite 205
Grand Rapids, MI
49505
616/364-3000

**National Dance
Association**
1900 Association Dr.
Reston, VA 22091
703/476-3436

**National Foundation
for Advancement in
the Arts**
800 Brickell
Suite 500
Miami, FL 33131
305/377-1140

**New England Theater
Conference**
c/o Dept. of Theater
Northeastern Univ.
360 Huntington Ave.
Boston, MA 02115
617/424-9275

**Producers Guild of
America**
400 S. Beverly,
Suite 211
Beverly Hill, CA 90212
310/557-0807

Screen Actors Guild
5757 Wilshire Blvd.
Hollywood, CA 90036
213/954-1600
(Write or call for local
offices.)

PERFORMING ARTS DIRECTORIES

*The Academy Players
Directories*
The Academy of
Motion Picture Arts
and Sciences
8949 Wilshire Blvd.
Beverly Hills, CA

90211
310/247-3000
(Listing for agented
SAG or AFTRA
members; distributed to
casting directors, etc.)

*American Dance Guild
Membership Directory*
American Dance Guild
31 W. 21st St.
New York, NY 10010
212/627-3790

Foundation Grants to Individuals; Foundation Directory; Corporate Foundation Profiles
Foundation Center
79 Fifth Ave.
New York, NY 10003-3076
212/620-4230
(The first directory is particularly valuable to artists seeking financial support from foundations.)

International Motion Picture Almanac; International

Television and Video Almanac
Quigley Publishing Company
159 W. 53rd St.
New York, NY 10019
212/247-3100
(Includes production companies and producers, agencies, affiliated firms and businesses, names and extra information on major film players.)

Regional Theater Directory; Summer Theater Directory
American Theater Works, Inc.

P.O. Box 519
Dorset, VT 05251
802/867-2223
(Theater companies listed by region, hiring information.)

Ross Reports Television
Television Index, Inc.
40-29 27th St.
Long Island City, NY 11101
718/937-3990
(Monthly directory listing major TV employers along with requirements, names of casting personnel, etc.)

PERFORMING ARTS MAGAZINES

American Cinematographer
American Society of Cinematographers
P.O. Box 2230
Hollywood, CA 90078
213/876-5080
(Monthly.)

Art Search
Theatre Communications Group
355 Lexington Ave.
New York, NY 10017
212/697-5230
(Lists artistic as well as administrative, production, and education job openings.)

Back Stage
1515 Broadway
New York, NY 10036

212/764-7300
(Weekly tabloid; a major source of ads and information, particularly for the East Coast.)

Billboard
P.O. Box 2011
Marion, OH 43305
1-800/669-1002
(Weekly tabloid of the music industry.)

The Chicago Reader
11 E. Illinois
Chicago, IL 60611
312/828-0350
(Weekly theater magazine listing Chicago theater productions.)

Daily Variety
5700 Wilshire Blvd.
Suite 120

Los Angeles, CA 90036
213/857-6600
(Daily paper covering film and TV production; along with *Hollywood Reporter,* it is *the* Hollywood source.)

Dance Magazine
33 W. 60th St.
New York, NY 10029
212/245-9050
(Monthly.)

Down Beat
102 N. Haven
Elmhurst, IL 60126
708/941-2030
(Monthly for jazz players and amateurs.)

Drama-Logue
1456 N. Gordon
Hollywood, CA 90028

213/464-5079
(Major source for
theater, film, and TV
jobs on the West
Coast.)

Emmy
5220 Lankershim Blvd.
N. Hollywood, CA
91601
818/754-2860

Hollywood Reporter
5055 Wilshire Blvd.
Los Angeles, CA
90036
213/525-2000
(Daily; along with
Daily Variety, it is *the*
major source of
Hollywood TV and film
production information.)

Variety
245 W. 17th St.
New York, NY 10011
212/337-7002
(Weekly; more East
Coast-oriented, more
theater and distribution
rather than the nitty-
gritty daily production
of *Daily Variety.*)

SALES AND MARKETING PROFESSIONALS

BRIEF BACKGROUND

▶ **Marketing employees position a product or a service—they develop a campaign that includes sales, advertising, and public relations. Then the sales force goes out and sells it. Those are the basics; everything else is changing.**

First, computers are entering the marketplace and are changing the time-worn ways of doing business. They are taking the administrative functions away from the sales force and freeing them to concentrate on sales.

Computers are giving retailers and buyers more information. For example, with computerized sales scanners, they have up-to-date inventory and sales figures. This makes selling more difficult. Today, if a product doesn't sell quickly, it is off the shelves quickly.

Also, more products or services are entering markets, competition is heating up both in the U.S. and abroad, and in many cases products and services are becoming more complex. Once, a salesperson would go out and sell a typewriter; now he or she must make sell a complicated, computerized word-processing system.

That's a big difference. This new complexity is creating a demand for more knowledgeable and technically oriented sales and marketing people. There is more interaction between sales and manufacturing, product development, and other corporate areas. In some areas there's more team selling, in other areas the emphasis is on more targeted sales drawn from sophisticated databases; but in all areas, it is clear that further change is ahead.

▶ **A consulting executive interviewed in *Sales & Marketing Management* put it this way: "Sales management will move from a game of checkers to a game of chess."**

As the corporate chess game intensifies, sales and marketing employees will play a key role. Already more top CEOs come from sales or marketing positions than from any other, and salaries average near the top. This is an increasingly open area to women, who make up over 50 percent of some sales categories.

But: recessions and industrial or corporate downturns can hurt sales and marketing people faster and often harder, and tough competition gets tougher. In the words of another sales and marketing executive to a new class of salespeople: "Welcome to the pressure cooker." Someone else, scarred a bit from the recession, put it differently: "It's a roller-coaster ride." [Note: for more specific information, see the various industry sections, and Managerial Careers section.]

EMPLOYMENT OUTLOOK: Good in long term.

▶ **Sales and marketing professionals should see relatively strong demand for their services for the rest of the 1990s—but, as always, should be aware that what comes up may come down during short-term recessions.**

The sales and marketing professions are very dependent on the state of the economy—more so than most professions. When boom times occur, salaries and opportunities very often greatly exceed the averages of other positions, but when inevitable downturns occur, the outlook can turn temporarily bad.

This is what happened in the 1980s, when it was not uncommon for young salespeople to take home pay in excess of $100,000 in the first few years. Then came the recession of the early 1990s and, along with it, layoffs and much lower paychecks. In those years, the number of people employed in sales declined by 2.1%. Among the hardest hit: newcomers, lower performers, and those in poorly performing industries. Sales reps in finance and business services saw a 4.3% decline; those in media sales fared worse. But as the economy improved, hiring began to inch up.

What's ahead? In general, expect a positive outlook for sales and marketing personnel. Even while certain industries are consolidating, others are expanding into new markets—or introducing new products and/or services in an effort to maintain market strength. One key point: Part of the "restructuring" of American corporations has resulted in focus on long-term growth, which means an emphasis on new product introduction. This, in turn, points to job opportunities in sales and marketing overall. A good note: According to the federal government, sales and marketing as a whole will increase fairly rapidly in the long term—projecting above-average growth of 38% to 2005. In general, opportunities look the strongest for sales professionals with several years experience; demand is not as strong for those at higher levels or entry levels.

As always, employment in sales and marketing is dependent upon the climate in a specific industry, company, or region. For more information, read the industry and regional sections in this book.

▶ **The best way to look for sales and marketing jobs: assess the top-performing industries, then look for corporations that have restructured successfully.**

Key point: Today, the marketplace changes far more rapidly than it did in the past. Management fads come and go, companies rise and fall swiftly. What to do: research for yourself the industries and companies carefully. Assess: is the industry strong and poised for continued growth, and is my target company a strong player? In general, look for: concentration on core businesses, strong sales support, lean staffing, a team approach with marketers, salespeople, and service/manufacturing personnel working together closely.

Here's a breakdown of employment outlooks in different specific areas:

▶ **Financial sales: as usual, tied to the overall strength of the economy.**

1996 and early 1997 were excellent times for most stockbrokers and other financial salespeople. Bonuses and total salary hit record highs. But expectations of a flat market for the next few years somewhat dampened enthusiasm. In the words of one broker, "The best times are over."

But that doesn't mean the outlook is gloomy.

On the plus side: over the long term, employment of financial and securities sales reps is expected to go up. As baby boomers age, investing for retirement will increase. In addition, personal income growth and increased inherited wealth should have a positive impact on the picture. However, economic ups and downs will, of course, affect short-term hiring. Keep in mind: Wall Street is much more economy-oriented than in the past, and new hires are expected to add value quickly. But if they can, the sky is often the limit. Compensation was up again last year, and average salaries are among the highest in the nation.

Key trends: the days of the old-fashioned stockbroker are over. Many firms are looking for salespeople who sell a firm's total financial service package (from insurance to stocks). Somewhat older or more experienced applicants are often preferred. Rationale: they can bring in more moneyed clients faster. Look for more attention to financial planning, etc.—more on *managing* assets as opposed to selling or trading them. Financial salespeople will be called "financial planners," and will try to sell *all* financial services, not just stocks and bonds. For details, see Financial Services, page 339.

▶ **Insurance agents and brokers: highly competitive. Good outlook for ambitious sales types, especially those with expertise in a range of insurance and financial services.**

Over the long term, insurance sales should be increasing. Key reasons: An aging population—which means increased demand for life insurance, long-term care insurance, and retirement investment vehicles; increasing demand for commercial insurance (such as liability, employee benefits, and the like).

This picture, however, *doesn't* necessarily translate into increased job opportunities. The reason? Computerization is enabling agents and brokers to do more than in the past—they can pinpoint client needs, craft tailor-made insurance packages, and so, handle a larger volume of sales. In addition, mutual fund companies and brokerage houses are getting into insurance sales, cutting out the independent broker. In the past ten years, for example, the number of insurance agents has dropped by 27,000 to 219,000.

But employment opportunities still will be there for people with strong sales skills and financial services expertise. The good news for a skilled, ambitious salesperson: With a high turnover rate—less than 20% remain after four years— there is still an ongoing need for new recruits. And many progressive companies are beefing up their compensation plans and salesman support programs, including backup teams to furnish technical assistance. And for job seekers—be ready to take specialized tests. Many companies are beginning to find that testing can predict who will stay in insurance, and so they can avoid paying for training only to find their new hire in the 80% who leave after a few years. Best areas: Specialists in financial planning, international, the relatively wealthy Asian market, and other relatively untapped sectors of new ethnics in the U.S. *Key trend:* Expect to see a growing number of "multiline" insurance agents—that is, agents who offer a range of insurance policies, including life, property/casualty, and health and disability policies.

▶ **Real estate sales: High turnover will create job opportunities.**

There are currently about 400,000 agents and brokers in the U.S.—but the number is elastic. According to a recent report by *Real Estate Today* and the National Association of Realtors, real estate companies reported an average turnover of about 20% in one year. Given this, tens of thousands of real estate sales jobs open up each year. However, the field is highly competitive. In other words, it's often tougher to keep a job than to obtain one.

What real estate firms want: A changing real estate market has changed the profile of the ideal job candidate. These days, many real estate companies are seeking candidates with experience in other careers. In other words, career changers are most definitely wanted. As the real estate market has gotten more complex, real estate companies want people with analytical skills, business experience in general, and the ability to make a commitment. This is especially crucial in the inevitable downturns that occur in real estate when the economy slows down. However, real estate firms are still hiring novices—the key is to prove sales ability and energy level.

Broad trend: there's a shift in focus away from the technical emphasis on law, finance, and accounting. The need for the future: the ideal real estate candidate should have a broad general education, enabling him or her to tackle the increasingly complex transactions of the future, involving foreign currencies, environmental problems, politics, and so on. Also, according to a major real estate study reported by Elizabeth Fowler in *The New York Times*, the real estate firm of the future will be larger—with larger staffs, possibly international branches, and more services. Needed: the multi-talented, multi-linguistic sales forces and, more particularly, sales managers of the future.

▶ **Manufacturers' and wholesale sales reps: a mixed bag. According to the federal government, manufacturers' and wholesale sales representatives should be in for stable job growth.**

In general, the outlook is a bit brighter for manufacturers' agents as opposed to sales representatives. The reason? More companies have consolidated their buying areas and computerized their supply chains. As a result, sales jobs have been eliminated. In addition, companies will continue to rely on outsourcing as a way of keeping costs down. As a result, instead of having an in-house sales or direct marketing staff, companies will hire manufacturers' agents to take over their sales duties.

The best opportunities should be with small wholesale and manufacturing firms. These firms typically rely more on both wholesalers and manufacturers' agents to market their products as a way of keeping costs under control while increasing their customer base.

Best job candidates: those people who combine strong selling skills with technical knowledge or product expertise, as well as good business experience. For example, a chemical manufacturing firm might hire a person with an engineering background; a pharmaceutical company, pharmacy grads or nurses. The good news? There is often a short supply of these technical types—which is good news for recruits with the right skills.

▶ **Service sales representatives: bright prospects.**

There are already well over 600,000 service sales representatives in the U.S.—people who sell a variety of services ranging from temporary help to computer services to engineering; from telephone services to automotive leasing to equipment rental. And this number should increase as services industries grow. Certain areas look better than others. Best bet: computer and data processing sales.

Training for these positions varies. Nontechnical service companies—such as linen supply, laundry, funeral services—often will hire people with a high school diploma as long as they have sales experience. Technical services typically require a college degree (and in some cases, even more)—and also offer intensive training programs. Recent college graduates usually will find better opportunities at larger companies, while people with experience are often in demand at smaller companies.

▶ **The outlook in marketing: prospects good.**

The government forecasts a positive long-term outlook for marketers—and the short term should be fairly strong as well. A key reason? Intense domestic and global competition for consumers has put marketing into the spotlight. As such, marketers will be in demand.

Key reasons: more of an emphasis on selling quality products, less on finance. And in the marketplace, there is increasing market segmentation, shorter life cycles for products, increasing demand for new and better-quality items—and more competition. All point to the new role of marketing as the focal point of the corporation in the future.

Be ready for some major changes in the field, including the rise of temporary, consultative marketing. And be ready for more marketers in CEO seats, and much more emphasis on international sales.

Marketing is an enormous field—well over 300,000 Americans work in some aspect of marketing. But growth in the coming years will be very strong—better than 44% by the year 2005, according to the Bureau of Labor Statistics. Competition will be tough, however, in particular for entry-level positions. Many qualified applicants will be competing for the same jobs.

▶ **Certain marketing areas will offer better opportunities than others.**

Given the highly competitive nature of the field, the best way to target a job is to pinpoint areas that are headed for future growth. Some good bets:

In many cases, outside marketing firms should see growth. Corporations that downsized often cut back on in-house marketing departments. As a result, they have been relying more on outside marketing firms. These firms—which may range from very small boutiques to larger full-service agencies—are a good bet for employment over the short term.

Other good areas include: *Direct marketing.* Retailers eager to regain market strength, catalogers, technological companies, and telecommunications firms, in particular, have been rolling out bid direct market pushes—and this trend should continue. As such, marketing experts who can effectively run these campaigns should be in strong demand. *Telemarketing* experts, as well, will continue to be needed as businesses continue their phone pitches to consumers. *Database marketing* has been heating up—as more consumer products companies turn to databases as a way of pinpointing possible consumers. Finally, as global marketing continues to grow, people with *international* expertise will continue to be in demand.

New opportunities to watch for: Keep an a eye on "interactive marketing"—new employment opportunities linked to the Internet and World Wide Web. This new area has been attracting corporate attention. Businesses are eager to find new ways to market their products or services on the Web—and so are looking for marketing professionals who can help. In many cases, businesses are interested in people with direct marketing experience—who can translate their direct marketing skills from mailings and letters to on-line direct marketing via a Web site.

In addition to developing marketing plans using the Internet, interactive marketers may do market research on how people surf the Net and the like. Finally, a niche area that has been seeing growth: *sports marketing*. Sports marketing firms, who develop advertising and public relations programs for sports teams, have been growing—up from only about 100 firms in 1980 to roughly 800 now. This area should remain hot over the long term.

▶ **Poised for long-term growth: franchise sales.**

According to some experts, salespeople who specialize in selling franchises can expect high pay and strong demand in the rest of the 1990s. A key reason: franchises will continue to proliferate (in spite of possible temporary lulls in economic downturns and job competition.

▶ **Retail sales: fair—sometimes poor—prospects in a changing category.**

Employment prospects in retail sales are, of course, directly linked to the economy. When the economy slows and consumer spending drops, retail sales positions dry up—and when times are better, jobs reemerge. However, over the long term, the federal government projects that retail sales positions will grow as fast as average for all workers through the year 2005.

For the short term, retail looks more iffy. As of early 1997, sales had been relatively healthy. But a mountain of consumer debt makes some experts worry that problems could be on the horizon. As one expert, Carl E. Steidtmann of Management Horizons, put it, "It's sort of like termites eating away at the porch. The porch looks okay until you step on it."

Another problem: America is still "over-stored"—expect more consolidations in the future, and some more layoffs as these occur.

As for upper level jobs, merchandise planners are seeing strong job growth, buyers are not. Reason: mergers of retail firms, reducing absolute demand for buyers. Moreover, merchandise planners track what buyers buy on computer, monitor trends, and keep inventory levels right—usurping in many instances the importance of buyers in the corporate hierarchy, as this sort of computer control of inventory becomes so much more important. Key skills: numbers orientation, and of course, good communications skill.

More generally, retail managers should be affected by the same factors that affect lower-level sales positions. Certain areas should offer more employment opportunities than others—directly based on the strength of the retail category. Upper-level and middle-level managers will be directly affected by consolidation in the retail industry. But store-level retail supervisors and managers may be in for a more stable ride, as corporate streamlining often occurs more at the headquarter level in retail companies than at the store level. The only problem: store closings, which, of course, often mean that store-level managers are laid off.

The key to successful job hunting in retail, overall: Target strong companies and strong categories. Best areas in the recent past: Home improvement, hard goods, electronics. Weakest: apparel specialty shops, regional discount department stores. For more information, see the Retailing section.

WHAT'S NEXT

▶ **Sales will become more complex, more knowledge-oriented.**

As a sales manager stated, "There's no longer a sort of homogenous sale. . . . It's no longer just a product and a program. Now it's starting to be product, program, the financial package around it, and how you can deliver it."

Translation: the demand for top-quality salespeople will go up. Markets are growing more competitive, average sales costs are going up, and the need for detailed, up-to-date product or service information is increasing.

In this line, expect:

1. **much greater demand for *specialist* sales representatives**—people with a specialized knowledge and background of products or services. This is already the case in many areas such as computers, banking, and particularly health care, where many salespeople have backgrounds in biology or chemistry. On the other hand, don't assume that product knowledge is everything. For example, if you're an expert in distribution channels, that knowledge is probably more valuable than your specific product knowledge. Key point: understanding a strategic area *extremely well*.

2. **much greater demand for highly skilled salespeople.** One trend: IQ *and other testing* for sales applicants, increased need for statistical, computer-oriented people, more thorough interviewing process for applicants. Another trend: testing for weaknesses—and specific programs to correct them.

3. **intensified competition for the top sales jobs.** Example: 28,000 people applied for 500 sales positions at Merck.

4. **selling will become more *information-oriented*.** People who can quickly master information in general, statistical data in particular, will prosper.

5. **fewer—but longer—sales calls** (already, average sales calls are down from eight to six a day) as time spent per customer goes up.

6. **hybrid reps**—particularly in media sales, salespeople are representing more than one media area.

7. more cross-training—salespeople going into marketing. With a strong background in sales, in knowing what the company wants, they have an edge in making strategic marketing decisions.

8. less sales support—In some ways the computer age has made more work for sales reps. Administrative people back at headquarters have been cut back, putting more of the onus on the sales rep.

9. more work at home—A growing trend—cutting back on field offices and letting sales reps operate out of home offices, linked to their corporation by computer. One problem: many people miss the camaraderie—trading war stories. One advantage: you can make your own hours (most people work *more*).

But the bottom line: there will always be a demand for top salespeople who can *sell*, with or without the right paper qualifications.

SALARIES

▶ **Sales and marketing middle managers make more *on average* than other middle managers. But they earn it with long hours and high pressure.**

Commissions, not base salary, are what motivate most salespeople. Marketing employees are paid on salary—but often with substantial bonuses.

But remember: what goes up must come down. A few top earners saw their incomes drop by 50% during the recession. Volatility is *not* uncommon.

RETAIL: Median salary, $300 per week, lower for certain areas like hardware; $700 and up for certain fields (automotive, boat, and electronics). For salespeople on *straight* commission, the range varies. In a department store, for example, a typical range would be from about 5% for low-ticket goods to 10% for high-ticket items. Partial commission would be around 2%, plus a base salary. Merchandising personnel earnings average about $35,000 to $65,000 range, depending on product lines. Merchandise managers can earn much more, ranging upwards of $140,000.

INSURANCE: One problem with average salaries: with the downsizing and changes in the insurance industry, increases in compensation in traditional areas—life, casualty, fire, and marine—may become iffy, unless the agent is a more aggressive producer. On average, begins with base salary of $18,000 to $20,000—lasting usually for a year and a half, provided the agent meets sales targets. Afterward, commissions provide income. Median income for an insurance agent with over five years experience is approximately $30,000, after ten years salaries can go up to $70,000. Twenty percent of all agents earn over $100,000. One major growth area in compensation: managed care policies—group health and employee benefits. Earnings average about $50,000; senior sales rep can earn up to $100,000; sales manager $150,000. Growing market niche: disability insurance sales.

REAL ESTATE: Agents and brokers usually depend entirely on commission. The *median* income for real estate agents is approximately $25,000. Real estate brokers, who also rent, manage properties, arrange real estate loans, etc., reported a higher median salary of over $35,000. However, in both cases, salaries of $200,000 or more are not uncommon. But in good years, successful real estate brokers can be among the highest paid salespeople in the U.S.

SECURITIES: Salespeople begin in a range from $35,000 to $40,000—usually paid as a base salary until certification requirements are met and commissions reach a certain amount. Experience counts: average earnings increase to $90,000 after several years; institutional account representatives averaged over $200,000.

Brokers typically earn an average upwards of $130,000. Key point: compensation for most brokers is tied to the commissions they generate for their firms, although firms are now beginning to change compensation plans.

FINANCIAL SERVICES: For salaries and other information, see the Banking and Financial Services section.

SERVICE SALES REPS: earn widely varied salaries, depending on the industry, region, and specific firm and type of payment and commission structure. Advertising salespeople earn a median salary of about $30,000; other business services a median salary of about $33,000. Above these medians, salaries can be very high—many advertising salespeople in New York easily earn over $100,000.

MANUFACTURING SALES REPS: also vary widely in earnings. Median income is approximately $33,000, the top 10% earn over $70,000. Upper-level sales executives averaged $105,000 in base salary in 1995, or $135,500 in total compensation, according to *Sales and Marketing Management.*

MARKETING: salaries vary widely as well—depending on the firm, the industry, and the individual. In manufacturing, salary increases in the 1990s will probably be higher in nondurables; but again, more depends on the specific industry.

Beginning marketing salaries averaged $23,000, rising to approximately $36,000 after several years. Many firms pay far more: a survey by the National Institute of Business Executives found that the median total compensation of all marketing executives was $90,000 in 1994. Top sales-and-marketing executives averaged over $180,000 in total compensation, top marketing executives over $130,000, and about $170,000 at larger firms. Often bonuses, stock options, and other nonsalary perquisites like company cars can raise incomes.

RETAIL SALES: Salaries for retail sales workers begin at the federal minimum wage level of $4.25 an hour and rise upward, depending on experience, type of store, and region. For example, average 1994 weekly earnings for a sales worker ranged from $427 for a furniture salesperson to $333 in building supplies, to $265 for apparel. As for retail managers, salaries also vary widely, depending upon job level, length of service, type of firm, region, and more. Average salary for assistant store managers was from $13,700 to $16,300 a year in 1994; store managers from $21,900 to $26,300. But higher salaries are very common—with salaries in the $100,000+ range not uncommon at higher levels for national store chains.

BEST BETS

NORTHWESTERN MUTUAL LIFE: A salesperson's dream company—this year and virtually every year. Not for the fainthearted job seeker. Northwestern Mutual Life is looking for independent starters with "strong business values" and ambitious goals (you get a forceful but sincere sales pitch just calling for information), but this sort of fervor pays off. Ranked number 2 last year by *Sales and Marketing Management* in their survey of the best sales forces of all kinds in America. And in the insurance business, Northwestern Mutual Life (NML) is number 1 in life insurance sales (in terms of value of policies sold) in the same year that its major competitors saw *declines*. Strong emphasis on training, customer service, and selling in a technical environment.

HEWLETT PACKARD: Sometimes nice guys finish first. Known industrywide as an innovative, supportive employer (with flex time; emphasis not on downsizing, but on keeping people with the company even during recessions; empathetic bosses), HP is also ranked as having the number 1 sales force in America—famed for its sales performance *and* its customer service. Early innovative uses of intranet and other forms of sales support allows sales reps to do what they do best—sell. It's no wonder that staff turnover is in the single digits.

SPECIAL EVENTS MARKETING: The job sounds fun—getting involved in sponsoring special events, usually sports-related, such as a golf match, a NASCAR race, or a tennis match. But it's big business too—corporations spend upwards of $4 billion sponsoring such huge events as the Olympics, and the job itself can be grueling and time-consuming. Marketers may do everything from selling the concept to making sure the lemonade or beer is cold to entertaining clients in a sky-box. But the growth is there—this is a very hot area of advertising and marketing. Pay potential is high as well; salaries begin in the $20s, average in the $40s, and can move up to $200,000 and more. And if you like sports, it's an interesting way to be involved.

WHERE TO GO FOR MORE INFORMATION

SALES AND MARKETING ASSOCIATIONS

(For advertising associations, directories, and magazines, see Advertising and Public Relations in the Industry section on page 215.)

American Marketing Association 250 S. Wacker Dr., Suite 200	Chicago, IL 60606-5819 312/648-0536 (Publishes periodicals	with job listings, directory, placement service.)

Bank Marketing Association
1120 Connecticut Ave., NW
Washington DC 20036
202/663-5268
(Affiliated with American Bankers Association; offers placement service, publishes directory, etc.)

Broadcast Promotion and Marketing Executives
2027 Century Park E.
Suite 555
Los Angeles, CA 90067

Direct Marketing Association
1120 Ave. of the Americas
New York, NY 10036
212/768-7277
(Publishes directory, periodical with some listings, offers placement service, etc.)

Electronic Representatives Association
20 E. Huron St.
Chicago, IL 60611
312/649-1333
(Covers multiline salespersons of electronic items, including consumer; publishes directory.)

Financial Marketing Association
401 N. Michigan Ave.
Chicago, IL 60601
312/644-6610

Hotel Sales and Marketing Association International
1300 L St., NW,
Suite 800
Washington, DC 20005
202/789-0089

Manufacturers' Agents National Association
P.O. Box 3476
Laguna Hills, CA 92654
714/859-4040
(Publishes magazine, *Agency Sales*, with many job listings, and directory.)

Marketing Research Association
2189 Silas Deane Hwy., Suite 5
Rocky Hill, CT 06067
203/257-4008

Meeting Professionals International
Infomart
1950 Stemmons Fwy., Suite 5018
Dallas, TX 75207-3109
214/712-7700
(Largest professional group in meetings industry.)

National Electrical Manufacturers Representatives Association
200 Business Park Dr.
Suite 301
Armonk, NY 10504
914/273-6780
(Association for independent sales reps for electrical manufacturers;

sponsors various programs.)

Newspaper Association of America
11600 Sunrise Valley Dr.
Reston, VA 22091
703/648-1177

Promotion Marketing Association of America
257 Park Ave. S.
New York, NY 10003
212/420-1100

Sales and Marketing Executive International
Statler Office Tower,
Suite 977
Cleveland, OH 44115
216/771-6650
(Huge group; involved in sales education programs, publishes directory, etc.)

Society of Corporate Meeting Professionals
1819 Peachtree
Atlanta, GA 30309
404/355-9932
(Provides scholarship money to members who wish Corporate Meeting Professional certification.)

Society for Marketing Professional Services
99 Canal Ctr. Plz.,
Suite 250
Alexandria, VA 22314
703/549-6117
(Placement and educational services; directory of members.)

| United Association
Manufacturers
Representatives | P.O. Box 986
Dana Point, CA 92629
714/240-4966 | (Publishes monthly
journal with many
situation listings, etc.) |

SALES AND MARKETING DIRECTORIES

(Many associations publish directories, as do some magazines listed below.)

Manufacturers' Agents
and Representatives
American Business
Directories
5711 S. 86th Cir.
P.O. Box 27347
Omaha, NE 68127
402/593-4600

(Twenty thousand
names, addresses, and
phone numbers
nationwide for $660;
sells a list of marketing
consultants for $330.)

The Salesman's Guide:
National Directory of

Corporate Meeting
Planners
P.O. Box 31
New Providence, NJ
07973
800/323-6772
(Also publishes related
directories.)

SALES AND MARKETING PERIODICALS

Agency Sales
Magazine
P.O. Box 3467
Laguna Hills, CA
92654
714/859-4040
(Monthly for
manufacturers reps.)

American Agent &
Broker
330 N. Fourth St.
St. Louis, MO 63102
314/421-5445
(Monthly magazine for
insurance agents and
brokers.)

Business Marketing
Crain Communications
740 N. Rush St.
Chicago, IL 60611
312/649-5200

Corporate
Meetings/Incentives
60 Main St.
Maynard, MA 01754
508/897-5552

(Monthly for business
meeting planners, etc.)

Direct Marketing
224 Seventh St.
Garden City, NY
11530-5771
516/746-6700
(Monthly; contains
some job listings.)

Industrial Distribution
Cahners Publishing
Circulation Department
8773 S. Ridgeline
Blvd.
Highlands Ranch, CO
80126
303/470-4000
(For sales reps, etc.;
carries some job
listings.)

Insurance Sales
98 Ennis Dr.
Lexington, KY 40503
606/277-6221
(Monthly for life
insurance agents, etc.)

Life Insurance
Selling
330 N. Fourth St.
St. Louis, MO 63102
314/421-5445
(Monthly magazine for
insurance agents and
brokers.)

Marketing News
250 S. Wacker Dr.,
Suite 200
Chicago, IL
60606-5819
312/648-0536
(Biweekly association
publication.)

Recreation
Resources
527 Marquette,
Suite 1300
Minneapolis, MN
55402
800/923-2326
(Nine-issue magazine
for recreation
managers.)

*Sales Manager's
Bulletin*
The Bureau of
Business Practice
24 Rope Ferry Rd.
Waterford, CT 06386
203/442-4365

*Sales & Marketing
Management*
355 Park Ave. S.
New York, NY 10010
212/592-6300
(Fifteen issues/yr.,
major magazine for
sales and marketing.)

Successful Meetings
355 Park Ave. S.
New York, NY 10010
212/592-6200
(Monthly; particularly
for managers who plan
and manage sales and
marketing meetings.)

SCIENTISTS

▶ **Although society is getting more technologically complex, scientists won't benefit as much as can be expected.**

At first glance, it would appear that a shortage of scientists is in the offing. The U.S. graduates only about 10,000 science Ph.D.s each year, and a proportionally larger (but still small) number of M.S. and B.S. students. Match a small number of graduates with an increasingly technical marketplace—and you'd think the result would be a shortage.

So far, though, this hasn't happened—and best indications are it won't happen soon. Why? Several reasons—first, many scientists are employed by federal government research institutions—and as government cuts continued, so did employment cuts or hiring freezes. Second, many companies also cut back on basic research, in turn reducing hiring of scientists. Finally, the opening up of Russia and Eastern Europe, along with the rise of East Asian economies has led to increased competition from scientists from these lower-priced areas. More to the point, there really is no one "scientific job market"; instead there are many smaller specialized employment markets.

EMPLOYMENT OUTLOOK: In general, fair.

Major areas of employment:

BIOLOGISTS: There are over 100,000 biologists working in the U.S.—half of whom work in colleges and universities. Much job growth in the remaining 1990s will be in private industry, particularly *biotechnology and environmental positions*, as well as with government and universities. Under a "moderate growth" scenario for the economy as a whole, the federal government projects employment to 2005 to increase by a substantial 25%; with medical scientists faring even better—growth approaching 70%. Some studies point to a probable shortage of biologists in the long term, but other experts point out that the biological forefront of bio-tech companies are not labor-intensive, and won't dramatically expand hiring no matter what miracles they manage. Another problem: federal cutbacks in basic research spending, resulting in layoffs, reduced hiring, reduced funding of university research.

Some more caveats: Biotechnology is entering an unpredictable growth phase; about the only thing that is certain is that *some* areas will be booming in the future. Some estimate that over 1,000 new positions will open each year for the next few years. From engineered plant genes to new medical technologies, job opportunities are available both at small firms and at the giants which have been entering the field in a big way. One drawback: the area is a volatile one, which makes job security often low.

What will be the best qualifications for a new career in this area? According to *Biotechnology* magazine, beyond the right academic background, the key will be laboratory skills—and this does *not* include school laboratory courses. Their recommendations: Get the relevant experience before applying for employment—through work, summer positions, research assistantships.

Environmental positions are becoming mainstream at many companies as they attempt to anticipate the problems of hazardous waste, chemical dumping, and the environmental consequences of industry. In addition, another growing area for the 1990s will be environmental renewal—as people seek to return the environment to its natural condition, with native plants and animals. However, much depends on the economy, and how much the federal government will require cleanups. Bottom line: expect strong long-term growth.

AGRICULTURAL SCIENTISTS: Fairly good opportunities. About 25% of all agricultural scientists work for the federal government, many also work for state and local governments. Government cutbacks could affect employment in this large sector, but in general, experts predict that job growth will match employment growth in the economy in general. Best opportunities for those with advanced degrees.

Best bets: Ph.D.s with backgrounds in molecular biology, microbiology, genetics or biotech; soil scientists; food technologist. BAs face a more difficult market, but may find opportunities in managerial jobs in businesses dealing with the agricultural community—feed, fertilizer, seed and farm equipment manufacturers.

CHEMISTS: There are 92,000 chemists in the U.S. Over half work for manufacturing firms—half of those for firms within the chemical industry. The single largest specialty is pharmaceuticals, which should experience relative strength throughout the 1990s despite recent problems within the industry. Key advantage: as biotechnology advances, these firms stand to gain tremendously in the sale of bio-engineered drugs. In addition, the aging of the population is increasing demand for drugs for this high-spending segment of the population.

In recent years employment outlooks have been relatively weak, particularly in 1995 for Ph.D.s and for B.S. chemists. The short-term outlook improved, particularly in late 1996 and early 1997, pointing to further improvements. Best areas for job hunters: small companies. Pharmaceutical hiring rebounded, as did hiring at large firms and even college campuses. For recent grads: summer and co-op programs were recruiting—and seen as almost essential for later jobs.

In general, jobs for chemists are expected to grow at the same rate as employment growth in the economy as a whole. Key reason for growth: technological advances spur more sales of specialty chemicals, which in turn spurs companies to do more research, particularly applied research—and hence, hire more chemists. Although areas other than pharmaceuticals will not grow as rapidly, the outlook is still relatively bright. Probable best areas: materials chemistry, analytical, environmental, and synthetic organic chemists. Another probable good area: scientific management—managing chemists in a lab research setting. As technical specialties increase, watch for a growth in consulting jobs as well. Already, chemical consulting occupies 3.5%–5% of the total U.S. consulting market.

For job openings: check with the American Chemical Society (address on page 167), which operates the Employment Clearing House; want ads in *Chemical and Engineering News* are another good bet.

PHYSICISTS: Experts see only fair to poor prospects in the short term. The number of physics Ph.D.s graduating each year exceeds the annual number of job openings. In addition, government cutbacks of funding point to reduced opportunities in universities, although in the longer term, some experts point out that a fairly large number of faculty retirements may open up many positions. However, other experts suggest that many of these openings may not be refilled. Another problem: most corporations are deemphasizing basic research, which tends to be where physicists are employed, in favor of applied research.

But another problem is defense related—although defense-related economic sectors have been picking up lately, the cutbacks in the earlier part of the decade are still being felt. Result: probable decline in employment opportunity in many areas, although accelerated civilian research in high-tech areas may raise employment. So far, however, universities, major sources of employment for physics Ph.D.s still aren't hiring in substantial numbers, making competition for low-security jobs fierce. The number of university openings has been stable since 1990; and with the number of Ph.D.s increasing, the university marketplace is grim. One employment specialist inquired, not without substance, whether graduate physics departments should be engaged in birth control. One bright spot: Enrollments in physics departments are already down—perhaps easing long-term employment procedures.

A good source of job leads, both academic and nonacademic, is the American Institute of Physics and its various publications, especially *AIP Notice* and *Physics Today.* The address is at the end of this section.

Other physical science areas:

METEOROLOGISTS: Sluggish job outlook. Previous estimates of strong job growth have changed, owing to the National Weather Service's extensive modernization of its equipment—leading to reduced need for human meteorologists. Some growth is expected in private industry—but prospects are dependent on the state of the economy.

GEOLOGISTS AND GEOPHYSICISTS: Generally good job outlook. Key reason: the petroleum industry, which is a major employer, is a cyclical industry that in the recent past was in the down part of its cycle. This led to such reduced numbers of college students entering geology and geophysics specialties that now job prospects are good for the fewer numbers of graduates coming onstream. Best bets: master's degree and Ph.D. holders, computer modeling familiarity. Other areas outside of petroleum that look good: environmental protection and reclamation—especially engineering geology, hydrology, and geochemistry. One potential problem: recent increased numbers of graduates specializing in these areas. For job openings, check with the Geological Society of America Matching Service (address is listed on page 168), which is a job bank run by the association listing current geological jobs.

MATHEMATICIANS: Job outlook is relatively poor—jobs should increase more slowly than average, according to government experts. Key problems: corporate research departments that employ mathematicians are reducing or freezing hiring in the wake of the continued defense cutbacks; the same is going on in the federal government. Also, many domestic mathematicians face competition from highly trained foreign mathematicians. According to the American Mathematical Society, 40% of last year's newly hired mathematics workers came from outside the United States.

One trend because of this: employment of mathematicians in areas other than basic mathematics—such as computer programming, systems design, etc. Here outlooks are much stronger. Check for openings with the American Mathematical Society and the Mathematical Association of America—addresses are listed at the end of this section.

WHAT'S NEXT

▶ **Although scientists rate high in career satisfaction surveys, various problems surface again and again:**

Inadequate career preparation: Many science students are not coached on employment prospects while in college. In many cases, this encourages the "postdoc" syndrome, where graduate students specialize in areas that condemn them to low-paid, low-prestige postdoctoral positions. They aren't steered toward research that will offer rewards once they've got their Ph.Ds. Worst for: physics Ph.D. graduate students; women—who also face lingering discrimination in some areas. The American Physical Society is focusing now on identifying alternative career paths for Ph.D. physicists, while the AIP is studying whether postdocs are having trouble finding permanent employment.

Inadequate use of scientific talent on the job; lack of communication between scientists and management: Some scientists in corporations complain they must sacrifice quick corporate profits for long-term advancement. In other words, the lack of R&D spending—and attention—can be very frustrating. A survey reported in *R&D Magazine* in 1992 found that the problem of inadequate communication was worst in government (66%), next in industry, and least serious in universities and consulting.

Lack of funding for young researchers: This is a major problem—consigning young scientists to post-doc positions.

Academic "inbreeding": Harvard graduates wind up with Harvard jobs, etc. Problem: not enough cross-fertilization, overreliance on "old boy" networks.

Scientists may be vital, but a lot of plumbers make more money: The average scientist with almost twenty years experience makes $45,000 to $50,000 a year. To make substantially more, a scientist must usually leave scientific work and become a manager or an entrepreneur.

Women are lagging behind in scientific jobs in industry: The bad news: women comprise 45% of the workforce, and only 12% of the workforce of engineers and scientists in industry. On average, they make less money: about 73% of the median male's salary for women with bachelor's degrees and two years of experience, 88% for women with Ph.D.s. Apparently, industry isn't helping; childcare is lacking, paternalism is common. On the bright side: corporations like Xerox, Alcoa, the Aerospace Corporation, AT&T, Bell Labs, Scios Nova and Barrios Technology were cited by the National Academy of Sciences as having positive programs for women.

Key new trends: Temp jobs for scientists, lab technicians. Major temp firms like On Assignment (offices nationwide) have been placing science grads in temp jobs. Numbers placed are increasing.

SALARIES

BIOLOGISTS: Beginning employees with a bachelor's or master's degree average $20,000 to $25,000; Ph.D.s $30,000 to $35,000. Experienced biologists average about $45,000 in government, $50,000 in private industry. Biotechnology Ph.D.s can make over $50,000 starting, $75,000 on up with several years of the right experience.

CHEMISTS: Median salaries, in 1996, according to *C&EN* (*Chemical & Engineering News*), were $68,200 for all chemists. Starting salaries for B.S. degree holders were $25,000; $31,000 for M.S. holders; and $46,000 for Ph.D. holders. In academia, highest salaries were for full professors of Ph.D.-granting schools. The median salary was $50,000, with $63,400 for full professors, $44,600 for associate professors, and $37,000 for assistant professors. Highest salaries for chemists in industrial firms, particularly those working as managers, with a median salary of over $80,000.

Chemical engineers received an average starting salary of about $33,000 in 1989.

PHYSICISTS AND OTHER PHYSICAL SCIENTISTS: Starting salaries in 1994, according to the American Institute of Physics, was about $30,000 for physicists in industry with a bachelor's or master's degree and $60,000 for Ph.D.s. Experienced Ph.D.s reported a median salary of $65,000; those employed in colleges reported $43,000, compared to $71,500 for those in industry and $78,000 for those in hospitals. On the bright side, these numbers were higher than those of the previous year. The average salary for **meteorologists** was $40,000. **Astronomy** postdoctoral applicants earned a median salary of $36,000.

MATHEMATICIANS: Starting salaries range from about $25,000+ for BAs to $40,000+ for Ph.D.s. According to the Bureau of Labor Statistics, median salaries for mathematicians with Ph.D.s ranged from about $42,000 in academics to over $50,000 in business in 1985. **Actuaries** earn from about $25,000 for entry-level positions to $100,000+ for experienced employees.

BEST BETS

ENVIRONMENTAL CAREERS: Despite downturns, this area should continue to expand along with the economy, as environmental clean-up (particularly as mandated by Superfund and related legislation), pollution prevention, and environmental management become crucial corporate and government concerns. In-demand areas: hydrogeologists, air-quality engineers, risk assessment specialists, industrial hygienists, and environmental engineers. Best route to a job: an appropriate undergraduate degree, graduate degree is probably better. Key point: more people are entering this specialty, so competition should be increasing. Jobs are available with corporations in chemical, petroleum, and manufacturing industries, and with specialty firms like Waste Management, for the smaller consulting and engineering firms. However, research prospects carefully.

For more information, contact specialty associations below and in Engineering and High-Tech section on page 50. Particularly for students, note that the Environmental Careers Organization offers careers conferences, special career publications, and other services. It also places students and recent graduates in short-term professional positions, serves as an on-the-job training organization, and gives associates an inside track for employment. For information and applications, see address on page 61.

WHERE TO GO FOR MORE INFORMATION

SCIENCE ASSOCIATIONS

American Academy of Actuaries
1100 17th St., NW
7th Fl.
Washington, DC 20036
202/223-8196
(Directory, introductory career guide, etc.)

American Anthropological Association
4350 N. Fairfax Dr.
Suite 640
Arlington, VA 22203

703/528-1902
(Publishes periodical with some job information and listings; sells booklets that list government employment opportunities; members' placement service, etc.)

American Association of Physical Anthropologists
Department of Anthropology

SUNY at Buffalo
365 MFAC
Buffalo, NY 14261
716/645-2414
(Publishes journal, etc.)

American Association of Zoological Parks and Aquariums
Oglebay Park
Wheeling, WV 26003
304/242-2160
(Publishes career guide, directory, periodical with job openings for members.)

American Chemical Society
1156 16 St., NW
Washington, DC 20036
1-800/227-5558
(Publishes various periodicals with job listings, such as the *Journal of Agricultural and Food Chemistry*—see separate listings for *Chemical & Engineering News*—career brochures, and salary surveys; maintains job clearinghouse, listing service, counseling services, etc.)

American Geological Institute
4220 King St.
Alexandria, VA 22302
703/379-2480
(Publishes magazine with job listings, etc.)

American Geophysical Union
2000 Florida Ave., NW
Washington, DC 20009
202/462-6900
(Publishes weekly newspaper with employment information and listings.)

American Horticultural Society
7931 E. Blvd. Dr.
Alexandria, VA 22308
800/777-7931
(Publishes magazine, offers placement service for members.)

American Institute of Architects
1735 New York Ave., NW
Washington, DC 20006
202/626-7300
(Publishes periodical with employment information, directory, etc.)

American Institute for Biochemistry and Molecular Biology
9650 Rockville Pike
Bethesda, MD 20814-3996
301/530-7145
(Offers placement service, etc.)

American Institute of Biological Sciences
1444 Eye St., NW
Suite 200
Washington, DC 20005
202/628-1500

American Institute of Physics
500 Sunnyside Blvd.
Woodbury, NY 11797
516/576-2200
(Publishes periodicals with job listings, surveys, etc.; affiliated members include American Physical Society, Acoustical Society, Association of Physics Teachers, and Geophysical Union.)

American Mathematical Society
P.O. Box 6248
Providence, RI 02940-6248

401/455-4000
(Publish periodical with job listings, directory, etc.)

American Meteorological Society
45 Beacon St.
Boston, MA 02108
617/227-2425
(Publishes journal with employment listings, educational programs, etc.)

American Society of Agronomy
677 S. Segoe Rd.
Madison, WI 53711
608/273-8080
(Operates placement service for members, etc.)

American Society for Microbiology
1325 Massachusetts Ave., NW
Washington, DC 20005-4171
202/737-3600
(Publishes periodical with employment listings; placement service.)

American Statistical Association
1429 Duke St.
Alexandria, VA 22314-3402
703/684-1221
(Publishes periodical with job openings, directory, etc.)

Archeological Institute of America
656 Beacon St.

Boston, MA 02215
617/353-9361
(Publishes periodical
with dig
information, small
directory, etc.)

**Association of
American
Geographers**
1710 16th St., NW
Washington, DC
20009-3198
202/234-1450
(Operates placement
service; sometimes
expedition
announcements, etc.)

**Botanical Society of
America**
1735 Neil Ave.
Columbus, OH
43210
614/292-3519
(Periodical, etc.)

**Center for American
Archeology**
P.O. Box 22
Kampsville, IL 62053
618/653-4316

**Federation of
American Societies
for Experimental
Biology**
9650 Rockville Pike
Bethesda, MD 20814
301/530-7020
(Runs job bank,
periodical with job
openings, directory.)

**Geological Society of
America**
3300 Penrose Pl.
Boulder, CO 80301
303/447-2020
(Publishes periodical
with a few job listings,
directory, etc.)

**Institute of
Mathematical
Statistics**
3401 Investment Blvd.,
Suite 7
Hayward, CA 94545
510/783-8141
(Publishes periodical
with job listings.)

**Minerals, Metals,
and Materials
Society**
420 Commonwealth
Dr.
Warrendale, PA 15086
412/776-9000
(Publishes periodical
with employment
listings, etc.)

**Society of
Actuaries**
475 N. Martingale Rd.
Suite 800
Schaumburg, IL 60173-
2226
708/706-3500
(Publishes free booklet
on careers, etc.)

**Society for American
Archeology**
900 2nd St., NE

Suite 12
Washington, DC 20002
202/789-8200
(Publishes periodicals
with some listings.)

**Society for Applied
Anthropology**
P.O. Box 24083
Oklahoma City, OK
73124
405/843-5113
(Three thousand
members work in
government and
business, applying
techniques of
anthropology to
development planning,
etc.)

**Society for Industrial
and Applied
Mathematics**
3600 University City
Science Center
Philadelphia, PA
19104-2688
215/382-9800
(Publishes periodical
with job listings, etc.)

**Society for Mining,
Metallurgy, and
Exploration**
P.O. Box 625002
Littleton, CO 80162-
5002
303/973-9550
(Publishes directory,
etc.)

SCIENCE DIRECTORIES, DATABANKS

(Many of the associations above publish directories; many are listed under the appropriate association.)

BIOSIS
2100 Arch St
Philadelphia, PA
19103-1399
1-800/523-4806
(Life-science database includes millions of addresses, job listings, etc.)

BioTron
(See listing under American Institute of Biological Sciences.)

Conservation Directory
National Wildlife Federation
Order Dept.
P.O. Box 8925
Vienna, VA 22183
703/790-4402
800/432-6564
(Lists hundreds of state and federal governments, nonprofit organizations, educational institutions, with addresses, names, etc., all involved in conservation.)

Peterson's Job Opportunities for Engineering, Technology
Peterson's
P.O. Box 2123
Princeton, NJ
08543-2121
609/243-9111
800/338-3282
(Lists hundreds of corporations and government agencies that are hiring; includes detailed information.)

SCIENCE MAGAZINES

American Laboratory
P.O. Box 870
Shelton, CT 06484
203/926-9300
(Monthly; particularly for research chemists and biologists.)

American Scientist
P.O. Box 13975
Research Triangle Park, NC 27709
919/549-0097
(For members of Sigma Xi.)

BioScience
American Institute of Biological Sciences
1444 Eye St., NW
Washington, DC 20005
202/628-1500

Chemical Engineering
P.O. Box 507
Princeton Rd.
Highstown, NJ 08526
609/426-7070
(Excellent industry roundups are particularly valuable as overviews for entry-level job hunters; classifieds include many job openings.)

CRM
U.S. Department of the Interior
National Park Service
P.O. Box 37127
Washington, DC
20013-7127
202/343-3395
(News of the Park

Service; gives a feel for the work, sometimes has paid intern information for arch., foresters, etc.)

Federal Archeology Report
Archeological Assistance Division
National Park Service
P.O. Box 37127
Washington, DC
20013-7127
202/343-4101
(Quarterly; sometimes includes information on volunteer programs, as well as training programs for government workers.)

High Technology Careers
Westech Publishing Company
4701 Patrick Henry Dr., Suite 1901
Santa Clara, CA 95054
408/970-8800
(High-tech industry tabloid with hundreds of high-tech job openings listed.)

Physics Today
500 Sunnyside Blvd.
Woodbury, NY 11797
516/576-2200
(Monthly association magazine; carries numerous job listings, a few state-of-the-profession articles, etc.)

Science
1333 H St., NW
Washington, DC 20008
202/326-6500
(Prestigious weekly science magazine; carries listings.)

Weatherwise
1319 18th St., NW
Washington, DC 20036
202/362-6445
(Bimonthly.)

SOCIAL SERVICES AND LEGAL PROFESSIONALS

▶ **As society grows more complex, as social institutions change or break down, the demand for social service workers and legal professionals is becoming ever more evident.**

To many of us, it seems that society is getting ever more complex—and ever more dangerous. Both trends point to increased demand for social service and legal professionals. More legal professionals will be called to take care of the increasing legal complexity of personal and corporate affairs, the increasing tendency to rely on legal experts to settle disputes. More social service professionals will be hired to help attack or ameliorate the social problems of crime, homelessness, and mental illness.

Of course, just because demand for these professionals will be rising for the next five years doesn't mean the employment picture is completely bright. Much depends on government funding of social programs, competition for the best jobs, and most important, what specific area you're most interested in. The rest of this section explores these aspects of employment

EMPLOYMENT OUTLOOK: In general, good. Strongest demand for paralegals, social workers in rural areas, correctional officers. Keen competition for many of the highest paid jobs.

▶ **The fastest-growing area: jobs for *paralegals*—expected to grow almost 60% by the year 2005.**

Paralegals will be one of the fastest growing occupations in the U.S. during the next ten years.

Paralegals, or legal assistants, work with lawyers in most areas of legal work, from researching and reporting to preparing legal arguments, helping to draft agreements, and preparing corporate tax returns.

Reason for growth in the 1990s: paralegals are a lower-cost alternative to lawyers, particularly useful as legal services become more generally used in society, and as corporations and individuals become more cost conscious.

Most paralegals are employed by private law firms, where employment prospects will increase. But as more and more people enter the field, expect increased competition for good jobs. Jobs in the public sector are expected to increase as well. Reason: the government now provides more legal and related services to the poor and elderly—and paralegals are a low-cost way of maintaining and expanding services. One caveat: over the long term, computers may replace paralegals in certain functions.

New trend: Paralegal *firms*, made up of independent paralegals, who offer legal services for lower prices. The number of such firms increased from 200 in 1985 to over 6,000 last year.

Best bet: While paralegals still are not required to be certified, it helps job prospects. The National Association of Legal Assistants (NALA, see address on page 178) sets experience and educational standards for a two-day qualifying exam, after which paralegals who pass are designated Certified Legal Assistants (CLAs). Education for paralegals is varied, from two months to two years, from general to specialized. Contact the NALA for ABA-approved schools and recommended programs; the association also offers a self-teaching cassette course, seminars, and library facilities.

Strong prospects in the field: *trusts and estates.* Reason: high demand, low numbers. According to one recruiter, "Most people want the glamour of litigation, not the more technical work of going through accounts." Paralegals must be familiar with accounting as well as legal issues. *Trademark law*—according to *Legal Professional* magazine, there is a current shortage of adequately trained paralegals. *Employee benefits* is another extremely strong hiring area, with demand expected to stay very high throughout the 1990s.

On the downside: As mentioned earlier, more and more people are entering this field, generating much competition for the best jobs. Best bet: get a B.A., good paralegal studies background.

▶ Outlook for attorneys—more jobs, but a lot of competition.

Like many corporations across the country over the past few years, law firms fell into a pattern of downsizing—including layoffs and hiring freezes. One reason: As corporations became more cost-conscious, they cut back on their use of outside legal services. Worst hit: young associates. Partnerships are becoming harder than ever to attain, and the job market for those looking for jobs as in-house counsel has shrunk. Reason: law firms—both big and small—are filled with young partners (around forty years old) who will stay partners for many years. And each year, more and more new lawyers come on board, competing for new positions.

The good news: government employment experts predict continued job growth for attorneys. Key reasons: growth of legal action in employee benefits, environment, health care, tort law, intellectual property, sexual harassment, real estate. More middle- and lower-income use of legal services, spurred by legal service plans and legal clinics.

Bottom line: growth in jobs—but somewhat offset by continued large numbers of law school graduates. About 36,000 new lawyers enter the job market each year. Although enrollments at law schools were down in 1995, enrollment is still very high, and some are projecting increases in the next few years. There are about 500,000 attorneys practicing law today.

Best areas: intellectual property law, corporate finance law, international law. Experts note that hiring is often best for those with advanced degrees, and experience in various specialties.

Where once the majority of lawyers in private practice were solo practitioners (67% new law grads chose this option back in 1957) today only 2% or so work alone. Reason: as law has become more complex, it is increasingly difficult to work alone. Best bets for solo lawyers just starting out: rural areas, expanding suburbs where competition for big firms is less.

About 18% of all private practitioners work in the large, big-name national firms. The majority of the rest work in government or with corporations as in-house counsel. Both areas are expected to increase hiring—particularly as corporations recognize the cost advantages of in-house counsel.

Two trends are affecting employment:

Cost consciousness hits the law: Many major corporations are tired of spending so much on legal help. New trend: they're consolidating legal work with a few firms and looking at costs carefully. Result: the high-flying days for lawyers are long past. Large legal firms are cutting back on salary increases (which rose 460% in the past 20 years) and scrutinizing promotion to partner much more carefully. Aiding and abetting this trend: the large number of lawyers. Comptition is even tougher than before at major law firms (although the associate salaries are still high—up to $85,000 or so at top firms), many associates don't have a chance at making partner as firms pick and choose among the best and the brightest from the best law schools.

Legal complexity is increasing. This will make lawyers specializing in certain areas more employable. Best bet for 1997 and beyond: Intellectual property lawyer. These lawyers in effect protect *ideas*—the products that come from the technological innovators, writers, etc. They're versed in patent, trademark, trade secrets, and copyright law. As the technological revolution continues, particularly in bio-tech and electronics, and along with the proliferation of entertainment in new multi-media environments, this area looks hot for the near and long-term future. Salaries look excellent as well—*starting* salaries for these experts at top firms in New York City topped $100,000.

But remember a general rule of thumb, according to a top legal recruiter: "Specialize in what you like. That way, you'll be the best, and get the best offer, even in a crowded field."

Two areas that almost always need law school graduates: public interest groups and government agencies. Reason: it is tough attracting top applicants when all you can offer is an average salary of $27,000 (versus an average starting salary of over $80,000 at top New York law firms). Check with the National Association of Public Interest Law, which sponsors a national job fair.

▶ **The job outlook for many social work and human services jobs will most likely improve.**

The bottom line is simple: governments are cutting back on social services, just as crime is getting out of control. And despite all the talk of more prisons, we all should realize that the best solutions come *before* the crimes are committed.

This points to a need for more social workers and their kin. Right now, job prospects are fair to good, but a lot depends on how much the government (and ultimately the taxpayer) is willing to fund various programs. And depending on the success of new initiatives in retraining and welfare reform, demand could pick up in the near term. Bottom line: keep an eye on initiatives in Washington. And look for jobs in the private sector (drug rehab, etc.) and public-sector jobs where the demand (and burn-out rate) is relatively stronger—in cities like New York, Washington, and Philadelphia.

Projected employment growth areas: practices centering on children or the elderly (particularly the over-eighty-fives), publicly funded community halfway houses, employee assistance programs, hospitals, Sunbelt states. Rural areas will have continued difficulty attracting social workers, due to low salaries and poorer facilities.

Human services workers—a catchall term referring to the employees who work under professional supervision in health agencies, halfway houses, group homes, prisons, and other organizations—will see their field grow at a very fast rate.

One reason: a high turnover rate as employees "burn out." Another reason: growth in various social programs, such as group counseling, day care for the elderly. The better jobs and advancement potential will go to those with college degrees; almost 500 colleges, institutes, or vocational schools offer courses.

▶ **In the protective and law enforcement professions, the fastest-growing areas will be in the private sector.**

The U.S. is still suffering from high crime—and corporations and individuals are willing to pay for extra security. But it's not just guard duty. Private security will become increasingly sophisticated, and trained employees will be needed to handle complex problems of computer fraud.

Already, private security companies employ about 1.5 million people and spend over $50 billion a year compared to 600,000 people and $30 billion by government, according to the National Institute of Justice. Look for that number to double by the year 2000—and watch employment figures jump as well.

The best areas: According to insiders, potential applicants should strongly consider specialized enforcement fields like telecommunications, computer security, planning in the private sector.

And what about the public sector?

Much depends on how much local communities are willing to pay for enforcement. Today, many communities are cutting back on social spending, and local police can be affected as well. Government experts predict applicants will find the best prospects in high-crime urban areas—although salaries are often lower. On the bright side: layoffs of police personnel are rare. Usually when municipalities cut jobs, they do so through attrition. And most communities offer police very attractive pension plans—many can retire at half pay after 20 or 25 years.

Bottom line: people are tired of crime, and in most cases seem willing to pay for more police to help reduce it.

Federal enforcement jobs are almost always tough to get—particularly in today's cost-cutting environment. Jobs can be found in various parts of the federal government: The Justice Department employs agents who work for:

• the Drug Enforcement Agency (DEA)

• the Federal Bureau of Investigation (FBI)

• the U.S. Border Patrol

• U.S. Marshal's Service

In addition, the Treasury Department employs agents who work for:

• the Bureau of Alcohol, Tobacco, and Firearms

• U.S. Customs Service

• Internal Revenue Service

• U.S. Secret Service

There are many other government agencies that also employ enforcement officers. The U.S. Department of State employs agents who work in the Diplomatic Security Service, the U.S. Mint has a special police force, as does the Government Printing Service. There's also the Federal Protective Service and the Central Intelligence Agency's Special Protective Service. For more on these jobs, check addresses in the Government and International sections, then call or write for more specific information.

Employment source for all law and security professionals: the NELS job listing. See page 179.

Employment Spotlight: Corrections

The numbers keep going up. Highlighted last year, this far from glamorous field—working in the prison system guarding or counseling inmates and offenders, or managing prison staff—will see job growth of 60%, one of the fastest-growing job categories in America.

Jobs will increase in most areas: for corrections officers, prison social workers and psychologists, and probation officers. According to *Corrections Today* magazine, the greatest growth in the history of the Bureau of Prisons will come in the next five years. Also looking strong: state corrections and private corrections (run by private corporations). In California, the number of corrections officers more than doubled in seven years. On the downside: corrections can be a dangerous profession, and salaries are lower than for others in law enforcement, ranging from $14,100 to $33,400, depending upon the state, for entry-level corrections officers, to a high of $58,800 for experienced officers; directors of corrections can make $120,000, wardens up to $80,000. At the federal level, the starting salary in 1993 was about $18,000; the average for nonsupervisory corrections officers was about $30,000, and about $53,000 for supervisors. For more information, contact: The American Correctional Association, address on page 177.

WHAT'S NEXT

▶ **Legal revolving door: as many people are leaving the law as entering. Most common leavers—new lawyers, corporate lawyers, more women than men.**

This trend will continue, as the thousands who enter law school discover it's not what they thought. Another growing trend: self-help groups for disgruntled, discouraged lawyers who want to switch careers.

▶ **Social workers will turn to the private sector in large numbers.**

Reasons: better pay, more personal autonomy. And a strong feeling that some of the major problems society faces begin with "normal" people. Major employment areas: corporations—employee assistance programs, private practice marriage psychotherapy, and family counseling.

SALARIES

LAWYERS: Average starting salary is about $37,000, more at top firms (up to $80,000), much less at smaller firms. Median salary of all lawyers is about $85,000. First-year law partners averaged about $100,000 to $150,000. Supervising attorneys in private industry averaged $55,100, with earnings to $100,000, depending upon experience and company size. Government lawyers average about $63,000; beginning salaries in the $30s.

LEGAL SUPPORT POSITIONS: Legal administrators earn between $35,000 and $100,000, depending on the size of the firm, more for top firms.

PARALEGALS: starting salaries in 1995 of around $25,000; with some experience, salaries from $27,000 to $43,000. In addition, many receive a bonus averaged about $1,800. Supervisors or specialists may earn from $48,000 up. Paralegal specialists in the federal government started at $18,000 to $23,000, depending on experience. Average salaries were $38,000.

SOCIAL WORK POSITIONS: beginning salaries average $27,000 (with an MSW, in 1993); the average for employees with fifteen years experience is around $40,000, according to the National Association of Social Workers.

HUMAN SERVICES WORKERS: salaries range around $18,000, more for experienced or educated workers.

SOCIAL SCIENTISTS: See "University Faculty," page 188.

POLICE AND PROTECTIVE PERSONNEL: starting salaries in the mid-$20,000s; mid-level in the $30s and $40s. One advantage: liberal benefits; retirement at half-pay after twenty years is common.

BEST BETS

CAREER COUNSELOR: Key point: people are changing jobs, losing jobs, looking for jobs—and other people are needed to help them make their choices. Career counselors are in increasing demand at colleges and universities, as well as at corporations and private practice. Requirements usually include a master's degree in counseling for university work; certification for private practice. Contact: American Counseling Association (see below).

WHERE TO GO FOR MORE INFORMATION

SOCIAL SERVICES AND LEGAL ASSOCIATIONS AND ORGANIZATIONS

American Counseling Association
5999 Stevenson Ave.
Alexandria, VA 22304
703/823-9800
800/545-2223
(Major association in certifying counselors; holds workshops, etc., for members; publishes periodical with job openings, educational information, etc.)

American Association for Marriage and Family Therapy
1133 15 St., NW
Washington, DC 20005
202/452-0109
(Publishes periodical with job listings, etc.)

American Association on Mental Retardation
444 N. Capitol St., NW
Suite 846
Washington, DC 20001
800/424-3688
202/387-1968
(Publishes periodicals with job listings, etc.)

American Correctional Association
4380 Forbes Blvd.
Lanham, MD 20706
301/918-1800

1-800/ACA-JOIN
(Publishes periodical, directories, etc.)

American Humantics
4601 Madison Ave.
Kansas City, MO 64112
816/561-6415
(For current college students interested in admin., etc., careers in social service attending various colleges, including UCLA, Pepperdine, High Point University (NC), etc. this group offers various orientation and training programs with organizations such as the Red Cross, Boy Scouts, and Girl Scouts.)

American Planning Association
1776 Massachusetts Ave., NW
Suite 400
Washington, DC 20036
202/872-0611
(Affiliated with American Planning Association, listed below.)

American Planning Association
122 S. Michigan Ave.

Suite 1600
Chicago, IL 60603
312/431-9100
(Publishes periodical with listings for members, directory.)

American Psychological Association
750 First St., NE
Washington, DC 20002
202/336-5500
(Publishes periodical with job listings, directories, etc.)

American Society of Criminology
1314 Kinnear Rd., Suite 212
Columbus, OH 43212
614/292-9207
(Publishes periodical with job openings, directory; placement service for members, etc.)

American Society for Industrial Security
1655 N. Ft. Myer Dr., Suite 1200
Arlington, VA 22209
703/522-5800
(Publishes periodical with job listings, placement for members, etc.)

American Speech-Language-Hearing Association
10801 Rockville Pike
Rockville, MD 20852
301/897-5700
(Publishes periodical with job listings, employment referral, career/educational information, etc.)

American Vocational Association
1410 King St.
Alexandria, VA 22314
703/683-3111

Association for Supervision and Curriculum
1250 N. Pitt St.
Alexandria, VA 22314-1493
703/549-9110
(Publishes periodical; educational programs; sponsors various members' professional networks, some of which publish newsletters and directories.)

Career Planning and Adult Development Network
4965 Sierra Rd.
San Jose, CA 95132
408/559-4946

(Career counselors, teachers, therapists, etc.)

Child Welfare League of America
440 First St., NW,
Suite 310
Washington, DC 20001-2085
202/638-2952
(Publishes periodical with some listings; placement service.)

EAPA
(Employee Assistance Professional Association)
2101 Wilson Blvd.
Suite 500
Arlington, VA 22201
703/522-6272

Legal Assistant Management Association
638 Prospect Ave.
Hartford, CT 06105
203/586-7507

Council on Social Work Education
1600 Duke St.
Alexandria, VA 22314-3421
703/683-8080
(Publishes journal with some listings.)

National Association of Legal Assistants
1516 S. Boston Ave.
Suite 200
Tulsa, OK 74119-4013
918/587-6828

National Association of Social Workers
750 First St., NE
Washington, DC 20002
202/408-8600
(Publishes periodicals with job listings, etc.)

National Court Reporters Association
8224 Old Courthouse Rd.
Vienna, VA 22182-3808
703/556-6272
(Publishes employment periodical with many job openings, directories; computerized job referral service for members, etc.)

National Rehabilitation Association
633 S. Washington St.
Alexandria, VA 22314
703/836-0850
(Publishes periodical with job listings; placement service, etc.)

SOCIAL SERVICES AND LEGAL DIRECTORIES

Law Firm Yellow Pages
Leadership Directories, Inc.
104 Fifth Ave.
2nd Fl.
New York, NY 10011
212/627-4140

National Paralegal Association
P.O. Box 406
Solebury, PA 18963
215/297-8333

(Publishes and sells many different directories, salary surveys; rental mailing lists, placement networks, etc.)

SOCIAL SERVICES AND LEGAL PERIODICALS

ABA Journal
750 N. Lake Shore Dr.
Chicago, IL 60611
312/988-6003
(Monthly to members
of the American Bar
Association.)

American Lawyer
600 Third Ave.
New York, NY 10016
212/973-2800
(Iconoclastic
"insider's" view of
legal industry—chock
full of ads as well; ten
issues a year.)

**American
Rehabilitation**
Rehabilitation Services
Administration
330 C St., SW
Washington, DC 20202-
2531

Business Law Today
750 N. Lake Shore Dr.
Chicago, IL 60611
312/988-6056
(Quarterly.)

Community Jobs
ACCESS
30 Irving Pl.
9th Fl.
New York, NY 10003
212/475-1001
(Monthly job magazine;
lists hundreds of jobs in
the nonprofit sector.)

Corrections Today
4380 Forbes Blvd.
Lanham, MD 20706
301/918-1800
800/222-5646
(Invaluable for anyone
considering a
corrections career.)

Law and Order
1000 Skokie Blvd.
Wilmette, IL 60091
708/256-8555
(Monthly journal for
police, etc.)

NASW News
750 First St., NE
Washington, DC
20002
202/408-8600
(Ten issues/year;
association social
worker magazine; many
job listings.)

**National
Employment Listing
Service**
Sam Houston State
University
Criminal Justice Center
Huntsville, TX
77341-2296
409/294-1692
(Monthly listing of job
openings in all areas of
law enforcement and
corrections; also social
work.)

**National and Federal
Legal Employment
Report**
Federal Reports
1010 Vermont Ave., NW
Suite 408
Washington, DC 20005
202/393-3311
(Monthly; lists hundreds
of legal jobs, primarily
government.)

National Law Journal
345 Park Ave. S.
New York, NY 10003
212/779-9200
(Weekly tabloid for
lawyers; many job
listings.)

**Opportunity in Public
Interest Law**
ACCESS
1001 Connecticut Ave,
NW
Suite 838
Washington, DC 20036
202/785-4233
(Lists hundreds of
government legal jobs.)

Social Service Jobs
10 Angelica Dr.
Framingham, MA 01701
508/626-8644
(Biweekly job listings in
social services—
counselors,
psychologists, etc.)

TEACHERS, EDUCATORS, AND SOCIAL SCIENTISTS

BRIEF BACKGROUND

▶ **Teaching and education are vital to the country's future: only now are we beginning to realize how essential an educated workforce and citizenry really are.**

In a nation where 23 million citizens are estimated to be functional illiterates, and where 40% of one high school class in a major city couldn't identify the U.S. on a map, obviously teaching is something we *should* emphasize.

But there is some good news: people are returning to the profession, and there is at least talk of salary hikes and better conditions for teachers and students. Job prospects are improving in many areas, from pre-school to college. Adults are also returning to college for retraining, and corporations are getting into the act as they train often undereducated workers in the complex skills they need performed. Already, corporations spend almost as much as the public sector in training workers. And adding to the possibility of good job prospects is the possibility of government sponsored job-retraining. But no matter what the government does, the outlook seems relatively bright.

EMPLOYMENT OUTLOOK: Fairly good in general over the long term, particularly as many current teachers retire. Librarians face a tougher job market due to probable continued budget constraints, but even here there has been improvement; educational administrators face substantial competition for these prestigious positions. Prospects for librarians in the private sector should be much better. Among social service jobs, psychologists will face the best long-term prospects.

▶ **Some experts are predicting a shortage of over 300,000 teachers by 2001, but others say this is far too optimistic.**

Key point: over half (51.6%) of current teachers are over forty—as many retire over the next ten years, job prospects will open further for applicants. Outlook will be best for mathematics, science and special-education teachers in particular.

Another major factor: teaching is a tough profession (ask any teacher)—and relatively low-paying considering the responsibilities. Some experts are concerned that not enough highly qualified individuals will be attracted to the profession—further increasing the potential shortage.

▶ So is the outlook good or bad for teachers? Answer: It depends on which survey you're reading. Our best guess: fairly good.

First, the good news: according to the federal government, teaching positions account for 3 of the top 20 jobs slated to add the most employees by 2005. More specifically, secondary school teachers come in at number 11, with nearly 400,000 new employees added; teachers aides and education assistants, number 13 with over 300,000; and elementary school teachers, number 20, with over 200,000.

Now for some bad news. According to the 1997 American Association for Employment in Education (AAEE) handbook, the predictions of a huge teacher shortage haven't turned out to be accurate so far because cities and municipalities have been cutting back on school budgets. In general, expect more static employment levels for elementary grades (pre-K to intermediate).

Key employment trends in terms of location: Highest demand and most employment opportunities for teachers will be in rural areas and inner cities. Expect hotter competition for fewer job openings in suburban and wealthy urban areas. *Subject areas in demand:* According to the AAEE, areas with a "considerable shortage" of teachers include: speech pathology, bilingual education, special education for the mentally handicapped and for those with behavioral disorders; areas with "some shortages" include other special education areas, most areas of science, math, Spanish, and Japanese. Also probably looking good: high school teaching, particularly as members of the "baby boomlet" move up to high school age. Strongest areas for job hunters: in general, the western and Pacific coast states.

Bottom line: Even with competition, short-term outlook is relatively good for determined job seekers.

New career possibility: Postschool tutoring. This is a relatively new job area that should be growing as Americans follow the Japanese model for after-school enrichment education. A postschool tutor teaches a specialized subject at a for-profit center—for example, a teacher could teach computer science at a computer center, ecology at a center specializing in the environmental sciences, and so forth. Typically, these centers attract higher-income students.

Weaker areas in terms of job prospects: Due to a general oversupply, general elementary education, physical education, and social studies teachers will face fewer employment opportunities—and more competition for positions.

▶ There is renewed emphasis on teaching as a career.

At Columbia's Teachers College, 15% of the entering class came from other jobs in finance, publishing, and other fields. And in the past few years, the number of education-degree candidates has jumped by over 60%. This is a far cry from the times when low pay and stories about lack of fulfillment, crime, and little autonomy discouraged many people from the profession.

One reason for the change: in at least twenty-six states, there are alternative certification programs, where people with mathematics, business, or other skills can be trained—and then allowed to teach. In New Jersey, whose Provisional Teacher Program has served as a model for other states, prospective teachers must first pass the National Teachers exam, and hold at least a BA or BS in the field they wish to teach. They are then put into the classroom with full pay, taking in addition 200 hours of instruction in teaching and child psychology. They are also rated periodically. After one year, the school principal decides whether to recommend permanent certification. So far, the programs have been extremely successful: the teacher dropout rate is far lower than normal, and the caliber of new teachers is high. For new grads in particular, another option includes signing up with Teach for America, which places grads in schools nationwide, and Recruiting New Teachers, which operates a referral service. Addresses and details on page 193.

Most teachers, however, are graduates of four-year colleges with degrees in education, and most have master's degrees (MATs, master's of arts in teaching, are offered at many colleges) as well. Each state has its own certification programs, usually requiring the applicant to pass the National Teachers exam (required in twenty-two states).

Best bets: minority, bilingual teachers. Math and science. Vocational education (particularly in larger, private, job-training programs). Lesson from the recession: the first areas to be cut are music, art, gifted and remedial programs.

Another good bet: special education. Recent employment numbers showed actual shortages in various areas. Also speech pathology.

▶ **Jobs for preschool teachers.**

With many parents working, demand for preschool teachers will continue. However, recent hiring data, despite earlier rosy predictions, look stable rather than increasing, with indications that there is "some surplus" of teachers—and hence, a fair amount of competition.

However, earlier predictions were very optimistic. Enrollment in formal preschool programs has jumped from 2.3 million in 1981 to 3.3 million in 1991, a 44% increase in ten years. According to *American School and University*, this growth rate will increase in the next ten years—pointing to strong job prospects. A good area: business day care centers.

There are currently about 1 million preschool workers. Although many are family day care providers, some are state-certified teachers eligible to teach at any level of public school. Many states require certification for preschool teachers: the CDA, or Child Development Associate. Many public schools require state certification for preschool workers. Contact: the National Association for the Education of Young Children (see page 192) and the Association for Childhood Education International (see page 192); and for more information on the CDA, the Council for Early Childhood Professional Recognition (page 192).

▶ **The employment outlook for librarians: improving.**

There are about 149,000 librarians nationwide, according to the Bureau of Labor Statistics; 75% of them are women. A master's in library science (MLS) is a requirement for most library jobs. Most librarians work as public and academic librarians, or as special librarians—for corporations, government agencies, or professional associations, and maintaining specialized collections of information. On the cutting edge of the field are database librarians, who manage computer information systems and those specializing in the Internet. These librarians are often actually working as systems analysts, researchers, and managers. While this area is still developing as the technology continues to evolve, it is a specialty to keep an eye on.

In general, the field is split into two main branches: user services (dealing with the public), and technical services (dealing primarily with acquisitions, cataloguing, etc.). In small libraries, these functions may be shared; in larger ones, librarians specialize.

Hiring was up for librarians recently: Recent figures, according to several surveys, showed both increased job openings and higher salaries—a change from the gloomier outlooks of the recent past.

Interestingly, while many experts were predicting a rise in "nontraditional" library jobs (with business, in the Internet, or other technical areas) the latest hiring figures showed increased hiring instead in "traditional" library jobs. One reason: As the economy improved, municipalities and schools had more money to spend on libraries.

On the downside, more new hires were put into part-time and temporary positions. Also on the downside: Libraries are often perceived by administrators as less essential than other areas—and they find it much easier to cut library staff than their own salaries or perks.

Also, with the increasing use of computers, some are saying that demand for librarians may decrease, as computers take the place of human catalogers, etc. However, if recent experience is anything, increased computerization may instead increase the need for technical librarians, and may not much affect demand for other librarians, who will still be needed for acquisitions and management of increasingly large collections.

Long-term outlook for librarians: Fair. Libraries are increasingly vital as the cliché of the "information age" becomes a reality and as the wide diversity of information sources becomes even more diverse.

Some good news for the future: Only half as many library students as in the past—pointing to less competition. For Ph.D.s: Jobs market may be brighter. Library school faculty is aging. Over half of all library school deans in a recent survey indicated concern over *"the dearth of Ph.D.-holding professors available to replace an aging professoriate."*

All in all, government statisticians predict employment growth between 3 and 19%. The most likely scenario: presuming a moderately growing economy, by the year 2005 job growth will be at about 11%. Better job prospects will come as funding increases can be sustained. Best way to look for jobs: check the many services of the American Library Association—see page 191. Or call the ALA hotline at 800/545-2433 ×4277 for a free pamphlet describing career opportunities.

Best bets for the rest of the decade: As mentioned earlier, librarians with computer skills and corporate librarians with technical skills. In general, librarians with scientific and technical backgrounds of any type should experience the least difficulty getting jobs, as will bilingual librarians, archivists, and systems analysts. Temping as a way of getting a foot in the door is frequently recommended; moreover, temp hiring was fairly strong even during the recession of the early 1990s. Other, nontraditional, routes to employment include work with CD-ROM companies, library sales, and independent work as information consultants.

▶ Tougher times ahead for college faculty:

The problem is simple: Job openings are scarce. For a long time, experts thought that this wouldn't be the case. Their rationale: A large number of professors, hired in the 1950s and 1960s were coming up for retirement—and so this would create a large number of job openings. But this hasn't happened. Why not? For several reasons. Enrollments to college are stable, but not increasing, costs are rising, and states and the federal government are cutting back on funding. Result: no increases in hiring, since universities can't or won't expand. Worst areas for job hunters: English, foreign languages, arts, social sciences, biology, education.

Is there any good news? Yes, for job hunters looking for faculty positions in business areas. Some bright spots: accounting, finance, management, marketing. Also, some regional areas look better, including California and Connecticut. Look for many changes in colleges and universities: a more "bottom line" emphasis, more part-time hires, more attention to teaching versus research, more emphasis on high-quality and "core" areas, with lower quality departments biting the dust.

▶ Social scientists and historians.

About 258,000 people work as some sort of social scientist—interestingly, about 25% are self-employed as consultants and so on. Outlook: fairly strong competition, best for those with advanced degrees; in the long term probably best for economists (see below). Psychologists will face the best job market—for more on this and similar "helping professions" see page 171.

For other areas, employment prospects are to a greater extent tied to the fate of universities, since many social scientists and historians are employed in academia.

Economists are employed by government, academia, business, financial services firms, and banks. *Typical career paths:* Generally speaking, in academia, a Ph.D. is required—one survey found that over 90% of academic economists had one. The second largest employer of economists is the federal government, which hires a wide range of backgrounds, from B.S. to Ph.D. See Government, page 66, for employers. A good specialty within government: international trade, finance. Vital as government is called upon to support U.S. exports in competitive world economy. See information on U.S. Department of State on page 113; U.S. Dept. of Commerce on page 77.

Outlook: Its's a mixed outlook for this profession: On one hand, the government predicts faster than average job growth through 2005, with strongest employment in private industry, especially in research, testing, and consulting firms. On the other hand, other industry experts see employment opportunities decreasing—as businesses downsize. The bottom line: In either scenario, consulting work is the best bet—either as an independent or with a firm. Key to success in this area: practical orientation. The new trend for business economists is solving specific problems as opposed to doing general forecasting or more arcane scholarly theorizing. Other possibilities: going the enterpreneurial route and writing a newsletter; switching to a Wall Street job; or opting for a marketing or finance position in corporate America.

For more information on a career as a business economist, write the National Association of Business Economists (address on page 192). Banking and finance: Master's degree usually required for analytical jobs—normal specialties include monetary and fiscal policy and theory; business economics and economic development.

Other employers: nonprofits, international organizations (see page 109), and state and local government.

▶ **Educational administration jobs are expected to grow at an average rate over the next several years.**

A lot depends on how states budget for education, and on enrollment levels. Right now, in a cost-cutting atmosphere, hiring can be expected to be sluggish— but on the other hand, highly qualified administrators with experience in budgeting may do well.

There are only about 400,000 educational administrators in the United States— ranging from elementary school principals to college presidents.

Requirements for jobs: For public schools, a master's degree or doctorate and a state teaching certificate. For universities and college, usually a doctorate in the appropriate field for deans, and a Ph.D. or Ed.D. for top general administrative posts, although many people enter with B.A.s and get the advanced degrees on the job.

Demand areas in the future: Principals of school systems, elementary school administrators, medical school deans, hospital med-center administrators, dentistry deans, law deans, administrators of college computer systems, labor relations managers (particularly as college workers unionize), publications administrators, housing officers.

In other auxiliary areas, assessment specialists who test, analyze, and track student performance will probably do well, as school systems become more performance-oriented.

One probable area in ascendence: college administration. It sounds paradoxical, but as colleges cut back on administrators, new types of administrators are needed who can straddle dual functions and who may have outside corporate experience in cost-cutting, fund-raising, or budgeting. Fund-raising, although a small field, has seen high growth rates in the past few years of 20%. Another good area: MIS. Colleges are in need of network specialists and systems administrators. And for those with experience in the stratosphere, the market for college presidents is very strong. The only problem: the job is extraordinarily difficult, balancing diverse constituencies such as students, faculty, alumni, and trustees.

▶ Corporate training prospects should remain fairly good.

According to experts, corporations train and retrain 10 million people a year—which is very close to the 12 million undergraduates that universities and colleges teach. According to a recent survey of 300 midwestern manufacturing firms, management is shifting emphasis (which means money) from automation to employee training. Reasons: business is becoming increasingly technical. Employees now must be trained how to run complicated machinery—or, in white-collar jobs, to manage complex transactions.

In addition, English skills are failing; at the same time, business needs people who can communicate well. Problem: only 10% of all U.S. employees now receive training from their companies—although estimates are that 50 million need it. In fact, many corporations have actually cut back on their training departments. However, this points to opportunities at independent training firms—who are picking up the outsourced work that used to be done in-house.

A little background on the field:

Corporate training runs the gamut from factory operations to accounting and computers to basic and remedial English, communication skills and sales training. In service industries, trainers may specialize in teaching basic business skills, sales techniques, or specialized skills; in manufacturing firms, they may instruct workers on machine or computer use. Generally corporate teachers come out of human resources departments; but former schoolteachers are being hired as well. Technical trainers may be technicians already, or specialists who design manufacturing teaching programs.

Best bets: Information technology is probably the hottest growth area, as well as offering some of the best opportunities. More specifically, hottest areas include Internet-related training, including working with the World Wide Web, Windows, and other applications.

Another area with potential: cross-cultural trainer. As Americans go overseas to work or trade, understanding foreign cultures becomes essential. These trainers do the job of translating overseas customs and mores, and help in marketing or, on the personal side, helping families relocate. For more information, contact the Society for Intercultural Education, Training, and Research in Washington, DC.

Many teachers are also hired as consultants (as with many bank-training programs which farm out basic accounting, banking, and finance to local university professors). According to *Money* magazine, this is a good area for entrepreneurs: *Fortune* 500 firms are increasingly hiring small outside training firms to handle many aspects of corporate training.

▶ In the *long term,* increases in the numbers of jobs for *museum curators, directors,* and *archivists*—and a lot of competition.

Curators are generally specialists in an academic field who manage museum collections and staff in that area. Major areas are art, archeology, science, technology, botany, zoology. Despite the tough times in recent years, the outlook for museums appears relatively bright, as interest and attendance increase. In all, museums account for one of the largest employment areas in the nonprofit sector, and are a reasonable employment goal for those with art or scientific backgrounds, as well as for those with business backgrounds and an interest in a particular field. This has led to a different trend: museum administrators coming from the ranks of business.

In spite of projected increases in jobs, however, there will still be only a very few openings. There are only about 10,000 professional-level museum jobs in the country, and the career is prestigious and interesting to many specialists. The Smithsonian Institution, for example, has one of the lowest turnover rates in government.

One problem is on the rise: "museum director burnout." According to the American Association of Museum Directors and *ARTnews* magazine, it is increasingly common, "almost an epidemic." The problems: not enough money from endowments to meet increasing costs, rising exhibition and fund-raising pressures, and not enough managerial expertise. The result: overworked museum directors—and burnout.

One solution, and a new trend: curators will be getting MBAs or business training along with a specialist degree. Increasingly, museum management is as much financial as curatorial. And so financially astute curators may be ahead of the competition. Already the American Federation of the Arts runs a summer program that trains curators in business administration. But the major trend is different: museums are looking for business types to work in museum administration. Key reason: the old days of government or philanthropic funding are waning. Now museums must hustle to get funds, and hustle to cut costs and stay afloat. New need: trained businesspeople, from legal experts to navigate the web of government regulations (and influence funding from state and federal governments) to public relations experts to help in lobbying for money, to finance types to manage cost-cutting and investments. Salary levels are lower but competitive with industry, depending primarily on the size of the museum. For more information: check *Jobs in Arts and Media Management,* published by the American Council for the Arts.

A good source for jobs: Check *Aviso,* the monthly magazine published by the American Association of Museums. Besides general museum news, it lists about fifty openings per issue for museum jobs across the country. See address on page 194.

WHAT'S NEXT

▶ Empowerment, professionalism, prestige . . . and dollars?

Calls for school reform, and the realization of the educational crisis facing the U.S., will speed changes in the school system.

Many ideas are already in place. More ease of entry for those with nonteaching backgrounds (in itself controversial with some), more control by teachers, and new "management team" administrative structures are already changing the face of education. The bottom line: administration is becoming more localized, more efficiency-based. Good teachers will increasingly be rewarded—and noticed. The profession itself is at long last gaining the prestige it deserves.

The rest of the decade will see action replacing talk. The key issue is raising standards—and a major way is to simply encourage teachers to teach. This will mean higher pay as a reward to good teachers (instead of a standardized pay schedule), "mentoring" (where good teachers teach other teachers), less administrative duties, more control over how they do their jobs. The buzzword in teaching is "empowerment"—meaning giving teachers the power to make the critical decisions. The big problem, of course, is getting the money.

▶ American education: getting some ideas from Japan?

Americans typically think of Japanese elementary schools as regimented places, when in fact the opposite is true. In many ways taking their ideas from the famed U.S. scholar John Dewey, the Japanese try to make elementary education exploratory and fun; young students start from the concrete and then move to the theoretical, they have short recesses between class, they are not divided into "tracked" classes of good and poor students, and in general feel less stress.

Some other ideas from the Japanese, as reported in *The New York Times*, which may trickle back to a concerned U.S.:

- **higher pay** for teachers

- **less time teaching;** more time to consult with students and to prepare classes

- **larger classes** (sounds bad, but gives teacher more time for all of the above)

Another trend: midmarket schools, or private schools for the middle class. These are "no frills" private schools—emphasis is on the basics. Salaries tend to be lower, but quality of teaching is high.

SALARIES

TEACHERS (KINDERGARTEN, PRESCHOOL): The average salary in 1995 was about $34,000. Preschool teachers with state certification earned roughly the same amount; much lower for day care workers.

TEACHERS (ELEMENTARY AND SECONDARY): According to the National Education Association, the average salary for elementary teachers was about $36,400 in 1995; the average secondary school teacher's salary was $37,800. Average beginning salary from $20,000 to $25,000. Private school teachers, however, generally earn less. These salaries also hold for *special education teachers.* What state offers the highest starting salary for a teacher in the U.S.? Alaska, with $31,709 (in 1995).

UNIVERSITY FACULTY: According to a salary survey by the American Association of University Professors, the average salary in 1994–1995 was $47,000 for an associate professor, $39,100 for an assistant professor, and $63,500 for a full professor.

Much more for top faculty: some professors earn well over $100,000. In keeping with supply and demand, science engineering faculty often earn more than liberal arts faculty; universities and top colleges more than others, four-year colleges more than two-year schools. The highest paid professors are usually found in business schools, where total compensation can reach $120,000 to $200,000. Consulting is the normal way to add-on base salary; the norm in colleges is not to require summer work.

EDUCATION ADMINISTRATORS (ELEMENTARY, SECONDARY SCHOOL): Senior high school principals in 1994–1995 earned an average of $66,600; junior high/middle school principals, $62,300; and elementary school principals, $58,600, according to the Educational Research Service. Assistant principal salaries at the senior high school level averaged $44,600; at the junior/middle school, $52,900; and $48,500 for elementary school.

EDUCATION ADMINISTRATORS (COLLEGE, UNIVERSITY): According to the College and University Personnel Association, median salaries in 1994 for administrators ranged from $28,800 for admissions counselors to $173,287 for medical school deans. Registrars earned $43,300; dean of students, $52,200; and dean of arts and sciences, $76,600.

LIBRARIANS: According to the American Libraries Association, the average salary of children's librarians in academic and public libraries was $35,000 in 1995; reference/information librarians, $35,600; catalogers and classifiers, $36,300; department heads, $42,000; library directors, $58,200. Starting salary for those with an M.L.A. but no experience is about $28,300. Corporate and collegiate librarians usually earn more, with the average salary at $45,912. Federal government librarians earn an average $48,200.

CURATORS AND ARCHIVISTS: Salaries vary; much higher for major museums, and in the western and mid-Atlantic states. Average starting salary in 1995 was $18,700 for those with a bachelor's degree, $23,200 for those with some experience; $28,300 for those with a master's, and more for those with doctorates. Average curator salary: about $51,600. For archivist $50,000. Museum specialists and technicians, $32,800.

CORPORATE TRAINING: The average salary is about $47,000. Executive-level training managers average in the $65,000 range; single-person department managers in the $40,000 range. Instructors and evaluators earn between $35,000 and $45,000. Trainers promoted within the human resources department to vice presidents or senior managers can make $100,000 to $200,000.

BEST BETS

LANGUAGE TEACHER: As borders open, and international careers become more important, the basic skill of speaking a foreign language obviously becomes more important. Already, enrollment is up in secondary schools and colleges. According to the Modern Language Association, college student enrollment exceeded 1 million a few years back—for the first time in fourteen years. That said, a lot depends on *which* language and *which* age level. In general, demand is best for "strategic languages" (German, Russian, Chinese, Japanese) and for people at secondary school levels. College-level foreign language teachers will find stiff competition in many areas.

According to the National Governors Association, twenty-six states reported shortages of qualified teachers recently. Shortages are worst in elementary and secondary schools, but openings will grow in other areas as business and academia finally address the problem. Some best bets for the 1990s: Japanese, German. On the downside, pay is still often low. And, despite a lot of lip service, many school systems still won't budget funds for language teaching.

Good source for jobs: Check the Job Information List of the Modern Language Association. It lists hundreds of jobs by geographic region, by college and university, by specialty, including related jobs ranging from comparative literature to linguistics, with sections for second-career job hunters. The address is on page 192.

WHERE TO GO FOR MORE INFORMATION

TEACHERS, LIBRARIANS, HISTORIANS, AND SOCIAL SCIENTISTS ASSOCIATIONS AND ORGANIZATIONS

Academy for Educational Development
1875 Connecticut Ave., 9th Fl.
Washington, DC 20009
202/884-8000
(Placement service, etc.)

African Studies Association
Credit Union Bldg.
Emory University
Atlanta, GA 30322
404/329-6410
(Publishes journal with some job listings, etc.)

American Alliance for Health, Physical Education, Recreation, and Dance
1900 Association Dr.
Reston, VA 22091
703/476-3400
(Publishes periodical with job listings, placement service.)

American Counseling Association
5999 Stevenson Ave.
Alexandria, VA 22304
703/823-9800
(Major association in certifying counselors; holds workshops, etc. for members; publishes periodical with job openings, etc.)

American Association for Employment in Teaching
820 Davis St.
Evanston, IL 60201
847/864-1999
(Publishes *Job Search Handbook,* with articles and job listings.)

American Association for Higher Education
1 Du Pont Circle, Suite 360
Washington, DC 20036
202/293-6440
(Publishes periodical, holds conferences, etc.)

American Association of Law Libraries
53 W. Jackson
Suite 940
Chicago, IL 60604
312/939-4764
(Publishes periodical with job openings, job database, and hot line, directory.)

American Association of Museums
1225 I St., NW
Suite 200
Washington, DC 20005
202/289-1818
(Publishes periodical with job openings, placement service, etc.)

American Association of School Administrators
1801 N. Moore St.
Arlington, VA 22209
703/528-0700
(Publishes periodical with listings, etc.)

American Association of School Librarians
50 E. Huron St.
Chicago, IL 60611
312/944-6780

American Association for State and Local History
530 Church St.,
Suite 600
Nashville, TN 37219
615/255-2971
(Publishes periodicals with job listings, etc.)

American Association of University Professors
1012 14th St., NW,
Suite 500
Washington, DC 20005
202/737-5900
(Publishes journal with occasional job listing, etc.)

American Council on Education
No. 1 Dupont Circle,
NW
Washington, DC 20036
202/939-9300
(Publishes journal, trends, etc.)

American Economic Association
2014 Broadway,
Suite 305
Nashville, TN 37203
615/322-2595
(Publishes periodical with job openings, operates placement service, etc.)

American Economic Development Council
9801 W. Higgins Rd.
Rosemont, IL

60018-4726
847/692-9944
(Publishes periodical, job referrals, etc., for members.)

American Federation of Teachers
555 New Jersey Ave.,
NW
Washington, DC 20001
202/879-4400

American Historical Association
400 A St., SE
Washington, DC 20003
202/544-2422
(Publishes periodical, etc.)

American Library Association
50 E. Huron Street
Chicago, IL 60611
1-800/545-2433
(Publishes periodicals with job listings. *Important Note:* The ALA maintains phone numbers and information on *state library job hot lines*— tape-recorded messages, periodically updated, that list library job openings for some states. Call for specific phone numbers. The ALA also maintains the special Grapevine job database. See also the Guide to Library Placement Sources, under "Directories.")

American Political Science Association
1527 New Hampshire

Ave., NW
Washington, DC 20036
202/483-2513
(Publishes periodical for members with job listings; sponsors fellowships, maintains job contacts for members, etc.)

American Society for Information Science
8720 Georgia Ave.,
Suite 501
Silver Springs, MD
20910
301/495-0900
(Periodical with job openings; members' placement service, etc.)

American Sociological Association
1722 N St., NW
Washington, DC 20036
202/833-3410
(Publishes periodical with job listings, directory, etc.)

American Vocational Association
1410 King St.
Alexandria, VA 22314
703/683-3111

Association of American Law Schools
1201 Connecticut Ave.,
NW, Suite 800
Washington, DC 20036
202/296-8851
(Publishes *Placement Bulletin,* which lists both faculty and admin. job openings.)

Association of American Universities
1 DuPont Circle, NW,
Suite 730
Washington, DC 20036
202/466-5030

Association for Childhood Education International
11501 Georgia Ave.
Suite 315
Wheaton, MD 20902
301/942-2443

Association of Christian Schools International
P.O. Box 4097
Whittier, CA 90607-4097
310/694-4791
(Placement service, etc.)

College and University Personnel Association
1233 20th St., NW,
Suite 301
Washington, DC 20036
202/429-0311
(Major salary survey, professional development programs, etc.)

College Music Society
202 W. Spruce St.
Missoula, MT 59802
406/721-9616

Council for the Advancement and Support of Education
11 Du Pont Circle, NW,
Suite 400
Washington, DC 20036
202/328-5900
(Publishes directory, etc.)

Council for Early Childhood Professional Recognition
1341 G St., NW
Suite 400
Washington, DC 20005
202/265-9090

Institute of International Education
809 United Nations Plz.
New York, NY 10017
212/883-8200
(Used to publish directory of international exchange programs and positions; at time of writing institute was unsure if publication would be resumed.)

Kennedy Center for International Studies Association
237 Herald Clark Bldg.
Brigham Young University
Provo, UT 84602
801/378-2695
(Publishes periodical with job listings.)

Modern Language Association
10 Astor Pl.
New York, NY 10003-6981
212/475-9500
(Publishes job listings for English- as well as foreign-language teachers.)

National Art Education Association
1916 Association Dr.
Reston, VA 22091

703/860-8000
(Placement service.)

National Association for the Education of Young Children
1509 16th St., NW
Washington, DC 20036
202/232-8777

National Association for Girls and Women in Sport
1900 Association Dr.
Reston, VA 22091
703/476-3450
(Also HQ of National Council of Athletic Training.)

National Association of Business Economists
1233 20th St., NW
Suite 505
Washington, DC 20036
202/463-6223
(Publishes periodical with job openings, career booklet, etc.)

National Association of College Admissions Counselors
1631 Prince St.
Alexandria, VA 22314
703/836-2222

National Association of College and University Business Officers
1 Du Pont Circle,
Suite 500
Washington, DC 20036
202/861-2500

National Association of Elementary School Principals
1615 Duke St.
Alexandria, VA 22314
703/684-3345

(Planning at time of writing to operate an electronic bulletin board for job listings, tie-in to state associations, etc.)

National Association of Secondary School Principals
1904 Association Dr.
Reston, VA 22091
703/860-0200

National Association for Sport and Physical Education
1900 Association Dr.
Reston, VA 22091
703/476-3410

National Association of Student Personnel Administrators
1875 Connecticut Ave., NW, Suite 418
Washington, DC 20009
202/265-7500

National Business Education Association
1914 Association Dr.
Reston, VA 20191
703/860-8300

National Council of Teachers of English
1111 W. Kenyon Rd.
Urbana, IL 61801
217/328-3870

National Council of Teachers of Mathematics
1906 Association Dr.
Reston, VA 22091
703/620-9840
(Publishes journal with listings, etc.)

National Science Teachers Association
1840 Wilson Blvd.
Arlington, VA 22201
703/243-7100
(Publishes periodical with job listings, directory, etc.)

Organization of American Historians
112 N. Bryan St.
Bloomington, IN 47408
812/855-7311
(Publishes periodical with some job listings for members.)

Recruiting New Teachers
385 Concord Ave., Suite 103
Belmont, MA 02178-9804
617/489-6000
(Has free referral service.)

Society of American Archivists
600 S. Federal St.,

Suite 504
Chicago, IL 60605
312/922-0140
(Publishes periodical with job listings, information; placement service, etc.)

Special Library Association
1700 18th St., NW
Washington, DC 20009
202/234-4700
(Periodical with job openings, resume referral service, tape-recorded job openings.)

Teach for America
20 Exchange Place
New York, NY 10050
212/425-9039
(Well-known new program that encourages and helps place new teachers; submit an application and recommendations, and demonstrate your teaching ability.)

Women's Resource Center
University of California
250 Golden Bear Ctr.
Berkeley, CA 94720-2440
510/642-4786

TEACHERS, LIBRARIANS, HISTORIANS, AND SOCIAL SCIENTISTS DIRECTORIES

American Library Association—Handbook of Organization and Membership Directory
American Library

Association
50 E. Huron St.
Chicago, IL 60611
1-800/545-2433

American Library Directory

Reede Reference Publishing
P.O. Box 31
New Providence, NJ 07974-9904
1-800/521-8110

*Directory of Federal
Libraries*
Oryx Press
4041 N. Central
Suite 700
Phoenix, AZ 85012-3397
1-800/279-6799

*Directory of Special
Libraries and
Information Centers*
835 Penobscot Bldg.
Detroit, MI 48226-4094
1-800/877-GALE

*Guide to Library
Placement Sources*
American Library
Association
50 E. Huron
St.Chicago, IL 60611
1-800/545-2433
(This is a valuable,
centralized source that
lists associations and
organizations nation-
wide that offer placement
services for librarians.)

*Opportunities Abroad
for Educators:
Fulbright Teacher
Exchange Program*

Teacher Exchange
Program
E/ASX, Room 353
U.S. Information Agency
Washington, DC 20547
202/619-4555
(Lists countries and
positions available;
includes application
and describes program;
updated yearly.)

*Patterson's American
Education*
Educational
Directories, Inc.
P.O. Box 199
Mount Prospect, IL
60056
708/459-0605

*Requirements for
Certification of
Teachers, Counselors,
Librarians,
Administrators, for
Elementary and
Secondary Schools
and Junior Colleges*
by **John Tryneski**
University of Chicago
Press

11030 S. Langley Ave.
Chicago, IL 60628
800/621-2736
312/702-7700
(Before you apply, it
might be best to know
if you can—this guide
lists certification
requirements state by
state.)

*WILSONLINE:
Education Index*
(**computer database**)
H. W. Wilson Company
950 University Avenue
Bronx, NY 10452
718/588-8400
1-800/367-6770
(On-line database
that extensively lists
many education
periodicals.)

*World Guide to
Libraries*
Reede Reference
Publishing
P.O. Box 31
New Providence, NJ
07974-9904
1-800/521-8110

TEACHERS, LIBRARIANS, HISTORIANS, AND SOCIAL SCIENTISTS MAGAZINES

American Educator
555 New Jersey Ave.,
NW
Washington, DC 20001
202/879-4420
(Quarterly general
magazine.)

American Libraries
50 E. Huron St.
Chicago, IL 60611
1-800/545-2433
312/944-6780

(Monthly association
magazine; job ads can
be obtained three
weeks in advance of
publication—call for
details.)

Aviso
American Association
of Museums
1225 I St., NW,
Suite 200
Washington, DC 20005
202/289-1818

(General museum
news, with job
listings.)

*Change: The
Magazine of Higher
Learning*
Heldre Publications
1319 18th St., NW
Washington, DC 20036
202/362-6445
(Prestigious journal of
higher education.)

Chronicle of Higher Education
1255 23rd St., NW
Washington, DC 20037
P.O. Box 1955
Marion, OH
43306-2055
202/466-1000
(Monthly for college faculty and administrators; many job listings.)

Education Week
Editorial Projects In Education, Inc.
4301 Connecticut Ave., NW
Ste. 432
Washington, DC 20008
202/364-4114

Educational Leadership
1250 N. Pitt
Alexandria, VA 22314
703/549-9110
(Eight-issue magazine for supervisors.)

Instructor
411 Lafayette St.
New York, NY 10003
212/505-4900
(Monthly primarily for elementary school administrators.)

Learning
P.O. Box 54293
Boulder, CO 80322
800/753-1843
(Nine-issue magazine for elementary and junior-high educators.)

Library Journal
249 W. 17th St.
New York, NY 10011
212/463-6819
800/842-1669
(Semimonthly magazine; has many job listings.)

NEA Today
1201 16th St., NW
Washington, DC 20036
202/822-7260
(Eight-issue tabloid for association members.)

Phi Delta Kappan
Phi Delta Kappa, Inc.
Box 789
Bloomington, IN
47402-0789
812/339-1156

School Library Journal
249 W. 17th St.
New York, NY 10011
212/463-6759
800/842-1669
(subscriptions number; Cahners Publishing in Ohio)
(Monthly journal specializing in school libraries; carries some job listings each month.)

Teacher
4301 Connecticut Ave., NW
Suite 432
Washington, DC 20008
202/686-0800
(Monthly.)

TECHNICAL CAREERS

BRIEF BACKGROUND

▶ **As society gets more technological, demand for technical workers should increase—but not in all areas.**

It seems obvious. Manufacturing is getting more complex, computers control more and more parts of our lives—and so more people with strong technical backgrounds are needed to control, run, and fix these increasingly complex machines.

To a degree, that's true. Demand will increase strongly or moderately for many technically oriented workers, including most types of health care technicians, computer repair, some types of machine and mechanical work, air-conditioning, and household appliance repair.

But there's another side to the story, too. Computers are becoming increasingly good at doing a lot of technical work without as much human input as before—and so in many cases, the demand for certain technical workers isn't increasing as fast as some experts predicted in the past. And as the economy goes international, some technical jobs are being transferred abroad—to places like Malaysia, India, and Ireland.

Bottom line: technical jobs will be there for the well-qualified applicant with good job-hunting skills. But a lot depends on what *type* of technical job you're looking for.

This section will focus primarily on the various types of engineering technicians, repair and mechanical technical workers, CAD/CAM technicians, broadcast technicians, mechanics, and airline-related professions, including pilots and air-traffic controllers.

For more on health care technical jobs, see Health Care and Medical Specialists section on page 94.

EMPLOYMENT OUTLOOK: Fair to good.

▶ **Engineering technicians—job growth somewhat offset by advances in technology.**

There are about 700,000 engineering technicians working in the U.S. today—but that large number covers a wide range of diverse jobs in both the public and private sectors. Basically, about 40% of all engineering technicians work in manufacturing, and about 20% work in services, usually with consulting firms. About 17% work for the federal, local, and state governments.

In general, the field can be split into five major catagories: electrical and electronics, industrial, mechanical, chemical, and civil engineering. Engineering technicians in all of these areas generally work on the more practical aspects of engineering jobs, helping engineers solve technical problems, and working with technical equipment, often under the supervision of senior technicians or engineers.

Outlook in general: slower than average job growth. Reasons: better computer technology is reducing demand for some technician jobs; defense cutbacks are affecting jobs in the huge aerospace/defense area.

► **Job prospects for computer repair technicians look very good; for electrical repair, fair.**

Computer repair jobs, according to the latest government projections, will grow much faster than average until 2005. Best guess: jobs for computer and office machine repairers will increase by about 24%. (But note that most of this increase comes from the computer side of things—jobs for office machine repairers won't increase very rapidly at all). The key reason for the good news: more computers than ever are being used, the number is still going up—and the machines sooner or later break down.

The outlook for electrical repair technicians is not as good. The government expects growth of around 2% by the year 2005—but given the large number of people in this job area, jobs will be there as workers retire, quit, or transfer. Best bets: electromedical and biomedical machine repair. These are the machines that keep us alive in hospitals—prospects look very good for specialists in this area.

Key to the best jobs: technical know-how, mathematical skills. Training can be obtained at vocational schools, technical schools, some colleges. The International Society of Certified Electronics Technicians and the Electronics Technicians Association offer certification tests for most areas of computer and electronic repair—those passing become Certified Electronics Technicians recognized by the Accreditation Board for Engineering and Technology. Better: get a four-year engineering background, and maybe a job as an applied engineer.

► **Outlook for machine tool workers, numerical control tool operators, CAM (computer-aided manufacturing) technicians and programmers is generally good.**

The key point: manufacturing machinery is increasingly computerized and very complex, and highly skilled technicians who use these machines that make parts are in short supply. For example, there are only about 10,000 numerical control workers—technicians who run the electronic controllers on machine tools—in the U.S. today. In all, there are about 380,000 people employed in all of these areas.

So what are the jobs exactly? Let's start with the area that had some of the best job prospects in 1997: numerical control tool operators and programmers.

In general, these jobs are concerned with the machine tools (lathes, drill presses, etc.) that manufacture precision machine parts out of metal. In more and more cases, these machine tools are *numerically controlled* (NC), that is, they have an electronic controller that tells the machine what to do. In most cases, this numerical controller is a computer, so the machines are called CNC machines—or computer numerically controlled machines. Technicians who are involved with these machines may be tool programmers—that is, they actually program the computer in the CNC machine, or they may be machinists who run the CNC machines. Increasingly, they may do both. And other machinists work at maintaining and repairing these complex machines. Naturally, a job doing these functions requires a relatively high level of skill. Because of this, the job outlook is quite good. Although the government projects that total employment for all machine operators will go down slightly by 2005 (slightly fewer operators are needed because computers can do more of the job, and some jobs are being transferred overseas), they also foresee *many* jobs for those with CNC experience. Reason: employers are still having trouble finding enough skilled workers. Moreover, as older workers retire, more jobs will open up.

Ways of getting a job: many move up from machine tool operator, others enter via a formal apprenticeship or job-training program. Increasingly, operators and programmers have formal training from a local or community college.

Because of the relative shortage, industry and industry associations are encouraging high school students to get the training and skills to enter the field. In the Chicago area, one association began a foundation a few years back to promote the field and provide assistance to area vocational colleges. For more information, contact: Tooling and Manufacturing Association, 1177 South Dee Road, Park Ridge, IL 60068.

Other related areas:

TOOL AND DIE MAKERS: These are workers and technicians who make tools, dies, and devices that are in turn used in machines to make many other products—consumer products like clothing or textiles, or industrial products like valves or bearings.

General outlook: good. Although employment as a whole will go down, according to government experts, job hunters shouldn't worry, say experts, because this is more than offset by the shortage of qualified workers. About 30% of tool and die workers are over 50—and as they retire even more severe shortages should occur.

METAL-WORKING AND PLASTICS WORKING MACHINE OPERATORS IN GENERAL. These workers set up and run the machines that make the metal and plastic parts of many industrial and consumer products. In general, outlook is not as good as other areas, except, as mentioned earlier, for those with CNC skills. Best area: plastics. One reason for poorer outlook: manufacturers are shifting production overseas. One worry: will this affect other areas as well.

▶ Outlook for aviation-related jobs: mixed.

In general, it's tough competition for jobs that involve aircraft or flying. There's one very basic reason: people like these "glamor" jobs, so in many cases, many more people apply for them than the number of jobs available. Here's a brief breakdown of job outlooks. For more, see Aviation section on page 249.

AIRCRAFT MECHANICS: Until fairly recently, the outlook was excellent. Then in the early 1990s, companies started cutting back on corporate flying, the government started cutting back on funding and the military, and the outlook got worse. In general, experts predict that job growth will be about average, with most job openings coming from replacement—that is, from openings created when mechanics retire or leave their current jobs. On the bright side: air travel is expected to increase, leading to more airplanes—and more need for mechanics to fix them. Best bets: commuter and regional airline, FAA repair stations. Key point: get the best technical background possible to be able to master increasingly computerized aircraft. According to workers, "they're not airplanes anymore, they're flying computers."

AIR TRAFFIC CONTROLLERS: tough competition for jobs. Key reasons: After Ronald Reagan fired air-traffic controllers during their strike in the 1980s, replacements were hired—and they're still young.

Important Note: Technical jobs require training—which can be obtained on the job, or at a university, college, two-year college—or trade or technical school. Although many of these trade or technical schools give you your money's worth and are excellent places to learn a trade, others aren't. *Before* enrolling in a school, check with local authorities, a trade association (addresses are listed below), and local employers. To learn what to look for (and look out for), ask for a free pamphlet: *Getting Skills, Getting Ahead.* Contact: Consumer Information Center, Dept. 574W, Pueblo, CO 81009.

WHAT'S NEXT

▶ **Employers are seeing the need for *increased education* for technicians—and are beginning to do something about it.**

There's no time to waste—and finally, people are catching on.

New programs are being offered, old ones revamped. For example: Tech Prep or TPAD, in which high school students take classes designed for them to enter a technical program at a community college. Community colleges are improving curricula—and linking their programs with local and national employers.

Some Department of Education award-winning examples:

Technical Training Winners

1. **Valencia Community College** (Orlando, FL, 407/299-5000) (computer training, with placement services; affiliated with major firms like Martin Marietta)

2. **Thief River Falls Technical College** (Thief River Falls, MN, 218/681-5424) (aviation maintenance technology, certification training, internships with Northwest)

3. **Longview Community College** (Lee's Summit, MO, 815/763-7777) (up-to-date automotive technology program, with partnerships with GM, Ford, Toyota; 95% placement rate)

4. Spokane Community College (Spokane, WA, 509/536-7148) (fluid power technology—hydraulics, pneumatics, in machinery—program; job placement rate for successful students is near 100%)

► **Apprenticeships—a new trend?**

In Europe (and in the U.S. in the past), an apprentice goes to work for a skilled craftsperson, and learns the skills he or she needs on the job. It's a good way for everyone—the craftsperson gets a cheap worker, the apprentice earns a living while learning. Today, only 2% of all U.S. high school grads get their start as apprentices—and this at a time when corporations are *rejecting* applicants in record numbers for not having the right skills.

Apprenticeships are an idea whose time has come again. Grants from the federal government are being provided to help the idea; for example, the Pennsylvania Department of Commerce is working on a program with the metalworking industry.

And giant German manufacturer Siemens AG has indicated it is interested in bringing in an apprenticeship program here in the U.S., where it already employs 30,000 workers.

SALARIES

► **General trend: salaries expected to increase for high-demand jobs as competition for scarce workers tightens.**

Salaries for some major areas:

AIR TRAFFIC CONTROLLERS: beginning salaries approximately $24,000; average about $54,000. Earnings can reach up to $75,000.

AIRCRAFT TECHNICIANS: median salaries $33,000, higher for skilled technicians in avionics. Average salary for *mechanics* between $15-$25/hour with experience.

AUTOMOTIVE MECHANICS: average starting earnings in 1994, $15,700; average earnings for experienced mechanics: $31,900.

COMMUNICATIONS TECHNICIANS: varies widely; around $26,000. Several years experience from $33,000 to $38,000; over $40,000 for supervisors or significant experience. Average annual salary increases in past two years: 10%.

COMPUTER SERVICE TECHNICIANS: earnings average around $29,000. Top earners can make over $40,000; more if they own a business.

ENGINEERING TECHNICIANS: earnings average around $29,000; top earners make over $45,000.

ENVIRONMENTAL CAREERS: 1993 starting salaries around $25,000–$35,000, starting in staff positions; supervisory positions up to $50,000; more for project managers.

BEST BETS

COOPERATIVE EDUCATION: Not a technical job, but a means to a full-time technical job; particularly good for those forced out of a profession by layoffs who need to find a new means of making a living. Cooperative education involves job-related classes and paid work, most often in alternating terms for two to four years. Pay is usually low, less than $5,000 (net of tuition and supplies), but the experience can be invaluable. Best area: *Cincinnati, Ohio,* which has five such programs, the most in the U.S. At *Cincinnati Technical College,* a whopping 98% of its co-op graduates found jobs last year; 600 businesses provided co-op jobs, including packaged-goods giant Procter & Gamble. Average age of students is twenty-nine, and students over forty are not uncommon. Students study such fields as engineering technology, nursing, landscape horticulture, medical records technology, etc.

WHERE TO GO FOR MORE INFORMATION

TECHNICAL ASSOCIATIONS AND GROUPS

(See listings also under "Science," page 161, and "Engineering," page 50. Medical specialties are covered on page 94.)

Aeronautical Repair Station Association
121 N. Henry St.
Alexandria, VA 22314
703/739-9543

Air Traffic Control Association
2300 Clarendon Blvd.,
Suite 711
Arlington, VA 22201
703/522-5717
(Publishes periodical, etc.)

American Congress on Surveying and Mapping
5410 Grosvenor Ln.
Suite 100
Bethesda, MD 20814
301/493-0200

American Society for Industrial Security
1655 N. Fort
Myer Dr., Suite 1200
Arlington, VA 22209
703/522-5800

Association of Manufacturing Technicians
7901 Westpark Dr.
McLean, VA 22102
703/893-2900

Computer-Aided Manufacturing International
1250 E. Copeland Rd.,
Suite 500
Arlington, TX
76011-8098
817/860-1654

Corporation for Public Broadcasting
901 E St., NW
Washington, DC 20004
202/879-9600
800/582-8220

Electronics Technicians Association International
602 N. Jackson St.
Greencastle, IN 46135

317/653-8262
(Publishes periodical with a few job openings and referral service for members, certification tapes, etc.)

Future Aviation Professionals of America
4971 Massachusetts Blvd.
Atlanta, GA 30337
800/JET-JOBS

International Society of Certified Electronics Technicians
2708 W. Berry
Fort Worth, TX 76109
817/921-9101
(Publishes periodical with job openings, etc.)

National Automotive Technician Education Foundation
13505 Dulles
Technology Dr.

Suite 2
Herndon, VA
22071-3421
703/713-0100
(Maintains listing of
certified automotive
technician schools.)

**National Tooling and
Machining
Association**
9300 Livingston Rd.
Fort Washington, MD

20744
301/248-6200

**Professional Aviation
Maintenance
Association**
1200 18th St., NW
Washington, DC
20036-2598
202/296-0545

**Society of Motion
Picture and Television
Engineers**

595 W. Hartsdale Ave.
White Plains, NY
10607
914/761-1100
(Publishes *SMPTE*
journal.)

**Tooling and
Manufacturing
Association**
1177 S. Dee Rd.
Park Ridge, IL 60068
708/825-1120

TECHNICAL PERIODICALS

*Airport Maintenance
Technology*
1233 Janesville Ave.
Ft. Atkinson, WI 53538
414/563-6388
(Bimonthly tabloid
covering aircraft
maintenance.)

*Computer-Aided
Engineering*
Penton Publishing
1100 Superior Ave.
Cleveland, OH
44114
216/696-7000

Professional Surveyor
2300 South 9th St.
Suite 501
Arlington, VA 22204
703/892-0733
(Bimonthly magazine;
carries some job
listings.)

OTHER TECHNICAL JOB SOURCES

InternAmerica
Ford Careerworks
105 Chestnut St.
Suite 34
Needham, MA 02192
800/456-7335
(Bimonthly newsletter
with many internships
listed for technical and
vocational grads as
well as liberal arts.)

**Federal Aviation
Administration**
Headquarters
800 Independence Ave.,
SW
Washington, DC 20591
202/267-8007
(Employs air traffic

controllers nationwide,
as well as electronics
specialists and
engineers, etc.
Regional offices are
listed below.)

Alaskan Region
Federal Aviation
Administration
222 W. 7th Ave.
Anchorage, AK 99513
907/271-5747

Central Region (KS,
MO, IA, NE)
Federal Aviation
Administration
601 E. 12th St.
Kansas City, MO

64106
816/426-4600

Eastern Region (DE,
MD, NJ, MY, PA, VA,
WV)
Federal Aviation
Administration
JFK International
Airport
Jamaica, NY 11430
718/995-7999

Federal Aviation
Administration
Mike Monroney
Aeronautical Center
P.O. Box 25082
Oklahoma City, OK
73125
405/954-3011

Federal Aviation Administration Technical Center
ACM 110
Atlantic City International Airport
Atlantic City, NJ 08405
609/485-4000

Great Lakes Region (ND, SD, IL, IN, MN, MI, OH, WI)
Federal Aviation Administration
2300 E. Devon
Des Plaines, IL 60018
708/294-7000

New England Region (CT, ME, MA, NH, RI, VT)
Federal Aviation Administration
12 New England Executive Park
P.O. Box 510
Burlington, MA 01803
617/238-7264

Northwest Mountain Region (CO, MT, UT, ID, OR, WA, WY)
Federal Aviation Administration
1601 Lind Ave., SW
Renton, WA 98055-4056
206/227-2014 (C-68966)
Seattle, WA 98618
206/227-1913

Southern Region (FL, AL, GA, KY, MS, NC, SC, TN, PR, VI)
Federal Aviation Administration
1701 Columbia Ave.
College Point, GA 30337
404/305-5330

Southwest Region (AR, LA, NM, OK, TX)
Federal Aviation Administration
2601 Meacham Blvd.
Ft. Worth, TX 76193
817/222-4000

Western-Pacific Region (AZ, CA, NV, HI)
Federal Aviation Administration
P.O. Box 92007
Worldway Postal Center
Los Angeles, CA 90009
310/725-3501

Office of Personnel Management
P.O. Box 52
Washington, DC 20415
202/606-2700
(The federal government hires many technicians, and one place to start is with the OPM. As mentioned in the "Government" section on page 66, the OPM in some cases fills the role of a government search firm; through its offices nationwide it can offer you information on technical careers in government, and explain what tests, if any, you must pass and where to take them. In general, you're best off contacting the OPM office nearest you— jobs of a technical nature and the requirements will be posted. Check the "Regional" section, for the office nearest you.)

WRITERS, EDITORS, AND JOURNALISTS

BRIEF BACKGROUND

▶ **Jobs involved with writing are widely diverse. However, almost all share the same general employment outlook: much competition.**

The problem, of course, is that the number of applicants is expected to more than keep up with the demand in most areas. Each year, colleges graduate thousands of English majors and minors; each year, thousands of people decide to "have more fun out of life" and switch into some "dream job" like freelance writing or editorial work. Each year, the competition stays tough, recession or not; and each year, thousands of dissatisfied applicants switch to other lines of work. But, at the same time, each year sees someone selling or editing a bestselling novel, someone winning a Pulitzer.

There are currently about 350,000 people working as writers, editors, journalists, and in related positions.

EMPLOYMENT OUTLOOK: Fair.

▶ **Overall, tough competition for many writing jobs.**

The 1990s have not been good years to be searching for a job as a journalist or editor, to say the least. But better times for many were here in 1996 and 1997, although competition was fierce, as always. In particular, opportunities are expected to be best for technical writers, people who can translate the complex jargon of a technical society into understandable English. In addition, better than average job growth over the long term will be found for public relations writers, journalists who can explore databases, as well as for magazine writers and editors, although competition will be particularly keen.

▶ **The rest of the 1990s should be better than the early years, when cost-cutting led to hiring freezes and layoffs.**

Look for a gradual recovery in hiring—and be aware of rapid changes, as various media formats compete.

A brief overview of the major job areas:

BOOK EDITORS: The early 1990s were tough years, and the trends of cost-cutting and much attention to the bottom line will continue. Editors are expected increasingly to understand the marketing aspects of the business, while marketing and financial employees are gaining in importance. On the other hand, a backlash is developing that emphasizes quality books over top-selling books (although sometimes the two are synonymous). Best way to enter the field: attend a publishing program (addresses of some of the most prominent are listed at the end of this section) and learn the basics of the industry, and most importantly, make valuable contacts. *On the bright side:* The book publishing industry is expected to grow, according to government experts. On the other hand, industry insiders are still concerned by soaring levels of "returns" (unsold books) and the difficulties of marketing in a superstore marketplace. Bottom line: Hiring will be very competitive. *Some growing areas:* Spanish language publishing, audio books (retail sales of audio books have increased by a numbing 480% in the past five years).

JOURNALISTS: Tough competition as always, but recently the oulook has been better. Job offerings increased last year, particularly with newspapers in the southern part of the country. Currently, over 75,000 people work as journalists—about 59,000 for newspapers, and the rest with magazines, TV, radio, and wire services such as the Associated Press. Long-term outlook is fair; most job growth will come from suburban papers, along with some growth from radio and TV. Key point: most openings will come from high turnover in the industry; journalism is a tough, difficult, hectic job and many find the reality far more taxing than the dream.

Best bets for employment: Think about *on-line* journalism. This is *the* story of recent years—a new area for journalism grads. Key point: Many old-timers don't have the on-line skills or inclinations, creating *new* openings for people working on electronic newspapers and magazines. One iffy question: Will these electronic media keep on growing—or is this just a flash in the pan? Time will tell.

Think small—smaller dailies, weekly newspapers, small radio and television stations historically offer more employment opportunities . . . but pay is typically low. Best bets last year: Newspapers in the Southeast; copy editor and page designer jobs, in broadcasting at network news magazines, and of course, with on-line services.

Many major dailies look for at least five years experience at a good daily; in addition, many require writing and other screening tests. As usual, the best preparation for a journalism career is prior experience. Employment trends, according to a Dow Jones Newspaper Fund survey:

- Almost 85% of new hires have mass communications or journalism degrees.
- Newspapers hire 25% of their staff out of college, 75% from other papers or media.
- 78% of those hired had worked on college newspapers, 83% had worked as interns.
- **Bottom line:** experience counts.

Ways to get a foot in the door: jobs at community papers, with on-line news services, internships (although sometimes they don't offer relevant experience), working initially as a copy editor, outside the field in newsletters, etc. Usual job path for entry-level person: the lucky get hired by a major daily or network directly; others start at a remote paper, television, or radio station with the expectation of waiting five, six, or seven years to make it to a major market. Many of the major dailies have "farm" papers where they do most of their hiring. Similarly, many of the flagship television and radio stations and networks hire from their smaller affiliates in minor markets. *One good bet:* Reporters with strong computer database skills, i.e., computer-assisted reporting specialists. *Key point:* analysis of huge amounts of data on the "information highway" can reveal patterns of fraud, waste, or discrimination—and help write prize-winning stories.

Key markets for recent journalism graduates: According to Columbia University's School of Journalism, on-line journalism or electronic reporting, especially on the Internet, is creating a healthy market for graduates, particularly with experience. On-line positions are generally in the large cities and at higher salaries than traditional positions. The only drawback? As this is a new area, expect volatility. Another entry-level job area looking strong: network news magazines. Finally, the key to landing a traditional reporting job (with a newspaper or television station)? Broaden your geographic horizons . . . or, in other words, be willing to move—and start your career in a smaller job market.

MAGAZINES: Competition will still be tough. *Best bet for employment, particularly for beginners:* trade magazines, the magazines geared to a specific industry. Also take a look at niche magazines, magazines geared to a specific small area of interest. If you can research this area well, you may have a leg up over competing candidates who don't know tropical fish, or trains, or whatever specific area, as well. *Another good area:* Spanish-language publishing. Expected to grow substantially in the next decade.

Another good area: association magazines—the magazines put out by various trade and professional associations. For years, these magazines were for the most part stodgy house organs; now the trend is to turn them into competitive profit makers. As they gain ad pages, they're getting glossier and more mainstream; this can mean employment opportunities.

PUBLIC RELATIONS WRITERS: The outlook was very good in 1997—best for PR pros with five or six years of experience. Best areas: pretty much across the board, ranging from pharmaceutical (PR pros with science backgrounds especially), high tech, service industries (law and accounting firms), advertising, Internet.

A major trend: Companies are choosing not to expand their own PR departments as much as depending on outside firms, where hiring is expected to be particularly strong. However, remember that PR is always the one area that executives find easy to downsize during recessions. *Best bets in terms of preparation:* strong industry knowledge, good technical skills (multimedia knowledge, database knowledge, audiovisual ability) strong writing skills. The last seems something of a misnomer, but recently recruiters have been complaining that many PR candidates are not up to par in grammar, clarity, and creativity.

COPYWRITERS: a varied field. Some copywriters specialize in print, writing advertising "copy" for promotions (pamphlets, brochures); others focus on direct mail; others work in the biggest print specialty: magazines and newspapers. Copywriters also work in radio, in television, in all or many of these specialties. Outlook in general: fair, highly variable, problems related to general state of the economy. Agencies with hot clients will pay top dollars for copywriters with experience. For more, see Advertising and Public Relations Section, page 215.

TECHNICAL WRITERS: Demand will increase throughout the 1990s, particularly as the need for well-written computer documentation increases. The job involves translating complex technical instructions into understandable English. Best areas: computers and pharmaceuticals. Get training in English, technical writing, and become moderately familiar with some growing area of technology. The job isn't just writing—senior writers may supervise other writers, running a department. For more information, contact: the Society for Technical Communication—address on page 211.

▶ **And, among the largely self-employed,**

AUTHORS: The bottom-line orientation at publishing houses is continuing—which means tougher times for writers. Publishers are reviewing proposals more carefully, cutting back on titles, and risking less money advances. And, as always, it is hard to break into full-time writing as a career, harder to make money, and almost impossible to make a lot of money. *Best advice*: start by writing for magazines. Check *Writers Digest, Writers Guide,* and *Literary Marketplace (LMP)* (which lists virtually every major magazine and book publisher, along with addresses, requirements)—addresses are listed at the end of this section. Also check such industry bibles as *Publishers Weekly,* which gives you an inside view of what publishers are buying, and current trends and fads in the industry.

SCREENWRITERS: Most screenwriters have other jobs—the odds of seeing a screenplay you write produced on the silver screen are close to zero. According to the Writers Guild of America, the minimum for an original script is $40,833 and $35,736 for an adaptation. But then again—the rewards are there if you make it. One screenplay by a first-time author sold for $500,000, before "points" or a percentage of the profits.

Best avenue to success? Comedy is king (and usually the hardest to write), television is usually the easiest place to start. Start by writing a complete script (story ideas or treatments are rarely bought from first-timers, according to insiders), then write another and another. Then meet with anyone you can, in order to sell it. The best way to get the right people interested is to find an LA agent who likes your script enough to push it—or *anyone* producing, directing, or acting in similar projects. Check the *LMP* for a listing of agents.

Other jobs in the field include **story editors** (who also usually double as writers) and **script readers**, who work for large studios reading and evaluating scripts submitted by agents and writers. Both can give you an inside track on contacts—and a good income while you learn and write. The name of the game in Hollywood, more than anywhere else, is just that: contacts. From several insiders: "And if you haven't read *Screenplay* [New York: Delta, 1982] by Syd Field, read it soon: sooner or later someone in 'The Business' will recommend it."

WHAT'S NEXT

▶ **Turbulent change: As technology improves, new opportunities and ways of working will open, and other avenues will close.**

In magazines: Continued shake-outs and ever fiercer competition will dominate. Only 20% of new magazines survive for more than four years—and the magazine start-ups often hire few people, relying instead on a lean staff of experienced personnel to keep costs down until the magazine clicks. Here, though, are some general forecasts:

• Specialty consumer and trade magazines will continue to offer opportunities for writers with background or experience to write about such topics as Hawaiian scuba diving, fine embroidery—or hog futures (one award-winning trade magazine is entitled *Pork 1997*).

• Consider this: by the year 2000, over 60% of the population of the U.S. will be over thirty-five. Look for magazines which specialize in this market—and think about this as a hot area. One prediction by *Folio*: the special interest magazines owned by the Reader's Digest Association may be a surprisingly big success.

• More decentralization, smaller offices, writers and editors working at home and "commuting" electronically with the home office via computer modems and networks.

• Readers may break the "printed-page barrier" and pick and choose types of articles from a computer at home, in effect creating their own magazines—although writer's ownership rights are as yet unresolved. So far, electronic magazines of any sort are experimental.

In newspapers: an acceleration of the big changes in the past fifteen years: computers will dominate the newsrooms even more than today.

• Better databases (and better ways of accessing them) will speed story and court research; voice-activated computers may change the way stories are written.

• More new beats: reporters will be assigned more special areas to focus coverage, e.g., ethics, family life, elderly, taxes—and journalists with such specialties will experience better employment prospects.

• Hiring of minorities, elderly, and the disabled will increase.

In general: For all writers, *increased* opportunities coupled with competition. Just as literacy is going down, the need for writers is going up. Some sources of jobs:

• Large corporations. From in-house corporate newsletters and video presentations, corporate speechwriting, corporate reports and public relations, corporate America will absorb a large number of writers each year.

• Television, video, film media. With all the lamenting about the decline of the written word, it is easy to forget that writers are busy *writing* the spoken word for actors, newspeople, and the like. As entertainment and news keeps rising in importance, so will the role of entertainment and news writers. On the horizon: computers for screenwriters which actually "picture" scenes for the writer on the screen—according to Syd Field, author of *Screenplay*.

▶ **We said it before, but we'll say it again. Journalists and writers, especially beginning ones, should take a look at hiring trends on-line. An area to keep an eye on: On-line media—or digital journalism.**

This is an area that has been growing as interest in the Internet surges. Many larger media companies are going on-line—publishing electronic editions of their magazines and newspapers—and many smaller companies are devising their own "cyberzines." The good news? Extensive computer knowledge is *not* necessarily required; good writing skills are. The reasoning: These on-line purveyors of the written word are usually more concerned about the ability to write and report well—and so are willing to train qualified candidates in HTML (hypertext markup language), the basic writing tool of the World Wide Web). The bad news? So far the jury is still out. Will these magazines succeed, or will some other form of "cyber-journalism" dominate?

SALARIES

BOOK AND MAGAZINE EDITORS: Variable. According to *Publishers Weekly,* average salary for a book editor was $44,100 in 1994; $21,000 for an editorial assistant. These salaries vary widely, however, depending on size of company, region, and experience. Salaries for editorial staffers in magazine publishing vary widely as well—with larger consumer magazines paying substantially more than trade magazines. Average salary for a consumer magazine editor is $45,000—but top editors at top magazines can make well over $100,000. Average trade magazine editor salary is $35,000.

JOURNALISTS: Beginning salaries in the high teens to low $20s in traditional print and broadcast media, while in on-line publications entry-level salaries were close to $30,000. According to a 1994 survey by Ohio State University and Dow Jones, college graduates received $18,500. Mid-level salaries are in the $30,000 range, and senior editors at large newspapers average $60,000 annually. Over 50% of journalists have incomes over $40,000, according to a *Los Angeles Times* poll. As for broadcast: In 1994, radio reporters earned an average of $18,600 a year at small stations, $29,000 at larger ones, according to the National Association of Broadcasters. As for television, salaries ranged from $17,435 at small stations to nearly $80,000 at larger stations, with salaries well over $100,000 not uncommon for reporters at stations in the largest markets, such as New York or L.A. A recent survey in the *Columbia Journalism Review* showed that salaries increased by about 7.6% in the past three years for newspaper reporters, and by 11.4% for TV journalists in one year alone. Rule of thumb: outside of TV, you shouldn't be in reporting for the money.

BOOKS, MAGAZINES, AND OTHER FREELANCE WRITING: Highly variable. Magazines may pay anywhere from zero to thousands of dollars. In general, small magazines pay from $250 to $1,000 for articles; some small fiction magazines pay 3–5 cents a word, more for experienced authors. Major magazines pay more. Book authors are usually paid an advance—a payment against projected royalties—generally half on acceptance and half on receipt. Often, the author is represented by an agent (who negotiates for and represents the author to the publisher); in return, the agent receives 10–15% of the advance and future royalties. Royalties for first-time novelists are usually several thousand dollars—on up to six figures and more for major authors or authors with hot ideas.

SCREENWRITING: The Writers Guild lists current minimums for screenplays, teleplays, rewrites, etc. Most film screenwriters are employed by the project; television writers are often employed by the production company. The money varies according to type of film or television feature, type of writing, and so on. According to the Writers Guild, in 1995, a feature-film writer working for scale earned between $26,512 and $54,267 for a draft, a set of changes, and polish, depending on the film's budget. For writing a screenplay adapted from an already existing work, the minimums in 1995 were: for a low-budget film, $21,575; for a high-budget film, $44,399.

The Guild also has minimums for rewrites, etc.—which can add more money to the totals. And writers may negotiate for more. Television writers earned median incomes from the mid- to high $20s to the high $30s—with major writers on major programs earning far more. In related fields: Story editors make about $2,000 a week; script readers for major studios usually earn about $40,000 a year.

BEST BETS

SPEECHWRITER: "The better you are, the more unnoticed you are," unless it is by the people who count, said one writer in *BusinessWeek* magazine. Speechwriting can be risky (if your boss is fired, you may go, too), annoying (often the speaker gets the credit), and boring (it's more fun writing novels). But it can also be lucrative—top corporate speechwriters can make over $100,000, freelancers even more. And it is important. Rhetoric is coming back into vogue. Speechwriters can make the difference between a win and a loss in elections, and can help set corporate agendas by the power of their writing. Speechwriters don't just make speeches, they write editorials, scripts for executives, and coach them as well. Way to break into the field: usually through corporate or government public relations.

ON-LINE CONTENT DEVELOPER: A high growth area, chiefly because it is so new. On-line developers are the people who produce on-line stories for electronic newspapers, magazines, newsletters, and other information sources. In effect, these people are a cross between television producers and print journalists—because their job is to both write (or oversee the writing of) news or entertainment text and incorporate video or audio material. Depending upon the specific position, an on-line content developer may produce a story for a publication by hiring and overseeing writers and designers, as well as repackaging previously published material in the on-line piece; or may do the actual writing and production herself. Salaries range from about $30,000 at the entry-level up to $80,000 for seasoned professionals. Best background? In addition to general communications skills, experience in multimedia programming or graphic design is a big plus.

WHERE TO GO FOR MORE INFORMATION

SPECIAL PUBLISHING PROGRAMS

Dow Jones Newspaper Fund
P.O. Box 300
Princeton, NJ
08543-0300
609/452-2820
(Offers various programs for young people interested in journalism; publishes career guides.)

The New York University Summer Publishing Institute
48 Cooper Sq.,
Room 108
New York, NY 10003
212/998-7215

The Radcliffe Publishing Procedures Course
6 Ash St.
Cambridge, MA 02138
617/495-8678

Rice University Publishing Program
School of Continuing Studies
MS 550
6100 Main St.
Houston, TX 77005
713/520-6022

University of Denver Publishing Institute
2075 S. University Blvd.
No. 0114
Denver, CO 80210
303/871-2570

WRITERS, EDITORS, AND JOURNALISTS ASSOCIATIONS

For more associations, directories, and periodicals, see the appropriate industry section; including "Advertising and Public Relations," and "Publishing."

Editorial Freelancers Association
71 W. 23rd St.
New York, NY 10010
212/929-5400
(For annual fee, members may use listing service which lists full time, part time jobs for editors, writers, indexers, etc.)

Investigative Reporters and Editors
138 Neff Annex
Columbia, MO 65211
314/882-2042

National League of American Pen Women
1300 17th St., NW
Washington, DC 20036
202/785-1997

Society for Technical Communication
901 N. Stuart St.,
Suite 904
Arlington, VA 22203
703/522-4114

Writers Guild of America, West
700 W. 3rd St.
Los Angeles, CA 90048
213/951-4000

WRITERS, EDITORS, AND JOURNALISTS DIRECTORIES

Children's Writers and Illustrator's Market; Guide to Literary Agents; Novel and Short Story Writer's Market; Poet's Market; Songwriter's Market; Writer's Market
Writer's Digest Books
1507 Dana Ave.
Cincinnati, OH 45207
1-800/289-0963
(All books are lists of prime markets for free-lance sale of written work, with names, addresses, requirements, etc.)

The Editor & Publisher Syndicate Directory
11 W. 19th St.
New York, NY 10011
212/675-4380
(This is the prime source of information about syndicates—the companies that syndicate writers' work to papers across the country. The directory includes contact names, etc.)

Foundation Grants to Individuals; Foundation Directory; Corporate Foundation Profiles
Foundation Center
79 Fifth Ave.
New York, NY 10003-3076
212/620-4230
(The first directory is particularly valuable for those seeking financial support from foundations.)

Writer's Guild Directory
Writer's Guild of America, West
700 W. 3rd St.
Los Angeles, CA 90048
213/951-4000

WRITERS, EDITORS, AND JOURNALISTS PERIODICALS

(For more, see "Publishing," page 416.)

Columbia Journalism Review
700A Journalism Bldg.
116 St. & Broadway
Columbia University
New York, NY 10027
212/854-2716
(Bimonthly magazine devoted to bettering journalism.)

Editor & Publisher
11 W. 19th St.
New York, NY 10011
212/675-4380
(Weekly magazine for newspaper editors; valuable in giving a "feel" for what editors want.)

The Writer
120 Boyleston St.
Boston, MA 02116
617/423-3157
(Monthly magazine designed primarily for freelance writers; also useful for agents, editors, etc.)

Writer's Digest
1507 Dana Av.
Cincinnati, OH 45207
513/531-2222
(Monthly magazine designed primarily for freelance writers. Includes monthly "markets" section, which lists currently buying magazines and book publishers and describes requirements.)

SECTION 2

INDUSTRY
FORECASTS 1998

ADVERTISING AND PUBLIC RELATIONS

INDUSTRY OUTLOOK: Hot competition ahead as downsized and newly consolidated firms attempt to improve market share in their core specialties, and aggressively pursue foreign markets.

As always, the strength of the industry will be directly tied to the health of the economy. Key trends to be aware of: *Trend number 1.* As companies focus on cost-cutting, watch for a growth in alternative marketing. In other words, ad agencies won't rely only on the old-fashioned straight consumer advertising, but will be heavily exploring other marketing and advertising areas such as direct mail, Internet and Web advertising, telephone marketing, and in-store marketing. *Trend number 2.* Increased moves overseas. Advertising of American products abroad should rise above domestic rates as the large less-developed economics show signs of strong consumer demand. Especially hot? The Asia-Pacific rim region, which has been a growing area for American product advertising. *Trend number 3.* New advertisers entering the marketplace. Industries that did little advertising in the past—such as utilities—will be increasing their advertising to cope with heated competition in their area. *Trend number 4.* An increase in consumers' skepticism of advertising. Agencies will be trying to buck this trend by turning out compelling campaigns. As a result, professionals skilled at creating believable materials may do well, as will research personnel to evaluate and steer advertising campaigns. Ad agencies should continue to feel pressure from clients reluctant to pay the traditional 15% commission on agency fees and shift to negotiated fees. As their margins are battered and better quality pressures increase, keep an eye on agency responses—expect to see increased cost efficiencies, including performance-based employee compensation. Other factors to be aware of: continued attention paid to "integrated marketing" (see following page for more details); increased competition across the board—and probably the emergence of new strategies—as different agencies try to attract and maintain clients.

As for **public relations,** performance will also be tied to the economy. Similarly, look for tough competition for clients, increased reliance on newer methods—such as utilizing the Internet as a public relations tool. Hottest areas in PR: health care, high tech, financial services, pharmaceuticals, the food and beverage industry, and telecommunications.

A LOOK BACK

▶ **The recent past in advertising: rising revenues—and the continued dominance of the mega-agencies.**

In 1996, advertising was on the move, with ad expenditures up, buoyed by the continued, slow expansion of the economy, the summer Olympics, the national and local election season, as well as increases in promotional activities by companies to support new product entries and improve revenue and profit performance. Advertising expenditures in 1997 improved despite the absence of the extra stimulus of the 1996 Olympics and political advertising, as the economy continued its slow expansion.

The big winners in the past few years: the huge mega-agencies. These multinational agencies were created when advertising giants swallowed other agencies. The resulting agency mega-groups—advertising/marketing communications conglomerates—kept up their merger and acquisitions activity and still dominate the industry.

WHAT'S NEXT

▶ Look for the "smaller is better" trend to continue.

It began as a backlash movement against the mega-agencies formed by the mergers. Now it has become an industry trend—and one that looks like it will continue.

Where employment is concerned, this points to potential opportunities at the smaller shops. Of course, keep in mind that competition for spots at small agencies is very tight, and positions may not be secure, as they depend upon the account. The focus may be on flexible talents with many skills.

▶ On the flip side, integrated services remain a player in the industry.

Integrated services—when an agency offers a coordinated package of advertising, sales, marketing and promotion—continues to be one of the ways larger agencies in particular try to attract and keep clients—and smaller agencies try to compete with the big guys.

The effect of this on employment: Some agencies are now looking for different types of account executives—people with more than straight ad experience, but with experience in a related field such as public relations, sales promotion, or packaging.

▶ Expect a growing focus on targeted advertising and marketing.

It's a way to break through the clutter—more agencies are and will be focusing on very specific markets and methods.

Expect to see attention paid to adveritsing and marketing outside of the traditional consumer advertising (on television, etc.). Instead, watch for growth in direct mail, telemarketing, and, most recently, Internet advertising.

In addition, niche markets will continue to be of increased importance to agencies—especially small agencies. Among the areas that will see growth: foreign-language programming and advertisements; advertising aimed at distinct ethnic groups; advertising aimed squarely at the over-fifty market. For example, Spanish language advertisements; ads aimed directly at the growing Asian population; etc.

Along these lines, there should be growth at small agencies that specialize in specific markets—which may translate into job opportunities.

▶ **The old New York/San Francisco dominance of the ad industry will continue to decline.**

Expect to see more agencies succeeding outside of the New York/San Francisco axis. One reason—the nationwide trend for businesses to move away from traditional urban areas to the outlying exurbs. Another reason—the shakeups in the ad industry, which led to smaller, less well known agencies winning high-visibility accounts.

This trend, which began in the '80s, will continue through the '90s. Agencies outside of New York and San Francisco have now established themselves and are coming on strong—winning awards, major clients, a great deal of attention, and a great deal of business. The leaders of the pack: Chiat/Day/Mojo in Los Angeles, Hill Holiday in Boston, The Martin Agency in Richmond, and Earle Palmer Browne in Maryland.

Where employment is concerned, this trend is good news. The industry is clearly becoming more regionally diverse, which means that job hunters may find opportunities springing up in different parts of the country.

EMPLOYMENT OUTLOOK: Fair—and highly competitive.

The long-term employment picture should be a fairly bright one, depending, of course, on the strength of the economy. In a strong economy, ad agency billings rise—which means that fewer small and midsized agencies will close, and more larger agencies will be hiring. The U.S. government forecasts an increase of more than 4% in employment over the next decade.

A good bet for employment? Smaller (and usually newer) "hot shops" or "creative boutiques." While these agencies usually have fewer staffers than the more established older shops, they are also raking in billings lately and adding new clients. One word of warning: Competition is *extremely* intense. A strong portfolio (of actual or spec work) is a must for creatives seeking employment in these agencies. On the account side, experience on their accounts or similar accounts is important.

Hot specialty: Computer graphics. Most agencies rely on computers for design—so people with specialized skills are in demand. Also hot: Internet-related ability. As more companies turn to the World Wide Web to advertise and market products and services, more agencies will be called upon to design and produce Web sites for their clients. As such, Web Site designers and producers are in demand both at the agencies and at the smaller computer shops set up to concentrate on this growing field. Only problem? High competition.

Also expect to see intense promotional/advertising activities from the players in the exploding telecommunications industry—which should lead to employment. (See Broadcasting, page 296.)

As for public relations: As with advertising, the employment picture is tied to the strength of the economy. And, in general, the outlook is a positive one, with hiring up in 1997—and probable strength over the long term.

Best areas for PR professionals? High-tech companies, which continue to grow, introduce new products and, as such, require PR and media relations staffers. Financial services companies have been adding investor relations specialists; the healthcare industry—both health services companies like HMOs and drug companies have been seeking PR pros with experience. In addition, many drug companies, after having trimmed in-house staff, are relying on outside agencies with PR practitioners specializing in pharmaceuticals. Other areas looking strong: law, accounting, architectual firms, high tech, biotech, Internet.

Best region: the Northeast—especially New York, as the home of many of the top PR firms and financial services companies; the Boston area, where many high-tech firms are located. Median salary for a PR professional at a public relations company: $64,000, $40,000 at an ad agency, $48,000 at a health care organization.

Keys to employment: Experience in a specific industry—or, at least, knowledge of that industry. Unlike the past when companies hired people with general PR skills, now employers are seeking specialized experience and knowledge. The best bet? Expertise, experience, or educational credentials beyond straight public relations. An MBA is especially helpful as is a background in areas like finance, marketing, international business, law, or science. Governmental experience can also be a help, depending on the particular company or agency clients. In addition, computer skills are most definitely an asset—especially hands-on on-line experience, as more companies look to the Internet to expand their corporate presence.

JOBS SPOTLIGHT

Advertising

INTERACTIVE MARKETING SPECIALISTS: This is a relatively new area that has emerged with the growth of the Internet and its graphical portion, the World Wide Web. As businesses turn to the Web as a new means of advertising and marketing their products or services, more agencies have been seeking people who specialize in on-line advertising and marketing. It's actually a high-tech spin on direct marketing—but instead of writing and sending out direct mail letters, interactive marketers write and transmit material on-line. Best background? On-line skills, writing skills, and a big plus, direct market experience.

Public Relations

PHARMACEUTICAL PUBLIC RELATIONS: It's tied to the boom in health care, fueled by the aging population—and it shows no sign of letting up in the near future. Demand for public relations professionals with experience in pharmaceuticals has been extremely high. As drug companies continue to introduce new products—and enter into heavy competition with others in the field—the need for strong public relations has increased. Best qualifications? Science degree and strong communications skills.

LEGAL PUBLIC RELATIONS SPECIALIST: This is a specialty that is growing swiftly at a number of agencies because the legal field has become more crowded and more competitive—and law firms want to win clients without resorting to advertising. To do this, they hire agencies to promote a law firm or its partners. The PR specialist must tread a fine line, promoting the firm without making it appear "pushy." Legal experience or a background in a related area is a big plus.

BEST BETS

Leo Burnett
125 E. Delaware St.
Chicago, IL 60601
312/220-5959

A Best Bet for the past five years, Leo Burnett continues to be a good choice for employment in the usually volatile ad industry. It is known for its traditional clients, traditional ways, and successful advertisements and, as such, keeps coming on strong in an understated way. One of the main reasons it's known as a good place to work: stability. Leo Burnett believes in long-term relationships—both with clients and with staff members.

TOP ADVERTISING AGENCIES

Admarketing, Inc.
1801 Century Park E.,
Ste. 2000
Los Angeles, CA
90067
213/203-8400

Alcone Sims & O'Brien
15 Whatney
Irvine, CA 92718
717/770-4400

Ammirati Puris, Lintas
1 Dag Hammarskjold Plaza
New York, NY 10017
212/605-8000

N.W. Ayer & Partners
825 Eighth Ave.
New York, NY 10019
212/474-5000

Backer Spielvogel Bates Worldwide
405 Lexington Ave.
New York, NY 10174
212/297-7000

BBDO Worldwide, Inc.
1285 Ave. of the
Americas
New York, NY 10019
212/459-5000

Bozell Worldwide, Inc.
40 W. 23rd St.
New York, NY 10010
212/727-5000

Leo Burnett Co.
125 E. Delaware St.
Chicago, IL 60601
312/220-5959

Cato Johnson Worldwide
675 Ave. of the
Americas
New York, NY 10010
212/941-3700

Chiat/Day/Mojo Advertising
340 Main St.
Venice, CA 90291
213/314-5000

Campbell-Mithun-Esty Advertising
222 S. 9th St.,
Minneapolis, MN
55402
612/347-1000

Dailey International Group
3055 Wilshire Blvd.
Los Angeles, CA
90010
213/386-7823

D'Arcy Masius Benton & Bowles
1675 Broadway
New York, NY 10019
212/468-3622

DDB Needham Worldwide, Inc.
437 Madison Ave.
New York, NY 10022
212/415-2000

W. B. Doner & Co.
25900 Northwestern
Hwy.
Southfield, MI 48075
313/354-9700

Earle Palmer Brown Cos.
6935 Arlington Rd.
Bethseda, MD 20814
301/986-0510

Fahlgren Martin
Rosemar Rd. and
Seminary Dr.
Parkersburg, WV
26102
304/424-3591

FCB/Leber Katz Partners, Inc.
150 E. 42nd St.
New York, NY 10017
212/885-3000

**Gage Marketing
Group LLC**
1000 Hwy. 55
Plymouth, MN 55441
612/595-3800

Gotham Inc.
260 Madison Ave.
New York, NY 10016
212/213-4646

**Grey Advertising,
Inc.**
777 Third Ave.
New York, NY 10017
212/546-2000

Griffin Bacal, Inc.
130 Fifth Ave.
New York, NY 10011
212/337-6300

GSD&M
1250 S. Capitol of
Texas Hwy.
Austin, TX 78746
512/327-8810

**Hill Holiday Connors
Cosmopulos**
200 Clarendon St.
Boston, MA 02116
617/437-1600

**Bernard Hodes
Advertising**
555 Madison Ave.
New York, NY 10022
212/758-2600

**The Interpublic
Group of Companies,
Inc.**
1271 Avenue of the
Americas
New York, NY 10020
212/399-8000

**Jordan McGrath Case
& Taylor**
445 Park Ave.
New York, NY 10022
212/326-9100

**Kallir, Phillips, Ross,
Inc.**
333 E. 38th St.
New York, NY 10016
212/856-8400

**Keller-Crescent Co.,
Inc.**
1100 E. Louisiana St.
Evansville, IN 47711
812/464-2461

**Ketchum
Communications, Inc.**
6 PPG Pl.
Pittsburgh, PA 15222
412/456-3500

**Kobs & Draft
Advertising**
142 E. Ontario
Chicago, IL 60611
312/944-3500

**Lavey Wolff Swift,
Inc.**
488 Madison Ave.
New York, NY 10022
212/593-3630

**Lord Dentsu &
Partners**
810 Seventh Ave.
New York, NY 10019
212/408-2100

**Lowe & Partners,
S. M. S.**
1114 Ave. of the
Americas
New York, NY 10036
212/403-7000

The Martin Agency
500 N. Allen Ave.
Richmond, VA 23220
804/254-3400

**McCann-Erickson,
Worldwide, Inc.**
750 Third Ave.
New York, NY 10017
212/697-6000

**Medicus Group
International**
1675 Broadway
New York, NY 10019
212/468-3100

**Nationwide
Advertising Service**
1228 Euclid Ave.
Cleveland, OH 44115
216/579-0300

**Ogilvy & Mather
Worldwide**
309 W. 49th St.
New York, NY 10019
212/237-4000

**Rapp Collins
Worldwide, Inc.**
488 Madison Ave.
New York, NY 10022
212/371-9100

Richards Group, Inc.
10000 N. Central Expy.
Dallas, TX 75231
214/891-5700

Hal Riney & Partners
735 Battery St.
San Francisco, CA
94111
415/981-0950

Ross Roy, Inc.
100 Bloomfield Hills
Pkwy.
Bloomfield Hills, MI
48034
313/433-6000

**Saatchi & Saatchi
Advertising**
375 Hudson St.
New York, NY 10014
212/463-2000

**Sudler & Hennessey,
Inc.**
1633 Broadway
New York, NY 10019
212/265-8015

Tatham Euro, RSCG
980 N. Michigan Ave.
Chicago, IL 60611
312/337-4400

TBWA Chiat-Day Advertising
180 Maiden Lane
New York, NY 10038
212/804-1000

J. Walter Thompson Co.
466 Lexington Ave.
New York, NY 10017
212/210-7000

Tracy-Locke, Inc.
200 Crescent Ct.
Dallas, TX 75201
214/969-9000

Warwick Baker & Fiore, Inc.
100 Ave. of the Americas
New York, NY 10013
212/941-4200

Wells Rich Greene BDDP, Inc.
9 W. 57th St.
New York, NY 10019
212/303-5000

Wunderman Cato Johnson
675 Avenue of the Americas
New York, NY 10010
212/941-3000

Wyse Advertising, Inc.
24 Public Sq.
Cleveland, OH 44113
216/696-2424

Young & Rubicam, Inc.
285 Madison Ave.
New York, NY 10017
212/210-3000

TOP PUBLIC RELATIONS AGENCIES

(*—advertising agency affiliate)

N.W. Ayer & Partners
825 8th Ave.
New York, NY 10019
212/474-5000

BmC Strategies, Inc.
100 Unicorn Park Dr.
Woburn, MA 01801
617/932-6844

Burson-Marsteller*
230 Park Ave. S.
New York, NY 10003
212/614-4000

Cerrell Associates, Inc.
320 N. Larchmont Blvd.
Los Angeles, CA 90004
213/466-3445

Charles Ryan Associates
1012 Kanawha Blvd. E.
Box 2464

Charleston, WV 25301
304/342-0161

Clarke & Co.*
535 Boylston St.
Boston, MA 02116
617/536-3003

CMF&Z Public Relations (Creswell, Munsell, Fultz, & Zirbel)*
600 E. Court Ave.
Des Moines, IA 50309-4807
515/246-3500

Cohn & Wolfe*
225 Peachtree St.
N.E., Ste. 2300
Atlanta, GA 30303
404/688-5900

Cone Communications
90 Canal St.
Boston, MA 02114
617/227-2111

Cunningham Communications, Inc.
3945 Freedom Circle, 9th Flr.
Santa Clara, CA 95054
408/982-0400

Aaron D. Cushman & Associates, Inc.
35 E. Wacker Dr.
Chicago, IL 60601
312/263-2500

DeVries Public Relations
30 E. 60th St.
New York, NY 10022
212/891-0400

Dewe Rogerson, Inc.
(U.S. office)
850 Third Ave.
New York, NY 10022
212/688-6840

Dix & Eaton
1301 E. 9th St.
Cleveland, OH 44114
216/241-0405

Dragonette, Inc.
200 W. Wacker Dr.
Chicago, Il 60606
312/424-5300

Dye, Van Mol, & Lawrence
209 7th Ave. N.
Nashville, TN 37219
615/244-1818

Earle Palmer Browne Public Relations*
6935 Arlington Rd.
Bethesda, MD 20814
301/657-6000

Edelman Public Relations Worldwide
211 E. Ontario St.
Chicago, IL 60611
312/986-0510

Financial Relations Board
675 Third Ave.
New York, NY 10017
212/661-8030

Fleishman-Hillard, Inc.
200 N. Broadway
St. Louis, MO 63102
314/982-1700

Foote Cone & Belding Communications
101 E. Erie St.
Chicago, IL 60611
312/751-7000

Franson, Hartery, & Associates
560 Waverly St.,
Ste. 200
Palo Alto, CA 94301
415/462-1605

GCI Group*
777 Third Ave.
New York, NY 10017
212/546-2200

Gibbs & Soell
600 Third Ave.

New York, NY 10016
212/697-2600

Gross Townsend Frank Hoffman, Inc.*
114 Fifth Ave.
New York, NY 10011
212/886-3000

E. Bruce Harrison Co.
1440 New York Ave.,
NW
Washington, DC 20005
202/638-1200

Hill & Knowlton*
466 Lexington Ave.
New York, NY 10017
212/885-0300

Holt, Ross & Yulish, Inc.
P.O. Box 127
Far Hills, NJ 07931
908/287-0045

Edward Howard & Co.
1 Erie View Plaza,
Cleveland, OH 44114-1716
216/781-2400

The Kamber Group
1920 L St., NW
Washington, DC 20036
202/223-8700

KCS&A Public Relations
820 Second Ave.
New York, NY 10017
212/682-6300

Ketchum Communications*
220 E. 42nd St.
New York, NY 10017
212/878-4600

Lobsenz-Stevens, Inc.
460 Park Ave. S.
New York, NY 10016
212/684-6300

Makovsky & Co.
575 Lexington Ave.
New York, NY 10022
212/508-9600

Manning, Selvage & Lee*
79 Madison Ave.
New York, NY 10016
212/213-0909

Morgen-Walke Associates, Inc.
380 Lexington Ave.
New York, NY 10168
212/850-5600

MWW/Strategic Communications, Inc.
70 Grand Ave.
Grand Four Office Center
River Edge, NJ 07661
201/342-9500

Nelson Communications Group
184-01 Van Karman Ave.
Irvine, CA 92715
714/957-1010

Ogilvy Adams & Rinehart Inc.
708 Third Ave.
New York, NY 10017
212/880-5200

Omnicom
437 Madison Ave.
New York, NY 10022
212/415-3600

Pacific-West Communications Group
3435 Wilshire Blvd.
Ste. 2850
Los Angeles, CA 90010
213/487-0830

Padilla Speer Beardsley
22 W. Franklin Ave.
Minneapolis, MN 55404
612/871-8877

PRX, Inc.
97 S. 2nd St.,
San Jose, CA 95110
408/287-1700

Public Communications, Inc.
35 E. Wacker Dr.
Chicago, IL 60601
312/558-1770

Robinson, Lake, Sawyer, Miller
75 Rockefeller Plz.
New York, NY 10019
212/484-7700

The Rockey Co.
2121 Fifth Ave.
Seattle, WA 98121
206/728-1100

Rowland Worldwide*
1675 Broadway
New York, NY 10019
212/527-8800

Ruder Finn
301 E. 57th St.

New York, NY 10022
212/593-6400

M. Silver Associates, Inc.
747 Third Ave.
17th Fl.
New York, NY 10017
212/754-6500

Stoorza, Ziegaus, & Metzger
555 Capitol Mall
Sacramento, CA 95814
916/446-6667

WHERE TO GO FOR MORE INFORMATION

ADVERTISING/PUBLIC RELATIONS ASSOCIATIONS

Advertising Research Foundation
641 Lexington Ave.
New York, NY 10022
212/751-5656

American Advertising Federation
1101 Vermont Ave.,
Ste. 500
Washington, DC 20005
202/898-0089
(Sponsors a special competition for students.)

American Association of Advertising Agencies
405 Lexington Ave.
New York, NY 10174
212/682-2500

Association of National Advertisers
155 E. 44th St.
New York, NY, 10017
212/697-5950

International Advertising Association
521 Fifth Ave.
New York, NY 10017
212/557-1133

Public Relations Society of America
33 Irving Pl.
New York, NY 10003
212/995-2230

Worldwide Partners
2280 South Xanadu Way
Aurora, CO 80014
303/671-8551

ADVERTISING/PUBLIC RELATIONS DIRECTORIES

AAAA Roster and Organization
American Association of Advertising Agencies
405 Lexington Ave.

New York, NY 10174
212/682-2500

Directory of Minority Public Relations Professionals

Public Relations Society of America
33 Irving Pl.
New York, NY 10003
212/995-2230

*O'Dwyer's Directory
of Corporate
Communications*
271 Madison Ave.
New York, NY 10016
212/679-2471

*O'Dwyer's Directory
of Public Relations
Executives*
271 Madison Ave.
New York, NY 10016
212/679-2471

*O'Dwyer's Directory
of Public Relations
Firms*
271 Madison Ave.
New York, NY 10016
212/679-2471

*Public Relations
Consultants Directory*
American Business
Directories, Inc.,
Division
American Business
Lists, Inc.

5711 S. 86th Circle
P.O. Box 27347
Omaha, NE 68127
402/593-4600

*Standard Directory of
Advertising Agencies*
Reede Reference
Publishing
121 Chanlon Rd.
New Providence, NJ
07974
800/521-8110

ADVERTISING/PUBLIC RELATIONS PERIODICALS

Advertising Age
220 E. 42nd St.
New York, NY 10017
212/210-0100
800/678-9595
(Weekly tabloid
covering the
advertising industry.
Excellent help-wanted
section.)

Adweek
1515 Broadway
New York, NY 10036
212/536-5336
(Weekly magazine
covering the
advertising industry.
Like *Ad Age,* this
publication has a strong
help-wanted section.)

*O'Dwyer's PR
Marketplace*
271 Madison Ave.
New York, NY 10016
212/679-2471
(Biweekly newsletter
listing job opening and
business opportunities
for PR practitioners.)

*Phillips Business
Information*
1201 Seven Locks Rd.
Potomac, MD 20854
800/777-5006
(Weekly newsletter sent
to corporate public-
relations executives,
PR agencies, etc.)

PR Reporter
PR Publishing

Company, Inc.
Box 600
Exeter, NH 03833
603/778-0514
(Weekly newsletter sent
to PR practitioners.)

*Public Relations
Journal*
Public Relations
Society of America
33 Irving Pl.
New York, NY 10003
212/995-2230
(Monthly magazine
sent free to PRSA
members but available
at a yearly subscription
price to nonmembers;
annual Register issue
lists members,
affiliations, addresses.)

AEROSPACE

INDUSTRY OUTLOOK: mixed. Continued pressure to reduce military/defense spending—but robust demand for commercial airliners. Expect more industry restructuring/consolidations as prime manufacturers and subcontractors shop for merger partners—and also expect continued hot competition.

The **defense aerospace** press is rife with rumors of candidates for divestiture, for acquisition, with more candidates regularly being identified. And with good reason. The defense market continues to shrink as the federal budget targets reduction in defense aerospace expenditures. Even increases in defense aerospace may not turn the tide, given the smaller market compared to 20 years ago. Profitability requires consolidations of product lines and reductions in overhead. Second-tier supplier companies and subcontractors will be—are—vulnerable for acquisition. The result: further layoffs. Also watch as defense companies continue to explore commercial areas, expanding into nondefense businesses based on space technology as the Federal Communications Commission (FCC) continues to open airwaves to commercial customers. Hot area: space satellites demand from communications companies.

As for **commerical aerospace:** here too, watch for merger activity, in some cases with defense companies. Two examples: the 1997 announcements of the Boeing–McDonnell Douglas (combined $48 billion revenues) and the Lockheed Martin–Northrup Grumman (combined $37 billion revenues) mergers. Also, expect increased competition in this field, especially between U.S. manufacturers and their foreign counterparts. The newest competitive threat: Asian manufacturers. In general, however, the industry looks like it is headed for a strong long term, especially since, by 2000, airlines will have to 1) replace a great deal of aging aircraft to meet federal noise standards and 2) add to their fleets to meet the soaring U.S. and global passenger traffic. Another factor that should help U.S. commercial manufacturers in their fight against foreign competitors: a successful conclusion to multilateral negotiations to reduce government supports to international aerospace industries. Also pointing to long-term growth: Added demand from Asia and the Pacific Rim in line with their economies.

A LOOK BACK

▶ Defense cutbacks change the face of the aerospace industry.

It started ten years ago—in 1987, when defense spending reached its peak. From that point on, spending began decreasing—and the defense industry began its downhill slide. To cope with the downturn, defense companies began downsizing, slashing jobs, instituting cost-cutting measures across the board, and merging with other companies.

The newer smaller industry—dominated by fewer larger companies—has been performing well for the past few years, racking up record profits. But, with overcapacity still a problem, the slimming down of the industry isn't over yet.

▶ **Commercial aerospace: a grim opening to the decade, but a strong finish.**

The early nineties weren't good years for commercial aerospace. The recession took its toll on airlines—which, in turn, impacted on aerospace companies. Travel dropped, airlines went bankrupt or out of business, and orders for new planes fell. Adding to the problem: increased competition from non-U.S. manufacturers, such as Airbus Industrie. But the slumping sales soared back up in the mid-nineties—as the economy rebounded. New orders started pouring in and the industry was on the move. The only problem: Competition for business has been hotter than ever, so many companies are cutting prices to win contracts. The result: more cost cutting . . . and a possible continuation of layoffs.

WHAT'S NEXT

▶ **Look for consolidation as companies adjust to the new competitive environment.**

It's the result of the reduced Pentagon spending in the past—and even if defense expenditures actually increase, as some experts have predicted, the consolidations should continue. The reason: companies selling to this market will seek to acquire complementary businesses and reduce costs. As one industry analyst stated, "Everyone is talking to everyone." Expect to see more consolidations. Employment opportunities will continue to suffer as these companies lay off personnel to achieve consolidation economies.

▶ **Long term bright for commercial aerospace—but here, too, expect consolidations.**

It looks like all systems are go where the long-term outlook is concerned.

The key reason? World air-traffic growth is expected to resume its upward climb, with some predicting that air traffic will *triple* by the year 2010. In addition, a high number of planes are due to be retired. The bottom line—a surge in new-plane orders. This will translate into employment opportunities in the long term, as aircraft manufacturers staff up to meet the production demands.

▶ **Expect tougher competition from foreign companies as they continue to grow in strength.**

European and Asian countries are beginning to take a bite out of U.S. exports of aircraft. Aerospace is the number-one U.S. export, responsible for $38 billion in overseas sales annually. The commercial aerospace sector has been particularly strong in exports, but foreign competition is beginning to weaken this strength.

Watch as foreign companies, particularly European ones, cut even more deeply into U.S. aerospace sales in the years ahead. One of the toughest competitors is Airbus Industries, the European consortium that is number two, behind Boeing, in worldwide orders. Other competitors include British Aerospace and Fokker Aircraft. But if the multilateral negotiations to reduce government supports to international aerospace industries pan out, it should level out the playing field for U.S. companies competing with foreign ones.

▶ **Along similar lines, watch as the U.S. aerospace industry becomes increasingly globalized.**

The globalization trend that is sweeping the rest of U.S. industry will affect aerospace as well. Some of the results: Expect to see more foreign investment in U.S. companies. In some cases, this will be a way of getting the funding that used to come from government contracts.

Also expect to see more U.S. companies turn to foreign companies for subcontract work and others team up with foreign manufacturers. There is already a rising number of international team arrangements in the aircraft engine area: General Electric is working with European and Japanese manufacturers on advanced engines such as the CFM56, CF6-80, and GE90; Pratt & Whitney is doing the same with the V2500, the JTD-8-200, and the PW4000. This trend should continue.

▶ **Watch defense aerospace manufacturers target themselves for nondefense projects, sometimes teaming up with former competitors to gain them.**

More manufacturers will seek different areas of business to compensate for the defense projects that have been cut. Some of the more prominent examples: Hughes Aircraft's highly successful satellite television service—DirecTV, which had over 1 million subscribers in its first year and will be going global now. TRW's Space and Defense Sector is producing tax-processing equipment for the IRS and is planning nuclear-waste disposal equipment for the Energy Department. Martin Marietta has begun managing research laboratories for the Energy Department and computer systems for the Department of Housing and Urban Development. Expect to see more actions like this as companies struggle to find new lines of business. An area that is seeing a great deal of action: Environmental technology. A number of companies have formed environmental subsidiaries, including General Dynamics, Lockheed, and Hughes. Expect more companies to focus on developing and marketing environmental products worldwide. One area that should see stiff competition is the space sector.

Similarly, watch as more companies team up to share expertise in an attempt to win new defense and nondefense government contracts—or commercial contracts. An example: Lockheed Martin, Raytheon, and other companies have teamed up to offer satellite images to farmers and real estate agents.

Expect more companies to aim their sights at projects unconnected with the government. For example, McDonnell Douglas has been exploring the market for and profitability of building bullet trains—high-speed rail transports, which are already widely used in Japan. Westinghouse Electronics Systems is making (among other products) security gear for home and commercial use and radar equipment.

The effect on employment? Limited at this time, as companies shop around for new work. The key to uncovering employment opportunities is keeping abreast of any developments and contracts awarded. However, don't expect miracles. According to a recent *BusinessWeek* report, experts say that over the short term, switching to nondefense projects will replace only 25 to 30% of the defense work that was cut.

EMPLOYMENT OUTLOOK: A split—stronger demand for workers in commercial aerospace, while defense jobs remain weaker.

It's a mixed picture for aerospace employment, mirroring the split in the industry: with a bright outlook for commercial, weaker—and much more competitive—for defense. In general, though, things are looking brighter than in the past. Most industry insiders believe that the days of downsizing are finally over—and employment has bottomed out . . . and will be increasing again.

More specifically, with the boom in commercial aerospace, the employment outlook here looks good. As commercial aerospace companies continue to meet increased production demands, expect to see continued employment opportunities for skilled production workers. In fact, many industry experts have predicted substantial job increases. Areas that look especially hot: Demand for hundreds of satellites as the satellite-based communications (telephone) and entertainment (direct broadcast TV) businesses mushroom.

The picture is not as bright for defense. Hot competition, lower government funding, and flat revenues will translate into a weaker employment market. Expect to see more consolidation—which may mean job cutbacks.

The key to employment opportunities in defense? Keeping abreast of new developments and projects. The companies that will eventually be hiring again will be those that find a means of replacing earnings lost in the defense cutbacks.

JOBS SPOTLIGHT

SOFTWARE ENGINEERS: Demand has been high in this area, particularly for engineers who can model physical systems. Many aerospace companies cite this as a strategic need.

BEST BETS

AlliedSignal Aerospace Co.
2525 W. 190th St.
Torrance CA 90504
213/321-5000

One of the best-performing aerospace companies, AlliedSignal actually increased sales at the same time the defense industry was struggling. Key to its success? Aggressive expansion into new areas and markets, emphasis on R&D—with attention to new product development, and application of aerospace technology into nonaerospace fields. More specifically, AlliedSignal has been expanding into repair work and spare parts production—targeting overseas markets such as Asia. In addition, it has been working in global-positioning satellite technology and applying aviation technology to automobiles. This attention to R&D, and key targeting of strong markets makes AlliedSignal look like a good employment bet.

Boeing
Box 3707
7755 E. Marginal Way S.
Seattle, WA 98124
206/655-1131

Ranked by fellow executives in the industry as the best aerospace company in terms of management, innovation, and financial soundness, Boeing is on a roll. In 1996, earnings were projected to increase by a whopping 31%. But all this hasn't been easy. Boeing has cut thousands of jobs over the past few years, in an effort to transform itself from a pilot-engineering-oriented company that focuses on making innovative planes to a manufacturing company that focuses on making cost-effective planes. Along with this will come more early retirements or layoffs of personnel, as the company transforms itself into a high-productivity giant. But innovation is still in the air. The new Boeing 777 has won a large share of orders, and Boeing engineers are already excited about a proposal for work on a second generation supersonic transport, the SST, that will be able to travel at 1,600 miles per hour.

Teleflex
630 W. Germantown Pike
Plymouth Meeting, PA 19462
610/834-8228

Not one of the big guys in aerospace, but one that is managing to move ahead with the times, Teleflex looks like it's laying the groundwork for long-term growth. Teleflex is actually a small conglomerate that, in addition to aerospace manufacturing, makes controls for boats and cars, as well as medical devices. It has translated its aerospace technology into other areas: for example, its jet-engine-blade technology is being used to make the blades for electricity-generating turbines. This type of crossover ability, plus its ability to compete with other companies, makes it look like a good bet for the future.

TOP AEROSPACE AND DEFENSE ELECTRONICS COMPANIES

(For related companies, also see "Top Electronics Companies," page 297.)

ABEX
Liberty Ln.
Hampton, NH 03842
603/926-5911

Alliant Techsystems, Inc.
200 2nd St. N.E.
Hopkins, MN 55343
612/931-6000

AlliedSignal Aerospace Co.
2525 W. 190th St.
Torrance, CA 90504-6099
310/323-9500

AlliedSignal Aerospace Co.
111 S. 34th St.
Phoenix, AZ 85034
602/231-1000

The Boeing Company
Box 3707
7755 E. Marginal Way S.
Seattle, WA 98124-2207
206/655-1131

Coltec Industries, Inc.
430 Park Ave.
New York, NY 10022
212/940-0400

**Delco Electronics
Corp.**
1 Corporate Center
Kokomo, IN
46904-9005
317/451-8400

E-Systems, Inc.
6250 LBJ Fwy.
Dallas, TX 75240
214/661-8500

**The Fairchild
Corporation**
300 W. Service Rd.
Box 10803
Chantilly, VA 22021
703/478-5800

**General Dynamics
Corp.**
3190 Fairview Park
Drive
Falls Church, VA
22042-4523
708/876-3000

**GE Aircraft
Engines**
1 Neumann Way
Cincinnati, OH 45215
513/243-2000

GenCorp
175 Ghent Rd.
Fairlawn, OH 44333
216/869-4200

**GM Hughes
Electronics Corp.**
7200 Hughes Terrace
Los Angeles, CA
90045
310/568-7200

**Gulfstream Aerospace
Corp.**
500 Gulfstream Rd.
Savannah, GA 31407
912/965-3000

Harris Corp.
1025 W. NASA Blvd.

Melbourne, FL 32901
407/727-9100

Honeywell, Inc.
2701 4th Ave. S.
Minneapolis, MN
55408
612/951-1000

Hughes Aircraft Co.
7200 Hughes Ter.
Los Angeles, CA
90045
310/568-7200

**ITT Defense &
Electronics, Inc.**
1000 Wilson Blvd.
Arlington, VA 22209
703/247-2942

Kaman Corp.
1332 Blue Hills Rd.
Bloomfield, CT 06002
203/243-8311

**Kollsman Instrument
Corp.**
220 Daniel Webster
Hwy.
Merrimack, NH 03054
603/889-2500

Litton Industries
21240 Burbank Blvd.
Woodland Hills, CA
91367-6675
818/598-5000

**Lockheed-Marietta
Corp.**
6801 Rockledge Dr.
Bethesda, MD 20817
301/897-6000

Loral Corp.
600 Third Ave.
New York, NY 10016
212/697-1105

The LTV Corp.
25 W. Prospect Ave.
Cleveland, OH 44115
216/622-5000

**McDonnell-Douglas
Corp.**
325 McDonnell Blvd.
St. Louis, MO 63042
314/232-0232

**McDonnell Douglas
Space Systems**
(Division of
McDonnell Douglas
Corp.)
5301 Balsa Ave.
Huntington Beach, CA
92647
714/896-3311

Northrop/Grumman
1111 Stewart Ave.
Bethpage, NY
11714-3580
516/575-0574

Northrop/Grumman
1840 Century Park E.
Century City
Los Angeles, CA
90067-2199
310/553-6262

**Parker Hannifin
Corp.**
17325 Euclid Ave.
Cleveland, OH 44112
216/531-3000

**Pratt & Whitney
Group**
400 Main St.
East Hartford, CT
06118
203/565-4321

Raytheon Co.
141 Spring St.
Lexington, MA 02173
617/862-6600

**Rockwell Systems
Development**
2600 Seal Beach Blvd.
Seal Beach, CA 90740
310/797-3311

Rockwell International Space Systems Division
3370 East Miraloma Ave.
Downey, CA 90242
310/922-2111

Rohr Industries, Inc.
850 Lagoon Dr.
Chula Vista, CA 91910
619/691-4111

Sequa Corp.
200 Park Ave.
New York, NY 10166
212/986-5500

Sundstrand Corp.
P.O. Box 7003
4949 Harrison Ave.
Rockford, IL 61108
815/226-8069

Teledyne, Inc.
1901 Ave. of the Stars
Los Angeles, CA 90067-3201
310/277-3311

Textron, Inc.
40 Westminster St.
Providence, RI 02903
401/421-2800

Thiokol Corp.
2475 Washington Blvd.
Ogden, UT 84401
801/629-2000

United Technologies Corp.
1 Financial Plz.
United Technologies Bldg.
Hartford, CT 06106
203/728-7000

Westinghouse Electronics Systems
7323 Aviation Blvd.
Baltimore, MD 21240
410/765-1000

WHERE TO GO FOR MORE INFORMATION

(For more information sources relating to the aerospace industry, also see "Engineering," page 50, "Aviation," page 249, and "Computers and Electronics," page 288.)

AEROSPACE ASSOCIATIONS

Aerospace Industries Association
1250 I St., NW
Washington, DC 20005
202/371-8400

American Institute of Aeronautics and Astronautics
370 L'Enfant Promenade, SW
Washington, DC 20024
202/646-7400
(Among other publications, puts out the *AIAA Bulletin,* which includes employment listings, and the *AIAA Student Journal,* which is aimed at aerospace students and includes articles on job hunting and entry-level career opportunities.)

Aviation Distributors and Manufacturers Association
1900 Arch St.
Philadelphia, PA 10103
215/564-3484

General Aviation Manufacturers Association
1400 K St., NW
Washington, DC 20005
202/393-1500

National Aeronautic Association
1815 N. Fort Meyer Dr.
Suite 700
Arlington, VA 22209-1805

AEROSPACE DIRECTORIES

Aerospace Facts & Figures
Aerospace Industry
Association
1250 I St., NW
Washington, DC 20005
202/371-8400

**Aerospace
Consultants Directory**
Society of Aerospace
Engineers
400 Commonwealth Dr.

Warrendale, PA 15096
412/776-4841

*World Aviation
Directory*
Aviation Week Group

McGraw Hill, Inc.
1200 G St., NW
Washington, DC 20005
202/383-3700

AEROSPACE PERIODICALS

Aerospace Daily
1200 G St., NW
Washington, DC 20005
202/383-3700
(Daily newsletter
circulated to
government officials
and aerospace
executives.)

*Aerospace
Engineering*
400 Commonwealth Dr.
Warrendale, PA 15096
412/772-7114

Monthly publication of
the Society of
Aerospace Engineers;
geared to design
engineers, technical
managers, etc.)

*Aviation Week and
Space Technology*
1221 Ave. of the
Americas
New York, NY 10020
212/512-4857
(Weekly magazine;
considered by many to

be the industry "bible";
covers all phases of the
aerospace industry—
commercial defense,
space, etc. Includes
classified ads.)

Defense News
and *Space News*
6883 Commercial Dr.
Springfield, VA 22159
703/658-8400
(Magazines covering
the defense industry
and space industry.)

AGRICULTURE

INDUSTRY OUTLOOK: generally good, with continued high world demand, particularly from Asia. Long-term mixed, as bioengineered insect- and herbicide-resistant seeds contribute to higher yields, with uncertain European response to such products. Decreased farming costs as chemical spraying decreases. On balance, the expanding developing-world economies should expand U.S. exports over 35% by 2006, according to farm industry experts.

The U.S. should be the major player in world markets. The plus side—increased yields and lower farming costs, low farm debt, low interest rates, and elimination of many government set-aside and farm acreage control programs, and strong exports to Japan and other Pacific Rim nations, as well as output drops in Russia—until now, America's major competitor. Potential problems—cuts in imports by cash-poor China, Russia, and Eastern Europe if U.S. government financing drops, and a possible backlash by Europe (led by Germany and Switzerland) to biotech farm products.

A LOOK BACK

▶ **The two major forces that affected agriculture: in the past decade the "Farm Belt Depression" of 1982 and the increasing subsidies from the federal government.**

It may now be ancient history, but these two forces are what made the U.S. agriculture industry what it is today. First came the Farm Belt Depression, when agriculture went into a free fall. The major culprits? Too-rapid expansion, which led to a heavy debt load for most farmers. Then came a drop in exports, a decline in crop prices and land prices—and a number of farms failing. Agriculture went into a steep decline in the early 1980s. A key cause was the fact that farmers had been expanding rapidly, buying land and equipment, taking on a heavy debt load in the process (about $183 billion at its peak in 1983). Next exports dropped consistently, reaching a low in 1986. At the same time, crop prices were declining, land prices were declining—and many farms failed.

To help farmers out of their financial straits, the government began to beef up its federal farm subsidy program. Payments to farmers skyrocketed, hitting $27.5 billion in 1986. The problem? Payments were often highest to the farms and farmers who needed them least. So even with the subsidy program, large numbers of smaller farms continued to fail or to lose money.

The farm depression ended, and farmers, aided by low debt and even lower interest rates, began seeing record incomes. But Mother Nature dealt a mean hand of cards in 1995: first came heavy rains in the Midwest; then a blistering summer heat wave; then a September frost—which led to record low crops. But 1996 looked better—and farmers were optimistic, especially faced with increased demand for exports. The final development in 1995 and 1996: proposed legislation that would eliminate government "set-aside" programs, under which farmers are paid for keeping land idle. Instead, the government would pay grain farmers at a fixed rate based on what they received in the past—and this amount would shrink each year. As a result, there would be an increase in land devoted to production of corn, wheat, and soybean—all big exports. (Cotton, rice, sugar, peanut and dairy farmers would not be affected by this proposal, as they would remain on the subsidy program.)

WHAT'S NEXT

▶ Look for the impact of the "new world order" on agriculture, specifically, on grain growers.

The collapse of communism in Eastern Europe continues to translate into an increase in the amount of grain grown and sold to Russia and Eastern Europe, particularly with the collapse of agricultural output in the region. This trend should continue in the short term as demand remains high and the region remains unsettled. Despite bumper crops in China, yields have not kept pace with demand and the country continues to seek supplies from abroad including the U.S., a low-cost producer.

▶ A growing trend: fewer—but larger—farms.

This has been happening for the past few years. Each year, the number of U.S. farms drops by about 30,000. This has resulted in a 61% decline in the number of farms over the past forty years. Department of Agriculture figures show 5,399,437 working farms in 1950 and only 2,104,560 in 1991.

But the amount of land used for agriculture hasn't dropped by the same degree. The reason? While the number of farms is decreasing, the size of farms is *increasing*.

Expect this to continue as the agriculture industry polarizes, with small "hobbyist" farms run by people whose primary sources of incomes are in nonfarming areas at one end, and large farms, with sales of more than $250,000 annually, dominating the picture. These larger farms are better equipped to stay financially sound without government help; they tend to be more profitable and so can invest in the machinery and other capital improvements that are becoming increasingly vital to modern farming.

▶ In line with the trend toward larger farms, midsized farms will fade out of the U.S. agriculture picture.

This, too, has been happening for the past few years. Farms with annual sales ranging from $40,000 to $250,000 have been unable to keep up with the financial realities of agriculture in the '80s and '90s. In short, their sales and profits aren't high enough to maintain their high equipment costs, and to endure marginal crops and weak prices, bad weather and possible natural disasters, or no subsidies. In addition, when farm land credits don't keep pace with inflation, banks tighten credit—which means lack of financing and possible failure. Over the next few years, watch for the continuing decline of the midsized farm.

▶ **Expect more farms to take advantage of technological breakthroughs.**

It's a growing trend: Large farms, in particular, are introducing high-tech methods to farming and are automating their cycle of crop production. The result? Farms that are run similarly to factories and are very profitable.

The use of technology has changed the employment picture at many of the larger farms. Employees, especially farm managers, must have some degree of technical skills and even better, experience with the new methods.

▶ **Farms will be adjusting their output to meet changing consumer demands.**

As with other industries, the agricultural industry will become more market-driven, tracking demographics and customer preferences to determine what will sell best. The key factor: a growing health-consciousness that is sweeping the nation. Given this, expect a growing number of organic and natural farms to keep up with the increasing demand for foods produced without the use of chemical pesticides. Similarly, there should be a growth in production of livestock that haven't been treated with hormones.

Also getting a great deal of attention: Genetic engineering and other facets of agriculture biotechnology. This is still a relatively young area in agriculture, but it will be taking off, as current research and development evolve into actual breakthroughs that can be adopted by more farmers. Keep an eye on this area—in the long term, it will have a huge impact on the agriculture field. For more information on ag biotech, see Chemicals, page 280.

EMPLOYMENT OUTLOOK: Fair.

According to the U.S. Bureau of Labor Statistics, farming is the occupational category with the largest projected numerical decrease in total employment over the next ten years—with over 250,000 jobs predicted to be lost.

In spite of these figures, however, job opportunities will remain. For example, in 1994, about 1,327,000 jobs were held by farm operators and managers. About 90 percent were self-employed farm operators. In 1988, about 1,272,000 jobs were held by farm operators and managers. Of these, roughly three out of five managed crop production; more than two out of five managed livestock production. The bottom line? While the field is shrinking, the slack is being taken up, in part, by the larger farms, with a rising demand for experienced farm managers. (See below.)

Agricultural scientists face about average job growth. As for agricultural technicians, the outlook is generally positive. Demand should be strongest for those working in biotech.

JOBS SPOTLIGHT

FARM MANAGERS: A position that has become more important as, on the one hand, farms grow larger and more technologically complex and, on the other, absentee ownership rises. Demand for experienced personnel continues. Salary levels depend upon the type and size of farm managed, and cover a wide range—

typically from $20,000 to $40,000—and usually with housing either provided or partially subsidized.

BEST BETS

"BRAND NAME" FARMS: There is a growing presence of brand-name farms—that is, farms that market their product like other manufacturers. For example, J.G. Boswell Company, a cotton farm, sells Boswell Cotton—at a higher price than the competition because of high quality and brand identification. Brand-name farms will continue to be a growing trend and should offer growing employment opportunities.

LEADING AGRICULTURE COMPANIES

(For related companies, also see listing under "Food," page 339.)

A & B-Hawaii, Inc.
822 Bishop St.
Honolulu, HI 96813
808/525-6611
(Sugar, molasses, etc.)

Ag Processing, Inc.
12700 W. Dodge Rd.
Omaha, NE 68154
402/498-2215
(Soybean oil, cake, meal, etc.)

Bud Antle, Inc.
315 Neponset Rd.
Marina, CA 93933
408/758-0540
(Vegetables.)

C. Brewer & Co. Ltd.
827 Fort St. Mall
Honolulu, HI 96813
808/536-4461
(Nuts, sugar cane, etc.)

Alfred Brubaker
21700 SW 252nd St.
Homestead, FL 33031
305/246-9969
(Produce.)

Cal-Maine Foods, Inc.
3320 Woodrow Wilson Ave.
Jackson, MS 39209

601/948-6813
(Eggs, etc.)

Campbell Soup Co.
Campbell Pl.
Camden, NJ 08103
609/342-4800
(Produce.)

Campbell's Fresh, Inc.
Maiden Creek Rd.
Blandon, PA 19510
215/926-4101
(Mushrooms.)

Cargill, Inc.
15407 McGinty Rd.
Minnetonka, MN 55440
612/742-7575
(Grain, food products.)

Central Soya Company, Inc.
110 W. Berry St.
Ft. Wayne, IN 46802
219/425-5100
(Livestock and poultry feeds, soybean meal, etc.)

Continental Grain
277 Park Ave.
New York, NY 10172

212/207-5100
(Grain, food products.)

DeKalb Genetic Corp.
3100 Sycamore Rd.
DeKalb, IL 60115
815/758-3461
(Corn, etc.)

Diamond Walnut Growers, Inc.
1050 Diamond St.
Stockton, CA 95205
209/467-6000
(Walnuts.)

Dole Food Co. Inc.
313555 Oak Crest Dr.
Westlake Village, CA 91361
818/876-6600
818/879-6600
(Fruits, vegetables.)

A. Duda & Sons
1975 W. State Rd.
Oviedo, FL 32765
407/365-2189
(Produce.)

Foster Poultry Farms
1000 Davis St.
Livingtons, CA 95334

209/394-7901
(Poultry hatchery.)

Fresh Express Inc.
P.O. Box 80599
Salinas, CA 93912
(Crops.)

Gilroy Foods, Inc.
1350 Pacheco Pass
Hwy.
Gilroy, CA 95020
408/842-3103
(Dehydrated garlic,
onion, etc.)

Harris Farms, Inc.
Rt. 1, Box 400
Coalinga, CA 93210
209/884-2435
(Crops.)

Hudson Foods, Inc.
1225 Hudson Rd.
Rogers, AR 72756
501/636-1100
(Poultry.)

Lykes Brothers, Inc.
111 E. Madison St.
Tampa, FL 33602
813/223-3981
(Fruits, cultivation
services.)

**Maui Land &
Pineapple Co., Inc.**
120 Kane St.
Kahului, HI 96732
808/877-3351
(Fruits.)

**Mid-America
Dairymen, Inc.**
3253 E. Chestnut
Expwy.
Springfield, MO 65802
417/865-7100
(Dairy products.)

**Monterey
Mushrooms, Inc.**
1500 41st Ave., Ste. 14
Capitola, CA 95010
408/475-1955
(Mushrooms.)

Murphy Farms, Inc.
Hwy. 117 S.
P.O. Box 759
Rose Hill, NC 28458
919/289-2111
(Hogs.)

Pilgrims Pride Corp.
110 S. Texas
Pittsburg, TX 75686
903/856-7901
(Broiler, fryer, and
roaster chickens.)

**Prairie Farms Dairy,
Inc.**
1100 N. Broadway
Carlinville, IL 62626
217/854-2547
(Milk processing.)

Riceland Foods
2120 Park Ave.
Stuttgart, AR 72160
501/673-5500
(Milled and polished
rice, vegetable
shortenings and oil—
except corn oil—etc.)

J. R. Simplot
P.O. Box 27
Boise, ID 83707
208/336-2110
(Potaotes and other
food products.)

**Sun World
International, Inc.**
5544 California Ave.,
No. 280

Bakersfield, CA 93309
805/833-6460
(Crop preparation
services for market
fruits, vegetables.)

**Townsend Farms,
Inc.**
Rte. 24
P.O. Box 468
Millsboro, DE 19966
302/934-9221
(Broiler, fryer, and
roaster chickens.)

Tyson Foods, Inc.
2210 W. Oaklawn Dr.
Springdale, AR 72762
501/290-4000
(Broiler, fryer, and
roaster chickens.)

**United States Sugar
Corp.**
111 Ponce de Leon
Ave.
Clearwater, FL 33440
813/983-8121
(Sugar, vegetables,
etc.)

**Wisconsin Dairies
Co-op, Inc.**
Rt. 3, Hwy. 12 W.
P.O. Box 111
Baraboo, WI 53913
608/356-8316
(Dairy products.)

Zacky Farms, Inc.
2000 N. Tyler
El Monte, CA 91733
818/443-9351
(Broiler, fryer, and
roaster chickens.)

WHERE TO GO FOR MORE INFORMATION

AGRICULTURE ASSOCIATIONS

**Agriculture Council
of America**
927 15th St., NW,
Ste. 800
Washington, DC 20005
202/682-9200

**Agricultural Research
Institute**
9650 Rockville Pike
Bethesda, MD 20814
301/530-7122

**American Farm
Bureau Federation**
225 Touhy Ave.
Park Ridge, IL 60068
312/399-5700

**American Feed
Industry Association**
1501 Wilson Blvd.,
Suite 1100
Arlington, VA 22209
703/524-0810

**American Society of
Agricultural
Engineers**
2950 Niles Rd.

St. Joseph, MI 49085
616/429-0300

**American Society of
Agronomy**
677 S. Segoe Rd.
Madison, WI 53711
608/273-8080
(Puts out monthly
magazine—also
available to
nonmembers for a low
subscription price—
that includes a help-
wanted section; also
offers a resume
bank/job placement
service—free for
members; low cost to
nonmembers.)

**American Society of
Farm Managers and
Rural Appraisers**
950 S. Cherry St.
Ste. 508
Denver, CO 80222
303/758-3513

**Future Farmers of
America**
P.O. Box 15160
Alexandria, VA 22309
703/360-3600

**National Corn
Growers Association**
201 Massachusetts
Ave., NE
Washington, DC 20002
202/546-7611

**National Council of
Agricultural
Employers**
1112 16th St., NW
Suite 920
Washington, DC 20036
202/728-0300

**National Grain and
Feed Association**
1201 New York Ave.,
NW, Suite 830
Washington, DC 20005
202/289-0873

AGRICULTURE DIRECTORIES

Farms Directory
American Business
Directory

P.O. Box 27347
5711 S. 86th Circle

Omaha, NE 68127
402/593-4600

AGRICULTURE PERIODICALS

(There are a number of agricultural magazines and newspapers focusing on
specific regional areas and specific crops or livestock. To find the appropriate
names, check a periodicals directory at the public library, such as *Business Publication Rates & Data,* published by Standard Rates & Data Service.)

Ag Consultant
37733 Euclid Ave.
Willoughby, OH 44094
216/942-2000
(Nine-issue magazine
on the agricultural
field, aimed at
agricultural advisers,
agri-fieldmen,
researchers, and
schools.)

Agri Finance
6201 W. Howard
Niles, IL 60714
708/647-1200
(Nine-issue magazine
on agricultural
financing, designed for
bank officers, farm
credit agencies,
management and
loan/mortgage firms,
etc.)

Farm Journal
1500 Market St.
Center Square W.
Philadelphia, PA 19102
215/557-8900
(Monthly magazine
covering many aspects
of farming.)

Feed Management
122 S. Wesley Ave.
Mt. Morris, IL 61054
815/734-4171
(Monthly magazine for
executives, managers,
manufacturers, etc., in
the feed industry.)

Successful Farming
1716 Locust St.
Des Moines, IA
50309-3023
515/284-2897
(Monthly magazine
covering farming,
aimed at a wide range
of readers, including
farmers, managers,
operators, bankers, and
business managers.)

Top Producer
1500 Market St.
Center Square W.
Philadelphia, PA 19102
215/557-8900
(Monthly magazine for
farmowners and farm
managers.)

AUTOMOTIVE

INDUSTRY OUTLOOK: Flat demand, increased competition and general sluggishness.

The auto industry has done everything right—but it faces a disappointing sales outlook. Over the past few years, it cut costs, upped productivity, improved quality—but sales haven't increased like the industry hoped. In fact, while total **vehicle** sales have been flat, with negligible annual increase, **automobile** sales in fact have been slipping, with the slack taken up by small pickup trucks, minivans, and sports utility vehicles—fortunately at higher profit margins. Key reasons: high prices, longer-lasting vehicles due to improved technology, a saturated car market, and a larger supply of good used cars. Another problem— the lack of new, innovative product to draw in consumers. Finally, the number of households (the major car-buying unit) is dwindling, especially those headed up by people from 35 to 44 years old, the prime car-buying age. The result: Experts predict a slowdown of sales that may continue over ten years. Adding to the woes: squeezed automobile profit margins, as consumers demand better deals and new model launch costs go up. Also expect prices and profit margins on pickups, minivans, and sports utility vehicles to drop as foreign manufacturers invade the U.S. market.

But the auto industry is far from dead. Even while unit sales should remain flat, people will continue spending the same percentage of their income on vehicles—in many cases, they'll be trading up. This points to stronger sales for pricier cars and for those with new accessories. In addition, minivans, pickups, and sports utility vehicles should continue selling well—although Japanese manufacturers are making inroads in this area. The industry response: introduction of upgraded production techniques and outsourced parts production to reduce production/parts costs. Long term, auto job prospects may improve with replacements for retiring auto workers.

The upshot? Over the short term, watch for hotter competition as manufacturers fight for consumers. In addition, expect to see the continued influx of foreign carmakers producing cars in the U.S. These transplants will be picking up some of the slack as the Big Three slow production.

A LOOK BACK

▶ The past few years: consolidation, competition, and cost-cutting.

The early '90s was a time for the auto industry to retrench. Hammered by competition from the Japanese carmakers in particular, the Big Three were forced to institute wide-ranging cost-cutting measures. These included closing factories and laying off both factory workers and middle-management staff—nearly 30 assembly and parts facilities have been scrapped by the Big Three since 1984.

General Motors alone announced the closing of eleven factories and the eventual loss of 80,000 jobs. By 1995, General Motors had disposed of parts operations for radiator caps, vacuum pumps, electric motors—over forty-one lines of business, with job shifts to non-GM companies, and was reorganizing its product development operations. One negative result: 5,000 engineering jobs cut. GM trails Chrysler and Ford in outsourced parts. GM announced plans to eliminate 30,000 parts and assembly jobs by 2000 as part of a pact with the United Auto Workers.

Manufacturing wasn't the only sector of the industry that was hard-hit. In 1991 645 dealers closed their doors, bringing the total up to 1,588 closed dealers since 1989. Dealers that survived were often forced to institute their own cost-cutting efforts, laying off staff and closing unprofitable operations. By 1997, the auto industry was lean and mean. Productivity was up, quality was up, and U.S. carmakers were competing successfully with the Japanese. The problem? Sales began to lag, profits drop, and automakers were beginning to steel themselves for a stagnant period.

WHAT'S NEXT

▶ **Intense competition ahead.**

With sales lagging, competition will heat up again. Adding to the competitive climate: a weak yen and increased cost-cutting has made the Japanese more competitive than ever. As a result, expect to see continued competition between different U.S. companies as well as against foreign companies. Some probable results: Unprofitable lines will be dropped; some companies will link up for cooperative manufacturing and marketing ventures (like GM and Toyota's 50-50 venture with the Geo); and joint R&D will increase. One area that should see especially intense competition: Minivans, pickups, and utility vehicles. While this has been one bright spot in terms of sales, the Japanese are now moving in—at the same time that the Big Three's capacity has increased. As a result, watch as manufacturers vie to keep their share of this stronger, more profitable area of the market.

▶ **Look for an increase in joint ventures between U.S. auto makers and their foreign counterparts.**

For all the competition, both U.S. manufacturers and their import counterparts realize they actually need one another. In 1996, Ford increased its investment in Mazda to over one-third, installing its own president. (The plant produces the Ford Probe.) It also linked up with Nissan to produce a minivan marketed by both companies under the Mercury and Nissan badges. General Motors has no intention of loosening its ties with Toyota, which led to the production of the Geo Prizm and the Toyota Corolla. Nor will it change the ventures that led to the Geo Metro and Geo Tracker, produced with Suzuki.

▶ Transplant production: still coming on strong.

Expect to see the continuing presence of non-U.S. auto manufacturers in the U.S. The Japanese manufacturers started the trend—with Nissan, Honda, Toyota, and Mazda, among others, setting up shop—and they have recently begun stepping up their production, and increasing their exports of American-built cars to 38 countries, including Japan. Now European manufacturers are following suit, with German automakers building factories and beginning production. The result: Even while Big Three production went down, transplant production kept the number of cars produced in the United States from declining, with only slight increases in total U.S. auto production capacity. And it's good news where employment is concerned as well—even while U.S. automakers were cutting jobs, transplants were creating them, keeping job loss from swamping the industry.

▶ Consolidation in the parts supply industry—even as auto companies depend more on suppliers instead of making their own parts.

Automakers have been moving away from the past ways of meeting parts requirements and instead are using outside parts suppliers to fulfill virtually every step of parts production—including design and engineering, integration into the assembly process, and delivery. But, because suppliers are handling so much of the development responsibility, U.S. auto manufacturers are cutting back on the number of suppliers they deal with. One example: Ford used to use 10,000 suppliers. As of early 1996, it had cut the number to 2,300—and announced plans to cut the number further still, to 1,150 by the year 2000.

Given this, expect to see consolidation in the industry. Most experts predict that the field will become a global one, as automakers want suppliers to supply their factories not only in the U.S. but also in other countries. Smaller companies will be swallowed by larger ones—or may wind up going belly-up, as the climate favors larger companies who can handle the growing demands of the business.

The impact on the employment picture: A mixed bag. On one hand, the shrinking number of suppliers may lead to job cuts. However, this could be offset by the increasing responsibilities of the larger suppliers. These companies may offer employment opportunities in many areas of the country. The emphasis will be on design/systems engineers and electronic specialists capable of developing and evaluating unique parts designs and engineering.

▶ Watch Japanese transplants increase their sourcing of U.S. parts and components.

The Japanese transplants are under intense political pressure to increase their use of U.S.–made parts and components in cars and trucks built in this country. As such, they will work closely with U.S. suppliers, particularly in systems engineering, development, and production. Expect to see more contracts given to U.S. suppliers, which will result in more jobs.

The big winners will be the super suppliers—giants like Dana Corp. and TRW, which can offer complete services. The key to working with the Japanese, however, is to understand their culture. This means it can be a wide-open area for even midsized suppliers.

Employment in the supplier area: There should be job opportunities as the Japanese start ordering both on the engineering and the production side. But don't expect to see suppliers overstaffing. The lessons of the '80s are still too fresh in their memories.

▶ In the face of a slowing U.S. market, watch U.S. manufacturers look for more overseas sales.

U.S. auto manufacturers have made no secret of the fact that they want to export their products overseas. General Motors reorganized its overseas sales units. Ford already plans to increase its export business, as does Chrysler. They are looking at both Europe and Japan.

The overseas markets are projected to grow faster than the U.S. market. Eastern Europe is especially promising: According to a forecast by Ford Europe, this market will account for about 7 million car sales in 2008. Add to this the 16 million projected for the Western European markets and the result is a strong market.

Japanese transplants are also looking hard at exporting. Honda already exports its Accord to Japan; expect to see others doing the same thing. This will enable them to free up their Japanese factories for other models and avoid duplication of effort. But the real exporting opportunity for the transplants will be Europe. Unlike the United States, Europe is not a totally free market. There are restrictions on Japanese automakers there. But the U.S. exports will receive more favorable treatment. On the employment side: If the Japanese succeed in exporting more products, they will have to expand their production, perhaps not by building new plants but by adding more shifts. And with Ford's increased interest in Japan's Mazda—a controlling interest because of Ford's veto power over board actions—the company has a strong Asian base, as Ford and the other of the Big Three explore investments in such disparate places as China, Thailand, India, Vietnam, Malaysia, Turkey, Brazil, and Argentina. GM's overseas plant strategy has cost over $2.2 billion.

▶ Expect increased emphasis on—and budgets for—research and development.

Domestic automakers are spending more on R&D. They must, to meet the competition as well as to comply with today's stiff environmental laws.

Japanese auto manufacturers have a shorter new-product cycle—about four years to design and build a new car. American manufacturers are on an eight-year cycle, although GM is trying to put a five-year product cycle in place.

U.S. automakers have invested heavily in new-product development. Buick alone introduced five new cars over two model years. Chrysler launched four.

While U.S. automakers are looking hard to cut their cycles, the Japanese have started to rethink their philosophy as well. In 1992 the unmentionable was finally mentioned: The Japanese product cycle doesn't do much for the bottom line. Several manufacturers, including Toyota, have said that they would like to see longer cycles. Expect the Japanese to meet the U.S. automakers somewhere in the middle.

But it's more than product cycle that is spurring R&D—it is also the need for new technology. Stricter air-pollution laws have pressured both U.S. and import automakers to rethink the automobile. Watch for new technology that will mean more electric cars and cars powered by alternative fuels such as natural gas.

Greater effort will also be put into the use of recyclable materials. New technologies will have to be developed, so expect to see expanded development and production of composite polymer materials and development of applications.

Car makers will also attempt to target specific markets for their products—for example, by manufacturing cars with features for older people in an effort to capitalize on the aging population.

The shift to R&D across the board to meet the changing demands of the market points to opportunities for design engineers.

▶ Traditional auto dealers will continue to retrench.

Even with sales picking up, dealers are not going to be anxious to increase their sales staffs—and when they do hire, they will be looking for experience and dedication. The biggest opportunity, however, remains in the service department. Service will be the name of the game in the '90s—and as such, dealers will want skilled service personnel more than ever.

Expect fewer auto dealers as automakers seek to focus on strong dealers requiring less servicing and as dealers combine into mini–retail chains. Today's auto dealer market is no longer the few square miles around the dealership showroom. Enter the Internet as dealers explore the expanded sales opportunities afforded by this new sales/marketing tool. Indeed, Internet buying services have developed, forcing dealers to compete with dealers in other cities. Some industry experts project that by 2000 possibly up to 20% of new automobiles may be bought through the Internet. Some experts forecast that today's 22,000 dealerships may drop to 8,000 within ten years, compared to 49,000 in 1949.

▶ Look for a growing category of auto dealers—used car megastore chains, now in its infancy, which may chip away at traditional auto dealers' used car (and high profit) markets.

With used car sales generating higher sales volume and profit margins than new cars, traditional dealers may be hard pressed to meet challenges from low-key, no-hassle specialist used car megastores. The fragmented used car market may well be reorganized, affecting local used car and new car dealers. In 1995 nearly 13 million vehicles came off 2- to 3-year leases, with dealers offering low interest rates and sweet deals to dispose of inventories. The megastores see an opportunity. Job outlook? Good for experienced salespeople skilled in high service levels.

EMPLOYMENT OUTLOOK: Fair—but very vulnerable to ups and downs in the economy. Relatively bright long-term picture, however.

In 1996, for the first time in 25 years, U.S. automakers began hiring in earnest. Key point: During the massive layoffs of the '80s, the workers that were kept on were those with most seniority. Given this, a huge number of employees are now reaching retirement age—according to one estimate as much as 42% of the total auto industry's workers will be retiring over the next seven years. In fact, according to the University of Michigan, the Big Three will hire up to 170,000 factory workers between now and 2003—with pay ranging from $25,500 to $46,500 a year—not counting often hefty overtime. But these jobs aren't going to just anyone. Ford and Chrysler both have announced that they expect to replace up to about 50% of their workforce over the next decade—which translates into 75,000 workers between them. The key element they're looking for in their new worker: Skills, skills, skills.

Highly skilled employees are the most likely to profit from the new strength of the auto industry. Both Ford and Chrysler are bullish on upgrading their workforce to better compete internationally. The result: In some cases, testing on everything from math to manual dexterity screens prospective employees; those who are hired have more responsibility for quality, and input on redesigning manufacturing and product improvement. There's an increase of college graduates and those with higher degrees at even the lower levels.

Engineers—mechanical, electrical, and industrial—will be in increased demand. At the entry level, requirements are fairly basic: a B.S. degree, gradepoint average above 3.0, and work or co-op experience at a major manufacturer.

Demand for higher-level engineering positions tends to be stable. The automakers, after all, are trying to gain a competitive edge.

As for nonengineering jobs: In the short term, expect to see employment opportunities arise as older blue-collar workers retire. And, in both cases, job opportunities with parts suppliers should be up—this may be one of the hotter areas in the industry.

Another area that looks good is purchasing. With manufacturers becoming extremely cost conscious, they want stable prices.

Jobs Spotlight

Design/Systems Engineers: These individuals are particularly valuable to original equipment suppliers. This is not a huge market, but suppliers who develop long-term relationships with manufacturers will continue to need design/systems engineering.

Automobile Service Personnel: As people hold onto their cars longer, these cars need maintenance. Dealers are also putting more emphasis on their service departments. The dealership and repair shops should enjoy a rise, and long-term prospects look good.

MIS/Factory Automation Personnel: This is not a huge market, but there is a constant need in the industry. Domestic manufacturers are focusing on automated systems, just as their Japanese and transplant counterparts have done, and they need trained people to operate those systems.

Quality Control Personnel: Producing a high-quality product is a key to success these days. Domestic manufacturers, transplants, and suppliers all need skilled manufacturing managers and other personnel skilled in this area.

BEST BETS

Chrysler Corp.
12000 Chrysler Dr.
Highland Park, MI 48288-0001
313/956-5741

Chrysler was tops in its industry on *Fortune* magazine's annual "Most Admired Companies" ranking, and was termed "Company of the Year" by *Forbes* magazine in 1997. Key reason for these kudos? Most experts believe Chrsyler's management is excellent—from the top on down. In addition, the company has a much envied production engineering ability—Chrysler beats out its competitors with quicker new model launches. And success means more than just speed—Chrysler is winning an increasing number of awards.

Chrysler is biggest and best in the fast-growing truck segment of the market; winning over its main rival Ford and GM in terms of sales and profits. Its car divisions aren't as strong—and its main challenge lies in upgrading this segment and working with manufacturing to improve quality across the board. Bottom line: Chrysler looks like it's on a roll.

LEADING AUTOMOTIVE COMPANIES

Acura Division
American Honda Motor Co.
1919 Torrance Blvd.
Torrance, CA 90501-2746
310/783-2000

American Honda Motor Co., Inc.
1919 Torrance Blvd.
Torrance, CA 90501-2746
310/783-2000

American Isuzu Motors, Inc.
2300 Pellisier Pl.
Whittier, CA 90601
310/699-0500

American Suzuki Motor Corp.
3251 E. Imperial Hwy.
Brea, CA 92621-6722
714/996-7040

Audi of America, Inc.
3800 Hamlin Rd.
Auburn Hills, MI

48326
313/340-5000

BMW of North America, Inc.
300 Chestnut Ridge Rd.
Woodcliff Lake, NJ 07675
201/307-4000

Buick Motor Division
General Motors
902 E. Hamilton Ave.
Flint, MI 48550
810/236-5000

Cadillac Motor Car Division
General Motors
4300 S. Saginaw St.
Flint, MI 48507
810/492-4324

Chevrolet Motor Division
General Motors
30007 Van Dyke Ave.
Warren, MI 48093
810/492-8822

Chrysler Corp.
12000 Chrysler Dr.
Highland Park, MI 48288-0001
313/956-5741

Dodge Car & Truck Division
Chrysler Motors Corp.
12000 Chrysler Dr.
Detroit, MI 48288
313/956-5741

Ford Motor Co.
American Road
Detroit, MI 48126
313/322-3000

General Motors Corp.
3044 W. Grand Ave.
Detroit, MI 48202
313/556-5000

Harley-Davidson Inc.
3700 W. Juneau Ave.
Milwaukee, WI 53208
414/342-4680

Honda of America Mfg., Inc.
24000 Honda Pkwy.

Marysville, OH 43040
513/642-5000

**Hyundai
MotorAmerica**
10550 Talbert Ave.
Fountain Valley, CA
92728
714/965-3508

Infiniti Division
Nissan Motor Co.
18501 S. Figueroa St.
Carson, CA 90248
310/532-3111

Jaguar Cars, Inc.
555 MacArthur Blvd.
Mahwah, NJ 07430
201/818-8500

Jeep/Eagle Division
Chrysler Motors Corp.
12000 Chrysler Dr.
Highland Park, MI
48288-1919
313/956-5741

Lexus Division
Toyota Motor Sales
U.S.A., Inc.
19001 S. Western Ave.
Torrance, CA 90501
310/328-2075

**Lincoln-Mercury
Division**
Ford Motor Co.
300 Renaissance Ctr.
Detroit, MI 48243
313/446-4450

**Mazda Motors of
America, Inc.**
7755 Irvine Center Dr.

Irvine, CA 92718
714/727-1990

**Mercedes-Benz of
North America, Inc.**
1 Mercedes Dr.
Montvale, NJ
07645-0350
201/573-0600

**Mitsubishi Motor
Sales of America, Inc.**
6400 W. Katella Ave.
Cypress, CA
90630-0064
714/372-6000

**Navistar International
Corporation**
455 N. City Front Plaza
Chicago, IL 60611
312/836-2000

Nissan Motor Corp.
18501 Figueroa St.
Carson, CA 90248
310/532-3111

Oldsmobile Division
General Motors
920 Townsend St.
Lansing, MI 48921
517/377-5000

Paccar, Inc.
777 106 Ave. NE
Bellevue, WA 98004
206/445-7400

Pontiac Division
General Motors
1 Pontiac Plz.
Pontiac, MI 48340
810/857-5000

**Porsche Cars North
America, Inc.**
100 W. Liberty St.
Reno, NV 89501
702/348-3000

**Range Rover of North
America, Inc.**
P.O. Box 1503
Lanham, MA 20706
301/731-9040

Saab Cars USA, Inc.
35 Executive Blvd.
Orange, CT 06477
203/795-2222

Saturn Corp.
100 Saturn Pkwy.
Spring Hill, TN 37174
615/486-5731

**Subaru of America,
Inc.**
2235 Rt. 70 W.
Cherry Hill, NJ 08002
609/488-8500

**Toyota Motor Sales
U.S.A., Inc.**
19001 S. Western Ave.
Torrance, CA 90501
310/618-4000

**Volkswagen of
America, Inc.**
3800 Hamlin Rd.
Auburn Hills, MI
48326
313/340-5000

**Volvo Cars of North
America**
7 Volvo Dr.
Rockleigh, NJ 07647
201/768-7300

WHERE TO GO FOR MORE INFORMATION

AUTOMOTIVE INDUSTRY ASSOCIATIONS

**American Automobile
Manufacturers**

Association, Inc.
7430 Second Ave.

Detroit, MI 48202
313/872-4311

**American
International
Automobile Dealers
Association**
8400 W. Park Dr.
McLean, VA 22102
703/821-7000

**American Society of
Body Engineers**
2127 15 Mile Rd.,
Ste. A
Sterling Heights, MI
48310
810/268-8360

**Automotive Parts and
Accessories**

Association
4600 E. West Hwy.
3rd Fl.
Bethesda, MD 20814
301/654-6664

**National Automobile
Dealers Association**
8400 Westpark Dr.
McLean, VA 22102
703/821-7000

**National Automotive
Parts Association**
2999 Circle 75 Pkwy.
Atlanta, GA 30339
770/956-2200

**National Independent
Automobile Dealers
Association**
2521 Brown Blvd.,
Ste. 100
Arlington, TX 76006
817/640-3838

**Society of Automotive
Engineers**
400 Commonwealth
Dr.
Warrendale, PA 15096
412/776-4841
(Puts out monthly
magazine, *Automotive
Engineering,* for
members.)

AUTOMOTIVE INDUSTRY DIRECTORIES

*Automotive News
Market Data Book*
1400 Woodbridge Ave.
Detroit, MI 48207
313/446-6000

(Annual, special issue
of *Automotive News;* in
addition to statistics,
includes extensive
listings of auto

manufacturers,
suppliers, etc., that
include addresses,
contact names.)

AUTOMOTIVE INDUSTRY MAGAZINES

Automotive Executive
National Auto Dealers
Association
8400 Westpark Dr.
McLean, VA 22102
703/821-7150
(Monthly paper sent to
members of NADA, as
well as financial
personnel.)

Automotive Industries
2600 Fisher Bldg.
Detroit, MI 48202

313/875-2090
(Monthly magazine for
design, management,
manufacturing, and
sales personnel.)

Automotive Marketing
1 Chilton Way
Radnor, PA 19089
610/964-4395
(Monthly magazine for
parts/accessories
retailers,
manufacturers.)

Automotive News
1400 Woodbridge Ave.
Detroit, MI 48207
313/446-6000
(Weekly newspaper
considered the industry
"bible"; covers all
phases of the
industry—
manufacturing,
marketing, sales, etc.;
includes extensive
help-wanted section.)

AVIATION

INDUSTRY OUTLOOK: good long-term prospects as domestic and foreign passenger travel shows steady increases and as the industry restructures itself into two distinct segments. Short term—hot competition, price wars.

Once again, commercial airlines are making money, as passengers flock into airline terminals. Traffic should show increases to 2005, with some experts projecting this to last to 2014. In general, expect moderate fare increases to boost earnings, supplementing domestic air growth and the even greater international air growth.

Increasingly, this is a two-segment industry, split between the few major carriers and the many smaller, newer, low-cost airlines.

Where the major carriers are concerned, expect to see continued retrenchment, emphasis on cost-controls, yield management policies (charging different prices for passengers on the same flight), concentration on key markets, and the abandoning of risky expansion. Along these lines, they will also continue to pull back from their head-to-head fight with their smaller competitors. In effect, instead of trying to imitate these low-fare airlines, the large airlines will get back to business as usual . . . before deregulation. Rumors of merger talks between the majors persist, as well as transatlantic alliances with European carriers.

The lower-cost airlines will remain on the move—expanding into new markets, adding routes, and generally beefing up business. In addition, expect to see new entrants into this market, increasing competition.

Job opportunities, albeit at lower salaries than the heretofore industry standard, may well be found with the expected flourishing of no-frills carriers. Also a source for job opportunities: commuter airlines which will move into the routes dropped by the larger airlines.

A LOOK BACK

▶ **The '80s were turbulent, taking the industry from deregulation, to heavy competition, to a frenzy of mergers and acquisitions.**

Deregulation brought about an increase in the number of airlines, including small upstarts that shook the larger established airlines. Competition was cutthroat as airlines entered into price slashing to attract passengers, and profits sank.

Then came consolidation: the upstarts were bought out; large airlines snapped up regional carriers; commuter airlines were swallowed.

▶ **Next it was high flying—as the emergence of the hub system and mergers ended the price wars—then a slump as the country entered a recession.**

By the end of the '80s, airlines were ringing up record profits, as mergers cut down on the number of competing airlines and the institution of the hub system (in which one or two airlines become primary carriers at an airport) eliminated route duplication.

But the recession caused a sharp downturn in air traffic, and in 1991 the industry went through the worst year it had faced since deregulation. The triple whammy of the Persian Gulf War, high fuel prices, and plunging tourism rates sent airlines into a tailspin. Some airlines, including Pan Am, Eastern, and Midway, went belly up, others filed for bankruptcy protection, and others just waited for the better times to return. Airlines had a grim year in 1992, as traffic dropped further, leading to industry losses of up to $1.7 billion. And a lukewarm 1993 saw airline industry leaders hoping the worst was over—but still facing numerous challenges, including supply in excess of demand.

By 1995 the industry was well into the black—for the first time since 1989—as the economy improved and passenger traffic increased. The trend appears to have continued through 1997. Analysts believe that this trend should proceed for the next few years, with a continuation of the economy's growth and, possibly, some fare stability.

WHAT'S NEXT

▶ Competition—always hot—will remain so.

It's a given in the airline industry—even when air traffic rises. Depending upon the state of the economy, expect to see the airlines duking it out as usual. One question: With air traffic up and profits following suit in the recent past, will airlines resurrect the fare wars of the past? Or will the newly retrenched industry stick to cost-cutting as a way of keeping profits up?

▶ Expect to see an influx of new low-fare airlines.

It's already happening: in 1994 and 1995, the U.S. Department of Transportation certified 22 new carriers. In early 1996 eight more were certified, and it looked like others were going to do so. The bottom line? This flurry of activity should continue over the short term. As such, there should be an increase in the number of low-fare airlines, flying point-to-point for relatively low fares. In addition, watch as the major airlines accommodate these new airlines, rather than compete head-on with them. For example, American has set up a consulting division to help newer, smaller airlines; in addition, it takes reservations, does maintenance work, and handles computing for them.

An employment note: Many of these upstarts will rely on outsourcing for much of their staffing—hiring companies to handle such duties as tickets, baggage, accounting, scheduling, arrival, departure information, and more. Given this, these outsourcing companies may offer better employment opportunities than the airlines themselves.

▶ International travel should remain strong for the larger carriers—but competition will be tough there as well.

The international market has been of increasing importance to U.S. airlines, with the giants like American, Delta, and United snapping up international routes.

Now competition is increasing, especially with the opening up of Europe's borders and the growing importance of the Asian market. Expect U.S. airlines to go head to head with their foreign counterparts, battling for customers, market share, and routes. Among their moves: the addition of European and Pacific Rim flights; improved passenger service to rival the service of foreign carriers.

This new internationalization of the airline industry is pointing to increased career opportunities for people with international business backgrounds and foreign-language ability.

▶ **Watch for continued industry globalization, marked by joint ventures, marketing agreements, and other team arrangements.**

Increased cooperation between companies is one way of coping with increased global competition. While early 1992 talks between British Airways, KLM Royal Dutch Airlines, and Northwest Airlines concerning a merger to form a global carrier went nowhere, the issue is far from dead. This remains an interesting long-term event to watch for.

Already, more carriers are becoming interdependent to maintain a competitive edge. Expect to see more companies enter into joint marketing arrangements, enabling them to offer their customers better service, enhanced routes, and the like.

EMPLOYMENT OUTLOOK: Hot competition expected.

Many experts, including the federal government, expect tough competition for jobs over the next few years—especially for pilots. Reasons: Mergers that affected the industry resulted in fewer carriers—and more out-of-work people looking for new jobs. In addition, with defense cutbacks, more pilots have left the armed forces. Finally, computerized flight management systems on new aircraft have cut back on the need for flight engineers—and the use of larger planes has increased productivity—and, again, cut back on the need for more pilots. The bottom line: More qualified pilots than there are available jobs. Nevertheless, with salaries for experienced pilots as high as $190,000, the profession retains an allure. Key to success: Experience—especially with the newer aircraft. Given this, pilots from the armed forces typically have an edge.

The outlook is brighter for flight attendants. This career has a high turnover rate, and while it has come down from the past, many people still leave their flight attendants' jobs each year, resulting in thousands of job openings. This is one reason the occupation should grow faster than average through the rest of the decade. Best qualifications to have: two years of college and experience dealing with the public in some capacity, such as sales.

As for aircraft mechanics, the outlook is varied. For more information, see page 199.

More generally: International opportunities may be stronger than those in other areas because of the international expansion so many domestic airlines have been going through. In addition, there may be new job opportunities arising due to the growth of the no-frills carriers. The only downside here: salaries will possibly be lower than previous industry standards at these lower-end airlines.

JOBS SPOTLIGHT

APPLICATIONS DEVELOPERS: More airlines are switching applications that don't require a centralized database (like crew scheduling, airport check-in, and dispatching) to PC local-area networks (LANs). Due to this, airlines are using applications developers with networking backgrounds to facilitate this changeover. Requirements: computer experience, network experience, general business skills, and airline experience (it is difficult to break in with experience from another industry).

BEST BETS

Southwest Airlines
PO Box 3661
2702 Love Field Dr.
Dallas, TX 75235-1611
214/904-4000

An airline that has carved out a niche for itself by offering frequent short-hop flights at low prices, Southwest looks like a winner. In 1997, it was chosen number one among airline companies in *Fortune* magazine's annual most-admired corporations survey, and for good reason. The past few years have seen it through a period of growth: It was one of the few airlines to pull out a profit in 1990; it has been expanding routes and adding flights; it keeps a tight rein on operating costs. Southwest also has an excellent reputation as an employer. Employee morale is consistently high; staffers talk about the camaraderie they feel between themselves and management. (It's so strong that a third of the employees actually took voluntary pay cuts to cover the high cost of airline fuel during the Gulf War.) One reason for this loyalty is job security. Management keeps staffing lean, so there is no need for layoffs. Finally, Southwest is well known for a sense of fun that runs through the company, from the CEO (who dropped in on maintenance hangars at 2:00 A.M. dressed like Klinger from "MASH") to flight personnel (who entertain passengers with skits, contests, and the like). The one drawback? Southwest is reportedly selective in its hiring practices.

TAKE A LOOK AT:

Western Pacific Airlines
2 So. Tejon St., #400
Colorado Springs, CO 80903
719/473-7737

Remember America West? Out of the failure of this small airline, comes its former founder with a new start-up airline called Western Pacific. It's now a 12-plane medium haul carrier. CEO and founder Edward Beauvais says he's learned from his mistakes in the past, and this time he's got some strong advantages. Western Pacific is based in Colorado Springs, near Denver, Colorado. Key advantage: many people are avoiding the expensive Denver International Airport (28 miles away from Denver) and opting for the Colorado Springs airport. Western Pacific is expanding into Atlanta, San Jose, San Antonio, and Nashville. Some more good news: the airline is hitting profitability—and in today's climate of high chief executive salaries and luxurious life-styles, you can say at least one thing about Western Pacific—its founder lives in a rented home—he's got his money in the company.

TOP NATIONAL AND REGIONAL AIRLINES

Alaska Airlines
19300 Pacific Hwy. S.
Seattle, WA 98188
206/433-3200

Aloha Airlines
371 Aokea Pl.
Honolulu, HI 96819
808/244-9071

American Airlines
Box 619616
Mail Drop 5106
Dallas Ft. Worth
Airport, TX
75261-9616
817/967-1234

Continental Airlines
2929 Allen Pkwy.
Houston, TX 77019
713/834-5000
Fax 713/590-2150

Delta Airlines
Building 2
Hartsfield-Atlanta
International Airport
Atlanta, GA 30320
404/715-2501

Northwest Airlines
Minneapolis-St.Paul
Airport
5101 Northwest Dr.
St. Paul, MN
55111-3034
612/726-2111

Southwest Airlines
2702 Love Field Dr.
Dallas, TX 75235-1611
214/904-4000

Tower Air
JFK International
Airport
Hangar 17
Jamaica, NY 11430
718/553-4300

**Transworld Airlines
Inc.—TWA**
1 City Centre
515 No. 6 St.
St. Louis, MO 63101
314/567-6778

**United Airlines—
UAL**
1200 Algonquin Rd.
Arlington Heights, IL
60005
708/952-4000

US Airways
2345 Crystal Dr.
Crystal Park Four
Arlington, VA 22227
703/418-5139

**Western Pacific
Airlines**
3 So. Tejon St., #400
Colorado Springs, CO
80903
718/473-7737

World Airways
13873 Park Center Rd.
Herndon, VA 22071
703/834-9200
(Contract flight, charter passenger, and cargo.)

TOP AIR FREIGHT AND FREIGHT FORWARDING COMPANIES

**Airborne Freight
Corp.**
3101 Western Ave.
Seattle, WA 98111
206/285-4600

**Air Express
International Corp.**
120 Tokeneke Rd.
Darien, CT 06820
203/655-7900

**Amerford
International Corp.**
21801 Merrick Blvd.
Jamaica, NY 11413
718/528-0800

**Burlington Air
Express**
18200 Von Karman
Ave.
Irvine, CA 92715
714/752-4000
**Continental Airlines
Cargo Division**
Gateway II, Suite 300
15333 JFK Blvd.
Houston, TX 77032
713/987-6661
Danzas-Northern Air
3650 131 Ave. SE
Newport Tower,
Ste. 700
Bellevue, WA 98006
206/649-9339

DHL Airways
333 Twin Dolphin Dr.
Redwood City, CA
94065
415/593-7474
**Emery Air Frieght
Corp.**
3350 W. Bayshore Rd.
Palo Alto, CA
94303-0986
415/855-9100
**Evergreen
International Airlines**
3850 Three Mile Ln.
McMinnville, OR
97128-9496
503/472-0011

Federal Express
2005 Corporate Ave.
Memphis, TN 38132
901/369-3600
**Southern Air
Transport**
6355 N.W. 36 St.
Miami, FL 33166
305/871-5171
United Parcel Service
55 Glenlake Pkwy. N.E.
Atlanta, GA 30328
770/828-6000
United Van Lines
One United Dr.
Fenton, MO 63026
314/326-3100

WHERE TO GO FOR MORE INFORMATION

(For more information sources relating to the Aviation industry, check listings under "Aerospace," page 225; "Technical Careers," page 196; and "Engineers," page 50. For information related to air cargo, also see listings under "Transportation," page 470.)

AVIATION INDUSTRY ASSOCIATIONS

**Aeronautical Repair
Station Association**
121 N. Henry St.
Alexandria, VA 22314
703/739-9543
**Air Line Employees
Association**
6520 Cicero Ave.
Bedford Park, IL 60638
708/563-9999
(Puts out *Job
Opportunity Bulletin,* a
monthly publication
listing job openings in
all areas of aviation.)
**Air Traffic Control
Association**

2300 Clarendon Blvd.,
Suite 711
Arlington, VA 22201
703/522-5717
**Air Transport
Association of
America**
1301 Pennsylvania Ave.
NW
Suite 1100
Washington, DC 20004
202/626-4000
**American Association
of Airport Executives**
4212 King St.
Alexandria, VA 22302
703/824-0500

(Puts out publications
including *Airport
Report* and *Airport
Report Express,* which
contain help-wanted
ads.)
**Future Aviation
Professionals of
America**
497 Massachusetts Blvd.
Atlanta, GA 30337
770/997-8097
(Offers a range of
career assistance for
members, including
putting out publications
that include job

listings, including *Pilot Job Reports* and *Flight Attendant Job Reports,* and maintaining computerized job banks for mechanics/technicians, etc., and for pilots.)

General Aviation Manufacturers Association
1400 K St., NW, Suite 801

Washington, DC 20005
202/393-1500

National Air Carrier Association
1730 M St., NW
Washington, DC 20036
202/833-8200

National Air Transportation Association
4226 King St.
Alexandria, VA 22302
703/845-9000

National Business Aircraft Association
1200 18th St., NW
Washington, DC 20036
202/783-9000

Regional Airline Association
1101 Connecticut Ave., NW
Washington, DC 20036
202/857-1170

AVIATION INDUSTRY DIRECTORIES

Annual Report of the Commuter Regional Airline Industry
Regional Airline Association
1101 Connecticut Ave., NW
Washington, DC 20036
202/857-1170

Official Airline Guide: North American Edition; Official Airline Guide: Worldwide Edition
Official Airlines Guides, Inc.
2000 Clearwater Dr.

Oak Brook, IL 60521
800/323-3537

World Aviation Directory
McGraw-Hill
1200 G St., 2nd Fl.
Washington, DC 20005
202/383-3700

AVIATION INDUSTRY MAGAZINES

Air Cargo News
P.O. Box 777
Jamaica, NY 11431
718/479-0716
(Monthly publication for those involved in cargo—freight forwarders, cargo airline personnel, customs brokers, etc.)

Air Line Pilot
P.O. Box 1169
Herndon, VA 22070
703/689-4182
(Monthly magazine sent to members of the

Air Line Pilots Association.)

Airport Press
P.O. Box 300879
Jamaica, NY 11430
718/244-6788
(Monthly aimed at airline officials, airport personnel, freight forwarders, etc.)

Air Transport World
1350 Connecticut Ave., NW
Suite 902
Washington, DC 20036

202/659-8500
(Monthly magazine designed for air transport executives and supervisors.)

Aviation Employment Monthly
Box 8286
Department A
Saddle Brook, NJ 07662
800/543-5201
(Lists job openings worldwide for pilots, engineers, technicians, A&Ps.)

Business &
Commercial Aviation
4 International Dr.
Rye Brook, NY 10573
914/939-0300
(Monthly publication
for airline owners and
operators, aviation

managers, operations
and maintenance
personnel, etc.)

Professional Pilot
3014 Colvin St.
Alexandria, VA 22314
703/370-0606

(Monthly publication
for pilots in all
phases of aviation—
commercial, commuter,
corporate, charter, and
military—as well as
airport operators.)

BANKING

INDUSTRY OUTLOOK: Short term: good with a continuation of a low-interest climate and high loan demand, as the industry reduces expenses, develops new, profitable, fee-based products—insurance, securities underwriting, and other financial services—and as mergers/acquisitions continue apace.

As noted, **commerical banks** in the short term seem likely to have good prospects. Merger activity should continue as they strive to reduce operational overhead and achieve economies of scale. Candidates: other commercial banks or savings and loan associations, with financial service firms as additional candidates as banks try to stem penetrations by these firms into the banks' primary markets. Commercial bank mergers will result in a two-tiered banking system: the giants and the much smaller regional and community banks. Look for further consolidations, more layoffs as banks seek to further lower costs, and more technological change as banks seek different ways of earning a dollar. Merger activity among **savings and loan associations** should continue, as the thrift segment of the banking industry feels the pressure of a dwindling market. Traditional borrowers—home owners—increasingly seek mortgages without regard to source, from such nonthrifts as commercial banks or mortgage brokers and bankers and often from outside their geographic service area. Merger candidates: other savings and loans, commercial banks, mortgage banks.

A LOOK BACK

▶ 1995–1997: merger years.

The merger between money-center banks Chemical Banking and the venerable Chase Manhattan symbolized that the old days of banking were truly gone forever. Among the other mergers making news in the past few years: Fleet Financial with Shawmut National and National Westminster, First Union with First Fidelity, PNC Bank with Midlantic, First Chicago with NBD Bancorp, National City with Integra Financial, CoreStates with Meridian Bancorp, Wells Fargo with First Interstate, Bank of Boston with Baybanks, NationsBank with Barnett Banks. Before this latest round, in other mergers Chemical had already absorbed Texas Commerce Bancshares, then Horizon Bancorps, then Manufacturers Hanover.

The rationale for these mergers? There are several. First, economy of scale. Banks can increase capital and simultaneously eliminate costly duplicate branches and functions. Also: diversification of assets and increase in market share—banks can enter more markets and spread their risks. In other words, banks can enter more markets more effectively—and position themselves for the very tough competition expected in the rest of the 1990s. However, in the short term, many of these mergers resulted in short-term cost increases, as banks paid the price of temporarily duplicated services, buy-out provisions, etc.

More to the point, what's good for the goose is not neccessarily so for the gander. Just as top banking executives applaud the merger moves, many employees are finding that megamergers mean megalayoffs. Bottom line: In 1995, 10 mergers alone resulted in announced 45,000 job cuts, an over 5% reduction in personnel, with the Chase Manhattan deal representing 12,000 jobs. For those remaining, there have been problems with the merging of different corporate cultures as well.

▶ **The 1990s have been, in general, good for banks.**

During the past several years, banks have seen substantial profit growth and improvement in assets—and coupled with this many have seen their stock prices soar.

How did all this happen? This certainly didn't seem to be the future back in 1991, when banks were said to be heading for the doldrums. Experts talked about the substantial number of bad loans on the books at banks, the consequence of heavy lending in oil, real estate and LBOs (leveraged buy-outs—whereby a buyer borrows the bulk of the money to purchase a company and promises to repay the loan out of revenues from the company.) By 1991, it had appeared that the drop in real estate and oil prices and faltering LBOs meant more bank failures would be the order of the day. Too many people and institutions wouldn't be able to repay their loans to the banks, and so many banks would go under, saddled under the weight of an increasing bad loan portfolio.

And to a degree, this began to happen. Bank failures reached 1,500 by 1992.

But thanks in part to Alan Greenspan at the Federal Reserve, the government kept interest rates low in the early 1990s—that made it easier for banks to weather the bad loans on their books. Meanwhile the "spread"—the difference between the interest rate at which banks get their money and the rate at which they lend it out—began to rise. And smart bank managers began charging more for banking services—as anyone who's ever bounced a check could tell you. Also, in the midst of the mergers came an increased emphasis on cost-control. Banks started emphasizing managing their capital cost-effectively, and as managers watched stock prices rise, they began emphasizing stockholder return.

The bottom line: bank profitablity started rising . . . and kept rising until those bad loan problems of the past looked very minor indeed. In fact, estimates were that banks had *billions* of extra dollars that they no longer needed to keep in reserve to meet those bad loans of the past.

Suddenly, many banks were faced with a nice new managerial problem—what to do with all that extra money. Of course, where there's good news, bad news often follows, and by 1996 some problems were once again on the horizon, particularly due to the closing of the short-term and long-term interest rate differences. That means banks have to borrow at money (at short-term rates) that's almost as costly as the money they're lending over the long term—leaving little room for more profit. But all in all, bankers could look back on the previous years as good ones—for the industry, that is.

WHAT'S NEXT

▶ Leaner, meaner banks will still be the order the year.

The banking watchwords will continue to be: watch your capital. Cut costs, raise fees. In some cases, another watchword will be *decrease* capital—as some banks continue to buy back stock using their profits to increase net shareholder returns. Other banks have been taking a more growth-oriented route—buying or merging with other banks, investing in new technologies.

But more changes are on the horizon . . .

▶ Will loan problems come back again?

For the short term, probably not in the commercial sector. And if they do, banks still have a lot of cash in reserve. But there are (slightly) nagging concerns again about loan quality. Commercial loans have been increasing rapidly, and although lending terms are much stronger than in the 1980s, more borrowers may default as the economy weakens.

Consumer credit looks weaker—consumer debt is near a 10-year high and any economic downturn could yield some problems. Bottom line: banking as a whole looks poised to weather any potential minor loan problems well.

▶ Regulatory barriers will continue to weaken over the long term, but look for short-term snafus.

The end of the Glass-Steagal Act, which long ago kept banking and most other financial services separate, is probably in the cards. The end result: Banks will participate more fully in the securities business and insurance. (They already do to some extent, especially via various legal artifices.) More importantly: look eventually at the legalization of insurance companies or securities firms purchase of banks—or vice versa.

On the other hand, it's not all over yet. In fact, look for some agitation for *more* regulation, as other industries seek to weaken banking's forays onto their turf. Already, the National Association of Securities Dealers put forth a proposal limiting securities sales in bank lobbies. And deregulation talks have been recently stymied by failure to agree on the lines between banking and insurance. Bottom line: the artificial barriers that have kept banking separate from other areas of finance will eventually disappear—but don't hold your breath for it to happen.

▶ Mergers will continue.

Even as banks digest their latest acquisitions, look for mergers to continue. The hottest targets: Midwestern banks and thrifts, other regional banks. Some predict that by the end of the 1990s, mergers will have changed the map of U.S. banking, with 50 banks controlling 80% of banking compared to 56% in 1995. Result: Maybe a dozen or so huge national banks and a larger number of regional and community banks.

The big players will operate—and advertise—nationwide, seeking, like a McDonald's or a Wendy's, to establish a national identity. Others, like Citicorp, with over 40,000 employees overseas in 3,300 worldwide branches, will seek an *international* brand identity. The super-regionals will operate on a slightly smaller scale—but don't forget the community banks. Some of these small banks, run by conservative old-line bankers, will do surprisingly well. Key: Making loans is a personal business. And local bankers, who *know* the local marketplace and local personalities, will more than likely weather any economic storms and benefit from economic recoveries of the future.

▶ Changing demand for bank services.

Banks used to be the major lenders to major corporations. Today that has changed. Healthy large corporations can raise money directly on the capital markets, bypassing banks and bypassing bank fees.

So what will banks do? Answer: go where the business is. Some banks are now specializing in niche markets. For example, Bankers Trust has transformed itself into something of a Wall Street firm, emphasizing wholesale banking and securities and derivatives trading. Others are focusing on retail mortgage lending, or an entire new range of retail services, going against finance companies in their quest for new business. And others are focusing on transactions processing—or in other words, the basic job of moving money. One prime player in this area is State Street Boston, which handles billions of dollars of mutual fund money.

And of course, banks are also beginning to move into the lucrative, fee-based mutual fund business themselves, banking on their customers' desire for convenience—being able to have both an account and investments under one roof. One key advantage for bank mutual funds: a built-in distribution network. So far, this foray into the mutual fund business appears to be working well.

▶ Look for more technological innovation—and employee layoffs.

Cost cutting to some degree means cutting human beings from employee payrolls. For example, retail bankers are anxiously trying to get customers to use electronic banking—and in so doing get them out of the expensive branch offices. Bottom line: look for more layoffs of tellers and bank clerks. Between 1990 and 1995, over 40,000 teller positions were eliminated; it is estimated that over 75% of cash is being dispensed by bank ATMs as the industry shifts to an emphasis on electronic/telephone transactions.

▶ More competition from nonbank financial services firms.

It almost goes without saying. Banks are entering a phase of heavy competition with insurance companies, financial services firms, and corporations. No area of banking seems safe—AT&T, GM, GE, Ford, Prudential, and Fidelity have entered the lucrative credit-card market—and many banks may end up selling off this business. Some mutual-fund companies, like Fidelity, also offer services such as check writing and loans against fund balances, which, barring some differences in terminology and mechanics due to law, sound very much like regular banking services. Even businesses that have been banking focal points, such as payment processing, are being invaded by nonbank companies.

EMPLOYMENT OUTLOOK: Mixed—some areas looking good; others (especially lower-level positions) look weaker.

First the bad news: In fact, according to Andersen Consulting and the Bank Administration Institute, by 2000 the number of bank jobs will drop by 250,000 from the current level of about 1.49 million. Half of these cuts will involve tellers and administrators, the other half will be certain technicians and managers. In addition to mergers, technology is leading to job cuts. As computerized banking and automatic teller machines are more commonly used, the old days of branch banks with their staffs of tellers and managers is over—which means, of course, a cut in jobs. In fact, some experts estimate that up to 450,000 banking jobs will disappear over the next five to ten years.

Now the good news. Since the banking industry is so huge, many jobs will open as workers simply retire or transfer to other jobs; moreover, certain areas are projected to grow substantially: these include computer, mathematical and operations research specialists, which the government projects will grow much faster than average by the year 2005. Best general area: mortgage banking and personal credit. Best nontechnical specialties: financial managers, loan officers.

As stated before, banks are looking for sales- and marketing-oriented people. Since the culture of banking will change, so too will the ideal candidates. According to *Banker's Monthly,* the old idea of a "tenure track" at a bank—safe, stable working conditions in exchange for loyalty and a "don't rock the boat" attitude—will change.

Opportunities are likely to increase in distribution (solicitation of new loans) and new product development, as banks aggressively seek new business. Therefore, look for an emphasis on more aggressive sales-oriented personalities, and greater flexibility, a willingness to learn new techniques and services. In addition, as more banks focus on mutual funds and other investment vehicles as a way of bringing in more money, expect to see a rise in demand for people with investment experience.

One advantage for liberal arts graduates: Banking is a field in which entry-level employees can get free training that almost matches a financial MBA. Competition is expected to remain extremely tough, however, as many people meet entry-level qualifications for banking positions. For example, according to *The New York Times*, the Bank of New York recently received 3,000 applications for 35 positions in its training program.

Bankers with strong credit experience will be increasingly in demand. Reason: When problems hit, banks become more concerned with creditworthiness.

JOBS SPOTLIGHT

SALES AND MARKETING SPECIALISTS: Increased competition and new services will make this area relatively strong for the long term. As financial service companies enter the banking area, banks must aggressively compete to increase—or maintain—market share. Key areas: brokerage and mutual-fund sales, as banks compete with mutual funds and brokerage houses; marketing research; product development. Investment Manager: As mentioned above, banks are competing with financial services companies—as such, are expanding their mutual fund and pension fund businesses. This means that investment managers are becoming increasingly in demand. One example: In 1995, J.P. Morgan Investment Management hired over 100 new investment managers, and planned to add even more. Key qualifications: At the minimum, a degree in economics or business; but an MBA gives candidates the edge.

▶ **Derivatives Trader:**

See page 343.

PRIVATE BANKING: This niche focuses on developing bank relationships with well-heeled individuals, entrepreneurs, principal stockholders, and others who may have specialized banking needs and large balances. So far this area has not grown as predicted, probably because the specialty is relatively new. This is a profitable and potentially high-growth situation, especially in many metropolitan areas where many wealthy individuals live—such as Florida's Palm Beach, California's Palm Springs, Georgia's Buckhead section of Atlanta, and the like. Some advantages: retail bank clients typically generate about $1,000 in annual revenue to a bank; private banking clients generate $5,000; it is not capital intensive but more fee-income oriented—and it's very customer-service oriented. Most major banks have now established private banking groups, which provide a good source of income and a targeted market for new bank services. Best for people with strong personal as well as banking skills.

BEST BETS

Norwest Corp
Norwest Ctr.
Minneapolis, MN 55479-1016
612/667-1234

A truly modern retail bank well-poised to handle the challenges of the late '90s. Norwest has been highly praised by many industry experts—and for good reason. In 1996, it ranked second only to J.P. Morgan among banks in *Fortune* magazine's most admired corporation survey. Key strength: Its strong focus on selling loans and other services, which has made Norwest come on very strong. When and if interstate banking gets approved, Norwest should be a big winner . . . which points to possible long-term employment possibilities. In addition, one of its subsidiaries, Norwest Financial, has also been growing and going strong. One final note—and a big plus for employees: managerial and nonmanagerial employees who have achieved certain goals are allowed to be part of the Invest Norwest program—which allows them to buy brokerage-fee-free stock. Over 28% of Norwest employees are part of this program, with employees owning about 9% of the bank's stock shares.

TOP BANKS

AmSouth Bancorp	Associated Banc-Corp	Banc One
1900 Fifth Ave.	112 N. Adams St.	100 E. Broad St.
Birmingham, AL 35203	Green Bay, WI 54301	Columbus, OH 43215
205/320-7151	414/433-3166	614/248-5944

BancOne
201 N. Central Ave.
Phoenix. AZ 85004
602/221-2900

Bancorp Hawaii
130 Merchant St.
Honolulu, HI 96813
808-537-8111

BankAmerica
555 California St.
San Francisco, CA
94104
415/622-3456

Bank of Boston
1 Financial Center
Boston, MA 02111
617/434-2200

Bank of New York
48 Wall St.
New York, NY 10286
212/495-1784

Bank South
55 Marietta St., N.W.
Atlanta, GA 30303
404/525-1859

Bankers Trust NY
280 Park Ave.
New York, NY 10017
212/250-2500

Barnett Banks
50 N. Laura St.
Jacksonville, FL 32202
904/791-7720

Baybanks
175 Federal St.
Boston, MA 02110
617/482-1040

**Boatmen's
Bancshares**
800 Market St.
St. Louis, MO 63101
314/466-6000

BOK Financial
1 Williams St.

Tulsa, OK 74172
918/588-6000

CCB Financial
111 S. Corcoran St.
Durham, NC 27701
919/683-7777

**Central Fidelity
Banks**
1021 E. Cary St.
Richmond, VA 23219
804/697-6700

Centura Banks
134 N. Church St.
Rocky Mount, NC
27804
919/977-4400

**Charter One
Financial**
1215 Superior Ave.
Cleveland, OH 44114
216/589-8320

**Chase Manhattan
Corp.**
270 Park Ave.
New York, NY 10017
212/270-6000

Citicorp
399 Park Ave.
New York, NY 10043
800/285-3000

City National Bank
400 N. Roxbury Dr.
Beverly Hills, CA
90210
310/550-5400

Collective Bancorp
716 W. White Horse
Pike
Cologne, NJ 08213
609/965-1234

Comerica
500 Wodward Ave.
Detroit, MI 48226
313/222-3300

**Commerce
Bancshares**
1000 Walnut St.
Kansas City, MO
64106
816/234-2000

Continental Bank
400 Skokie Blvd.
Northbrook, IL 60002
708/559-1226

CoreStates Financial
13 Chestnut St.
Philadelphia, PA 19107
215/973-3827

Crestar Financial
919 E. Main St.
Richmond, VA 23219
804/782-5000

Cullen/Frost Bankers
100 W. Houston St.
Houston, TX 78205
210/220-4011

Dauphin Deposit
213 Market St.
Harrisburg, PA 17101
717/255-2121

Fifth Third Bancorp
38 Fountain Sq. Plz.
Cincinnati, OH 45202
513/579-5300

**First Alabama
Bancshares**
P.O. Box 10247
Birmingham, AL 35202
205/326-7060

**First of America
Bancorp**
211 S. Rose St.
Kalamazoo, MI 49007
616/376-9000

First American Corp.
300 Union St.
Nashville, TN 37237
615/748-2000

Firstar
777 E. Wisconsin Ave.
Milwaukee, WI 53202
414/765-4321

First Bank System
90 S. 6 St.
Minneapolis, MN
55402-4302
612/973-1111

First Chicago
1 First National Plz.
Chicago, IL 60670
312/732-4000

First Commercial
400 W. Capitol Ave.
Little Rock, AR 72201
501/371-7000

First Empire State
1 M&T Plz.
Buffalo, NY 14203
716/842-5445

**First Fidelity
Bancorporation**
Church & Elm Sts.
New Haven, CT 06510
203/929-5552

First Financial Corp.
1305 Main St.
Stevens Point, WI
54481
715/341-0400

First Hawaiian
1132 Bishop St.
Honolulu, HI 96813
808/525-6386

**First Interstate
Bancorp**
633 W. 5 St.
Los Angeles, CA
90071
213/614-3001

First Merit
106 S. Main St.
Akron, OH 44308-1444
216/996-6300

**First Tennessee
National**
165 Madison Ave.
Memphis, TN 38103
901/523-4444

First Union
301 S. College St.
Charlotte, NC 28202
704/374-6565

First Union Bank
30 S. Jefferson St.
Roanoke, VA 24011
703/563-7000

First Virginia Banks
6400 Arlington Blvd.
Falls Church, VA
22042-2336
703/241-4000

Fleet Financial Group
50 Kennedy Plz.
Providence, RI 02903
401/278-5800

Hibernia
313 Carondelet St.
New Orleans, LA
70161
504/533-3333

**Huntington
Bancshares**
41 S. High St.
Columbus, OH 43215
614/480-8300

**Integra Financial
Corp.**
4 PPG Pl.
Pittsburgh, PA
15222-5408
412/644-7669

Key Bank
66 S. Pearl St.
Albany, NY 12207
518/486-8500

**Key Bank of
Washington**
1119 Pacific Ave.

Tacoma, WA 98411
206/593-3600

KeyCorp
127 Public Sq.
Cleveland, OH
44114-1306
216/689-3000

La Salle Bank FSB
55 S. Kedzie St.
Chicago, IL 60629
312/726-8915

Magna Group
1401 S. Brentwood
Blvd.
St. Louis, MO
63144-1401
314/963-2500

Marshall & Illsley
770 N. Water St.
Milwaukee, WI 53202
414/765-7899

Mellon Bank
1 Mellon Bank Ctr.
Pittsburgh, PA
15258-0001
412/234-5000

**Mercantile
Bancorporation**
721 Locust St.
St. Louis, MO 63101
314/425-2525

**Mercantile
Bankshares**
2 Hopkins Plz.
Baltimore, MD 21201
410/237-5900

Meridian Bancorp
35 N. 6 St.
Reading, PA 19601
610/655-2000

Midlantic
505 Thornall St.
Edison, NJ 08837
908/321-8000

J. P. Morgan
60 Wall St.
New York, NY
10260-0060
212/483-2323

National Bank of South Carolina
1426 Main St.
Columbus, SC 29226
803/765-3000

National City
1900 E. 9th St.
Cleveland, OH
44114-3484
216/575-2000

National City Bank of Indiana
101 W. Washington St.
Indianapolis, IN 46204
317/267-7000

NationsBank
101 S. Tryon St.
Charlotte, NC 28255
704/386-5000

NBD Bancorp
611 Woodward Ave.
Detroit, MI 48226
313/225-1000

NBD Bank
1 Indiana Sq.
Indianapolis, IN 46266
317/266-6000

Northern Trust
50 S. LaSalle St.
Chicago, IL 60603
312/630-6000

Norwest
90 S. 7 St.
Minneapolis, MN
55402
612/667-1234

Old Kent Financial
111 Lyon St. N.W.
Grand Rapids, MI
49503
616/771-5000

Old National Bancorp
420 Main St.
Evansville, IN 47708
812/464-1200

OnBancorp
101 S. Salina St.
Syracuse, NY 13202
315/424-4400

PNC Financial
101 S. Tryon St.
1 PNC Plz.
Fifth Ave. & Wood St.
Pittsburgh, PA 15265
412/762-2666

Provident Bancorp
1 E. 4th St.
Cincinnati, OH 45202
513/579-2000

Regions Financial
417 20 St. N.
Birmingham, AL 35203
205/326-7060

Republic New York
452 Fifth Ave.
New York, NY 10018
212/525-6000

Riggs National
1503 Pennsylvania Ave.
NW
Washington, DC 20005
202/835-6000

Roosevelt Financial Group
900 Roosevelt Pkwy.
Chesterfield, MO
63017
314/532-6200

Shawmut National
1 Federal St.
Boston, MA 02210
617/292-2000

Signet Banking Corp.
7 N. 8 St.
Richmond, VA 23219
804/747-2000

Society Bank
127 Public Sq.
Cleveland, OH 44114
216/689-3000

Southern National Corp.
200 W. 2 St.
Winston-Salem, NC
27101
910/671-2000

SouthTrust Alabama
420 20 St. N.
Birmingham, AL
35203
205/254-5000

Star Banc Corp.
425 Walnut St.
Cincinnati, OH 45215
513/632-4000

State Street Boston Corp.
225 Franklin St.
Boston, MA 02110
617/786-3000

Sumitomo Bank of California
320 California St.
San Francisco, CA
94104
415/445-8000

Summit Bancorporation
1 Main St.
Chatham, NJ 07928
201/701-6200

SunTrust Banks
P.O. Box 4418
Atlanta, GA 30302
404/588-7711

Synovus Financial Corp.
901 Front St.
Columbus, GA 31901
706/649-2387

Texas Commerce Bank
712 Main St.
Houston, TX 77002
713/216-4865

Trustcorp Bank Ohio
N. Shoup & Parkview
Wauseon, OH 43567
419/259-6977

UJB Financial
301 Carnegie Ctr.
Princeton, NJ
08540
609/987-3200

UMB Financial Corp.
1010 Grand Blvd.
Kansas City, MO
64106
816/860-7000

Union Bank
350 California St.
San Francisco, CA
94104
415/705-7000
Fax 415/705-7399

United Carolina Bancshares
127 W. Webster St.
Whiteville, NC 28472
910/642-5131

U.S. Bancorp
111 S.W. 5 Ave.
Portland, OR 97204
503/275-6111

U.S. Trust
114 W. 47th St.
New York, NY 10036
212/852-1000

Wachovia Bank
100 N. Main St.
Winston-Salem, NC
27171
910/770-5000

Wells Fargo
420 Montgomery St.
San Francisco, CA
94163
415/396-3814

Wilmington Trust
1100 N. Market St.
Wilmington, DE
19890-0001
302/651-1000

TOP THRIFT INSTITUTIONS

H. F. Ahmanson & Co.
4900 Rivergrade Rd.
Irwindale, CA 91706
818/960-6311

American Capital Asset Management, Inc.
2800 Post Oak Blvd.
Houston, TX 77056
713/993-0500

American Savings of Florida FSB
17801 NW Second Ave.
Miami, FL 33169-5089
305/653-5353

Bay View Capital
2121 S. El Camino Real
San Mateo, CA
94403-1897
415/573-7300

CalFed Bank
5700 Wilshire Blvd.
Los Angeles, CA
90036
213/932-4200

Coast Savings Financial
1000 Wilshire Blvd.
Los Angeles, CA
90017-2457
213/362-2000

Commercial Federal
2120 S. 72nd St.
Omaha, NE 68124
402/554-9200

CSF Holdings
1221 Brickell Ave.
Miami, FL 33131
305/577-0400

Dime Bancorp Inc.
EAB Plaza
Uniondale, NY 11556
516/745-2831

Downey Financial
3501 Jamboree Rd.
Newport Beach, CA
92660
714/854-3100

First Fed Financial
401 Wilshire Blvd.
Santa Monica, CA
90401-1490
310/319-6000

FirstFed Michigan
1001 Woodward Ave.
Detroit, MI
48226-1967
313/965-1400

First Nationwide Bank
88 Kearny St.
San Francisco, CA
94108
415/995-5800

Glendale Federal Bank
700 N. Brand Blvd.
Glendale, CA 91203
818/500-2000

Golden West Financial Corp.
1901 Harrison St.
Oakland, CA 94612
510/446-3420

GP Financial
41-60 Main St.
Flushing, NY 11355-3820
718/670-7600

Great Western Financial
9200 Oakdale Ave.
Chatsworth, CA

91311-6519
818/775-3411

People's Bank
850 Main St.
Bridgeport, CT 06604
203/338-7171

Rochester Community Savings Bank
40 Franklin St.
Rochester, NY 14604
716/258-3000

St. Paul Bancorp
6700 W. North Ave.
Chicago, IL 60635
312/622-5000

Sovereign Bancorp
P.O. Box 12646
Reading, PA 19612
610/320-8400

Standard Federal Bancorp
2600 W. Big Beaver Rd.
Troy, MI 48084
810/643-9600

TCF Financial Corp.
801 Marquette Ave.
Minneapolis, MN 55402
612/661-6500

Washington Federal Inc.
425 Pike St.
Seattle, WA 98101
206/624-7930

Washington Mutual Savings Bank Inc.
PO Box 834
Seattle, WA 98111
206/461-2000

WHERE TO GO FOR MORE INFORMATION

BANKING INDUSTRY ASSOCIATIONS

American Bankers Association
1120 Connecticut Ave., NW
Washington, DC 20036
202/663-5000
(Publishes *American Banker* magazine; see below for more information.)

American League of Financial Institutions
1709 New York Ave., NW, Suite 801
Washington, DC 20006
202/628-5624
(Offers career placement assistance.)

Bank Marketing Association

1120 Connecticut Ave. NW
Washington, DC 20036
202/663-5268

The Bankers Roundtable
805 15th St. NW
Suite 600
Washington, DC 20005
202/289-4322

Credit Union Executives Society
P.O. Box 14167
Madison, WI 53714
608/271-2664
800/252-2664
(Puts out *Credit Union Management,* also available to nonmembers.)

Financial Institutions Marketing Association
401 N. Michigan Ave.
Chicago, IL 60611
312/644-6610

Independent Bankers Association of America
1 Thomas Cir., NW, Suite 950
Washington, DC 20005
202/659-8111
(Publishes monthly magazine *Independent Banker.*)

Mortgage Bankers Association of America
1125 15th St., NW
Washington, DC 20005

202/861-6500
(Publishes monthly
magazine *Mortgage
Banking* for members.)

**National Association
of Federal Credit
Unions**
3138 N. 10th St.,
Suite 300
Arlington, VA 22201

703/522-4770
(Publishes monthly
Jobs/OPS, which lists
job opportunities;
available, free, to
members only.)

**National Bankers
Association**
1802 T St., NW
Washington, DC 20009

202/588-5432
(Operates job referral
service for members.)

**America's
Community Bankers**
900 19th St. NW
Suite 400
Washington, DC 20006
202/857-3100

BANKING INDUSTRY DIRECTORIES

***American Banker
Yearbook***
American Banker, Inc.
1 State St. Plz.
New York, NY 10004
212/803-6700

***American Financial
Directory***
1770 Breckenridge
Pkwy.
Suite 500
Duluth, GA 30136
770/381-2511
800/247-7376

***American Savings
Directory***

1770 Breckenridge
Pkwy.
Suite 500
Duluth, GA 30136
770/381-2511

***Business Week*—Top
200 Banking
Institutions Issue**
McGraw-Hill, Inc.
1221 Ave. of the
Americas
New York, NY 10020
212/512-2641

***Moody's Bank and
Financial Manual***
Moody's Investors

Services, Inc.
99 Church St.
New York, NY 10007
212/553-0300

Polk's Bank Directory
R. L. Polk & Co.
P.O. Box 3051000
Nashville, TN
37230-5100
615/889-3350
800/827-2265
(Two different editions:
North American edition
and International
edition.)

BANKING INDUSTRY MAGAZINES

ABA Banking Journal
345 Hudson St.
New York, NY 10014
212/620-7200
(Monthly for bank and
S&L officers, financial

executives, insurance
firm executives, etc.)

American Banker
1 State St. Plz.
New York, NY 10004
212/803-6700

(Daily newspaper for
senior executives and
bank officers; often has
good help-wanted
section.)

BROADCASTING

INDUSTRY OUTLOOK: Hot competition—and probable consolidation—ahead.

First, a quick look at the playing field: The television, cable, and radio broadcasting industries continue to be dominated by a few majors, with the money and muscle to acquire, restructure, and absorb the weaker sisters in their expansion drives. In television, the Big Three account for 40% of annual industry ad revenues; in cable, despite the several hundred cable system operators, the five largest companies account for about 70% of the country's cable subscribers; and in radio, the ten largest broadcasters account for about 25% of industry ad revenues.

More specific outlooks:

Television: Still fighting the turf wars, the Big Three networks continue to lose share of the prime-time audience and ad revenues with the aggressive competitive efforts from the UPN, WB, and Fox television networks, from cable television companies, and from the new alternative viewing choices afforded by new cable technologies, and likely later, from the Internet. With the relaxation of governmental regulations, watch as broadcast companies scoop up properties and extend their ownership in different markets. Their prevailing belief? Bigger is better.

Also keep an eye on changes resulting from to the mega-merger of Capital Cities/ABC and Disney, and the CBS/Westinghouse merger. This type of monolithic entertainment company may be a sign of the future where media in general and broadcast in particular are concerned.

1998 ushers in the digital—high-definition—television (HDTV) industry as 22 stations were scheduled to begin regular broadcasting, with the rest of the country's stations broadcasting by 2003. Technical personnel will be needed to produce receivers and to produce and install transmitter and production equipment to enable broadcast of digital signals. And watch for cable's countermeasures. HBO, in fact, announced plans to begin transmitting HDTV programming in mid-1998—the first national cable network to announce entry and support of this new standard.

Cable: Competition should heighten as satellite TV, wireless cable, and telephone companies step up their participation in the area. Expect to see cable companies continue growing, though—but instead of adding new subscribers, companies will be adding on services—such as cable modem services, cable telephony, and digital set-top boxes. Some industry experts see higher cable rates and better financial results by 1999 as the industry approaches deregulation. Moreover, cable companies are attractive acquisition candidates for their superior state-of-the-art two-way data transmission technology.

Radio: Looking better than in the past. A key reason: Consolidation—multistation ownership has helped keep costs down, which in turn makes each station more profitable. Add to this the fact that radio advertising has increased, and radio talk shows are still gaining in popularity—and the result is a fairly strong outlook for this broadcasting area.

A LOOK BACK

▶ Megamergers changed the face of the broadcast industry.

The biggest broadcast news of 1995—the merger activity that changed the face of the industry. First it was Capital Cities/ABC and Disney who merged, creating a huge entertainment company that would take advantage of cross-pollination of products. Second, CBS was acquired by broadcast giant Westinghouse while Time Warner's acquisition of Ted Turner's empire, including CNN, was pending final approvals in late 1996. The result? The jury was still out at the time of writing, but expect to see a realignment of the industry, especially as the new huge entertainment companies take advantage of their vertical integration capabilities.

▶ The past few years saw bad times for radio, resulting in consolidation—which, ultimately, strengthened the industry.

Stagnant audience numbers and dropping advertising dollars caused the industry to slump. AM stations were especially hurt. As a result, the radio industry went through a period of consolidation. Adding to the rush to consolidate: the government lifted restrictions on the number of stations one company can own in a single market. As a result, takeover mania hit the industry, with larger broadcasting companies gobbling up stations. An example of how heated the environment was: In the first two months of 1996, over 80 radio stations were sold. And experts predict that this activity will continue over the short term—as radio revenues stay high and listeners keep tuning in. The end result: a smaller, more cost-effective industry.

WHAT'S NEXT

▶ The sweeping Telecommunications Act of 1966 will affect the industry's structure as cable and telephone companies eagerly eye expansion opportunities in each other's territories.

Phone companies will now be operating in a more deregulated arena, permitting them immediately to enter cable markets outside their home market and, within their own region, if they can prove their phone business faces competition. Phone companies may try to outdo cable companies by offering new features. And look for more alliances such as the Disney-GTE-Ameritech-Bell South pact providing programming for a new cable channel . . . with matching employment opportunities. And the U.S. West acquisition of Continental Cablevision, the industry's number 3 supplier, suggests other likely affiliations between cable and telephone companies.

► **Competition will still be setting the scene for television broadcasters.**

It's business as usual—which means hot competition as usual—among the original networks, the new upstarts, cable TV, and independent programmers. Even though most new shows introduced in 1996 fared poorly, expect to see the networks—and the fledgling networks like UPN—continue pushing out new programming in an effort to grab audience share. The problem for the networks: viewership has been declining for years, with audience members tuning into cable—or sitting in front of their PC. An example: ten years ago, when cable was new, network prime-time shows drew 76% of the viewing audience. In 1995, the number dropped to 57%; in 1996, to 53%. And with the new kids on the block expanding their programming into more nights, prime-time television has been glutted with new shows . . . that many people weren't watching. But the networks will keep on swinging, hoping for a hit along the lines of *Friends* to bolster their audience share.

One possible outcome of the hot competition: the newer, weaker networks that are trying to establish themselves as players may wind up teaming up.

► **Along the same lines, watch the growth of niche networks in cable.**

With fierce competition for advertising dollars, the broad-based cable networks will be spending more money for original programming, sports, series development, and the like.

The winners may well be the cable networks that aim at a very targeted audience or that offer "narrowcasted" programming, such as MTV, CNN, and Court TV. Expect the continued success and growth of these networks—and possibly the development of spin-off networks, similar to MTV's development of VH-1 for older viewers. This area will be ripe for employment opportunities in the long term as the number of narrowcast cable networks increases.

Cable's Top 10 (RANKED BY NUMBER OF SUBSCRIBERS)	Radio's Top 10 (RANKED BY NUMBER OF STATIONS)
Tele-Communications, Inc.	Westinghouse/CBS/Infinity
Time-Warner Cable	Jacor Communications
U.S. West Media Group	Clear Channel Radio
Comcast Corp.	Evergreen Media
Cox Communications, Inc.	Disney/ABC
Cablevision Systems Corp.	American Radio Systems
Adelphia Cable Communications	SFX Broadcasting
Jones Intercable, Inc.	Cox Communications
Marcus Cable	Chancellor Broadcasting Network
Falcon Cable Systems	Bonneville International
SOURCE: *Broadcasting*	SOURCE: *Duncan's Radio Market Guide*

Note: Rankings will change due to forthcoming mergers.

► **It will be a two-tier picture for radio: Larger stations, or those owned by one owner, will continue to hold their own or do better; smaller, independent stations will fall by the wayside or be swallowed up.**

Expect the largest radio stations to continue performing well but the smaller stations to fall victim to high operating costs—and be swallowed up in the takeover frenzy that has been sweeping the industry.

One probable result? The number of "robot" stations will increase—that is, stations that act, in effect, as transmitters for larger stations instead of offering up their own programming.

On the flip side, because owning a large number of stations keeps costs down, the large broadcast companies will strengthen—and may in fact, add more programming to be able to offer a wide range of demographics to advertisers.

Where employment is concerned, then, it points to a mixed picture: On one hand, as the number of independent stations decrease, jobs will be lost. However, on the other hand, opportunities will continue to be found at the larger stations—especially in programming, as broadcasting companies beef up original programs to be played on their group stations.

▶ **Watch for rapid growth in satellite-to-home broadcasting.**

Satellite-to-home broadcasting (or direct satellite broadcasting) is a simple idea: High-powered direct broadcast satellites orbit the earth, beaming television programming directly into viewers' homes.

With over 2 million subscribers after a rocky start, experts forecast that service will grow to as much as 11 million by the end of this decade, with possible negative impacts for network television. The jury is still out with regard to the effect upon cable television; early signs are that each time a satellite broadcasting service gets a new subscriber, such pay services as HBO and TMC are likely to acquire a new subscriber as well. Merger activity threatened cable operators, with the 1997 announcement of ambitious plans to enter the growing direct satellite–TV market, which would cover 75% of the country's TV markets. Subsequent scrapping of these plans did not allay concerns of cable operators that similar plans may surface at a later date. Another threat: wireless cable systems with multichannel services.

▶ **A growth niche market to keep an eye on: Hispanic radio, television, and cable.**

This is one of the hottest areas in all phases of broadcasting—and may offer promising employment opportunities for Spanish-speaking job seekers.

Hispanic broadcasting is growing across the board. Spanish-language TV networks have been pulling in higher ratings—and more advertising—as the Hispanic marketplace in the United States continues to increase. An example of how large the Spanish-speaking television audience is? Recent numbers show that market share among Spanish speakers is up to 60% to 70%. Cable networks are also targeting this market. Witness, for example, the recent announcement of a planned new Spanish language cable channel beamed to U.S. and Latin American viewers. In addition, Spanish-language radio has been hot, with every major Hispanic market now supporting two or more FM stations. A major player in this market is the Spanish Broadcasting System, ranking tenth in U.S. radio listenership in 1996, compared to fourteenth in 1995. The bottom line? This is an area that should show healthy growth over the long term—and may be a hot spot for employment.

▶ Look at the Internet niche market.

Think of a superstation without a satellite—that is the lure of Internet. With over 30 million people in 200 countries connected to Internet, allowing a PC user to hear audio coming through his modem and speakers, attractive opportunities exist for some entrepreneurs.

Although audiences may be low at present, entry costs are very low—with sound quality improving—as firms enter into this unregulated business to tap such small niche markets as Ethiopian Online Radio.

Broadcasting and communications companies are eyeing this market cautiously. By late 1996, fourteen cable companies were offering cable Internet services, either on a trial or fully commercial basis. While Internet ad revenues are still small—less than $2 million in 1996—one industry analyst projects this to soar to $5 billion by 2000.

▶ Another growth niche market to look at: the religious cable, television, and radio markets.

Starting in 1973, several networks have been establishing to serve this market with wholesome and uplifting programming. With subscriber enrollments of 2–3 million per year for each of the major religious networks, this growing market may offer significant opportunities.

EMPLOYMENT OUTLOOK: Like the industry itself, very competitive.

Broadcast is historically a tough field to break into and stay afloat in, and this won't change.

As network fortunes go up and down, expect periodic hiring freezes depending upon business at the moment. As always, the easiest way to break into television is to work at a local independent station. Hiring in news, especially at local stations, should remain stable. Best qualifications: a B.A. or B.S. in science, political science, or other specialty area. Undergraduate journalism degrees are not necessary or even desirable at many stations. In addition, many executives don't think internships are all that valuable, but work experience is always a plus.

As for sales, the outlook is varied. Expect ups and downs depending upon the specific time, but in general the outlook is favorable.

Area to keep an eye on: Cable stations. With hundreds of new—and more established—cable stations, there are often numerous job opportunities in a range of specialties.

JOBS SPOTLIGHT

DIRECTOR OF MARKETING/ASSISTANT DIRECTOR (IN RADIO): These two promotion department positions are of increasing importance at radio stations as competition remains high. Most radio stations have a two-person promotion department, consisting of a director and an assistant. Among the areas that radio promotion staffers are involved in, depending on the size of the station and of the department: advertising, direct mail, promotional copy, public relations (in terms of developing an image for the station), special events, publicity, promotional events such as on-air contests. Experience in radio is a definite plus, as are writing, promotion, and marketing experience or skills. Salaries depend on the station size and market.

TOP TELEVISION COMPANIES

(including networks, group television station owners)

ABC
77 W. 66th St.
New York, NY
10023-6298
212/456-7777
West Coast office:
2040 Ave. of the Stars
Century City, CA
90067
310/557-7777

A. H. Belo Corp.
400 S. Record St.
Dallas, TX 75202
214/977-6600

**Bonneville
International Corp.**
Broadcast House
55 N. Third
Salt Lake City, UT
84180
801/575-7500

CBS
51 W. 52nd St.
New York, NY 10019
212/975-4321
West Coast office:
7800 Beverly Blvd.
Los Angeles, CA
90036
213/852-2345

**Chris-Craft
Industries**
767 Fifth Ave.
New York, NY 10153
212/421-0200

City Casters
1 East 4 St.
Cincinnati, OH 45202
513/562-8000

**Cox Communications,
Inc.**
1400 Lake Hearn Dr.,
NE
Atlanta, GA 30319
404/843-5000

**Fox Broadcasting
Company**
10201 W. Pico Blvd.
Los Angeles, CA
90064
310/277-2211
East Coast office:
1211 Avenue of the
Americas
New York, NY 10036
212/556-2400

**Gannett Broadcasting
Group**
1100 Wilson Blvd.
Arlington, VA 22209
703/284-6000

**LIN Broadcasting
Corp.**
5295 Carillon Pt.
Kirkland, WA 98033
206/828-1902

**Multimedia
Broadcasting Co.**
1000 Market St.
St. Louis, MO 63101
314/444-5266

NBC
30 Rockefeller Plz.
New York, NY 10112
212/664-4444
West Coast office:
3000 Alameda Ave.

Burbank, CA 91523
818/840-4444

**Park
Communications, Inc.**
333 W. Vine St.
Lexington, KY 40507
606/252-7275

**Post/Newsweek
Stations, Inc.**
3 Constitution Plz.
Hartford, CT 06103
860/493-6530

**Providence Journal
Broadcasting Co.**
75 Fountain St.
Providence, RI 02902
401/277-7000

**Pulitzer Broadcasting
Co.**
515 N. 6 St.
St. Louis, MO 63101
314/231-5969

**Schurz
Communications, Inc.**
225 W. Colfaz Ave.
South Bend, IN 46626
219/287-1001

**Scripps-Howard
Broadcasting Co.**
312 Walnut St.
Suite 2800
Cincinnati, OH 45202
513/977-3000

**Telemundo Group,
Inc.**
1740 Broadway
New York, NY 10019
212/492-5500

Time Warner
75 Rockefeller Plz.
New York, NY 10019
212/484-8000

Tribune Broadcasting
435 N. Michigan Ave.
Chicago, IL 60611
312/222-3333

Turner Broadcasting System
190 Marietta St., NW
Atlanta, GA 30303
404/827-1700

Univision Station Group
605 3rd Ave.,
12th Flr.
New York, NY 10158
212/455-5200

Viacom
1515 Broadway
New York, NY 10036
212/258-6000

Westinghouse/CBS-Group W Broadcasting
685 3rd Ave.
New York, NY 10017
212/916-1000

TOP CABLE NETWORKS AND PAY TV SERVICES

A&E—Arts & Entertainment Cable Network
235 E. 45th St.
New York, NY 10017
212/661-4500

ACTS Satellite Network
6350 W. Fwy.
Fort Worth, TX 76116
817/737-3241

Adelphia Communications Corp.
5 W. 3rd St.
Coudersport, PA 16915
814/274-9830

American Movie Classics; Bravo Rainbow Programming Service
3 Crossways Pk. W.
Woodbury, NY 11797
516/364-1160

BET—Black Entertainment Television
1899 9 St. NE
Washington, DC 2001
202/608-2000

Cablevision Systems Corp.
1 Media Crossways
Woodbury, NY 11747
516/364-8450

CNBC Consumer News and Business Control
2200 Fletcher Ave.
Ft. Lee, NJ 07024
201/585-2622

CNN; CNN Headline News
Box 105366
CNN Ctr.
Atlanta, GA
30348-5366
404/827-1500

Comcast Corp.
1234 Market St.
Philadelphia, PA 19107
215/665-1700

Continental Cablevision, Inc.
The Pilot House
Boston, MA 02110
617/742-9500

Cox Cable Communications
1400 Lake Hearn

Dr., NE
Atlanta, GA 30319
404/843-5000

Country Music Television
2806 Opryland Dr.
Nashville, TN 37214
615/871-5830

C-SPAN (Cable Public Affairs Network)
400 N. Capitol St.,
NW, Suite 650
Washington, DC 20001
202/737-3220

The Discovery Channel
7700 Wisconsin Ave.
Bethesda, MD
20814-3522
301/986-1999

The Disney Channel
3800 W. Alameda Ave.
Burbank, CA 91505
818/569-7701

E! Entertainment Television
5670 Wilshire Blvd.,
2nd Flr.
Los Angeles, CA 90036
213/954-2400

**ESPN—
Entertainment and
Sports Programming
Network**
ESPN Plz.
Bristol, CT 06010
203/585-2000

Falcon Cable Systems
10900 Wilshire Blvd.
Los Angeles, CA
90024
310/824-9990

Family Channel
2877 Guardian Ln.
Virginia Beach, VA
23452
804/459-6000

Home Box Office, Inc.
(includes HBO and
Cinemax)
1100 Ave. of the
Americas
New York, NY 10036
212/512-1000

**Home Shopping
Network, Inc.**
2501 118 Avenue No.
St. Petersburg, FL
33716
813/572-8585

Jones Intercable, Inc.
9697 E. Mineral Ave.
Englewood, CO 80111
303/792-3111

Lifetime Television
309 W. 49th St.

New York, NY 10019
212/424-7000

Marcus Cable
205 Industrial St.
Dallas, TX 75065
817/321-6464

MTV Networks, Inc.
(inc. MTV,
Nickelodeon, Nick at
Nite, VH-1)
1515 Broadway
New York, NY 10036
212/258-8000

**The Nashville
Network**
2806 Opryland Dr.
Nashville, TN 37214
615/871-5830

**Playboy; Playboy at
Night (pay-per-view)**
Playboy Enterprises,
Inc.
9242 Beverly Blvd.
Beverly Hills, CA
19380
215/430-1000

QVC Network, Inc.
Goshen Corporate Pk.
1365 Enterprise Dr.
West Chester, PA
19380
215/430-1000

**Showtime/The Movie
Channel, Inc.**
1633 Broadway,
37th Fl.

New York, NY 10019
212/708-1600

**Tele-Communications
Inc.**
5619 DTC Pkwy.
Englewood, CO 80111
303/267-5500

Time Warner Cable
300 1st Stamford Plaza
Stamford, CT 06902
203/328-0600

**TNT—Turner
Network Television**
190 Marietta St., NW
Atlanta, GA 30303
404/827-1700

The Travel Channel
2690 Cumberland
Pkwy.
Suite 500
Atlanta, GA 30339
404/801-2400

USA Network
1230 Ave. of the
Americas
New York, NY 10020
212/408-9100

**U.S. West Media
Group**
7800 E. Orchard Rd.
Englewood, CO 80111
303/793-6500

The Weather Channel
2600 Cumberland Pky.
Atlanta, GA 30339
404/434-6800

TOP RADIO COMPANIES

ABC Radio Networks
New York office:
125 West End Ave.
New York, NY 10023
212/501-9700

ABC Radio Networks
Chicago office:
333 N. Michigan Ave.
Suite 1615
Chicago, IL 60601
312/984-0890

ABC Radio Networks
Los Angeles office:
3321 S. La Cienega
Los Angeles, CA
90016
310/840-4900

American Radio Systems Corp.
116 Huntington Ave.
Boston, MA 02116
617/375-7500

Associated Press Radio Division
1825 K St., NW
Washington, DC
20006-1253
202/736-1100

Bonneville International Corp.
55 N. 300 West
Broadcast House
Salt Lake City, UT
84180
801/575-7500

Business Radio Network
5025 Centennial Blvd.
Colorado Springs, CO
80918
719/528-7040

CBS Radio Division
New York office:
51 W. 52nd St.
New York, NY 10019
212/975-4321

CBS Radio Division
Los Angeles office:
7800 Beverly Blvd.
Los Angeles, CA 90036
213/852-2345

Chancellor Broadcasting Network
749 E. Pine St.
Central Point, OR
97502
503/664-5673

Clear Channel Radio, Inc.
200 Concord Plaza
San Anotonio, TX
78216
210/822-2828

CNN Radio Network
1 CNN Ctr.
Box 105366
Atlanta, GA
30348-5366
404/827-2500

Disney/ABC
77 W. 66 St.
New York, NY 10023
212/456-7777

Evergreen Media Corp.
433 E. Las Colinas
Blvd.
Irving, TX 75039
214/869-9020

Gear Broadcasting International, Inc.
Box 23172
Weybosset St.
Providence, RI 02903
401/331-6072
800/468-8424

Jacor Communications Inc.
201 E. 5 St.
Cincinnati, OH 45202
513/621-1300

Moody Broadcasting Network
820 N. LaSalle Dr.
Chicago, IL 60610
800/621-7031

National Public Radio
635 Massachusetts
Ave., NW
Washington, DC 20001
202/414-2000

NBC Radio Network
1755 S. Jefferson Davis
Hwy.
Arlington, VA 22202
703/413-8300

NBC Radio Network
Los Angeles Office:

3000 W. Alameda Ave.
Burbank, CA 91523
818/840-4444

SFX Broadcasting Inc.
150 E. 58 St.
New York, NY 10155
212/407-9191

UPI Radio Network
1400 I St., NW,
9th Fl.
Washington, DC 20005
202/898-8111

USA Radio Network
2290 Springlake Rd.,
Suite 107
Dallas, TX 75234
214/484-3900

Wall Street Journal Radio Network
200 Liberty St.,
14th Fl.
New York, NY 10281
212/416-2380

Westinghouse Broadcasting
888 7 Ave.
New York, NY 10106
212/307-3000

Westwood One, Inc.
9540 Washington Blvd.
Culver City, CA 90232
310/840-4000

Westwood One, Inc.
New York office:
1675 Broadway
New York, NY 10019
212/641-2000

Westwood One, Inc.
Washington, DC,
office:
1755 S. Jefferson
Davis Hwy.
Arlington, VA 22202
703/413-8300

Westwood One, Inc.   111 E. Wacker Dr.   312/938-0222
Chicago office: Chicago, IL 60601

WHERE TO GO FOR MORE INFORMATION

BROADCASTING INDUSTRY ASSOCIATIONS

Academy of Television Arts & Sciences
5220 Lankershim Blvd.
N. Hollywood, CA 91607
818/754-2800

Broadcast Promotion and Marketing Executives
6255 Sunset Blvd.
Los Angeles, CA 90067
213/465-3777
(Operates job referral bank for members.)

Corporation for Public Broadcasting
901 E St., NW
Washington, DC 20004
202/879-9600
(Maintains a computerized job referral service for public television and radio stations nationwide—Employment Outreach Project Talent Bank.)

International Radio and Television Society
420 Lexington Ave., Suite 1714
New York, NY 10170
212/867-6650
(Sponsors summer internships for college communications majors.)

International Television Association
6311 N. O'Connor Rd. LB51
Irving, TX 75039
214/869-1112

National Academy of Television Arts and Sciences
111 W. 57th St.
New York, NY 10019
212/586-8424

National Association of Black-Owned Broadcasters
1333 New Hampshire Ave., NW
Washington, DC 20036
202/463-8970
(Maintains placement service and offers workshops. Puts out annual *Black-Owned Station Directory*.)

National Association of Broadcasters
1771 N St., NW
Washington, DC 20036
202/429-5300
(Publishes career brochures; *Careers in Radio* and *Careers in Television;* maintains placement service for minorities and job clearinghouse.)

National Association of Public Television Stations
1350 Connecticut Ave., NW
Washington, DC 20036
202/887-1700

National Cable Television Association
1724 Massachusetts Ave., NW
Washington, DC 20036
202/775-3550

Personal Communications Industry Association
500 Montgomery St.
Suite 700
Alexandria, VA 22314
703/739-0300

Radio Advertising Bureau
304 Park Ave. S.
New York, NY 10010
212/254-4800

Radio-Television News Directors Association
1000 Connecticut Ave. NW
Suite 615
Washington, DC 20036
202/659-6510
(Puts out a newsletter listing job opportunities free to members, but also available to nonmembers for a subscription price.)

**Satellite Broadcasting
& Communications
Association**
225 Reinekers Ln.,

Suite 600
Alexandria, VA 22314
703/549-6990

**Television Bureau of
Advertising**
850 Third Ave.
New York, NY 10022
212/486-1111

BROADCASTING INDUSTRY DIRECTORIES

*Broadcasting & Cable
Marketplace*
P.O. Box 31
New Providence, NJ
07974-9903
800/323-4345

*Broadcasting & Cable
Yearbook*
Broadcasting & Cable,
Inc.
P.O. Box 31
121 Chanlon Rd.
New Providence, RI
07974
800/521-8110

*Gale Directory of
Publications and
Broadcast
Media*
Gale Research, Inc.
835 Penobscot Bldg.
Detroit, MI
48226-4094
800/877-4253

*International
Television and Video
Almanac*
159 W. 53rd St.
New York, NY 10019
212/247-3100

*Standard Rate & Data
Service
Spot Radio Rates &
Data and Spot
Television Rates &
Data*
SRDS
3004 Glenview Rd.
Wilmette, IL 60091
708/375-5000

*World Radio TV
Handbook*
Billboard Publications,
Inc.
1515 Broadway
New York, NY 10036
212/764-7300

BROADCASTING INDUSTRY MAGAZINES

Broadcasting & Cable
1705 DeSales St., NW
Washington, DC 20036
202/859-2340
(Weekly magazine
covering the broadcast
industry; aimed at
network and station
personnel, broadcast
advertisers, etc. Good
help-wanted section.)

CableVision
825 Seventh Ave.
New York, NY 10019
212/887-8400
(Biweekly publication
covering developments
in cable television.)

Electronic Media
740 N. Rush St.
Chicago, IL 60611
312/649-5200
(Weekly publication on
all aspects of the
broadcast industry; for
personnel at stations,
networks,
manufacturers, etc.)

Radio Business Report
6208-B Old Franconia
Rd.
Alexandria, VA 22310
703/719-9500
(Weekly news
publication of the radio
industry.)

Television Broadcast
2 Park Ave.
New York, NY 10016
212/779-1919
(Monthly publication
covering radio and
television broadcasting;
for engineering and
production staffs,
management.)

Video Week
Television Digest, Inc.
2115 Ward Court NW
Washington, DC 20037
202/872-9200
(Weekly publication
covering the television
industry.)

CHEMICALS

INDUSTRY OUTLOOK: Appears to be heading for a cyclical downturn, with capacity outstripping demand.

Many companies have anticipated the likely decline and improved manufacturing efficiencies and decreased costs, but those that manage to keep their capacity in check may do better, albeit at lower profit levels.

In general, the strength of the chemical industry—particularly commodities chemicals—will, as always, be tied to both the global and the domestic economies. More specifically, organic chemicals will perform in step with the world economy; inorganic chemicals with the U.S. economy. Problems: The European economy has been slowing, which will have a negative impact on specialty chemical companies with European operations. As for the domestic picture, the key players to watch are the automotive and housing construction industries. If they fare poorly, expect to see a negative impact on the chemical industry. Over the short term growth should be steady. Look for consolidations/mergers as chemical companies ally themselves with suppliers or end-use producers. The bright spot: Asia and Latin America with rising demand because of rapid population growth, increasing living standards, and rapid industrialization. Strongest probable chemical sectors? Industrial gases, selected specialty chemicals, and biotechnological applications of agricultural chemicals. One possible problem: If the economy slows suddenly, the chemicals industry may be forced to deal with oversupply, particularly as new overseas facilities enter the market.

A key factor in the long-term outlook for the chemical industry is the "greening" of American industry. This will force the industry to choose new plant sites, change manufacturing processes and increase R&D expenditures.

A LOOK BACK

▶ **The heavy expense of expansion, plus overcapacity and slow demand due to a slumping economy, led to an industry downturn, and then a slow increase as the economy improved.**

The chemical industry is a cyclical one, and the 1990s opened with chemical companies facing the low end of their cycle. In 1991 earnings dropped about 15%. Hardest hit were the commodity chemicals producers. One bright spot remained: chemical exports, which continued to grow—up 10% in 1991. As recession hit, chemical companies went through downsizing, restructuring, cost-cutting and debt control. And, when domestic demand increased as the economy began recovering, companies were poised for a brighter future. By 1996, with a return in the economy and a sharp increase in export markets, chemical industry shipments increased 5%. Capital and R & D spending was scheduled to rise to meet projected industry growth. With improving cash flow many companies set up aggressive programs to improve operations and cut costs to better weather downturns.

WHAT'S NEXT

▶ **Of key importance for the continuing growth of the U.S. chemical industry: international competitiveness.**

Strong international sales have kept many areas of the U.S. chemical industry strong, even through domestic economic downturns. (The U.S. chemical industry is the largest in the world, responsible for about 30 percent of the worldwide chemical markets.) To date it has frequently been a case of markets hungry to buy and of U.S. producers eager to sell, with success.

This won't change in the future, but there are several challenges and changes on the horizon. Chief among them: the changing chemical investment policies of much of the world. This will result in a rise in the number of new companies, partnership agreements between existing companies, and the like, which will create more competition in the world markets. Among the specific areas that should show increased competition in the near future are South Korea, Taiwan, and Mexico. Asia, in general, is gearing up for competition. Over the next few years, a number of new facilities should begin production. In addition, Japan has been making inroads into the U.S.–dominated advanced composites industry.

On the plus side where the international markets are concerned are Eastern Europe and the former Soviet Union. The emerging nations in these areas have already signed contracts with U.S. companies, which will mean increased business.

Where employment is concerned, this international focus points to an increasing need for people with backgrounds in international business.

▶ **Expect continued restructuring.**

This is a trend that should continue through the next few years as the industry remains cost conscious.

Also watch as small and midsize chemical companies increase their production of both specialty and commodity chemicals for the domestic market and for export.

▶ **Look for increased environmental awareness to continue having a strong impact on the chemical industry, helping some companies, hurting others.**

Companies that have already developed chemicals that can replace those that deplete the ozone layer will benefit from this "greening of America." Among them are Allied-Signal, Dow, and du Pont. Similarly, expect to see a push in R&D in environment-friendly chemicals, especially fuel additives such as methanol and methyl tertiary butyl ether.

This points to employment opportunities over the long term, as companies are forced to increase production of these chemicals, either through development of new processing technologies or through plant expansion. Keep in mind, however, that there will also be strong competition emerging from foreign companies, which may directly affect the U.S. companies' health.

▶ **Expect a slowdown in environmental services.**

The predicted boom hasn't panned out, so expect to see more companies scaling back on their announced movements into this area. Overall, the field looks flat for the short term. Some experts are still holding out for growth in environmental consulting and remediation, but many others expect little activity.

▶ **There will be a continued emphasis placed on research and development.**

It's the keystone to the long-term success of the chemical industry—and chemical producers are aware of it. So they are making sure that they stay technologically in step with their competitors, both domestic and overseas. Adding to the renewed focus on R&D are the new environmental regulations and concerns.

A positive outcome of this emphasis where workers are concerned: The heavy focus on technology has translated into higher salaries paid to nonproduction workers, including technicians, chemists, and engineers.

▶ **Keep an eye on biotechnology.**

Biotechnology is slowly making inroads into the marketplace, accounting for $10 billion sales in 1996 with volume of over $30 billion by 2006. Human therapeutics dominate this chemical group, with over 150 drug candidates in human clinical trials.

Agricultural/plant technology research, until recently a minor player in the biotech field, is being conducted in a number of areas, including development of BST (a milk-production hormone), PST (a lean pork hormone), and insect and herbicide–resistant cotton, with some genetically engineered products ready for commercialization by 1997. Many experts predict the plant biotech market will boom over the next five years. One downside: Watch for a possible continuation of recent serious negative public reaction to American biotech crops by such western European countries as Switzerland and Germany.

Among the companies involved in ag biotech are industry giants American Cyanamid, Ciba-Geigy, and Monsanto, as well as the lesser-known DNA Plant Technology, Ecogen, Biotechnical International, Calgene, and Hoechst and Schering's joint venture, AgrEvo.

EMPLOYMENT OUTLOOK: Fair; stronger in some areas than in others.

The chemical industry remains a large employer—currently employing over 850,000 people. About five percent of all U.S. manufacturing workers and about ten percent of all U.S. scientists and engineers work for chemical companies. Most of these jobs should remain fairly stable as the U.S. government has forecast that the chemical industry should continue growing slightly faster than the U.S. economy as a whole.

More specifically: Petrochemical producers, which account for roughly 30% of the total chemical industry employment, should continue to offer job opportunities, however, its performance is tied to its end-user industries. If the automotive, electronic, and construction materials industries falter, it will have a negative impact on chemical companies—and, thus, on employment opportunities.

The inorganic chemicals industry is headed for flat times, according to the U.S. Department of Commerce. The long-term employment picture shows little growth, perhaps even losses. As for organic chemicals, the picture is a bit brighter as new plants are being added on line, particularly to keep up with demand for ethanol.

Good bets for employment: keep an eye on smaller firms. Many emerging firms offer the best prospects for jobs. For example, in 1996, Furane Products (a unit of Ciba) projected increases of 49%. The problem, of course, is that these firms typically don't have large staffs, so the actual number of available jobs still is often low. However, these companies are good bets in general. Key areas: biotech, research services.

BEST BETS

Du Pont Company
1007 Market Street
Wilmington, DE 19898
302/774-1000
Fax 302/774-7321

Chosen the most admired chemicals company in *Fortune* magazine's 1996 Corporate Reputations survey, Du Pont has gone through layoffs and restructurings, and looks as if it might offer good employment prospects in the long term. One area to keep an eye on: Environmental services. Du Pont has been very bullish on this hot area and is planning to continue emphasizing and expanding its business in environmental services. Among its areas of interest: wastewater management, soil and groundwater cleanup, and consulting. A good choice for those in the environmental field, such as industrial hygienists and the like.

Eastman Chemical
100 N. Eastman Rd.
Kingsport, TN 37660
423/229-2000

If the name sounds vaguely familiar, that's because this chemical company used to be a division of Eastman Kodak Company. Split off in 1994, this chemical giant looks poised for growth. Already, it's beating industry averages, and now it's expanding overseas, to Latin America, Spain, and the Netherlands. For employees, it's strongly success oriented. *All* employees get a bonus based on return on capital. Last year, that meant cash amounting to 17% of base pay. Not bad. But on the downside, employees have to put up 5% of their own pay—and in a bad year, they forfeit it. Managers have more spice in their lives—more potential bonus, more to lose if the company doesn't perform well. So far, the strategy appears to be working. Employees are motivated, the company is growing—and bonuses keep coming.

TOP CHEMICAL COMPANIES

Air Products and Chemicals, Inc.
7201 Hamilton Blvd.
Allentown, PA
18195-1501
610/481-7435

Albemarle Corp.
330 S. 4 St.
Richmond, VA 23219
804/788-6000

American Cyanamid Co.
1 Cyanamid Plz.
Wayne, NJ 07470
201/831-2000

American International Chemical, Inc.
17 Strathmore Rd.
Natick, MA 01760
508/655-5805

Arcadian Corp.
6750 Poplar Ave.
Memphis, TN 38138
901/758-5200

Arco Chemical Co.
3801 W. Chester Pike
Newton Square, PA 19073
215/359-2000

Aristech Chemical Corp.
600 Grant St.
Pittsburgh, PA 15319
412/433-2747

Ashland Chemical, Inc.
3849 Fisher Rd.
Columbus, OH 43228
614/276-6143

BASF Corporation
3000 Continental Dr., N.

Mt Olive, NJ 07828
210/426-2600

Betz Laboratories, Inc.
4636 Somerton Rd.
Langhorne, PA 19053
215/355-3300

Cabot Corp.
75 State St.
Boston, MA 02109
617/345-0100

Cargill
P.O. Box 5697
Mail Stop 10
Minneapolis, MN 55440
612/742-2888

CF Industries, Inc.
1 Salem Lake Dr.
Long Grove, IL 60047
708/438-9500

Crompton & Knowles Corp.
1 Station Pl., Metro Ctr.
Stamford, CT 06902
203/353-5400

Dexter
1 Elm St.
Windsor Locks, CT 06096
203/627-9051

Dow Chemical USA
2030 Willard H. Dow Ctr.
Midland, MI 48674
517/636-1000

Dow Corning Corp.
2200 Salzburg St.
Midland, MI 48640
517/496-4000

Dresser Industries
3000 N. Sam Houston Pkwy., E.

Houston, TX 77032
713/987-4000

Du Pont Co.
1007 Market St.
Wilmington, DE 19898
302/774-1000

Eastman Chemical
100 N. Eastman Rd.
Kingsport, TN 37660
423/229-2000

Engelhard Corp.
101 Wood Ave.
Iselin, NJ 08830
201/205-6000

Ethyl Corp.
330 S. 4 St.
Richmond, VA 23219
804/788-5000

Ferro Corp.
P.O. Box 2189
Richmond, VA 23217
216/641-8580

First Chemical Corp.
(subs. of First Mississippi Corp.)
700 North St.
Jackson, MS 39202
601/949-0246

First Mississippi Corp.
700 North St.
Jackson, MS 39215
601/948-7550

FMC Corp.
200 E. Randolph Dr.
Chicago, IL 60601
312/861-6000

Freeport McMoRan-Agrico
1615 Poydras St.
New Orleans, LA 70112
504/582-4000

H. B. Fuller Co., Inc.
2400 Energy Pk. Dr.
St. Paul, MN 55108
612/645-3401

GAF Chemicals Corporation
1361 Alps Rd.
Wayne, NJ 07470
201/628-3000

Georgia Gulf Corporation
400 Perimeter Ctr Terr.
Atlanta, GA 30346
770/395-4500

B. F. Goodrich Company
3925 Embassy Pkwy.
Akron, OH 44333-1799
216/374-2000

W. R. Grace
One Town Center Rd.
Boca Raton, FL 33486-1010
407/362-2000

Great Lakes Chemical Corp.
1 Great Lakes Blvd.
W. Lafayette, TN 47906
317/497-6100

M. A. Hanna
200 Public Square
Cleveland, OH 44114
216/589-4000

Hercules, Inc.
Hercules Plz.
1313 N. Market St.
Wilmington, DE 19894-0001
302/594-5000

Hoechst Celanese Corp.
3 Park Ave.
New York, NY 10016
212/251-8000

Huntsman Chemical
500 Huntsman Way
Salt Lake City, UT 84108
801/532-5200

IMC Fertilizer Group, Inc.
1 Nelson C. White Pkwy.
Mundelein, IL 60060
708/970-3000

International Flavors & Fragrances
521 W. 57th St.
New York, NY 10019
212/765-5500

Loctite Corp.
Ten Columbus Blvd.
Hartford, CT 06106
203/520-5000

The Lubrizol Corp.
29400 Lakeland Blvd.
Wickliffe, OH 44092-2298
216/943-4200

Lyondell Petrochemical
1221 McKinney St.
Houston, TX 77010
713/652-7200

Monsanto Chemical Co.
800 N. Lindbergh Blvd.
St. Louis, MO 63141
314/694-1000

Morton International, Inc.
100 N. Riverside Plz.
Chicago, IL 60606-1596
312/807-2000

Nalco Chemical Co.
1 Nalco Ctr.
Naperville, IL 60563-1198
708/305-1000

Olin Chemicals
P.O. Box 4500
Norwalk, CT 06856
203/750-3000

PPG Industries Chemicals Group
1 PPG Pl.
Pittsburgh, PA 15222
412/434-3131

Praxair
39 Old Ridgebury Rd.
Danbury, CT 06810-5113
203/794-3000

Rexene Corp.
5005 LBJ Fwy.
Occidental Tower
Dallas, TX 75244
214/450-9000

Rohm and Haas Company
100 Independence Mall W.
Philadelphia, PA 19106-2399
215/592-3000

A. Schulman, Inc.
3550 W. Market St.
Akron, OH 44313
216/666-3751

Sherwin-Williams Co.
101 Prospect Ave., NW
Cleveland, OH 44115-1075
216/566-2000

Sterling Chemicals, Inc.
1200 Smith St.
Houston, TX 77002
713/650-3700

Union Carbide Corp.
39 Old Ridgebury Rd.
Danbury, CT 06817-0001
203/794-2000

Valhi, Inc.
3 Lincoln Ctr.
5430 LBJ Fwy., Suite 1700
Dallas, TX 75240
214/233-1700

Valspar Corp.
1101 S. Third St.

Minneapolis, MN 55415
612/332-7371

Vista Chemical Co.
P.O. Box 19029
900 Threadneedle
Houston, TX 77079
713/588-3000

Wellman, Inc.
1040 Broad St.
Shrewsbury, NJ 07702
908/542-7300

Witco Corp.
1 American Lane
Greenwich, CT 06831-2559
203/552-2000

WHERE TO GO FOR MORE INFORMATION

CHEMICAL INDUSTRY ASSOCIATIONS

American Association of Textile Chemists and Colorists
P.O. Box 12215
Research Triangle Park, NC 27709
919/549-8141
(Publishes *Textile Chemist & Colorist*—free to members, also available at a subscription price for nonmembers—which contains help-wanted ads.)

American Chemical Society
1155 16th St., NW
Washington, DC 20036
202/872-4600

(Publishes *Chemical & Engineering News,* listed below, as well as *Environmental Science & Technology,* both of which contain help-wanted ads; also offers helpful employment-related programs—including career counseling and a job clearinghouse—to members.)

American Institute of Chemists
501 Wythe St.
Alexandria, VA 22314
703/836-2090
(Publishes *The Chemist*—free to

members, available for $25/yr. to nonmembers—which includes employment listings; also maintains a job placement service.)

Chemical Manufacturers Association
1300 Wilson Blvd.
Arlington, VA 22209
708/741-5000

Chemical Specialties Manufacturers Association
1913 Eye St., NW
Washington, DC 20006
202/872-8110

CHEMICAL INDUSTRY DIRECTORIES

Chem Sources—International and *Chem Sources—USA*
Chemical Sources International
Box 1824
Clemson, SC 29633
803/646-7840

Chemicals Directory
275 Washington St.
Newton, MA 02158
617/964-3030
(Relatively low-cost—$40 in 1992—making this a good basic source for a resume mailing list.)

Directory of Chemical Producers U.S.A.
Stanford Research Institute International
333 Ravenswood Ave.
Menlo Park, CA 94025
415/859-3627

CHEMICAL INDUSTRY PERIODICALS

(Also see listings under "Scientists," page 161.)

Chemical Engineering
P.O. Box 507
Highstown, NJ
08520-1450
609/426-7070
(Monthly magazine for chemical engineers and technical executives.)

*Chemical &
Engineering News*
1155 16th St., NW
Washington, DC 20036
202/872-4600
(Weekly magazine put out by the American Chemical Society. Annual jobs outlook coverage is especially helpful for the recent graduate.)

*Chemical Marketing
Reporter*
80 Broad St.
New York, NY 10004
212/248-4177
(Covers industry marketing programs.)

Chemical Processing
301 E. Erie St.
Chicago, IL 60611
312/644-2020
(Fifteen-issue magazine aimed at executives and managers in chemical processing. Puts out annual Directory issue.)

Chemical Week
888 Seventh Ave.
New York, NY 10019
212/621-4900
(Weekly magazine for chemical processing executives and technical managers.)

Modern Plastics
P.O. Box 601
Highstown, NJ
08520-1450
609/426-7070
(Monthly magazine covering the plastics industry; for engineers, developers, designers, technicians, etc.)

Plastics Technology
355 Park Ave. S.
New York, NY 10010
212/592-6570
(Monthly magazine for plastics industry personnel, including engineers, managers, and factory supervisors.)

Plastics World
PTN Publishing
445 Broad Hollow Rd.
Melville, NY 11747
516/845-2700
(Monthly magazine on the plastics industry; aimed at a range of professionals, including those in engineering, technical areas, design, production, and management.)

COMPUTERS AND ELECTRONICS

INDUSTRY OUTLOOK: Volatility, hot competition, and continued growth ahead.

The industry appears poised to resume its historic growth rates after an apparently relatively good 1997. With only 30% to 40% of U.S. households owning a PC, compared to almost 90% owning a TV and VCR, industry experts project PC ownership to reach up to 70% by 2000. And with Asian and Latin American demand continuing to soar, PC sales should continue to grow, especially as attractive, well-priced innovations are offered via the "more bang for the buck" strategy—frequently a decisive buying motivation.

In addition, corporate demand is improving with the development of corporate networking systems, including downsizing—moving application from mainframes to PCs—or client/server systems—connecting the organization's network computers (NC) (lower cost computers without hard drive storage or floppy disks) to a file server that stores data and processes requests. The hardware trend is supported by moves to new operating systems capable of handling 32 bits of data at a time compared to the previous 16 bits.

In general, then, the picture is one of continued overall growth. However, the high tech area has always been competitive, largely due to the emphasis on innovation—and it will stay as competitive as ever, if not more so. Mergers and acquisitions will continue. Everyone is talking to everyone; it is a characteristic of this industry and it will not stop.

Shrinking profits in the hardware area have made companies more bottom-line oriented. Expect volatility and intense warfare—some companies may wind up going belly up.

Software should face volatility as well. But software related to the Internet should remain hot. In general, certain industry areas should see growth, particularly emerging technologies such as Web software, network servers, image processing, multimedia, document scanning, and collaborative computing.

Certain industry areas should see growth, particularly emerging technologies such as multimedia, work stations, document scanning, and collaborative computing.

A LOOK BACK

▶ **Hot times for the computer industry in the recent past—marked by restructuring, consolidation, downsizing, and, as always, tight competition.**

The computer industry is known for its volatility—and the past few years have seen evidence of it. In the early nineties, the industry saw heavy layoffs due to competition—and even IBM broke with its long-held tradition and began instituting layoffs for the first time. But smaller companies were on the move—taking the industry by storm. Companies such as Packard Bell grabbed market share with high sales of IBM clones; mail-order companies were growing steadily.

In the past few years, sales skyrocketed. The PC market, representing over 40% of total computer sales, leaped up as consumers snapped up the newest models—spurred by such introductions as Intel's Pentium chip, bundling in of CD-ROMs and faster fax/modems. And, in 1995, the introduction of Microsoft's Windows 95 further spurred new hardware model and software sales. Also adding to the sales—and volatility—in the industry: the Internet. By 1996, though, the picture was shifting a bit: the home/small office PC market appeared to be saturated, so sales looked as though they would slow in this area. Aggressive computer pricing, introduction of faster computer chips for desktops and laptops by year's end kept sales at relatively strong levels. And into 1997 the industry introduced faster multimedia-capable models to buoy sales. The still strong business market began shifting to the purchase of systems combining improved computer chips and operating systems better suited to their operations. So ultimately, although the playing field has changed somewhat, the general trends should persist: new technology still drawing consumers, continued growth overall . . . but heavy competition as always.

WHAT'S NEXT

▶ **The industry landscape is changing.**

Early in the 1990s a software revolution started that may well change the industry. The name of the new game is Internet and the World Wide Web. Internet established a computer standard enabling computers anywhere to communicate with each other regardless of their operating systems. The Web gave computers a common language for display in graphical "pages." Software and data could be transmitted and downloaded seamlessly, without concerns about operating platforms.

The results? 1) Scrambling by hosts of companies to serve the Internet market. In 1994 only 1,000 Websites were established, compared to 200,000 in 1995; and, in 1996, Website applications reached over 7,000 per week. 2) Software on demand. Instead of waiting for distribution through retail outlet, software and updates will be readily available on the Net. 3) Data on demand; Net users can tap into thousands of databases and information sources. A probable outcome: Client-server computing software may grow subsequently for the next several years.

Impact on employment: Experienced software designers should find employment opportunities with firms serving the Net markets that may exceed $4 billion annually by 2000.

▶ **The bywords of the computer industry:** *tougher, meaner, and leaner.*

In other words, competition will stay hot; companies will continue fighting to maintain customer bases; and the industry will continue to restructure.

Expect the price-cutting warfare that computer and electronics manufacturers have been engaged in for the past year or so to continue. A key reason: the commoditization of the computer and electronics industry. That is, computer systems, parts, semiconductors, and other products on the market appear interchangeable to the consumer—which means that brand names mean less and less and price and value mean more.

In addition to fighting by price slashing, companies will be trying to come up with ways to distinguish their products from the competition. Among the methods they will use: added features, software, and intensive marketing. This will have repercussions where employment is concerned. Product and software development will be highlighted by many companies, which points to opportunities in product development and software engineering. Also, the emphasis on marketing and product-line branding has made marketing and product management staffs crucial employees. This points to opportunities for product managers and marketing experts.

▶ Competition in worldwide markets will also increase.

In the past few years, as the U.S. market slowed, attention turned abroad. And even with a resurgence in domestic sales, companies—both hardware and software—will continue to target worldwide markets, especially as the Asian and European markets keep growing.

The U.S. and Japan in particular will be competing head-to-head for the upper hand in the world market, especially Europe. One problem that will continue to hammer at U.S. producers: the low-cost, high-volume capability of many foreign computer companies.

▶ There will be a rising number of joint agreements between companies and industry consolidation.

This is a way of boosting competitive edge and gaining access to new technology, R&D funding, and marketing muscle.

Joint ventures and consolidation will have a particularly strong impact on software companies because of the high number of small companies (those with one hundred employees or less). While teaming up will give smaller companies access to capital they would otherwise lack, or broaden the products they can offer, those that are unable to link up or gain the backing of a larger company will be unable to keep up. The possible result? A shakeout and eventual industry consolidation.

Joint ventures will also be used to maintain U.S. competitive edge in relation to foreign computer companies. As such (according to the U.S. Department of Commerce Office of Computers and Business Equipment) they may go beyond linkages between computer companies into broader associations between computer companies, telecommunications companies, semiconductor producers, and other parts and subassembly suppliers.

▶ Software: a hot spot as consolidation and competition increase and new markets explode.

It's a case of the big guys beating the little guys—a new story for such an entrepreneurial business. More specifically, it's the dominance of Microsoft pitted against upstarts that can't match its might and muscle. But not so with the exploding Internet/Web software market, which may make dramatic inroads into Microsoft's position.

So it will be a mixed picture in the industry: on one hand, certain small companies will be forced to link up to compete—and to compete globally and support R&D on small profit margins. Many will seek a small niche to stay alive or will become suppliers to the larger companies. On the other hand, there should be a rise in new entrepreneurial companies supplying Internet-related and multimedia software—some of whom may even be able to take on the industry giants.

This points to mixed employment opportunities—sometimes rougher with old line software companies, but strong with Internet software companies. On the plus side, even if the industry shakeout occurs, those companies that survive the competition should face a strong marketplace—with increased sales and growth. The bottom line? Personnel should choose their job targets carefully—and must stay on top of cutting edge technology. One hot region for Internet-related software and service companies: New York City. For more on this, see Northeast, page 506. On the plus side, though, while fewer companies may wind up sticking it out through the competition, those that do survive face a strong marketplace—with increased sales and growth.

▶ Continued activity in network computing.

There will be action both on the LAN front and in the area of larger, enterprise-wide networks. Industry experts see LAN vendors growing as much as 20 to 30% a year. Similarly, there should be growth in wide-area networks (WANs) and integrated network management. Watch for the impact of Intel and Microsoft's development of "NetPCs"—conventional PCs with networking abilities.

In terms of employment, this points to good opportunities for information systems (IS) staffers in industries such as insurance and banking, as well as employees of network companies, such as software engineers and designers.

▶ A growing trend: offering comprehensive services, including training, setup information, and field support.

This is part of the overall shift from being a technology-driven industry to being a service-driven one—and is another way that companies worried about commoditization hope to attract and keep customers.

Among the services companies will be offering: system setups, consulting, training, and general support.

This trend will open up a range of increased field-support positions, from computer trainers, to customer service experts, to technical support staffers, to technicians skilled in systems setup.

▶ Keep an eye on the growing importance of computer-services companies.

This is partly due to the increasing use of computerized networks by companies. The result? A growing number of companies that work with corporations to help with the network in a range of areas, including data transmission, retrieval, coordination, and general consulting work. This translates into a growth area where jobs are concerned.

EMPLOYMENT OUTLOOK: Overall, looking good—although industry volatility will continue to have an impact on jobs.

It's a fact of life: the computer industry will continue to go through shake-outs—which means layoffs and cutbacks are inevitable. But this doesn't mean the job picture is a bad one. Even while companies cut back, they're hiring. For example, in early 1996, Microsoft laid off 120 workers—but they added another 2,500 new employees. The bottom line, then: The computer industry, in general, is one of the hottest employment areas and should continue to be in the future.

One reason for this: the Internet—and its World Wide Web. The huge growth in Internet usage and the new technologies and specialties connected with it are increasing the employment opportunities in the computer industry. Many of the hottest jobs are Internet related. But it's not only the Internet that's causing all the growth. As more companies and individuals use computers, there's a resulting need for new applications, new software, and new technology in general. So computer jobs should remain on the upswing over the long term. In particular, keep an eye on smaller and midsize companies that often specialize in specific industries and are beginning to steal business away from giants like EDS or Computer Sciences.

Information services—both at specific information-services companies, such as database providers, and at general corporations with information-service departments. On-line information services are growing in importance, with more companies relying on computerized information sources. As such, there should be job opportunities in this field in all areas, including technical, customer service and sales and marketing.

As for specific career areas: the long-term forecast looks the strongest for software engineers, web site designers, systems architects, database and tool developers, experienced project leaders, relational database experts. (For more information on these, see Computers, page 50.) On the nontechnical side, opportunities continue to increase for skilled professionals with computer-help desks at hardware and software companies and at technical support companies. Salespeople, as well, are in for a positive employment outlook—as competition for consumers heightens in the computer industry. Applications software, middleware, and systems software companies have been hiring, as have hardware manufacturers. Best qualified: people with technical undergrad degrees and strong communications skills.

JOBS SPOTLIGHT

SOFTWARE ENGINEER: A field that has been hot for the past few years, software engineering remains strong. Salaries cover a wide range—from about $30,000 for entry-level workers up to the mid-$60,000s at the top of the scale.

BEST BETS

Hewlett-Packard Co.
3000 Hanover St.
Palo Alto, CA 94304
415/857-1501

Well known for its team orientation and "management by walking around" policies, H-P has long had an excellent reputation as a place to work. One example of how highly it is regarded by executives and business experts: In 1996, H-P was voted most admired corporation in the Computers and Office Equipment Industry in *Fortune* magazine's annual survey, as well as the ninth most admired company overall. All in all, H-P is a great place to work . . . but, of course, competition for a job here is usually quite tough.

Microsoft Corp.
1 Microsoft Way
Redmond, WA 98052-6399
206/882-8800

Consistently ranked by fellow executives among the US's best run corporations in *Fortune* magazine's annual listings (and in 1996 ranked number one among major computer firms), Microsoft is a software powerhouse that's the major force in the market. It's also well known for its innovative hiring program, which includes asking applicants unusual questions (alleged example: How would you weigh an airplane without a scale?) to assess their creativity and drive. Each month Microsoft gets about 12,000 resumes—all are logged into their computers along with other data; key-word oriented search programs sort them out—and if you're right for the job, Microsoft will give you a call.

TOP COMPUTER COMPANIES

Adobe Systems
1585 Charleston Rd.
Mountain View, CA 94039-7900
415/961-4400

Alltell Information Services, Inc.
4001 Rodney Parham Rd.
Little Rock, AR 72212
501/220-5100

Amdahl Corp.
1250 E. Arques Ave.
Sunnyvale, CA 94086
408/746-6000

America Online
8619 Westwood Center Dr.
Vienna VA 22182-2285
703/448-8700

American Management Systems
4050 Legato Rd.

Fairfax, VA 22033
703/841-6000

American Telephone & Telegraph Co.
295 N. Maple Ave.
Basking Ridge, NJ 07920
908/221-2010

Andersen Consulting
35 W. Monroe St.
Chicago, IL 60603
312/372-7100

Apple Computer, Inc.
1 Infinite Loop
Cupertino, CA 95014
408/996-1010

Applied Materials
3050 Bowers Ave.
Santa Clara, CA 95054
408/727-5555

ASK Computer Systems, Inc.
2880 Santa Clara Blvd.

Santa Clara, CA 95052
415/969-4442

AST Research, Inc.
16215 Alton Pkwy.
Irvine, CA 92718
714/727-4141

Atari Corp.
1196 Borregas Ave.
Sunnyvale, CA 94088
408/745-2000

Atmel
2125 O'Nel Dr.
San Jose, CA 95131
408/441-0311

AT&T Global Information Solutions
1700 S. Patterson Blvd.
Dayton, OH 45479
513/445-5000

Autodesk, Inc.
111 McInnis Pkwy.
San Rafael, CA 94903
415/507-5000

Automatic Data Processing, Inc.
1 ADP Blvd.
Roseland, NJ 07068
201/994-5000

Bay Networks
4401 Great American Pkwy.
Santa Clara, CA 95054
408/988-2400

Bell Atlantic Business Systems Services
50 E. Swedesford Rd.
Frazer, PA 19355
215/296-6000

BMC Software
2101 Citywest Blvd.
Houston, TX
77042-2827
713/918-8800

Boeing Information Services, Inc.
7990 Boeing Ct.
Vienna, VA 22182
703/847-1100

Bolt Beranek and Newman, Inc.
150 Cambridge Pk. Dr.
Cambridge, MA 02140
617/873-2000

Cabletron Systems Inc.
35 Industrial Way
Rochester, NH 03867
603/332-9400

Cadence Design Systems, Inc.
555 River Oaks Pkwy.
San Jose, CA 05134
408/943-1234

Ceridian Corp.
8100 34 Ave. S.
Minneapolis, MN
55425
612/853-8100

Cincom Systems, Inc.
2300 Montana Ave.
Cincinnati, OH 45211
513/662-2300

Cisco Systems
170 W. Tasman Dr.
San Jose, CA
95134-1706
408/526-4000

Compaq Computer Corp.
555 St. Hwy 249
Houston TX 77070
713/370-0670

Computer Associates
2400 Cabot Dr.
Lisle, IL 60532
708/505-6000

Computer Associates International, Inc.
1 Computer Associates Plz.
Islandia, NY
11788-7000
516/342-5224

Computer Sciences Corp.
2100 E. Grand Ave.
El Segundo, CA 90245
310/615-0311

Computer Task Group, Inc.
800 Delaware Ave.
Buffalo, NY 14209
716/882-8000

Concurrent Computer Corporation
2 Crescent Pl.
Oceanport, NJ 07757
908/870-4500

Convex Computer Corp.
3000 Waterview Pkwy.
Richardson, TX 75080
214/497-4000

Corel-U.S.A.
1555 N. Technology Way
Orem, UT 84057
801/225-5000

Cray Research, Inc.
655A Lone Oak Dr.
Eagan, MN 55121
612/452-6650

Data General Corp.
4400 Computer Dr.
Westborough, MA
01580
508/898-5000

Datastorm Technologies
3212 Lemoine Industrial Blvd.
Columbia, MO 65201
314/443-3282

Dell Computer Corp.
2214 W. Braker Lane
Austin, TX 78758
512/338-4400

Diebold, Incorporated
818 Mulberry Rd., SE
Canton, OH 44711
216/489-4000

Digital Equipment Corp.
111 Powder Mill Rd.
Maynard, MA
01754-2571
508/493-5111

Dun & Bradstreet Software Services, Inc.
3445 Peachtree Rd. NE
Atlanta, GA 30326
404/239-2000

Electronic Data Systems Corp.
5400 Legacy Dr.
Plano, TX 75024
214/604-6000

EMC
171 South St.
Hopkinton, MA
01748-9103
508/435-1000

Everex Systems, Inc.
5020 Brandon Court
Fremont, CA 94538
510/498-1111

Gateway 2000
610 Gateway Dr.
No. Sioux City, SD
57049
605/232-2000

**General Electric
Information
Systems**
401 N. Washington St.
Rockville, MD 20850
301/340-4000

Hewlett-Packard Co.
3000 Hanover St.
Palo Alto, CA 94304
415/857-1501

**IBM—International
Business Machines
Corp.**
Old Orchard Rd.
Armonk, NY 10504
914/765-1900

**Information Builders,
Inc.**
1250 Broadway
New York, NY 10001
212/736-4433

Informix
4100 Bohannon Dr.
Menlo Park, CA 94025
415/926-6300

Intel Corp.
P.O. Box 58119
2200 Mission College
Blvd.
Santa Clara, CA 95054
408/765-8080

Intergraph Corp.
8252 Hwy. 20 W.
Huntsville, AL 35894
205/730-2000
(Workstations and
applications.)

**International Game
Technology**
520 S. Rock Blvd.
Reno, NV 89502
702/688-0365

Intuit
2535 Garcia Ave.
Mountain View, CA
94043
415/994-6000

Iomega Corp.
1821 W. Iomega Way
Roy, UT 84067
801/778-1000

Itel
2 N. Riverside Plz.
Chicago, IL 60606
312/902-1515

**Lexmark
International Groupo**
55 Railroad Ave.
Greenwich, CT 06836
203/629-6700

Linear Technology
1630 McCarthy Blvd.
Milpitas, CA 95035
408/432-1900

**Lotus Development
Corp.**
55 Cambridge Pkwy.
Cambridge, MA 02142
617/577-8500

MAI Systems Corp.
9600 Geronimo Rd.
San Jose, CA 95134
408/432-1700

**McDonnell Douglas
Systems Integration
Co.**

P.O. Box 516
St. Louis, MO 63166
314/232-0232

Merisel
200 Continental Blvd.
El Segundo, CA 90245
310/615-3080

Micron Technology
P.O. Box 6
Boise, ID 83707-0006
208/368-4000

Micropolis Corp.
21211 Nordhoff St.
Chatsworth, CA 91311
818/709-3300

Microsoft Corp.
1 Microsoft Way
Redmond, WA
98052-6399
206/882-8080

NCR Corp.
1700 S. Patterson Blvd.
Dayton, OH 45479
513/445-5000

**Netscape
Communications**
501 E. Middlefield Rd.
Moutain View, CA
94043
415/254-1900

Novell, Inc.
122 E. 1500 S.
Provo, UT 84606
801/429-7000

Oracle Corp.
P.O. Box 659506
500 Oracle Pkwy.
Redwood Shores, CA
90465
415/506-7000

**Parametric
Technology**
128 Technology Dr.
Waltham, MA 02154
617/398-5000

PeopleSoft
4440 Rosewood Dr.
Pleaston, CA 94588
510/225-3000

Pyramid Technology Corp.
3860 N. First St.
San Jose, CA 95134
408/428-9000

Quantum Corp.
500 McCarthy Blvd.
Milpitas, CA 95035
408/894-4000

Recognition Equipment, Inc.
2701 E. Grauwyler Rd.
Irving, TX 75061
214/579-6000

Reynolds & Reynolds Company
800 Germantown St.
Dayton, OH 45407
513/443-2000

SAS Institutes, Inc.
SAS Campus Dr.
Cary, NC 27513
919/677-8000

SCI Systems, Inc.
2101 Clinton Ave.
Huntsville, AL 35805
205/882-4800

Science Applications International Corp.
10260 Campus Pt. Dr.
San Diego, CA 92121
619/546-6000

Seagate Technology
920 Disc Dr.
Scotts Valley, CA 95066
408/438-6550

Shared Medical Systems Corp.
51 Valley Stream Pkwy.
Malvern, PA 19355
610/219-6300

Silicon Graphics, Inc.
2011 N. Shoreline Blvd.
Mountain View, CA 94043-1389
415/960-1980

Sybase
6475 Christie Ave.
Emeryville, CA 94608
510/658-3500

Software AG of North America, Inc.
11190 Sunrise Valley Dr.
Reston, VA 22091
703/860-5050

Sterling Software, Inc.
11050 White Rock Rd., Suite 100
Rancho Cordova, CA 95670
916/635-5535

Storage Technology Corp.
2270 S. 88th St.
Louisville, CO 80028
303/673-5151

Stratus Computer, Inc.
55 Fairbanks Blvd.
Marlboro, MA 01752
508/460-2000

Sun Microsystems, Inc.
2550 Garcia Ave.
Mountain View, CA 94043-1100
415/960-1300

Tandem Computers, Inc.
19191 Vallco Pkwy.
Cupertino, CA 95014-2599
408/285-6000

Tech Data
5350 Tech Data Dr.
Clearwater, FL 34620
813/539-7429

Tektronix, Inc.
26600 SW Parkway Ave.
Wilsonville, OR 97070
503/627-7111

Tellabs
4951 Indiana Ave.
Lisle, IL 60532
708/969-8800

Teradyne
321 Harrison Ave.
Boston, MA 02118
617/482-2700

Texas Instruments, Inc.
13500 N. Central Expy.
Dallas, TX 75243
214/995-2011

3Com Corp.
5400 Bayfront Plaza
Santa Clara, CA 95052-8145
408/764-5000

TRW, Inc.— Information Systems and Services
1900 Richmond Rd.
Cleveland, OH 44124
216/291-7000

Unisys Corp.
Townshipline and Union Meeting Rds.
PO Box 500
Blue Bell, PA 19424-0001
215/986-4011

U.S. Robotics
8100 N. McCormick Blvd.
Skokie, IL 60076
847/982-5010

Wang Laboratories, Inc.
1 Industrial Ave.
Lowell, MA 01851
508/459-5000

Western Digital Corp.
8105 Irvine Center Dr.

Irvine, CA 92718
714/932-5000

Wyse Technology
3471 N. First St.
San Jose, CA 95134
408/922-4300

Xerox Corp.
800 Long Ridge Rd.

Stamford, CT 06902
203/968-3000

Xilinx
2100 Logic Dr.
San Jose, CA
95124-3450
408/559-7778

TOP ELECTRONICS AND PRECISION INSTRUMENTS COMPANIES

(For related companies, also see "Top Aerospace Companies," page 229.)

Advanced Micro Devices, Inc.
1 AMD Pl.
Sunnyvale, CA 94086
408/732-2400

American Annuity Group
250 E. Fifth St.
Cincinnati, OH 45202
513/357-3307

Ametek, Inc.
Station Sq.
Paoli, PA 19301
215/647-2121

AMP, Inc.
P.O. Box 3608
Harrisburg, PA
17105-3608
717/564-0100

Analog Devices
1 Technology Way
Norwood, MA 02062
617/329-4700

Applied Magnetics Corp.
75 Robin Hill Rd.
Goleta, CA 93117
805/683-5353

Arrow Electronics
25 Hub Dr.

Melville, NY 11747
516/391-1300

Avnet, Inc.
80 Cutter Mill Rd.
Great Neck, NY 11021
516/466-7000
Fax 516/466-1203

AVX Corp.
750 Lexington Ave.
New York, NY 10022
212/935-6363

Beckman Instruments, Inc.
2500 Harbor Blvd.
Fullerton, CA 92634
714/871-4848

Chips & Technologies, Inc.
2950 Zenker Rd.
San Jose, CA 95134
408/434-0600

Cypress Semiconductor Corp.
195 Champion St.
San Jose, CA 95134
408/943-2600

Dynatech Corp.
3 New England
Executive Pk.
Burlington, MA 01803
617/272-6100

Eastman Kodak Co.
343 State St.
Rochester, NY 14650
716/724-4000

EG&G, Inc.
45 William St.
Wellesley, MA 02181
617/237-5100

Fujitsu Microelectronics, Inc.
3545 N. First St.
San Jose, CA 95134
408/922-9000

Imo Industries, Inc.
1009 Lenox Dr.
Lawrenceville, NJ
08648
609/896-7600

Johnson Controls, Inc.
5757 N. Green Bay
Ave.
Glendale, WI 53209
414/228-1200

LSI Logic Corp.
1551 McCarthy Blvd.
Milpitas, CA 95035
408/433-8000

Memc Electronic Materials, Inc.
501 Pearl Dr.
St. Peters, MO 63376
314/279-5000

Millipore Corp.
80 Ashby Rd.
Bedford, MA 01730
617/275-9200

Molex, Inc.
2222 Wellington Ct.
Lisle, IL 60532-1682
708/969-4550

Motorola, Inc.
1303 E. Algonquin Rd.
Schaumburg, IL 60196
708/576-5000

National Semiconductor Corp.
1090 Kifer Rd.
Sunnyvale, CA 94086
408/721-5000

Perkin-Elmer Corp.
761 Main Ave.
Norwalk, CT 06859
203/762-1000

Polaroid Corp.
549 Technology Sq.
Cambridge, MA 02139
617/386-2000

Raychem Corp.
300 Constitution Dr.
Menlo Park, CA 94025
415/361-3333

Tektronix, Inc.
26600 SW Parkway Ave.
Wilsonville, OR 97070
503/627-7111

Thermo Electron Corp.
81 Wyman St.
Waltham, MA 02154
617/622-1000

Thomas & Betts Corp.
1555 Lynnfield Rd.
Memphis, TN 38119
901/682-7766

Varian Associates
3050 Hansen Way
Palo Alto, CA 94304
415/493-4000

Vishay Intertechnology, Inc.
63 Lincoln Hwy.
Malvern, PA 19355
215/644-1300

VLSI Technology, Inc.
1109 McKay Dr.
San Jose, CA 95131
408/434-3000

Western Digital Corp.
8105 Irvine Center Dr.
Irvine, CA 92718
714/932-5000

WHERE TO GO FOR MORE INFORMATION

(For more information sources related to the computers/electronics industry, see "Engineers," page 50; "Technical Careers," page 196; "Aerospace," page 225; and "Telecommunications," page 456.)

COMPUTER/ELECTRONICS INDUSTRY ASSOCIATIONS

American Electronics Association
5201 Great American Pkwy.
Suite 520
Santa Clara, CA 95054
408/987-4200

Association for Computing Machinery
1515 Broadway
New York, NY 10036
212/869-7440
(Runs resume databank for members.)

Computer and Automated Systems Association of SME
1 SME Dr.
Dearborn, MI 48121
313/271-1500

Computer & Business Equipment Manufacturers Association
1250 Eye St. NW
Suite 200
Washington, DC 20005
202/737-8888

Computer & Communications Industry Association
666 11th St., NW
Washington, DC 20001
202/783-0070

Computer Dealers and Lessors Association
1200 19 St., NW
Suite 300
Washington, DC 20036
202/429-5150

Electronics Industries
Association
2500 Wilson Blvd.
Arlington, VA 22201
703/907-7500

IEEE Computer
Society
1730 Massachusetts
Ave., NW
Washington, DC 20036
202/371-0101

Information Industry
Association
555 New Jersey Ave.,
NW

Washington, DC 20001
202/986-0280

Information
Technology
Association of
America
1616 N. Ft. Myer Dr.,
Suite 1300
Arlington, VA 22209
703/522-5055

Robotics
International of
SME
P.O. Box 930
1 SME Dr.

Dearborn, MI 48121
313/271-1500

Semiconductor
Equipment and
Material Institute
805 E. Middlefield Rd.
Mountain View, CA
94043
415/964-5111

Semiconductor
Industry Association
181 Metro Dr.
Suite 450
San Jose, CA 95110
408/436-6600

COMPUTER/ELECTRONICS INDUSTRY DIRECTORIES

*Computer Industry
Almanac*
The Reference Press
6448 Highway 290 E.
Suite E-104
Austin, TX 78723
512/454-7778

*Computing & Software
Design Career
Directory*
Gale Research

P.O. Box 33477
Detroit, MI 48232
800/877-4253

*Directory of Top
Computer Executives*
Applied Computer
Research
P.O. Box 82266
Phoenix, AZ 85071
602/995-5929

*Hoover's Guide to
Computer Companies*
The Reference Press
6448 Highway 290 E.
Suite E-104
Austin, TX 78723
512/454-7778

*Women in Technology
Directory*
http://www.sdsu.edu/wit

COMPUTER/ELECTRONICS INDUSTRY PERIODICALS

*Computer Reseller
News*
600 Community Dr.
Manhasset, NY 11030
516/562-5000
(Weekly tabloid for
systems personnel,
engineers,
manufacturers, etc.)

Computer World
500 Old Community
Pass

Framingham, MA
01701
508/879-0700
(Weekly tabloid
covering all phases of
the computer industry.)

Corporate Computing
60 E. 42nd St.
New York, NY 10065
212/682-1717
(Monthly magazine

sent to corporate
computer executives.)

Data Communications
1221 Ave. of the
Americas
New York, NY 10020
212/512-6950
(Monthly magazine for
professionals involved
in computer network
integration and
implementation.)

Datamation
275 Washington
Newton, MA 02158
617/964-3030
(Semimonthly
magazine aimed at IS
managers,
manufacturers, etc.
Annual *Datamation
100* issue lists the top
companies in the field
and includes addresses
as well as company
profiles. This may be
useful in a resume
mailing campaign.)

Digital News
Conners Publications
275 Washington St.
Newton, MA 02158
617/964-3030
(Biweekly publication
for hardware and
software
manufacturers, dealers,
retailers, etc.)

**ECN Electronic
Component News**
Chilton Way

Radnor, PA 19089
610/964-4000
(Monthly publication
for design engineers,
engineering managers,
etc.)

EDN
275 Washington St.
Newton, MA 02158
617/964-3030
(Biweekly for
electronics engineers,
product designers,
systems designers,
etc.)

Electronic Business
275 Washington St.
Newton, MA 02158
617/964-3030
(Semimonthly
magazine covering the
computer and
electronics industry.
Annual *Electronic
Business 200* issue runs
down the top
companies in the
industry.)

Electronic Design
611 Rte 46 W.
Hasbrouck Heights, NJ
07604
201/393-6060
(Biweekly magazine
for engineers and
design managers.)

**Electronic
Engineering Times**
600 Community Dr.
Manhasset, NY 11030
516/562-5000
(Weekly publication
aimed at engineers,
managers, supervisors,
and marketing and
research staffers.)

Electronic News
475 Park Ave. S.
New York, NY 10016
212/736-3900
(Weekly newspaper for
computer/electronics
industry professionals,
including engineers and
sales and marketing
managers.)

CONGLOMERATES

INDUSTRY OUTLOOK: Continued focusing and strengthening—with particular emphasis on establishing specific core businesses.

Conglomerates—diversified companies with unrelated businesses—should continue changing their operating and financial strategies. Since market values of such companies tend to be lower than the sum of their individual businesses, expect continued focus on improving market values.

The key elements to expect: Recapitalizing the company (including stock buybacks and revaluations), spinoffs of subsidiaries, and divestiture (selling off a portion of a subsidiary). Other efforts include more attention paid to cost-cutting, focus on fewer lines of business, and general streamlining. In the long term, there may be renewed merger activity.

Aside from this, specific outlooks depend upon the specific industries a conglomerate is involved in. For more specific forecasts, see the various industry chapters to find outlooks and trends for the different areas of business held by a conglomerate.

A LOOK BACK

▶ **The past few years: Conglomerates refocus and restructure—and some fall by the wayside.**

The number of conglomerates has been shrinking. Some companies (such as Insilco, Amfac, and Pullman) fell victim to the mergers-and-acquisition fever that swept the country. Others refocused on one area or a group of related areas instead of maintaining holdings in a broad range of industries. The prime example: Gulf & Western, long the epitome of a traditional U.S. conglomerate, shed its noncommunications holdings to become Paramount Communications.

The key trend of the recent past: refocusing corporate aims to center around a single industry or group of related industries, with the aim of dominating niches. In addition, some larger conglomerates began to look for suitors for unprofitable subsidiaries. For example, in 1992 LTV put its aerospace and missile divisions up for sale. Allied-Signal cut its business units to 32 from 49 from 1990 to 1994. The '90s, then, have been a period of change for conglomerates—as they retrenched and restructured, emerging leaner and less diversified than in the past.

WHAT'S NEXT

▶ **The general trend affecting conglomerates: like the U.S. economy as a whole, expect to see continued cost cutting, streamlining, and close attention to the bottom line.**

Conglomerates will remain somewhat cautious, careful to avoid the excesses of the '80s. Expansion will be balanced by consolidation; conglomerates will avoid taking on the heavy debt that characterized the "go-go" years in the past.

▶ Single-industry or related-industry holding companies will continue to replace the traditional conglomerates.

The years ahead should bring more of the same activity that marked the past few. The days of the old-fashioned conglomerate with holdings in a range of industries appear to be over for the time being. Instead, it looks like there will be an increase in the number of industry-specific conglomerates, like Paramount Communications and other communications giants.

Along these lines, expect to see sell-offs of subsidiaries unrelated to core businesses, consolidation activity, and a refocusing of business among some of the giants. Similarly, expect more conglomerates to follow ITT's lead—which, in 1995, announced it would split into three separate companies with three distinct core focuses.

▶ As for the conglomerates that remain, their overall performance will depend on the strengths and weaknesses of their subsidiaries.

It's the obvious rule of thumb: A conglomerate is as strong or as weak as the sum total of its parts. Certain conglomerates may be vulnerable in the short term if their subsidiaries are involved in slumping or excessively competitive industries.

EMPLOYMENT OUTLOOK: Varies according to the specific company and subsidiaries.

In line with the new streamlined, cost-aware conglomerate of the '90s, corporate staffs have been pared—and it's unlikely that there will be a major increase in terms of employment opportunities. But, on the plus side, the renewed attention to shareholder return and emphasis on revenues is forcing conglomerates to somehow create opportunities for employees. The upshot? Opportunities will exist, even in this leaner, meaner environment.

Employment opportunities at conglomerates are directly related to the particular industries the company is involved in. For forecasts, then, check the specific industry section that correlates with the company or subsidiary that interests you. Also check the Careers section, such as Managers (page 128) or Sales and Marketing Professionals (page 148).

BEST BETS

General Electric
3135 Easton Turnpike
Fairfield, CT 06431
203/373-2211

One of the biggest and the best, General Electric is consistently a best bet for employment. Among the reasons? Its extensive training programs and attention to continued employee development. Entry-level employees get immediate attention and intensive training, and it continues all the way up the ladder to upper-level seminars for managers. Another strong point for GE is its recent push for innovation. Even though the company has a reputation for being traditional, its managers are open to flexible working methods, like team manufacturing. Even better, GE isn't forcing the issue. It lets each plant decide what methods it wants to use.

3M (Minnesota Mining & Manufacturing)
3M Center
St. Paul, MN 55144-1000
612/733-1110

3M is known as a company that believes in career employees. As such, it is big on promoting from within. And to help new employees, it has developed a mentor program, in which new employees can go to a mentor who will help them, answer work-related questions, and so forth. Another 3M trait: rewarding employees for jobs well done, with everything from parties to pizza to bonuses. This type of attention to employees is one of the reasons 3M was chosen in *Fortune* magazine's 1996 survey, one of the ten most admired companies in the United States in terms of its ability to attract, develop and keep talented people. The company has long had a reputation for providing job security for workers and a history of maintaining a no-layoff policy even in tough times. The downside? Lagging sales have been plaguing the industry giant. If sales don't increase, 3M may be forced to trim its work force. However, in line with its corporate policy, it will try to avoid layoffs and rely instead on early retirement and attrition. The bottom line? While hiring activity might not be hot, this is a great bet if you can land a job here.

TOP CONGLOMERATES

(Also see company listings in other industries.)

The Actava Group
133 Peachtree St., NE
Atlanta, GA 30303
404/658-9000

Alco Standard Corporation
825 Duportail Rd.
Wayne, PA 19087
610/296-8000

Allied-Signal, Inc.
101 Columbia Rd.
Morristown, NJ 07960
201/455-2000

Ametek, Inc.
Station Square

Paoli, PA 19301
610/647-2121

Anixeter International Inc.
2 N. Riverside Plaza
Chicago, IL 60606
312/902-1515

Dial Corp.
1850 Central Ave.
Phoenix, AZ 85077
602/207-4000

Figgie International, Inc.
4420 Sherwin Rd.

Willoughby, OH 44094
216/946-9000

General Electric Co.
3135 Easton Tpke.
Fairfield, CT 06431-0001
203/373-2211

Harcourt General Corp.
27 Boylston St.
Chestnut Hill, MA 02167
617/232-8200

Itel Corp.
2 N. Riverside Plz.
Chicago, IL 60606
312/902-1515

ITT Corp.
1330 Ave. of the
Americas
New York, NY
10019-5490
212/258-1000

Kaman Corp.
1332 Blue Hills Ave.
Bloomfield, CT
06002
203/243-8311

**MacAndrews &
Forbes Holdings**
36 E. 63rd St.
New York, NY 10021
212/688-9000

Mark IV Industries
501 John James
Audubon Pk.
Buffalo, NY 14228
716/689-4972

Marmon Group
225 W. Washington St.
Chicago, IL 60606
313/372-9500

**Minnesota Mining &
Manufacuring Co.
(3M)**
3M Ctr.
St. Paul, MN 55144
612/733-1100

Ogden Corporation
2 Pennsylvania Plz.
New York, NY 10121
212/868-6100

**The Penn Central
Corp.**
1 E. Fourth St.
Cleveland, OH 45202
513/579-6600

**Philip Morris Cos.,
Inc.**
120 Park Ave.
New York, NY 10017
212/880-5000

Pittway Corp.
200 S. Wacker
Suite 700
Chicago, IL
60606-5802
708/498-1261

**Premark
International, Inc.**
1717 Deerfield Rd.
Deerfield, IL 60015
708/405-6000

**Rockwell
International
Corp.**
2201 Seal Beach Blvd.
Seal Beach, CA 90740
310/797-3311

Sequa Corp.
200 Park Ave.
New York, NY 10166
212/986-5500

**Standex International
Corp.**
6 Manor Pky.
Salem, NH 03079
603/893-9701

Tenneco, Inc.
1010 Milam St.
Houston, TX 77002
713/757-2131

Textron, Inc.
40 Westminster St.
Providence, RI 02903
401/421-2800

Thermo Electron Corp.
81 Wyman St.
Waltham, MA 02154
617/622-1000

Triarc Cos., Inc.
900 Third Ave.
New York, NY 10022
212/230-3000

TRW, Inc.
1900 Richmond Rd.
Cleveland, OH
44124-3760
216/291-7000

Valhi Group, Inc.
5430 LBJ Fwy., Suite
1700
Dallas TX 75240
214/233-1700

Whitman Corp.
3501 Algonquin Rd.
Rolling Meadows, IL
60008
708/818-5000

CONSUMER PRODUCTS

INDUSTRY OUTLOOK: Extremely competitive.

Package goods: Brand names are back with a vengeance. Brand loyalty isn't dead as many had predicted, and as a result, competition is hotter than ever. Expect it to continue, as package goods companies try to seize market share. Key problem: Limited retail shelf space. Look for marketers to seek out new avenues to growth—to chain drug stores, to specialty shops, to home improvement centers, and to warehouse clubs. Key consumer concerns driving new product development: environmental awareness and cost-consciousness. Over the long term: Keep a lookout for an increase in mergers and acquisitions as companies try to increase market share the least expensive way—by taking over other companies instead of investing in developing and marketing new products. Watch U.S. manufacturers jump into rapidly expanding overseas markets as foreign per capita incomes continue to increase.

Cosmetics: Expect long-term growth, an increase in mergers and acquisitions, movement into new distribution channels, and tighter competition in foreign markets. In addition, as a result of changing consumer demand and increased environmental awareness, cosmetics companies will be pumping more into R&D to come up with new products that are environmentally safe and that meet the needs of specific consumer niches. Hot areas: Products aimed at aging baby boomers, preteens, teenagers, and minorities.

Appliance manufacturers: Positive trends pointing to a bright long-term outlook include expected increases in home building and buying, an aging population, a high level of two-income families, and increases in spending. Good short-term potential: cooking products and personal care appliances. Keep an eye on retailers who are insisting on "just-in-time" delivery from manufacturers in order to reduce inventories and operating costs. Impact will be increased manufacturer inventory holding costs.

A LOOK BACK

► **The key trends of the '90s: mergers, competition, and an increase in consumer price consciousness.**

Mergers in the consumer products industries resulted in a smaller industry—populated by large giants. Then a weak economy led to increased price awareness on the part of consumers which led, in turn, to hotter competition than ever. Adding to the industry turmoil: the erosion of brand loyalty. Consumers sought bargains, and switched brands to get them. As a result, the consumer products industry reacted with price wars, heavy promotional activity, and a flurry of new product introductions, all in an effort to attract—and keep—customers. But brands regained footing in 1995 and 1996. And the consumer products industry reacted by reinstituting their usual brand warfare—battling for shelf space and trying to keep prices attractive.

WHAT'S NEXT

▶ **Cutthroat competition will continue to have a marked effect on all areas of the consumer products industry.**

It's a given in the consumer products industry. Competition will remain as hot as ever—and may, in fact, increase. It's a cutthroat environment. Expect to see smaller consumer products companies falter, as they lack the brand awareness to compete effectively. Also watch for pricing wars as established brands vie for consumer dollars. Finally, expect to see some companies compete by cutting *back* on products and focusing only on their most successful core products. This way they can pump advertising and marketing dollars into a select few products—and win market share.

▶ **To compete well in this tough marketplace, companies will continue consolidating and streamlining.**

It's one way to keep lean and mean. Over the long term, expect to see a limited continuation of merger activity—larger companies swallowing up smaller ones to expand market reach, add products, and increase global market share.

Similarly, keep an eye out for consolidation within companies. The recession made it look more attractive to other companies, and it looks like this trend will keep going strong. Specifically, more companies will be setting up smaller teams within their operations and focusing on working closely with their retail customers. These teams will be made up of specialists from different areas, including logistics, finance, information, and sales. In many cases, salespeople will have responsibility for an entire sector or category, as opposed to just one or two brands.

Problems: Some manufacturers will be relying increasingly on distributors, wholesalers, and retailers for sales and marketing while they concentrate on production. Moverover, in an effort to streamline and make systems more efficient manufacturers and distributors and retailers are beginning to use electronic inventory/ordering systems at manufacturers and distributors/retailers—which may result in cuts in sales jobs. But in the long term, this trend points to opportunities in broad-based product management, customer support, and logistics.

▶ **A long-term trend that will keep growing: industry globalization.**

More companies will be setting up international marketing networks to penetrate different parts of the world. U.S. companies are particularly interested in penetrating Eastern Europe, the Pacific Rim, and Latin America.

There's a flip side to this as well: Foreign companies, particularly European ones, are entering into joint ventures with U.S. companies to gain a toehold in the American marketplace. The long-term bottom line? By the year 2000, expect to see multinational giants dominate the worldwide consumer products industry.

In general, this attention to world markets points to employment opportunities for people with international experience, especially product managers and international marketing experts.

▶ A new reality—big retailers call the tune.

With the advent of mass merchandising, cost and service considerations play major roles for the major retailer in selecting manufacturers/vendors. The big retailers established just-in-time inventory policies—little on-premises inventories—forcing suppliers to maintain inventories with almost immediate shipment-to-store capabilities. Impact: Only major manufacturers with strong cost controls may be able to absorb the inventory holding costs. Smaller manufacturers may need to consolidate with others to achieve economies, particularly as retailers also reduce the number of suppliers, and to give them clout in the fight for retail shelf space.

▶ Keep an eye on efforts to target and reach niche markets.

It's one way of reaching new customers and getting a foothold in a new market. More companies will be targeting specific consumer sectors—such as blacks, Hispanics, and Asians—not only by introducing advertising and promotion directly aimed at these groups but also by introducing new products developed especially for them.

Cosmetics and health and beauty aids manufacturers have already made inroads in this area. Product lines such as Estée Lauder's Prescriptives All Skins and Maybelline's Shades of You are selling strong. Expect more companies to enter this field with complete lines. This should translate into employment opportunities both in new product development and sales and marketing.

▶ Keep an eye on the baby boomlet marketplace.

Health and beauty aids (HBA) manufacturers are examining and testing the opportunities in this 38 million–person market—children born in 1977–1994—with attractive growth rates to 2030. Traditionally, highly competitive HBA products earn low profit margins, with the child segment achieving better returns. Fueling this growth: dual-income families, with money to spend on their children; women waiting longer to have children; plus more effective family planning and greater ability to spend on children. One industry expert characterized the two major segments of this market as: the "I want that" preteenager and the "Have money, will spend" teenager.

▶ Watch for more industry developments and changes due to environmental issues.

Environmental issues will continue to have a strong impact on consumer products companies. Soap and detergent manufacturers will continue to come out with products that are environmentally sound—such as concentrated detergents, products with less packaging, and natural (as opposed to petrochemical-based) soaps and detergents. The R&D area will heat up as tougher environmental regulations are instituted and manufacturers look for new ways to produce products that conform to the new laws. This means opportunities for scientists and chemical engineers.

Appliance manufacturers will also be developing new products in response to concerns about environmental and health issues—such as chlorofluorocarbons (CFCs) and their impact on the ozone layer, electromagnetic fields (EMFs) and their effects on health, and appliance disposal and recycling. The result: the necessity for more R&D. In certain ways, concerns about the environment will have a positive impact on the appliance industry. With increased environmental awareness and new legislation, watch for refrigerator and air-conditioner companies to reap the rewards. Why? To combat a depleted ozone layer, consumers and industries will have to replace their existing appliances for new, environment-friendly ones.

EMPLOYMENT OUTLOOK: Directly affected by competition.

First the bad news: With such hot competition, profit margins have been shrinking . . . which means that some companies may resort to layoffs to keep costs down. In addition, the cost-consciousness that has been affecting the industry may translate into less money devoted to new product development—which, again, translates into fewer employment opportunities.

But it's not all grim. With this intense competition comes increased attention to targeted sales and marketing and focused brand development. This means that brand managers and senior brand managers will continue to see employment opportunities. Hot jobs: trade marketers and category managers (see below for more information). Interactive marketing is also hot for computer-savvy marketers.

On the technical side, logistics engineers will be in demand. A key reason: "Just-in-time" manufacturing—whereby factory orders are received at the time they are needed, rather than weeks or months in advance—is making the logistics of factory work a more vital concern. People with strong organizational and computer skills should do well.

JOBS SPOTLIGHT

PRODUCT MANAGERS: The backbone of most consumer products companies and as such always needed. Lately, with more brands on the shelves competing head to head, this area is becoming more visible—and more competitive. Salaries generally begin in the low $40s and can reach well over $90,000, with salaries in the six-figure range not uncommon at some of the larger companies.

CATEGORY MANAGERS: The newest twist on product and brand managers, they are becoming more common—and, as competition grows, more in demand. Category managers (also called trademark managers) are responsible for an entire category of products (such as soaps or laundry detergents) as opposed to a specific brand. They create long-term marketing plans for that category and work closely with retailers. Salaries are similar to those paid to product managers, ranging from the low $40s up to the mid-six figures, depending on experience, category, and company.

TRADE MARKETER: A great spot for salespeople who want to break into marketing. Trade marketers act as a sort of bridge between sales and marketing departments. Their key role: determining how to utilize a promotions budget for products to increase sales. This position has been seeing some heavy hiring activity over the past year, and should continue to come on strong.

BEST BETS

S. C. Johnson & Son
1525 Howe St.
Racine, WI 53403
414/631-2000

Long a powerhouse in certain niche markets, this maker of such products as Glade air freshener, Raid bug spray and Pledge furniture polish, is growing larger, facing more competition . . . and appears to be meeting the challenge. S. C. Johnson has had a reputation for being paternalistic and for offering its employees virtual lifetime employment. While this hasn't changed, the workstyle has. Management is shifting the use of self-directed work teams, making this company able to meet the competition and increase productivity. As a result, employees set up their own leadership, training, and budgets, and are encouraged to share ideas with management. This type of employee motivation and empowerment makes this a good bet.

Procter & Gamble Co.
1 Procter & Gamble Plz.
Cincinnati, OH 45202
513/983-1100

The ubiquitous package goods company, Procter & Gamble has been making a number of changes to face the '90s—including partnerships with retailers, a revamped brand management system, and streamlined product development. And, on the employment side, it announced plans to reduce its work force by 12% within four years. However, especially at the entry levels, P&G is still a good bet. Even during the recession, it continued college recruitment for its well-known training programs. Competition, as always, is high for a spot at P&G, but if you've got the right combination of skills, it's a good spot for the future.

TOP CONSUMER PRODUCTS COMPANIES
(PERSONAL PRODUCTS, COSMETICS, SOAP AND DETERGENTS, ETC.)

Alberto-Culver Co.
2525 Armitage Ave.
Melrose Park, IL 60160
708/450-3000

American Brands, Inc.
1700 E. Putnam Ave.
Old Greenwich, CT
06870
203/698-5000

Avon Products, Inc.
9 W. 57th St.
New York, NY
10019-2683
212/546-6015

Carter Wallace, Inc.
1345 Ave. of the
Americas
New York, NY 10105
212/339-5000

Church & Dwight Co., Inc.
469 N. Harrison St.
Princeton, NJ
08543-5297
609/683-5900

Clairol, Inc.
345 Park Ave.
New York, NY 10154
212/546-5000

Clorox Co.
1221 Broadway
Oakland, CA
94612-1888
510/271-7000

Colgate-Palmolive Co.
300 Park Ave.
New York, NY
10022-7499
212/310-2000

Helene Curtis, Inc.
325 N. Wells St.
Chicago, IL 60610
312/661-0222

Dial Corp.
1850 Central Ave.
Phoenix, AZ
85077-2315
602/207-4000

Estée Lauder, Inc.
767 Fifth Ave.
New York, NY 10153
212/572-4600

Gillette Co.
800 Boylston St.
Boston, MA 02199
617/421-7000

**International Flavors
& Fragrances**
521 W. 57th St.

New York, NY 10019
212/765-5500

Andrew Jergens Co.
2535 Spring Grove
Ave.
Cincinnati, OH 45214
513/421-1400

Johnson & Johnson
1 Johnson & Johnson
Plz.
New Brunswick, NJ
08933
908/524-0400

S. C. Johnson and Son
1525 Howe St.
Racine, WI 52403
414/631-2000

Kimberly-Clark
351 Phelps Dr.
Dallas, TX 75261-9100
214/830-1200

**Mary Kay Cosmetics,
Inc.**
8787 Stemmons Fwy.
Dallas, TX 75247
214/630-8787

Maybelline Co.
3030 Jackson Ave.
Memphis, TN 38112
901/320-2011

Mennen Co.
5 E. Hanover Ave.
Morristown, NJ 07960
201/631-9000

NCH Corp.
2727 Chemsearch
Blvd.
Irving, TX 75062
214/438-0211

**Proctor & Gamble
Co.**
1 Procter & Gamble
Plz.
Cincinnati, OH 45202
513/983-1100

**Proctor & Gamble
Cosmetic and
Fragrance Products**
11050 York Rd.
Hunt Valley, MD 21030
410/785-7300

Revlon, Inc.
625 Madison Ave.
New York, NY 10022
212/527-4000

**Service Corp
International**
1929 Allen Pkwy.
Houston, TX
77219-0548
713/522-5141

Tambrands
777 Westchester Ave.
White Plains, NY
10604
914/696-6000

Unilever US, Inc.
390 Park Ave.
New York, NY 10022
212/888-1260

TOP APPLIANCE/CONSUMER ELECTRONICS COMPANIES

Bissell, Inc.
2345 Walker Rd., NW
Grand Rapids, MI 49504
616/453-4451

Black & Decker Corp.
701 E. Joppa Rd.

Towson, MD 21286
410/716-3900

Conair Corp.
150 Milford Rd.
E. Windsor, NJ 08520
609/426-1300

Duracell International
4 Berkshire Blvd.
Bethel, CT 06801
203/796-4000

Electrolux Corp.
2300 Windy Ridge

Pkwy.
Marietta, GA 30067
404/933-1000

Matsushita Electronic Corporation of America
1 Panasonic Way
Secaucus, NJ 07094
201/348-7000

Maytag Corp.
1 Dependability Sq.
Newton, IA 50208
515/792-8000

North American Philips Corp.
100 E. 42nd St.
New York, NY 10017
212/850-5000

Philips Consumer Electronics
1 Philips Dr.
Knoxville, TN 37914
615/521-4316

Remington Products, Inc.
60 Main St.

Bridgeport, CT 06604
203/367-4400

Royal Appliance Manufacturing
650 Alpha Dr.
Cleveland, OH 44143
216/449-6150

Scott & Fetzer Company
28800 Clemens Rd.
Cleveland, OH 44145
216/892-3000

Sharp Electronics Corp.
Sharp Plz.
P.O. Box 650
Mahwah, NJ 07430
201/529-8200

Sony Corp. of America
1 Sony Dr.
Park Ridge, NJ 07656
201/930-1000

Sunbeam-Oster
200 E. Las Olas Blvd.
Suite 2100
Ft. Lauderdale, FL

33301
305/767-2100

Thomson Consumer Electronics
103-30 N. Meridian St.
Indianapolis, IN 46290
317/267-5000

The Toro Co.
8111 Lyndale Ave. S.
Minneapolis, MN 55420
612/888-8801

Toshiba America, Inc.
1251 Ave. of the Americas
New York, NY 10020
212/596-0600

Whirlpool Corp.
2000 M63 N.
Benton Harbor, MI 49022-2692
616/923-5000

White Consolidated Industries, Inc.
11770 Berea Rd.
Cleveland, OH 44111
216/252-3700

WHERE TO GO FOR MORE INFORMATION

CONSUMER PRODUCTS INDUSTRY ASSOCIATIONS

Association of Home Appliance Manufacturers
20 N. Wacker Dr.
Chicago, IL 60606
312/984-5800

Cosmetic Toiletry and Fragrance Association
1101 17th St., NW,
Suite 300
Washington, DC 20036
202/331-1770

Independent Cosmetic Manufacturers and Distributors
1220 W. Northwest Hwy.
Palatine, IL 60067
708/991-4499

Electronic Industries Association
2500 Wilson Blvd.
Arlington, VA 22201
703/907-7500

National Housewares Manufacturers Association
6400 Shafer Ct., Suite 650
Rosemont, IL 60018
708/292-4200

Soap and Detergent Association
475 Park Ave. S.
New York, NY 10016
212/725-1262

**Society of Cosmetic
Chemists**
120 Wall St.

New York, NY 10005
212/668-1500

(Offers job placement
service to members.)

CONSUMER PRODUCTS INDUSTRY DIRECTORIES

*Appliance
Manufacturer Annual
Directory*
Corcoran
Communications, Inc.
5900 Harper Rd.,
Suite 105
Solon, OH 44139
216/349-3060

*Electronic Market
Data Book*
Electronic Industries
Association
2500 Wilson Blvd.
Arlington, VA 22201
703/907-7500

*Household and
Personal Products
Industry Buyers Guide*
Rodman Publishing
Corp.
17 S. Franklin Turnpike
Ramsey, NJ 07446
201/825-2552

CONSUMER PRODUCTS INDUSTRY MAGAZINES

Appliance
Dana Chase
Publications
1110 Jorie Blvd.
Oak Brook, IL
 60522
708/990-3484

*Appliance
Manufacturer*
5900 Harper Rd.,
Suite 105
Solon, OH 44139
216/349-3060

*Cosmetic Insiders
Report*
Advanstar
Communications
7500 Old Oak Blvd.
Cleveland, OH 44130
216/243-8100

*Drug & Cosmetic
Industry*
Advanstar
Communications
7500 Old Oak Blvd.
Cleveland, OH
44130
216/243-8100

*Household and
Personal Products
Industry*
Box 555
Ramsey, NJ 07446
201/825-2552
(Monthly magazine
covering the soap,
detergent, cosmetics,
toiletries, and fragrance
industries. Good help-
wanted section.)

*Product Design and
Development*
Chilton Book Co.
Chilton Way
Radnor, PA 19089
215/964-4000

*Soap/Cosmetics/
Chemical Specialties*
445 Broad Hollow Rd.
Melville, NY 11747
516/845-2700
(Monthly magazine for
professionals involved
in all aspects of the
soap, cosmetics, and
chemicals industry—
including production,
management,
formulation,
purchasing, marketing,
and packaging.)

ENERGY

INDUSTRY OUTLOOK: Long term probably good, as the industry restructures and slims down, and as demand—espeically foreign demand—continues to expand; but outside factors may affect results.

In general, keep an eye on five main factors that will impact the overall energy industry: domestic economic growth, OPEC planning, production and export rates from former Soviet republics, increased environmental concerns and regulations, and economic growth in Asia.

Coal: Probable long-term steady growth ahead—but only if there are no changes in current laws or regulations. If, however, environmental legislation cuts back on coal usage, expansion plans, or costs, the industry will pay the price. The future is tied also to the growth of electric utilities—a stable customer base—which absorb 80% of domestic coal output. Watch for the fallout from deregulated electric utilities. (See page 487 for more specifics.)

A key growth factor: overseas markets, especially Asia's huge requirements to increase their power generation and Europe's need to replace scheduled closings of outmoded and uneconomic state-subsidized mines with other sources.

Natural Gas: A bright long-term outlook, with long-term growth in this industry sector expected to be higher than other energy sources. Key reasons: Environmental concerns, the desire to rely less on foreign concerns, and new technology plus better management to develop new supplies at lower costs. As with coal, expect to see changes due to the deregulation of utilities. Key trend: increased competition between smaller, lower-cost suppliers and the big guys. Watch as larger oil and gas companies team up with smaller companies to try to grab a piece of the entrepreneurial pie.

Oil: As always, the outlook for oil depends upon OPEC actions and world crude-oil production. For the near term the outlook is good. As the industry expands abroad, the risk persists of possible negative effects of dealing with unstable host governments.

As for **oilfield services**: The long-term outlook looks good and should benefit from increased exploration offshore and overseas.

A LOOK BACK

▶ The '90s: a time to regroup for the oil industry.

In the early '90s, refining and marketing slumped, petrochemicals declined, and the industry regrouped. Crude prices rose again and oil companies began putting money into exploration—chiefly targeting overseas areas, especially Canada. Then came the recession, and with it a drop in oil consumption and massive restructuring that left 500,000 American oil industry workers without jobs. This, combined with the successful push for world market share by OPEC nations, brought about a drop in the price of crude oil—and a bleak beginning to the '90s.

1995, however, proved to be the start of industry recovery, as European and Japanese demand improved, in addition to a strong cyclical recovery in petrochemicals. And, as 1996 opened, the industry was on stable ground—headed for healthy profits, continuing through 1997.

▶ **Natural gas went through a series of disappointing years.**

The key problem: Too much gas and not enough demand, which has been termed the "natural gas bubble." For a short time, the bubble burst—in a good way. Demand increased due to environmental concerns and a resurgence in manufacturing activity. But the turnaround was short lived, and the industry sector began sputtering again. The industry went through a cost-cutting phase—and everyone hoped that the day would finally come when natural gas took off the way experts have predicted. And, while gas didn't skyrocket, demand *did* increase—and was predicted to reach a ten-year high in 1997—leading experts to predict that demand would remain relatively healthy over the long term.

As for coal, the combination of lower-cost foreign competitors, declining exports, falling prices, and costly environmental standards hammered the industry. Added to the industry woes: deregulation in the utilities, which may lead to consolidation in the coal industry over the long term.

WHAT'S NEXT

▶ **A key trend for oil and gas producers: looking well beyond mainland United States for the next big find.**

The mainland United States is already well-tapped where oil and gas fields are concerned. So companies—hoping to cash in on a large discovery—will be forced to look elsewhere. To this end, companies will continue stepping up offshore and overseas exploration. Areas that will continue seeing action: the Gulf of Mexico, the Gulf of Thailand, as well as Asia, Africa, and South America.

▶ **Technological breakthroughs and increased usage of high-tech methods will be more crucial than ever.**

New methods of exploration and extraction are making it possible for companies to expand their efforts offshore and abroad—and to locate energy reserves in the United States as well. Given this, expect to see continued emphasis placed on development of new location, exploration, and extraction methods. Among the methods and equipment developed over the past few years: computer software that simulates oil-fields; specially designed high-speed computers and seismic gauges to locate oil; horizontal drilling (as opposed to standard vertical drilling), which reaches a much larger percentage of a reservoir.

An employment note: The increased importance of technological developments and equipment may point to a growing demand in the industry for software and research engineers.

▶ **Over the long term, natural gas will see increasing demand.**

One key reason: Environmental concerns. Natural gas has so-called clean fuel characteristics. Sulfur, which helps cause acid rain, can be removed from it easily, and it releases fewer toxic emissions like sulfur dioxide (which contributes to the greenhouse effect) than do either coal or oil.

▶ Expect to see the continued impact of utilities deregulation on different sectors of the energy industry.

As the huge utilities companies deregulate, energy companies are feeling the result of the changes.

Examples: Since electric utilities are the largest buyer of coal (buying over 80% of the coal produced), anything that happens to them is felt in the coal industry. Probable scenario: increased utility competition will lead to consolidation—which, in turn, will lead to the larger utilities pressuring coal companies to sell at a lower price. The outcome may well be a consolidation in the coal industry, then, with smaller companies falling by the wayside.

As for natural gas companies: deregulation of the utilities is leading to competition—and so, is leading to a flurry of marketing efforts. One development: natural gas companies are "unbundling"—that is, the cost of gas on a customer's bill is separated from the cost of its delivery. The picture now: Gas suppliers use the pipelines of a local utility to deliver the gas, and, as in the past, the utility will handle customer service, but the supplier is otherwise not related to the utility. The result: Gas companies have jumped onto the sales and marketing bandwagon, trying to sell their gas to customers—and, in many cases, they're going head to head with the larger utilities, selling their gas at a lower price. It's already happening with businesses, and, in some states, homeowners will be able to choose their gas supplier much as they choose a long distance telephone company. The logical extension of this trend? One monthly bill from a vendor offering energy service, satellite TV, long-distance service, and Internet access, as is being offered by KE Energy of Colorado under its Simple Choice brand name. The bottom line: Expect the sales and marketing push to continue—which points to employment opportunities for sales and marketing personnel—and, along the same lines, expect to see an increase in the number of smaller gas suppliers.

▶ Environmental legislation will continue to change much of the energy industry—particularly oil refining and coal.

The entire energy industry will feel the impact of environmental concerns and legislation such as the Clean Air Act, but these two sectors will be particularly affected.

Oil refiners will be forced to spend money on reconfiguring their refineries to produce the new, cleaner types of gasoline, in line with government regulations. This may translate into problems for smaller companies with simpler refineries and financial resources. Upgrading may be too expensive for them, yet if they don't upgrade, they will fall behind—and possibly go out of business. The probable outcome, then, will be the further consolidation of the refining industry.

As for coal: While coal production will be increasing over the next few years, the industry will be forced to deal with the environmental side effects of coal use. One probable outcome will be increased use of low-sulfur coal. This will mean increased output from the low-sulfur coal reserves in central Appalachia and the Powder River Basin in Wyoming; decreased output from high-sulfur reserves, primarily those in the Midwest.

▶ **Environmental concerns—and the push to move away from volatile oil—will bring about renewed emphasis on developing new energy products.**

An area that has been seeing a great deal of action is the development of alternative fuels, such as methanol, to replace gasoline. As more companies devote time, effort, and funding to developing replacement fuels, this may translate into opportunities for chemical engineers and others involved in the research and development of these fuels. In addition, many refiners will be setting up distribution systems for the new fuels, which may point to sales and marketing opportunities. On the down side, however, it may cut deeply into the earnings of petroleum refiners and even bring about the collapse of independents and smaller companies.

EMPLOYMENT OUTLOOK: Varied.

The energy industry has restructured—it has consolidated, cut back on costs and employees, and is generally leaner and meaner . . . which actually makes the employment picture fairly positive.

The key: companies have already slashed jobs where they had to—and barring a complete collapse in energy prices, probably won't be consolidating much more. While the Bureau of Labor Statistics projects that the crude oil and petroleum industry is in for a period of slow job growth, there are opportunities developing. Key reason? The previous job cuts. To point out just how deep these cuts were: Currently, the oil and gas industry employs about half as many people as it did ten years ago. And now that's causing some problems . . .

In many cases, with the renewed emphasis on exploration, companies that had downsized in the past are now facing a shortage of experienced workers. So the resurgence in exploration and extraction activity may mean hiring opportunities in a range of job categories, including petroleum engineers, geologists, and geophysicists.

Draftspeople, science technicians, engineering technicians, and surveyors, as well as other exploration jobs, look strong in the long term but are subject to sporadic ups and downs.

As for the coal industry: Increased use of labor-saving machinery will cut into the employment numbers. As such, the government forecasts a drop in employment over the next decade—from about 148,000 employees to 113,000. Employment in the coal industry declined steadily through the 1980s and is expected to continue to decline. In addition, look for employment shifts as new low-sulfur mines open and high-sulfur mines close in an effort to meet the 1990 Clean Air Act Amendments.

JOBS SPOTLIGHT

PETROLEUM ENGINEER: Employment growth in this field is projected at about 1% to year 2005, up to 3% if the economy is strong. But where actual hiring is concerned, the outlook may be brighter. The key reason? Since 1983 the number of students enrolled in petroleum engineering has dropped 80%, according to the Society of Petroleum Engineers. This means that as people retire or leave the field, the pool of qualified replacements is small.

BEST BETS

Consolidated Natural Gas
CNG Tower
625 Liberty Ave.
Pittsburgh, PA 15222-3199
412/227-1000

A leading natural-gas producer with a healthy amount of gas reserves, CNG should have a bright long-term future, once natural gas starts taking off as has been predicted . . . and perhaps before. One reason: "co-firing"—a new technology it is developing that reduces environmentally damaging emissions from coal-burning plants by burning gas with coal. With environmental legislation plus heightened awareness, this can be a winner for CNG.

Lyondell Petrochemical Corp.
1221 McKinney
Houston, TX 77010
713/652-7200

Oil refinery and petrochemical producer Lyondell is a small, scrappy company that looks like it is headed for a relatively bright future in the often-troubled energy industry. Among the reasons—technological advances have made the refinery capable of processing any crude oil at all, making it perhaps the only refinery in the world able to do so. In addition, the company is run with an open management style. Teams of managers and workers work together on projects and ideas. If a new proposal is instituted, the entire team gets a bonus. Another plus: The majority of its employees are shareholders in the company—something that aids both productivity and morale. Adding to the morale is the anonymous hotline via which employees are encouraged to make complaints or suggestions. Each month, these are printed in a newsletter along with the corresponding management reaction. All of this adds up to a best bet for employment in the energy industry.

TOP COAL COMPANIES

Amax Coal Industries, Inc.
20 NW First St.,
Evansville, IN
47708-1258
812/421-3900

Consol, Inc.
1800 Washington Blvd.
Pittsburgh, PA 15241
412/831-4000

Cyprus Amax Minerals Corp.
9100 E. Mineral Cir.
Englewood, CO
80155
303/643-5000

Drummond Co., Inc.
530 Beacon Pkwy.
Birmingham, AL 35209
205/387-0501

Peabody Coal Co., Inc.
1951 Barrett Ct.
Henderson, KY 42420
502/827-0800

**The Pittston
Company**
100 First Stamford Pl.
Stamford, CT 06912
203/978-5200

**Westmoreland Coal
Co., Inc.**
200 S. Broad St.
Philadelphia, PA 19102
215/545-2500

TOP OIL & GAS COMPANIES

Amerada Hess Corp.
1185 Ave. of the
Americas
New York, NY 10036
212/997-8500

Amoco Corp.
200 E. Randolph St.
Chicago, IL 60601
312/856-6111

Anadarko Petroleum
17001 Northchase Dr.
Houston, TX 77060
713/875-1101

Ashland Oil, Inc.
P.O. Box 391
Ashland, KY 41114
606/329-3333

**Atlantic Richfield
Co.**
515 S. Flower St.
Los Angeles, CA
90071
213/486-3511

BP America, Inc.
200 Public Sq.
Cleveland, OH 44114
216/586-4141

**Burlington
Resources**
5051 Westheimer Rd.
Houston, TX 77056
713/624-9000

Chevron Corp.
225 Bush St.
San Francisco, CA
94104-04289
415/894-7700

**Citgo Petroleum
Corp.**
6100 S. Yale Ave.
Tulsa, OK 74136
918/495-4000

Conoco, Inc.
600 N. Dairy Ashford
Rd.
Houston, TX 77079
713/293-1000

**Consolidated Natural
Gas**
CNG Tower
625 Liberty Ave.
Pittsburgh, PA 15222
412/227-1000

**Crown Central
Petroleum Corp.**
P.O. Box 1165
Baltimore, MD 21203
410/539-7400

**Diamond Shamrock,
Inc.**
P.O. Box 696000
San Antonio, TX
78269-6000
210/641-6800

DukeEnergy
5400 Westheimer Ct.
Houston, TX 77056
713/627-5400

DuPont Co.
1007 Market St.
Wilmington, DE 19898
302/774-1000

Exxon Corp.
225 E. Carpenter Fwy.

Irving, TX 75062-2298
214/444-1000

**Fina Oil & Chemical
Co.**
P.O. Box 2159
Dallas, TX 75221-2159
214/760-2399

Kerr-McGee Corp.
Kerr-McGee Ctr.
P.O. Box 25861
Oklahoma City, OK
73125
405/270-1313

**Louisiana Land &
Exploration Co.**
909 Poydras St.
New Orleans, LA
70112
504/566-6500

**Lyondell
Petrochemical Corp.**
1221 McKinney
Houston, TX 77010
713/652-7200

Mapco, Inc.
1800 S. Baltimore Ave.
Tulsa, OK 74119
918/581-1800

Marathon Oil Co.
555 San Felipe St.
Houston, TX 77056
713/629-6600

Maxus Energy Corp.
717 N. Harwood St.
Dallas, TX 75201
214/953-2000

Mobil Corp.
3225 Gallows Rd.
Fairfax, VA
22037-0001
703/846-3000

Murphy Oil Corp.
200 Peach St.
P.O. Box 7000
El Dorado, AR
71731-7000
501/862-6411

NorAm Energy
P.O. Box 2628
Houston, TX
77252-2628
713/654-5100

Occidental Petroleum Corp.
10889 Wilshire Blvd.
Los Angeles, CA 90024
310/208-8800

Oryx Energy Co.
13155 Noel Rd.
Dallas, TX 75240
214/715-4000

Pennzoil Co.
1 Pennzoil Pl.

Houston, TX 77002
713/546-4000

Phillips Petroleum Co.
1250 Adams Bldg.
Bartlesville, OK 74004
918/661-6600

Quaker State Corp.
255 Elm St.
Oil City, PA 16301
814/676-7676

Shell Oil Co.
1600 Smith St.
Houston, TX 77002
713/241-6161

Sun Company, Inc.
10 Penn Center Plz.
Philadelphia, PA 19103
215/977-3000

Texaco, Inc.
2000 Westchester Ave.
White Plains, NY 10650
914/253-4000

Tosco
72 Cummings Pt. Rd.
Stamford, CT 06902
203/977-1000

Union Texas Petroleum Holdings, Inc.
1330 Post Oak Blvd.
Houston, TX 77056
713/623-6544

Unocal Corp.
1201 W. 5 St.
Los Angeles, CA 90017
213/977-7600

USX-Marathon Group
600 Grant St.
Pittsburgh, PA 15219-4776
412/433-1121

Ultramar
2 Pickwick Plz.
Greenwich, CT 06830
203/622-7000

UtilCorp United
P.O. Box 132-87
Kansas City, MO 64199-3287
816/421-6600

TOP PETROLEUM SERVICES COMPANIES

Baker Hughes, Incorporated
3900 Essex Ln.
Houston, TX 77027
713/439-8600

CBI Industries
800 Jorie Blvd.
Oak Brook, IL 60521
708/572-7000

Cameron Corp.
P.O. Box 1212
Houston, TX 77251
713/939-2211

Cooper Oil & Tool
P.O. Box 1212
Houston, TX 77251
713/939-2211

Dresser Industries, Inc.
2001 Ross Ave.
Dallas, TX 75201
214/740-6000

Halliburton Co.
500 N. Akard St.
Dallas, TX 75201-3391
214/978-2600

Helmerich & Payne, Inc.
1579 E. 21st St.
Tulsa, OK 74114
918/742-5531

Noble Affiliates, Inc.
110 W. Broadway
Ardmore, OK 73401
405/223-4110

Noble Drilling Corporation
10370 Richmond Ave.
Houston, TX 77042
713/974-3131

Rowan Company, Inc.
2800 Post Oak Blvd.
Houston, TX 77056
713/621-7800

Schlumberger Ltd.
277 Park Ave.

New York, NY 10172
212/350-9400

Smith International Inc.
16740 Hardy St.
Houston, TX 77032
713/443-3370

Western Atlas
360 N. Crescent Dr.
Beverly Hills, CA
90210-4867

WHERE TO GO FOR MORE INFORMATION

ENERGY INDUSTRY ASSOCIATIONS

American Gas Association
1515 Wilson Blvd.
Arlington, VA 22209
703/841-8600

American Petroleum Institute

1220 L St., NW, Suite 900
Washington, DC 20005
202/682-8000

National Mining Association
1130 17th St., NW

Washington, DC 20036
202/463-2625

National Petroleum Council
1625 K St., NW
Washington, DC 20006
202/393-6100

ENERGY INDUSTRY DIRECTORIES

Brown's Directory of North American & International Gas Companies
7500 Old Oak Blvd.
Cleveland, OH 44130
800/225-4569

Oil & Gas Directory
P.O. Box 130508

Houston, TX 77219
713/529-8789

Refining & Natural Gas Processing
Midwest Register
1120 E. 4th St.
Tulsa, OK 74120-3220
918/582-2000

West Coast Petroleum Industry Directory
Pacific West Oil Data
15314 Devonshire St.
Suite D
Mission Hills, CA
91345-2746
818/892-1121

ENERGY INDUSTRY PERIODICALS

Coal
29 N. Wacker Dr.
Chicago, IL 60606
312/726-2802
(Monthly magazine for coal industry executives in all areas, including administrative, engineering, and operating.)

National Petroleum News
2101 S. Arlington Rd.
Arlington Heights, IL 60005
847/427-9512
(News publication dealing with petroleum transportation and storage issues.)

Oil and Gas Journal
P.O. Box 1260
Tulsa, OK 74101
918/835-3161
(Weekly magazine for those involved in oil production, exploration, and marketing.)

Petroleum Marketing Management
1801 Rockville Pike
Suite 330
Rockville, MD 20852
301/984-7333
(Bimonthly for petroleum marketing professionals,

including major company executives, independent marketers, distributors, etc.)

World Oil
P.O. Box 2608
Houston, TX 77252
713/529-4301

(Monthly magazine covering the oil industry; for company owners, operating managers, geologists, production engineers, and drilling contractors.)

FASHION

INDUSTRY OUTLOOK: Certain areas stronger than others.

As always, the health of the fashion industry is directly linked to the retail industry, as well as the strength of the economy and consumer confidence. Given this, expect the fashion industry to go through ups and downs in line with the economy. When the economy dips, look for belt tightening, and a return to basics; when the economy grows, expect more innovation and, of course, stronger sales as consumers begin spending more on fashion items. A key trend: Watch more apparel manufacturers jump on the outsourcing bandwagon—allowing their products to keep pace with consumer demand and changing tastes. Specifically, Mexico may become an attractive outsource because of NAFTA and proximity to the U.S. markets. Larger apparel manufacturers should do well because they can commit to the large orders from the major store chains (the big players in the fashion industry) and can respond quickly to changes in quantities, delivery dates, and styles. Also looking good: higher priced fashion apparel. This area has done well in the recent past, primarily because it has dedicated consumers who aren't as affected by swings in the economy. Given this, more retailers should continue devoting more floor space to premium brands—which, in turn, will create more demand. The bottom line? Expect the recognizable names, the brand leaders, to continue strong. Another growth area: Private label fashions, as department and specialty stores develop their own lines to increase profits—and meet specific consumer demands.

A LOOK BACK

▶ **Recent years were tough ones for the fashion industry—but hopes were lifted in 1997.**

It was a relatively rough time for the fashion industry. Consumer confidence was low, sales dropped, retailers began to cut back on inventory to avoid being stuck with racks of unsold merchandise—and the fashion industry suffered. Cost-cutting became common, as apparel companies tightened their belts and shed workers in an effort to remain profitable. But consumers simply weren't buying. Instead of spending their money on clothing, most shoppers instead turned to computers, sports and fitness equipment, and home furnishings. By the beginning of 1996, there was hardly any significant improvement with no clear fashion trends or hot items to give consumers a reason to buy. Price remained king, with continued discounting. Shifts in fashion direction—plus a strong economy and increased consumer confidence—improved the outlook for 1997.

But as of this writing, the jury was still out as to whether the improved outlook would continue.

WHAT'S NEXT

▶ **Designers and manufacturers have learned the lessons of the last few years. The result? They're following demographic trends, trying different approaches to market research, and sticking close to what the consumer wants.**

Apparel manufacturers and designers have learned the hard way—people won't buy whatever the fashion world dictates. Those days are long over. So now the fashion industry is closely tracking consumer preferences and demographics through a variety of market research methods.

Among them is the focus-group method used by other marketing-driven manufacturers (especially package-goods companies). In this case, manufacturers are developing satellite research operations, pulling together a selection of styles, and then showing the different styles to test subjects around the country. One result: this is creating employment opportunities for market research personnel.

Another method that will be growing in use: Producing limited runs of items as a test to gauge consumer reaction. These runs are often sold in outlet stores or in stores chosen as test-market labs. It's a way of testing different styles, colors, and price points while avoiding disastrous overruns of unwanted merchandise. Items that sell well are then mass-produced; those that don't are cut from production.

▶ **Technological changes will continue to affect the manufacturing process.**

It's the best way to keep costs down, productivity up, and excessive inventory (especially unfinished products) in check. An increasing number of apparel manufacturers have been automating, investing in new equipment and computer systems to design products, to determine how to cut costs in fabric by making pattern layout more efficient, and, ultimately, for use in sales presentations, to enable buyers to see the product. To accommodate the new equipment, companies are updating old factories or building new ones, and switching over to new production methods, such as modular manufacturing systems.

By switching from the traditional labor-intensive methods to robotics and automation, apparel manufacturers can react more quickly to changes in style based on consumer demand. (For more on this, see the section on Quick Response below.) In addition, automation enables domestic manufacturers to compete with the low-cost foreign producers.

In the short term, however, there is a high price to pay for these changes. Because modernization is so expensive, small and midsized companies are being forced to merge. The outcome? A shift in the makeup of the industry. Once comprised of a large number of small, specialized companies, the apparel industry is switching to one comprised of larger, more diverse corporations. The end result, clearly, is a consolidated industry of fewer manufacturers with larger product lines.

Technological breakthroughs are also affecting the employment picture. Traditional production jobs are being cut and will probably not be replaced. On the other hand, however, there is an increasing demand for people skilled in advanced manufacturing techniques.

▶ **An important trend: the growing use of "Quick Response," which allows designers and manufacturers to respond quickly to customer preferences.**

This may be one of the most important factors affecting the apparel industry. Basically, Quick Response is a production concept that allows manufacturers to quickly produce and deliver products that are in high demand, at the same time that they avoid producing products that are in low demand. In so doing, QR allows manufacturers and designers to react to changing customer demand. Color, style, trim—virtually any aspect of a garment or accessory can be swiftly changed in line with what is selling most.

QR typically relies on computerization—automated checkouts with bar-code scanners. The system allows retailers to track inventory, identify strong sellers, and know when to replenish stock. QR can cut the time between the order of goods and delivery of those goods from an average of sixty-six weeks to as little as twenty-one weeks.

Expect the use of QR to continue—and increase—as the need for shorter lead times, coupled with a rising consumer demand for quality and an increasing concern for trend tracking, make automation more necessary.

▶ **Foreign sourcing and foreign production will continue—and increase.**

It's partially a reaction to the high cost of automation, partially a way of keeping costs down. Even as the Made in the USA sentiment remains high, manufacturers and designers will continue looking overseas for low-cost production.

As such, expect increased competition between U.S. and foreign manufacturers as those domestic manufacturers continue to fight for higher market share.

Another interesting development to keep an eye on: U.S. companies are targeting overseas markets for their products, especially men's outerwear and home furnishings. The biggest markets so far have been Southeast Asia, Latin America, and Japan, but there is also increasing activity in South Korea, Hong Kong, Taiwan, and even Europe. This may translate into interesting international sales and marketing opportunities. Expect to see stepped-up efforts to increase market share abroad as this trend continues.

▶ **The result of increased attention to customers? Interesting shifts in focus for designers and apparel manufacturers.**

In the short term, expect to see the continued strength of "bridge lines." Also called secondary lines or diffusion lines, these are lower-priced lines of designer clothing. The trend began to a great degree when consumers started to cut back on higher-priced purchases, and it also cashed in on the growing number of affluent baby boomers.

In the longer term, expect to see the continued growth of lines aimed at aging baby boomers. Environmental awareness is getting a push, with lines such as Esprit, catalog house Smith & Hawken, and others offering natural-dyed clothing and the like. Manufacturers are also eager to tap the growing market of older Americans, many of whom will have high disposable incomes. Another hot target is children's wear, because of the mini–baby boom that has been happening.

The target markets may be different, but the bottom line is clear: Designers and companies that track demographic trends and come up with the product lines that meet the demands of a changing marketplace will be the winners. The losers? Those that don't change with the times.

EMPLOYMENT OUTLOOK: Competitive.

The apparel industry is traditionally a very labor-intensive one, employing about 6% of all employees in the U.S. manufacturing industry while accounting for only about 2% of the products. But in the recent past, the industry shrank. According to the Bureau of Labor Statistics, 1,000 apparel manufacturers closed since 1986—for a loss of about 20,000 jobs. On the production side, the growing use of automation is cutting back on jobs, which account for about 85% of all jobs in the industry. The keys to securing a job in today's apparel industry are computer skills, and computerized manufacturing experience.

On the nonproduction side, the fashion industry has always been competitive. Skills, contacts, and just plain luck are, to a great degree, the key factors in landing a design job. Several interesting employment trends: While New York remains the seat of the U.S. fashion industry, its dominance is less strong than in the past. Los Angeles, in particular, is growing in importance as a fashion capital, as are San Francisco and Chicago.

JOBS SPOTLIGHT

PRODUCT MANAGER: A growing area as retailers switch to centralized marketing. Product managers in the fashion industry work with buyers from retail stores to determine what the store wants; then they do "sourcing"—finding producers and production areas (often overseas) to make the item. Product managers sometimes offer design input. Salaries range from the low to mid $20s for assistant product managers to the mid $60s for senior product managers.

BEST BETS

Donna Karan Co.
550 7th Ave.
New York, NY 10018
212/789-1500

A star of the sportswear field, Donna Karan is one of the driving forces behind the trend toward bridge lines. The key to her success? Understanding her customer and aiming her clothing directly at the 30+ woman. Bridge line DKNY has been a brilliant success since it was introduced—and her forays into other areas seem equally profitable. The only questions: Can this success be sustained against hotter competition? So far the answer has been yes.

Levi Strauss & Co.
1155 Battery St.
San Francisco, CA 94111
415/544-6000

Levi Strauss has a reputation for having its workers participate in the management process. The management sponsors a number of programs designed to promote positive change in the company, such as CORE Curriculum, a training program covering such subjects as leadership, ethics, and diversity. This type of attention to employees, and a product line that has been evolving to keep up with its customers, make Levi Strauss a positive bet for the future.

Nine West Group Inc.
9 W. Broad St.
Stamford, CT 06902
203/324-7567

Nine West is a shoemaker that knows how to spot trends—and deliver them quickly to its customers. This ability has made it one of the largest and most successful companies that can knock off high fashion shoes and sell them for less. In addition, it recently created two new divisions: 9&Co, a line aimed at younger consumers, and Enzo Angiolini, an upscale, pricier fashion line. And the company hasn't stopped at producing shoes. It has also spread into retail, with over 500 in-store boutiques and about 200 stand-alone stores—including stores for the newer brands. It's also moving overseas, with retail agreements set up in Hong Kong, Canada, Mexico, and Australia. All in all, Nine West looks like it's headed up.

TOP FASHION COMPANIES

Harve Bernard Ltd.
225 Meadowlands Pkwy.
Secaucus, NJ 07094
201/319-0909

Bill Blass Ltd.
550 Seventh Ave.
New York, NY 10018
212/221-6660

Bon Jour Group Ltd.
1411 Broadway
New York, NY 10018
212/398-1000

Bugle Boy Industries, Inc.
2900 N. Madera Rd.
Simi Valley, CA 93065
805/582-1010

Byer California
66 Potrero Ave.
San Francisco, CA 94103
415/626-7844

Z. Cavaricci Inc.
2535 E. 12th St.
Los Angeles, CA 90221
213/629-1988

Bernard Chaus, Inc.
1410 Broadway
New York, NY 10018
212/354-1280

Cherokee, Inc.
9545 Wentworth St.
Sunland, CA 91040
818/951-1002

Liz Claiborne, Inc.
1441 Broadway
New York, NY 10018
212/354-4900

Donna Karan Co.
550 7th Ave.
New York, NY 10018
212/789-1500

Donnkenny, Inc.
1411 Broadway
New York, NY 10018
212/730-7770

Esprit
900 Minnesota
San Francisco, CA
94107
415/648-6900

Gant Corp.
2645 Mitchell Ave.
Allentown, PA 18103
215-797-6200

Guess, Inc.
1444 S. Alameda St.
Los Angeles, CA
90021
213/765-3100

Hartmarx Corp.
101 N. Wacker Dr.
Chicago, IL 60606
312/372-6300

Jantzen, Inc.
411 NE 19 St.
Portland, OR 97232
503/238-5000

JH Collectibles
1411 Broadway
New York, NY 10018
212/944-6644

Jones Apparel Group
250 Rittenhouse Cir.
Bristol, PA 19007
215/785-4000

Jordache Enterprises, Inc.
226 W. 37th St.
New York, NY 10018
212/643-8400

Jou Jou Designs, Inc.
525 Seventh Ave.
New York, NY 10018
212/997-0230

Kenar Enterprises, Ltd.
530 Seventh Ave.
New York, NY 10018
212/944-5300

Anne Klein & Co.
205 W. 39th St.
New York, NY 10018
212/221-7880

Calvin Klein Ltd.
205 W. 39th St.
New York, NY 10018
212/719-2600

Michael Kors, Inc.
550 7th Ave.
New York, NY
10221-1950
212/221-1950

Ralph Lauren Womenswear
550 Seventh Ave.
New York, NY 10018
212/857-2500

Levi Strauss & Co.
1155 Battery St.
San Francisco, CA
94111
415/544-6000

Maggy London International Ltd.
530 Seventh Ave.
New York, NY 10018
212/944-7199

Necessary Objects
503 Broadway
New York, NY 10012
212/334-9888

Nine West Group, Inc.
9 W. Broad St.
Stamford, CT 06902
203/328-4383

Phillips-Van Heusen Corp.
1290 Ave. of the
Americas
New York, NY 10104
212/541-5200

Polo Ralph Lauren Corp.
650 Madison Ave.
New York, NY 10022
212/318-7000

Russ Togs, Inc.
1450 Broadway
New York, NY 10018
212/626-5800

Ellen Tracy, Inc.
575 Seventh Ave.
New York, NY 10018
212/944-6999

U.S. Colors
501 English Rd.
Rocky Mount, NC
27804
919/937-6883

VF Corp.
1047 N. Park Rd.
Reading, PA 19610
215/378-1151

Warnaco Group, Inc.
90 Park Ave.
New York, NY 10016
212/661-1300

Woolrich, Inc.
Mill St.
Woolrich, PA 17779
717/769-6464

Yes Clothing Co.
1380 W.
Washington
Los Angeles, CA
90007
213/742-0201

TOP TEXTILE MANUFACTURING
AND HOME FASHIONS COMPANIES

Albany International
1373 Boadway
Albany, NY 12204
518/447-6400

Belding Heminway
1430 Broadway
New York, NY 10018
212/944-6040

**Burlington
Industries, Inc.**
3330 W. Friendly Ave.
Greensboro, NC 27410
910/379-2000

**Collins and
Aikman**
210 Madison Ave.
New York, NY 10016
212/578-1200

Concord Fabrics
1359 Broadway
New York, NY 10018
212/760-0300

Dan River, Inc.
111 W. 40th St.
New York, NY 10018
212/554-5531

Delta Woodside
233 N. Main St.
Greenville, SC 29601
803/232-8301

**Fieldcrest
Cannon**
326 E. Stadium Dr.
Eden, NC 27288
919/627-3000

**Hoechst Celanese
Corporation**
3 Park Ave.
New York, NY 10016
212/251-8000

Liberty Fabrics
295 5th Ave.
New York, NY 10016
212/684-3100

**Milliken and
Company**
920 Milliken Rd.
Spartanburg, SC 29301
706/278-3812

Shaw Industries
616 E. Walnut Ave.
Dalton, GA 30720
706/278-3812

Springs Industries
205 N. White St.
Fort Mill, SC 29715
803/547-1500

West Point-Pepperell
507 W. 10th St.
West Point, GA 31833
706/645-4000

**Westpoint Stevens
Company, Inc.**
1185 Ave. of the
Americas
New York, NY 10036
212/930-2000

WHERE TO GO FOR MORE INFORMATION

(For more information sources in related areas, also see "Designers," page 39, and "Retailing," page 442.)

FASHION INDUSTRY ASSOCIATIONS

**Affiliated Dress
Manufacturers**
500 7th Ave.
New York, NY 10018
212/819-1011

**American Apparel
Manufacturers
Association**
2500 Wilson Blvd.,
Suite 301
Arlington, VA 22201
703/524-1864

**Clothing
Manufacturers
Association of the USA**
730 Broadway
New York, NY 10010
212/529-0823

**Footwear Industries
of America**
1420 K St., NW,
Suite 600

Washington, DC
20005
202/789-1420

**International
Association of
Clothing Designers**
475 Park Ave. S.
New York, NY 10016
212/685-6602

| **Men's Fashions Association of America** | 475 Park Ave. S., 17th Flr. | New York, NY 10016 212/683-5665 |

FASHION INDUSTRY DIRECTORIES

AAMA Directory
American Apparel
Manufacturers
Association

2500 Wilson Blvd.
Arlington, VA 22201
703/524-1864

Apparel Trades Book
Dun & Bradstreet, Inc.
1 Diamond Hill Rd.
Murray Hill, NJ 07974
908/665-5000

FASHION INDUSTRY PERIODICALS

Apparel Industry Magazine
6255 Barfield Rd.
Suite 200
Atlanta, GA
30328-4300
404/252-8831
(Monthly magazine for staffers in all aspects of the apparel industry—designers, manufacturers, contractors, suppliers.)

Bobbin
P.O. Box 1986
Columbia, SC 29202
803/771-7500
(Monthly magazine for executives in apparel manufacturing, textile milling, retailing.)

California Apparel News
110 E. Ninth St.
Los Angeles, CA
90079
213/627-3737
800/360-1700
(Weekly covering California-based fashion industry.)

Daily News Record
7 W. 34th St.
New York, NY 10001
212/630-4000
(Daily newspaper for apparel manufacturers, wholesalers, buyers, retailers, and jobbers.)

Footwear News
7 W. 34th St.
New York, NY 10001
212/630-4230
(Weekly newspaper covering the footwear industry; for designers, buyers, wholesalers, suppliers, etc.)

Women's Wear Daily
7 W. 34th St.
New York, NY 10001
800/289-0273
(Daily newspaper, women's clothing industry "bible," for designers, wholesalers, retailers, etc.)

FILM AND ENTERTAINMENT

INDUSTRY OUTLOOK: Extremely competitive.

Film: While the film industry saw improvements each year since 1991 and should continue to stay on this track, the general long-term outlook through 1998 is for modest growth alone. The government predicts an increase of about 1 to 2% in box office receipts per year. Two key factors: a strong foreign market that snaps up Hollywood productions, and an increasing number of cable stations. But growth may be offset by declining profit margins and a sharp increase in the cost of production. Due to the soaring film production and promotion costs, film companies need to meet two major requirements: 1) wide product distribution in the United States and abroad to achieve even a modicum of profitability and 2) development of a stream of products to further absorb joint overhead and promotion costs. The impact: only big players can play the game successfully over the long term. Given this, there may be a continuation of mergers and acquisitions with distribution firms (TV and theaters) or other film production companies. On the flip side, independent productions have gotten new attention—given their performance in the 1997 Oscars. Expect to see more of the big players try to move into this turf by scooping up independent companies, setting up joint alliances, or establishing smaller, independent-like subsidiaries of their own.

Expect mergers and acquisitions activity to affect the industry, as other companies may follow the lead of Disney and hook up with related companies and as foreign companies descend on Hollywood looking to buy a piece of the American entertainment industry. Also watch as more film companies extend their reach into book publishing and film-related spin-offs, such as toys and computer games.

Music: Watch as the industry becomes increasingly globalized with the United States representing only one-third of the global pie. Hottest areas: Latin America, especially Mexico and Brazil; eastern Europe; and Asia. Also expect competition to heat up with the coming changes from analog to digital technology, such as digital video disc (DVD) and MiniDisc (MD). Look for aggressive market moves as distribution moves into grocery stores, airport vending machines, and the Internet.

A LOOK BACK

▶ **It was a ten-year run of record earnings for the film industry—matched by skyrocketing costs.**

There were some ups and downs, but overall the past decade was a great time for Hollywood. From 1989 on, the film industry was hitting box office bonanzas.

But it hasn't been all bright. In spite of the earnings, Hollywood has been getting a little nervous. The reasons? Profit margins have shrunk—and costs per film have skyrocketed, with films averaging $30 million. Add to this the fact that the major studios have reported less-than-stellar results on high-cost films. Even so, the high costs show few signs of diminishing. 1997 saw spending records hit new highs—with over $100-million budgets attached to a number of films. The bottom line: Tinseltown remained tense, hoping for box office bonanzas . . . and counting, at least, on the foreign and home video markets to bail them out if disaster struck.

▶ **For the music industry, the past few years saw industrywide merger and acquisition activity, the emergence of new labels, sales gains, and, most recently, a bit of a slowdown.**

The '90s opened with a flurry of mergers and acquisitions. The large companies bought up smaller companies, often combining different labels into one operation. But at the same time the industry was consolidating, new small labels began entering the marketplace—many of them fueled by the success of rap music. And by 1996 competition was having a real impact on the music industry. The double-digit U.S. sales that had been going strong for nearly a decade started drying up in 1996—with growth slowing down dramatically. Adding to industry concerns: increased competition for young adult and youth dollars from computers and other nonmusic entertainment sources; trouble—even bankruptcy—for record chain stores; disappointing sales for previously strong acts (like Hootie and the Blowfish and Pearl Jam); and an erosion in sales for back catalog standards.

By 1997, the industry was going through another shakeout—complete with job cuts and massive corporate reorganizations. But optimism remained high, with many experts and insiders believing that the worst was over. Key hope: strong international sales, plus refocused attention on newer (cheaper) talents.

WHAT'S NEXT

▶ **Foreign markets will continue to be of vital importance to the film industry.**

This is due partly to the international focus of U.S. business and partly to simple economics: About 80% of all films don't earn enough to cover their costs through U.S. distribution. Producers count on ancillary markets—cable, broadcast television, video cassettes, and especially foreign distribution—to make more money. Demand is high overseas for American films—high enough to make film one of the country's most successful exports. One problem, however: demand has eroded a bit—as foreign television and film production increases in quantity and quality, more international viewers are turning to products of their own country. But American productions still pull them in, even if it is at a lower rate than in the past. So, for the short term, the foreign market remains strong.

A key reason for the lucrative foreign market is the fact that cable and broadcast television are being expanded overseas. The results? More U.S. companies will be producing shows with foreign sales potential firmly in mind. And shows that may pull only fair ratings domestically can stay in production due to a strong foreign showing.

However, in addition to slightly eroding demand, the U.S. film industry faces a growing backlash against American film exports. Some foreign governments, primarily European Community members, have instituted quotas limiting both television broadcast and theater screen time of foreign films, as well as restrictions on imports. This situation may worsen as the U.S. seeks to penetrate the international market further.

▶ **"Vertical integration"—entertainment companies occupying several different niches in the entertainment business—will still play a major role in the industry, even as mergers slow down.**

It's connected with the general trend that swept American industry—a movement away from traditional conglomerates to newer ones formed of subsidiaries in related areas. Some examples of vertically integrated entertainment companies include Viacom, which is involved in television production, cable TV, and syndication; Fox, which has a film studio, television stations, and television production units; Sony, which has a film studio, recording labels; and, of course, Disney, which merged with Capital Cities/ABC and became more of an entertainment titan, adding television and radio to its range of businesses and increasing its ability to cross-pollinate.

While mergers between companies won't be occurring as rapidly as in the past, these companies will still make their mark on the industry. The key reason? They can dominate through sheer size and diversity. In the case of a Viacom or Fox, they can produce shows, distribute them, then broadcast or syndicate them. A Sony or an MCA can promote new music artists by recording a music video, then running the video as an opener to a movie. The possibilities are numerous—and, in these days of hot competition, they give the large companies an edge over their smaller competitors.

Watch for continued linkages and periodic spurts of merger activity as the industry goes through its usual ups and downs, with outsiders such as the Baby Bells getting into the industry.

▶ **The key trend to watch in the music industry: digital technology.**

It's the wave of the future—and one that many industry insiders are pinning their hopes on.

The old analog technology is quickly fading out, as audiotape cassette sales continue slipping. CDs, of course, got most of the business in the recent past. And now the music industry is focusing a lot of attention on digital video discs (DVDs) and MiniDiscs, a recordable 2.5-inch optical discs.

Expect the most action on the MiniDisc front. Designed primarily as a replacement for tapes, MiniDiscs already are beginning to win over consumers in a big way—with 3.5 million units sold in 1996 compared to 1.2 million in 1995.

As for DVDs, they will be focused chiefly on the home video and computer product, but even here the music industry is hoping to cash in on the new technology. Expect to see more record companies offering DVDs of concerts and the like, in an attempt to sell an MTV-like product directly to the consumer.

▶ **Changing consumer buying habits and heated competition are forcing music companies to try new ways of attracting attention and customers.**

The two main reasons for this trend? First, music-buying consumers are older than in the past and are less likely to buy a new release automatically or to walk into a music store at all. Second, it's harder to get radio airplay for a new (or even an old) act because of the intense competition. As a result, companies will be exploring new ways of marketing and promoting their wares.

Expect to see increased use of such methods as direct-mail catalogs from which a consumer can order by mail or by calling an 800 or 888 number; advertisements of new releases that include an 800 or 888 number; mail-order advertising in consumer magazines.

Record companies will also be exploring nontraditional retailing; with the decline of so many record chain stores, it's time for record companies to seek out different ways of selling to their customers. Along these lines, watch for record sales in such places as supermarkets, movie theater lobbies (especially those connected with the large entertainment giants that also own record divisions), even vending machines in airports and the like.

On the marketing and promotion side, expect to see record companies increasing their attention to the Internet. Already they're using it as a way to promote sales, by setting up live events, offering on-line chats with artists, and providing downloadable clips. This type of activity should increase as Internet access becomes more common—and as more young adults log on.

Other methods record companies will be using to reach more consumers: increased television advertising, particularly on cable; mass-transit and outdoor advertising; and (more common with labels that are part of a larger entertainment conglomerate) showing music videos in movie theaters before the main feature; arranging promotional tours of in-store appearances for new artists.

This activity in promotion and advertising points to *increased employment opportunities for sales and promotional staffers,* especially those with direct mail backgrounds, and advertising personnel.

▶ **The outlook for another area of the entertainment field: An aging population will mean bright days ahead for leisure companies— sporting goods manufacturers, recreational services, and the like.**

An older population means more money will be spent on leisure activities. Sporting goods companies, amusement parks, playgrounds, and other recreational services companies are all poised for a run of good years.

What does this mean in terms of employment? There may be opportunities in a range of areas, from recreational services to health clubs to sporting goods companies. Looking particularly strong: those companies or services that target families. This is a result of the large number of baby boomers having children themselves. The focus is now on family entertainment. In light of this, there may be a number of employment opportunities in companies that offer goods or services directly aimed at families, such as playground or "play-care" service franchisers and companies, amusement parks, and the like.

EMPLOYMENT OUTLOOK: Competitive, as always.

Entertainment companies are always competitive—but they're also always hiring. The trick, of course, is managing to land a job in spite of the intense competition. Generally, it's a combination of timing and luck.

More specifically: Film production jobs generally depend on specific companies and shows. However, given the recent influx of competition in television production, expect more of a squeeze than ever in this area.

A good bet: Because of growing competition and a blockbuster focus in the film industry, prerelease publicity and marketing are becoming more important. These areas will offer employment opportunities in the short term, but competition will be stiff.

An Employment Tip: The best way to get a job in Hollywood is to know someone. But for those who don't have that in, there is another way to break into directing. The Directors Guild offers a formal training program for assistant directors for individuals with a BA or a minimum of three years' experience. Applicants must take an all-day written test and oral exam. An example of how competitive it is: Only a little more than 1% of the applicants pass.

Contact:

> Assistant Director's Training Program
> Directors Guild of America
> 14144 Ventura Blvd.
> Sherman Oaks, CA 91423
> 213/289-2000

BEST BETS

HBO
1100 Avenue of the Americas
New York, NY 10036
212/512-7400

More than just a cable company, HBO is moving strongly into production—producing shows as well as a number of pilots, specials, and made-for-TV movies. In a crowded field, HBO Productions is carving out a niche for itself and looks headed for a bright future. An additional plus: HBO has a reputation for being a "family-friendly" company and was chosen one of the best companies for parents in various surveys.

Walt Disney Co.
500 S. Buena Vista St.
Burbank, CA 91521
818/560-1000

Disney has long been considered one of the entertainment industry's powerhouses and, in recent years, has been growing and going strong. Of course, the biggest sign of Disney's strength: its 1995 merger with media giant Capital

Cities/ABC. With only one major financial failure in years (Euro Disney Park), Disney has been introducing new products, shows, and more. One key to its continued success: Attention to merchandising. Disney knows how to get the most out of its product. Film features, such as *The Lion King,* spawn videos, soundtracks, toys, books, and many other products. This type of money-making ability makes Disney a strong choice for the future.

TOP FILM & VIDEO PRODUCTION COMPANIES

Buena Vista Home Video
500 S. Buena Vista St.
Burbank, CA 91521
818/560-0044

Stephen J. Cannell Productions
7083 Hollywood Blvd.
Los Angeles, CA 90028
213/856-7955

Cannon Pictures
1875 Century Park E.
Los Angeles, CA 90067
310/772-7764

Carolco Pictures, Inc.
8800 Sunset Blvd.
Los Angeles, CA 90069
213/850-8800

Castle Rock Entertainment
335 N. Maple Dr., No. 135
Beverly Hills, CA 90210
310/550-0388

Dick Clark Productions, Inc.
3003 W. Olive Ave.
Burbank, CA 91505
818/841-3003

Columbia Pictures— TV
10202 W. Washington Blvd.
Culver City, CA 90232
310/280-8000

Walt Disney Co.
500 S. Buena Vista St.
Burbank, CA 91521
818/569-1000

Walt Disney Pictures & TV
500 S. Buena Vista St.
Burbank, CA 91521
818/560-1000

Fries Entertainment, Inc.
6922 Hollywood Blvd.
Los Angeles, CA 90028
213/466-2266

Group W Productions, Inc.
10877 Wilshire Blvd.
Los Angeles, CA 90024
213/446-6000

Hanna Barbera Productions, Inc.
3400 W. Caheunga Blvd.
Los Angeles, CA 90068
213/851-5000

Hemdale Film Corp.
1640 S. Sepulveda Blvd.
Los Angeles, CA 90025
310/445-4460

Imagine Films Entertainment, Inc.
1925 Century P. E., No. 2300
Los Angeles, CA 90067
310/552-0057

Kushner-Locke Co.
11601 Wilshire Blvd.
Los Angeles, CA 90025
310/445-1111

Lorimar Productions; Lorimar Telepictures Corp.
4000 Warner Blvd.
Burbank, CA 91522
818/954-6000

Lucasfilm Ltd.
P.O. Box 2009
San Rafael, CA 94912
415/662-1700

MCA, Inc.
100 Universal City Plz.
Universal City, CA 91608
818/777-1000

MGM-Pathé Communications Co.
2500 Broadway
Santa Monica, CA 90404
310/449-3000

New Line Cinema Corp.
888 7th Ave.
New York, NY 10106
212/649-4900

New World Entertainment Ltd.
1440 S. Sepulveda Blvd.
Los Angeles, CA 90025
310/444-8100

Orion Pictures Corp.
304 Park Ave. S.
New York, NY 10010
212/505-0051

Paramount Pictures Corp.
5555 Melrose Ave.

Hollywood, CA 90038
213/956-5000

Prism Entertainment Corp.
1888 Century Pk. E.,
Los Angeles, CA 90067
310/277-3270

Aaron Spelling Productions
5700 Wilshire Blvd.
Los Angeles, CA 90036
213/965-5888

Twentieth Century-Fox Film

10201 W. Pico Blvd.
Los Angeles, CA 90035
310/277-2211

Universal City Studios, Inc.
100 Universal City Plz.
Universal City, CA 91608
818/777-1000

Warner Brothers/Warner TV, Inc.
4000 Warner Blvd.
Burbank, CA 91522
818/954-6000

TOP RECORD COMPANIES

A&M Records
1416 North La Brea
Hollywood, CA 90028
213/469-2411
New York office:
825 8th Ave.
New York, NY 10019
212/333-1328

Arista Records, Inc.
6 W. 57th St.
New York, NY 10019
212/489-7400

Atlantic Recording Corp.
75 Rockefeller Plz.
New York, NY 10019
212/275-2000

BMG Music (RCA Records)
1540 Broadway
New York, NY 10036
212/930-4000
Los Angeles office:
6363 Sunset Blvd.
Los Angeles, CA 90028
213/468-4000
Nashville office:

1 Music Circle N.
Nashville, TN 37203
615/664-1200

Capitol-EMI Music, Inc.
1750 N. Vine St.
Hollywood, CA 90028
213/462-6252
Nashville office:
Liberty Records
3322 West End Ave.
11th Fl.
Nashville, TN 37203
615/269-2000

Columbia Records
(c/o Sony Music Entertainment Inc.)

Elektra Entertainment
385 N. Maple Dr.
Suite 123
Beverly Hills, CA 90210
310/288-3800
New York office:
75 Rockefeller Plz.
New York, NY 10019
212/275-4000

EMI Music Worldwide
152 W. 57th St.
New York, NY 10019
212/261-3000

EMI Records Group
(Chrysalis & SBK)
1290 Ave. of the Americas
New York, NY 10104
212/492-1700

Epic Records
(c/o Sony Music Entertainment Inc.)
550 Madison Ave.
New York, NY 10022
212/833-8000
Los Angeles office:
2100 Colorado Ave.
Santa Monica, CA 90404
213/449-2100
Nashville office:
34 Music Sq. E.
Nashville, TN 37203
615/742-4321

Island Records, Inc.
825 8th Ave.
New York, NY 10019
212/333-8000

MCA Records
70 Universal City Plz.
N. Hollywood, CA
91608
818/777-1000

Motown Records
575 Wilshire Blvd.
Los Angeles, CA
90036
213/634-3500

Polygram Records, Inc. (Mercury and Polydor)
825 Eighth Ave.
New York, NY 10019
212/333-8000
Los Angeles office:
11150 Santa Monica

Blvd.
Ste. 1100
Los Angeles, CA
90025
310/996-7200

Sire Records
(c/o Warner Brothers Records)
75 Rockefeller Plz.
New York, NY 10019
212/275-4560

Sony Music Entertainment, Inc.
550 Madison Ave.
New York, NY 10022
Attn: Recruitment 51/3
212/833-8000
Los Angeles office:
2100 Colorado Ave.
Santa Monica, CA
90404
310/449-2100

Nashville office:
34 Music Sq. E.
Nashville, TN 37203
615/742-4321

Sun International
3106 Belmont Blvd.
Nashville, TN 37212
615/385-1960

Warner Brothers/ Reprise Records
3300 Warner Blvd.
Burbank, CA 91505
818/846-9090
New York office:
75 Rockefeller Plz.
New York, NY 10019
212/275-4500
Nashville office:
20 Music Sq. E.
Nashville, TN 37203
615/320-7525

WHERE TO GO FOR MORE INFORMATION

ENTERTAINMENT INDUSTRY ASSOCIATIONS

Academy of Motion Picture Arts and Sciences
8949 Wilshire Blvd.
Beverly Hills, CA
90211
310/247-3000

American Film Marketing Association
10850 Wilshire Blvd.
Los Angeles, CA 90024
310/446-1000

American Society of Cinematographers
1782 N. Orange Dr.
Hollywood, CA 90028
213/876-5080
800/448-0145

Association for Independent Video and Film
304 Hudson St.
6th Fl. North
New York, NY 10014
212/807-1400

Directors Guild of America
7920 Sunset Blvd.
Hollywood, CA 90046
310/289-2000

National Academy of Recording Arts and Sciences
3402 Pico Blvd.
Santa Monica, CA
90405
310/392-3777

Producers Guild of America
400 S. Beverly Dr.
Ste. 211
Beverly Hills, CA
90212
310/557-0807

Recording Industry Association of America
1020 19th St., NW
Washington, DC 20036
202/775-0101

Society of Motion Picture and Television Engineers
595 W. Hartsdale Ave.
White Plains, NY 10607
914/761-1100

ENTERTAINMENT INDUSTRY DIRECTORIES

Billboard
International
Recording Studio &
Equipment Directory
Billboard Publications,
Inc.
1515 Broadway
New York, NY 10036
212/764-7300

International Motion
Picture Almanac
Quigley Publishing Co.
159 W. 53rd St.
New York, NY 10019
212/247-3100

Radio & Records
Ratings Report &
Directory
Radio and Records, Inc.
10100 Santa
Monica Blvd.
Los Angeles, CA 90067
310/553-4330

ENTERTAINMENT INDUSTRY MAGAZINES

Back Stage
1515 Broadway
New York, NY 10036
212/764-7300
(Weekly newspaper
covering film
production,
entertainment, and
television commercial
production. Includes
help-wanted ads.)

Billboard
Billboard Publications,
Inc.
1515 Broadway
New York, NY 10036
212/764-7300

(Covers the music
industry.)

Box Office
6640 Sunset Blvd.
Suite 100
Hollywood, CA 90028
213/465-1186
(Aimed at theater
owners, managers,
operators, etc.—people
involved in film
production and distri-
bution.)

Daily Variety
5700 Wilshire Blvd.
Los Angeles, CA

90036
213/857-6600

Film Journal
244 W. 49th St.
New York, NY 10019
212/246-6460

Hollywood
Reporter
5055 Wilshire Blvd.
Los Angeles, CA
90036
213/525-2000

Variety
245 W. 17th St.
New York, NY 10011
212/337-7002

FINANCIAL SERVICES

INDUSTRY OUTLOOK: Fair but guarded—much depends on the state of the stock market and consumer credit.

Financial services firms cover a broad spectrum of markets that serve the financial and investment needs of the public.

Securities firms, which are the main focus of this section, perform various functions. They act as agents for buyers on securities exchanges like the New York Stock exchanges; as dealers, by making markets (buying or selling on their own accounts to preserve liquidity); as underwriters, by marketing and selling new stock and bond issues to finance clients; as lenders to giant institutional customers (and to individuals via margin accounts); and as advisors in mergers and acquisitions.

There are about 8,000 security firms today, ranging from giants like Merrill Lynch, which carries out virtually every function, to medium- and small-size specialty firms.

What's ahead for the securities industry? The near term, nevertheless, appears good as the persistence of low interest rates spurs investments into the securities markets and increases corporate refinancing, including mergers and acquisitions. Excess capacity still faces the brokerage business with consolidations likely to continue into 1997.

A LOOK BACK

► The 1995–early 1997 period was excellent for Wall Street.

Two major trends made Wall Streeters happy for much of the 1995–1997 period.

First, an unprecedented amount of consumer money flowed into Wall Street brokerage houses and mutual funds. Partly because of the aging of the huge baby-boomer population bulge—who are now older and in their peak earning years—and partly because low interest rates made stocks, not bank savings accounts or CDs the best place to put their investment dollars, Wall Street saw a large surge in activity. And the stock market reflected this by going up—and up. Brokerage houses earned large revenues from commissions on buying and selling stocks, and further gains from managing assets.

In turn, low interest rates spurred more debt and equity underwriting, keeping investment bankers happy, as companies issued stocks and bonds to support new or increased business activity. Meanwhile, mergers and acquisitions activity (companies buying or merging with other companies) reached extremely high levels in 1995, topping $450 billion domestically. Driving this trend: globalization, increased competition, and deregulation. In other words, big companies see the advantage of being even larger in today's worldwide markets—and with interest rates down and governments allowing them—they merged or acquired other firms.

Big mergers in 1995 centered on commercial banking and media; in early 1996 defense, telecommunications, mining and energy were keeping investment bankers talking. As one major industry insider noticed, major merger and acquisitions activity normally centers around one major industry in a year—but in 1995 and 1996 it seemed that every quarter a major upheaval was occurring. On the downside: in early 1996 it appeared that some of this activity was slowing, and although a record number of new issues of stock was ready in the pipeline, and although brokerage houses were staffed for peak business, always on the horizon was the question: what happens if the market falls? Which it did in mid '96, ushering in a roller coaster ride for the industry; and a recovery by year's end and into 1997.

This sort of concern was also on the minds of the purveyors of credit: credit card companies and consumer finance giants like American Express, Advanta, Dean Witter Discover, and Household International. Credit was very easy to get in recent years. In an effort to attract more customers, many credit card companies lowered standards, increased mailings and advertising—and already in early 1997, credit delinquencies were on the rise. Not that this was a major problem . . . yet.

1997 saw the announcement of a merger between Morgan Stanley and Dean Witter Discover to create the industry's number 5 firm in terms of issues underwritten. And most industry insiders saw this as a sign that other companies might follow suit in the future—either taking over other companies . . . or being taken over themselves.

▶ **The 1980s were one of the longest and strongest "up cycles" in the history of the business, and although it's all memory, it's important to understanding the business today.**

The '80s started slow but built momentum, as investors—both private and institutional—poured money into stocks, bonds, and other securities. Wall Street firms changed. The industry moved away from small partnerships to large corporations, hiring increased dramatically, and branch offices opened here and abroad. New investment vehicles were created or marketed more aggressively, including mortgage-backed securities (Fannie Maes, Freddie Macs, etc.) and junk bonds (bonds rated Ba or less, offering higher yields). Meanwhile, an unprecedented wave of mergers and acquisitions revolutionized the marketplace—and earned investment bankers fat fees.

Then, in October 1987, the stock market plunged. The result? A drop in earnings and the beginning of layoffs. But the economy, contrary to predictions, remained strong, and merger activities, which had slowed briefly, picked up. Late '80s mergers brought large fees to some big players, including Morgan Stanley, Bear Stearns.

In 1989, however, two of Wall Street's major money-makers turned sour. Merger activity slowed and junk-bond financing stopped almost completely, culminating in the closure of Drexel Burnham Lambert, the junk-bond king. Liquidity problems at other firms, which occurred as business dried up, prompted a Street-wide cost-cutting purge. Layoffs dominated the news. It has been estimated that over the next three years, 70,000 employees were laid off; one-fifth of the total pre-1987 crash work force.

But by 1991, as the recession made front-page news, things started looking up on Wall Street (except for the investment firm Salomon Brothers, which admitted to bidding illegally on the U.S. Treasury markets). The stock market entered into another long bull market, and it became evident that Wall Street was on a different cycle from the rest of the economy. It had entered into the recession first, trimmed its fat earlier, and resumed hiring earlier.

All this 1980s history was to illustrate a point: employment levels on Wall Street are cyclical, and more so than many other industries. For the past three years Wall Street was a good place to be—hiring was fairly strong, profits were good. But a downturn can result in hefty downsizing. But for those who are strong, and who can weather the storm, the good times return; and apparently relatively quickly, if recent history is any lesson.

WHAT'S NEXT

▶ **The key in the next years: fierce competition for the same customer.**

The financial marketplace is becoming crowded, as banks, insurance firms, and other giants seek to offer the same services to the same customer. Expect more competition in the near future—and various changes.

Many non-financial companies have already acquired securities subsidiaries, while the weakening of regulatory barriers has brought banks such as Citicorp into the mutual-fund business.

Three major results: pricing pressures, emphasis on sales, and emphasis on service.

Responding to these challenges, securities firms are postioning themselves in various ways. Some firms are emphasizing across-the-board financial services, while others take the opposite tack and opt for specialization. Various investment banks are transforming themselves into old-line merchant banks. Other investment firms are beefing up their trading arms, reducing customer contacts, and trading their own accounts. The key strategy is concentration on "core" areas—where they do business best.

▶ **Companies will continue to expand geographically or into businesses that relate to core areas.**

Key: Telecommunications advances and declining regulatory barriers have increased the flow of investments across international borders. U.S. firms have expanded abroad, where their branches buy foreign investments for U.S. portfolios as well as participate in foreign domestic market—giving others access to U.S. sources of finance. Expect to see more brokerages follow in the footsteps of companies like Merrill Lynch—which has bought firms around the world. Other brokerages will expand internationally by setting up joint ventures with foreign firms. At the same time, foreign firms will further increase their presence in this country. The bottom line? Finance has become truly global, and U.S. investment and securities firms realize it.

▶ Health care underwriting and counsel—a growth niche market.

1996 saw over $3.9 billion of health care products and services initial public offerings (IPOs), excluding biotech or pharmaceutical IPOs or secondary health care offerings. *Modern Healthcare,* an industry trade journal, reported that health care is one of the two primary areas for financing by emerging finance companies; the other area is technology.

▶ Two key elements that should be a main focal point for the securities industry: derivatives, fee-based business, and money management.

As the market changes, so does the focus of the financial services industry. It has changed course as a result of the lean years of the late '80s. Due to this, the following key elements should receive special emphasis:

1. A move to fee-based business as opposed to commission-based. This should grow as financial services firms seek to keep costs and earnings more stable.
2. Increased attention to money management. As a result of the massive moves of money into mutual funds, financial services firms are recognizing the importance of individual investors and should continue to increase efforts to reach and maintain this customer base.
3. Cross-selling: much of what was discussed in the above two trends translates into a much-used term: cross-selling. Many retail firms are trying to be all things to all people—taking in investment money from a consumer, giving him or her a mortgage, managing his or her savings, selling insurance. A big mover in this realm: giant Merrill Lynch.
4. More consolidations. The giants will get bigger, and the smaller Wall Street firms will offer specialized services—but the middle level is fast disappearing. Example: Dean Witter, Discovery & Company's announced merger with Morgan Stanley Group Inc. to surpass Merrill Lynch as the largest securities company. *Key point:* in today's global marketplace, it's tough for the medium-size Wall Street firm, starved of resources, to compete effectively.

Look also for firms to explore innovative new ways of reaching the customer. A pioneer in this area is the discount brokerage giant Charles Schwab, which sells over 900 no-load mutual funds, and now is selling its brokerage services on the Internet.

▶ In the short term, expect much volatility.

Several trends point to a short term time of more than normal volatility. First, unprecedented amounts of money won't keep coming into the market—and a major market downturn—if it hasn't already happened by the time you read this, could be in the offing. On the other hand (and on Wall Street, there's always an "on the other hand"), some experts point out that interests rates are possibly going to go lower in the next few years—and that means a continuing rise of the stock market. *Bottom line:* this could mean higher than average layoffs. Secondly, consumer credit delinquencies have been rising to troubling record highs. If the economy falters, expect even more of the same—and major trouble for consumer finance and credit companies.

EMPLOYMENT OUTLOOK: Fair to good over the long term.

It's difficult to make short-term predictions on financial hiring—so much depends on the current state of the always fluctuating financial markets. 1996 and 1997 were, of course, very good years—fueled by the skyrocketing stock market. The outlook for the future, then, is, as always, dependent on the strength of the financial markets.

That said, it's probable that hiring will continue to be fair to strong overall . . . as long as the economy remains healthy.

Over the long term, one of the best areas for employment may still be financial sales. The federal government is predicting that employment of securities and financial sales representatives will grow faster than the average through 2005. Why?

Key long-term trend: more money into the financial services industry will generate demand for more financial salespeople and advisors. Rationale: as baby boomers age (the 45–64 age group saves the most of any group on average), even more money will come into the securities markets as their incomes rise, they inherit money, and they save for retirement. Also, with the increasing array of investment products and options, more investment advisors will be needed to guide investors through a bewildering array of options—from IRAs, SEPs and Keoghs to REITs, annuities and mutual funds.

Key point: in many cases financial sales is being transformed into financial *planning* sales. Brokerages and other financial services companies are starting to act more like banks—the traditional function of investing a client's money isn't enough; now they also want to satisfy his or her *credit* needs as well. Retail brokers are increasingly acting as firm point men—not only advising clients on specific investment vehicles, but also steering them to the firm's mortgage bankers, savings institutions, etc. This points to increased hiring over the long term in many areas of financial sales and planning—and work in these areas will span a wide range of institutions—from commercial banks, to brokerage houses, to investment banks. On the downside: some are speculating that increased computerization will spawn more home banking and home investing, somewhat offsetting projected strong growth. And, as always, expect fluctuations in the markets to give a see-saw pattern to the generally upward hiring trends.

JOBS SPOTLIGHT

The often arcane world of Wall Street has spawned many diverse jobs. Here are two that look good in the next few years:

DERIVATIVES SALES; DERIVATIVES CONSULTANT: Derivatives are options and futures; in effect bets placed on the movements of currencies and other assets. They're increasingly used in today's global marketplace as a hedging technique by companies—to offset any potential loss in a business transaction or investment due to foreign currency fluctuations. Because of this ever increasing use, look for employment growth in *derivative sales positions*—at commercial and investment banks, financial houses; also *derivatives consultant* positions, advising companies using these financial instruments of the best risks and strategies. Best bet for a job: an MBA, experience.

BEST BETS

Merrill Lynch
World Financial Center North Tower
New York, NY 10281-1331
212/449-1000

As the premier retail house, it is still expanding into such quasi-banking practices as business lending and insurance. According to an insider, "anyone contemplating a career at Merrill Lynch should expect that an increasing share of his income will be derived from nontraditional investment areas, such as insurance, and business lending, instead of the traditional stocks and bonds."

A. G. Edwards & Sons
1 N. Jefferson Ave.
St. Louis, MO 63103
314/289-3000

This is the broker's brokerage house. It consistently wins accolades from brokers as *the* place for ethics and honesty as well as quality work. It has a conservative approach to the business, it doesn't pressure its brokers to sell the latest hot investment product but rather lets them pick what *they* feel objectively suits their clients' investment objectives. It has high payouts for brokers, and possibly the best retirement package in the business. Branches in New York, New Jersey, Washington, DC, Colorado, California and Florida.

Another best bet is the premier investment firm **Goldman Sachs.**

TOP SECURITIES COMPANIES

Bear Stearns Cos., Inc.
245 Park Ave.
New York, NY 10167
212/272-2000

Donaldson Lufkin & Jenrette, Inc.
277 Park Ave.
New York, NY 10172
212/892-3000

A. G. Edwards & Sons
1 N. Jefferson Ave.
St. Louis, MO 63103
314/289-3000

Equitable Life Assurance Society of the U.S.
787 Seventh Ave.
New York, NY 10019
212/554-1234

C.S. First Boston Corp.
55 E. 52nd St.
New York, NY 10055
212/909-2000

Goldman Sachs & Co.
85 Broad St.
New York, NY 10004
212/902-1000

Legg Mason, Inc.
111 S. Calvert St.
Baltimore, MD 21203
410/539-3400

Lehman Bros. Holdings
3 World Financial Center
New York, NY 10285
212/526-7000

Marsh & McLennan Cos.
1166 Ave. of the Americas
New York, NY 10036-2774
212/345-5000

Merrill Lynch
North Tower
World Financial Ctr.
New York, NY 10281-1331
212/449-1000

Morgan Stanley, Dean Witter, Discover & Co., Inc.
1581 Broadway
New York, NY 10036
212/761-4000

Oppenheimer & Co., Inc.
Oppenheimer Tower
World Financial Ctr.
New York, NY
10281
212/667-7000

PaineWebber
1285 Ave. of the
Americas
New York, NY 10019
212/713-2000

Piper Jaffrey & Hopwood Incorporated
222 S. Ninth St.
Minneapolis, MN
55402
612/342-6000

Prudential Securities
1 Seaport Plz.
New York, NY 10292
212/214-1000

Salomon Brothers, Inc.
7 World Trade Ctr.
New York, NY 10048
212/783-7000

Charles Schwab Corp.
101 Montgomery St.
San Francisco, CA
94104
415/627-7000

Smith Barney
388 Greenwich St.
New York, NY 10013
212/816-6000

TOP CREDIT AGENCIES, LEASE & FINANCE COMPANIES, AND OTHER FINANCIAL COMPANIES

Advanta
200 Tournament Dr.
Horsham, PA 19044
215/657-4000

Ambac
One State Street Plaza
New York, NY 10004
212/668-0340

American Express
American Express
Tower
World Financial Center
New York, NY
10285-4805
212/640-2000

Beneficial Corp.
301 N. Walnut St.
Wilmington, DE 19801
302/425-2500

Countrywide Credit Ind.
155 N. Lake Ave.
Pasadena, CA 91101
818/304-8400

The Dreyfus Corporation
200 Park Ave.
New York, NY 10166
212/922-6000

Equifax
1600 Peachtree St.,
NW
Atlanta, GA 30309
404/885-8000

Federal Home Loan Mortgage Corp.
8200 Jones Branch Dr.
McLean, VA 22102
800/336-3672

Federal National Mortgage Association
3900 Wisconsin Ave.,
NW
Washington, DC
20016-3808
202/752-7000

Fidelity Investments
82 Devonshire St.
Boston, MA 02109
617/570-7000

Finova Group
1850 N. Central Ave.
Phoenix, AZ 85004
602/207-6900

First USA
1601 Elm St.
Dallas, TX 75201
214/849-2000

Franklin Resources
777 Mariners Island
Blvd.
San Mateo, CA 94404
415/312-2000

GATX
500 W. Monroe
Chicago, IL
60661-3676
312/621-6200

Household International, Inc.
2700 Sanders Rd.
Prospect Heights, IL
60070-2799
708/564-5000

H&R Block
4410 Main St.
Kansas City, MO
64111
816/753-6900

MBIA
113 King St.
Armonk, NY 10504
914/273-4545

MBNA Corp.
400 Christiana Rd.
Newark, DE 19713
302/453-9930

Mercury Finance
40 Skokie Blvd.
Northbrook, IL 60062
708/564-3720

MGIC Investments
250 E. Kilbourn Ave.
Milwaukee, WI 53202
414/347-6480

Primerica
61 Broadway
New York, NY 10006
212/248-0600

Student Loan
Marketing Association
(Sallie Mae)
1050 Jefferson St. NW

Washington, DC 20007
202/333-8000

Travelers
250 West St.
New York, NY 10013
212/723-3900

WHERE TO GO FOR MORE INFORMATION

(For more information sources in related areas, also see "Banking," page 257.)

FINANCIAL SERVICES INDUSTRY ASSOCIATIONS

Association for
Investment
Management and
Research
P.O. Box 3668
Charlottesville, VA
22901
804/977-6600
804/980-3688
(Operates free twenty-
four-hour job
opportunities hot line,
for members only.)

Commercial Finance
Association
225 W. 34th St.,
Suite 1815
New York, NY 10122
212/594-3490

Financial Analysts
Federation
5 Boar's Head Lane
Charlottesville, VA

22903
804/980-3688
(Operates free twenty-
four-hour job
opportunities hot line,
for members only.)

Financial Executives
Institute
10 Madison Ave.
P.O. Box 1938
Morristown, NJ 07962
201/898-4600
(Offers members free
job-hunting services,
including career
counseling and job
referrals.)

Financial Managers
Society
8 S. Michigan Ave.
Suite 500
Chicago, IL 60603
312/578-1300

National Association
of Real Estate
Investment Trusts
1129 20th St. NW
Washington, DC 20036
202/785-8717

International Credit
Association
243 N. Lindbergh Blvd.
St. Louis, MO 63141
314/991-3030

National Association
of Credit
Management
8815 Centre Park Dr.
Columbia, MD 21045
410/740-5560

Securities Industry
Association
120 Broadway
New York, NY 10271
212/608-1500

FINANCIAL SERVICES INDUSTRY DIRECTORIES

Corporate Finance
Sourcebook
Reede Reference
Publishing Co.

121 Chanlon Rd.
New Providence, NJ
07974
800/323-6772

Directory of American
Financial Institutions
Thomson Financial
Publications

1770 Breckenridge
Pkwy.
Suite 500
Duluth, GA 30136
770/381-2511

***Moody's Bank and
Finance Manual***
Moody's Investor
Service
99 Church St.
New York, NY 10007
212/553-0300

***Securities Industry
Yearbook***
Securities Industry
Association
120 Broadway
New York, NY 10271
212/608-1500

FINANCIAL SERVICES INDUSTRY MAGAZINES

***Barron's National
Business and
Financial Weekly***
200 Liberty St.
New York, NY 10281
212/416-2000
(Weekly newspaper for
finance executives,
investors, etc.)

***Financial Services
Report***
Philips Publishing
1201 Seven Locks Rd.
Suite 300
Potomac, MD 20854
301/340-2100

Financial World
Financial World
Partners
1328 Broadway
New York, NY 10001
212/594-5030
(Monthly magazine
aimed at commodity
and options traders.)

***Institutional
Investor***
488 Madison Ave.
New York, NY 10022
212/224-3300
(Monthly magazine for
a range of people

involved in the
investment area,
including brokers,
portfolio managers,
bankers, financial
consultants, and
professional investors.)

***Pensions & Investment
Age***
220 E. 42nd St.
New York, NY 10017
212/210-0100
(Biweekly newspaper
for pension plan
managers, executives,
and administrators.)

FOOD AND BEVERAGE

(including Food Processing, Beverage Processing, and Food Retailing)

INDUSTRY OUTLOOK: Continued hot competition ahead as food and beverage firms scramble to meet changing requirements from new and growing demographic groups; an intensive international focus.

Key trends: Aging of baby boomers with changing health and nutrition attitudes, growth of ethnic groups with related food interests, and dual-income/single-parent families, all with different food packaging requirements.

Food Processing: Expect to see product innovations reflecting a change in focus, cost awareness, globalization. Watch as the industry promotes nutrition and convenience and attempts to spread costs as well as to attract new incremental revenue by adding private label lines and products targeted to niche markets. The name of the promotion game will continue to be brand awareness and pricing. Winners: companies pushing big-name brands with high perceived quality and who have a high enough volume to deliver good prices; smaller or housebrand companies who can deliver lower cost goods as well. Losers: lesser-known brands. Manufacturing efficiency should receive increased emphasis as companies try to keep costs down—and beat the competition's price. Finally, expect more companies to push overseas to expand their hold on foreign markets.

Beverages: Hot competition—but growth as well. Soft-drink companies such as Coke and Pepsi will be jumping on the promotions and packaging bandwagons, trying to increase market share. In addition, they'll be moving heavily overseas, especially into Third World countries. Smaller firms may lag, unable to compete with the marketing muscle of the big guys. One question: Are so-called "alternative beverages" (such as Fruitopia and Snapple) a thing of the past . . . or will planned image changes make them take off the way companies had hoped? Bottled water should continue to grow in line with consumers' healthy lifestyle attitudes and some concerns with municipal water safety.

Alcoholic Beverages (beer and spirits): Not a promising outlook, as the industry faces a number of key challenges—such as a drop in consumer demand, intensifying competition at home, and problems arising in the international marketplace. Wine: some growth, although healthy lifestyle attitudes may be a growth deterrent.

Food Retailers: Slow, steady growth forecast over the long term. Key challenge: hot competition, especially from nonsupermarket chains and price discounters.

A LOOK BACK

▶ **The key trends of the recent past: cost cutting, consumer cost consciousness, and consolidation.**

Like many U.S. industries, food processors went through a period of restructuring—complete with mergers and cost cutting—including several plant closings and a flurry of layoffs. Consumer cost consciousness led to an erosion in brand loyalty, with consumers switching from their usual brands to whatever was the least expensive. And often the least expensive comparable product was a store brand or a smaller, lesser known brand. The result: food processors fought back, trying to shore up market share with new product introductions to regain growth, increasing promotions and price cutting, and generally trying anything to woo consumers. By 1995, the trend had shifted again. With a recovering economy, brands resurged . . . but the competition stayed tough. By early 1997, with inflation low, companies couldn't raise prices—so had to focus on keeping costs down, brand awareness up—and continuing to focus overseas for growth.

▶ **A battery of changes had a strong impact on the food retailing business.**

The changes were as follows: a shifting marketplace with fewer housewives, more working women, and a bulge of aging baby boomers; increasing operational costs; stronger competition from smaller regional stores. The result of these changes was a round of mergers and takeovers, and restructuring and refocusing as companies tried to adapt to their changing customers. The recession hit food retailers fairly hard, leading to a period of low sales. In a double whammy, supermarkets also faced hotter competition from such competitors as warehouse clubs and other discount stores.

WHAT'S NEXT

▶ **Watch for a continued emphasis on brand image—and, on the flip side, the emergence of smaller niche players.**

With the resurgence in brand loyalty, the big-name food processing companies are going at it as they did in the past—promoting brand names, cautiously extending brand franchises, and emphasizing marketing and advertising. The result: hot competition continues as the brands slug it out for shelf space and consumer dollars. Price wars may be ahead, as well, as larger brand names cut prices to compete with their higher-priced competitors and lower-priced store brands. Case in point: Philip Morris's Post cereal brand, number 3 among cereal brands, cut prices 20% in April 1996 in an effort to boost sales at the expense of established brands Kellogg and General Mills, and Kellogg followed suit a month later. This type of competitive pricing may continue into a long-term trend in the battle between the brands.

The overall impact on employment: This points to probable employment opportunities for brand and category managers—as well as for staffers in packaging and promotions. Because the big brands will be dominating the marketplace, expect to see activity on the other end: in niche markets. To avoid head-to-head competition, companies—especially smaller ones that lack the capacity and money to compete—will be bringing out products to fit into a narrow niche (health foods, gourmet foods, international foods, etc.). This action may lead to employment opportunities, as the smaller companies continue to grow.

▶ **New product development will center around the needs of a changing marketplace.**

It's the only way to keep—and grow—market share. Expect to see competitive lines introduced by most major companies that are directly targeted to distinct niches in the marketplace: for example, dual-income families, single-parent families, aging baby boomers, Hispanic and African-American ethnic groups.

For example, "better for you" foods lower in sodium, calories, or carbohydrates are aimed at newly health-conscious baby boomers and their elders. Ethnic packaged foods are aimed at the diverse ethnic groups in the country. Look for more product developments along these lines—and more head-to-head competition between companies eager to cash in on the different markets. Still continuing to be the hottest area for new products: "light" foods and drinks. Hispanics will represent 40 million by 2010, a sizable target market for distinctive food lines. Higher incomes of those in the middle age group may result in more upscale food packages and more dining in white-cloth restaurants. With the new lifestyles—more women at work, dual-income families, and single-parent families—watch for further growth in convenience food packaging.

The impact on employment? More action—and possibly more job opportunities—in R&D in particular, as competing companies work to develop new products. There should be similar emphasis on product management and brand development. And finally, sales and marketing staffers will be needed to push the new products.

▶ **With competition so strong in the U.S., food and beverage companies will keep pushing aggressively overseas.**

Food processors and beverage companies have been going global for the past few years—and this sort of activity will continue. Key reason: the huge potential marketplace, especially in developing countries. Example: Coca Cola and Pepsi have been particularly strong in this area, moving into newly opened markets such as Eastern Europe and China. In addition, food giants CPC International, Kellogg, and Sara Lee are also expanding overseas.

Along the same lines, watch for an increase in joint ventures between U.S. companies and their foreign counterparts—one of the safest ways for domestic companies to expand overseas. A common scenario: A U.S. company supplies the technology or product formulation, and the foreign company supplies sales distribution, warehousing, production facilities—and, most important, marketing.

The effect of this on employment? An increased demand for food marketing specialists with international experience. The companies expanding overseas are emulating their work in the U.S.—building up brand image and recognition to ensure market share. As such, people with the marketing know-how as well as international expertise will continue to be in demand.

▶ **Alcoholic beverage producers will be facing strong competition and a continuing drop in demand.**

With the national interest in health and fitness still going strong, alcohol companies will continue to suffer a decline in consumer demand. This will result in stronger competition, as companies fight for a piece of the shrinking market. As with food products, "light" will be the focus of most new alcoholic beverages—light and dry beers, alcoholic cooler-type drinks, etc.

▶ **Food retailers will be trying to keep up with the demands and desires of the changing marketplace.**

This is the chief way of beating the competition and keeping customers coming in. With the population growing more slowly than in the past, food retailers will be carefully focusing their products and promotional efforts to fit the specific demographics of their customers. An aging, health-conscious population will mean that many food retailers will be paying special attention to produce. Also coming on strong: organic and natural foods supermarkets. This looks like an area with hot growth prospects. It's a fact. In today's flat market, food retailing growth results from superstore remodeling and more larger units, with increased product lines and services—with pharmacies, health and beauty care, florists, as well as expanded produce sections. The idea? To lure shoppers with a wide selection and specialty services all in one place—one stop shopping. And watch as retailers open restaurants within supermarkets to capitalize on the eating away from home trend and to boost profit margins.

▶ **Another major trend in the food industry: the emergence of a new relationship between food processors and food retailers.**

This is a trend that should be growing in the long term. Advances in technology and competitive pressures will be forcing retailers and suppliers to work more as partners than in the past. This will mean different things to different companies. For example, food processors and distributors may ship directly to a supermarket; in other cases they will set up Electronic Data Interchange (EDI) programs to reduce paperwork and allow better inventory control; in other cases they will arrange special promotion deals or the like.

This may change the employment picture to some degree, as field salespeople may have more responsibility in terms of working out alliances with the supermarkets to which they sell. Customer support services will become a hotter area. Another probability: the growth of "category managers," people responsible for an entire category of product as opposed to one or two brands. This is an interesting area to keep an eye on.

▶ **Also expect to see merger activity between food wholesalers.**

This will probably occur as parts of their important customer base—independent grocery stores—wither or go out of business. The problem? The independents will be feeling the squeeze due to the growth of the major food chains and supercenters.

EMPLOYMENT OUTLOOK: Fair, but like the industry itself, competitive.

As the food and beverage industry steels itself for stiff competition, many companies are cutting back on jobs, trying to streamline operations and restructure. This should stabilize in the long term, however.

With more new-product introductions expected as companies try to keep attracting new customers, employment opportunities may be found in product management. Probable hot areas: brand and category managers. Similarly, expect to see an emphasis on new packaging and promotions—which will lead to employment opportunities. Another area that looks good in the long term is advertising.

With so much attention turned toward overseas expansion, employment opportunities should be stronger for people with international backgrounds.

As for food retailers, in spite of hot competition and resulting consolidation, employment opportunities remain fairly good. A key reason: Companies that have already stripped down to the bone are able to expand and upgrade stores. Hottest job: category managers. Recently, produce, meat, and other specialty managers have been in demand. Key qualification: hands-on experience. In addition, more supermarkets are moving into private-label merchandise. This fast growing area is producing a demand for private-label buyers and marketers. Finally, as more food retailers step up the competition for take-home food money, expect to see a rising demand for food service managers, even chefs and bakers.

JOBS SPOTLIGHT

FOOD MARKETING SPECIALISTS: A growing field that hasn't peaked yet, food marketing is looking hot. A key reason for this is the internationalization of the U.S. food industry. Now that fast food has made inroads abroad and (literally) whet the appetites of a huge new market, food-processing companies are moving in to sell their products to that overseas market. Requirements vary, but a marketing degree and related experience are a definite plus. Best—a degree in food service or food marketing.

FOOD SCIENTISTS: New-product development—especially fat-free, sugar-free, and other "nutrition-sensitive" products—will create a long-term need for food scientists. The career track for food scientists (especially those involved in product R&D) often leads to managerial positions. Salaries reach the high $50s for people with B.S. and M.S. degrees, higher for those with Ph.Ds.

BEST BETS

The Coca-Cola Co.
Coca-Cola Plz.
Atlanta, GA 30313
404/676-2121

Number 1 on *Fortune* magazine's 1997 "Most Admired Company" list, and number 1 among beverage companies (with PepsiCo coming in at number 2), Coca-Cola is a perennial best bet for employees. Among the reasons: a reputation for good management and training programs, an attention to innovation (but not at the expense of established products—a lesson learned after the New Coke debacle) and a continued strong presence in the marketplace. Making the picture good over the long term: aggressive moves into the global marketplace.

PepsiCo, Inc.
700 Anderson Hill Rd.
Purchase, NY 10577
914/253-2000

Chosen as one of the best companies for blacks by *Black Enterprise* and a Best Bet in *Jobs '96*, PepsiCo has a reputation for being a good place to work, with an ability to attract, develop, and keep talented people. The key reason for this? Policies that treat employees well. For example, in 1989 Pepsico began the practice of giving each employee stock options equal to 10% of his or her salary. It operates a mentor program for minority employees and has a good reputation for hiring and promoting minorities and women. And now the best news: PepsiCo has been on a growth surge—and has announced plans to add new staff . . . 30,000 to 40,000 a year.

TOP FOOD COMPANIES

Agway, Inc.
P.O. Box 4933
Syracuse, NY 13221
315/449-6127

American Crystal Sugar Co.
101 N. Third St.
Moorhead, MN 56560
218/236-4400

American Maize-Products Co.
250 Harbor Dr.
Stamford, CT 06902
203/356-9000

Archer-Daniels-Midland Co.
P.O. Box 1470
4666 Faries Pkwy.
Decatur, IL 62525
217/424-5200

Beatrice Co.
2 N. LaSalle St.
Chicago, IL 60602
312/558-4000

Ben & Jerry's Homemade, Inc.
P.O. Box 240
Waterbury, VT 05676
802/244-5641

Borden, Inc.
180 E. Broad St.
Columbus, OH 43215
614/225-4000

Campbell Soup Co.
Campbell Pl.
Camden, NJ
08103-1799
609/342-4800

Chiquita Brands International, Inc.
250 E. Fifth St.
Cincinnati, OH 45202
513/784-8000

ConAgra, Inc.
1 ConAgra Dr.
Omaha, NE
68102-5001
402/595-4000

CPC International, Inc.
700 Sylvan Ave.
Englewood, NJ 07632
201/894-4000

Dean Foods Co.
3600 N. River Rd.
Franklin Park, IL 60131
312/625-6200

Del Monte Foods
1 Market St.
San Francisco, CA 94105
415/247-3000

Dole Food
31355 Oak St. Blvd.
Westlake Village, CA 01361
818/879-6600

Doskocil Companies, Inc.
321 N. Main St.
S. Hutchinson, KS 67505
316/663-1005

Erly Industries Inc.
10990 Wilshire Blvd.,
Suite 1800
Los Angeles, CA
90024
213/879-1480

**Flowers Industries,
Inc.**
200 U.S. Hwy. 19 S.
Thomasville, GA 31799
912/226-9110

General Mills, Inc.
1 General Mills Blvd.
Minneapolis, MN
55426
612/540-2311

Gerber Products Co.
445 State St.
Fremont, MI 49412
616/928-2000

Gold Kist, Inc.
244 Perimeter Ctr.
Pkwy., NE
Atlanta, GA 30346
404/393-5000

H. J. Heinz Co.
600 Grant St.
Pittsburgh, PA 15219
412/456-5700

Hershey Foods Corp.
100 Crystal A. Dr.
Hershey, PA
17033-0810
717/534-6799

Hormel Foods
One Hormel Pl.
Austin, MN 55912
507/437-5611

Hunt–Wesson Foods
1645 W. Valencia Dr.
Fullerton, CA 92633
714/680-1000

**Interstate Brands
Corp.**
12 E. Armour Blvd.

Kansas City, MO
64111
816/561-6600

IBP, Inc.
Highway 35
Dakota City, NE 68731
402/494-2061

Imperial Holly Corp.
8016 Hwy. 90-A
Sugarland, TX 77487
713/491-9181

**International
Multifoods Corp.**
Multifoods Tower
33 S. 6th St.
Minneapolis, MN
55402
612/340-3300

Kellogg Co.
1 Kellogg Sq.
Battle Creek, MI
49016-3599
616/961-2000

**Kraft General Foods,
Inc.**
Three Lakes Dr.
Northfield, IL 60093
847/646-6383

Lance, Inc.
8600 S. Blvd.
Charlotte, NC 28273
704/554-1421

Land O'Lakes, Inc.
P.O. Box 116
Minneapolis, MN
55440
612/481-2222

**Thomas J. Lipton,
Inc.**
(subs. of Unilever PLC
Lipton)
800 Sylvan Ave.
Englewood Cliffs, NJ
07632
201/567-8000

Mars
6885 Elm St.
McLean, VA 22101
703/821-4900

**McCormick & Co.,
Inc.**
P.O. Box 6000
Sparks, MD 21152
410/771-7301

Michael Foods
5353 Wayzata Blvd.
Minneapolis, MN
55416
612/546-1500

**Morningstar Foods,
Inc.**
5956 Sherry Ln.,
Suite 1100
Dallas, TX 75225
214/360-4700

**National Grape Co-op
Association, Inc.**
2 S. Portage St.
Westfield, NY 14787
716/326-3131

Nestlé Food Company
800 N. Brand Blvd.
Glendale, CA 91203
818/549-6000

Pillsbury Co.
200 S. Sixth St.
Minneapolis, MN
55402
612/330-4966

**Pioneer Hi-Bred
International**
400 Locust St.
Des Moines, IA 50309
515/245-3500

**The Procter &
Gamble Co.**
1 Procter & Gamble
Plz.
Cincinnati, OH 45202
513/983-1100

The Quaker Oats Co.
321 N. Clark St.
Chicago, IL 60610
312/222-7111

Ralston Purina Co.
Checkerboard Sq.
St. Louis, MO 63164
314/982-1000

RJR Nabisco, Inc.
1301 Ave. of the
Americas
New York, NY
10019-6013
212/258-5600

Sara Lee Corp.
700 W. Madison Ave.
Chicago, IL 60602
312/726-2600

**Savannah Foods &
Industries, Inc.**
2 E. Bryan St.
Savannah, GA 31402
912/234-1261

Seaboard Corp.
200 Boylston St.
Chestnut Hill, MA
02167
617/332-8492

**Smithfield Foods,
Inc.**
501 N. Church St.
P.O. Box 447
Smithfield, VA 23430
804/357-4321

J. M. Smucker Co.
Strawberry Ln.
P.O. Box 280
Orrville, OH 44667
216/682-0015

**Thorn Apple Valley,
Inc.**
18700 W. Ten
Mile Rd.
Southfield, MI
48075
810/552-0700

**TLC Beatrice
International
Holdings**
9 W. 57th St.
New York, NY 10019
212/756-8900

Tri-Art Corp.
280 Park Ave.
New York, NY 10017
212/451-3000

Universal Foods Corp.
433 E. Michigan St.
Milwaukee, WI 53202
414/271-6755

WLR Foods, Inc.
800 Coop Dr.
Timberville, VA 22853
540/896-7001

Wm. Wrigley Jr., Co.
410 N. Michigan Ave.
Chicago, IL
60611-4287
312/644-2121

TOP BEVERAGE COMPANIES

American Brands, Inc.
1700 E. Putnam Ave.
Old Greenwich, CT
06870-0811
203/698-5000

**Anheuser-Busch
Companies, Inc.**
1 Busch Pl.
St. Louis, MO 63118
314/577-2000

Bacardi Imports
2100 Biscayne Blvd.
Miami, FL 33137
305/573-8511

Brown-Forman Corp.
850 Dixie Hwy.
Louisville, KY
40201-1080
502/585-1100

**Canandaigua Wine
Co.**
12667 Road 24
Madera, CA 93937
209/673-7071

The Coca-Cola Co.
1 Coca Cola Plz., NW
Atlanta, GA 30313
404/676-2121

**Coca-Cola Bottling
Co. of Chicago**
1440 W. Carmak Rd.
Chicago, IL 60608
312/226-3299

**Coca-Cola Bottling
Co. Consolidated**
1900 Rexford Rd.
Charlotte, NC 28211
704/551-4400

**Coca-Cola
Bottling Co. of New
York**
20 Horseneck Ln.
Greenwich, CT
06830
203/625-4000

**Coca-Cola
Enterprises**
(bottling company
group)
P.O. Drawer 1734
Atlanta, GA 30301
404/676-2100

Adolph Coors Co.
12th & Ford Sts.
Golden, CO 80401
303/279-6565

Dr Pepper/Seven UP Companies, Inc.
8144 Walnut Hill Ln.
Dallas, TX 75231
214/360-7000

E&J Gallo Winery
600 Yosemite Blvd.
Modesto, CA 95353
209/579-3111

G. Helleman Brewing Co.
100 Harborview
LaCrosse, WI 54601
608/785-1000

Johnston Co.
1 Union Sq.
Chattanooga, TN 37402
615/756-1202

John Labatt Ltd.
Labatt House
181 Bay St.
Suite 200

Toronto, Ont. M55 2TC
Canada
519/667-7500

Miller Brewing Company
3939 W. Highland Blvd.
Milwaukee, WI 53201
414/931-2000

The Molson Companies Ltd.
Scotia Plz.
40 King St. W.
Ste. 3600
Rexdale, Ont.
M5H 3Z5
Canada
416/360-1786

Ocean Spray Cranberries, Inc.
1 Ocean Spray Dr.
Middleboro, MA

02346
508/946-1000

PepsiCo, Inc.
700 Anderson Hill Rd.
Purchase, NY 10577
914/253-2000

Joseph E. Seagram & Sons
375 Park Ave.
New York, NY 10152
212/572-7000

The Stroh Brewing Co.
100 River Pl.
Detroit, MI 48207
313/446-2000

Whitman Corp.
(Pepsi-Cola General Bottlers)
3501 Algonquin Rd.
Rolling Meadows, IL 60008
708/818-5000

TOP FOOD RETAILERS

Acme Markets, Inc.
75 Valley Stream Pkwy.
Malvern PA 19355
215/889-4000

American Stores Co.
708 E. S. Temple
Salt Lake City, UT 84102
801/539-0112

Bruno's, Inc.
800 Lake Shore Pkwy.
Birmingham, AL 35211
205/940-9400

Circle K Corp.
3003 N. Central
Phoenix, AZ 85012
602/437-0600

Dominick's Finer Foods

505 Railroad Ave.
Northlake, IL 60164
708/562-1000

Flagstar Cos.
203 E. Main St.
Spartanburg, SC 29319-0001
803/597-8000

Food Lion, Inc.
2110 Executive Dr.
Salisbury, NC 28147
704/633-8250

Furr's Inc.
1730 Montano Rd., NW
Albuquerque, NM 87107
505/344-6525

Giant Eagle, Inc.
101 Kappa Dr.

Pittsburgh, PA 15238
412/963-6200

Giant Food, Inc.
P.O. Box 1804
Washington, DC 20013
202/234-0215

Grand Union Co.
201 Willowbrook Blvd.
Wayne, NJ 07470
201/890-6000

Great Atlantic & Pacific Tea Co.
2 Paragon Dr.
Montvale, NJ 07645
201/573-9700

Hannaford Bros. Co.
145 Pleasant Hill Rd.
Scarborough, ME

04074
207/883-2911

Hy-Vee Food Stores
2001 Court Ave.
Chariton, IA 50049
515/774-2121

Kroger Co.
1014 Vine St.
Cincinnati, OH
45202-1100
513/762-4000

Fred Meyer, Inc.
3800 SE 22nd Ave.
Portland, OR 97202
503/232-8844

The Penn Traffic Company
1200 State Fair Blvd.
Syracuse, NY 13209
315/457-9460

Publix Super Markets
1936 George Jenkins Blvd.
Lakeland, FL 33802
813/688-1188

Ralph's Supermarkets Inc.
1100 W. Artesia Blvd.
Compton, CA 90220
310/884-9000

Red Apple Companies Inc.
823 11th Ave.
New York, NY 10019
212/956-5803

Safeway Stores, Inc.
201 Fourth St.
Oakland, CA 94660
510/891-3000

Shaw's Supermarkets
140 Laurel St.
East Bridgewater, MA 02333
508/378-7211

Southland
2711 N. Haskell Ave.
Dallas, TX 75204
214/828-7011

Stop & Shop Companies
1385 Hancock St.
Quincy, MA 02169
617/380-8000

Supermarkets General Corp.
301 Blair Rd.
Woodbridge, NJ 07095
908/499-3000

The Vons Companies, Inc.
P.O. Box 3338
Arcadia, CA 90051-1338
818/821-7000

Weis Markets
1000 S. Second St.
Sunbury, PA 17801
717/286-4571

Winn-Dixie Stores, Inc.
5050 Edgewood Ct.
Jacksonville, FL 32254
32205-0297
904/783-5000

WHERE TO GO FOR MORE INFORMATION

FOOD AND BEVERAGE INDUSTRY ASSOCIATIONS

American Bakers Association
1350 Eye St., NW
Washington, DC 20005-3305
202/789-0300

American Frozen Food Institute
2000 Corporate Ridge
Suite 100
McLean, VA 22102
703/821-0770

Biscuit & Cracker Manufacturers

Association
1400 L. St., NW,
Ste. 400
Washington, DC 20005
202/898-1636

Distilled Spirits Council of the United States
1250 Eye St., NW,
Suite 900
Washington, DC 20005
202/628-3544

Grocer Manufacturers

Association
1010 Wisconsin Ave., NW,
Suite 900
Washington, DC 20007
202/337-9400
(Puts out free annual directory.)

American Frozen Food Association
2000 Corporate Ridge
Ste. 1000
McLean, VA 22102
703/821-0770

**Milk Industry
Foundation**
1250 H St., NW
Suite 900
Washington, DC 20005
202/737-4332

**National Food
Brokers Association**
2100 Reston Pkwy.

Suite 400
Reston, VA 22091
703/758-7790

**National Food
Processors
Association**
1401 New York Ave.,
NW

Suite 400
Washington, DC 20005
202/639-5900

**National Soft Drink
Association**
1101 16th St., NW
Washington, DC 20036
202/463-6732

FOOD AND BEVERAGE INDUSTRY DIRECTORIES

---

*Adams Handbook of
Wine*
*Adams Handbook of
Beer*
*Adams Handbook of
Spirits*
Jobson-Adams
Publishing
1180 Avenue of the
Americas
New York, NY 10036
212/827-4700

*American Frozen Food
Institute Membership
& Buyers Guide*
American Frozen Food
Institute
2000 Corporate Ridge
Suite 100
McLean, VA 22102
703/821-0770

*Hereld's 5000: The
Directory of Leading
U.S. Food,
Confectionary,*

*Beverage and Petfood
Manufacturers*
The Hereld Org.
200 Leeder Hill Dr.
Ste. 341
Hamden, CT 06517
203/281-6766

*Progressive Grocer's
Marketing Guidebook*
263 Tresser Blvd.
Stamford, CT
06901-3218
203/325-3500

FOOD AND BEVERAGE INDUSTRY PERIODICALS

Beverage Industry
1935 Shermer Rd.
Northbrook, IL 60062
847/205-5660
(Monthly trade
magazine covering
current trends and
issues related to the
U.S. beverage
industry.)

Beverage World
150 Great Neck Rd.
Great Neck, NY 11021
516/829-9210
(Monthly magazine for
beverage industry
executives. Puts out

annual leading
companies issue, which
may be useful for
targeting a résumé
mailing list.)

*Convenience Store
News*
233 Park Ave. S., 6th
Flr.
New York, NY 10013
212/979-4800
(Tabloid for executives
in the convenience
store industry, as well
as suppliers and
distributors.)

Food Business
301 East Erie Street
Chicago, IL 60611
312/644-2020
(Monthly magazine
covering food
industry.)

Food Engineering
Chilton Way
Radnor, PA 19089
610/964-4000
(Monthly magazine for
food industry personnel,
including food
processors, equipment
manufacturers and
distributors, retailers, etc.)

Frozen Food Digest
Magazine
271 Madison Ave.
New York, NY 10016
212/557-8600

Frozen Food Report
2000 Corporate Ridge
Suite 100
McLean, VA 22102
703/821-0770

Natural Foods
Merchandiser
New Hope
Communications Inc.
1301 Spruce St.
Boulder, CO 80302
303/939-8440

Prepared Foods
1350 E. Touhy Ave.
Des Plaines, IL 60018
847/635-8800
(Monthly publication
covering current trends
in the U.S. packaged
food and beverage
industries.)

Progressive Grocer
263 Tresser Blvd.
Stamford, CT 06901
203/325-3500
(Monthly magazine for
grocery/supermarket
executives, owners,
operators, etc.)

Snack Food
1935 Shermer Rd.,
Suite 100
Northbrook IL 60062
708/205-5660
800/346-0085
(Monthly magazine
covering the snack food
industry.)

Supermarket News
7 W. 34th St.
New York, NY 10001
212/630-4204
800/247-2160
(Weekly tabloid for
food store executives,
managers, owners, etc.)

HEALTH SERVICES AND PHARMACEUTICALS

INDUSTRY OUTLOOK: Still feeling the impact of industry-wide changes—watch for consolidation and increased competition and be on the lookout for legislation to blunt some market forces.

Health services: Experts predict industry-wide consolidation over the short term—resulting in a more streamlined industry with fewer health care facilities . . . and, so, fewer jobs in some cases. But some areas should go against the wave and stay strong. Probable winners? Home health care providers, nursing homes, HMOs and other managed-care companies, and well-managed hospitals. Possible losers? Smaller or less profitable hospitals. In addition, many small niche providers (such as surgery centers) may feel a pinch and be forced to cut costs. Also expect to see HMOs face hotter competition than in the past from hospital chains.

Pharmaceuticals: Facing considerable change—due to price discounting, increased use of generic and over-the-counter drugs, and government mandates. In addition, the growth in managed-care health plans has cut into drug company growth. Expect hot competition. A bright spot for the major drug companies: new proprietary drugs in the R&D pipeline should contribute to growth through the end of the decade.

A LOOK BACK

▶ **The past few years have brought a number of changes to the health services industry, new competition, and growth.**

The biggest change has been the emergence of health maintenance organizations (HMOs) as major players in the health care industry. Many individuals and employers, concerned about the high cost of health care, have opted for HMOs over other forms of medical care. As a result, the HMO industry took off, while hospitals started to feel the pinch.

HMOs went through rapid growth—but also through rapid changes: Intense competition and overexpansion led to mergers and industry consolidation as smaller or mismanaged plans were squeezed out of the picture. By 1996 the HMOs had nearly 60 million subscribers. Hospitals, in the meantime, went through a period of restructuring as well, to counteract several years of slumping profits and dwindling patient admissions. They cut back on beds, beefed up outpatient services, and began trying to learn how to compete with their new rivals. But not enough. Despite the hundreds of mergers in the past few years, 40% of hospital beds are not occupied, and industry experts see this increasing to 55% by 2000 as HMOs reduce hospital utilization further.

▶ **Strong growth was the byword for pharmaceutical companies.**

The past few years were good ones for pharmaceutical companies. A run of successful drug introductions, heavy investment in R&D, and a growing number of older Americans combined to make the late '80s and early '90s high-earning years for drug companies. Among the key trends of the period: the emergence of small biotechnology companies as industry growth spots; and, on the other hand, a rash of mergers that resulted in a number of mega-companies dominating the industry. But 1994 brought a new change to the industry: prescription sales fell because of cost-containment pressures and a governmental push to cut drug costs. In response, drug companies started cutting costs (and employees)— and began preparing for leaner times. Other companies responded by diversification—acquiring companies that handle prescription and drug purchases by patients. Next came a wave of mergers and megamergers, with larger companies taking over smaller ones and larger companies linking up with other large companies. This was a way of putting themselves in a better position to compete globally, find higher funding for R&D, and have the ability to bargain more with HMOs, one of their largest markets. By 1997, the merger frenzy had slowed, but the industry was still flying high, coming off of high profits in 1996—and the promise of only slightly lower profits for the year ahead.

WHAT'S NEXT

▶ **Increased competition among health care providers ahead.**

The competition may occur in all levels of the industry. HMOs, currently the industry leaders, will be facing competition from modified HMOs called Preferred Provider Organizations (PPOs), which allow a patient to see a doctor outside of the network; from hospitals and physicians that have jumped on the managed-care bandwagon; and from corporations that are setting up their own health network plans.

As for hospitals, they are competing not only with HMOs or PPOs but also with specialized health care providers, such as psychiatric institutions or institutions offering care to substance abusers.

The result of this competition? More mergers and consolidations probable. Hospital chains will be fighting back against the HMOs by continuing to consolidate—in an effort to up efficiency and lower prices and costs. Hurt by the fallout: smaller hospitals, those in poorer areas, and teaching hospitals. Similarly, as HMOs face more vigorous competition from these larger hospital companies, they too may continue consolidating as they've done in the recent past. The biggest examples: In 1996, the Aetna Life and Casuality-U.S. Health Services merger established Aetna, Inc. as the country's third largest HMO, and early 1997 saw the announcement of Cigna's agreement to acquire HealthSource—creating the largest HMO in the country.

Although the current market forces are HMOs and traditional insurers, industry experts project that long term, physician/hospital managed care (PHOs) will bypass middleman HMOs and deal directly with employers or patients.

Another result of the competition will be changes in the services HMOs and hospitals offer. A few trends for HMOs: shifting away from flat fee coverage and charging for items such as prescriptions or office visits; partial or full coverage of alternative medicine (including chiropractic, massage therapy, homeopathy, accupuncture, even yoga); offering "open-ended plans" that allow patients to receive partial reimbursement when receiving treatment outside the HMO.

A new development: Expect to see a rise in the number of physician practice–management companies (PPM)—companies that manage doctors and their back-office chores and so enable them to negotiate contracts with insurers and health care companies. PPMs may capture as much as 50% of the physician services market by 2001; and one long-term scenario sees them evolving into the major and alternative health care provider to HMOs.

Top 10 Managed Health Plan Companies
(PUBLICLY TRADED, BY NUMBER OF SUBSCRIBERS)

Cigna/HealthSource*
United Healthcare
Aetna
PacifiCare
Health System
Wellpoint
Humana
Oxford Health Plans
Physician Corp. of America
Medica
*pending

SOURCE: Sanford Bernstein & Co.

▶ Home health care: a hot industry growth spot.

This area of health services has been coming on strong for the past decade and will continue to do so. In fact, it may grow even more rapidly than before. Experts predict the home health care business will take a 10% share of health spending within five years, up from the current 2% levels. As the population ages and as health costs rise, watch home health care take off. As mentioned above, hospitals are adding home health care services to the outpatient services they offer. In addition, the number of home health care companies, many with specific specialties such as brain rehabilitation, is growing. One cautionary note: The optimistic growth scenario may change with respect to the Medicare segment of home health care. Patients will continue to be pushed by their health insurers to leave the hospital early as a cost reduction measure, creating a demand for nursing services, hospital equipment, and other goods and services. While non-Medicare patients may receive these at-home services, it is likely that Medicare will reduce this coverage severely, forcing them to either pay for them out-of-pocket or just forego them.

The impact on the employment picture: If present trends continue, home health aides will be in increasing demand, with growth rates predicted up to 96% over the next twelve years. There will also be increased opportunities for nurses, health consultants, physical therapists, health managers, and others involved in the field.

▶ **The growing sales of generic drugs are adding to the already competitive nature of the drug industry.**

As with health services, the drug industry is headed for a period of heightened competition. Domestic pharmaceutical companies will be competing with one another, with foreign manufacturers, and with the newest competitors—generic drug producers. Today 40% of all prescriptions are filled with generic drugs. This may rise to 60% within five years.

Generic drug producers are posing new challenges for traditional pharmaceutical companies. One is the fact that generic drug producers have been advertising directly to consumers. As a result, the traditional pharmaceutical companies are stepping up their marketing efforts to stem the flow away from their competitors' products, while some add their own generic drug divisions. The outcome? Opportunities in both areas, for pharmaceutical advertising staffers and pharmaceutical marketing professionals.

Another challenge posed by generic drugs is their lower cost. The rising cost of drugs has already upset a great number of consumers—and state and federal government legislators. One development: As patents expire on important drugs, pharmaceutical companies will come out with their own lower-cost generic version to compete with the generic producers—and with their own higher-priced brand-name version.

▶ **U.S. companies will continue their push overseas, especially in Europe.**

The U.S. already has a strong stake in the international market, accounting for about 42% of the major drugs sold worldwide, according to the U.S. Department of Commerce, Office of Chemicals and Allied Products. But competition from foreign companies is increasing, and factors such as price controls and foreign regulations are making things even more difficult for U.S. drug manufacturers. In addition, U.S. government regulations in the pharmaceutical industry are often considered the toughest in the world, a fact that is affecting U.S. pharmaceutical companies' performance in the international market.

Even so, expect to see increased attention to worldwide markets. Also probable: an increase in joint ventures and licensing agreements with European and Japanese companies, or mergers, such as the Pharmacia/Upjohn merger. This will help both parties gain new products without the usual high development costs.

▶ **Now past its infancy, biotechnology will continue to grow but will face certain challenges.**

Individual companies will have their ups and downs depending on the results of research and drug testing, but the industry sector as a whole will keep booming. Several factors, however, will continue to affect the industry.

One of the most important: the time lag between product development and product introductions. Only after a product is brought to market does it generate any income for the company. But because biotechnology is still relatively young and is research driven, a large number of biotech firms—for example, Pfizer with investments in four small biotechnology companies, have no sales at all—

all of their work is currently centered around R&D. The result: The need to raise capital to meet high R&D costs will probably push some firms into mergers or joint ventures with larger, established pharmaceutical companies.

This is a beneficial arrangement to both parties: The large companies get the benefit of innovative products and cutting edge technology; the small companies get financial benefits, and, once the products have been tested and are ready for commercial use, a stronger marketing push and preestablished sales and distribution networks.

EMPLOYMENT OUTLOOK: Mixed—some areas strong, others weak. In general, expect changes, volatility and competition.

Health care has been one of the hottest spots for job opportunities for a few years—adding well over 1 million jobs since the beginning of the decade. More specifically, employment has grown in all health services sectors, especially home care, nursing, and personal care facilities, medical doctors' and dentists' offices and clinics and hospitals. Highest growth rate? Home health care services. Hospitals, on the other hand, had the lowest growth rate. But that doesn't mean opportunities aren't there—hospitals alone account for over half of all employment in the health services industry.

The overall problem where employment is concerned? The changeability in both the health services and pharmaceuticals industries, particularly health services. In general, expect fluctuations in employment opportunities as the industries continue to go through this period of changes.

Outlook for health services: Expect changes as the industry continues expanding, diversifying, and, in some cases, consolidating. While the government projects continued strong employment opportunities in the field, other experts think otherwise. The reasons? Health organizations have been merging and consolidating—and, as a result, one job exists where several once did. In addition, hospitals have been cutting back as they feel the pinch from HMOs. And finally, while HMOs have been growing, they often use fewer staffers per patient than traditional health care arrangements. The bottom line, then? A changing employment picture, and probably, increased competition in many areas. In general, certain areas are much stronger than others. *Strongest industry areas:* HMOs, home health agencies, offices of other health practitioners, nursing homes, and personal care facilities. *Slower growth:* hospitals. *A new employment area:* hospital management companies, which provide such services as emergency department assistance, information management systems, managed care contract negotiations, physician recruiting, even consulting services. *Hot jobs:* home health care aides, physical therapists, medical scientists, medical assistants, occupational therapists, speech-language pathologists, and in some cases, general managers. For more information on health care occupations, see Health Care and Medical Specialists section, page 94.

Pharmaceutical industry: Competition here as well as the changing face of the health service industry affects drug companies.

More specifically, expect field sales forces to decrease as pharmaceutical companies refocus their sales efforts away from smaller doctor's offices to a few thousand managed care buyers. But there's a flip side: with drug companies cutting their sales forces because of managed care, managerial jobs have actually increased—chiefly because larger medical center accounts require more attention than the smaller doctor's office accounts of the past. A good example: American Home Products cut its sales force by 30% in late 1995—but *quadrupled* the number of managers overseeing medical center accounts. *Keep an eye on:* smaller biotech companies. While the number of people these companies have on staff is relatively low, the growth rate is often very high—with staff increases of over 40% not uncommon. Good spots for people in R&D, scientists, lab technicians, even marketers.

Medical instruments and supplies industry: should mirror the rest of the health care industry. In other words, will be coping with the changing marketplace. Good bet? Companies involved in new technologies, such as low-invasive surgical procedures, or computerized surgery. In addition, companies that are pushing into international markets may offer opportunities for marketers who are willing to travel extensively.

JOBS SPOTLIGHT

CLINICAL RESEARCH ASSOCIATE: The boom in drug research is causing a boom in this area. CRAs are employed by pharmaceutical and biotech companies to work with the medical centers that are conducting tests of new drugs. Generally, a B.S. degree in a related area (chemistry, biology, pharmacy, nursing, etc.) is required, as is experience in a laboratory, hospital, or related field, although specific requirements may vary. Pay ranges from the mid-$20s for entry-level workers, up to the high $60s for upper-level positions.

NURSING HOME/LONG-TERM CARE FACILITIES MANAGEMENT: As the population of the country ages, demand grows for managers of facilities aimed at senior citizens. This area should show long-term opportunity. The downside? Salaries are often lower than those paid to management at hospitals. But the pluses are definitely there, including the opportunity for rapid career advancement, as well as career stability.

HEALTH CARE INFORMATION SPECIALIST: A field that is expected to skyrocket as more hospitals, HMOs, and other health service providers switch from paper to computer databases for their patient records. In fact, some estimate that the demand will exceed supply of qualified candidates by 54% by 2000. Health care information specialists (formerly called medical records administrators) are the staffers who ensure that patient records are accurate and organized. They coordinate all patient records generated by different members of a health care team, oversee all such records, and interact with the medical and nursing staff, updating records, answering queries, pulling records for research and the like. Qualifications: A two- or four- year degree in health information management, as well as a passing grade on the national certification exam. In addition, communications skills, knowledge of medical information and computer databases are required. Those with an associate's degree become Accredited Record Technicians (ARTs); bachelor's degree, Registered Record Administrators (RRAs). Salaries begin at an average $27,500 and rise to the high $30s with experience. Directors earn an average $70,000–75,000.

BEST BETS

Amgen
1840 DeHavilland Dr.
Thousand Oaks, CA 91320-1789
805/447-1000

This biotechnology firm has been growing at a rapid pace—as of April 1992, it employed 1,900 people and was growing at the rate of 50% a year. But it's not just a good bet because of the job prospects. It's also reportedly a great place to work because of the work style. Projects are developed and introduced through a team system. Product Development Teams (PDTs) are reponsible for R&D; task forces handle other aspects of work. Both deal directly with upper management and have members from all departments in the company. This type of work environment, plus an emphasis on building a family atmosphere through cook-offs, whale-watching and other trips, and the like, make Amgen an excellent choice.

Coram Healthcare Corp.
1121 Alderman Dr.
Alpharetta, GA 30202
404/442-2160

With the explosive growth in home health care, Coram is a company that is cashing in on this trend. CEO James Sweeney says that his goal is to make Coram the one-stop spot for any home health care need—and, along these lines, has lined up agreements with providers of everything from wheelchairs to hospital beds to IV units and intravenous drugs. And it has been signing contracts with major insurers and HMOs. For example, the giant Cigna has chosen Coram to supply all home health care (including nurses, prosthetics, and more) to its Houston HMO members. Another big move: Coram plans to offer total health care coverage to patients with AIDS or cancer in certain health plans. The bottom line? As home health care surges, so too should Coram.

Forest Laboratories
909 Third Ave.
New York, NY 10022
212/421-7850

A relatively small pharmaceutical company, Forest Labs's outlook looks anything but small. Unlike many of its larger competitors, Forest Labs doesn't do basic research. Instead it develops drugs that it has bought or licensed from other companies. This keeps costs down, and keeps the company growing. The key reason Forest is a best bet? Its sales force is among the highest paid in the industry, with salaries reaching up to $200,000 or more. And top earners also are eligible for stock options. Of course, the sales force has to work for the money—they log about 60% more calls a day than competitors. In addition, competition for jobs here is tough. As of 1995, Forest Labs employed only 450 people. But for those who have what it takes, Forest Labs looks like a great bet.

Stryker
P.O. Box 4085
Kalamazoo, MI 49003-4085
616/385-2600

A medical supply company that is known for its aggressive sales force, new product development, and decentralized management, Stryker is posed for long-term growth. It has been on the climb for the past five years, and looks as though it will keep on going up. One key to its success: its management style. It is set up into nine competing profit centers, each run by its own manager who is responsible for all aspects of that center—from growth to profitability to product development. The bottom line: Stryker is competitive, but, for people who can produce, it's a solid spot for the future.

TOP HEALTH SERVICES COMPANIES

Aetna, Inc.
151 Farmingdale Ave.
Hartford, CT 06156
203/273-0123

Beverly Enterprises, Inc.
1200 S. Waldron Rd.
Fort Smith, AR 72903
501/452-6712

Charter Medical Corp.
577 Mulberry St.
Macon, GA 31201
912/742-1161

Cigna/HealthSource
1 Liberty Pl.
Philadelphia, PA 19192
215/761-1000

Columbia/HCA Healthcare
One Park Plz.
Nashville, TN 37203
615/327-9551

Community Psychiatric Centers
24502 Pacific Pk. Dr.
Laguna Hills, CA

92656
714/831-1166

FHP International Corp.
9900 Talbert Ave.
Fountain Valley, CA
92708-8000
714/963-7233

Foundation Health Corp.
3400 Data Dr.
Rancho Cordova, CA
95670
916/631-5000

Health Care & Retirement Corp.
1 Seagate
Toledo, OH
43604-2316
419/247-5000

Healthsource
Two College Park Dr.
Hooksett, NH 03106
603/268-7000

HealthSouth
Two Perimeter Park
South

Birmingham, AL
35243
205/967-7116

Health Trust
4525 Harding Rd.
Nashville, TN 37205
615/383-4444

Hillhaven Corporation
1148 Broadway Plz.
Tacoma, WA 98401
206/572-4901

Hospital Corp. of America
1 Park Plz.
Nashville, TN 37202
615/327-9551

Humana, Inc.
Box 1438
Louisville, KY
40201-1438
502/580-1000

Laboratory Corp. of America
4225 Executive Sq.
La Jolla, CA 92037
619/550-0600

Manor Care, Inc.
10750 Columbia Pike
Silver Spring, MD
20901
301/681-9400

Med Partners Inc.
3000 Galleria Tower
Birmingham, AL 35244
205/733-8996

Nu-Med, Inc.
16633 Ventura Blvd.
Encino, CA 91436
818/990-2000

Olsten Corp.
175 Broadhollow Rd.
Melville, NY 11747
516/844-7800

Ornda Health
Corp.
2600 W.
Magnolia Blvd.
Burbank, CA 91505
818/841-8750

Oxford Health Plans
800 Connecticut Ave.
Norwalk, CT 06854
203/852-1442

PacificCare Health
Systems
5995 Plaza Dr.
Cypress, CA
90630-5028
714/952-1121

Regency Health
Services
2742 Dow Ave.
Tustin, CA 92680
714/544-4443

Tenet Healthcare
2700 Colorado Ave.
Santa Monica, CA
90404
310/998-8000

United HealthCare
9900 Bren Rd. E.
Minnetonka, MN

55343
612/936-1300

Universal Health
Services, Inc.
P.O. Box 61558
King of Prussia, PA
19406
610/768-3300

Value Mark Health
Care Systems, Inc.
300 Galleria Pkwy.
Atlanta, GA 30339
770/933-5500

Vencor
400 W. Market St.
Louisville, KY 40202
502/569-7300

WellPoint Health
Networks
21555 Oxnard St.
Woodland Hills, CA
91367
818/703-4000

TOP PHARMACEUTICAL COMPANIES

Abbott Laboratories
100 Abbott Park Rd.
Abbott Park, IL 60064
708/937-6100

Allergan, Inc.
2525 Dupont Dr.
Irvine, CA 92715
714/752-4500

ALZA Corp.
950 Page Mill Rd.
Palo Alto, CA 94304
415/494-5000

American Home
Products Corp.
5 Giralda Farms
Madison, NJ 07940
201/660-5000

AmeriSource Health
P.O. Box 959
Valley Forge, PA
19482-0959
610/296-4480

Amgen
1840 DeHavilland Dr.
Thousand Oaks, CA
91320-1789
805/447-1000

Baxter Healthcare
Corp.
1 Baxter Pkwy.
Deerfield, IL 60015
708/948-3746

Baxter International,
Inc.
1 Baxter Pkwy.

Deerfield, IL 60015
708/948-2000

Bergen Brunswig
4000 Metropolitan Dr.
Orange, CA
92668-3510
714/385-4000

Bindley Western
Industries
10333 N. Meridian St.
Indianapolis, IN 46290
317/298-9900

Block Drug Company,
Inc.
257 Corneilson Ave.
Jersey City, NJ 07302
201/434-3000

Bristol Myers-Squibb
Co.
345 Park Ave.
New York, NY
10154-0037
212/546-4000

Burroughs Wellcome
Co.
3030 Cornwallis Rd.
Research Triangle
Park, NC 27709
919/248-3000

Cardinal Health
655 Metro Place South
Dublin, OH 43017
614/761-8700

Chiron
4560 Horton St.
Emeryville, CA
94608-2916
510/655-8730

Ciba-Geigy Corp.
444 Saw Mill River Rd.
Ardsley, NY 10502
914/479-5000

DuPont-Merck
Pharmaceutical Co.
Barley Mill Plz.
Wilmington, DE 19880
302/992-5107

Forest Laboratories
909 Third Ave.
New York, NY 10022
212/421-7850

FoxMeyer Health
1220 Senlac Dr.
Carrollton, TX 75006
214/446-4800

Genentech, Inc.
460 Pt. San Bruno
Blvd.
South San Francisco,
CA 94080
415/225-1000

Glaxo-Wellpoint Inc.
5 Moore Dr.
Research Triangle
Park, NC 27709
919/248-2100

Hoechst Celanese
Corp.
1041 U.S. Hwy.
202/206 S.
Somerville, NJ 08876
908/231-2000

Hoffman-LaRoche,
Inc.
340 Kingsland St.
Nutley, NJ 07110
201/235-5000

Imcera Group, Inc.
2315 Sanders Rd.
Northbrook, IL 60062
708/564-8600

IVAX
8800 NW 36th St.
Miami, FL 33178-2404
305/590-2200

Eli Lilly & Co.
Lilly Corporate Ctr.
Indianapolis, IN 46285
317/276-2000

Mallinckrodt Group
7733 Forsyth Blvd.
St. Louis, MO 63105
314/854-5200

Marion Merrell Dow,
Inc.
9300 Ward Pkwy.
Kansas City, MO
64114
816/966-4000

McKesson
One Post St.
San Francisco, CA
94104
415/983-8300

Merck & Co., Inc.
P.O. Box 100

Whitehouse Station, NJ
08889-0100
908/423-1000

Miles, Inc.
1127 Myrtle St.
Elkhard, IN 46515
219/264-8111

Mylan Laboratories
1030 Century Bldg.
Pittsburgh, PA 15222
412/232-0100

Novartis Corp.
608 Fifth Ave.
New York, NY 10020
212/307-1122

Ortho-McNeil
Pharmaceutical Corp.
P.O. Box 300
Raritan, NJ 08869
201/218-6000

Pfizer, Inc.
235 E. 42nd St.
New York, NY
10017-5755
212/573-2323

Pharmacia & Upjohn
Co.
7000 Portage Rd.
Kalamazoo, MI 49001
616/323-4000

Rhone-Poulenc-Rorer
500 Arcola Rd.
Collegeville, PA 19426
610/454-8000

Richardson-Vicks,
Inc.
1 Procter & Gamble
Plz.
Cincinnati, OH 45202
513/983-1100

Sandoz Foundation
608 Fifth Ave.
New York, NY 10020
212/307-1122

Sandoz
Pharmaceuticals
Corp.
Rte. 10
East Hanover, NJ
07936
201/503-7500

Schering-Plough
Corp.
1 Giralda Farms
Madison, NJ
07940-1000
201/822-7000

G. D. Searle & Co.
5200 Old Orchard Rd.
Skokie, IL 60077
708/982-7000

SmithKline Beecham
Corp.
1 Franklin Plz.
Philadelphia, PA 19101
215/751-4000

Syntex Corp.
3401 Hillview Ave.
Palo Alto, CA 94304
415/855-5050

Warner-Lambert Co.
201 Tabor Rd.
Morris Plains, NJ
07950
201/540-2000

Whitehall
Laboratories

5 Giralda Farms
Madison, NJ 07940
201/660-5000

Whitehall Robins Co.,
Inc.
1407 Sherwood Ave.
Richmond, VA 23220
804/257-2000

Wyeth-Ayerst
Laboratories Division
(American Home
Products Corp.)
555 Lancaster Ave.
P.O. Box 8299
Radnor, PA 19087
215/688-4400

TOP MEDICAL SUPPLY COMPANIES

Acuson Corp.
1220 Charleston Rd.
Mountain View, CA
94043
415/969-9112

C. R. Bard, Inc.
730 Central Ave.
Murray Hill, NJ 07974
908/277-8000

Bausch & Lomb, Inc.
One Bausch & Lomb
Pl.
Rochester, NY 14604
716/338-6000

Baxter International,
Inc.
1 Baxter Pkwy.
Deerfield, IL 60015
708/948-2000

Beckman
Instruments, Inc.
2500 Harbor Blvd.
Fullerton, CA 92634
714/871-4848

Becton Dickinson &
Co.
1 Becton Dr.
Franklin Lakes, NJ
07417-1880
201/847-6800

Biomet, Inc.
P.O. Box 587
Warsaw, IN 46581
219/267-6639

Boston Scientific
1 Boston Scientific Pl.
Natick, MA
01760-1537
508/650-8000

Guidant
P.O. Box 44906
Indianapolis, IN 46244
317/971-2000

Hillenbrand
Industries, Inc.
700 State Rt. 46 E.
Batesville, IN
47006-8835
812/934-7000

Johnson & Johnson
1 Johnson &
Johnson Plz.
New Brunswick, NJ
08933
908/524-0400

Medtronic, Inc.
7000 Central Ave., NE
Minneapolis, MN
55432-3576
612/574-4000

Owens & Minor
4800 Cox Rd.
Glen Allen, VA 23060
804/747-9794

Pall
2200 Northern Blvd.
East Hills, NY 11548
516/484-5499

Perkin-Elmer
Corp.
761 Main Ave.
Norwalk, CT 06859
203/762-1000

St. Jude Medical, Inc.
1 Lillehi Plz.
St. Paul, MN 55117
612/483-2000

Stryker
P.O. Box 4085
Kalamazoo, MI
49003-4085
616/385-2600

U.S. Surgical Corp.
150 Glover Ave.
Norwalk, CT 06856
203/845-1000

WHERE TO GO FOR MORE INFORMATION

HEALTH CARE INDUSTRY ASSOCIATIONS

American Association of Homes for the Aging
901 E St. NW, Suite 500
Washington, DC 20004-2037
202/783-2242

American Health Care Association
1201 L St., NW
Washington, DC 20005
202/842-4444

American Hospital Association
1 N. Franklin
Chicago, IL 60606
312/422-3000

American Medical Association
515 N. State St.
Chicago, IL 60610
312/464-5000

American Pharmaceutical Association
2215 Constitution Ave., NW
Washington, DC 20037
202/628-4410

Drug, Chemical and Allied Trades Association
2 Roosevelt Ave., Suite 301
Syosset, NY 11791
516/496-3317

Group Health Association of America
1129 20th St., NW, Suite 600
Washington, DC 20036
202/778-3247

Health Industry Distributors Association
66 Canal Ctr. Plz.
Suite 520
Alexandria, VA 22314
703/549-4432
(Puts out low-cost—$35 in 1992—annual directory.)

Health Industry Manufacturers Association
1200 G St., NW
Suite 400
Washington, DC 20005
202/783-8700

Healthcare Financial Management Association
2 Westbrook Corporate Ctr.,
Suite 700

Westchester, IL 60154
800/252-4362
708/531-9600

National Association for Home Care
228 7th St., SE
Washington, DC 20003
202/547-7424

National Association of Private Psychiatric Hospitals
1319 F. St., NW
Washington, DC 20004
202/393-6700

National Pharmaceutical Council
1894 Preston White Dr.
Reston, VA 22091
703/620-6390

Nonprescription Drug Manufacturers Association
1150 Connecticut Ave., NW
Washington, DC 20036
202/429-9260

Pharmaceutical Manufacturers Association
1100 15th St., NW
Washington, DC 20005
202/835-3400

HEALTH CARE INDUSTRY DIRECTORIES

AHA Guide to the Health Care Field
American Hospital Association
1 N. Franklin
Chicago, IL 60606
312/422-3000

Hospital Blue Book
2100 Powers Ferry Rd.
Atlanta, GA 30339
770/955-5656
(Affordable price; possibly useful for mailing lists.)

Drug Topics Red Book
Medical Economics Co.
5 Paragon Dr.

Montvale, NJ 07645
201/358-7200

Dun's Guide to Healthcare Companies
Dun's Marketing Services
3 Sylvan Way
Parsippany, NJ 07054-3896
201/605-6000

Medical and Health Information Directory
Gale Research Co.
835 Penobscot Bldg.
Detroit, MI 48226
800/877-4253
313/961-2242

National Directory of Health Maintenance Organizations
Group Health Association of America
1129 20th St., NW, Suite 600
Washington, DC 20036
202/778-3247

Peterson's Job Opportunities in Health Care
P.O. Box 2123
Princeton, NJ 08543-2121
609/243-9111
800/338-3282

HEALTH CARE INDUSTRY PERIODICALS

Biomedical Products
Box 650
Morris Plains, NJ 07950
201/292-5100
(Monthly tabloid for those involved in biopharmaceutical research and development.)

Biotechniques
154 E. Central St.
Natick, MA 01760
508/655-8282
(Monthly magazine for bioresearch scientists.)

Contemporary Long Term Care
355 Park Ave. S.
New York, NY 10010
212/592-6200
(Monthly magazine for professionals in the

long-term care health-services industry, covering hospitals, nursing homes, retirement and assisted living centers, etc.)

Healthweek
7500 Old Oaks Blvd.
Cleveland, OH 44130
216/243-8100
(Biweekly publication for health service professionals—personnel at hospitals, nursing homes, HMOs, suppliers, nurses, physicians, etc.)

Hospitals
737 N. Michigan Ave.
Chicago, IL 60611
312/440-6800
(Semimonthly

magazine for hospital management personnel.)

Long-Term Care News
2 Northfield Plaza, Suite 300
Northfield, IL 60093
708/441-3700
(Monthly publication for nursing home personnel—administrators, managers, nursing directors, etc.)

Modern Healthcare
740 Rush St.
Chicago, IL 60606
312/649-5341
(Biweekly magazine for health care professionals—including health care

administrators, purchasing agents, medical staffs.)

Pharmaceutical Executive
858 Williamette St.
Eugene, OR 97401
800/341-0085
(Monthly magazine for professionals in the pharmaceutical industry.)

Pharmaceutical Processing
Box 650
Morris Plains, NJ 07950
201/292-5100
(Monthly magazine for people in pharmaceutical production, research & development, quality control, engineering, etc.)

Pharmaceutical Technology
Box 10460
Eugene, OR 97401
503/343-1200
(Monthly magazine for people in pharmaceutical production, research & development, quality control, and related areas.)

HOSPITALITY

(including Hotels and Restaurants)

INDUSTRY OUTLOOK: Challenges still ahead.

Hotels: Expect continued slow growth, as the demand for rooms continues to exceed the rate of new rooms available—especially in key business markets. However, this trend of supply far exceeding demand has been slowing down over the past year. And, should the economy slow down, the hotel industry will, of course, feel the impact. In general, look for a number of changes in the industry. Among them: Expect to see more hotels affiliating with a national or regional chain and a rise in cooperative arrangements with other areas of the travel industry—such as airlines, destinations, rental car companies, and the like. In addition, watch for high growth in the economy and mid-priced hotel market.

Restaurants: Highly competitive but a generally good outlook—again, dependent on the strength of the economy. Over the long term, the restaurant industry should perform well. Key reason: As the population gets older, more people dine out. Over the short term, watch the industry coping with hot competition. In addition, expect to see an industry shakeout and consolidation due to overbuilding. Chains will continue battling for market share, relying on increased service, low prices. Keep an eye out for innovations in the industry—restaurants will compete by offering different products; expanding their franchises; opening up entirely new franchises; coming up with new places for outlets—including overseas, in hotels, in supermarkets, in discount retailers, and more. *The bad news:* wage costs may rise if unemployment rates remain low. *And the good news:* employment opportunities—at higher salaries—for seasoned personnel and managers.

A LOOK BACK

▶ **The past few years saw the hotel and motel industry rebuilding, retrenching, and gearing up for economic recovery.**

First, a quick look at some ancient history: In the 1980s, hotel companies went in for the largest building boom in recent history. And the boom went bust . . . Hotels overbuilt, and with too many rooms and not enough demand, they slumped.

But the industry has learned from the tough times. It has consolidated—with some companies merging, others falling by the wayside. And after several years of slow growth, it emerged stronger than in the recent past. Occupancy rates were up, and the hotel industry was reaping the benefits of cost-cutting and increases in daily rates. By 1996 profits were up about 41% over 1995's—and it looked as though the industry was headed for stable, steady growth through 1997.

▶ **The restaurant industry's fortunes also went through a sharp up-and-down cycle.**

For much of the '80s, the restaurant industry was in high gear—eating out was in vogue, fast-food chains were raking in money, new restaurants were opening and prospering. But the number of restaurants ultimately grew faster than demand. Added to the oversupply were a labor shortage, high food costs, and a sudden rise in stay-at-home consumers. The '90s—and the recession—brought about the beginnings of a shakeout. Weaker restaurants were forced out of business by the heavy competition; stronger ones began seeking new ways to increase market share.

The retrenched industry, then, began coming on strong. The past three years saw one of the strongest growth periods in terms of sales—as customers began dining out in high numbers. Higher ticket restaurants benefited as more members of affluent households ate meals away from home—accounting for nearly 50% of all diners in 1995. And fast-food outlets were predicted to reach a record $103.5 billion in sales in 1997.

But now it looks like the cycle is beginning to repeat itself: Restaurant companies began building heavily again—and, as of early 1997, were beginning to feel the pressures of overbuilding. Many chains have scaled back on their building; others have been selling off less profitable chains and refocusing on the stronger ones; still others are trying to draw in consumers through remodeling and new food offerings. And, finally, others, usually smaller chains, have been forced into bankruptcy. So now the question for 1998: How big a shakeout will the industry have—and who will survive the inevitable consolidation process?

WHAT'S NEXT

▶ **The key trend still affecting the hotel industry: consolidation.**

It originally happened in reaction to overbuilding—and it's still a prime factor in the industry. In the U.S., over 60% of the industry's rooms are affiliated with a chain. About 50% of all rooms worldwide are controlled by the top 25 chains. The result: Watch as the familiar brand names in the hotel industry get even larger—and put marketing muscle behind their already familiar names. To compete with them, more independent hotels have followed the lead of travel agencies and formed networks with their fellow independents. These consortiums of hotels can then act like chains by combining marketing strengths and budgets, instituting centralized reservation systems, and doing cooperative advertising. As a result, these smaller hotels can keep from being swallowed up by their larger competitors—who, instead of building new rooms, will grow through takeovers. One exception to this rule: Certain areas, such as hot travel spots like Las Vegas, Atlantic City, and Orlando, may still see new construction of hotels—which will result in increased employment opportunities. Overall, expect most of the new hotel construction to be in the economy or limited-service area and the extended stay area—not at the luxury level.

▶ Over the long term, expect increasing specialization in the hotel/motel industry.

In an effort to keep up with changing demographics and to differentiate themselves from the competition, hotel companies will be seeking out market niches and clearly positioning their hotels to meet the needs of the markets they have targeted. Categories that will continue strong are corporate meeting/convention, budget, and luxury.

Market specialization and the development of promotional packages should translate into some limited employment opportunities for sales, marketing, and promotions staffers.

▶ The hottest area of the hotel industry: time shares.

The days when time-share operators were a low-rent, dubious bunch luring unsuspecting consumers into less-than-good deals are long over. Legislation cleaned up the act—and the big hotel companies have moved into the time-share market. It's now the fastest growing segment of the hotel industry—with record sales being produced each year since 1995—and it looks like it will keep coming on strong.

Marriott, Disney, Hyatt, Radisson, and Hilton are at the top of the heap where time shares are concerned, and they should continue to pursue this business aggressively. Expect to see hot action in this area, particularly as these large American hotel companies target Europe as the newest market for time shares. This may translate into good employment opportunities—for salespeople as well as managers.

▶ Increased international travel is translating into increased internationalization of U.S. hotels.

In other words, U.S. hotels are offering special amenities and services to make foreign guests feel at home. This is another example of the niche marketing that is taking hold of the industry. One way of beating the competition where international travelers are concerned is to "internationalize"—which includes serving international foods, and offering more visible concierges, multilingual staffers, and room directories and information in different languages. Especially hot: offering services to attract Pacific Rim travelers.

Employment note: Excellent opportunities exist for people with language skills and those with foreign experience. As hotels rush to prove how international they are, they will be seeking people who can promote this global image. Best language skill: Japanese.

▶ Also increasing: the use of technology at hotels.

Even through the recession and the corresponding cost cuts, hotels were introducing technological methods and equipment to their properties. In many cases, they help keep costs down and enhance customer service. The innovations already catching on include "smart card" room keys; televisions allowing in-room checkout. On the horizon are computerized services that will allow for remote check in; robotic cleaning.

▶ **A growing segment of the hospitality industry: communities and food services aimed at the elderly.**

As Americans age, the hospitality industry is keeping up with them. One key way it is doing so is through the development of life-care or assisted-living residences: living complexes that offer full service (housing, meals, and, in some cases, nursing care) to senior citizens. Marriott has announced plans to invest $1 billion in life-care community development and hopes to have 150 such communities. And the boom in demand has generated new players in the field—companies whose sole focus is on assisted living for seniors. In general, this market segment looks extremely strong for the future. The facts: Experts predict that the industry should grow about 20% a year for the next three to five years. By 2000, forecasts are there will be almost 1.5 million beds in assisted living complexes, compared to less than 800,000 today.

This developing area will offer wide employment opportunities—from nutritionists to geriatric care specialists to hotel managers or nursing home managers.

▶ **Heavy competition in the restaurant industry will lead to a flurry of new-product introductions and increased attempts by restaurants to position themselves for the changing marketplace.**

The key challenges facing the restaurant industry? Competition, price wars, rising labor costs, and consumers seeking value for their dining-out dollars. These trends haven't died down. And at the same time, restaurants are facing competition from new players: gourmet take-out shops, supermarkets offering take-home food, delis, and food delivery companies (especially common in urban areas).

Restaurants will be responding by offering new products that fit in with the changing marketplace and stepping up advertising and marketing campaigns that position them as price or value leaders. Where products are concerned, more restaurants will be leaping on the nutrition-conscious bandwagon, offering lower-fat foods, salads—anything that seems likely to appeal to older baby boomers and their families. Also looking hot: "gourmet" products (international foods and the like), as fast-food restaurants try to get away from the "burgers only" image. In addition, there may be an increase in regional fare, with national chains offering certain foods only in specific regions.

Look for expansion of the Boston Market "home meals" concept—completely prepared take-out foods similar to meals that otherwise would be prepared at homes—as KFC, McDonalds, Wal-Mart, and others test this new baby-boomer market. This trend should accelerate with the increase in two-wage earner families.

At the same time, expect periodic resurgences in the price wars between the big chains, and numerous short-run promotions, tied in to new-product introductions, as well as general promotions.

All of this activity points to opportunities in sales and marketing and promotion, as new products and new campaigns become vital to restaurant companies trying to regain their customer base.

▶ **The fast-food industry will be expanding into more overseas markets.**

From Paris to Moscow to Beijing, American fast-food restaurants are attracting attention and customers. This is a growing area for U.S. restaurant companies and one that is proving very profitable. Watch for a continued push, especially into Eastern Europe, Southeast Asia (especially Vietnam), Canada, and Mexico.

International marketing specialists will be in increased demand, due to this attention.

EMPLOYMENT OUTLOOK: Mixed for hotels, long-term outlook bright for restaurants.

First the good news: According to the Bureau of Labor Statistics, the need for hospitality managers—both in restaurants and hotels—should increase 44% by 2005—with 232,000 new positions being created. And the picture is also favorable over the long term for other areas, including marketing and certain lower-level areas. In fact, one industry expert estimated that the hospitality industry would need another *3 million* employees over the next 10 years, with half of them in management and the rest in varied fields. Here's the outlook in the different industry areas:

Hotel and motel industry: Increased business travel and increased foreign and domestic tourism should have a positive impact on hiring. The only problem: Much of the industry growth should be in economy hotels. This isn't great news for managers, as economy hotels usually have fewer on-site managers than full-service hotels. But management trainee positions will remain good employment opportunities at the larger full-service hotels. As for nonmanagerial positions, including hotel and motel desk and reservation clerks, other administrative jobs, and housekeeping staffers: While there won't be many new jobs created because of the rise in economy hotels and the increased use of automated guest registration, high turnover as people leave their jobs will create job openings. In fact, many hotel executives complain that it's getting tougher to find people to fill lower-level jobs—which means that employment opportunities should remain strong.

Restaurant and food service industry: A generally good outlook—as long as the economy doesn't sag. Key reason: as the population gets older, more people dine out . . . which means more restaurant workers are needed. For example, an additional 449,000 jobs for waiters and waitresses are expected to be added by 2005. The food service portion of the industry—hospitals, schools, and other institutions—should be offering employment opportunities, particularly in areas catering to the older population. One of the hottest areas in terms of hiring? Chain restaurants, which have been going through a labor shortage. To attract workers, many are upping their pay scale, offering bonuses for employees who bring in new staffers—both hourly employees and managers, and trying to "grow" employees from hourly workers to managerial staff. The hiring boom should continue, as the typical labor pool of young workers (16 to 24) shrinks, even while jobs increase. See the Jobs Spotlight below for more information.

The result? Increasing attempts on the part of fast-food restaurants to target nontraditional employees such as senior citizens and the disabled.

On the managerial level, restaurant hiring should remain fair to good, primarily because of the high turnover and shortages in the industry. Best background: experience or degree in restaurant management or food service. As for cooks, the long-term outlook is good with the number of jobs projected to grow about 42% by 2005.

Hiring at independent restaurants will depend primarily on the specific region of the country in which they are located and the type of food/service offered. In general, expect an improvement over the past two years, as the economy strengthens and people begin to eat out more.

JOBS SPOTLIGHT

FOOD SERVICE DIRECTORS/MANAGERS (also called Food Distribution Managers): A growing area, primarily because of the increase in nursing homes, retirement communities, and senior citizens centers offering food services, as well as programs such as Meals on Wheels. Food service directors are employed by food service companies to work with the nursing home, social welfare program, or retirement community that has contracted the food service company. A food service director will often work on site at the nursing home, retirement community, etc. In addition, food service managers are in demand by supermarket companies. As more customers opt for take-out food, supermarkets are beefing up their offerings—adding prepared food counters, in-store coffee bars, and the like—and are hiring food service managers to oversee them. Best background? A degree and/or experience in hotel/restaurant management, dietetics/nutrition, or, in some cases, general business administration. Salaries range from the low $20s for entry-level staffers up to the high $40s for upper-level employees.

BEST BETS

Host Marriott Corp.
1048 Fernwood
Bethesda, MD 20817
301/380-9000

The past few years have brought about tough times for this hotel giant resulting in layoffs and cost-cutting, but the long-term outlook for Marriott is a good one. Two reasons: its focus on niche markets in its domestic business, and its international expansion. These, plus its heavy investment in and development of senior-citizen life-care communities, make Marriott look well poised for the future. Add to this the fact that Marriott has a reputation as a good employer. It offers such things as "fast-track" management development programs to encourage career advancement for minorities and women, day-care discounting for working parents, elder-care programs, and other family-friendly benefits.

Mirage Resorts
3400 Las Vegas Blvd. S.
Las Vegas, NV 89177
702/791-7111

The casino business is booming in much of the U.S., and Mirage is booming along with them. But Mirage is going a bit further, ranking in *Fortune* magazine's 1996 listing of America's most admired corporations. Reason: quality of management; excellent customer service. And maybe that's why employees stay put. All in all, casinos average about 43% turnover annually in Nevada—but Mirage averages only about 12%. Management encourages employees to stay, sponsoring employee education programs, etc.

TOP HOTEL, MOTEL, AND CASINO COMPANIES

Aztar Corp.
2390 E. Camelback Rd.
Phoenix, AZ 85016
602/381-4100
(Casino hotels.)

Best Western International
6201 N. 24 Pkwy.
Phoenix, AZ 85016
602/957-5700
(Hotels, motels.)

Caesars NJ, Inc.
2100 Pacific Ave.
Atlantic City, NJ 08401
609/348-4411
(Casino hotel.)

Caesars World, Inc.
1801 Century Park E.,
No. 2600
Los Angeles, CA
90067
310/552-2711
(Resort hotels,
casinos.)

Carlson Hospitality Group, Inc.
700 Lake Shore Pkwy.
Minnetonka, MN
55305
612/540-5275
(Hotels/motels—
Radisson Hotels

International; Colony
Hotels & Resorts;
Country Lodging by
Carlson.)

Choice Hotels International
10750 Columbia Pike
Silver Springs, MD
20901
301/593-5600
(Hotels/motels—
Comfort Inns/Suites;
Quality Inns/Hotels/
Suites; Clarion Hotels/
suites/resorts—
Carriage House Inns;
Sleep Inns; Rodeway
Inns; Econo Lodges;
Friendship Inns.)

Circus Circus Enterprises
2880 Las Vegas
Blvd. S.
Las Vegas, NV 89109
702/734-0410
(Casino hotel.)

Days Inns of America
339 Jefferson Rd.
Parsipanny, NJ 07054
201/428-9700
(Motels—Days Inn;
Daystop.)

Desert Palace, Inc.
3570 Las Vegas
Blvd. S.
Las Vegas, NV 89109
702/731-7110
(Casino hotel.)

Forte Hotels, Inc.
1973 Friendship Dr.
El Cajon, CA 92020
619/448-1884
(Hotels/motels—
Travelodge; Travelodge
Hotels; Thriftlodge;
Forte Hotels.)

Golden Nugget, Inc.
129 Fremont St.
Las Vegas, NV 89101
702/385-7111
(Casino hotel.)

HFS, Inc.
339 Jefferson Rd.
Parsippany, NJ 07054
201/428-9700
(Hotels/motels)

Harrah's Entertainment
1023 Cherry Rd.
Memphis, TN
38117-5423
901/762-8600

Hilton Hotels Corp.
9336 Civic Ctr. Dr.
Beverly Hills, CA
90210
310/278-4321
(Hotels—Hilton
Hotels; Hilton Inns;
Hilton Suites; Conrad
Hotels—overseas.)

Hilton International Co.
1 Wall St.
New York, NY 10005
212/820-1700
(International hotels.)

Holiday Inns Worldwide
3 Raviana Dr.
Atlanta, GA 30346
770/604-2000
(Hotels/motels—
Holiday Inn Hotels;
Holiday Inn Crowne
Plaza; Holiday Inn
Express; Holiday Inn
Garden Court.)

Host Marriott Co.
10400 Fernwood Rd.
Washington, DC 20058
301/380-9000

Hyatt Hotels Corp.
200 W. Madison St.
Chicago, IL 60607
312/750-1234
(Hotels—Hyatt Hotels;
Hyatt International.)

ITT—Sheraton Corporation
60 State St.
Boston, MA 02109
617/367-3600
(Hotels/motels—
Sheraton Hotels;
Sheraton Inns;
Sheraton Resorts;
Sheraton Suites.)

Kyo-Ya Co. Ltd.
2255 Kalakaua Ave.
Honolulu, HI 96815
808/931-8600
(Hotels.)

La Quinta Motor Inns, L.P.
112 E. Pecan
San Antonio, TX 78205
210/302-6030
(Motels.)

Marriott International Corp.
1 Marriott Dr.
Washington, DC
20058
301/380-3000
(Hotels/motels—
Marriott Hotels/
Resorts/Suites;
Residence Inns;
Fairfield Inns;
Courtyard.)

MGM Grand, Inc.
3799 Las Vegas Blvd.
Las Vegas, NV 89109
702/891-3333
(Casino hotel.)

Mirage Resorts
3400 Las Vegas
Blvd. S.
Las Vegas, NV 89177
702/791-7111
(Casino hotel.)

Motel 6, LP
14651 Dallas Pkwy.,
Suite 500
Dallas, TX 75240
214/386-6161
(Motels.)

Omni Hotels Management Corp.
500 Lafayette Rd.
Hampton, NH 03842
603/926-8911
(Hotels.)

Prime Motor Inns, Inc.
700 Rte. 46 E.
Fairfield, NJ 07007
201/882-1010
(Motels.)

Promus Hotels, Inc.
850 Ridge Lake Rd.
Memphis, TN 38120
901/680-7200
(Hotels, motels—
Embassy Suites;
Hampton Inns;
Homewood Suites;
Harrah's.)

Radisson Hotels International, Inc.
Carlson Pkwy.
P.O. Box 59159
Minneapolis, MN 55459
612/540-5526
(Hotels.)

Red Lion Hotels and Inns, L.P.
4001 Main St.
Vancouver, WA 98663
206/696-0001
(Hotels/motels.)

Red Roof Inns, Inc.
4355 Davidson Rd.
Hilliard, OH 43026
614/777-1070
(Motels.)

Renaissance Hotel Co.
29800 Brainbridge Rd.
Solon, OH 44139
216/248-3600
(Hotels—Stouffer
Hotels; Stouffer
Resorts; Stouffer
Presidente Hotels/
Resorts.)

Super 8 Motels, Inc.
1910 Eighth Ave., NE
Aberdeen, SD 57401
605/225-2272
(Motels.)

**Trump Plaza
Associates**
Boardwalk and
Mississippi Ave.
Atlantic City, NJ 08401
609/441-6000
(Casino hotel.)

**Trump Taj Mahal
Associates, Inc.**
1000 Boardwalk
Atlantic City, NJ 08401
609/449-1000
(Casino hotel.)

**Westin Hotel &
Resorts**
Westin Bldg.
2001 Sixth Ave.
Seattle, WA 98121
206/443-5000
(Hotels.)

TOP RESTAURANT/FOOD SERVICE COMPANIES

ARA Services, Inc.
ARA Tower
1101 Market St.
Philadelphia, PA 19107
215/238-3000

**Baskin-Robbins USA
Co.**
31 Baskin-Robbins Pl.
Glendale, CA 91201
818/956-0031

Boston Chicken
14103 Denver W.
Pkwy.
Golden, CO 80401
303/278-9500

**Burger King
Corporation**
1777 Old Cutler Rd.
Miami, FL 33157
305/378-7011

**Caterair International
Corporation**
6550 Rockspring Dr.
Bethesda, MD 20817
301/897-7800

Church's
352 Spencer Ln.
San Antonio, TX 78210
210/737-5088

**Darden Restaurants,
Inc.**
P.O. Box 593330
Orlando, FL 32859
407/245-4000

Denny's, Inc.
3545 Michelson,
Suite 350
Irvine, CA 92715
714/251-5000

Domino's Pizza, Inc.
30 Frank Lloyd
Wright Dr.
Ann Arbor, MI 48105
313/930-3030

Dunkin' Donuts, Inc.
P.O. Box 317
Randolph, MA 02368
617/961-4000

**Flagstar Companies,
Inc.**
203 E. Main St.
Spartanburg, SC 29319
803/597-8000

Foodmaker
9330 Balboa Ave.
San Diego, CA 92113
619/571-2121
(Jack in the Box,
Chi-chi's)

**Hardee's Food
Systems, Inc.**
1233 Hardee's Blvd.
Rocky Mount, NC
27804
919/977-2000

Host Marriott Services
10400 Fernwood Rd.
Bethesda, MD 20817
301/380-9000

**International Dairy
Queen, Inc.**
7505 Metro Blvd.
Edina, MN 55439
612/830-0020

KFC Corp.
1441 Gardiner Ln.
Louisville, KY 40213
502/456-8300

**Little Caesar
Enterprises, Inc.**
2211 Woodward Ave.
Detroit, MI 48201
313/983-6000

Long John Silver's
101 Jerrico Dr.
Lexington, KY 40579
606/263-6000

McDonald's Corp.
McDonald's Plz.
Oak Brook, IL 60521
708/575-3000

Morrison, Inc.
4721 Morrison Dr.
Mobile, AL 36625
205/344-3000

Pizza Hut, Inc.
9111 E. Douglas
Wichita, KS 67207
316/681-9000

Shoney's, Inc.
1727 Elm Hill Pike
Nashville, TN 37202
615/391-5201

Taco Bell Corp.
17901 Von Karman
Ave.
Irvine, CA 92714
714/863-4500
**Thompson
Hospitality LP**

1191 Freedom Dr.
Reston, VA 22090
703/709-0145
TW Services, Inc.
203 E. Main St.
Spartanburg, SC 29302
803/597-8000

**Wendy's
International, Inc.**
4288 W. Dublin-
Granville Rd.
Dublin, OH 43017
614/764-3100

WHERE TO GO FOR MORE INFORMATION

HOSPITALITY INDUSTRY ASSOCIATIONS

**American Hotel and
Motel Association**
1201 New York
Ave., NW
Washington, DC 20005
202/289-3100
(Publishes monthly
Lodging Magazine,
which includes help-
wanted listings.)

**Hotel Sales and
Marketing
Association**
1300 L. St., NW,
Suite 800
Washington, DC 20005
202/789-0089
**International Food
Service Executives
Association**

1100 S. State Rd. 7,
Suite 103
Margate, FL 33068
305/977-0767
**National Restaurant
Association**
1200 17th St., NW,
Washington, DC 20036
202/331-5900

HOSPITALITY INDUSTRY DIRECTORIES

*Chain Restaurant
Operators; High
Volume Independent
Restaurants*
Lebhar-Friedman, Inc.
425 Park Ave.
New York, NY 10022
212/756-5000

*Directory of Hotel and
Motel Systems; Hotel
and Motel Red Book*
American Hotel
Association Directory
Corp.
1201 New York
Ave., NW
Washington, DC 20005
202/289-3162

*Directory of
Hotel/Motel
Management
Companies*
Advanstar
7500 Old Oak Blvd.
Cleveland, OH 44130
216/243-8100

HOSPITALITY INDUSTRY PERIODICALS

*Cornell Hotel and
Restaurant
Administration
Quarterly*
Cornell University
School of Hotel
Administration

327 Statler Hall
Ithaca, NY 14853
607/255-5093
*Hotel and Motel
Management*
7500 Old Oak Blvd.

Cleveland, OH 44130
216/243-8100
(Twenty-one-issue
magazine aimed at
hotel/motel industry
executives.)

Hotels
1350 E. Touhy Ave.
Des Plaines, IL 60018
708/635-8800
(Monthly magazine
aimed at hotel industry
executives, developers,
management firms,
etc.)

Lodging Hospitality
1100 E. Superior Ave.
Cleveland, OH 44114
216/696-7000
(Monthly magazine for
lodging/food service
managers, owners, etc.)

**Nation's Restaurant
News**
425 Park Ave.
New York, NY 10022
212/756-5200
(Weekly tabloid for
restaurant owners and
food service managers.)

Restaurant Business
355 Park Ave. S.
New York, NY 10010
212/592-6500
(Eighteen-issue
magazine for food
service organization
executives,
manufacturers, and
restaurant food
distributors.)

Restaurant Hospitality
1100 E. Superior Ave.
Cleveland, OH 44114
216/696-7000
(Monthly magazine for
restaurant owners,
managers, etc.; aimed
chiefly at table-service
establishments.)

**Restaurant
Management**
Advanstar Publications
7500 Old Oak Blvd.
Cleveland, OH 44130
216/243-8100

**Restaurants and
Institutions**
1350 E. Touhy Ave.
Des Plaines, IL 60618
708/635-8800
(Biweekly publication
for hospitality industry
managers.)

**Vacation Industry
Review**
Worldex Corp.
6262 Sunset Dr.
Penthouse 1
Miami, FL 33143
305/667-0202

INSURANCE

INDUSTRY OUTLOOK: Changes ahead—in a period marked by consolidation and hot competition from both domestic and foreign firms.

Life Insurance: Slow growth ahead, with most products continuing to show low margins. But expect the times to be changing fast. Watch for mergers, management shifts, sell-offs of nonessential businesses and cost-cutting. The reason? Increased competition for these markets from banks, mutual funds and other financial firms, and from foreign insurers. Also watch more life insurance companies, chiefly through holding companies, compete with financial firms by moving into other financial services, such as securities and real estate. In addition, expect more U.S. life insurers to tap expanding foreign markets. Finally, expect to see more insurers team up with their outside competition—that is, set up deals with banks and securities firms to sell their life insurance products.

Health Insurance: Headed for changeable times. Expect to see an industry shake-out, with some companies leaving the business, multiline insurers selling their health line to other companies, and other companies seeking new ways to hold old customers and win new ones or developing new market niches such as disability insurance or annuities. Effective cost controls will continue to be a key to success. Best positioned? Insurers that run large managed-care networks.

Property/Casualty Insurance: Relatively fast growth. Fierce competition and decreasing rate levels should translate into continued industry restructuring, with stronger companies grabbing market share and weaker companies streamlining, merging with their better-off competitors, or going belly up. In addition, the trend of insurance giants selling off property/casualty units may continue—resulting in further industry consolidation.

A LOOK BACK

▶ The past few years: merger mania as competition increased.

It has been a busy few years—with the insurance industry coping with numerous changes in the marketplace, hotter competition than in the past—from outside players as well as other companies in the industry and weaker earnings than hoped for.

The key result of this climate: Industrywide consolidation. Some insurance companies went on a buying spree; others sold off units not attached to their core business; still others were swallowed by stronger competitors. Over the past few years a number of huge mergers changed the face of the insurance industry. For example, General Re bought National Re, Munich Re bought American Re, Aon Corp. announced plans to buy Alexander & Alexander Services,

Met Life and New England Mutual announced a merger, Marsh & McLennan and Johnson & Higgins announced a merger . . . the list goes on and on. Other companies stepped up sell-offs of noncore businesses; still others streamlined in an effort to keep up in the highly competitive market. Add to this the fact that health insurance companies were feeling the pinch from the staggering rise in HMO growth. And the upshot as the entire insurance industry enters 1998? More of the same.

WHAT'S NEXT

▶ **Expect to see more competition in the life and health insurance industry over the next few years.**

Not only will insurers be competing with one another, they will also be facing increased competition from nontraditional sources. Regulations may allow banks to sell and underwrite insurance. Already, banks and other financial institutions, such as mutual funds, are offering investment and savings vehicles that compete head-to-head with insurance offerings. As for health insurance providers (often life insurers), with the increase in managed-care services, employer-funded health plans, demand may drop and the market for private health insurance shrink. The winners may be the well-funded life insurance—sponsored health maintenance organizations. Industry experts predict managed care will make up 80% of the health insurance market this year.

The outcome? A competitive push to hold on to old customers and win new ones.

▶ **To keep earnings up, watch more companies target the needs of the changing (aging) population.**

Insurance companies are focusing on two key areas: senior citizens and aging baby boomers.

As the American population grows older and senior citizens control about 50 percent of all U.S. discretionary income, it's no wonder that insurance companies will be emphasizing products and services aimed directly at this market segment. These include long-term care policies that pay for nursing homes or in-home medical assistance, "last-to-die" life insurance policies that can be used to pay off estate taxes; "living benefits" policies that allow holders to receive a portion of their benefits before death.

Along the same lines, aging baby boomers represent a huge bulge in the population. Insurance companies will therefore be targeting them with products such as health insurance and services such as financial planning and retirement planning.

Employment note: This points to increased opportunity for agents with specialized retirement or financial planning training, as well as certified financial planners. An offshoot of this: Since agents moving into retirement and financial planning need upgraded training, this will also mean increased opportunities for trainers and other human-resources personnel in this area.

▶ **Another growing trend: life insurance companies will be moving into other financial services fields.**

New regulations on insurance, increased competition, and diminished returns on life insurance will force insurance companies to come up with new ways of making money. Watch for an increase in the number of life-insurance holding companies entering other financial services areas, such as banking, real estate, and securities.

One specific area that's attracting a lot of attention: Derivatives. The financial services industry moved into derivatives sales in the past few years—and made a bundle. As a result, watch as insurance companies try to cash in on this business as well, steeping up their participation in the risk management business. Already, AIG had moved aggressively, offering new policies covering business risk. Expect other insurance companies to follow suit.

▶ **Expect life insurance companies to try new sales and marketing methods.**

Belt-tightening on the part of life insurers will lead to the exploration of different ways of selling insurance. Watch for an increase in joint ventures between insurers and banks, brokers or, as mentioned earlier, foreign insurers. Also increasing: using direct mail to reach customers, and establishing marketing ties with funeral directors, financial advisers and consultants, etc.

The effect on employment? In the short term, insurance agents may face increased competition, but these changes also point to new employment opportunities as the industry expands its sales and marketing efforts. One area that should see growth: Direct marketing. More companies will be shifting away from direct selling and moving into direct marketing instead. As such, life insurers have been looking for entry-level people with direct marketing skills.

▶ **Consolidation and competition ahead for independent agencies.**

Independent agencies have already been forced in increasing numbers to consolidate so they can better compete with the larger agencies. Consolidation also enables them to afford the usually expensive automation that agencies need to keep up. Another problem for independent agents: Compensations are being cut.

▶ **Watch for the increased globalization of the insurance industry.**

Watch as American companies continue their push into overseas markets, through branches, subsidiaries, joint ventures, and reinsurance. Companies will be offering straight insurance packages, as well as claims processing, investment services, actuarial services, and information services. In addition to Canada, Europe, and Japan, South Korea, Taiwan, and other Asian markets are seeing a great deal of action.

Employment note: This trend points to increasing opportunities for people with international backgrounds. Foreign-language ability is a definite plus. Companies will also be looking for people who understand the cultural differences involved in working in a foreign country, as well as the political and economic situation there—in other words, anything that will enable them to meet the client's needs more easily.

Another sign of the increasing globalization of the industry? Increased competition from foreign companies moving into the U.S. marketplace. Over the past few years, global companies have been aggressively pushing into the American market—and this trend shows no signs of stopping. The result? Hotter competition than ever.

▶ Insurance companies will be cutting back on their offerings and seeking more specialized niches.

To a great degree, this will be occurring as a result of problems with automobile insurance, worker's compensation, and health care. More specifically: More states will be reducing automobile insurance rates; similarly, worker's compensation insurance is becoming increasingly unprofitable as medical costs rise and pressure to keep rates down increases. In addition, increased competition makes cutting back more cost-effective. As a result, expect to see more companies cut back and concentrate on core businesses. For example, The Continental Corporation has dropped life and health insurance to concentrate on P/C to midsized manufacturers and shipping companies. Allstate sold off its reinsurance division, and Chubb announced plans to sell its life insurance and real estate operations. Other companies will seek to cash in on the burgeoning managed care field. Most notably, in 1996, the Aetna Life and Casualty—U.S. Health Services merger established Aetna, Inc., as the country's fourth largest HMO. This type of activity will continue.

One negative outcome: The move away from multiline insurance companies has led to employment cuts. But on the plus side, lower-cost/high-volume companies may be expanding to pick up the slack—and will be adding workers, as well.

The effect on employment: As insurance companies attempt to carve out market niches, specialist insurance professionals should see employment opportunities, for example, medical and hospital casualty underwriters, self-insurance program developers, long-term-care insurance sales personnel, and malpractice insurance sales personnel.

▶ The P/C insurance industry will be in for a shakeout.

Larger, financially strong companies will win larger and larger market shares, while smaller, weaker companies will lag behind. Their only chance for survival will be to find other capital sources—very possibly from foreign investors—or to link up with one of the stronger companies.

This type of activity should continue for the next few years, resulting in a more streamlined industry. Depending on the particular company, this may affect employment opportunities. The key to a stable job outlook? Sticking with the larger companies that will weather the shakeout.

EMPLOYMENT OUTLOOK: Extremely competitive, as the industry continues changing.

Insurance sales should be increasing over the long term because the population is aging, which translates into increased demand for life insurance, long-term care insurance, and retirement investment vehicles. In addition, there has been an increasing demand for commercial insurance (such as product liability, employee benefits, and the like).

But this *doesn't* necessarily translate into increased job opportunities. The reasons? Computerization, competition, and consolidation. With increased automation, agents and brokers can do more than in the past—which means fewer people can do the job that many did before. Add to this the fact that financial services firms like mutual fund companies and brokerages are getting into insurance sales and so competing with insurance firms and brokers. As a result, many insurance firms have become increasingly cost-conscious and are outsourcing many tasks—and industry-wide consolidation is stepping up. The bottom line: A tighter job market.

Weak areas: claims and underwriting, and data processing, as these tasks are increasingly outsourced; actuaries, as new product development slows.

Stronger career areas: In life insurance, executives with financial backgrounds and analytic skills are increasingly in demand, since more companies are offering more complex investments—such as mortgage-backed securities. Life insurance and long-term-care underwriters saw increased demand in 1996. Also promising: environmental claims specialists. As for the more promising industry areas: HMOs are a fairly good bet, especially for people with strong financial backgrounds and managed care experience. In addition, smaller and mid-sized insurance firms should offer decent opportunities, since most of the growth in sales is taking place at these types of companies.

Best background to have in today's insurance industry: In general, most insurance firms are looking for people with a combination of sales, marketing, and people skills. More specifically, the following are in demand: Direct marketing skills—especially at the entry level in both life and property/casualty—as more companies are opting out of direct selling and into direct marketing programs. Financial skills—to deal with increasingly complex investment vehicles. (In fact, many insurance companies recruit from banks and brokerage houses.) Computer skills, as the industry becomes more automated.

For more information, see Sales & Marketing Professionals, page 148.

JOBS SPOTLIGHT

INFORMATION SYSTEMS (IS)/TECHNOLOGY EXPERTS: As the insurance industry becomes more technology-driven—and as existing technologies used in the industry are replaced by newer ones—there is a growing need for information systems personnel in the industry. Insurance companies are shifting from the use of older mainframe systems to a number of new technologies—including LANs, CASE (computer-aided software engineering) tools, laptop and pen-based computers, open systems, client/server environments, image processing, even artificial intelligence. Along these lines, opportunities are opening up for people with expertise in these areas—and, in many cases, people with the ability to integrate the older systems with the new ones. The best qualifications—technological skills, as well as knowledge of (or even better, experience in) the insurance industry.

TOP INSURANCE COMPANIES

Aflac
1932 Wynton Rd.
Columbus, GA 31999
706/323-3431

Alleghany
375 Park Ave.
New York, NY 10152
212/752-1356

Allstate Insurance Co.
Allstate Plz.
Northbrook, IL 60062
708/402-5000

American Bankers Insurance Group, Inc.
11222 Quail Roost Dr.
Miami, FL 33157
305/253-2244

American Family Corp.
1932 Wynnton Rd.
Columbus, GA 31999
706/323-3431

American Financial
1 E. Fourth St.
Cincinnati, OH 45202
513/579-2121

American General Corp.
2929 Allen Pkwy.
Houston, TX 77253
713/522-1111

American International Group, Inc.
70 Pine St.
New York, NY 10270
212/770-7000

American National Insurance Co.
1 Moody Plz.
Galveston, TX 77550-7999
409/763-4661

American Re
555 College Rd. East
Princeton, NJ 08543-5241
609/243-4200

Aon Corp.
123 N. Wacker Dr.
Chicago, IL 60606
312/701-3000

W. R. Berkley
165 Mason St.
Greenwich, CT 06830
203/629-2880

Berkshire Hathaway, Inc.
3555 Farnam St.
Omaha, NE 68131
402/346-1400

Capital Holding Corp.
400 W. Market
Louisville, KY 40202
502/560-2000

CCP Insurance
11825 N.
Pennsylvania St.
Carmel, IN 46032
317/817-6100

Chubb Corp.
15 Mountain View Rd.
Philadelphia, PA 19103
908/903-2000

Cigna Corporation
1 Liberty Pl.
Philadelphia, PA 19192-1550
215/761-1000

Cincinnati Financial Corp.
6200 S. Gilmore Rd.
Fairfield, OH 45014
513/870-2000

CNA Financial Corp.
333 S. Wabash Ave.

Chicago, IL 60604
312/822-5000

Commerce Group Inc.
211 Main St.
Webster, MA 01570
508/943-9000

Conseco
11825 N.
Pennsylvania St.
Carmel, IN 46032
317/817-6100

Empire Blue Cross & Blue Shield
622 Third Ave.
New York, NY 10017
212/476-1000

Equitable of Iowa Cos.
P.O. Box 1635
Des Moines, IA 50306-1635
515/245-6911

Equitable Life Assurance Society
787 Seventh Ave.
New York, NY 10019
212/554-1234

Fireman's Fund Insurance Co.
777 San Marin Dr.
Novato, CA 94498
415/899-2000

The First American Financial Corp.
114 E. 5 St.
Santa Ana, CA 92701
714/558-3211

First Colony
900 E. Bundt St.
Richmond, VA 23219
804/775-0300

Foremost Corp. of America
5600 Beach Tree Ln.

Caledonia, MI 49316
616/942-3000

Geico Corp.
1 Geico Plz.
Washington, DC
20076-0001
301/986-3000

General Re
695 E. Main St.
Stamford, CT 06905
203/328-5000

**Hanover
Insurance Co.**
100 N. Pkwy.
Worcester, MA 01605
508/853-7200

**Hartford Steam
Boiler Inspection &
Insurance Co.**
1 State St.
Hartford, CT 06102
203/722-1866

**Horace Mann
Educators**
1 Horace Mann Plz.
Springfield, IL
62715-0001
217/789-2500

**Independent
Insurance Group**
1 Independent Dr.
Jacksonville, FL 32202
904/358-5151

**ITT Hartford
Insurance Group**
7 World Trade Center
New York, NY
10048-1198
212/553-8000

Jefferson-Pilot Corp.
100 N. Greene St.
Greensboro, NC 27421
910/691-3000

Kemper Corp.
Kemper Ctr.

Long Grove, IL
60049-0001
708/320-2000

Leucadia National
315 Park Ave. S.
New York, NY 10010
212/460-1900

Liberty Corp.
Wade Hampton Blvd.
Greenville, SC 29602
803/268-8111

Life Partners Group
7887 E. Belleview Ave.
Englewood, CO 80111
303/779-1111

Life USA Holding
P.O. Box 59060
Minneapolis, MN
55459-0060
612/546-7386

**Lincoln National
Corp.**
200 E. Berry
Fort Wayne, IN
46801-2706
219/455-2000

**Metropolitan Life
Insurance Co.**
1 Madison Ave.
New York, NY 10010
212/578-2211

**Mutual of Omaha
Insurance Cos.**
3301 Dodge St.
Omaha, NE 68131
402/342-7600

Nationwide Corp.
1 Nationwide Plz.
Columbus, OH 43216
614/249-7111

**Northwestern Mutual
Life Insurance Co.**
720 E. Wisconsin Ave.
Milwaukee, WI 53202
414/271-1444

**NWNL Companies
Inc.**
**Northwestern National
Life Insurance Cos.**
20 Washington Ave. S.
Minneapolis, MN
55401
612/372-5432

Ohio Casualty Corp.
136 N. Third St.
Hamilton, OH 45011
513/867-3000

**Old Republic
International**
307 N. Michigan Ave.
Chicago, IL 60601
312/346-8100

Orion Capital Corp.
600 5th Ave.
New York, NY 10020
212/332-8080

Progressive Corp.
6300 Wilson Mills Rd.
Mayfield Village, OH
44143
216/461-5000

Protective Life
2801 Hwy 280 S.
Birmingham, AL 35223
205/879-9230

**Provident Mutual Life
Insurance Co.**
1600 Market St.
Philadelphia, PA 19103
215/635-5000

Providian
400 W. Market St.
Louisville, KY 40202
502/560-2000

**Prudential
Insurance Co. of
America**
213 Washington St.
Newark, NJ 07101
201/802-6000

Reliance Group Holdings
55 E. 52nd St.
New York, NY 10055
212/909-1100

ReliaStar Financial
20 Washington Ave. S.
Minneapolis, MN 55401
612/372-5432

Safeco Corp.
Safeco Plz.
Seattle, WA 98185
206/545-5000

St. Paul Companies Inc.
385 Washington St.
St. Paul, MN 55102
612/221-7911

Southwestern Life
500 N. Akard St.
Dallas, TX 75201
214/954-7111

Sun America
One Sun America Ctr.
Los Angeles, CA 90067-6022
310/772-6000

TIG Holdings
65 E. 55th St.
New York, NY 10022
212/446-2700

Torchmark Corp.
2001 Third Ave. S.
Birmingham, AL 35233
205/325-4200

Transamerica Corp.
600 Montgomery St.
San Francisco, CA 94111
415/983-4000

Transatlantic Holdings
80 Pine St.
New York, NY 10005
212/770-2000

The Travelers Corp.
1 Tower Sq.
Hartford, CT 06183
203/277-0111

Travelers Group
388 Greenwich St.
New York, NY 10013
212/816-8000

USF&G Corp.
100 Light St.

Baltimore, MD 21202
410/547-3000

US Life
125 Maiden Ln.
New York, NY 10038
212/709-6000

United Service Life Insurance Co.
4601 Fairfax Dr.
Arlington, VA 22203
703/875-3400

Unitrin, Inc.
1 E. Wacker Dr.
Chicago, IL 60601
312/661-4600

UNUM Corp.
2211 Congress St.
Portland, ME 04122
207/770-2211

Wausau Insurance Comps.
2000 Westwood Dr.
Wausau, WI 54401
715/845-5211

Western National
5555 San Felipe Rd.
Houston, TX 77056
713/888-7800

WHERE TO GO FOR MORE INFORMATION

INSURANCE INDUSTRY ASSOCIATIONS

Alliance of American Insurers
1501 Woodfield Rd.
Schaumburg, IL 60173
708/330-8500
(Members are property and casualty insurance companies, not individuals.)

American Council of Life Insurance
1001 Pennsylvania Ave., NW, Suite 500-S

Washington, DC 20004
202/624-2000

American Insurance Association
85 John St.
New York, NY 10038
212/669-0400

Health Insurance Association of America
555 13th St., NW
Suite 600 E.
Washington, DC 20004
202/824-1600

Insurance Information Institute
110 William St.
New York, NY 10038
212/669-9200
(Members are property and liability insurance companies. This group provides information services to the public, schools, etc.; sponsors seminars; and has a library.)

Life Office Management Association
2300 Windy Ridge Pkwy.
Suite 600
Atlanta, GA 30339
770/951-1770

National Association of Independent Insurers

2600 River Rd.
Des Plaines, IL 60018
708/297-7800

National Association of Mutual Insurance Companies
3601 Vincennes Rd.
P.O. Box 68700
Indianapolis, IN 46268
317/875-5250

Reinsurance Association of America
1301 Pennsylvania Ave., NW,
Suite 900
Washington, DC 20004
202/638-3690

Risk and Insurance Management Society
655 Third Ave.
New York, NY 10017
212/286-9292

INSURANCE INDUSTRY DIRECTORIES

Best's Insurance Reports
(See listing for *Best's Review* in "Insurance Industry Periodicals.")

Insurance Almanac
Underwriter Printing & Publishing Co.
50 E. Palisade Ave.
Englewood, NJ 07631
201/569-8808
(Lists more than three thousand insurance companies; national, state, and local insurance associations; and agents, brokers, etc.)

Insurance Phone Book & Directory
Reede Reference Publishing
121 Chalon Rd.
New Providence, NJ 07974
800/323-6772

Who's Who in Insurance
Underwriter Printing & Publishing Co.

50 E. Palisade Ave.
Englewood, NJ 07631
201/569-8808
(Lists more than five thousand individuals involved in the insurance industry, such as officials, brokers, etc. Includes title, company affiliation and address, biographical information, and more. May be useful to prepare for interviews.)

INSURANCE INDUSTRY PERIODICALS

American Agent & Broker
330 N. 4th St.
St. Louis, MO 63102
314/421-5445
(Monthly magazine for insurance agents, brokers, department heads, and adjusters.)

Best's Review
Ambest Rd.
Oldwick, NJ 08858

908/439-2200
(Monthly magazine; there are two different editions, *Life and Health* and *Property and Casualty*. Both are aimed at insurance executives and often include good help-wanted sections. The annual *Best's Insurance

Reports is a directory of companies.)

Business Insurance
740 Rush St.
Chicago, IL 60611
312/649-5200
(Weekly tabloid for those involved in corporate property, casualty, and employee insurance protection.)

Insurance Review
110 William St.
New York, NY 10038
212/669-9200
(Monthly magazine for
insurance industry

managers and
executives.)

National Underwriter
43–47 Newark St.
Hoboken, NJ 07030
201/963-2300

(Weekly tabloid; there
are two editions,
Property & Casualty
and *Life & Health
Insurance*, both aimed
at management.)

MANUFACTURING

INDUSTRY OUTLOOK: Tied to the performance of other industries and on foreign economic development. As such, will mirror the economic times.

The key trends: continuing cost consciousness, increased attention to international markets, particularly Asia (outside of Japan) and Latin America. The benefit of the growing international markets: should a slowing domestic economy have a negative impact on manufacturing demand, foreign demand should ease matters a great deal.

A LOOK BACK

▶ **The watchwords for the past few years: cost-cutting, competition, and globalization.**

Manufacturing in general has been maintaining a lean and competitive shape—and was rewarded, on the whole, with growth and profits. Key points: business investment increased in the economy, so shipments of industrial machinery and equipment were high. Growth overseas further fueled expansion.

From 1993 through 1995, manufacturing rode the recovering economy to a strong overall performance. There were problem areas, of course, but machinery orders from farms, aerospace, and many other basic industries looked strong. But by 1996 the days of strong growth had tapered off. Manufacturing leveled off, with only modest growth in 1997. The problem? Even though the economy continued to be strong, businesses weren't adding new capacity, so orders remained somewhat flat. In addition, the troubled European economy affected manufacturing companies that deal heavily overseas. All in all, the outlook for 1998 appears to be more of the same—no huge shakeout likely, but no great gains either.

WHAT'S NEXT

▶ **Key long-term trend: cutting costs and increasing market share.**

This is the key to success in 1998 and beyond. Equipment manufacturers are focusing on improving their bottom line.

Expect to see continued, but much slower, restructuring and consolidation.

In addition, there may be an increase in joint ventures between companies, particularly in the research and development areas. Linking up with another company helps a manufacturer defray the high cost of research while still allowing the benefit of innovation. Similarly, there will be some merger activity and increased industry consolidation.

▶ Manufacturing is still expanding overseas.

U.S. manufacturers are continuing to expand overseas. Many have set up foreign subsidiaries or have entered into joint-venture agreements with a manufacturer from the area. Among the reasons for establishing a physical presence in a foreign market: companies gain a market advantage by being able to adapt their products more easily to the market's specific needs; they can avoid trade barriers and negative fallout from a fluctuating dollar. Hottest areas? China, Southeast Asia, Latin America. More specifically:

Construction machinery companies will be targeting the former Soviet Union, Asia, and Eastern Europe, in particular, to capitalize on the development that will be occurring in these areas. Companies such as Ingersoll Rand are focusing on China, planning on three additional joint ventures (it already has three in-country)—in general, most of East Asia looks very strong; as does India.

One caveat: Global manufacturing also means increased competition *from* abroad. Witness the transfer of some manufacturing to such economic powerhouses as South Korea and Taiwan, and the rise of manufacturing in China and Thailand. Bottom line: Expect strong competition in the years ahead—but expect U.S. firms to maintain their competitive edge in many areas.

▶ A growing trend: the use of team manufacturing.

This method is called by many names—including worker participation, employee involvement (EI), and self-managed team manufacturing—but whatever the name used, it describes the same method, and it is a rapidly growing trend in the manufacturing industry.

A brief explanation: With self-managed team manufacturing, a group of workers forms a team that is responsible for the production of an entire product, not just a single part. Every team member is trained in every step of the manufacturing process; in some cases, members rotate through each position. Members are also trained to handle problems such as production bottlenecks and equipment failures and to do their own production scheduling. At many companies, teams elect a team leader who, along with a plant supervisor, represents the only management at the facility.

The team manufacturing method has been credited with improving productivity—with increases up to 30 percent, according to some reports. In addition, workers often report higher morale and improved working conditions.

The impact on employment? A need for more skilled workers. Companies that use the team method generally seek highly motivated individuals and say that attitude is important. On the down side, the team method may point to cutbacks in lower-management and supervisory positions.

▶ Another growing trend, and one that fits in with team management: increased use of automation.

Automation has become crucial to maintain a competitive edge. For example, many manufacturers have instituted concurrent engineering (also called design-integrated manufacturing or simultaneous engineering). This method relies on the use of integrated networks of personal computers, mainframes, and other systems—in effect, a web of computerized systems. Some of the individual automated systems that can be linked up through the network include expert systems (ES) software, used to streamline the manufacturing process; computer-aided design and manufacturing (CAD/CAM) systems; and electronic data interchange (EDI) systems, often used in ordering materials.

By using concurrent engineering, manufacturers can raise productivity, cut costs (after the initial capital outlay), and reduce time lags in product development and production. In some cases, it dovetails into a version of team manufacturing, as a team of workers from different departments—design, manufacturing, purchasing, etc.—work together to develop the specific concurrent engineering program for a new project.

In line with automation, there is also an increased use of "just-in-time" (JIT) manufacturing, in which manufacturing supplies reach the factory as needed, rather than in prescheduled shipments, and "small batch" manufacturing, in which manufacturers customize products to meet specific customer needs and demands, and an emphasis on "total quality management" (TQM) techniques.

These changes in manufacturing methods are having a major impact on employment. First of all, there is a growing need for IS (Information Systems) staffers to develop the software and hardware used in the manufacturing process (although a number of companies use outside firms for this). There are also employment opportunities for workers skilled in computerized manufacturing, CAD/CAM technicians, mechanical engineers, software engineers, and skilled craftspeople. A strong demand is expected for technical professionals who can increase plant efficiency by installing/maintaining plant machinery. One result: More highly educated workers, such as those with college or graduate degrees, are opting for these lucrative and challenging factory jobs.

▶ **One result of the streamlining that has been going on in manufacturing: there has been an increase in the use of outside contractors to supply part-time and temporary workers.**

This is a way of keeping costs down and permanent staffing lean.

And manufacturers have found that relying on a part-time or temporary work force to meet demands when orders are high means they can avoid layoffs and furloughing of workers during slack periods. One result—higher productivity and higher morale among permanent employees.

Employment note: Typically, a company uses a contractor to provide temporary workers. Agencies specialize in different fields and often make efforts to keep their temp employees working year-round, by finding them positions at different companies when one company doesn't need them. Well-paid, high-level technical and engineering personnel are frequently sought after for three- to six-month projects as contract employees.

EMPLOYMENT OUTLOOK: Affected by automation and other corporate innovations. As such, expect increased hiring in some areas, decreased in others.

Over the past five years, manufacturers slashed over 1.4 million jobs. And technological breakthroughs, automation and a shift in the economy will continue to result in a long-term drop in manufacturing jobs. The federal government predicts the decline to continue—with 1.3 million jobs lost between 1994 and 2005. Operators, fabricators, precision production, craft and repair occupations should account for about 1 million of these jobs. Key point: Even though declines are projected in the long term, and despite short-term declines due to possible recession, many experts say that many thousands of jobs, particularly in the industrial Midwest, are vacant and waiting—for *skilled* workers.

So generally speaking, this is part of the overall trend shifting employment from goods-producing to service-producing areas. For example, in 1920, manufacturing accounted for about 27% of those working; in 1990, the number dropped to 17%. And by 2005, experts predict the number will drop even lower, to about 12%.

But there will be employment opportunities. First, increased automation is actually *increasing* the demand for skilled workers and engineers. Projections show that there may be a shortage of these people, so training programs for machinists and craftspeople are increasing. In addition, about 7 million people will land jobs that replace workers who retire or otherwise leave manufacturing. In addition, the outlook for industrial engineers is a favorable one—given the greater use of automation in factories; and it's a similar picture for mechanical engineers as manufacturing processes become more complex. The picture in sales and marketing isn't quite as good, as many companies rely on outsourcing as a way of keeping costs down. However, this will increase demand for manufacturers' agents, especially with small and midsized firms.

JOBS SPOTLIGHT

"GENERALIST" ENGINEERS: Companies employing the team manufacturing method often need "generalist" engineers—that is, manufacturing engineers who understand an entire manufacturing process. These engineers often lead teams and must be able to supervise a variety of operations and maintenance workers. As such, both technical and strong interpersonal skills are a necessity.

TECHNICAL TRAINERS: This is a growing area as companies increase automation and workers need to upgrade skills or learn new skills to work with the new technologies. Technical trainers often work in the human resources department of a company, although some are contracted on a per-project basis and, as such, work for a training firm. Requirements vary but may include manufacturing experience, a degree in engineering or another technical area, and course work in education. Salaries range from about $30,000 for an entry-level position up to the six figures for senior management.

BEST BETS

Baldor Electric Co.
5711 RS Boreham Jr. St.
Fort Smith, AR 79201
501/646-4711

This small powerhouse is committed to doing several things well while growing at a fast and powerful clip. Baldor competes successfully against much larger firms, as the leading manufacturer of electric motors and other automated components that keep factories humming. The key to Baldor's success? Flexibility, extensive stock, and, most importantly, attention to customer service, especially when industrial customers run into emergencies and need a product immediately. This ability for quick service lies in Baldor's setup. Baldor warehouses are owned and operated by independent Baldor sales reps who stay in contact with the other reps around the country. The setup has worked. With no pink slips at its major plants during the major 1991 recession, Baldor has grown consistently stronger, with steady sales and profit increases. A plus for employees: a portion of their pay is tied to profit sharing and stock options—so the better the company performs, the better their pay. All in all, a good long-term bet.

TOP GENERAL MANUFACTURING COMPANIES

Avery Dennison Corp.
150 N. Ocean Grove Blvd.
Pasadena, CA 91103
818/304-2000

Blount, Inc.
4520 Executive Pk. Dr.
Montgomery, AL 36116
205/244-4000

Corning, Inc.
1 Riverfront Plz.
Corning, NY 14831
607/974-9000

Crane Co.
100 First Stamford Pl.
Stamford CT 06902
203/363-7300

Duracell International
Berkshire Corporate Pk.
Bethel, CT 06801
203/796-4000

Exide Corp.
645 Pennsylvania St.
Reading, PA 19601
215/378-0500

First Brands Corp.
83 Wooster Heights Rd.
Danbury, CT 06813
203/731-2300

Great American Management
2 N. Riverside Pl.
Chicago, IL 60606
312/648-5656

Harsco Corp.
350 Poplar Church Rd.
Camp Hill, PA 17011
717/763-7064

Hillenbrand Industries, Inc.
700 State Rt. 46 E.
Batesville, IN 47006-8835
812/934-7000

Illinois Tool Works, Inc.
3600 W. Lake Ave.
Glenview, IL 60625-5811
708/724-7500

Jostens, Inc.
5501 Norman Ctr. Dr.
Minneapolis, MN 55437
612/830-3300

Mark IV Industries, Inc.
501 John James Audubon Pkwy.
Amherst, NY 14228
716/689-4972

Minnesota Mining & Manufacturing Co. (3M)
3M Center
St. Paul, MN 55144-1000
612/733-1110

Rubbermaid, Inc.
1147 Akron Rd.
Wooster, OH 44691
216/264-6464

Trinova Corp.
3000 Strayer
Maumee, OH 43537
419/867-2200

TOP INDUSTRIAL MACHINERY, MACHINE, AND HAND TOOLS MANUFACTURING COMPANIES

Amsted Industries
205 N. Michigan Ave.
Chicago, IL 60601
312/645-1700

Baldor Electric Co.
5711 RS Boreham Jr. St.
Fort Smith, AR 79201
501/646-4711

Black & Decker Corp.
701 E. Joppa Rd.
Towson, MD 21286
410/716-3900

Briggs & Stratton Corp.
3300 N. 124 St.
Milwaukee, WI 53222
414/259-5333

Case Corp.
700 Racine St.
Racine, WI 53404
414/636-6011

Caterpillar, Inc.
100 NE Adams St.
Peoria, IL 61629-1425
309/675-1000

Cincinnati Milacron, Inc.
4701 Marburg Ave.
Cincinnati, OH 45209
513/841-8100

Clark Equipment Co.
100 N. Michigan St.
South Bend, IN 46601
219/239-0100

Cummins Engine Co.
P.O. Box 3005
500 Jackson St.
Columbus, IN 47201
812/377-5000
812/397-7373

Danaher Corp.
1250 24th St., NW
Washington, DC 20037
202/828-0850

Deere & Co.
John Deere Rd.
Moline, IL 61265-8098
309/765-8000

Dover Corp.
280 Park Ave.
New York, NY
10017-1292
212/922-1640

Dresser Industries
2001 Ross Ave.
Dallas, TX 75221
214/740-6000

FMC Corp.
200 E. Randolph Dr.
Chicago, IL 60601
312/861-6000

General Signal Corp.
1 High Ridge Pk.
Stamford, CT 06904
203/357-8800

Harnischfeger Industries, Inc.
13400 Bishops Ln.
Brookfield, WI 53005
414/671-4400

Ingersoll-Rand
200 Chestnut Ridge Rd.
Woodcliff Lake, NJ
07675
201/573-0123

Interlake Corp.
550 Warrenville Rd.
Lisle, IL 60532
708/852-8800

Johnson Controls
5757 N. Green Bay Ave.
Milwaukee, WI 53201
414/228-1200

Nacco Industries, Inc.
5875 Landerberook
Dr., Suite 300
Mayfield Heights, OH
44124
216/449-9600

Pall Corp.
2200 Northern Blvd.
East Hills, NY 11548
516/484-5400

Parker Hannifin Corp.
17325 Euclid Ave.
Cleveland, OH
44112-1290
216/531-3000

Pentair, Inc.
1500 Country Rd.,
B2 West
St. Paul, MN 55113
612/636-7920

Snap-On Tools Corp.
2801 80th St.
Kenosha, WI 53141
414/656-5200

SPX Corp.
100 Terrace Plz.
Muskegon, MI 49443
616/724-5011

Stanley Works, Inc.
1000 Stanley Dr.
New Britain, CT 06053
203/225-5111

Tenneco, Inc.
1010 Milam St.
Houston, TX 77002
713/757-2131

Terex Corp.
500 Post Rd. E.,
Suite 225
Westport, CT 06880
203/222-7008

Timken Co.
1835 Dueber Ave., SW
Canton, OH 44706
216/438-3000

Trinity Industries, Inc.
2525 Stemmons Fwy.
Dallas, TX 75207-2401
214/631-4420

Tyco Laboratories, Inc.
1 Tyco Pk.
Exeter, NH 03833-1108
603/778-9700

WHERE TO GO FOR MORE INFORMATION

(For more information sources in related areas, also check listings under "Engineers," page 50, and "Technical Careers," page 196.)

MANUFACTURING ASSOCIATIONS

American Hardware Manufacturers Association
801 N. Plz. Dr.
Schaumburg, IL 60173
708/605-1025

American Production and Inventory Control Society
500 W. Annandale Rd.
Falls Church, VA 22046
703/237-8344

Construction Industry Manufacturers Association
111 E. Wisconsin Ave.
Milwaukee, WI 53202
414/272-0943

Fabricators & Manufacturers Association International

833 Featherstone Rd.
Rockford, IL 61107
815/399-8700

Industrial Research Institute
1550 M St., NW
Washington, DC
20005-1712
202/296-8811

Institute of Industrial Engineers
25 Technology Park
Norcross, GA 30092
770/449-0460
(Puts out monthly publication *Industrial Engineering*.)

National Association of Manufacturers
1331 Pennsylvania Ave., NW,
Suite 1500, North Lobby
Washington, DC

20004-1703
202/637-3000

Paradine Design Group
801 18th St., NW
Washington, DC 20036
202/331-8430

Society of Manufacturing Engineers
P.O. Box 930
1 SME Dr.
Dearborn, MI 48121
313/271-1500

Tooling & Manufacturing Association
1177 S. Dee Rd.
Park Ridge, IL 60068
708/825-1120
(Offers job referral information and resume bank service.)

MANUFACTURING DIRECTORIES

American Manufacturers Directory
American Business Directories
P.O. Box 27347

5711 S. 86th Cir.
Omaha, NE 68127
402/593-4600

Moody's Industrial Manual
Moody's Investors

Service, Inc.
99 Church St.
New York, NY 10007
212/553-0300

Thomas Register of American Manufacturers; Thomas Register

Catalog File
Thomas Publishing Company

1 Penn. Plz.
New York, NY 10119
212/290-7200

MANUFACTURING MAGAZINES

Design News
275 Washington St.
Newton, MA 02158
617/964-3030
(Semimonthly magazine for design and technical engineers, managers, etc.)

Machine Design
1100 E. Superior Ave.
Cleveland, OH 44114
216/696-7000
(Primarily biweekly magazine aimed at design and technical engineers, managers, etc.)

Manufacturing Engineering
Box 930
1 S.M.E. Dr.
Dearborn, MI 48121
313/271-1500
(Monthly magazine put out by the Society of Manufacturing Engineers; aimed at manufacturing engineers as well as plant managers, designers, technicians, and researchers.)

Material Handling Engineering
1100 E. Superior Ave.
Cleveland, OH 44114
216/696-7000
(Thirteen-issue magazine for executives, chief engineers, technicians, foremen, etc.)

Plant Engineering
1350 E. Touhy Ave.
Des Plaines, IL 60018
708/635-8800
(Twenty-two-issue magazine for personnel in plant engineering.)

Plant Services
301 E. Erie St.
Chicago, IL 60611
312/644-2020
(Monthly magazine for plant personnel in a range of fields, including maintenance, engineering, materials handling, environment, sites.)

Quality
191 S. Gary Ave.
Carol Stream, IL 60188
708/665-1000
(Monthly magazine for manufacturing/ engineering managers, quality assurance managers and inspectors, etc.)

Quality Progress
611 E. Wisconsin Ave.
Milwaukee, WI
53202-4606
414/272-8575
(Monthly magazine for quality assurance/ quality control engineers, inspectors, etc.)

METALS AND MINING

INDUSTRY OUTLOOK: In many areas, a relatively flat short-term outlook, some very heavy competition. Increased competition—and continued consolidation.

Steel is headed for hot competition. First, there's the head-to-head combat between the larger and smaller steelmakers. In 1997, about 5 million new tons of mini-mill capacity came onstream. And foreign steel producers will continue making inroads into the U.S. market as well. As a result, the big steel companies will be fighting it out with lower cost competitors. Along these lines, expect to see the larger companies keep on exploring new markets.

Aluminum should be headed for long-term growth, especially as aluminum makers make inroads into new areas—including automobiles—and as they develop new materials employing aluminum. But there may be short-term problems—specifically, periodic price drops.

As for other metals, the picture, as always, is mixed. **Nickel,** a major component in stainless steel, has the best outlook: the increases in demand, reflecting improvements in stainless steel, was double the increase in production; **copper** was more problematic, although copper producers are continuing to seek new applications, such as in construction, telecommunications, and automotive electronics. As for **gold,** expect to see this segment continue consolidating, as mine companies opt for buying companies rather than for exploring for gold reserves.

A LOOK BACK

▶ **The mid 1990s—not the best of times for steel and some other metals sectors.**

In the bad old days, metals companies learned from competition—and modernized metals mills and built back their industries. But this restructuring and increased efficiency in some cases was too much of a good thing—many mills increased their ability to produce their metal so much that they threatened the level of prices they wanted to charge. They had too much capacity.

Adding to this home-grown capacity problem is the problem of metals imports. There's always the problem of foreign competition as well.

The aluminum industry faced this problem a few years ago, when Russian imports flooded the market. Result: a sort of mini-OPEC in aluminum in 1994, where aluminum manufacturers closed down 30% of their production and divided up rights to produce among themselves. In 1995, steel began facing a similar problem of overcapacity, and prices began to drop.

▶ **The challenge in the past two years: with short-term overcapacity, problems appeared to be looming ahead.**

With the strikes, weather, and production problems of 1996 behind them, steelmakers faced 1997–1998 with good news and bad news. The good news: heavy domestic orders and record exports to feed domestic auto production and other products sold abroad. And the bad news: To meet competition, mills improved efficiencies—and capacity—by restructuring and modernizing, while new mills were scheduled to come on stream, adding to capacity.

WHAT'S NEXT

▶ **For big steel, heavy competition ahead.**

As mentioned above, steel is facing an overcapacity challenge in the short term. Key problem: The improvement of the steel industry over the past 10 years has dramatically improved production capacity—particularly from mini-mills (mills which use scrap steel instead of iron-ore), which will have over 10 million tons of capacity coming on stream in the next few years. Any demand drop will create price and profit pressures—and ultimately employment problems.

▶ **Watch for the increased use of aluminum in motor vehicles.**

This, clearly, points to a very positive development for aluminum producers. Aluminum is already being used more and more in cars—for example, more than 30% of the Acura NSX's weight, or 941 pounds, is aluminum—and its use is expected to increase dramatically in the future. Experts predict that over the next five years, Japan's use of aluminum in its cars will more than double. Similar developments may occur with U.S. car manufacturers and Japanese transplants in the U.S. One result? Watch for joint ventures and agreements between steel companies and aluminum companies.

All in all, the next few years should be good for the aluminum industry. Demand is increasing at about 3.5% a year, Russia appears to be producing at capacity, aerospace demand looked to be picking up, and prices rose last year. One fear: what will happen if aluminum makers reopen the smelters they closed back in 1994, under the agreement to limit capacity? That original agreement expired in 1996.

▶ **Expect mini-mills to still pose a definite competitive threat for the larger steel makers.**

While they may face short-term downslides, mini-mills (low-cost steel producers using smaller furnaces and, usually high-tech methods) are in for a very promising future. The reasons for their strength? An emphasis on cost-efficiency—instead of more costly iron ore, they usually use scrap, labor costs are lower, etc.; and streamlined operations typically utilizing technologically advanced methods and equipment. These efficient and low-cost mini-mills have been able to successfully compete head-to-head with the larger integrated steel producers. As such, expect to see further growth in the area. A competitive reaction: mini-grated mills: integrated steel-makers challenging mini-mills with a new cost-competitive steelmaking technology, producing high-quality steel in 90 minutes, compared with the present ten days.

▶ On the horizon: aluminum mini-mills.

The use of continuous casting to produce sheet aluminum for beverage cans may make aluminum mini-mills another success story. While the recent poor performance of aluminum has slowed the industry down, this is an area that may see growth over the long term. A leading proponent of the mini-mill is Golden Aluminum in Elmendorf (San Antonio), Texas. If this method of producing sheet aluminum works efficiently, it should have far-reaching effects on the industry.

▶ Increased automation and the use of manufacturing methods such as "just in time" will be key to staying competitive.

Like most other manufacturers, metals producers will try to remain cost-efficient by using "just in time" manufacturing, keeping finished-goods, in-process goods, and raw-material inventory in check. Similarly, more mills and service centers will be computerizing, linking systems by computer networks to keep track of all phases of production. Another trend to watch for is the development of strategic partnerships between producers and customers.

▶ Similarly, watch for continued technological breakthroughs to change the industry.

In general, companies will follow in the path of the mini-mills and continue to come up with new methods of producing metals. For example, MicroMet Technology Inc. introduced Rhondite, a new type of steel with a different structure than that of regular steel. The key pluses? It is stronger than conventional steel, and it reportedly can be produced at the same or lower cost than mini-mill—produced steel. Another example: Republic Engineered Steels, a bar and specialty steel manufacturer, has come up with a quality-verification system called the Quality Verification Line. According to *Industry Week,* this is an integrated system that inspects and verifies the quality of bar steel and so assures customers of high quality.

These types of breakthroughs will bring about shifts in the industry power balance—and may, in the long term, result in a shakeout among companies. Those unable to keep up technologically due to the high cost of modernizing will risk failure.

▶ Expect the mining industry to move toward further globalization.

This will occur in a number of ways. First of all, watch as more companies step up global activity. As a result, the number of joint ventures between domestic and foreign companies will increase. One reason? Joint ventures will enable companies to get involved in expensive overseas mining projects without taking on too much of a financial burden. With the rise in joint ventures, there also will be an increase in multiple-country ownership of companies.

▶ A growing trend: Metals companies are developing new markets and new products.

They are doing so to help the cyclical industry cope with the inevitable drops in demand. The different segments of the industry will continue to search for new areas in which to market their traditional products and will be developing new products as well.

A few examples: Aluminum producers are making efforts to sell aluminum packaging for products not traditionally packaged in aluminum. They also are modernizing and developing new products. One of the most promising is a composite incorporating aluminum but reinforced with lightweight, high-strength materials, which increases its applications.

Titanium producers, facing cutbacks in a prime market, thc defense sector, are exploring alternative industrial markets, including hole oil drilling applications and tubing for desalinization plants. Lead producers are researching and testing different uses for lead-acid batteries, including using them as computer and communication systems backup and as a power source for industrial trucks and electric cars. Copper producers, facing a decrease in demand from telecommunications companies due to the growth of fiber optics, are targeting the construction, roofing, and automotive electronics industries.

In short, the metals industry is staying as flexible as possible to ensure strong performance in the years ahead.

One key trend: Metals companies are increasingly competing among themselves. Look for heated battles over what metal such seemingly minor products as car tailpipes or beer cans should be made of.

EMPLOYMENT OUTLOOK: Fair to poor.

Between 1979 and 1995, there was an over 50% drop in employment in mining. Although the pace may slow, this trend should continue over the long term in both the metals and mining industries. The key reason? Technological breakthroughs. Today's labor-saving equipment doesn't require the same number of hourly production workers as in the past. At the same time, the new technology has created a greater need for administrative and managerial personnel. The result? An increase in the number of supervisors and engineers. This trend should continue as technological breakthroughs continue to affect the industry.

JOBS SPOTLIGHT

METALLURGISTS/METALLURGIC ENGINEERS: While overall employment in this specialty is expected to increase more slowly than average, there actually should be good employment opportunities, especially at the entry level. The reason? A relatively low number of new graduates in the discipline. As a result, demand for new employees should at least equal the number of qualified professionals . . . if not exceed it.

BEST BETS

Inland Steel Industries
30 W. Monroe St.
Chicago, IL 60603
312/346-0300

Now that the steel industry has transformed itself, it appears that one of the smartest players was Inland Steel. During the worst years, its competitors got rid of their materials distribution service centers—huge storage depots that supply industrial customers with all sorts of steel—and other—products. Inland Steel kept on supplying, and now that it's making profits at home, it's expanding abroad. Inland Steel aims at supplying U.S. and other firms overseas the same quality materials they can get at home. And it looks as if this strategy is paying off. They're in Mexico already (linked to the U.S. by computer) and they're looking to expand into China and India. All in all, this hard-charging company looks like a winner.

Worthington Industries Inc.
1205 Dearborn Dr.
Columbus, OH 43085
614/438-3210

One of the strongest performers in the metals industries, and one that may offer employment opportunities over the long term. The reason? Worthington is on an expansion drive, planning to build new plants (such as a $72 million steel processing plant in Delta, Ohio) and acquire existing plants from other companies. Experts predict that this company will continue growing through 2000—which could well translate into positive job opportunities.

TOP METALS & MINING COMPANIES

Acme Steel Co.
13500 S. Perry Ave.
Riverdale, IL 60627
708/849-2500

AK Steel Holding
703 Curtis St.
Middletown, OH
45043-0001
513/425-5000

Alcan Aluminum Corp.
100 Erieview Plz.
Columbus, OH 44114
216/523-6800

ALCOA—Aluminum Co. of America
1501 Alcoa Bldg.
425 Sixth Ave.
Pittsburgh, PA 15219
412/553-4545

Allegheny Ludlum Corp.

1000 Six PPG Pl.
Pittsburgh, PA 15219
412/394-2800

Alumax
5655 Peachtree Pkwy.
Norcross, GA
30092-2812
404/246-6600

Armco, Inc.
2 Oxford Bldg.,
15th Fl.
301 Grant St.
Pittsburgh, PA 15219
412/255-9800

Asarco, Inc.
180 Maiden Ln.
New York, NY
10038-4991
212/510-2000

Bethlehem Steel Corp.
1170 8th Ave.
Bethlehem, PA

18016-7699
610/694-2424

Chaparral Steel
300 Ward Rd.
Midlothian, TX 76065
214/775-8241

Commercial Metals Co.
7800 Stemmons
Freeway
Dallas, TX 75247
214/689-4300

Cyprus Amax Minerals Co.
P.O. Box 3299
9100 E. Mineral Cir.
Englewood, CO
80155
303/643-5000

Engelhard Corp.
101 Wood Ave.
Iselin, NJ 08830-0770
908/205-6000

Freeport McMoRan Copper Co.
1615 Poydras St.
New Orleans, LA
70112
504/582-4000

Homestake Mining Co.
650 California St.
San Francisco, CA
94108-2788
415/981-8150

Inco United States, Inc.
1 New York Plz.
New York, NY 10004
212/612-5500

Inland Steel Industries
30 W. Monroe St.
Chicago, IL 60603
312/346-0300

Kaiser Aluminum Corp.
5847 San Felipe
Houston, TX 77057
713/267-3777

Kennecott Corp.
10 E. S. Temple St.
Salt Lake City, UT
84133
801/322-7000

The LTV Corp.
25 W. Prospect Ave.
Cleveland, OH 44115
216/622-5000

Magma Copper Co., Inc.
P.O. Box M
Hwy. 76
San Manuel, AZ 85631
602/385-3100

Maxxam, Inc.
5847 San Felipe St.
Houston, TX 77057
713/975-7600

National Steel
4100 Edison Lakes Pkwy.
Mishawaka, IN
46545-3440
219/273-7000

Newmont Gold
1700 Lincoln St.
Denver, CO 80203
303/863-7414

Newmont Mining Corp.
1700 Lincoln St.
Denver, CO 80203
303/863-7414

Nucor Corp.
2100 Rexford Rd.
Charlotte, NC 28211
704/366-7000

Phelps Dodge Corp.
2600 N. Central Ave.
Phoenix, AZ
85004-3014
602/234-8100

Reynolds Metals
6601 W. Broad St.
Richmond, VA 23230
804/281-2000

Rouge Steel
3001 Miller Rd.
Dearborn, MI
48121-1699
313/390-6877

USX-U.S. Steel Group
600 Grant St.
Pittsburgh, PA
15219-4776
412/433-1121

Weirton Steel Corp.
400 Three Springs Dr.
Weirton, WV 26062
304/797-2000

Wheeling-Pittsburgh Steel Corp.
1134 Market St.
Wheeling, WV 26003
304/234-2400

Worthington Industries, Inc.
1205 Dearborn Dr.
Columbus, OH 43085
614/438-3210

WHERE TO GO FOR MORE INFORMATION

METALS AND MINING INDUSTRY ASSOCIATIONS

American Institute of Mining, Metallurgical, and Petroleum Engineers
345 E. 47th St.,
14th Fl.
New York, NY 10017
212/705-7695

American Iron & Steel Institute
1101 17th St., NW,
13th Fl.
Washington, DC 20036
202/452-7100

ASM International (American Society for Metals)

9639 Kinsman
Materials Park, OH
44243-0002
216/338-5151
(Publishes *Advanced Materials and Processes* and *ASM News* magazines, which

include help-wanted ads.)

Association of Iron and Steel Engineers
3 Gateway Ctr., Suite 2350
Pittsburgh, PA 15222
412/281-6323

Association of Steel Distributors
401 N. Michigan Dr.
Suite 2200
Chicago, IL 60611
312/644-6610

Minerals, Metals and Materials Society
420 Commonwealth Dr.
Warrendale, PA 15086
412/776-9080

National Mining Association
1130 17th St., NW
Washington, DC 20036
202/861-2800

Society of Mining Engineers
P.O. Box 625002
Littleton, CO

80162-5002
303/973-9550
(Puts out monthly
Mining Engineering
magazine.)

Steel Manufacturers Association
1730 Rhode Island Ave., NW
Suite 907
Washington, DC 20036
292/296-1515

METALS AND MINING INDUSTRY DIRECTORIES

Directory of Iron and Steel Plants
Association of Iron and Steel Engineers
3 Gateway Ctr., Suite 1900
Pittsburgh, PA 15222
412/281-6323

Directory of Steel Foundries in the United States, Canada and Mexico
Steel Founders' Society of America
455 State St.

Des Plaines, IL 60016
708/299-9160

Dun's Industrial Guide: The Metalworking Directory
Dun's Marketing Services
3 Sylvan Way
Parsippany, NJ 07054-3896
201/455-0900

Iron & Steel Works of the World
Metal Bulletin Inc.

220 Fifth Ave.
New York, NY 10001
212/213-6202

Western Mining Directory
Howell Publishing Company
Box 370510
Denver, CO 80237
303/770-6795
(Lists about fourteen hundred firms and organizations involved in the mining industry in the West.)

METALS AND MINING INDUSTRY PERIODICALS

Engineering & Mining Journal
29 N. Wacker Dr.
Chicago, IL 60606
312/726-2802
(Monthly magazine covering the mining industry; for mining and processing production and

engineering staffs, executives, etc.)

Mining World News
100 W. Grove St.
Suite 240
Reno, NV 89509
702/827-1115
(Monthly tabloid for professionals involved in mining, including

mining engineers, geologists, geophysicists, metallurgists, etc.)

New Steel
191 S. Gary Ave.
Carol Stream, IL 60188
708/462-2286
(Monthly magazine covering the iron industry.)

PAPER AND FOREST PRODUCTS

INDUSTRY OUTLOOK: Mixed.

Paper: Probably faces fairly flat growth. Still facing the challenges of weak prices, oversupply in some segments, and increased competition. Key to continued strength: keeping excess capacity in check. Long term: probably more of the same, unless foreign mills' expansion plans materialize.

Forest Products: Split. As goes housebuilding, so goes lumber. If moderate residential construction growth continues, the industry should see at least stable, slow growth. But with housebuilding expected to slow, expect this to impact the lumber industry. Some firms are suffering from overseas competition, particularly from Canada, Southeast Asia, and South America.

A LOOK BACK

▶ The paper industry saw a boom in 1995—followed by a slowdown.

1995 was one great year. Prices skyrocketed—newsprint rose 39%, to almost $800 a ton. As domestic and world economies improved, so did demand for packaging, newsprint, and office paper. Plants operated at near capacity. And profits naturally soared. Flush with cash, many companies went on a buying binge. Kimberly-Clark bought Scott Paper, International Paper signed an agreement to buy Federal Paper Board, Canada's Stone Consolidated bought Boise Cascade's Rainy River Forest Products unit. *But,* paper firms learned from the slump of the early '90s, and instead of investing in more plant and equipment only to create too much production capacity, they bought back stock and paid down debt—all in an effort to stay strong should prices tumble. And sure enough, as 1995 price highs started dropping, and as 1995 turned into 1996 and prices and demand looked to be dropping further, it was clear that the companies had done well by their conservative approach.

Meanwhile, on the forest products front, things weren't as rosy. Housing starts weren't all that strong, and demand for lumber wasn't that great. Worse yet, Canadian timber sales increased to a third of the U.S. market—making them a fierce competitor to U.S. companies. Lumber represented the weak link in the forest products industry as housing starts continued at near flat levels. But when paper began falling into a slump, forest products took off. Buoyed by a strong domestic economy, housing starts increased, construction in general perked up—and lumber companies enjoyed increased demand. The only potential problems on the horizon? A slowdown of the housing boom and increased competition from foreign imports.

WHAT'S NEXT

▶ **In spite of some fluctuations in the worldwide marketplace, expect to see a growing push into international markets.**

There will be increased international opportunities for paper companies due to a number of factors, among them the unification of Western Europe, the democratization of Eastern Europe, the U.S.-Canada Free Trade Agreement and NAFTA. In addition, in spite of tough competition, paper and paperboard manufacturers will be targeting Japan and other Pacific Rim countries.

Expect to see activity in a number of different ways. Some companies will enter the international marketplace as general paper and paperboard producers, others with more specialized products targeted to niche markets. Competition should be intense as U.S. manufacturers already entrenched go head to head with new arrivals, as well as with their foreign competitors. In many cases, companies are entering into joint ventures with their foreign counterparts—and in so doing, have the advantage of in-country facilities, distribution networks, and market position. Others are buying local operations or building new plants.

▶ **The flip side of internationalism—much competition at home.**

Both paper and the forest products industry will increasingly feel the effects of international competition.

For example, earlier we explained how U.S. paper companies were weathering a downturn in prices and demand by keeping U.S. capacity low. Normally, that would be enough to stabilize the market—but then, along came foreign competition, like lower-priced European newsprint and Asian hardwood pulp. Predictably, prices began to drop. The wild card is the expansion planned by Asia-Pacific–Latin American–Nordic countries to meet their own internal market demands. Any cancellations could create export opportunities. For lumber, the threat seemed more serious, as Canadian lumber companies increased their sales to the American market.

▶ **Paper and pulp companies will increasingly rely on automation and technological advancements to keep costs down and productivity high.**

Like most other U.S. industries, the paper and pulp industry is increasingly automating and computerizing. Plant automation will be one of the most significant technological changes for the industry. Expect to see the development and implementation of systems that will allow for a completely automated mill—from setting production schedules to measuring and controlling quality.

But like other manufacturing industries, the paper industry may be feeling the results of the skilled labor shortage and will be setting up retraining programs to prepare workers to use the new high-tech equipment.

▶ **A few more trends affecting the paper and forest products industries—with potentially major repercussions.**

Trend 1—Upcoming fiberboard wars: Lumber companies have developed a new kind of fiberboard (called oriented strand board) that looks like it will take up 50% of total fiberboard capacity nationwide. Prediction: A huge battle over fiberboard will erupt as companies fight over who will control this large sector.

Trend 2—Wood and Paper replacements: It's not that earth-shattering now, but the housing industry is increasingly using steel instead of wood to build house frames. Over the past four years, steel-frame housing has risen from 500 to 80,000 houses.

▶ Dealing with environmental issues will be a key challenge for the paper industry.

As in the past, preventing water pollution will be a prime focus for the paper industry. Expect to see continued heavy cash outlays by companies to upgrade plants to meet more stringent pollution levels.

Concern about air pollution will also be affecting numerous paper and pulp mills. Under the Clean Air Act Amendments, mills in areas that do not meet national standards for clean air will have to demonstrate either that they are in compliance with air standards or that the benefits of having the mill in the area outweigh the pollution concerns. The possible outcome in these cases? Costly renovations or plant closings.

More generally, expect to see paper and pulp companies do further research into wastewater management, emissions control, waste recycling, and energy recovery. More plants will increase their use of recycled materials as part—or all—of their raw materials. Along related lines, expect to see more research into and development of paper products in synch with environmental consciousness: more biodegradable paper products, more recyclables, etc.

Environmental awareness is also leading to *new employment opportunities,* specifically for environmental specialists at paper and pulp companies, and in the areas of R&D and product development and management.

▶ Along the same lines, forest products companies will also be coping with pressure from environmental groups and changes in federal legislation.

Expect continued efforts on the part of environmentalists and preservationists to stop or modify lumber-cutting in the Pacific Northwest. The U.S. Fish and Wildlife Service has designated 8.1 million acres as proposed critical habitat areas due to the presence of the northern spotted owl, an endangered species. Timber harvesting will probably be severely cut back or eliminated in these areas.

More developments like this are expected, especially as environmentalists continue to win an increasing number of forest protection cases. For example, in 1991 the Seattle Audubon Society won a case barring the U.S. Forest Service from offering timber sales on about 66,000 acres. The result? Tight log supplies and the closing of more than fifty lumber and panel mills.

EMPLOYMENT OUTLOOK: Fair to poor.

In the paper industry, employment continues to drop. Since employment reached a record high in 1989 of 630,000, it has dropped consistently every year since then, losing thousands of jobs each year, for a total of over 10,000 jobs cut. Reasons for the decline? Mergers and acquisitions, consolidations, and the phase-out of less efficient machinery and operations and the resulting phase-in of more streamlined, automated systems. And this should continue. Over the long term, the trend toward automation will continue to cut into employment prospects. Hiring will be centering primarily around filling replacement positions.

A few brighter areas: With international expansion so strong, there may be more positions in sales and marketing. Furthermore, the push for new product development at many paper companies may translate into product management and marketing positions. As for wood products, even as demand for timber rises, the employment picture will remain flat.

TOP PAPER & FOREST PRODUCTS COMPANIES

Boise Cascade Corp.
1111 W. Jefferson St.
Boise, ID 83728
208/384-6161

Bowater, Inc.
1120 Post Rd.,
Darien, CT 06820
203/656-7200

Champion International Corp.
1 Champion Plz.
Stamford, CT 06921
203/358-7000

Chesapeake Corp.
1021 E. Cary St.
Richmond, VA 23219
804/697-1000

Consolidated Papers, Inc.
231 First Ave. N.
Wisconsin Rapids, WI 54495
715/422-3111

Federal Paper Board Co.
75 Chestnut Ridge Rd.
Montvale, NJ 07645
201/391-1776

Ft. Howard Corp.
1919 S. Broadway

Green Bay, WI 54304
414/435-8821

Gaylord Container Corp.
500 Lake Cook Rd.
Deerfield, IL 60015
708/405-5500

Georgia-Pacific Corp.
133 Peachtree St., NE
Atlanta, GA 30348-5605
404/652-4000

P. H. Glatfelter Co.
228 S. Main St.
Spring Grove, PA 17362
717/225-4711

International Paper Co.
2 Manhattanville Rd.
Purchase, NY 10577
914/397-1500

James River Corp. of Virginia
120 Tredegar St.
Richmond, VA 23219
804/644-5411

Jefferson-Smurfit Corp.
8182 Maryland Ave.

St. Louis, MO 63105
314/746-1100

Kimberly-Clark Corp.
545 E. John Carpenter
Irving, TX 75062
214/830-1200

Louisiana-Pacific Corp.
111 SW Fifth Ave.
Portland, OR 97204
503/221-0800

Mead Corp.
Mead World
Headquarters
Courthouse Plz. NE
Dayton, OH 45463
513/222-6323

Potlatch Corp.
1 Maritime Plz.
San Francisco, CA 94111
415/576-8800

Rayonier, Inc.
1177 Summer St.
Stamford, CT 06905
203/348-7000

Scott Paper Co., Inc.
1 Scott Plz.
Philadelphia, PA 19113
610/522-5000

Union Camp Corp.
1600 Valley Rd.
Wayne, NJ 07470
201/628-2000

Westvãco Corp.
299 Park Ave.

New York, NY 10171
212/688-5000

Weyerhaeuser Co.
Weyerhaeuser Bldg.
Tacoma, WA 98477
206/924-2345

Willamette Industries, Inc.
1300 SW Fifth Ave.
Portland, OR 97201
503/227-5581

TOP PACKAGING COMPANIES

Bemis Co., Inc.
222 S. Ninth St.
Minneapolis, MN 55402
612/376-3000

Crown Cork and Seal Co.
9300 Ashton Rd.
Philadelphia, PA 19136
215/698-5100

Owens-Illinois
One Seagate

Toledo, OH 43666
419/247-5000

Longview Fibre Co.
P.O. Box 639
Longview, WA 98632
206/425-1550

Sonoco Products Co.
1 N. 2nd St.
Hartsville, NC 29550
803/383-7000

St. Joe Paper Co.
1650 Prudential Dr.

Jacksonville, FL 32207
904/396-6600

Stone Container Corp.
150 N. Michigan Ave.
Chicago, IL 60601-7568
312/346-6600

Temple-Inland, Inc.
303 S. Temple Dr.
Diboll, TX 75941
409/829-2211

WHERE TO GO FOR MORE INFORMATION

PAPER AND FOREST PRODUCTS ASSOCIATIONS

American Forest & Paper Association
1111 19th St., NW
Suite 800
Washington, DC 20036
202/463-2700

Forest Products Research Society
2801 Marshall Ct.
Madison, WI 53705
608/231-1361
(Puts out *Forest Products Journal.*)

National Hardwood Lumber Association
P.O. Box 34518

Memphis, TN 38184
901/377-1818

National Paper Trade Association
111 Great Neck Rd.
Great Neck, NY 11021
516/829-3070

Paper Industry Management Association
1699 Wall St.
Suite 212
Mt. Prospect, IL 60065
708/956-0250
(Publishes *PIMA Magazine*, which

includes good help-wanted section.)

Paperboard Packaging Council
888 17th St.
Suite 900
Washington, DC 20006
202/289-4100

Technical Association of the Pulp and Paper Industry
15 Technology Pkwy. S.
Norcross, GA 30092
770/446-1400
(Puts out monthly magazine *TAPPI.*)

PAPER AND FOREST PRODUCTS INDUSTRY DIRECTORIES

International Pulp and Paper Directory
Miller Freeman Publications, Inc.
6600 Silacci Way
Gilroy, CA 95020
408/848-5296

Lockwood-Post's Directory of the Paper, Pulp, and Allied Trades

Miller Freeman Publications, Inc.
6600 Silacci Way
Gilroy, CA 95020
408/848-5296

Walden's ABC Guide and Paper Production Yearbook
Walden-Mott Corp.
225 N. Franklin Tnpk.
Ramsey, NJ

07446-1600
201/818-8630

Who's Who in Paper Distribution
(special issue of *Management News*)
National Paper Trade Association
111 Great Neck Rd.
Great Neck, NY 11021
516/829-3070

PAPER AND FOREST PRODUCTS INDUSTRY PERIODICALS

Forest Industries
600 Harrison St.
San Francisco, CA 94107
415/905-2200

Logger and Lumberman
P.O. Box 489
Wadley, GA 30477
912/252-5237
(Monthly magazine for forest industry professionals, including manufacturers, loggers, pulp and paper mills personnel, lumber fabricators, processors, etc.)

Pulp & Paper
600 Harrison St.
San Francisco, CA 94107
415/905-2200
(Monthly magazine for pulp and paper industry managers, technicians, supervisors, etc.)

Wood Technology
600 Harrison St.
San Francisco, CA 94107
415/905-2200
(Monthly magazine for forest industry executives, logging managers, superintendents, manufacturers, and processors.)

PUBLISHING

(including Books, Magazines, and Newspapers)

INDUSTRY OUTLOOK: Mixed, depending on the industry, but all marked by intense competition and the need to meet changing consumer demands.

As with the broadcast industry, expect this media industry to be marked by consolidation, competition, forays into new media areas. Expect to see cross-cutting—with broadcasters venturing into book publishing; newspaper and magazine companies such as Hearst doing the same; and print companies across the board exploring cyberspace and other nonprint media. More specifically:

Books: Still coping with the changes in the industry brought about by the dominance of the book superstores. Watch the industry go through shakeups, including consolidation, the closing down of some imprints, possible cutbacks on the number of titles published each year, and trimming of staff. On the flip side, though, the government projects a bright long-term outlook due to demographic trends, including the aging population and increasing school enrollments. Watch for increased emphasis on electronic products (books on tape, multimedia, on-line services, Internet, etc.).

Magazines: Extremely competitive—between different magazines and between magazines and other media—in battling for audience and for advertisers. To attract readers (and in so doing, attract advertisers), watch more magazines aim at a clearly identified audience or narrowly defined interest area. Expansion into electronic forms (videos, Internet, etc.) also expected.

Newspapers: Expect upturn in prospects as advertising linage improves with a stable economy. But hot competition from other media will force newspapers to emphasize meeting both advertisers' and consumers' wants and needs. Watch for new electronic products, including supplying news and information databases for on-line network and CD-ROM markets and newspaper coverage aimed at specific groups (such as women, minorities, young adults). Also expect some companies to explore foreign markets.

A LOOK BACK

▶ **Mergers, shakeouts, and a new emphasis on the bottom line were the key factors in the recent past for book publishers.**

The volatile period began with a series of mergers in the media industry. A number of large companies went on a buying spree, scooping up other media companies and growing into even larger conglomerates.

The outcome? A consolidated industry, in which many publishers were owned by a single larger company; and, more importantly, a new industry outlook, in which the bottom line became more important than ever.

This new emphasis led to management changes, restructurings, and wide shifts in company focus. Now parts of mega-companies, book publishers were pressed to show profitability. To do this, they cut back on the number of titles printed, changed top executives, and cut staff—or, in some cases, entire departments and imprints.

The improving economy of 1993—1996, the changing demographics, and the proliferation of retail megabookstores came to the rescue, as adult trade book and mass market paperback book sales increased. The problem? The superstores also are creating difficulties for publishers. Key among them: an increasing number of returns. As a result, 1997 saw publishers trying to determine how to cope with the new book marketplace. And the same climate should persist through 1998.

▶ **Magazines: The '90s have been volatile years, resulting in consolidation and restructuring.**

The early '90s were a period of cutbacks, streamlinings, and shakeouts. The magazine company Family Media went belly-up, leaving more than 250 employees jobless. Cahners Magazine company laid off 200 people. Time Warner laid off more than 600 employees, from both the business and editorial sides. The list of casualties continued to grow as budget cuts streamlined departments and new magazines and weaker magazines shut down. But the last few years have been better ones—while competition has stayed high, ad revenues have improved, and magazines have been coming on stronger. The past few years saw a flurry of new magazine introductions, particularly those aimed at specialty markets, and experts were optimistic about the 1998 outlook.

▶ **Newspapers were plagued by declining ad pages, declining readership, rising newsprint costs, and intense competition.**

It wasn't an easy time for newspapers. Competition from other media cut into circulation and advertising; advertising sales were sluggish, paper prices high, and readership declining. The result? The industry went through cost-cutting, consolidation, and restructuring. Weaker newspapers went belly-up; stronger papers automated to keep labor costs down and began exploring new areas of the media—and a number of newspaper companies bolstered their position by scooping up radio and television companies or, as in the case of Gannett, which bought Multimedia in 1996, buying other newspaper companies. And many newspapers, in search of new markets and higher readerships, went electronic—setting up Web sites and on-line editions of their print product.

By 1997, newspapers were feeling more confident—and hoping that their outlook would continue to be fairly bright.

WHAT'S NEXT

▶ **Key trend: Print publishers across the board will be exploring multimedia products.**

It's a reaction to the growth of the Internet, as well as a way of gaining an edge on competition. Over the past year or so, more publishing companies have been exploring alternative areas. Some didn't pan out as well as hoped—such as book publishers' forays into CD-ROMs. But others are still seeing growth. Hot areas: virtually anything connected to the Internet. Newspapers and magazines are offering on-line versions of their publications; some are developing special cyber publications only offered to subscribers of a particular on-line service. It's a growing field and one to keep an eye on over the long term. The Internet is a double-edged sword, giving newspapers a growth opportunity through new on-line ventures, while potentially cutting into their classified-advertising revenues as job seekers and employers utilize the Internet for job searches.

For information on employment prospects in this area, see Employment Outlook, page 290.

▶ **Intense competition will keep newspapers on the ropes.**

Although the newspaper industry has been cautiously optimistic in the recent past, it's not going to be easy street for a while where newspaper publishing is concerned. The good news: Some experts say that newspaper readership is finally up—as the U.S. population ages and more Americans are 35 and older, which is the prime newspaper reading audience. But competition for advertising revenues will come from the traditional sources—radio, television, magazines, the yellow pages, and direct mail—and from some newer sources, like electronic yellow pages, targeted cable programming, interactive telemarketing, and home shopping.

To fight back, newspapers will take a number of moves. A few to keep an eye out for: To attract both readers and advertisers, many newspapers will be redesigning, trying more sophisticated layouts and increasing the use of color and graphics. This will mean opportunities for layout specialists, graphic designers, and design consultants.

Newspapers will also be targeting growing ethnic groups by adding coverage or special sections. This will attract both new readers and advertisers eager to reach a targeted market—and may increase employment opportunities, both on sales and editorial staffs.

Similarly, some newspaper publishers will try to gain both new readership and increased ad revenues by putting out publications in addition to their regular newspapers—covering such subjects as health care, business, hobbies, and lifestyle. This may point to increased employment opportunities in a range of positions, as newspaper companies may need to add staff to put out these publications.

▶ **A growing trend: treating magazines as brands and developing a variety of spin-off businesses around them.**

It began during the recession when magazines started to suffer from lower ad revenues. Publishers wanted to come up with ways of generating income from a specific magazine other than the two traditional sources: circulation and ad revenues. The result? A number of large companies started looking into other ways of maximizing the profitability of magazines, and they came up with several workable ideas.

Among the related areas magazines are already trying: movies and television shows, audiotapes, international editions, books, home videos, spin-off titles (for example, *Ladies' Home Journal* developed *Ladies' Home Journal Parents Digest,* first as an insert, then as an individual magazine), subscriber clubs, even mail-order merchandise (such as Times-Mirror's hats, T-shirts, and other items bearing the *Golf* magazine or *Salt Water Sportsman* logo).

▶ **Specialization: the name of the game in magazine publishing.**

It's a growing trend—magazines that are aimed at a narrow audience—and it will continue growing. Narrow-focus magazines can attract strong newsstand sales, a devoted readership, and an advertiser pool that is targeted to that specific market niche.

A related note: Publishers will remain cautious. As a result, expect to see most new magazines start out as inserts in an existing magazine, as spin-offs of popular titles, or as quarterlies as opposed to monthlies.

▶ **The two groups most affecting the direction magazines will be taking are aging baby boomers and senior citizens.**

It's part of the old rule of thumb: Give the public what it wants. In this case, the reading public is getting older, and a traditionally prime magazine audience—young adults (ages eighteen to thirty-four) should shrink about 11% by the end of the decade.

As a result, watch more magazines redirect their editorial content to appeal to an older audience. Similarly, in line with the specialization trend, expect to see the continued success of new magazines aimed directly at the interests of older readers. *Walking* and *American Woodworker* are good examples of magazines that have skewed a basic area—in this case, sports and hobbies respectively—toward an older audience. Areas that should stay popular are parenting and grandparenting, health care, hobbies, travel, and the home.

▶ **The aging marketplace will also have a strong impact on book publishers.**

And it appears that it will be a positive impact. The strongest book-buying segment of the population is people aged thirty-five to fifty-four—a segment that is forecast to increase by 9.5 million (bringing the total to 84.6 million) this year. The result? A huge surge in potential book buyers. As such, expect book publishers to continue focusing their sights on this market and on senior citizens. Watch for trends in book topics that parallel the interests of both aging baby boomers and their parents. Probable winners: child rearing, children's books, retirement planning. On the flip side, publishers will keep trying for the under-35 market. Many new books will be targeted specifically to reach this younger crowd, and, in some cases, will be tied to other media companies such as broadcasters.

Also growing in popularity, perhaps as a function of the number of older Americans and two-income families with less time to read, is the audio book. This area will stay red-hot.

▶ **The new baby boom market will improve the book publishing outlook.**

By 2006—less than eight years away—the country may have almost 55 million school-age children, according to the U.S. Department of Education, reflecting the extension of the 1986–1996 trend. Impact: increasing demand for school textbooks, especially high school texts. High school enrollment is expected to increase by 15% in the next decade. And with the changing ethnic mix—more children of Hispanic, African, and Asian extraction—expect book publishers to focus on this market. Job outlook: attractive for specialists.

▶ **A growing internationalization will mean different things to the different publishing industries.**

In general, the print media industries have been increasing their international focus. One reason for this is the fact that many U.S. publishing companies have become part of larger multinational media companies. For example, German giant Bertelsmann owns the book publishing group Bantam Doubleday Dell, among others; French-owned Hachette Filipacchi Communications owns a number of magazines including *Elle* and *Woman's Day*. This trend, clearly, has encouraged a global emphasis among publishing companies.

The international picture in each area of publishing:

Book publishers will continue to expand their push into international markets, especially Spanish-language markets. As the world's fifth largest Spanish language market behind Spain, Mexico, Argentina, and Colombia, this segment will show significant increases. Mexico now represents the nation's sixth-largest book market. Over the past twenty years, the percentage of exports has nearly doubled. Watch for increased emphasis on international markets, which will create stronger visibility for staffers in the foreign rights areas, as well as agents with foreign experience.

Magazine publishers aggressively targeted international markets in the past few years, in part to compensate for the lagging business in the United States. Examples of successful international penetration include McGraw-Hill's *BusinessWeek*, which was recently launched in Hungarian and Russian language editions; *Forbes,* which is now published in a Chinese language edition; Hearst Magazines International, with sixty-four foreign language magazines distributed in 80 countries; and the International Data Group's corral of more than 100 computer magazines, which are now distributed in more than 40 countries. This activity will continue in a number of different ways. Some magazine companies will establish foreign-language editions of U.S. magazines on their own; to do this, a number may set up separate international divisions. But expect to see the majority of magazine companies enter into joint ventures with foreign publishers or set up licensing agreements.

As for *newspaper publishers:* Several of the larger newspapers will continue a global orientation, hoping to cash in on the rising number of Americans abroad (due to other industries' globalizing efforts) as well as capture foreign readers interested in U.S. coverage. A number are already pushing international editions, including *USA Today International,* the *Wall Street Journal,* as well as the more established *Asian Wall Street Journal* and the *International Herald Tribune*. Depending on the global economy, there may be a rise in new entrants in the international newspaper field. On the other side, expect to see an increase in foreign ownership of U.S. newspapers.

EMPLOYMENT OUTLOOK: Mixed.

Book Publishing

Cost-cutting has taken a toll on book publishing employment. With mergers and general streamlining, employment has dropped consistently each year since its peak of 77,300 in 1991. Most cuts were in marketing, administrative, and editorial positions, although production also saw some cutbacks. In addition, the high number of returns in 1996 and the uncertainty about the health of the industry due to the superstores has increased talk about more cutbacks in the short term, as book publishers make an effort to stay lean and mean in the face of the changing retail marketplace. But over the long term, there may be some improvement, especially as book publishers begin to reap the benefits of an aging, book-buying population. The field is always competitive, however, and this will continue. Another drawback: The historically low salaries paid by publishers, especially to entry-level employees. One area to keep an eye on: *Audio books.* This segment of book publishing houses has been growing, and may offer employment opportunities.

Magazine Publishing

Magazine hiring improved over the past few years, following several years of downsizing. But there is a catch in this picture: To keep costs down, many publishers are targeting people who can perform a number of jobs to keep budgets down. Other than this general outlook, it's a mixed bag: Large, established magazines continue to offer a range of opportunities, but, as always, competition will be tough. As the industry improves, new magazine launches will increase, which will lead to the creation of new jobs. The drawback? These jobs may be risky in terms of job security, as many magazine launches fail. Also a decent bet for employment opportunities: trade publications, the magazines that cover different industries. These are often good stepping-stone positions to consumer publications. One hot spot: magazine design and art direction. See Artists and Designers, page 39. *Keep an eye on:* magazine jobs connected to the Internet. Many magazines are going on-line—posting sections of their publication or developing new magazines or "cyberzines" for the Internet. It's a growing field as interest in the Internet increases, and may offer new employment opportunities—in writing, editorial, art direction, and sales.

Newspaper Publishing

The outlook here is better than in the past, when mergers and layoffs made the job-hunting climate very tough. Newspapers have been hiring again. And, while it's still as competitive as it's always been, the employment outlook is a fairly good one. Some areas that deserve special attention: To boost readership, more papers have been trying special sections—especially ones geared to younger readers, and different ethnic groups. This means employment opportunities for people with specialized backgrounds. Another area to keep an eye on: on-line newspaper jobs. As with magazines, newspapers are going on-line, either editing their regular copy for their on-line edition or coming up with new material. On-line experience or knowledge is a plus—but not a necessity. Many on-line news services are more interested in hiring people with strong news skills—and are willing to train them in the technological side.

For more information on jobs in the editorial side of publishing, see Writers, Editors, and Journalists, page 204; on graphic artists, see Artists and Designers, page 39; and on advertising space sales, see Sales and Marketing Professionals, page 148.

JOBS SPOTLIGHT

ON-LINE MARKETER: A new twist on regular magazine sales pros—in this case, the new "cyberzines" that have been popping up on the Internet need sales-people to sell advertising pages and even subscriptions via the computer. Skills required: As with the old-fashioned magazine ad sales rep position, candidates need strong sales and communications skills. In addition, on-line expertise is required.

BEST BETS

Gannett Co., Inc.
1100 Wilson Blvd.
Arlington, VA 22234
703/284-6000

Gannett, the largest U.S. newspaper company, has long had a reputation for being committed to equal opportunity for its workers and for treating employees fairly. And the reputation is well-founded. Chosen as one of the best places to work by *Black Enterprise,* Gannett offers a number of programs that encourage nondiscrimination and push for advancement of women and minorities, such as the Partners in Progress program. In addition, it provides all workers with extensive seminars and training, and has instituted a "management-by-objective" program, under which managers are judged by merit and goal-achievement.

McClatchy Newspapers
2100 Q St.
Sacramento, CA 95816
916/321-1850

Even with the slump in newspapers, McClatchy is a good choice for employment. The reasons? This newspaper chain is big on promotion from within and emphasizes management training. To coordinate promotion between the different papers, it has developed a Management Development Plan, in which top managers meet semimonthly to discuss who has executive potential and what training he or she will need to advance. Their chosen executives will take different positions at the different papers, working their way to the top. It's this type of program that makes McClatchy a good choice for fast-trackers on the business side of newspapers.

TOP BOOK PUBLISHING COMPANIES

Adams Publishing
260 Center St.
Holbrook, MA 02343
617/767-8100

Addison-Wesley Publishing Co., Inc.
1 Jacob Way
Reading, MA 01867
617/944-3700

**Avon Books
The Hearst Corporation**
1350 Ave. of the Americas
New York, NY 10019
212/261-6800

Ballantine—Del Ray—Fawcett—Ivy
(div. of Random House)
201 E. 50th St.
New York, NY 10022
212/751-2600
(Imprints: Ballantine Books, Del Ray Books, Fawcett, Ivy Books.)

**Bantam Books
Bantam Doubleday Dell Publishing Group, Inc.**
1540 Broadway
New York, NY 10036
212/354-6500

Basic Books
(div. of HarperCollins)
10 E. 53rd St.
New York, NY 10022
212/207-7057

The Berkley Publishing Group
200 Madison Ave.
New York, NY 10016
212/951-8800
(Imprints: Berkley, Berkley Trade Paperbacks, Jove, Charter, Diamond, Pacer, Ace Science Fiction.)

Carol Publishing
600 Madison Ave.
New York, NY 10022
212/486-2200
(Imprints: Lyle Stuart, Birch Lane Press, Citadel Press, University Books.)

Chronicle Books
275 Fifth St.
San Francisco, CA 94103
415/777-7240

Collins Publishers San Francisco
(div. of HarperCollins)
1160 Battery St., 3rd Fl.
San Francisco, CA 94111
415/788-4111

Contemporary Books
186 N. Stetson Ave.
Chicago, IL 60601
312/782-9181

The Crown Publishing Group
201 E. 50th St.
New York, NY 10022
212/751-2600
(Imprints: Crown Publishers, Inc., Clarkson Potter/Publishers, Orion Books, Harmony Books, Bell Tower, Living Language, Prince Paperbacks.)

Dell Publishing
(div. of Bantam Doubleday Dell)
1540 Broadway
New York, NY 10036
212/354-6500
(Imprints: Delacorte Press, Delta, Laurel.)

Doubleday
(div. of Bantam Doubleday Dell)
1540 Broadway
New York, NY 10036
212/354-6500
(Imprints: Dolphin Books, Double D Western, Spy Books, Zephyr Books.)

Harcourt General, Inc.
27 Boyleston St.
Chestnut Hill, MA 02167
617/232-8250

HarperCollins Publishers
10 E. 53rd St.
New York, NY 10022
212/207-7000
(Imprints: Harper Business, Harper Perennial, Harper References, Collins Publishers San Francisco.)

Houghton Mifflin Company
222 Berkeley St.
Boston, MA 02116
617/351-5000
(Imprints: Clarion Books)

Hyperion Press Inc.
114 5th Ave.
New York, NY 10011
212/633-4400

Little, Brown and Company
34 Beacon St.
Boston, MA 02108
617/227-0730
New York office:
1271 Ave. of the Americas
New York, NY 10020
212/522-8700

McGraw-Hill, Inc.
1221 Ave. of the Americas
New York, NY 10020
212/512-2000

W. W. Norton & Company, Inc.
500 Fifth Ave.
New York, NY 10010
212/354-5500

Penguin USA
375 Hudson St.
New York, NY 10014
212/366-2000
(Imprints: E. P. Dutton, Plume/Meridian.)

Pocket Books
Simon & Schuster
1230 Ave. of the Americas
New York, NY 10020
212/698-7000

Putnam Publishing Group, Inc.
200 Madison Ave.
New York, NY 10016
212/951-8400

Random House, Inc.
201 E. 50th St.
New York, NY 10022
212/751-2600
(Imprints: Alfred A. Knopf, Pantheon Books, Vintage Books, Villard Books, Times Books, Schocken Books, Random House Reference.)

Simon & Schuster
1230 Ave. of the Americas

New York, NY 10020
212/698-7000
(Imprints: Simon & Schuster, Inc., Touchstone Books, Fireside Books, Meadowbrook Press, Washington Square Press, Macmillan General Reference, Free Press, Scribner.)

St. Martin's Press Inc.
175 Fifth Ave.
New York, NY 10010
212/674-5151

Viking
Penguin USA
375 Hudson St.
New York, NY 10014
212/366-2000

Warner Books, Inc.
Time-Warner Bldg.
Rockefeller Center
New York, NY 10210
212/522-7200

John Wiley & Sons, Inc.
605 Third Ave.
New York, NY 10158
212/850-6000

TOP NEWSPAPER COMPANIES

Affiliated Publications
135 Morrisey Blvd.
Boston, MA 02107
617/929-2000

American Publishing Co.
111–115 S. Emma St.
West Frankfort, IL 62896
618/932-2146

ABC
77 W. 66th St.
New York, NY 10023
212/456-7777

Central Newspapers, Inc.
135 N. Pennsylvania St.
Indianapolis, IN 46204
317/231-9201

Chicago Tribune Co.
435 N. Michigan Ave.
Chicago, IL 60611
312/222-2222

The Chronicle Publishing Co.
901 Mission St.
San Francisco, CA 94103
415/777-1111

Cowles Media Company
329 Portland Ave.
Minneapolis, MN 55415
612/673-7100

Cox Newspapers
P.O. Box 105357
Atlanta, GA 30348
404/843-5000

Donrey Media Group
P.O. Box 17017
Fort Smith, AR 72917-7017
501/785-7815

Dow Jones & Co., Inc.
200 Liberty St.
New York, NY 10281
212/416-2000

Freedom Communication, Inc.
17666 Fitch
Irvine, CA 92714
714/553-9292

Gannett Co., Inc.
1100 Wilson Blvd.
Arlington, VA 22209
703/284-6000

Harte-Hanks Communications
200 Concord Plz. Dr.
San Antonio, TX 78216
210/829-9000

Hearst Newspapers
Hearst Magazine Bldg.
959 Eighth Ave.
New York, NY 10019
212/649-2000

Howard Publications
171 S. Freeman St.
Oceanside, CA 92054
619/433-5771

Journal Register Company

State St. Sq.
50 W. State St.
Trenton, NJ 08608-1298
609/396-2200

Knight-Ridder, Inc.
1 Herald Plz.
Miami, FL 33132-1693
305/376-3800

Landmark Communications, Inc.
150 W. Brambleton Ave.
Norfolk, VA 23501
804/446-2030

Lee Enterprises, Inc.
215 N. Main St.,
Suite 400
Davenport, IA 52801
319/383-2100

Macromedia, Inc.
150 River St.
Hackensack, NJ 07601
201/646-4545

McClatchy Newspapers
2100 Q St.
Sacramento, CA 95816
916/321-1850

Media General, Inc.
333 Grace St.
Richmond, VA 23292
804/649-6000

Media News
4888 Loop Central Dr.
Houston, TX 77081
713/295-3800

Multimedia Newspapers
305 S. Main St.
Greenville, SC 29601
803/298-4373

New York Times Co.
229 W. 43rd St.
New York, NY

10036 3959
212/556-1234

Newhouse Newspapers
140 E. 45th St.
New York, NY 10017
212/697-8020

News America Publishing, Inc.
1211 Ave. of the Americas
New York, NY 10036
212/852-7000

Park Communications, Inc.
Terrace Hill
P.O. Box 550
Ithaca, NY 14851
607/272-9020

Pulitzer Publishing Co.
900 N. Tucker Blvd.
St. Louis, MO 63101
314/340-8000

E. W. Scripps
P.O. Box 5380
Cincinnati, OH 45201
513/977-3000

Seattle Times Co.
1120 John St.
Seattle, WA 98109
206/464-2329

Thomson Newspapers
Metro Ctr.
1 Station Pl.
Stamford, CT 06902
203/425-2500

Times Mirror Co.
Times Mirror Sq.
Los Angeles, CA 90053
213/237-3700

Tower Media Group
21221 Oxnard St.
Woodland Hills, CA
91367
818/673-7100

Washington Post Co.
1150 15th St., NW
Washington, DC 20071
202/334-6000

TOP MAGAZINE PUBLISHING COMPANIES

The Condé Nast Publications, Inc.
Condé Nast Bldg.
350 Madison Ave.
New York, NY 10017
212/880-8800
(Publishes *Vogue, Glamour, Mademoiselle, GQ, Self, Vanity Fair, Bride's & Your New Home, Gourmet,* etc.)
6300 Wilshire Blvd.,
12th Fl.
Los Angeles, CA 90048
213/965-3700
(Publishes *Architectural Digest, Bon Appetit*)

Enquirer/Star Group
600 S.E. Coast Ave.
Lantana, FL 33462
407/586-1111
(Publishes *National Enquirer, Star Magazine.*)

Forbes, Inc.
60 Fifth Ave.
New York, NY 10011
212/620-2200
(Publishes *Forbes.*)

General Media Entertainment
277 Park Ave.
New York, NY 10023
212/702-6000
(Publishes *Penthouse,* etc.)

Hachette Filipacchi Magazines, Inc.
1633 Broadway
New York, NY 10019
212/767-6000
(Publishes *Elle, Mirabella, Woman's Day, Popular Photography,* etc.)

Hearst Magazine Division
The Hearst Corporation
959 8th Ave.
New York, NY 10019
212/649-2000
(Publishes *Cosmopolitan, Good Housekeeping, Harper's Bazaar, Popular Mechanics, House Beautiful, Redbook, Country Living.*)

Johnson Publishing Co.
820 S. Michigan Ave.
Chicago, IL 60605
312/322-9200
(Publishes *Ebony, Jet,* etc.)

K-III Holdings Corporation
717 Fifth Ave.
New York, NY 10022
212/745-0500
(Publishes *Seventeen,*

Soap Opera Digest, New York, New Woman.)

McGraw-Hill, Inc.
McGraw-Hill Bldg.
1221 Ave. of the Americas
New York, NY 10020
212/512-2000
(Publishes *Business Week, Byte.*)

Meredith Corp.
1716 Locust St.
Des Moines, IA 50336
515/284-3000
(Publishes *Better Homes & Gardens, Ladies' Home Journal.*)

National Geographic Society
1145 17th St., NW
Washington, DC 20036
202/857-7000
(Publishes *National Geographic.*)

The New York Times Company Magazine Group
1120 Ave. of the Americas
New York, NY 10011
212/789-3000
(Publishes *Tennis, Golf Digest.*)

Newsweek, Inc.
251 W. 57th St.
New York, NY 10019
212/445-4000
(Publishes *Newsweek.*)

Playboy Enterprises, Inc.
680 N. Lakeshore Dr.
Chicago, IL 60611
312/751-8000
(Publishes *Playboy.*)

Reader's Digest Association
Reader's Digest Rd.
Pleasantville, NY
10570-7000
914/238-1000
(Publishes *Reader's Digest.*)

Rodale Press
33 E. Minor St.
Emmaus, PA 18098
215/967-5171
(Publishes *Prevention, American Woodworker,* etc.)

Straight Arrow Publishers
1290 Ave. of the
Americas
New York, NY 10104
212/484-1616
(Publishes *Rolling Stone, US.*)

Time, Inc., Magazine Company
Time-Warner
Time & Life Bldg.
Rockefeller Ctr.
New York, NY
10020-1393
212/522-1212
(Publishes *People, Sports Illustrated, Time, Fortune, Money, Southern Living, Life.* etc.)

Times-Mirror Magazines
2 Park Ave.
New York, NY 10016
212/779-5000
(Publishes *Outdoor Life, Popular Science, Field & Stream, Golf Magazine.*)

U.S. News & World Report
2400 N St., NW
Washington, DC 20037
202/955-2000
(Publishes *U.S. News & World Report.*)

Ziff Communications
1 Park Ave.
New York, NY 10016
212/503-3500
(Publishes *PC, PC Week, MACuser,* etc.)

(*Note:* In many cases, specific magazines have addresses or telephone numbers different from those of their parent company. It's often best to call to check what the address and number of the particular magazine is. Another way: Check the masthead—the staff listings—in an issue of the magazine.)

WHERE TO GO FOR MORE INFORMATION

PUBLISHING ASSOCIATIONS

American Business Press
675 3rd Ave.,
Suite 415
New York, NY 10017
212/661-6360
(Puts out monthly *Employment Roundup* listing employment opportunities for members.)

Association of American Publishers
71 Fifth Ave.
New York, NY 10003
212/255-0200

Magazine Publishers Association
919 Third Ave.
New York, NY 10022
212/752-0055

National Newspaper Association
1525 Wilson Blvd.,
Suite 550
Arlington, VA 22209
703/907-7900

Newspaper Association of America
11600 Sunrise
Valley Dr.
Reston, VA 20191
703/648-1000

PUBLISHING DIRECTORIES

American Book Trade Directory
Reede Reference Publishing
121 Chanlon Rd.
New Providence, NJ 07974
908/464-6800

Bacon's Publicity Checker
Bacon's Publishing Company
332 S. Michigan Ave., Suite 900
Chicago, IL 60604
312/922-2400
(Lists newspapers and magazines)

Burelle's New England Media Directory; New Jersey Media Directory; New York State Media Directory; Pennsylvania Media Directory; Minnesota Media Directory; Texas Media Directory
Burelle's Media Directories
75 E. Northfield
Livingston, NJ 07039
201/992-7070

Editor & Publisher International Yearbook
11 W. 19th St.
New York, NY 10011
212/675-4380

Editor & Publisher Market Guide
Editor & Publisher Company, Inc.
11 W. 19th St.
New York, NY 10011
212/675-4380

Gale Directory of Publications and Broadcast Media
Gale Research, Inc.
835 Penobscot Bldg.
Detroit, MI 48226-4094
800/877-4253

The Journalist's Road to Success
The Dow Jones Newspaper Fund
Box 300
Princeton, NJ 08543
609/452-2820

Literary Marketplace: The Directory of American Book Publishing; International Literary Marketplace
Reede Reference Publishing
121 Chanlon Rd.
New Providence, NJ 07974
908/464-6800

National Directory of Magazines
Oxbridge

Communications
150 Fifth Ave.
New York, NY 10011
212/741-0231 (in New York)
800/955-0231

Publishers Directory
Gale Research, Inc.
835 Penobscot Bldg.
Detroit, MI 48226-4094
800/877-4253

Standard Periodical Directory
Gale Research, Inc.
835 Penobscot Bldg.
Detroit, MI 48226-4094
800/877-4253

Standard Periodical Directory
Oxbridge Communications
150 Fifth Ave.
New York, NY 10011
212/741-0231 (in New York)
800/955-0231

Ulrich's International Periodicals Directory
Reede Reference Publishing
121 Chanlon Rd.
New Providence, NJ 07974
908/464-6800

PUBLISHING PERIODICALS

Editor & Publisher
11 W. 19th St.
New York, NY 10011
212/675-4380
(Weekly magazine with in-depth coverage of the newspaper industry; extensive help-wanted section.) (Monthly magazine for magazine publishing managers and editors.)

Folio
11 Riverbend Dr., S.
P.O. Box 4949
Stamford, CT
06907-0949
203/358-9900
(Biweekly, for professionals in the magazine industry.)

Magazine & Bookseller
322 Eighth Ave.
New York, NY 10001
212/620-7330
(Monthly magazine for people in magazine and book retailing and wholesaling.)

Publishers Weekly
249 W. 17th St.
New York, NY 10011
212/645-9700
800/278-2991
(Weekly magazine, considered the industry "bible," covering all phases of book publishing, including production and design, book selling, rights, new book forecasts, and more; good help-wanted section.)

REAL ESTATE AND CONSTRUCTION

INDUSTRY OUTLOOK: Mixed, with certain sectors stronger than others.

Real estate and construction companies will continue to face challenges, including growing foreign competition, high liability insurance.

Real estate: Expect steady growth in most cases, as office vacancy rates continue dropping—especially as new high-tech companies continue emerging, expanding . . . and needing office space. If the economy stays healthy, expect commercial real estate to continue going strong. One trend: With suburban office space tightening up—and going up in price—watch for more activity in the real estate markets in a number of downtown city areas. A possible weak spot: older commercial space, chiefly because it doesn't offer modern communications systems or workspace that can be adapted to meet multiple uses. Along these lines, watch for developers to convert this space to other uses, such as hotels. Another possible problem, especially over the long term: the rise in 1) telecommuting and "hoteling"—where a number of employees use the same office space at different times—and 2) "cave and commons" office arrangements—mobile, small work stations that can be moved for conference meetings. Should these alternate forms of work really catch on, there may eventually be a negative impact on commercial real estate. As for retail real estate, the picture looks relatively flat. Problems with an overabundance of retail stores may cause problems in the long term, however, should the economy falter, as department stores and category stores begin to show some signs of weakness—and experts predict a 15% to 20% possible failure rate for malls by the year 2000. Overall, the long-term outlook appears to be a fair to good one, provided a growing economy generates demand for office and industrial space.

Construction: On the **residential** side: Should be leveling off after the four-year surge through 1996. However, over the long term, single-home construction looks positive because of aging baby boomers—who will be in the market for trade-up houses. In addition, multifamily housing looks good over the long term, as more people opt for rental housing—and as the percentage of elderly people increases. On the **nonresidential** side: Over the short term, expect slow growth with renovation or upgrading of properties rather than new construction becoming a key construction activity. Estimates are that for the near term as much as 80% of all construction activity will be renovations. The retail boomlet is slowing, with traditional stores being converted to supercenters. Fewer freestanding hospitals are scheduled. As for the hospitality industry, except for some few full-service hotels as well as modest-size facilities and activity in a few areas—such as Las Vegas and Atlantic City—property renovations and upgrading will continue. The office building market, however, should continue to show growth, with experts projecting this market segment to represent almost 25% of the total nonresidential building market over the next few years, compared to only 16% in the 1991–1995 period. The prevailing office building may not be the high-rise skyscraper of the past, as developers complete more modest buildings to meet current demand rather than long-term—and possibly elusive—demand. Experts indicate that emerging companies in the high-tech areas should represent a relatively strong demand for office buildings. Plant construction and public works spending looks somewhat flat. But prison construction should be up. As a result, expect to see industrial developers setting their sights overseas.

The key to long-term prospects lies, of course, in the economy. If the manufacturing sector remains stable and high tech continues its growth, expect to see facilities renovated to keep in line with technological breakthroughs and environmental legislation, and new plant/office facility construction.

A LOOK BACK

▶ **The past few years: relatively good ones for real estate and construction.**

Both industries suffered greatly in the late '80s and early '90s—with real estate prices plummeting and construction spending dropping its most since 1944. But then it was time for restructuring and retrenching—and better times came back. The general economic recovery saw the industries going through a steady, slow recovery. In real estate, vacancies fell and rents increased in many cases. As for the construction industry, it was time for a boomlet: with retail construction up, apartment construction up, home building up. And by 1997 the overall picture was one of caution: real estate companies enjoying resurgent demand, but wary of winding up with oversupply; construction companies seeing strength in residential but weaknesses in industrial building.

WHAT'S NEXT

▶ **Still some changes ahead.**

Many industry experts predict a drop in the number of real estate developers and the emergence of two tiers in the industry. The top tier will be the larger, well-financed firms that can take the downturns in the cyclical industry best because of size, geographic diversity, and access to capital. The other tier will consist of smaller developers that are attuned to local markets and can be more flexible because of their size. Squeezed out of the picture? Midsized developers.

Keep an eye on the National Association of Realtors' plans to organize a secondary market for commercial real estate loans. Under the plan, lenders would pool and sell mortgages on existing buildings to investors. If successful, this could help the commercial real estate industry avoid a repeat of the early '90s by lessening its reliance on its traditional finance sources (banks, thrifts, and insurance companies) and so encourage long-term stability.

▶ **Foreign investment will continue to play a role in real estate and construction.**

The past five years have seen substantial foreign real estate investment. Japan, West Germany, Canada, and France have been the most visible foreign presences, scooping up property in such cities as Boston, New York, and Los Angeles.

Japanese investors have began to pull back from the U.S. real estate market, but there's still a great deal of interest and investment coming from foreign sources—other Pacific Rim countries such as Taiwan, Hong Kong, Singapore, and South Korea, in particular, as well as European pension funds. A key reason for the continued interest? The weak real estate market of the past few years led to bargain prices, often as low as 35% of replacement cost. Even so, the influx of foreign investment acts as a safety net against a larger drop in real estate value (like the one that hit Texas in the '80s).

Similarly, expect to see increased foreign investment in U.S. engineering and construction firms. As of 1990, foreign companies owned 15% of the top 400 U.S. construction companies. This percentage will increase, especially as Japanese and European companies attempt to penetrate the U.S. market in terms of winning contracts. The outcome? Increased competition between U.S. and foreign firms for domestic nonresidential projects.

► **On the flip side, there will be new opportunities and challenges ahead for U.S. companies in international engineering and construction.**

Changes in the global economy—such as the democratization of Eastern Europe and the former Soviet Union, the U.S.-Canada Free Trade Agreement, developments in the European Community (EC), and growing opportunities in Asia and other developing areas—are creating new opportunities for U.S. engineering and construction firms.

Billings have already been increasing annually. The reason for this success? Providing quality service and staying technologically ahead of foreign competition. But for future success, these companies must actively promote and market their services.

One way to maintain their position in the international marketplace is to enter into joint ventures with local (foreign) companies. This strategy has worked successfully for Japanese companies, in particular, as have their other strategies: investing in other countries, and allowing subsidaries to operate independently. The outcome of these strategies? Stronger ties with local experts and the ability to identify potential projects.

As the U.S. construction industry tries to become more international, expect to see it take similar tacks. Watch for a rise in the number of joint ventures between U.S. firms and their foreign counterparts, especially in developing countries, where U.S. firms can share their technological expertise.

The following areas look especially strong for U.S. business abroad: environmental projects; industrial construction—such as chemical plants and refineries; infrastructure. The countries that should remain strong prospects include Hong Kong, South Korea, Taiwan, Malaysia, Indonesia, and Thailand, Saudi Arabia, and Kuwait. Over the long term, opportunities should be developing in Eastern Europe and the former Soviet Union.

This overall trend toward internationalization points to **expanded employment opportunities,** particularly for those with international experience. Foreign language skills are a help.

▶ Infrastructure renovation and replacement will mean long-term activity for construction and engineering firms.

Aging infrastructure will be creating opportunities over the long term for heavy construction and engineering firms. While many projects are pending due to legislation, expectations in this industry sector are high, chiefly because so many roads, bridges, and other infrastructure are in such urgent need of repair or replacement that it is unlikely that projects can be put off. For example, financially strapped New York City is currently repairing the Williamsburg Bridge— a ten-year project.

This type of activity will have **positive effects on employment.** As outlined below in Employment Outlook, heavy construction should offer strong employment opportunities over the long term.

▶ A restructuring in the real estate agency business is ahead.

It's already happening, and as with developers, the midsized firms are falling by the wayside. The industry is shaping up into a top tier of large national agencies that primarily service institutions, and a lower tier of small agencies specializing in local markets.

EMPLOYMENT OUTLOOK: Long-term outlook looks good; but expect ups and downs in line with moves in the economy.

Both real estate and construction are tied closely to the economy—in good times, the industries do well and employment opportunities are strong; in bad times, both perform more weakly. Some general trends: Even though the number of first-time home buyers is shrinking, the baby boomers are entering their high earning years—which means that trade-up homes will be in demand . . . and means that both home construction and real estate sales should perform well over the long term. In addition, the government forecasts an increase in demand for commercial buildings over the long term—even though there still is a glut of office space. As a result, the long-term picture in both real estate and construction looks generally positive. More specifically:

Real estate: Brokers and agents should face increasingly hot competition. Good news—many firms now hire people with non-real estate experience, as the field has gotten more complex and requires financial skills. As for real estate and property managers, the outlook seems good overall, although commercial real estate will be tied to the performance of the economy. In general, though, certain areas look good: Apartment management, as more people stay in rental housing; retirement community/assisted living housing management, as the number of elderly people rises; housing development management, as more new home developments elect to be governed by a community association and require professional management of jointly owned areas. (For more information see Managers, page 128, and Sales & Marketing Professionals, page 148.)

As for *construction*: According to the U.S. Bureau of Labor Statistics, construction is a field with a good long-range outlook. The key reason for this projected growth, as mentioned before, is the need to replace aging infrastructure, such as bridges and roads. This will also bring about an increase in job opportunities for civil and consulting engineers. Similarly, as industrial businesses replace or add plants and facilities, employment opportunities will increase for industrial construction staffers, engineers, and those in architectural services. Also adding to the employment picture: environmental legislation that will force manufacturers to retrofit plants and facilities to stay in line with new legislation will result in an increase in repair and renovation work.

As for housing and commercial construction: Over the short term, these areas will mirror the economy. In general, expect to see a weakening in housing—as the surge in homebuilding eases off. However, should the economy remain strong, expect to see strength in the "trophy home" market—trade-up homes for the well-off. As for commercial: There should be an increase in demand for construction managers and, in many cases, for construction workers in general. A plus for managers: Many construction projects have become increasingly complex, using advanced building materials and innovative construction methods. In addition, there is a rise in electronically operated "smart" buildings, energy-efficient building, and multipurpose buildings—all of which require the work of more construction managers. For more information on construction managers, see below.

Architects and engineers also have a positive employment outlook—with an increase in construction and rehabilitation of urban areas. Downside: Competition may be high—and will, as always, increase, in poor economic times.

Keep an eye on: International opportunities. The industrial construction industry has a global focus, with more companies expanding into international markets there will be more employment opportunities for people with international experience. Hottest markets: Asia, Latin America, the Middle East, while Eastern Europe may heat up over the long term.

JOBS SPOTLIGHT

CONSTRUCTION MANAGERS: The federal government predicts a faster-than-average growth rate in construction management. Construction managers oversee different aspects of a construction project—they determine construction methods, do time estimates, determine labor requirements, and, in some cases, supervise workers, including engineers, designers, clerks, estimators, and equipment operators. During a project, construction managers supervise construction supervisors and monitor all construction activities. In other words, it's their job to keep the construction job going smoothly. Starting salaries range from the mid-$20s to the mid-$30s. Salaries for experienced construction managers cover a wider range: from the low $40s to over $100,000. For more information, contact:

Construction Management Association of America
12355 Sunrise Valley Drive
Reston, VA 22091
703/904-9731

DESIGN/BUILD SPECIALISTS: A new specialty emerging at architectural firms—and one that should see rapid growth. Briefly, design/build architects do building design, then work with the contractor through the design execution process—amending the design when necessary and generally overseeing the process. This replaces the traditional set-up in which an architect simply designed a building, then handed off the blueprints to a contractor, who then built it. A sign of the rapid growth in this field: In 1985 only about 10% of new non-residential buildings were built under this system; the number more than doubled up to 28% by 1995, and is projected to reach nearly 50% by 2005. Qualifications: a degree in architecture; successful completion of the architect registration exam. Construction-related experience a plus.

BEST BETS

Fluor Corp.
333 Michelson Dr.
Irvine, CA, 92730
714/975-2000

Despite some ups and downs in the industry, this engineering and construction services giant is on the move. Over the last five years, its engineering projects have grown over 230%. One reason? A willingness to innovate. Fluor is big on electronic worksharing—employees work via computer and e-mail on projects far removed from their base of operations. The result is high productivity . . . and more clients. Maybe that's why industry executives ranked this firm the top in the industry in *Fortune* magazine's 1996 annual most admired corporation survey. All in all, Fluor looks like a good bet for the future.

TOP REAL ESTATE DEVELOPERS

The Alter Group
3000 Glenview Rd.
Wilmette, IL 60091
708/256-7700

Betawest, Inc.
1999 Broadway,
Suite 1900
Denver, CO 80202
303/292-7000

Breslin Realty Development Corp.
500 Old Country Rd.
Garden City, NY 11530
516/741-7400

The Cafaro Co.
2445 Belmont Ave.
Youngstown, OH
44504
216/747-2661

The Oliver Carr Co.
1700 Pennsylvania Ave., NW
Washington, DC 20006
202/624-1700

Carter
1275 Peachtree St., NE
Atlanta, GA 30309
404/888-3138

Catellus Development Corp.
201 Mission St.
San Francisco, CA 94105
415/974-4500

CBL & Associates, Inc.
1 Park Pl.
6148 Lee Hwy.
Chattanooga, TN 37421
615/855-0001

Cousins Properties, Inc.
2500 Windy Ridge Pkwy.,
Suite 1600
Marietta, GA 30067
404/955-2200

Crown American Corp.
Pasquerilla Plz.
Johnstown, PA 19901
814/536-4441

The Edward J. DeBartolo Corp.
7620 Market St.
Youngstown, OH 44513
216/758-7292

Donahue Schriber
3501 Jamboree Rd.,
Suite 300, S. Tower
Newport Beach, CA 92660
714/854-2100

Duke Associates
8888 Keystone Crossing,
Suite 1200
Indianapolis, IN 46240
317/846-4700

Forest City Enterprises, Inc.
10800 Brookpark Rd.
Cleveland, OH 44130-1199
216/267-1200

The Galbreath Co.
180 E. Broad St.
Columbus, OH 43215
614/460-4444

General Growth Cos.
215 Keo Way
Des Moines, IA 50309
515/281-9140

Gosnell Builders
2728 N. 24th St.
Phoenix, AZ 85008
602/956-4300

J. J. Gumberg Co.
1051 Brinton Rd.
Pittsburgh, PA 15221-4599
412/244-4000

The Hahn Co.
4350 La Jolla
Village Dr.,
Suite 700
San Diego, CA

92122-1233
619/546-1001

Henley Group
Liberty Ln.
Hampton, NH 03842
603/772-0631

Hillman Properties
450 Newport Center Dr.,
Suite 304
Newport Beach, CA 92660
714/640-6900

Hines Interests Limited Partnership
2800 Post Oak Blvd.
Houston, TX 77056-6110
713/621-8000

Homart Development Co.
(subs. of Sears, Roebuck & Co.)
55 W. Monroe St.,
Suite 3100
Chicago, IL 60603-5060
312/551-5000

Industrial Developments International, Inc.
950 E. Paces Ferry Rd.,
Suite 875
Atlanta, GA 30326
404/233-6080

Kornwasser & Friedman Shopping Center Properties
145 S. Fairfax Ave.
Los Angeles, CA 90036
213/937-8200

The Kroenke Group
1001 Cherry St. Centre,
Suite 308
Columbia, MO 65201
314/449-8323

The Landmarks Group
5 Concourse Pkwy.,
Suite 2000
Atlanta, GA 30328
404/698-2200

Lefrak Organization
97–77 Queens Blvd.
Rego Park, NY 11374
718/459-9021

Lincoln Property Co.
500 N. Akard,
Suite 3300
Dallas, TX 75201
214/740-3300

Maguire Thomas Partners
355 S. Grand Ave.,
Suite 4500
Los Angeles, CA 90071
310/453-4471

Manulife Real Estate
200 Bloor St. E.
South Tower, 10th Fl.
Toronto, Ont.
M4W 1E5
Canada
416/926-5500

The McGuire Group
212 S. Tryon St.,
Suite 800
Charlotte, NC 28281
704/334-9735

Melvin Simon & Assocs., Inc.
P.O. Box 7033
Indianapolis, IN 46207
317/636-1600

Metropolitan Structures
111 E. Wacker Dr.,
Suite 1200
Chicago, IL 60601
312/938-2600

Mills Corp.
3000 K St., NW
Washington, DC 20007
202/965-3600

The Morris Cos.
535 Secaucus Rd.
Secaucus, NJ 07094
201/863-0900

New England Development
1 Wells Ave.
Newport, MA 02159
617/965-8700

New Market Cos.
3350 Cumberland Circle,
Suite 1300
Atlanta, GA 30339
404/612-1700

Opus Cos.
9900 Bren Rd. E.
Minnetonka, MN 55343
612/936-4444

Prentiss Properties Limited, Inc.
1717 Main St.,
Suite 5000
Dallas, TX 75201
214/761-1440

The Prudential Property Co.
751 Broad St.
Newark, NJ 07102
201/802-4990

The Pyramid Cos.
The Clinton Exchange
4 Clinton Sq.
Syracuse, NY 13202-1078
315/422-7000

Edward Rose Building Enterprise
23999 W. Ten Mile Rd.
P.O. Box 937
Southfield, MI 48037
313/352-0952

Richard I. Rubin & Co., Inc.
200 S. Broad St.
Philadelphia, PA 19102
215/875-0700

Charles E. Smith Cos.
2345 Crystal Dr.
Arlington, VA 22202
703/920-8500

Spaulding and Slye Co.
25 Burlington Mall Rd.

Burlington, MA 01803
617/270-9595

Stein & Co.
227 W. Monroe St.,
Suite 3400
Chicago, IL 60606
312/372-4240

Trammel Crow Co.
2001 Ross Ave.,
Suite 3500
Dallas, TX 75201-2997
214/979-5100

Trammel Crow Residential
2859 Paces Ferry Rd.,
Suite 2100
Atlanta, GA 30339
404/801-1600

Westcor Partners
11411 N. Tatum Blvd.
Phoenix, AZ 85028
602/953-6200

Wright Runstad & Co.
1201 Third Ave.,
Suite 2000
Seattle, WA 98101
206/447-9000

TOP CONSTRUCTION COMPANIES

Apogee Enterprises, Inc.
7900 Xerxes Ave. S.
Minneapolis, MN 55431
612/835-1874
(Commercial construction.)

APAC
900 Ashwood Pkwy.
Atlanta, GA 30338-4780

404/261-2610
(Engineering services.)

Guy F. Atkinson Co.
1001 Bayhill Dr.,
2nd Fl.
San Bruno, CA 94066
415/876-1000
(Industrial and heavy construction.)

Bechtel Group, Inc.
50 Beale St.

San Francisco, CA 94119
415/768-1234
(Heavy construction.)

B E & K, Inc.
2000 International Park Dr.
Birmingham, AL 35243
205/972-6000
(Industrial construction, engineering, etc.)

Blount, Inc.
4520 Executive Park Dr.
Montgomery, AL
36116
205/244-4000
(Commercial
construction.)

Brown & Root, Inc.
4100 Clinton Dr.
Houston, TX 77020
713/676-3011
(Heavy construction,
engineering, etc.)

**Butler Manufacturing
Co.**
BMA Tower
Kansas City, MO
64108
816/968-3000
(Commercial
construction.)

CBI Industries, Inc.
800 Jorie Blvd.
Oak Brook, IL 60521
708/572-7000
(Commercial
construction.)

Centex Corp.
P.O. Box 19000
3333 Lee Pkwy.
Dallas, TX 75219
214/559-6500
(Residential and
nonresidential
construction.)

Ebasco Services, Inc.
(subs. of Enserch)
2 World Trade Ctr.
New York, NY 10048
212/839-1000
(Heavy construction,
engineering services.)

Fluor Corp.
3333 Michelson Dr.
Irvine, CA 92730
714/975-2000

(Nonresidential
construction.)

Foster Wheeler Corp.
Perryville Corporate Pk.
Clinton, NJ
08809-4000
908/730-4000
(Engineering services.)

**Granite Construction,
Inc.**
P.O. Box 50085
Watsonville, CA 95077
408/724-1011
(Heavy civil
construction.)

ICF Kaiser Engineers
1800 Harrison St.
Oakland, CA 94612
510/419-6000
(Engineering, design,
and construction.)

**Jacobs Engineering
Group, Inc.**
251 S. Lake Ave.
Pasadena, CA 91101
818/449-2171

**Kaufman & Broad
Home Corp.**
10877 Wilshire Blvd.
Los Angeles, CA 90024
213/443-8000
(Operative builder.)

M. W. Kellogg Co.
(subs. of Dresser
Industries)
601 Jefferson
Houston, TX 77002
713/960-2000
(Heavy construction.)

**Kiewit Construction
Group, Inc.**
1000 Kiewit Plz.
Omaha, NE 68131
402/342-2052
(Nonresidential
builders.)

Lennar Corp.
700 NW 107th Ave.
Miami, FL 33172
305/559-4000
(Operative builder.)

William Lyon Co.
4490 Von Karmen Ave.
Newport Beach, CA
92660
714/833-3600
(Operative builder.)

MK-Ferguson Co.
(subs. of Morrison-
Knudsen)
1500 W. 3rd St.
Cleveland, OH 44114
216/523-5600
(Nonresidential
builder, engineering
services.)

**Morrison-Knudsen
Corp.**
Morrison-Knudsen Plz.
P.O. Box 73
Boise, ID 83729
208/386-5000
(Heavy construction.)

NVR L.P.
7601 Lewinsville Rd.,
No. 300
McLean, VA 22102
703/761-2000
(Residential builder.)

Parsons Corp.
100 W. Walnut St.
Pasadena, CA 91103
818/440-2000
(Heavy construction,
engineering services.)

Perini Corp.
73 Mount Wayte Ave.
Framingham, MA
01701
508/628-2000
(Commercial
builder.)

PHM Corp.
33 Bloomfield Hills
Pky.
Bloomfield Hills, MI
48304
313/644-7300
(Residential builder.)

Ryland Group, Inc.
1100 Broken

Land Pkwy.
Columbia, MD 21044
410/715-7500
(Operative builder.)

**Turner
Construction**
375 Hudson St.
New York, NY 10014
212/229-6000

(Nonresidential
construction.)

**Wheelabrator
Technologies, Inc.**
3003 Butterfield Rd.
Oak Brook, IL 60521
708/218-1700
(Heavy construction,
engineering services.)

TOP ENVIRONMENTAL SERVICES/
WASTE MANAGEMENT COMPANIES

**Air & Water
Technologies Corp.**
Route 22 West and
Station Rd.
Branchburg, NJ 08876
908/685-4600

**Browning-Ferris
Industries, Inc.**
P.O. Box 3151
Houston, TX 77253
713/870-8100

**Chemical Waste
Management, Inc.**

(subs. of Waste
Management, Inc.)
3003 Butterfield Rd.
Oak Brook, IL 60521
708/218-1500

**ICF International,
Inc.**
9300 Lee Hwy.
Fairfax, VA 22031
703/934-3000

**Thermo Electron
Corp.**
P.O. Box 9046

81 Wyman St.
Waltham, MA
02254-9046
617/622-1000

**WMX Technologies
Inc.**
3003 Butterfield Rd.
Oak Brook, IL 60521
708/572-8800

Zurn Industries, Inc.
1 Zurn Pl.
Erie, PA 16505
814/452-2111

TOP CONSTRUCTION MATERIALS COMPANIES

**American Standard,
Inc.**
1 Centennial Ave.
Piscataway, NJ 08855
908/980-6000

**Armstrong World
Industries, Inc.**
P.O. Box 3001
313 W. Liberty St.
Lancaster, PA
17604-3001
717/397-0611

Holnam, Inc.
61211 N. Ann Arbor Rd.
P.O. Box 122

Dundee, MI 48131
313/529-2411

LaFarge
11130 Sunrise
Valley Dr.
Reston, VA 22091
703/264-3600

Masco
21001 Van Born Rd.
Taylor, MI 48180
313/274-7400

**Owens-Corning
Fiberglas Corp.**
Fiberglas Tower

Toledo, OH 43659
419/248-8000

PPG Industries
1 PPG Pl.
Pittsburgh, PA 15272
412/434-3131

Tecumseh Products
100 E. Patterson St.
Tecumseh, MI 49286
517/423-8411

USG Corp.
P.O. Box 6721
Chicago, IL
60680-6721
312/606-4000

Vulcan Materials Co.
P.O. Box 530187
Birmingham, AL
35253-0187
205/877-3000

**York International
Corp.**
P.O. Box 1592-3648
York, PA 17405-1592
717/771-7890

WHERE TO GO FOR MORE INFORMATION

REAL ESTATE & CONSTRUCTION INDUSTRY ASSOCIATIONS

**American Society of
Professional
Estimators**
11141 Georgia Ave.,
Suite 412
Wheaton, MD 20902
301/929-8849

**American
Subcontractors
Association**
1004 Duke St.
Alexandria, VA 22314
703/684-3450

**Associated Builders
and Contractors**
1300 N. 17 St.
Rosslyn, VA 22209
703/812-2000

**Associated General
Contractors of
America**
1957 E St., NW
Washington, DC 20006
202/393-2040

**Institute of Real
Estate Management**
710 E. Ogden Ave.
Naperville, IL 60563
630/369-2406
(Puts out publication
*Journal of Property
Management* for
members only; includes
good help-wanted
section.)

**International
Association of
Corporate Real Estate
Executives; National
Association of
Corporate Real Estate
Executives**
440 Columbia Dr.,
Suite 100
West Palm Beach, FL
33409
407/683-8111
(Puts out newsletters
for members only;
contains job
opportunities.)

**National Association
of Home Builders**
1201 15th St., NW
Washington, DC 20005
202/822-0200
(Puts out monthly
magazine *Builder,*
semimonthly *Nation's
Building News.*)

**National Association
of Minority
Contractors**
1333 F St. NW,
Suite 500
Washington, DC 20004
202/347-8259

**National Association
of Realtors**
430 N. Michigan Ave.

Chicago, IL 60611
312/329-8200
(Puts out ten-issue
magazine *Real Estate
Today.*)

**National Association
of Real Estate
Appraisers**
8383 E. Evans Rd.
Scottsdale, AZ
85260
602/948-8000

**National Association
of Women in
Construction**
327 S. Adams St.
Fort Worth, TX 76104
817/877-5551
800/552-3506
(Publishes a monthly
job openings listing for
members.)

**National
Constructors
Association**
1730 M St., NW
Suite 530
Washington, DC 20036
202/466-8880

**Society of Industrial
and Office Realtors**
700 11th St., NW
Washington, DC
20001-4511
202/737-1150

REAL ESTATE AND CONSTRUCTION INDUSTRY DIRECTORIES

Executive Guide to Specialists in Industrial and Office Real Estate	Society of Industrial and Office Realtors 700 11th St., NW Suite 510	Washington, DC 20001-4511 202/737-1150

REAL ESTATE AND CONSTRUCTION INDUSTRY PERIODICALS

Building Design and Construction
P.O. Box 5080
Des Plaines, IL 60017
708/635-8800
(Monthly magazine for those involved in commercial building, including engineers, general contractors, subcontractors, and architects.)

Buildings
P.O. Box 1888
Cedar Rapids, IA 52406
319/364-6167
(Monthly magazine for developers, building managers and owners, building management firms, etc.)

Engineering News-Record
1221 Ave. of the Americas
New York, NY 10020
212/512-3549

(Weekly magazine covering engineering, heavy and industrial construction, etc., aimed primarily at construction executives, engineers, architects, and contractors. Good help-wanted section.)

Environmental Protection
Box 2573
Waco, TX 76702
817/776-9000
(Magazine for professionals in pollution control and waste control management and hazardous waste disposal.)

Construction Equipment
P.O. Box 5080
Des Plaines, IL 60017-5080
708/635-8800

(Monthly magazine for contractors and engineers involved in highway and heavy construction.)

Professional Builder/Remodeler
P.O. Box 5080
Des Plaines, IL 60017-5080
708/635-8800
(Eighteen-issue magazine for professionals in construction, contracting, architecture, etc.)

Water Engineering & Management
380 E. Northwest Hwy.
Des Plaines, IL 60016
708/298-6622
(Monthly publication for designers, construction personnel, and others in waste water/water engineering.)

RETAILING

INDUSTRY OUTLOOK: Hot competition, possible continued consolidation—and changing consumer demands.

As always, the outlook for retail depends squarely on the economy. Given this, expect to see a continuation of modest growth rates. However, even in a strong economy, don't expect a major surge for retailers. The reasons? Slow population growth, aging of the baby boomers, and saturation of retailers in most markets. In addition, price-slashing sales of the past have turned many customers into bargain-hunting monsters—they just won't pay full price, but will wait for the price reductions. Add to this the ever-increasing rate of consumer debt—which means many consumers may be forced to back off of buying. Another potential problem: too many stores. Overexpansion may hurt different segments of the retail industry.

In addition, retailers are coping with marketplace changes. A key one: The end of the "shop till you drop" pattern now that baby boomers have aged and most families have become busy, two-income families. The result? Intensified competition for customers and shifts in retail strengths. Key to staying alive in this marketplace: cost-cutting, increased automation, strict inventory controls, ability to quickly react to trends, and lower prices to attract cost-conscious consumers used to paying sale prices.

Certain retail segments should perform more strongly than others—and, in addition, there should be shakeouts within the different sectors. In general, expect apparel stores to continue posting mixed results. Home furnishings and hard-goods chains should perform well over the long term, as baby boomers shift priorities; however, expect to see larger retailers push into this area—and so possibly hurt the smaller companies. Department stores should be regaining strength against their chief competitors of the recent past, outlet stores and off-price retailers, as they focus on value. Finally, watch for more activity in the megastores area, for example, Sports Authority, Home Depot, Staples, Barnes and Noble, and similar retailers—may expand to cover other merchandise categories, for example, used cars and health care products. However, watch for a shakeout, as certain category killers lose ground by overexpanding and by inroads from very specialized superstores. Changes ahead? Megastore chain consolidations: Will there be too many stores, offering too much merchandise and too few customers, as with office supply megastore chains? There were fifteen such chains within three years of the establishment of Staples in 1986; by 1997, there were only three; it could have been two chains if not for the government's blocking of a merger attempt. Watch for a possible backlash to the megastore concept by consumers who do not want a selling experience, walking across huge parking lots and through mall-size stores merely to make a small purchase. Given this, look for an increase in small single-category specialty shops.

Also expect to see mall consolidations. Some experts suggest that by the end of this decade as many as 20% of conventional malls will be out of business.

Over the short term, expect continued attention to cost containment—including adding more laborsaving automation. The bad news? This means jobs cut over the past few years may not be re-added, even as stores improve.

A LOOK BACK

▶ Consolidation, bankruptcies, and heavy competition marked the past few years in the retail industry.

It was a case of the survival of the fittest over the past few years. The retail industry went through major restructuring; as consumer confidence dipped, customers stopped buying—or simply waited for promotional price cutting, and certain stores began feeling the pinch. A sign of how tough the times were: in 1995, about 15,000 retail companies went into Chapter 11 filings. Others shut down some of their stores, such as Ann Taylor, and others simply liquidated—such as Merry-Go-Round stores. In addition, once seemingly invulnerable category killers, stores with dominance in a specific market sector, started faltering as well—typically due to overenthusiastic expansion as well as too much merchandise and not enough customers. Among those with troubles: Today's Man.

Some companies, of course, did better than others, such as discount giant Wal-Mart. But, here again, Wal-Mart's success was the downfall of others, especially regional discounters like Bradlees and Caldor (both of whom went Chapter 11), and Jamesway, which liquidated. The year 1997 also saw the end of an era—that of the 5-and-10-cent store—with the liquidation of Woolworth's, after unsuccessful attempts to emulate, via Wool-Mart, the transformation of Kresge's into K-Mart.

But 1996–1997 showed an improvement in sales—with consumer confidence, along with consumer spending, up. Even so, industry experts were cautious—and remained aware of the problems a weaker economy and the skyrocketing consumer debt could cause.

WHAT'S NEXT

▶ Look for continued industry consolidation.

A survival-of-the-fittest mode will continue changing the face of the retail industry. The strongest companies will keep getting stronger; the weaker ones will either be swallowed or will fall by the wayside.

The result? A few companies will be controlling the majority of the retail business. For example, retail consultants predict that over the next ten years, the top ten specialty retailers will control 40% of the market, and the top ten discount chains will control a whopping 90% of their market.

Where employment is concerned, this trend paints a clear picture: Opportunities will remain strong for healthy retailers like Wal-Mart, while retailers that have been suffering will be less likely to offer jobs or will be more likely to institute hiring freezes or layoffs.

▶ **On the flip side, expect to see a long term increase in the number of specialty stores.**

The consolidation trend won't cancel out the emergence of new specialty stores aimed at specific customer niches. Specialization is hitting a number of other industries as well and is developing into one of the best ways for companies to stay competitive. For example, the Kids "R" Us megastores have seen inroads by Noodle Kidoodle superstores catering to the upscale educational toy market. Smaller stores will focus in on narrow market niches—in many cases, ones that until now have been filled by catalog sales. The result? Increased competition for mail-order companies and more competition for department stores as well.

In a related trend, expect to see a number of the stronger mail-order houses build on their popularity and name recognition and move into regular retail. Both trends point to increased employment opportunities over the long term in retail management and merchandising.

▶ **Watch for a continued decline in sales and a focus on providing "everyday value."**

In other words, retailers will keep moving away from the traditional method of marking prices up, then slashing them during seasonal promotions or sales. The everyday-value method not only makes customers feel that they are getting the merchandise at a fair price, it also stabilizes the industry by steering it away from the damaging price wars of recent years. This method has worked successfully at Wal-Mart and at specialty stores like The Gap, which has also moved heavily into the "value-priced" category with its highly successful Old Navy Stores.

▶ **To compete with one another and with specialty stores, department stores will try to develop distinct images.**

Positioning to keep up with a changing customer has already made a number of specialty stores the big success stories of the past few years. For example, The Gap experienced a growth surge when it grew up with its customers and moved away from a jeans-only (primarily Levi's) image to become a fashion merchandiser.

Now department stores will be following suit.

Watch as department stores determine ways to distinguish themselves from the competition. One method that more stores will be trying: managing the store as if it were a group of specialty stores. This makes the individual departments stronger and more focused to their particular customers. Similarly, expect more department stores to emphasize private label lines—for example, Macy's I.N.C. sportswear line. This increases profits—and allows them to offer merchandise that no other stores have.

▶ **Along the same lines, watch as stores (and departments within stores)—especially those aimed at trendy, younger customers—micromanage for success.**

It's the most crucial factor in keeping and attracting customers—giving them what they want, as quickly as possible. In other words, specialty stores have been focusing carefully on emerging trends and quickly translating into product for the store—this, instead of testing, reordering, and the usual more drawn-out cycle of the past. And department stores have been following suit in some limited cases.

In addition, watch as more store chains tailor their products to specific markets. Instead of relying on a merchandise mix that every store across the country has, these chains play to the demographics of a region—and match the merchandise to match it. This sort of activity is what enabled certain stores—such as Contempo Casuals, a junior clothing chain—to stay strong when the times were rough—and it's becoming one of the key ways stores can grow, and increase profits. Expect to see more attention paid to this sort of micromanaging in the future—with department stores also jumping onto the targeted merchandise bandwagon. The growing and attractive preteen/teenager market appears ripe for development by retailers. The so-called "I want that"/"Have cash, will spend" purchasing patterns of the 2–12/13–19-year-old age group may provide attractive to retailers. Watch as they create a destination area within their stores featuring music, jewelry, accessories, and health and beauty aids.

▶ Increasing at a rapid pace: the use of technological systems.

Computerized sales and inventory systems are making retailers more efficient, better able to meet the demands of their customers, and more cost-effective.

The most commonly used: Quick Response or QR (also discussed in Fashion, page 322). QR computers analyze sales data, enabling retailers to track items, and to determine what's selling and what isn't, what modifications should be made on merchandise, and more. QR is typically used in conjunction with Electronic Data Interchange (EDI), which allows retailers to automatically record sales information at the point of sale. EDI can also automatically place orders, track shipments, and pay vendors for merchandise.

The bottom line of these systems: retailers can act more quickly, reordering merchandise without fear of time lags, adjusting merchandise orders according to consumer preferences (such as style changes, color changes, etc.), as demonstrated by sales, and trend-tracking. Look for more stores with on-line credit authorization, bar coding utilization, full-price lookups, and, as a result, better in-store service.

▶ Health care—a new niche market.

With managed care driving pharmacy sales and the erosion of retail drug margins, watch stores develop adjunct health care departments—with higher margins—catering to the health conscious, the aging baby boomers, and the growing senior citizen markets. A bellwether: The category killer may have arrived in the health care marketplace, with several superstore chains debuting in 1996–1997 promoting wellness and fitness.

▶ The Internet—a new retail outlet.

More retail companies will explore the Internet as a new way of reaching customers.

It's already happening with bookstores. Book sales have soared via the Internet. For example, book sales over the Internet by privately held Amazon.com—

established only in July 1995—achieved almost $16 million in sales in 1996, with little sign of any significant change in growth rates. The company offers over 2.5 million book titles. Two megastore chains responded with entry on-line in 1997, each initially offering 1 million titles. A book publisher followed suit with 350,000 titles, projecting first sales to reach $15 million.

And other retailers are following suit. Retail giant Wal-Mart set up Web sites; catalog companies are selling on-line; the trend has been set and most think this area will boom: on-line sales hit $518 million in 1996, and experts predicted the number could reach $7 billion by 2000.

▶ **The job of buyer is changing—for the better, according to many insiders.**

With automated systems, basic items are automatically reordered and re-stocked. So buyers are freed from spending time on the basics, and can devote more time to the creative side of merchandising: shopping the vendors, planning ahead, forecasting trends, and the like. And since automation cuts the time between ordering and the delivery date, buyers can buy merchandise closer to the season and so target their consumer more precisely.

Another offshoot of the increased use of technology: centralized buying responsibility. Instead of being responsible for only one store, or one store chain, buyers at the larger department store companies will buy merchandise in their category for all the stores and chains nationwide. Then the buyers at the specific stores can adjust the merchandise mix according to the needs of their particular region. The result? The emergence of a new career path, and higher visiblity for certain buyer positions.

▶ **As with other industries, expect to see increased internationalization of retailing.**

U.S. retailers will be expanding overseas, not in a huge rush, but steadily. Among the areas targeted: Europe, Japan, and other Pacific Rim countries, and, over the long term, Eastern Europe and the former Soviet Union (both of which are particularly interesting to department stores).

Different companies will try different approaches. Watch as some retailers, particularly upscale specialty stores, open international subsidiaries. Some examples: Tiffany & Co. already has subsidiaries in a number of countries and is planning moves into Spain and the Pacific Rim countries; the women's apparel store Talbot's has opened in Tokyo, as has the specialty housewares store Williams-Sonoma. Another tactic: entering into joint ventures with already-established foreign retailers.

EMPLOYMENT OUTLOOK: Fairly strong over the long term; ups and downs over the shorter term.

Over the short term, employment opportunities will depend to a great extent upon the state of the economy and, along with this, consumer confidence. Employment opportunities will also vary according to the specific retail niches and the specific stores. In general, the best short-term outlook looks to be with strong stores in strong industry sectors, such as category killers (giants focusing on one single category), and certain specialty stores. With certain changes and trends in retailing, people with distinct skills may find more opportunities than others. Some examples: The switchover to more centralized buying has created a demand for merchandise planning and distribution specialists. As stores focus more on private label goods, buyers with product development experience are needed—and knowledge of overseas markets is a definite plus.

Beyond this, the real key to hiring will be individual store strength. Over the long term, the retail industry will grow, making it the second largest source of employment in the United States by the end of the decade. The long-range outlook for managers is good, with stable employment projected. In fact, many retail companies—even those that have cut back on staff—have been reporting a strong demand for managers and management trainee staffers. The problem? Retailers often offer lower pay than that offered by other industries. So there's often a need for people to fill the top jobs for college graduates. One final tip: Industry experts say that best bets for employment opportunities are often offered by companies that are about to go public or have recently done so. The reason? They're often about to undertake expansion plans and consequentially open new stores.

BEST BETS

The Gap, Inc.
1 Harrison St.
San Francisco, CA 94105
415/952-4400

The Gap has had its shares of ups and downs over the past few years, but it's still a definite winner where employment is concerned. The reason? It's still on the move—seeking out new retail opportunities. It is expanding into new areas—for example, it became the first major apparel retailer to locate in an airport when it opened a shop in the Pittsburgh International Airport. Its lower-priced spin-off Old Navy chain has been packing them in. And it has expanded its traditional product line from khakis and jeans to more fashion-forward merchandise, even shoes, soap and perfumes. The bottom line? The Gap is coming on strong and looks like a great bet for employment on a variety of levels.

Nordstrom, Inc.
1501 Fifth Ave.
Seattle, WA 98101-1603
206/628-2111

No one ever said working at retailing giant Nordstrom is easy. It's famous for providing excellent service to customers—but it pushes employees hard. There's a quota system for sales employees—and if you miss your quota three months in a row, you're not a sales employee at Nordstrom's any more. That climate of success and fear of failure extends all the way to the top. And that, perhaps, is the key to the success of Nordstrom as a whole. Its sales per square foot are about double its leading competitors. And that gets down to the people who work there. Nordstrom's likes the commission system, and that means the best salespeople can make good money, in some cases, the best salespeople have brought home pay of $75,000. Bottom line: if you're looking to succeed in retailing sales or management, Nordstrom's is probably one of the best training grounds.

Urban Outfitters
1801 Walnut St.
Philadelphia, PA 19103
215/564-2313

A specialty store chain that knows how to target merchandise to its target customers, Urban Outfitters has been coming on strong—and looks like it's headed for even more growth. As of 1995, it had twenty stores across the country selling both clothing and housewares. It carries its own clothing designs under the Anthropologie label, and recently spun off a new division of stores with the same name to capture its customers as they grow older, get married, and have children. These new Anthropologie stores also carry baby clothes, furniture, and other wares. The key to Urban Outfitters success? Keeping on top of trends and being able to react quickly. The company keeps a team of fashion "spies" whose job is to spot and track trends in hip, stylish neighborhoods, report them back to the company—which, in turn, can bring out the style for the stores in a short amount of time. This type of quick response makes Urban Outfitters look like a real winner in the tough fashion retail game.

Wal-Mart Stores
702 SW Eighth St.
Bentonville, AR 72716
501/273-4000

Most experts agree that Wal-Mart remains a winner. It's known for excellent management, and a strong belief in employee motiviation and in innovation. It not only is considered one of the best managed companies in the industry, it also consistently performs—even during the recession, Wal-Mart was posting high sales. It encourages input from employees and is committed to automation.

TOP DEPARTMENT STORES
AND DEPARTMENT STORE COMPANIES

Belk Stores
2801 W. Tyvola Rd.
Charlotte, NC 28217
704/357-1836

Boston Department Stores
331 W. Wisconsin Ave.
Milwaukee, WI 53203
414/347-4141

Bloomingdale's, Inc.
59th St. and Lexington Ave.
New York, NY 10022
212/705-2000

Bon Marché
1601 Third Ave.
Seattle, WA 98101
206/506-7409

Broadway Stores
3880 N. Mission Rd.
Los Angeles, CA 90031
213/227-2000

Burdine's, Inc.
7 W. 7th St.
Cincinnati, OH 45202
513/579-7000

Carson, Pirie, Scott & Co.
331 W. Wisconsin Ave.
Milwaukee, WI 53203
414/347-4141

Dayton-Hudson Corp.
777 Nicollet Mall
Minneapolis, MN 55402
612/370-6948

Dillard's Department Stores, Inc.
1609 Cantrell Rd.
Little Rock, AR 72203
501/376-5200

The Elder-Beerman Stores Corp.
3155 El-Bee Rd.
Dayton, OH 45439
513/296-2700

Famous-Barr
601 Olive St.
St. Louis, MO 63101
314/444-3111

Federated Department Stores
7 W. 7th St.
Cincinnati, OH 45202
513/579-7000

Filene's
426 Washington St.
Boston, MA 02108
617/357-2100

Foley's, Inc.
1110 Main St.
Houston, TX 77002
713/651-7038

Gayfer's
3250 Airport Blvd.
Mobile, AL 36606
205/471-6000

Hecht's
685 N. Glebe Rd.
Arlington, VA 22203
703/558-1811

Jacobson's
3333 Sergeant Rd.
Jackson, MI 49201
517/764-6400

Jordan Marsh Stores Corp.
450 Washington St.
Boston, MA 02111
617/357-3000

K Mart Corp.
3100 W. Big Beaver Rd.
Troy, MI 48084
810/643-1000

Kaufman's
400 Fifth Ave.
Pittsburgh, PA 15219
412/232-2000

Kohl's Department Stores, Inc.
N54 W13600 Woodale Dr.
Menomonee Falls, WI 53051
414/783-5800

Lazarus Stores
699 Race St.
Cincinnati, OH 45202
513/774-5980

Liberty House
1450 Ala Moana Blvd., 1300
Honolulu, HI 96814
808/941-5247

Lord & Taylor
424 Fifth Ave.
New York, NY 10018
212/391-3344

Macy's California, Inc.
170 O'Farrell St.
San Francisco, CA 94102
415/954-6000

Macy's Northeast, Inc.
151 W. 34th St.
New York, NY 10001
212/695-4400

Macy's South, Inc.
180 Peachtree St., NW
Atlanta, GA 30303
404/221-7221

Maison Blanche, Inc.
1500 Main St.
Baton Rouge, LA 70802
504/389-7318

Marshall Field & Company
111 N. State St.
Chicago, IL 60602
312/781-1000

The May Department Stores Co.
611 Olive St.
St. Louis, MO 63101
314/342-6300

McAlpin Co.
2301 Richmond Rd.
Lexington, KY 40502
606/269-3611

McRae's Inc.
P.O. Box 20080
Jackson, MS 39289
601/968-4400

Mercantile Stores
9450 Seward Rd.
Fairfield, OH 45014
513/881-8000

Mervyn's
25001 Industrial Blvd.
Hayward, CA 94545
510/785-8800

Neiman-Marcus
1618 Main St.
Dallas, TX 75201
214/741-6911

Nordstrom, Inc.
1501 Fifth Ave.
Seattle, WA 98101
206/628-2111

Parisian, Inc.
750 Lakeshore Pkwy.
Birmingham, AL 35211
205/940-4000

JC Penney Company, Inc.
6501 Legacy Dr.
Plano, TX 75024-3698
214/431-1000

Rich's
223 Perimeter Ctr. Pkwy.
Atlanta, GA 30346
770/913-4000

Robinson's May Company
6160 Laurel Canyon Blvd.
N. Hollywood, CA 91606
818/980-2340

Saks Fifth Avenue
611 5th Ave.
New York, NY 10017
212/753-4000

Sears Roebuck & Co.
3333 Beverly Rd.
Hoffman Estates, IL 60179
708/286-2500

Stern's
Bergen Mall Shopping Center
Rte. 4
Paramus, NJ 07652
201/845-8400

Strawbridge & Clothier
801 Market St.
Philadelphia, PA 19107
215/629-6000

Target Stores
33 S. 6 St.
Minneapolis, MN 55440
612/304-6073

Wal-Mart Stores
702 SW Eighth St.
Bentonville, AR 72716
501/273-4000

Woodward & Lothrop, Inc.
1025 F St., NW
Washington, DC 20051
202/879-8000

TOP SPECIALTY STORES

Autozone, Inc.
3030 Poplar Ave.
Memphis, TN 38111
919/537-0426
(Auto parts.)

J. Baker, Inc.
65 Sprague St.
Readville, MA 02137
617/364-3000
(Footwear.)

Barnes & Noble Inc.
122 Fifth Ave.
New York, NY 10011
212/633-3300
(Books.)

Best Buy Co., Inc.
P.O. Box 9312
Minneapolis, MN 55440
612/947-2000
(Consumer electronics.)

Burlington Coat Factory Warehouse Corp.
1830 Rte. 130 N.
Burlington, NJ 08016
609/387-7800
(Apparel.)

Charming Shoppes, Inc.
450 Winks Ln.
Bensalem, PA 19020
215/245-9100
(Apparel.)

Circuit City Stores, Inc.
9950 Mayland Dr.
Richmond, VA 23233
804/527-4000
(Consumer electronics.)

CompUSA
14951 N. Dallas Pkwy.
Dallas, TX 75240
214/383-4000
(Computers and electronics.)

Consolidated Stores Corp.
300 Phillipi Rd.
Columbus, OH 43228
614/278-6800
(Closeout merchandise.)

B. Dalton Bookseller, Inc., and Barnes & Noble
120 Fifth Ave.
New York, NY 10111
212/633-3300
(Books.)

Eddie Bauer, Inc.
15010 NE 36th St.
Redmond, WA 98052
206/882-6100
(Apparel.)

Edison Bros. Stores, Inc.
501 N. Broadway
St. Louis, MO 63102
314/331-6000
(Apparel.)

Egghead Software, Inc.
22011 SE 51st
Issaquah, WA 98029
206/391-0800
(Software.)

Gap, Inc.
1 Harrison St.
San Francisco, CA 94105
415/952-4400
(Sportswear.)

Home Depot Inc.
2727 Paces Ferry Rd.
Atlanta, GA 30339
770/433-8211

Intelligent Electronics
411 Eagleview Blvd.
Exton, PA 19341
610/458-5500
(Electronics.)

Kay Jewelers, Inc.
375 Ghent Rd.
Akron, OH 44333
214/668-5000
(Jewelry.)

Kay-Bee Toy Stores
100 West St.
Pittsfield, MA 01201
413/499-0086
(Toys.)

Kinney
233 Broadway
New York, NY 10279
212/720-3700
(Shoes, sporting apparel.)

Lechmere, Inc.
300 Mishawaka Rd.
Woburn, MA 01801
617/938-5959
(Hard goods.)

Levitz Furniture Corp.
6111 Broken Sound Pkwy.
Boca Raton, FL 33487
407/994-6006
(Furniture.)

The Limited, Inc.
3 Limited Pkwy.
Columbus, OH 43230
614/479-7000
(Apparel.)

Marshall's
200 Brickstone Sq.
Andover, MA 01810
508/474-7000
(Apparel.)

Melville Corp.
1 Theall Rd.
Rye, NY 10580
914/925-4000
(Apparel.)

Michaels Stores, Inc.
5931 Campus Circle Dr.
Irving, TX 75063
214/580-8242
(Arts and crafts and hobby supplies.)

Micro Age, Inc.
2400 S. Micro Age Way
Tempe, AZ 85282
602/804-2000
(Computers and electronics.)

Musicland Group, Inc.
7500 Excelsior Blvd.
Minneapolis, MN 55426
612/932-7700
(Entertainment software.)

Office Depot, Inc.
2200 Old Germantown Rd.
Delray Beach, FL 33445
407/278-4800
(Office supplies.)

OfficeMax
P.O. Box 228070
Shaker Heights, OH 44122-8070
216/921-6900
(Office supplies.)

Payless Cashways
P.O. Box 419466
Kansas City, MO 64141-0466
816/234-6000
(Home improvement.)

Pep Boys Manny Moe & Mack
3111 W. Allegheny Ave.
Philadelphia, PA 19132
215/229-9000
(Auto supplies.)

Petrie Stores Corp.
70 Enterprise Ave.
Secaucus, NJ 07094
201/866-3600
(Apparel.)

PetsMart, Inc.
10000 N. 31 Ave.
Phoenix, AZ 85051
602/944-7070
(Pet foods, supplies.)

Pic N' Save Corp.
2430 E. Del Amo Blvd.
Rancho Dominguez, CA 90220
310/637-5097
(Closeout merchandise.)

Pier 1 Imports, Inc.
301 Commerce St.
Fort Worth, TX 76102
817/878-8000
(Home furnishings.)

Price/Costco
999 Lake Dr.
Isaquah, WA 98027
206/313-8100
(Discount superstore.)

Radio Shack
1800 1 Tandy Ctr.
Fort Worth, TX 76102
817/390-3205
(Consumer electronics.)

Ross Stores, Inc.
8333 Central Ave.
Newark, CA 94560
510/505-4400
(Apparel.)

Silo Electronics
6900 Lindbergh Blvd.
Philadelphia, PA 19142
215/365-2148
(Consumer electronics.)

Sports Authority, Inc.
3383 N. State St.
Ft. Lauderdale, FL 33319
954/735-1701
(Sporting goods.)

Staples, Inc.
100 Pennsylvania Ave.
Framingham, MA 01701-9328
508/370-8500
(Office supplies.)

T. J. X. Cos.
770 Cochituate Rd.
Framingham, MA 01701
508/390-1000
(Apparel.)

Tower Records
2500 16 St.
Sacramento, CA 95818

916/373-2500
(CDs, tapes, etc.)

Toys "R" Us
461 From Rd.
Paramus, NJ 07652
201/262-7800
(Toys.)

U.S. Shoe Corp.
1 Eastwood Dr.
Cincinnati, OH 45227-1197
513/527-7000
(Shoes.)

Urban Outfitters
1801 Walnut St.
Philadelphia, PA 19103
215/564-2513
(Specialty clothing store.)

Waban Inc.
1 Mercer Rd.
Natick, MA 01760
508/651-6500
(Home improvement stores.)

Walden Books Co., Inc.
201 High Ridge Rd.
Stamford, CT 06905
203/352-2000
(Books.)

F. W. Woolworth Co.
233 Broadway
Woolworth Bldg.
New York, NY 10279-0003
212/553-2000
(Discount stores.)

Zale Corp.
901 W. Walnut Hill Ln.
Irving, TX 75038
214/580-4000
(Jewelry.)

TOP DRUG & DISCOUNT STORES

Caldor
20 Glover Ave.
Norwalk, CT 06856-5620
203/846-1641

CVS Corp.
One CVS Dr.
Woonsocket, RI 02895
401/765-1500

Dollar General Corp.
104 Woodmont Blvd.
Nashville, TN 37205
615/783-2000

Eckerd Corp.
P.O. Box 4689
Clearwater, FL 34618
813/399-6000

Long Drug Stores
P.O. Box 5222
Walnut Creek, CA 94596
510/937-1170

Fred Meyer
3800 SE 22 Ave.
Portland, OR 97202
503/232-8844

Revco DS Inc.
1925 Enterprise Pkwy.
Twinsburg, OH 44087
216/425-9811

Rite Aid
P.O. Box 3165
Harrisburg, PA 17105
717/761-2633

Venture Stores Inc.
2001 E. Terra Ln.
O'Fallon, MO 63366
314/281-5500

Wal-Mart Stores
702 SW 8th St.
Bentonville, AR 72716-8001
501/273-4000

Walgreen
200 Wilmot Rd.
Deerfield, IL 60015
708/940-2500

F. W. Woolworth Co.
233 Broadway
New York, NY 10279
212/553-2000

WHERE TO GO FOR MORE INFORMATION

(Also see listings under "Fashion," page 322. For more general business information sources, see listings in "Managers," page 128, and "General Business Sources," page 502.)

RETAIL INDUSTRY ASSOCIATIONS

International Council of Shopping Centers
665 Fifth Ave.
New York, NY 10022
212/421-8181

International Mass Retail Association
1700 N. Moore St.

Suite 2250
Arlington, VA 22209
703/841-2300

National Retailers Association
325 7th St., NW
Suite 1000
Washington, DC 20004
202/783-7971

RETAIL INDUSTRY DIRECTORIES

Directory of Department Stores
Chain Store Guide Information
Services

3922 Coconut Palm Dr.
Tampa, FL 33619
800/927-9292

Directory of General Merchandise/Variety Chains and Specialty Stores
3922 Coconut Palm Dr.
Tampa, FL 33619
800/927-9292

Retail Stores Financial Directory
Fairchild Publications
7 W. 34th St.
New York, NY 10001
212/630-4000

RETAIL INDUSTRY PERIODICALS

Chain Store Age Executive
425 Park Ave.
New York, NY 10022
212/756-5252
(Monthly magazine aimed at retail executives, managers, buyers, etc., at general merchandise, department, and specialty chain stores. Annual roundups include rankings of top stores in different retail categories.)

Children's Business
7 W. 34th St.
New York, NY 10001
212/630-4230
(Monthly tabloid covering children's apparel and accessories.)

Discount Merchandiser
233 Park Ave. S.
New York, NY 10003
212/979-4800
(Monthly magazine for executives, managers, buyers, etc., at discount stores.)

Discount Store News
425 Park Ave.
New York, NY 10022
212/756-5100
(Biweekly for merchandisers, discount store managers, and operators, planners, etc., at discount stores.)

Drug Store News
425 Park Ave.
New York, NY 10022
212/756-5220
(Biweekly publication for chain and independent drugstore executives, managers, pharmacists, and manufacturers.)

HFN Home Furnishings News
7 W. 34th St.
New York, NY 10001
212/630-4230
(Weekly tabloid covering the home furnishings retail industry.)

Kids Fashions Magazine
485 Seventh Ave.
New York, NY 10018
212/594-0880
(Monthly magazine for children's clothing and accessories retailers and manufacturers.)

Mass Market Retailers
220 Fifth Ave.
New York, NY 10001
212/213-6000
(Biweekly for headquarters executives of chain drugstores, discount stores, and supermarkets.)

Sportstyle
7 W. 34th St.
New York, NY 10001
212/630-4230
(Semimonthly publication for sporting goods and activewear retailers, wholesalers, and manufacturers.)

Supermarket News
7 W. 34 St.
New York, NY 10001
212/630-4230
(Weekly magazine covering trends in the supermarket industry.)

TELECOMMUNICATIONS

INDUSTRY OUTLOOK: A period of change due to emerging technologies and new deregulation—expect restructuring, mergers and acquisitions, and extremely heavy competition.

The telecommunications industry is in for a volatile period, marked by intense competition and the emergence of new businesses, products and services. Key reason: the rush to cash in on new technologies and possible restructuring of local services markets to allow for competition between local carriers and long distance companies, and loosening of other regulatory constraints. Key development: passage of the Telecommunications Act of 1996 ending barriers between local telephone service, long-distance service, cable television, and broadcasting. Implementation of the early 1997 announcement of the British Telecommunications acquisition of MCI Communications—a $21 billion transaction—may change the telecom landscape. Now even the giants will have difficulty participating without seeking merger partners. Expect changes in the competitive landscape as these telecom companies move into each other's markets, with accompanying alliances, mergers, and heavy capital expenditures. Hottest areas: markets involved with the Internet (already AT&T has moved aggressively into this area), wireless communications, including cellular phones and service and, even newer, PCS (personal communications service—in effect, pocket-sized wireless telephones). Also emerging as a very hot spot: digital interactive telecommunications services—which will result in more partnerships between telecommunications companies and cable TV companies (such as the 1996 pairing of US West and Continental Cablevision). Long term: Keep an eye on the Internet as a major communications medium once newer technology becomes available to improve speed and capacity of data/voice transmissions. Merger/acquisitions are likely between telephone and wireless telephone companies. Telecommunications equipment manufacturers are in for continued growth—with new services, companies and consumers need new equipment, but also face possible mergers-and-acquisitions activity.

A LOOK BACK

▶ **The past has seen major changes in the telecommunications industry.**

Since the divestiture of Bell Telephone—which resulted in seven Bell regional companies and about 1,500 independent local carriers, and the emergence of competing long-distance carriers—the telecommunications industry has been through a number of changes.

Among them: Hot competition between long-distance carriers led to consolidation, as weaker companies were swallowed by larger ones. The growth of local-access lines slowed. Local carriers increased their offering of private networking services. And while the industry was still dominated by the Baby Bells, competitive access providers continued chipping away at the market—increasing competition and, in some cases, forcing consolidation.

Then came a major event affecting the industry—the biggest since the break up of Ma Bell: The Telecommunications Act of 1996. And one of the first events following the passage of the act? The merger of regional Bells, Nynex and Bell Atlantic—the second largest merger in American history—creating the second largest telephone company after AT&T. Finally, the industry has been changing due to new technologies—cellular service, personal communications services, and the Internet all have been affecting telecommunications—as new companies began emerging and the older giants began testing the waters in the new market segments as well.

WHAT'S NEXT

▶ **The Telecommunications Act of 1996 is changing the entire telecommunications scene. Watch for continued fallout from this act.**

The act, signed in February 1996, deregulated the communications industries, and in the process set the stage for a building of the country's 21st century information economy—affecting phone companies, broadcasters, and cable television companies, and ultimately the related communications industries, for example, publishing companies, motion picture firms, information-technology companies, and others, who will be scrambling also to seize a piece of the others' markets.

The country will be shifting from a hard wired (rotary phone) system to a microchip system, putting all telecom services on the same digital footing.

What will happen due to the act: Expect to see industry restructuring, megadeals, mergers, and alliances as the industry norm as companies strive for position to become supercarriers, offering a full roster of telecom services—from telephone to video to high-speed data transmission. In time it may be possible to secure any or all of these services with one call and pay one bill: one stop telecom shopping.

The act also permits the regional Bells to provide long-distance services outside their operating regions and sets up guidelines under which they can continue to provide these within their regions with conditions for entry by others—as a result, look for more competition here as well, and merger activity. Expect others to follow in the footsteps of Bell Atlantic and Nynex, whose merger formed the second largest telephone company. Their key reason for teaming up: a huge potential long-distance market and a large customer base—in other words, a hefty competitive advantage . . . which other companies will want to emulate.

The bottom line, then? The act will be the prime shaper of the new telecommunications industry—and should continue having impact over the next few years.

▶ **Technological advances will continue having a major impact on the telecommunications industry.**

Experts predict that in five to ten years, both private and public telecommunications services will have changed dramatically as hard wire/mechanical switching systems are replaced by the digital wireless age.

The key trends that are emerging: the growth of high-speed data services, resulting from the range of broadband options now available, including fast-packet switching, high-speed frame-relay data services, Switched Multimegabit Data Service (SMDS), Fast Ethernet, ATM (asynchronous transfer mode) services within their regions, and transaction processing services such as electronic data interchange (EDI). An important area as the use of LANs (local area networks) increases the need for high-speed data communications is Integrated Services Digital Networks (ISDNs), and specialized data services being introduced over ISDN.

Although still in its infancy and experimental stage, expect to see development of voice communications over the Internet, with its possible threat to the long-distance telephone company business. The corporate data communications scene is especially hot. Data networks linking employees within companies—via the Internet —were in place with over half of the Fortune 1000 companies at the end of 1996, with annual Internet software sales likely to reach slightly more than $1 billion.

This area, in particular, has had an impact on the job market, creating opportunities for telecommunications professionals with experience in both voice and data communications and knowledge in both the telecommunications field and in other industries.

▶ **The effect of these technological trends on the telecommunications equipment industry? Increased R&D budgets, consolidation, and competition.**

Keeping up with technological advances has become the only way to survive in the telecommunications equipment industry. As such, companies will continue to pour money into R&D. This may point to continued employment opportunities for those involved in product and systems development.

Companies that previously only manufactured switches may be forced to expand their product lines, as the emerging technology requires that the new switches, software, and systems work together. One result of this climate will be industry consolidation. This should take place over the next decade, as smaller companies find themselves unable to keep up with the high cost of development and either fall by the wayside or are bought by other companies. The large companies with the financing capability will be the winners, but even they may be squeezed by price competition and the race to be on the cutting edge with new equipment.

▶ **Adding to the competition in the domestic telecommunications equipment area: the influx of foreign competitors.**

Already a number of international telecommunications equipment companies have expanded into the U.S. market, among them NEC, Fujitsu, Siemens, Alcatel, and Ericsson. The reason? The United States is deregulated and offers strong telecommunications services.

The flip side to this is the fact that U.S. equipment companies are pushing into foreign markets. Two examples: AT&T has already successfully penetrated the telecom equipment markets in the Netherlands, Spain, South Korea, and Japan; Motorola is one of the two leaders in the worldwide cellular market. This activity should continue.

▶ **Keep an eye on: the regional Bell companies striving to qualify for equipment manufacturing under the terms of the Telecommunications Act.**

The act continues the ban on equipment manufacturing by the regional Bells, except when they are given permission to provide certain long-distance services within their regions and meet other conditions. When—not if—the Bells are successful in this endeavor, competition in the telephone equipment area will even be hotter. AT&T, as the chief supplier to the Baby Bells, will be especially affected. The company has already evolved into three independent companies, one of which is equipment manufacturing and sales oriented. Another possible outcome: The regional Bell companies may enter into joint ventures with foreign manufacturers to make entering the equipment business smoother and less costly. This, too, would increase competition and might give foreign competitors a push into other areas of the marketplace as a result of their partnership with the regional Bells.

▶ **Telecommunications services companies will be aggressively expanding into a range of international markets.**

This expansion is vital to stay competitive in today's telecommunications industry. The key reason? As corporations increasingly turn to international markets for business, they need international suppliers of telecommunications services. In addition, international markets are getting more open than ever. Government controlled PTT (post, telephone, and telegraph) monopolies are crumbling—and the European Union has stated that free-market communications must begin by 1998.

As a result, U.S. telecommunications companies are targeting and penetrating international markets in a variety of ways, and this activity will continue.

Both telecommunications services and equipment manufacturers are targeting foreign markets—in some cases, competing with foreign rivals, in other cases linking up in joint ventures and arrangements. Some examples: Expect an increase in international private networks, such as U.S. Sprint's optical fiber network (linking Europe to Asia through its U.S. network), which was completed in 1991. Multinational corporations can use this type of private network to link their headquarters office with their foreign branches. Due to the increasing number of multinationals and the overall globalization of the corporate world, demand for private networks should be increasing.

The growth of private global networks will result in a corresponding growth in the services that support these networks. The major U.S. carriers have already introduced Virtual Private Network (VPN) services. AT&T has service agreements with six countries, and U.S. Sprint and Cable & Wireless have teamed up in service agreements with seven countries. Expect to see further increases in the next few years.

Another growing area: supplying services to the domestic international markets. The Baby Bells in particular are moving heavily into this area, investing in cellular and paging services. They have also been investing in foreign telephone companies. The region that looks especially interesting is Eastern Europe.

Other areas the Baby Bells have been targeting in the international marketplace are directory publishing, cable television, network management, voice mail, packet-switched data communications, and Personal Communications Networks.

▶ **Local telephone business: headed for increasing competition as the monopoly of Baby Bells starts crumbling?**

Opening up local service to competition is the final step to the complete deregulation of telecommunications services—and, as such, it will transform the telecommunications industry as much as the deregulation of AT&T did. For the short term, then, this is the area of telecommunications that many people are watching closely.

How it has developed: Recently, there has been a growth in the number of competitive access providers (CAPs), companies offering private communications services to corporations, usually over local fiber optics lines. State officials have begun loosening restrictions against allowing these smaller independents to connect their lines and switches to the existing public networks. The result? CAPs are then able to access the entire phone system and so provide services to low-volume users (typically not the large corporations that use CAPs).

The outcome of this? A completely deregulated local phone service system, in which a number of local telephone services providers form a phone network and compete for customers.

Local telephone services providers are already feeling the competition for corporate clients and are instituting such services as disaster avoidance which keeps telephone lines working even during black-outs and the like. This is especially important given the growing use of telephone lines for data transmission. But as a result of the deregulation, competition should get more intense, as high-technology services are offered at a lower cost. The probable bottom line? A highly volatile industry with tough competition and a period of shakeouts, mergers, and consolidation, similar to what the long-distance services industry went through.

▶ **Cellular telecommunications: still hot—but increasingly competitive, and with new competitive technologies on the move.**

Cellular telecommunications services is still on a roll—25–30 million subscribers are estimated to have signed on as of 1997. But as the industry grows older, it is becoming more competitive. A sign of the increasing competition: The regional Bell telephone companies already have been scooping up cellular properties.

Also on the scene where cellular properties are concerned: cable companies, who are hoping to challenge the Baby Bells' dominance of the market.

The regional Bells will also be looking beyond cellular telecommunications to the newer wireless technology: personal communications services (PCS). PCS systems may eventually be used for local telephone service instead of traditional phones. With wireless rates about ten times higher than cellular rates, this may take years, and the competitive players may well be stronger by then.

The bottom line? Keep an eye on this area. The jury is out as to which service, cellular or PCS, will provide the best service and the lower price—and so, which service will take off. But one thing is clear: wireless technology will stay hot; breakthroughs will continue being made—and employment opportunities may well be increasing in this growth area.

Even so, expect to see more companies entering the cellular services field as the market continues to grow. A recent development to keep abreast of: Motorola Inc. has proposed a global cellular network, called Iridium. It will use seventy-seven satellites and more than twenty ground stations to provide worldwide cellular telephone services. It has already received the radio frequencies it needs to operate and is scheduled to be operational in 1997.

▶ A potentially hot area in the long term—information services.

The jury is still out—but most experts point to Internet services as the coming hot spot. MCI was the first major phone company to test the waters—and has been pulling in $100 million in a year in revenues. AT&T followed suit with WorldNet, an Internet access service, then began offering a consumer version of WorldNet to its long-distance customers in 1996—and insiders estimated that it may win over 10 million users. And Sprint also has moved into the area, with Sprint Intranet Dial Service.

And smaller players should be entering the field as well, as several Baby Bells have been eyeing the turf. As of this writing, most experts predicted that the newly merged Bell Atlantic/Nynex would be the next to take the plunge. Bottom line? As the Internet remains an emphasis in the communications industry, telecom companies will be developing ways to incorporate it into their businesses. Some experts see the Internet phone market soaring, with 16 million persons regularly using the Internet by 1999 compared to about 400,000 persons in 1995. Expect more action over the long term.

EMPLOYMENT OUTLOOK: New opportunities emerging as the industry changes.

With so many rapid changes in the telecommunications industry, the action where employment is concerned tends to be in the newest areas.

Even while the telecommunications giants cut staff due to mergers and consolidations, other segments of the industry kept coming on strong—and it looks like this should continue. For example, employment opportunities have been strong at medium-sized and small companies, especially those in newer technologies such as wireless. Case in point: NexTel Communications, a small wireless firm, had only a few hundred employees in 1990. The number has grown to nearly 2,000. The bottom line? Think smaller and target new technologies, especially wireless companies. In addition, given the competitive climate in the industry as well as the new services and products being offered, sales and marketing personnel are in the spotlight. Qualifications: sales skills, of course, but also technical expertise is a plus.

Final note: keep an eye on industry developments for job opportunities. For example, if voice communications over the Internet takes off, long distance companies will suffer—and job opportunities will dry up. On the other hand, companies that have established themselves in niche markets will take off. The best advice: keep on top of industry news.

For more information, see Technical Careers, page 196.

JOBS SPOTLIGHT

WIRELESS SALES: A hot area, as wireless technology continues on its growth track. Personal communications services (PCS) companies are emerging to compete with the older cellular firms. The upshot? Salespeople will be needed to spearhead the fight, selling the new mobile technology—including phones, fax machines, and pagers. A plus: Candidates don't necessarily have to know the new technology; because it is so new, companies are often willing to train qualified people. What companies want: sales experience or a technical background—an engineering degree is a big plus.

WIRELESS DESIGNERS/TECHNICIANS: Again, the growth of wireless technology has created this new employment opportunity. Both PCS and cellular companies have been pushing to introduce new products—as such, demand for wireless specialists is on the upswing.

BEST BETS

LDDS
515 E. Amite St.
Jackson, MS 39201-2702
601/360-8060

The fourth largest long-distance telephone company in the United States, LDDS looks like a long-term winner. One key reason: Unlike its larger competitors, LDDS has focused on small companies rather than big ones. Its salespeople rely heavily on in-person calls on customers rather than just telemarketing—and the personal touch has been paying off. Another good sign for the future: With its acquisition of Wiltel Network Services, LDDS will own one of only four national fiber optic networks. Plus, it is aggressively spreading into global arrangements, including a direct United States to Cuba phone service via satellite, set up in late 1994. The bottom line? LDDS might be a lot smaller than AT&T, but it's coming on strong.

MCI Communications
1801 Pennsylvania Ave., NW
Washington, DC 20006
202/872-1600

A company that keeps introducing new brands in a usually somewhat stodgy industry, MCI is well known for encouraging innovation and flexibility. This free-spirited attitude comes from the top. Management wants its employees to come up with fresh ideas, rather than sticking with the tried and true. This, plus the fact that it hires extensively from *outside* the company to bring in new blood, makes MCI look like an interesting employment prospect.

TOP TELECOMMUNICATIONS AND DATA COMMUNICATIONS EQUIPMENT COMPANIES

ADC Telecommunications, Inc.
4900 W. 78th St.
Minneapolis, MN 55435
612/835-6800

Alltel Corp.
One Allied Dr.
Little Rock, AR 72202
501/661-8000

Ameritech Corp.
20 S. Wacker Dr.
Chicago, IL 60606
312/750-5000

Ameritech Information Systems
500 W. Madison
Chicago, IL 60606
312/906-4000

AT&T Global Information Systems
1700 S. Patterson Blvd.
Dayton, OH 45479
513/445-5000

AT&T Network Systems
475 South St.
Morristown, NJ 07960
201/606-2000

AT&T Paradyne Corp.
8545 126th Ave.
Largo, FL 34643
813/530-2000

Comdial Corporation
1180 Seminole Trail
Box 7266
Charlottesville, VA 22901
804/978-2200

Communications Systems, Inc.
213 S. Main St.
Hector, MN 55342
612/848-6231

DSC Communications Corp.
1000 Coit Rd.
Plano, TX 75075-5813
214/519-3000

Dynatech Corporation
40 Richards Ave.
Norwalk, CT 06854
203/866-2500

Executone Information Systems Inc.
6 Thorndal Cir.
Darien, CT 06820
203/655-6500

General Datacomm Industries, Inc.
1579 Straits Tpke.
Middlebury, CT 06762
203/574-1118

GTE
1 Stamford Forum
Stamford, CT 06901
203/965-2000

Harris Corp./Digital Telephone Systems Div.
300 Bel Marin Keys Blvd.
Novato, CA 94949
415/382-5000

Intellicall Inc.
2155 Chenault
Suite 410
Carrolltown, TX 75006
214/416-0022

IPC
88 Pine St.
Wall St. Plz.
New York, NY 10005
212/825-9060

Motorola-Codex Corp.
20 Cabot Blvd.
Mansfield, MA 02048
508/261-4000

Motorola-Universal Data Systems, Inc.
5000 Bradford Dr.
Huntsville, AL 35805
205/430-8000

Network Systems Corporation
7600 Boone Ave. N.
Minneapolis, MN 55428
612/424-4888

Northern Telecom, Inc.
Northern Telecom Plaza
Nashville, TN 37228
615/734-4000

Northern Telecom, Inc.
Integrated Network Systems Group
4300 Emperor Blvd.
Research Triangle Park, NC 27709
919/992-5000

Octel Communications Corp.
100 Murphy Ranch Rd.
Milpitas, CA 95035
408/321-2000

Racal DataCom, Inc.
1601 N. Harrison Pkwy.
Sunrise, FL 33323
305/846-1601

Reliance Electric Co.
24701 Euclid Ave.
Cleveland, OH 44117
216/266-7000

Ricoh Corp.
5 Dedrick Pl.
West Caldwell, NJ 07006
201/882-2000

Siemens Stromber-Carlson
900 Broken Sound Pkwy.
Boca Raton, FL 33487
407/955-5000

Symmetricom
85 W. Tasman Dr.
San Jose, CA 95134
408/943-9403

TIE/Communications, Inc.
8500 110th St., Suite 200
Overland Park, KS 66210
913/344-0400

Tellabs, Inc.
4951 Indiana Ave.
Lisle, IL 60532
708/969-8800

3Com Corp.
5400 Bayfront Plaza
Santa Clara, CA 95054
408/764-5000

TOP TELECOMMUNICATION SERVICES COMPANIES

(including local carriers, long-distance carriers, and cellular telephone services)

Airtouch Communications
2999 Oak Dr.
Walnut Creek, CA 94596
510/210-3900

Alltel Corporation
1 Allied Dr.
Little Rock, AR 72202
501/661-8000

American Telephone & Telegraph (AT&T)
32 Ave. of the Americas
New York, NY 10013-2412
212/387-5400

AT&T Wireless
5000 Carillon Pt.
Kirkland, WA 98033
206/827-4500

Ameritech Corp.
(Bell Regional Holding Company)
30 S. Wacker Dr.
Chicago, IL 60606
312/750-5000

Ameritech Michigan
(subs. of Ameritech)
444 Michigan Ave.
Detroit, MI 48226
313/223-9900

**Ameritech Mobile
Communications**
(cellular subs. of Ameritech)
1515 Woodfield Rd.
Schaumburg, IL 60173
708/706-7600

Ameritech Ohio
(subs. of Ameritech)
45 Erieview Plz.
Cleveland, OH 44114
216/822-4242

Bell Atlantic Corp.
(Bell regional holding company)
1717 Arch St.
Philadelphia, PA 19103
215/963-6000

Bell Atlantic Corp./Maryland
(subs. of Bell Atlantic)
1 E. Pratt St.
Baltimore, MD 21202
410/539-9900

Bell Atlantic Corp./New Jersey
(subs. of Bell Atlantic)
540 Broad St.
Newark NJ 07101
201/649-2841

Bell Atlantic Corp. of Pennsylvania
(subs. of Bell Atlantic)
1 Parkway—16th fl.
Philadelphia, PA 19102
215/466-9900

Bell Atlantic Corp./Virginia
(subs. of Bell Atlantic)
310 N. Courthouse Rd.
Arlington, VA 22201
804/225-6300

Bell Atlantic Corp./West Virginia
(subs. of Bell Atlantic)
1500 MacCorkle Ave., SE
Charleston, WV 25314
304/343-9911

**Bell Atlantic Network
Services, Inc.**
(subs. of Bell Atlantic)
1310 N. Court House Rd.
Arlington, VA 22201
703/974-3000

Bell Atlantic/Nynex Mobile Co.
(cellular sub of Nynex)
2000 Corporate Dr.
Pearl River, NY 10962
914/365-7200

Bellcore (Bell Communications
Research)
290 W. Mount Pleasant Ave.
Livingston, NJ 07039
210/740-3000

Bell South
675 W. Peachtree St., NE
Atlanta, GA 30375
404/529-8611

BellSouth Corp.
(Bell regional holding company)
1155 Peachtree St., NE
Atlanta, GA 30309
404/249-2000

C-Tec Corp.
46 Public Sq.
Box 3000
Wilkes-Barre, PA 18701
717/825-1100

**Century Telephone
Enterprises, Inc.**
100 Century Pk. Dr.
Monroe, LA 71203
318/388-9000

Cincinnati Bell, Inc.
201 E. Fourth St.,
Suite 700
Cincinnati, OH 45202
513/566-5050

Citizens Utilities Co.
3 High Ridge Rd.
Stamford, CT 06905
203/329-8800

Communications Systems, Inc.
213 Main St.
Hector, MN 55342
612/848-6231

COMSAT World Systems
6560 Rockspring Dr.
Bethesda, MD 20817
301/214-3000

Frontier Communications Group
180 S. Clinton Ave.
Rochester, NY 14606
716/777-1000

GTE Corporation
1 Stamford Forum
Stamford, CT 06904
203/965-2000

GTE Mobile NET
P.O. Box 105194
Atlanta, GA 30348
770/391-8000

Illinois Bell
(subs. of Ameritech)
225 W. Randolph St.
Chicago, IL 60606
800/257-0902

Indiana Bell
(subs. of Ameritech)
240 N. Meridian St.
Indianapolis, IN 46204
317/265-3600

LDDS Communications
515 E. Amite St.
Jackson, MS 39201
601/360-8600

Lucent Technologies
600 Mountain Ave.
Murray Hill, NJ 07974
908/582-8500

MCI Communications Corp.
1801 Pennsylvania Ave., NW
Washington, DC 20006
202/872-1600

MFS Communications
3555 Farnam St.
Omaha, NE 68131
402/271-2890

Nevada Bell
(subs. of Pacific Telesis)
1450 Vassar St.
Reno, NV 89502
702/333-4939

NYNEX
1095 Ave. of the Americas
New York, NY 10036
212/395-2121

Nynex Corp.
(Bell regional holding
company)
335 Madison Ave.
New York, NY 10017
212/370-7400

**Nynex Mobile
Communications Co.**
(cellular subs. of Nynex)
200 Corporate Dr.
Pearl River, NY 10962
914/365-7200

Nynex-New England
(subs. of Nynex)
125 High St., 30th Fl.
Boston, MA 02110
617/743-6000

Pacific Bell
(subs. of Pacific Telesis)
140 New Montgomery St.
San Francisco, CA 94105
415/542-9000

Pacific Telecom, Inc.
805 Broadway
P.O. Box 9901
Vancouver, WA 98660
206/696-0983

Pacific Telesis Group
(Bell regional holding
company)
130 Kearny St.
San Francisco, CA 94108
415/394-3000

Rochester Telephone Corp.
180 S. Clinton Ave.
Rochester, NY 14604
716/777-9800

SBC Communications, Inc.
175 E. Houston
San Antonio, TX 78205
210/821-4105

SLT Communications, Inc.
P.O. Box 650
Sugar Land, TX 77487
713/491-2131

SNET
227 Church St.
New Haven, CT 06506
203/771-5200

Southwestern Bell Corporation
(Bell regional holding company)
175 E. Houston St.
San Antonio, TX 78299-2933
210/821-4105

Southwestern Bell Mobile Systems, Inc.
(subs. of Southwestern Bell)
17330 Preston Rd.
Dallas, TX 75252
214/733-2000

Southwestern Bell Telephone Co.
(subs. of Southwestern Bell)
1010 Pine St.
St. Louis, MO 63101
314/235-9800

Southwestern Bell Telephone Co.—Arkansas Division
(subs. of Southwestern Bell)
1111 W. Capitol
Little Rock, AR 72201
501/324-1191

Southwestern Bell Telephone Co.—Missouri Division
(subs. of Southwestern Bell)
1 Bell Ctr.
St. Louis, MO 63101
314/235-9800

Southwestern Bell Telephone Co.—Oklahoma Division
(subs. of Southwestern Bell)
800 N. Harvey
Oklahoma City, OK 73102
405/236-6611

Southwestern Bell Telephone Co.—Texas Division
(subs. of Southwestern Bell)
1 Bell Plz.
Dallas, TX 75202
214/464-4934

SPRINT Cellular
8725 Higgins Rd.
Chicago, IL 60631
312/399-2500

Telephone & Data Systems, Inc.
30 N. LaSalle St.
Chicago, IL 60602
312/630-1900

Telephone Electronics Corporation
236 E. Capital St.
Jackson, MS 39201
601/354-9066

US Sprint Communications
2330 Shawnee Mission Pkwy.
Westwood, KS 66205
913/624-3000

US West Communications
(Bell regional holding company)
7800 E. Orchard St.
Englewood, CO 80111
303/793-6500

US West Communications Services, Inc.
(subs. of US West)
1801 California St.
Denver, CO 80202
303/391-8300

US West Communications— Pacific Northwest Bell
(subs. of US West)
1600 7th Ave.
Seattle, WA 98191
206/345-3230

US West New Vector Group
(US West cellular subsidiary)
3350 161 Ave., SE
Box 7329
Bellevue, WA 98008
206/747-4900

Worldcom, Inc.
515 E. Amiti St.
Jackson, MS 39201
601/360-8600

WHERE TO GO FOR MORE INFORMATION

(For more information sources in related areas, see "Engineers," page 50, "Technical Careers," page 196, and "Computers/Electronics," page 288.)

TELECOMMUNICATIONS INDUSTRY ASSOCIATIONS

Competitive Telecommunications Association
1140 Connecticut Ave., NW,
Suite 220
Washington, DC 20036
202/296-6650

International Communications Association
12750 Merrit Dr.,
Suite 710 Lb89
Dallas, TX 75251
214/233-3889

Telecommunications Association
74 New Montgomery
Suite 230
San Francisco, CA 94105
909/945-1122

United States Telephone Association
1401 H St., NW, Suite 600
Washington, DC 20005
202/326-7300

TELECOMMUNICATIONS INDUSTRY DIRECTORIES

Telecommunications Directory
Gale Research, Inc.
835 Penobscot Bldg.
Detroit, MI 48226-4094
800/877-4253

Telephone Engineer & Management Directory
7500 Old Oak Blvd.
Cleveland, OH 44130
800/225-4569

Telephone Industry Directory and Sourcebook
Phillips Publishing, Inc.
1201 Seven Locks Rd., Suite 300
Potomac, MD 20854
301/340-2100

Statistics of the Local Exchange Carriers
United States Telephone Association
1401 H St., NW, Suite 600
Washington, DC 20005
202/326-7300
(Lists top 150 U.S. telephone companies, and over 600 local exchange carriers.)

The Wireless Industry Directory
Phillips Publishing Inc.
1201 Seven Locks Rd., Suite 300
Potomac, MD 20854
301/340-2100

TELECOMMUNICATIONS INDUSTRY PERIODICALS

America's Network
7500 Old Oak Blvd.
Cleveland, OH 44130
800/225-4569
(Semimonthly magazine for telephone company managers, engineers, executives, etc.)

Communications Week
600 Community Dr.
Manhasset, NY 11030
516/562-5000
(Weekly news magazine covering the entire telecommunications industry.)

Telecommunications
685 Canton St.
Norwood, MA 02062
617/769-9750
(Monthly magazine for telecommunications engineers, and managers involved in telecommunications buying or specifications.)

Telephony
55 E. Jackson Blvd.
Chicago, IL 60604
312/922-2435
(Weekly magazine for engineers, specifiers, buyers, etc.)

TRANSPORTATION

INDUSTRY OUTLOOK: Tight competition likely. In the short term, overcapacity—too many truckers chasing too little business—means a shakeout is likely. Expect improvement to occur relatively soon, as truckers cut back and others go out of business.

Trucking: Watch for hot competition with other trucking firms and with railroads. Long term, merged railroads offering seamless product movement may capture additional market share from trucks. Crucial to be able to compete—using information-systems applications to automate shipping, track vehicles, manage data, etc. Those companies that don't keep up with the technological breakthroughs will fall behind. Key problem: driver shortages. In the long term, expect to see movement into niche markets and international areas as a result of growing global production and trade.

Railroads: The early 1997 announcement of the Conrail takeover by CSX and Norfolk Southern leaves two major eastern railroads and two major western railroads. The next steps may be additional mergers between the eastern and western lines, creating two railroads spanning the country, offering movement of goods without transfers and improved transit times, presumably at lower rates. Look for railroads to continue to gain business and compete with trucks, although in the short term, growth will probably be slowed if the economy slows down as seems likely.

Water: International shipping will be directly tied to the health of the world economy—bright spots include Southeast Asia and other areas of Asia. As for domestic shipping, as always it will mirror the national economy. Two key issues that may have an effect on the industry: environmental legislation and the need for capital improvements on the inland waterways system.

A LOOK BACK

▶ **Truckers were faced with several changes and challenges over the past few years.**

Deregulation in 1980 sent the trucking industry into a slump because of the high number of new entrants into the marketplace and the resulting oversupply of carriers. Then came price slashing, consolidation, and—for a while—improved earnings. Even the recession and the Persian Gulf War didn't hurt the industry all that much. While diesel prices rose, truck companies were able to pass the costs along to shippers. But 1991 saw a drop in shipments, a slump in operating and income levels, and a decline in earnings. It was a matter of waiting for other industries to improve before the trucking companies could pull out of the downslide. As the economy rebounded in 1994, trucking revenues climbed. Then came 1995, which, to put it mildly, was not a good year. Increased costs in certain sectors of the industry, coupled with rising labor rates, and then some price competition, reduced profits. Add to that overcapacity—and you have a fairly bad year. Bottom line: expect improvement as a company shakeout occurs and other firms reap the benefits of improvements in operations.

▶ Railroad mergers mean stronger—and more competitive railroads.

Not so long ago, railroads seemed to be a dying industry—or at least, not particularly dynamic. Bankruptcies were common, transport was inefficient. Then, in 1980, the railroad industry was deregulated under the Staggers Rail Act—and the industry climbed out of its long slump—and began consolidating.

Over the past few years, the railroad industry saw three major mergers occur: Burlington Northern/Santa Fe, Union Pacific/Southern Pacific, and, in early 1997, the announcement of the Conrail takeover by CSX and Norfolk Southern. Mergers allow for more cost-effective transportation—and decreased government regulation has allowed the mergers and efficiencies to continue.

Bottom line: U.S. trains deliver more cargo with a third less equipment than in 1980. Cash-richer giants are better able to innovate and buy modern equipment. Intermodal transport—linking trucks and trains, is becoming a byword.

But there has been an employment cost, too. Although employees are better paid, fewer employees are needed—management layers have been cut and train crews have been reduced. This raises the issue of "captive shippers"—with one railroad setting prices, this may mean higher prices without competition, and thus, ironically, maybe a call for *more* government regulation over the long term. In addition, opposition has been raised on economic grounds, concerns that single railroads would control most of the traffic in specific geographic areas.

But for now, the future seems clear. Railroads will continue to grow larger, more profitable, and more able to compete with their main transport rivals and colleagues—the trucking companies.

What's Next

▶ The railroad mergers of the past few years—as well as new mergers—will continue to improve rail operations.

As we said earlier, the railroad mergers have reduced overcapacity, cut back on employment—including both management and staff. The railroads are now better financed, able to make capital improvements, and are delivering more cargo with less equipment. One problem: excess capacity still persists. In the short term, expect the railroad industry to continue to do well, although growth will be somewhat slow. Best area: container shipping—since export markets are strong. Intermodal shipping (see page 473) will increase more slowly. Besides mergers, look for railroads to continue to seek to streamline operations. Example: Conrail, which is cutting back on its least-used routes. Another possibility—Conrail itself is a candidate for merger—possibly with Norfolk Southern or Burlington Northern Santa Fe.

One possibility: given all these mergers and more "one train" towns—higher costs could be in the offing given less competition.

▶ **The trucking industry will continue to be highly competitive.**

It's an inevitability—competition in all four areas of service in the trucking industry: truckload (TL) carriers, less-than-truckload (LTL) carriers, small package, and package express. In both the LTL and TL areas, expect to see a continued dominance by the large carriers, with small and midsized carriers feeling the pinch.

▶ **To succeed in today's climate, trucking companies will turn to technological methods and applications.**

The use of technology is crucial for success in today's trucking industry, for three reasons: first, international production of goods is creating a need for precise coordination between production and distribution; second, the growth of "just-in-time" manufacturing is creating a need for precisely timed delivery of components; third, automation improves efficiency and keeps costs in check.

As such, expect the use of technological applications and systems to grow over the next few years. The chief use of automation will continue to be freight-transport management and integration. Among the advances already being used in this area: bar-code technology, satellite tracking of individual trucks, shipment tracking, computerized route selection. Companies already using systems such as these will expand their use; those without automation will be forced to upgrade—or lose market share rapidly.

▶ **Hottest trend in transportation? Logistics.**

Many of the large transportation companies will continue setting up logistics subsidiaries—and other independent logistics companies have begun emerging. Among the leading logistics companies: Skyway (a subsidiary of Union Pacific), Expeditors International, Fritz Cos., Harper Group, Eagle USA Air Freight, UPS Worldwide Logistics, Mark VIII, and Ryder Systems. It's all part of the impact of technology, especially the Internet, on the shipping and transportation businesses in general, and should remain a hot area where profits—and employment—are concerned.

An example of how hot this area is: In 1996, logistics companies made about $25 billion in revenues. That figure is expected to double by 2000. To tap this market, watch as more of the trucking companies get into warehousing, in an effort to offer integrated logistics to its customers.

Where employment is concerned: This is a good area to keep an eye on. Expect employment opportunities to remain good to strong over the long term.

▶ **Another way to beat the competition: positioning a company for a specific marketplace.**

The large companies will be establishing a national presence through industrial advertising and marketing campaigns. Smaller companies will focus on specialized fields and niche markets. Two of the main growth areas are commodity-specific hauling, and "just-in-time" delivery services, in which a carrier guarantees a delivery time.

In general, this attention to marketing points to new opportunities for trucking-company sales representatives and marketing professionals. Both areas will be more visible than in the past.

▶ Railroads will compete with trucking and barge companies by stepping up rail intermodal service, double-stack trains, and computerized systems.

Like trucking companies, railroads will be coming up with ways of cutting costs, expediting shipments, and the like.

One of the most common of these methods will be intermodal transportation. The concept—trailers and containers are moved by more than one transport method—isn't new, but as competition in the transportation industry stays hot, intermodal transportation is heating up again. As container shipments from the Far East increase, expect to see more rail companies increase the use of piggybacks, in which trailers or containers are placed on flatbed cars. Double-stack trains, which carry containers stacked two high, are also increasing in use; they now account for about 25% of all intermodal capacity.

To keep costs down and to enhance competitive reach, there should be a rise in cooperative ventures—marketing and joint-usage agreements between rail companies. Most commonly, companies share terminals and tracks. Among the companies already involved in cooperative ventures are Burlington Northern, Santa Fe Pacific, and Consolidated Rail.

Also watch for increasing computerization of the railroad industry. For example, both the U.S. and Canadian railroads have been developing integrated telecommunications and microelectronic systems that control train operations—Advanced Train Control Systems (ATCs). These systems can monitor a train's performance, manage maintenance crews, and more. When the systems are fully operational, they should create "smart trains"—trains that are more efficient and safer than regular trains and can detect any malfunctions and mechanical problems. The bottom line: Costs will be cut, productivity and efficiency increased, and customer service more easily ensured.

▶ A related trend: the emergence of multimodal companies that encompass different types of transportation.

It's a way of beating the competition, by being able to offer all forms of transportation to a customer. Multimodal companies—mergers of trucking, railroad, and water freight companies—first appeared in 1984, when CSX Corporation acquired controlling interest in American Commercial Lines and its subsidiary, American Barge Lines, and later, container ship company SeaLand Corporation. Rail companies in particular have been buying trucking companies while divesting themselves of nontransportation businesses.

Expect this type of across-the-board transportation merging to continue at a slower pace and to heat up when the national economy forces another industry shakeout.

▶ Water transportation faces challenges ahead.

Deep-sea foreign shipping will, as always, be dependent to a great degree on the performance of international shipping markets. The two keys to success: keeping shipping capacity in line with the supply of global merchandise that will be shipped by water; and keeping costs down—especially problematic because of the Oil Pollution Act of 1990, which will require the replacement of older tankers and tank barges.

Similarly, domestic carriers are tied to the health of the national economy—in particular, to the performance of steel, crude oil, coal, chemicals, and grain. The challenges ahead for this sector of the industry? The threat of more demanding government regulations regarding hazardous waste, waste disposal, and vessel inspection, among other things.

Overall, however, the picture is stable for water transportation.

EMPLOYMENT OUTLOOK: Variable.

Trucking industry: All in all, the government predicts about average job growth for truck drivers through the year 2005—although because the absolute number of drivers is so huge, and because so many leave or retire, generally speaking the number of job openings every year will be relatively high. On this basis, the government Bureau of Labor Statistics says the outlook is favorable. But never forget that trucking is very dependent on the state of the economy—and with recent downturns the outlook in the short-term is probably not as good, particularly for independents or those not in essential industries.

Rail industry: In general, although the rail business is expected to continue its long-term growth, job growth will be low, as railroad mergers and increased computerization reduce demand for workers. Expect a decline in transportation managerial jobs as well as general transportation jobs. New rules allowing two- or three-man crews instead of the traditional five are now widespread, leading to further decreases in employment. Best areas: locomotive and yard engineers. Key point: even with technological changes they can't be replaced. Worst area: brake operators. Looking good: subway and streetcar employment. Cities such as Los Angeles are building new systems or adding to their old as a way of off-setting increases in traffic jams.

Water transportation: Much competition for jobs over the next several years. Job growth will be probably static. About 50,000 people are employed in this area; about 40% as seamen and marine oilers; another 40% as captains, pilots, and engineers; and about 20% as mates. Key points: The U.S. proportion of deep-sea shipping is very small and getting smaller; new ships are technologically advanced and need less crew. Bottom line: Competition will continue for the small number of jobs, the overwhelming proportion of which will be replacement positions.

BEST BETS

Norfolk Southern
3 Commercial Pl.
Norfolk, VA 23510-2191
804/629-2600

Number one among railroad companies in *Fortune* magazine's "1996 Most Admired Corporations" survey, Norfolk Southern has big plans for the future, chief among them, a push to globalize. One aspect of this: selling international transport services. It's all part of Norfolk Southern's plan to provide complete transportation services. Closer to home, it has been a leader in intermodal transporation. This makes Norfolk Southern look like a long-term winner.

TOP TRANSPORTATION COMPANIES

ABF Freight System, Inc.
P.O. Box 10048
Fort Smith, AR 72917
501/785-8700
(Trucking)

Alexander & Baldwin, Inc.
822 Bishop St.
Honolulu, HI 96813
808/525-6611
(Shipping.)

Allied Van Lines, Inc.
215 W. Diehl Rd.
Naperville, IL 60563
708/717-3000
(Trucking.)

American President Cos. Ltd.
1111 Broadway
Oakland, CA 94607
510/272-8000
(Shipping.)

Arkansas Best Corp.
3801 Old Greenwood Rd.
Fort Smith, AR 72903
501/785-6000
(Trucking.)

Burlington Northern Santa Fe Inc.
777 Main St.
Fort Worth, TX 76102
817/333-2000
(Railroad.)

Carolina Freight Corp.
1201 E. Church St.
Cherryville, NC 28021
704/435-6811
(Trucking.)

Consolidated Freightways, Inc.
3240 Hillview Ave.
Palo Alto, CA 94304-1297
415/494-2900
(Trucking.)

Conrail Corp.
1401 Walnut St.
Philadelphia, PA 19101
215/977-4000
(Railroad.)

CSX Corp.
901 E. Cary St.
Richmond, VA 23219
804/782-1400
(Railroad.)

Florida East Coast Railway Co.
9955 NW 116 Way
Miami, FL 33178
305/887-4388
(Railroad.)

Grand Trunk Western Railroad
1333 Brewery Pk. Blvd.
Detroit, MI 48207
313/396-6000
(Railroad.)

J. B. Hunt Transport Services, Inc.
P.O. Box 130
Lowell, AR 72745
501/820-0000
(Trucking.)

Illinois Central Railroad
455 N. Cityfront Plaza Dr.
Chicago, IL 60611-5504
312/755-7500
(Railroad.)

Kansas City Southern Industries, Inc.
114 W. 11th St.
Kansas City, MO 64105
816/556-0303
(Railroad.)

Leaseway Transportation Corp.
3700 Park East Dr.
Cleveland, OH 44122
216/765-5500
(Trucking.)

Mayflower Transit, Inc.
9998 N. Michigan Rd.
Carmel, IN 46032
317/875-1000
(Trucking.)

Norfolk Southern Corp.
3 Commercial Pl.
Norfolk, VA 23510-2191
804/629-2600
(Railroad.)

North American Van Lines, Inc.
5001 U.S. Hwy 30 W.
Fort Wayne, IN 46818
219/429-2511
(Trucking.)

Overnite Transportation Co.
1000 Semmes Ave.
Richmond, VA 23224
804/231-8000
(Trucking.)

Preston Trucking Co., Inc.
151 Easton Blvd.
Preston, MD 21655
410/673-2900
(Trucking.)

Roadway Express, Inc.
1077 Gorge Blvd.
Akron, OH 44310

216/384-1717
(Trucking.)

Schneider National, Inc.
3101 Packerland Dr.
Green Bay, WI 54313
414/592-2000
(Trucking.)

Soo Line Railroad
105 So. 5 St.
P.O. Box 530
Minneapolis, MN 55440
613/347-8209
(Railroad.)

TNT Red Star Express, Inc.
24 Wright Ave.
Auburn, NY 13021
315/253-2721
(Trucking.)

Union Pacific Railroad Co.
1416 Dodge St.
Omaha, NE 68102
402/271-3530
(Railroad.)

United Parcel Service
55 Glenlake Pkwy. NE
Atlanta, GA 30328
404/828-6000
(Trucking.)

United Van Lines, Inc.
1 United Dr.
Fenton, MO 63026
314/326-3100
(Trucking.)

Yellow Freight System, Inc.
10990 Roe Ave.
Box 7563
Overland Park, KS 66211
913/345-3000
(Trucking.)

WHERE TO GO FOR MORE INFORMATION

TRANSPORTATION INDUSTRY ASSOCIATIONS

American Bureau of Shipping
2 World Trade Ctr.
106th Fl.
New York, NY 10048
212/839-5000

American Institute of Merchant Shipping
1000 16th St., NW,
Suite 511
Washington, DC 20036
202/775-4399

Association of American Railroads
American Railroad Building
50 F St., NW
Washington, DC 20001
202/639-2100

Industrial Truck Association
1750 K St., NW,
Suite 460
Washington, DC 20006
202/296-9880

National Association of Fleet Administrators; National Association of Fleet Managers
100 Wood Ave.
Iselin, NJ 08830
908/494-8100

National Association of Marine Services
1900 Arch St.
Philadelphia, PA 19103
215/564-3484

National Association of Waterfront Employers
2911 Pennsylvania Ave.
Washington, DC 20006
202/296-2810

National Motor Freight Traffic Association
2200 Mill Rd.
Alexandria, VA 22314
703/838-1821

National Tank Truck Carriers
2200 Mill Rd.
Alexandria, VA 22314
703/838-1960

National Private Truck Council of America
66 Canal Center Plz.,
Suite 600
Alexandria, VA 22314
703/683-1300

Transportation Institute
5201 Auth Way
Camp Springs, MD 20746
202/347-2590

TRANSPORTATION INDUSTRY DIRECTORIES

American Motor Carrier Directory
K-111 Press, Inc.
10 Lake Dr.
Hightstown, NJ 08520
609/371-7700

Moody's Transportation Manual
Moody's Investors Service, Inc.
99 Church St.
New York, NY 10007
212/553-0300

National Tank Truck Carrier Directory
2200 Mill Rd.
Alexandria, VA 22314
703/838-1960

Official Railway Guide—North American Freight Service Edition
K-111 Press Inc.
10 Lake Dr.
Hightstown, NJ 08520
609/371-7700

TRANSPORTATION INDUSTRY MAGAZINES

American Shipper
P.O. Box 4728
Jacksonville, Fl 32201
904/355-2601
(Monthly magazine aimed at those
involved in the shipping industry,
including ship and barge operators,
traffic and export managers,
manufacturers, service agencies, etc.)

Commercial Carrier Journal
201 King of Prussia Rd.
Radnor, PA 19089
610/964-4523
(Monthly publication for executives
involved in truck fleets, long and
short haul, volume buses, etc.)

Distribution
201 King of Prussia Rd.
Radnor, PA 19089
610/964-4000
(Monthly magazine for traffic and
transportation managers and
executives, shippers, packers, etc.)

Heavy Duty Trucking
P.O. Box W
Newport Beach, CA 92658
714/261-1636
(Monthly magazine aimed at
managers, maintenance and
specifications personnel, etc., at
companies with fleets over 26,000
pounds.)

Inbound Logistics
5 Penn Plz.,
8th Fl.
New York, NY 10001
212/629-1560

(Monthly magazine aimed at people
involved in inbound freight
transportation.)

Owner-Operator:
The Business Magazine of
Independent Trucking
201 King of Prussia Rd.
Radnor, PA 19089
610/964-4262
(Nine-issue magazine for small-fleet
operators and independent truckers.)

Pro Trucker
610 Colonial Park Dr.
Roswell, GA 30075
770/587-0311
(Monthly magazine for professional
drivers, fleet operators, etc.)

Progressive Railroading
230 W. Monroe, Suite 2210
Chicago, IL 60606
312/629-1200
(Monthly magazine aimed at railroad
operations and maintenance officials,
etc.)

Railway Age
345 Hudson St.
New York, NY 10014
212/620-7200
(Monthly magazine covering
railroads and rapid transit systems.)

Shipping Digest
51 Madison Ave.
New York, NY 10010
212/689-4411
(Weekly magazine aimed at
executives involved in overseas
export of U.S. goods.)

TRAVEL

INDUSTRY OUTLOOK: Hot competition for tourist dollars ahead.

Key challenges for the travel industry? Responding to the changing demands of the consumer and facing increasing competition. In line with this, watch companies aim at niche markets (such as the elderly, the environmentally aware or the health-conscious). Also watch for shifts in marketing strategies, promotion and advertising. A likely development—an increase in cooperative programs between travel industry companies (including agencies, tour operators, etc.), destinations, attractions, cities and states.

A LOOK BACK

▶ Good times for the travel industry.

The past years have been good ones for the travel industry—starting in 1992, when travel reached a record, with Americans taking nearly 1.4 billion trips a year. While there were periodic weak spots, the overall trend was one of moderate growth. International travel to the U.S. increased, domestic business travel increased, and in step with the improving economy, travel for pleasure increased. Key factors affecting the industry: easing of government regulation of air fares and routes—which resulted in lower ticket prices; the introduction of larger, more efficient planes; the explosive growth of the cruise industry; and the growing percentage of white-collar workers, who represent the largest segment of business travelers. The overall picture: a climate of moderate growth.

WHAT'S NEXT

▶ Competition will stay hot across the board.

Expect to see continued tight competition, not only between travel agencies but between agencies and suppliers and between the different segments of the travel industry.

The competition between agencies and suppliers—cruise lines, airlines, and the like—began following deregulation and has continued—as airlines and other sectors geared up to attract customers any way they could . . . and to avoid paying high commissions to agents. Expect this type of activity to keep growing, with suppliers increasing their advertising, marketing, and promotional campaigns, and packages aimed directly at consumers. And watch the Internet. Increasingly, consumers are bypassing travel agents to purchase air travel via the Internet. Travel agents will have to offer clients new values to keep them as customers.

One final area affected by competition: reduced commission paid to travel agents. Airlines, in an effort to keep costs down, first instituted this practice in 1995—putting a cap on the amount of commissions they will pay. The jury is still out as to how strongly this capping of prices will affect agencies. However, many believe that over the long term it will have a strong impact on travel agencies—and could spell real problems for the smaller agencies in particular, who may respond with fees for services.

▶ A continuing trend: industry consolidation.

The travel industry is increasingly being dominated by large agencies and agency networks—consortiums of smaller agencies that link up to remain competitive with the big guys like Carlson, Thomas Cook, and American Express.

This type of activity will continue as smaller independent agencies face stiffer competition from other agencies, particularly chains and franchises, and, as outlined above, from suppliers. By linking up with a network, even a small agency can gain the resources needed to stay alive in this competitive field. Among them: cooperative personnel recruiting, centralized computer systems, increased cooperative advertising and marketing and collective purchasing.

▶ Also increasing: specialization and targeted marketing.

This, too, is a result of competition in the field. Some developments to be on the lookout for: In the business travel segment, watch small and midsized corporate agencies target their services specifically to small and midsized corporations as the large chains will dominate much of the business travel segment.

Similarly, in the general travel field, local and regional agencies will rely on focused marketing to compete with the large agencies and chains. They will develop packages and services to meet the very specific needs of their so-called mini-markets.

An employment note: This emphasis on marketing and sales may translate into new opportunities for marketing and sales personnel in the travel industry.

▶ Similarly, the travel industry will be shifting focus and marketing to keep up with changing demographics.

It's the logical way for the industry to continue growing. And the general demographic picture is a positive one, chiefly because of the increasing number of older Americans and those with higher levels of education and income—all positive traits where travel is concerned.

Other key "people trends" that the travel industry will be tracking: The increase in two-income families will mean an increase in "short stay" travel—that is, trips of two to seven days. As a result, cruise lines and tour companies—even international tour companies—will emphasize shorter trip packages. The increasing number of baby boomers having babies—and so, the increase in the number of grandparents—will result in the growth of the family travel area. Again, tour operators and cruise lines will be developing special packages to accommodate these changes—and the related trend of families accompanying business travelers.

Another hot area: adventure-type trips, as the population ages and has more disposable income. Adventure trips—trekking, scuba diving, and other active trips—as well as trips to exotic locations are especially hot areas for entrepreneurs and small tour operators. A related travel segment that should remain strong in the short term is package tours or trips aimed at environmentally aware travelers: "ecotourism" or "low-environmental-impact-travel."

▶ The travel industry will continue strong in the international arena.

With an increase in international business—especially to Europe as a result of the EC and the changes in Eastern Europe—and the growing internationalization of U.S. companies, foreign business travel will remain strong over the long term.

Also pointing to growth in international travel: the changes in Eastern Europe and the former Soviet Union are opening up new markets. The U.S. already has bilateral tourism agreements with Poland, Hungary, Argentina and Venezuela. NAFTA and GATT should both help reduce travel barriers and facilitate business and investment in tourism as well.

▶ Cruise lines: in for competition.

The cruise industry may be headed for a shakeout—with the big players, like Carnival and Royal Caribbean emerging the winners, and smaller, privately owned fleets the losers. To stay alive, smaller operators may merge with competitors or simply go belly-up.

The reasons for the shakeout: In 1995, the number of cruise passengers declined for the first time in years. In addition, a number of smaller fleets hit the water, eager to cash in on the cruise business, which increased competition. Finally, as many as 25 new ships with over 40,000 new berths should hit the sea by 1998. So some experts worry that overcapacity may hit the cruise business.

But there is good news. First, many industry insiders believe that the industry is not saturated. Industry experts estimate that less than 7% of the American traveling public has ever taken a cruise. Second, as mentioned above, the population is growing older—and the traditional cruise customer is over forty-five. Aging baby boomers and senior citizens are likely cruise customers. In addition, the growing value-consciousness of the American consumer fits in with the cruise industry as cruises are all-inclusive vacations. Finally, the Cruise Line International Association predicts that by the year 2000 passenger lists may hit up to 8 million a year.

The bottom line, then—while the industry may be headed for choppy water and smaller companies feel the pinch, the larger cruise companies should continue coming on strong. Key reasons: young fleets, and brand name identity. As such, expect the industry to continue to pursue strong marketing efforts, including deep discounts to build volume.

Some other developments to watch for: Expect the evolution of a two-tier industry, with larger lines offering diversified services and smaller cruise lines finding niche markets (such as windjammer cruises, hands-on cruising, or special destinations) and offering specialized services.

Also expect to see more cruise lines linking up with other travel companies. Some will buy up or enter joint ventures with resorts or hotels and offer "land-sea" packages. For example, Cunard already owns seven hotels. Other cruise lines will develop arrangements and packages with tour operators and airlines. These collaborative arrangements will increase competitive power and attract more customers.

As for employment: The cruise lines offer good employment prospects. Salespeople are in for a relatively bright future as cruise lines beef up sales forces. Similarly, advertising and marketing will be heating up. As the cruise industry matures, more lines are pumping money into advertising to establish brand identity.

EMPLOYMENT OUTLOOK: Positive.

The long-term picture is a good one where jobs are concerned. The travel and tourism industry already employs more than 9 million people, and that number should increase over the next ten years. Already there's an upward trend. For example, from 1992 to 1993 employment increased only 1.3%, but from 1993 to 1994, it jumped 3.9%, and employment increased again from 1994 through 1996. And the travel industry isn't region-specific. In fact, it is the largest employer in thirty-nine of the fifty states.

The bottom line: Job opportunities will be there for people in the travel industry. *Travel agents* have a particularly strong picture, with the government predicting that their employment will grow faster than average through 2005. The reason: increased spending on travel in general; increased business travel; a larger percentage of older people in the population . . . who are more likely to spend money on travel; affordable airline rates; and so on. At the same time, travel agencies have been faced with a *shortage* of job applicants. So there's a strong demand for travel agents and salespeople—from the entry-level on up. An added plus of this demand: Salaries are going up as demand increases. In addition, many agencies are targeting women, minorities, senior citizens, and foreign-born people. And many are also starting to offer flexible work arrangements: seasonal work schedules, part-time schedules, temporary assignments, and the like. The only possible downside in this field: the growth in nontraditional ways of making travel arrangements. For example, on-line computer services allow people to make travel arrangements via PC; some travel companies make their services available through such new ways as electronic ticket machines and remote printers. But so far, this hasn't hurt the demand for travel agents. If these methods catch on, though, the long-term picture may worsen. In the meantime, however, the outlook is a bright one.

It's similarly bright for cruise line staffers—as people continue to opt for cruises as their vacation of choice; tour operators; and the like.

Corporate travel managers and staffs should also be increasing as business becomes more internationalized. Travel industry placement executives indicate that specialists selling to corporate accounts may average up to a 20% salary premium over leisure-market specialists.

JOB SPOTLIGHT

ADVENTURE TRAVEL SPECIALIST: An especially hot job for adventurous entrepreneurs, this travel specialty has been growing as more people seek thrills on their vacation. Adventure travel specialists act as tour guides and/or agents, Setting up higher-risk vacations for travelers—rock or mountain climbing, whitewater rafting, even bungee jumping. A background in leisure services management is a plus—as is experience in any of the high-risk activities involved.

BEST BETS

Carlson/Wagonlit Travel
P.O. Box 59159
Minneapolis, MN 55459
612/540-5000

The base of U.S. operations for the world's largest travel operator, with over 4,000 offices around the world, Carlson/Wagonlit is a consistent good bet for employment opportunities. It offers extensive in-house training programs for new agents. In addition, it's known as a worker-friendly place. Among the reasons: it offers flexible schedules to attract nontraditional workers, such as single parents and the elderly. In addition, Carlson/Wagonlit places a high premium on employee recognition—and rewards employees, both informally and formally, with everything from thank-you notes to bestowing Royal Honor awards (including checks, special prizes, and trips) for meeting certain criteria. All in all, Carlson/Wagonlit is considered a top choice for employment—by industry experts as well as employees themselves.

Carnival Cruise Lines, Inc.
3655 NW 87th Ave.
Miami, FL 33178
305/599-2600

Known for aggressive marketing and advertising, Carnival remains the top cruise line in the country and should keep coming on strong. There are expansion plans in the works, including zeroing in on a hot growth area: short-term cruises. A good bet for the future.

TOP TRAVEL COMPANIES

(including agencies, cruise lines, and tour operators)

American Express Travel Group, Inc.
American Express Tower
World Financial Ctr.
New York, NY 10285
212/640-2000
(Diversified travel services.)

Beehive Business and Leisure Travel
419 Wakara Way
Salt Lake City, UT 84108
801/583-0273
(Travel agency.)

Carlson/Wagonlit Travel
P.O. Box 59159
Minneapolis, MN 55459
612/540-5000
(Travel agencies.)

Carnival Cruise Lines Inc.
3655 NW 87th Ave.
Miami, FL 33178
305/599-2600
(Cruise line.)

Commodore Cruise Line
800 Douglas Rd.,
Suite 700
Coral Gables, FL 33134
305/529-3000
(Cruise line.)

Thomas Cook Travel
100 Cambridge Park Dr.
Cambridge, MA 02138
617/868-9800
(Travel agency.)

Cunard Line
555 Fifth Ave.
New York, NY 10017
212/880-7500
(Cruise line.)

Garber Travel Service, Inc.
1406 Beacon St.
Brookline, MA 02146
617/734-2100
(Travel agency.)

Holland America Line
300 Elliott Ave. W.
Seattle, WA 98119
206/281-3535
(Cruise line.)

IVI Travel, Inc.
400 Skokie Blvd.
Northbrook, IL 60062
708/480-8783
(Travel agency.)

Kloster Cruise Ltd.
95 Merrick Way
Miami, FL 33134
305/447-9660
(Cruise line.)

Morris Travel Express Corp.
240 E. Morris Ave.
Salt Lake City, UT 84115
801/483-6441
(Travel agency.)

Northwestern Travel Service, Inc.
7250 Metro Blvd.
Minneapolis, MN 55439
612/921-3701
(Travel agency.)

PS Group, Inc.
4370 La Jolla Village, Suite 1050
San Diego, CA 92122
619/546-5001
(Travel agency.)

Pleasant Travel Service, Inc.
2404 Townsgate Rd.
Westlake Village, CA 91361
818/991-3390
(Travel agency.)

Princess Cruises
10100 Santa Monica Blvd.
Los Angeles, CA 90067
310/553-1770
(Cruise line.)

Rosenbluth Travel Agency, Inc.
2401 Walnut St.
Philadelphia, PA 19103
215/977-4000
(Travel agency.)

Royal Caribbean Cruises, Ltd.
1050 Caribbean Way
Miami, FL 33132
305/539-6000

SATO Travel (Scheduled Airline Traffic Offices) Inc.
1005 N. Glebe Rd.
Arlington, VA 22203
703/358-1200
(Travel agency.)

Travel, Inc.
3680 N. Peachtree Rd.
Atlanta, GA 30341
770/455-6575
(Travel agency.)

US Travel Systems, Inc.
1401 Rockville Pike, Suite 300
Rockville, MD 20852
301/251-9450
(Travel agency.)

Vista Tours
1923 N. Carson St.,
Suite 105

Carson City, NV 89710
800/647-0800
(Tour operator.)

WHERE TO GO FOR MORE INFORMATION

TRAVEL INDUSTRY ASSOCIATIONS

American Society of Travel Agents
1101 King St.
Alexandria, VA 22314
703/739-2782

Association of Retail Travel Agents
845 Sir Thomas Ct.
Harrisburg, PA 17109
717/545-9613
800/969-6069

Association of Travel Marketing Executives
257 Park Ave. South

New York, NY 10010
212/598-2472

Institute of Certified Travel Agents
148 Linden St.
P.O. Box 812059
Wellesley, MA 02181
617/237-0280

International Association of Tour Managers
64 Charnes Dr.
East Haven, CT 06513
203/466-0425

TRAVEL INDUSTRY DIRECTORIES

World Travel Directory
Travel Weekly
Reed Travel Group

500 Plz. Dr.
Secaucus, NJ 07096
201/902-2000

TRAVEL INDUSTRY PERIODICALS

Travel Agent
801 Second Ave.
New York, NY 10017
212/370-5050
(Weekly magazine aimed at travel agents and others in the travel industry, including tour operators, executives, etc.)

Travel Trade
15 W. 44th St.
New York, NY 10036
212/730-6600
(Weekly periodical for travel agency personnel—salespeople, executives, reservation clerks—as well as tour operators, resort personnel, etc.)

Travel Weekly
500 Plz. Dr.
Secaucus, NJ 07096
201/902-2000
(Weekly tabloid covering all aspects of the travel industry, aimed at agency personnel, sales and promotion staffers, tour operators, hospitality industry personnel, etc.)

Travelage MidAmerica
Official Airlines Guide, Inc.
320 North Michigan Ave., Suite 601
Chicago, IL 60601
708/574-6871
(For travel agents in the mid-
American states, Ontario, and
Manitoba.)

Travelage West
Reed Travel Group
49 Stevenson, No. 460
San Francisco, CA 94105-2909
415/905-1155
800/446-6551

UTILITIES

INDUSTRY OUTLOOK: Slow growth, but many changes in this mature industry.

Partial and likely full deregulation is coming—state by state—with a changing landscape, as utilities shed transmission properties and become vendors of purchased power, as they invade other industries or explore foreign markets, as mergers continue apace, and as they adopt new operating/selling methods.

With a slow-growth customer base, from a slow-growing consumer market and a low-power-demand service industry base supplanting manufacturing, power needs will continue to decline. In response, watch the industry move into foreign markets, explore nonelectric markets, and merge with competitors and with firms in other industries. California will start the deregulation process in 1998, permitting electric utility customers to choose their own suppliers, with Pennsylvania and Massachusetts enacting similar legislation, and others considering moves. Watch as the old rules become obsolete, as consumers begin to shop for electricity the way they now shop for long distance phone service.

Utilities companies will be locked in a competitive battle with independents—both over power-plant construction and over customers. One possible development—an increase in agreements between utilities and independents. The utilities companies are locked into another vise: major customers are fighting for and getting deep discounts, while increasing deregulation is allowing customers to shop for electricity service from other areas and from independents. As a result, the utilities are scrambling to cut costs and improve operations and service. The ultimate decision may be to shed operations, electing to purchase power from others and to market/merchandise electricity to different market segments, with different needs, at rate differences. Instead of being considered as rate payers, purchasers will now become customers and offered service and value. Affected? Jobs—fewer jobs in operations but strong need for professionals with merchandising experience. In addition, it's causing increased merger activity. This activity should continue for the balance of this decade, as a result of both competition and a rise in construction costs needed to comply with Federal clean air and other regulations. Another activity to keep an eye out for: electric utilities getting into fiber-optics networks, and so competing on new territory with cable and telephone companies.

A LOOK BACK

▶ **The most important factor in the utilities industry in the past—and the future: partial deregulation.**

Utilities had always existed in a regulated environment in which regulating authorities balanced the risks of energy production and distribution against the rewards and then established consumer and commercial rate structures based on their estimates of a fair return. In other words, utilities were classic, regulated monopolies.

Then, in the late '70s, came the changes. Some of the impetus came from the push to build and finance nuclear power plants. Building these huge and costly plants resulted in large losses for the utilities industry. This forced the industry and its state and federal regulators to reexamine the traditional operating environment. One conclusion: In some situations it would be necessary for power utilities to go beyond the regulatory systems and into the marketplace to obtain financing.

The Public Utilities Regulatory Act of 1978 opened another wedge in the regulated marketplace by allowing the creation of small power-production and co-generation plants (which produce electricity from the steam released by factories and plants). The result? The beginning of competitive pressures in the industry—a trend that is continuing to affect the industry. In 1995 California set the stage for a new phase in the deregulation process, establishing guidelines to allow some customers to choose their electricity suppliers starting in 1998. Several New England and Midwestern states, seeing the inevitability of competition in the heavily regulated electric industry, have similar proposals. Industry leaders are developing and publicizing their own deregulation plans. The issue is no longer will there be regulation, but when and under what conditions.

WHAT'S NEXT

▶ **A continuing trend: an increasing number of non-utility generators and a rise in "retail wheeling."**

Independently owned generators will continue to play an increasingly important role, particularly where new capacity is concerned. One energy consultant predicts that independents will add more than six to seven thousand megawatts each year. Estimates are that by the year 2000, the amount of power produced by independents will double—from about 6% of the total power used to 12%.

The key reason for the continuing inroads being made by independents is low rates. Independents can afford to offer lower rates than the utilities because their overhead is lower and, perhaps the biggest advantage of all, because they are free of many of the regulations under which the large utilities must operate and so can raise capital more easily. As such, independents pass along the savings to their customers, usually industrial users. As for "retail wheeling," this is the practice of allowing utilities or independents to sell power directly to big customers—and, by so doing, cutting in on the business of other utilities which used to automatically service these customers. The result? Head-to-head competition, which is usually won by the utility or independent offering the lowest rates. This will force the large utilities into cost-cutting—so they can afford to offer lower rates. As a result, jobs may be cut, mergers may become necessary, and the once-stable industry will be facing numerous changes.

▶ **Given the new look of the utilities marketplace, watch for aggressive utility marketing.**

It's one of the best ways to compete in an increasingly competitive market.

Some utilities are experimenting with flexible or hourly pricing to attract additional volume; some offer development rates for new customers. As one industry leader stated, "We're marketing electricity like crazy."

It's happening with gas utilities as well. In many cases, independent gas companies use the utilities' pipelines to deliver gas to customers, but the bill is "unbundled"—customers see the cost of gas separate from the cost of the delivery. Often the cost is lower than that which the utilities have charged—so the utilities are forced into a competitive posture and cut prices as well, to try to win back or retain their customers. This has already been happening with business utility customers and, in some states, should soon be the case for homeowners as well. With homeowners able to pick their gas or electric supplier much like they are now able to choose a long-distance telephone carrier, the outlook is for extreme competition—complete with price-cutting and major marketing pushes.

Another marketing strategy of the utilities is the smorgasbord approach, offering customers one monthly bill for energy, long-distance phone service, Internet service, and satellite TV. Customers can choose one or a combination of services as offered by Colorado-based KN Energy. Texas-based Enron Corp. is spending millions to build a brand-name image to sell a variety of energy services to individual homeowners as well as to big energy customers, including multistate manufacturers. In fact, according to persistent but unconfirmed rumors, such major brand names as AT&T, General Electric, American Express, and CitiCorp may be considering entry into the huge, deregulated energy business, raising the spector of even more serious competition from these experienced, hard-hitting, marketing-oriented giants.

▶ **More large utilities will follow the "if you can't beat 'em, join 'em" strategy with independents.**

In other words, expect to see a growing number of large utilities entering into agreements with the independent power companies.

With the need for power up, and the cost of building plants to add capacity extremely high, more utilities companies will be buying power from independents, then selling that power to their own customers. These contracts will become more common as customer usage continues on its upward path. Along similar lines, watch for more utilities to buy smaller independents.

▶ **With competition increasing in the U.S., expect utilities companies to set their sights overseas.**

This is a way of grabbing higher returns as the U.S. utilities market becomes increasingly pinched by price-conscious consumers. Already 29 companies have been in the market for foreign utilities and some have closed deals. One example: Central & South West, the Dallas-based utility, agreed to purchase United Kingdom utility Seeboard Plc. Expect this sort of activity to increase as the domestic utilities field remains highly competitive.

▶ **Environmental concerns and legislation will continue affecting the industry.**

Electric utilities companies are the nation's largest consumer of coal—which, in turn, produces sulfur oxide and other hazardous air pollutants. According to the Clean Air Act Amendments, utilities plants must control their sulfur emissions. Some utilities companies can comply by burning low-sulfur coal. Others face a choice: either to install "scrubbers" (flue gas desulfurizers) or to retrofit their plants to run on natural gas. Either way, the cost is high.

▶ **Over the long term, there should be a rise in natural gas usage.**

Federal regulations passed in April 1992 changed the way in which gas pipelines sold natural gas to utilities. In brief, instead of being forced to pay pipelines one flat fee that included shipping and storage as well as the cost of the gas, utilities can now bargain directly with the producers and marketers of the natural gas. The result? Lower prices and less seasonal fluctuation. This, combined with the fact that natural gas is a clean fuel in line with the Clean Air Act Amendments, should lead to greater usage of natural gas by utilities.

▶ **There will be continued research into alternative forms of energy and use of renewable energy.**

Attempts to find alternative forms of energy are increasing as environmental pressures and legislation keep nuclear power from expanding in use and the use of high-sulfur coal is being phased out. While natural gas use may increase, many companies will still be looking into other energy sources. For example, there has recently been research into utility-scale applications of photovoltaic cells, which create solar-generated electricity. While the price of these is still too high for utility use, further research should result in a price drop. Watch for more developments along these and other lines.

EMPLOYMENT OUTLOOK: In spite of the layoffs, active hiring persists.

The bad news: The government projects that the total number of people employed in the power industries will decline in the years to 2005. Key reasons: some overcapacity resulting from overbuilding in the past means that new plant construction will be moderate—this means fewer new plants hiring employees. Also, the increased computerization and efficiency of systems will result in less need for more personnel at new and existing plants. In fact, as utilities streamline operations, they tend to be laying off more people than they hire. Finally, deregulation, causing consolidation in this once-sleepy industry, is resulting in layoffs of overlapping positions, with possibly up to 18% jobs cut.

More importantly, work in the utility industry is relatively high-paid—and so turnover is low: few people leave the industry to work elsewhere. This means high competition for the few job openings there are. The same relative decline is expected for gas and petroleum plant and systems operators.

However, *Electric Light and Power* magazine reported recently that the average age of workers in the utility industry is high and increasing—this means that over the long term, more replacement positions should open up.

And now the good news: Although the industry has certainly consolidated and jobs were cut, there are still a number of job opportunities out there—especially on the executive level. One key reason: As the utilities industry changes, there's a growing need for a different type of executive than in the past. So utilities companies have been actively seeking managers in new areas. Where in the past, utilities companies hired only from within the industry, they've recently been looking for people with experience in other fields, people who can help the companies manage through these turbulent, entrepreneurial times. Key qualities: people with backgrounds in competitive fields or related industries, such as telecommunications, natural gas or oil, metals and mining.

One especially hot area: marketing. As competition among the utilities heats up, the job outlook for marketing managers is looking up, as utilities search for ways to sell power to new customers.

JOBS SPOTLIGHT

MANAGEMENT INFORMATION SYSTEMS (MIS) PERSONNEL: The utilities industry is one of the best-paying fields for MIS staffers. Several recent studies show that utilities pay information-systems professionals the most of seven industries. And as utilities continue to emphasize cost control and automation, the need will remain constant. But there's a downside: career advancement has been slowing. With automation, MIS positions have been cut, and entry-level openings are tighter. The general outcome: MIS people are needed, they're well paid, and their positions in utilities companies are secure—but competitive.

TOP ELECTRIC AND WATER UTILITY COMPANIES

Allegheny Power System
12 E. 49th St
New York, NY 10017-1028
212/752-2121

American Electric Power Inc.
1 Riverside Plz.
Columbus, OH 43215-2373
614/223-1000

Baltimore Gas & Electric
Charles Ctr.
P.O. Box 1475
Baltimore, MD 21203-1475
410/234-5000

Boston Edison
800 Boylston St.
Boston, MA 02199-2599
617/424-2000

CMS Energy Corp.
330 Towncenter Dr.
Dearborn, MI 48126
313/436-9200

Carolina Power & Light
411 Fayetteville St.
Box 1551
Raleigh, NC 27602-1551
919/546-6111

Centerior Energy
6200 Oak Tree Blvd.
Cleveland, OH 44131
216/447-3100

Central & South West
1616 Woodall Rodgers Fwy.
Dallas, TX 75202
214/777-1000

CINergy Corp.
139 E. 4th St.
Cincinnati, OH 45202
513/381-2000

Commonwealth Edison Co.
10 S. Dearborn
Chicago, IL 60603
312/394-4321

Consolidated Edison Co. of New York
4 Irving Pl.
New York, NY 10003
212/460-4600

DPL
1065 Woodman Dr.
Box 8825
Dayton, OH 45432
513/224-6000

DQE Inc.
1 Oxford Ctr.
301 Grant St.
Pittsburgh, PA 15219
412/393-6000

Delmarva Power & Light Co.
800 King St.
Wilmington, DE 19801
302/429-3376

Detroit Edison Co.
2000 Second Ave.
Detroit, MI 48226
313/237-8000

Dominion Resources Inc.
P.O. Box 26532
Richmond, VA 23261
804/775-5700

Duke Power Co.
422 S. Church St.
Charlotte, NC 28242
704/373-4011

Entergy Group
639 Loyola Ave.
New Orleans, LA 70113
504/529-5262

FPL Group Inc.
700 Universe Blvd.
Juno Beach, FL 33408
407/694-6300

Florida Progress Corp.
1 Progress Plz.
St. Petersburg, FL 33701
813/824-6400

General Public Utilities
100 Interpace Pkwy.

Parsippany, NJ 07054-1149
201/263-6500

Gulf States Utilities Co.
350 Pine St.
Beaumont, TX 77701
409/838-6631

Hawaiian Electric Industries
900 Richards St.
Honolulu, HI 96813
808/543-5662

Houston Industries Inc.
440 Post Oak Pky.
Houston, TX 77027
713/629-3000

Idaho Power Co.
1220 W. Idaho St.
Box 70
Boise, ID 83702
208/383-2200

Illinova
500 S. 27th St.
Decatur, IL 62521
217/424-6600

Ipalco Enterprises Inc.
25 Monument Ctr.
Indianapolis, IN 46204
317/261-8261

Kentucky Utilities Co.
1 Quality St.
Lexington, KY 40507
606/255-2100

Louisville Gas & Electric Co.
200 Main St.
Louisville, KY 40202
502/627-2000

Long Island Lighting Co.
175 E. Old Country Rd.
Hicksville, NY 11801
516/755-6000

Montana Power
40 E. Broadway
Butte, MT 59707
406/723-5421

New England Electric System
25 Research Dr.

Westborough, MA 01582-0001
508/366-9011

New York State Electric & Gas
P.O. Box 3287
Ithaca, NY 14852-3287
607/347-4131

Niagara Mohawk Power
300 Erie Blvd. W.
Syracuse, NY 13202
315/474-1511

Nipsco Industries
5265 Hohman Ave.
Hammond, IN 46320
219/853-5200

Northeast Utilities
400 Sheldon St.
Hartford, CT 06106
203/665-5000

Northern States Power Co.
414 Nicollet Mall
Minneapolis, MN 55401
612/330-5500

Ohio Edison Co.
1919 W. Market St.
Akron, OH 44313
330/384-5151

Oklahoma Gas & Electric Co.
101 N. Robinson Ave.
Oklahoma City, OK 73101
405/553-3000

PECO Energy Co.
2301 Market St.
Philadelphia, PA 19103
215/841-4000

PSI Resources Energy, Inc.
1000 E. Main St.
Plainfield, IN 46168
317/839-9611

Pacific Gas & Electric Co.
525 Market St.
San Francisco, CA 94105
415/973-7000

Pacificorp
700 NE Multnomah St.
Portland, OR 97232
503/731-2000

Pennsylvania Power & Light
2 N. Ninth St.
Allentown, PA 18101
610/774-5151

Pinnacle West Capital Corp.
400 E. Van Buren St.
Phoenix, AZ 85004
602/379-2500

Portland General Corp.
121 SW Salmon St.
Portland, OR 97204
503/228-6322

Potomac Electric Power Co.
1900 Pennsylvania Ave., NW
Washington, DC 20068
202/872-2000

Public Service Co. of Colorado
1225 17 St.
Denver, CO 80202
303/571-7511

Public Service Enterprise Group
P.O. Box 570
80 Park Plz.
Newark, NJ 07102
201/430-7000

Puget Sound Power & Light Co.
411 108th Ave., NE
Bellevue, WA 98004
206/454-6363

SCEcorp
2244 Walnut Grove Ave.
Rosemead, CA 91770
818/302-2222

San Diego Gas & Electric Co.
101 Ash St.
San Diego, CA 92101
619/239-7500

Scana Corp.
1426 Main St.
Columbia, SC 29201
803/748-3000

Southern Co.
64 Perimeter Ctr. E.
Atlanta, GA 30346
404/393-0650

TECO Energy Inc.
P.O. Box 111
702 N. Franklin St.
Tampa, FL 33601
813/228-4111

Texas Utilities Co.
1601 Bryan St.
Dallas, TX 75201-3411
214/812-5600

Unicom
1 First National Plz.
Chicago, IL 60690
312/394-7399

Union Electric Co.
1901 Chouteau Ave.
St. Louis, MO 63103
314/621-3222

Western Resources, Inc.
818 S. Kansas Ave.
Topeka, KS 66612
913/575-6300

Wisconsin Energy Corp.
231 W. Michigan St.
Milwaukee, WI 53219
414/221-2345

TOP GAS & TRANSMISSION UTILITY COMPANIES

Arkla, Inc.
525 Milam St.
Shreveport, LA 71101
318/894-9165

Atlanta Gas Light Co.
303 Peachtree St., NE
Atlanta, GA 30308
404/584-4000

Brooklyn Union Gas
1 Metrotec Center
Brooklyn, NY 11201
718/403-2000

The Coastal Corp.
9 E. Greenway Plz.
Houston, TX 77046-0995
713/877-1400

The Columbia Gas System Inc.
20 Montchanin Rd.
Wilmington, DE 19807
302/429-5000

Consolidated Natural Gas Co.
625 Liberty Ave.
Pittsburgh, PA 15222-3199
412/227-1000

Enron Corp.
1400 Smith St.
Houston, TX 77002
713/853-6161

Enserch Corp.
300 S. St. Paul St.

Dallas, TX 75201
214/651-8700

MCN Corp.
500 Griswold St.
Detroit, MI 48226
313/256-5500

Nicor Inc.
1844 W. Ferry Rd.
Naperville, IL 60563
708/305-9500

Pacific Enterprises
633 W. Fifth St.
Los Angeles, CA 90071
213/895-5000

Panhandle Eastern Corp.
5400 Westheimer Ct.
Houston, TX 77056
713/627-5400

Peoples Energy Corp.
130 E. Randolph Dr.
Chicago, IL 60601
312/431-4000

Sonat Inc.
1990 5 Ave., N.
Birmingham, AL 35203
205/325-3800

Southwest Gas Corp.
5241 Spring Mountain Rd.
Las Vegas, NV 89150
702/876-7011

Transco Energy Co.
2800 Post Oak Blvd.
Houston, TX 77056
713/439-2000

The Williams Cos.
1 Williams Ctr.
Tulsa, OK 74172
918/588-3900

WHERE TO GO FOR MORE INFORMATION

UTILITIES INDUSTRY ASSOCIATIONS

American Public Gas Association
P.O. Box 11094D
Lee Hwy., Suite 102
Fairfax, VA 22030
703/352-3890

**American Public Power
Association**
2301 M St., NW

Washington, DC 20037
202/467-2970

**National Utility Contractors
Association**
4301 N. Fairfax Dr.
Suite 360
Arlington, VA 22203-1627
703/358-9300

UTILITIES INDUSTRY DIRECTORIES

*American Public Gas Association
Directory*
American Public Gas Association
P.O. Box 11094D
Lee Hwy., Suite 102
Fairfax, VA 22030
703/352-3890

Directory of Gas Utility Companies
P.O. Box 50350
Tulsa, OK 74150-0350
918/582-2000

*Electrical World Directory of
Electric Utilities*
UTI–McGraw-Hill
1200 G St., Ste. 250
Washington, DC 20005
202/942-8788

Moody's Public Utility Manual
Moody's Investors Service, Inc.
99 Church St.
New York, NY 10007
212/553-0300

UTILITIES INDUSTRY PERIODICALS

Electrical World
11 W. 19th St.
New York, NY 10011
212/337-4069
(Monthly magazine for electric
utility executives and managers,
engineers, and other related areas,
including students.)

Public Power
2301 M. St., NW

Washington, DC 20037
202/467-2900
(Bimonthly published by the
American Public Power Association.)

Transmission & Distribution
707 Westchester Ave., Suite 101
White Plains, NY 10604
610/566-7080
(Monthly magazine for electric
utilities executives, engineers, etc.)

SECTION 3

REGIONAL ROUNDUP 1998

NATIONAL OUTLOOK

MAJOR TRENDS

▶ **Over the long term, more jobs will continue to shift from goods-producing areas, such as manufacturing, to service industries.**

This is a trend that has been affecting the U.S. employment outlook for the past few years—and it's one that will continue. As the economy shifts from being manufacturing- to service-driven, so too will employment opportunities. For example, in three of the goods-producing industries—manufacturing, agriculture, and mining—employment has changed very little in over twenty years. Yet service industries have been job-creation engines. For example, according to the federal government's Bureau of Labor Statistics, over the 1994—2005 employment period, total U.S. employment is projected to increase by 17.7 million—or 14%. Of this total, the services and retail trade industries will account for 16.2 million jobs.

More specifically, expect to see strength in the following industry areas over the long term:

1. *Health services:* This area was hot for the early part of the '90s and, in spite of shakeouts caused by industry streamlining and changes, it still looks like it's coming on strong. The government estimates that about one-fifth of all the job growth from 1994 to 2005 will be in this field. Especially hot? Home health care and related areas. But it's not all smooth sailing. Certain segments—such as hospitals—will probably be weaker than others, as the health care industry shifts gears. The bottom line: Health services will offer strong employment opportunities, but only in specific areas.
2. *Retail trade:* Another of the service industries that is predicted to grow over the next decade. Restaurants in particular should be strong. The federal government predicts employment growth of almost 2.2 million in this area, making it the strongest segment of retail trade. One note: these jobs won't only be at the lowest level, as many had feared. Instead, there should also be a growth at the managerial level. But a word of caution: This area is particularly sensitive to the ups and downs of the economy. As such, expect periodic dips in employment opportunity during economic rough times.
3. *Business services:* This industry, which includes temporary help, computer, and information services, is another area that should grow over the long term and provide numerous employment opportunities. But it's also another industry that is very economy-sensitive, so expect ups and downs.

On the plus side: In economic downturns, the temp industry tends to do quite well, as downsizing corporations seek temporary rather than permanent help. All in all, business services in general, should prove a strong sector for the future.

▶ **Across the board, from lower levels to upper levels, training is often the key to employment.**

Training has always been important, but it's becoming increasingly so—especially as technology continues to change the different industries.

Technical ability, computer skills, and higher education are all becoming virtual necessities for landing a job in the late 1990s.

With increasing automation and heavier use of technological breakthroughs, technical skills are especially in demand. According to the Bureau of Labor Statistics, technicians will represent over one-fifth of the total workforce over the next decade. Even while manufacturing jobs shrink in comparison to service jobs, there should continue to be numerous opportunities for skilled technicians.

And on the nontechnical side, specialization is definitely a plus. According to numerous surveys, college students with liberal arts degrees are often at a disadvantage compared to those with specialized degrees, such as in business administration, accounting, engineering, computer science, and the like. Of course, job opportunities will still exist for liberal arts students—often, however, even these will require some technical ability, such as computers. In fact, no matter what the field, because of the rising use of technology in nontechnical fields, computer skills are becoming more of a plus than ever in terms of hirability.

The bottom line: In general, more companies will be seeking job candidates with technical or specialized skills and concentrations.

▶ **The federal government has pinpointed several jobs that should see the highest growth over the next decade.**

These jobs may see short-term lags; however, their long-term outlook seems bright. These jobs are:

1. Teachers
2. Nurses
3. Executives
4. Systems analysts
5. Truck drivers
6. Skilled secretarial and administrative assistant positions
7. Social workers
8. Lawyers
9. Financial managers
10. Computer engineers
11. Accountants
12. Physicians

13. Marketing managers
14. Physical therapists
15. Product designers
16. Paralegals
17. Medical records technicians
18 Occupational therapy assistants
    and aides
19. Personal, home-care, and
    home-health aides

▶ **The above specific jobs aside, expect to see the fastest growing jobs in two areas: health services and computer technology.**

These are the two industry areas that have been growing—and, as such, should see strong employment opportunities over the long term. Health services looks strong in the long run due to a number of factors, key among them: the aging of the country. As Americans grow older, a higher percentage of the population will require health care services, especially home care. In addition, the changing health care services industry is creating a higher need for certain personnel.

As for the computer industry, this area has been a hot spot for a number of years. Software engineers and systems analysts are two of the fastest growing job segments—and with the rise in interactive media and the Internet, new jobs should be created over the long term.

▶ **Certain metropolitan areas have been seeing particularly strong job growth.**

The following metropolitan areas saw the fastest job growth in the 1991–1996 period, according to the latest figures compiled and analyzed by the U.S. Bureau of Labor Statistics and Regional Financial Association.

Top 10 Metro Areas by Job Gain 1991–1996

METRO AREA	5-YEAR JOB GAIN (IN THOUSANDS)	ANNUAL GROWTH RATE (%)
Atlanta, GA	371.3	4.5
Chicago, IL	296.4	1.6
Phoenix, AZ	243.1	4.4
Dallas, TX	223.0	3.0
Detroit, MI	197.5	2.0
Minneapolis/St. Paul, MN	178.4	2.5
Boston, MA	174.0	2.5
Houston, TX	162.3	1.9
Denver, CO	160.5	3.5
Las Vegas, NV	157.5	6.6

The next list points out the areas with the highest job *rate* gain:

Top 10 Metro Areas by Growth Rate 1991–1996

METRO AREA	5-YEAR JOB GAIN (IN THOUSANDS)	ANNUAL GROWTH RATE (%)
Las Vegas, NV	157.5	6.6
Austin, TX	139.3	6.2
Boise, ID	46.9	6.0
Fayetteville, AK	31.6	5.6
Provo, UT	28.9	5.3
Killeen-Temple, TX	21.8	5.3
Salt Lake City, UT	134.0	4.8
Albuquerque, NM	68.9	4.7
Boulder, CO	30.2	4.6
Atlanta, GA	371.3	4.5

Can any conclusions be drawn from this data? One general trend much talked about in the past—of jobs and population moving down south—seems to be borne out at first glance. But the West (outside California) did well too; Rocky Mountain states were booming. In fact, in 1996–97, this region led the country in the number of start-up businesses—which fueled a 32% increase in jobs. But also booming was Minneapolis/St. Paul, with an unemployment rate last year around 3%, and other Central states such as Nebraska, which boasted the lowest unemployment rate in the country—2.4%. In general, then, fastest job growth took place in the West and the Sunbelt, with lowest unemployment rates in the Midwest. But the good news isn't confined to these areas.

Even the two weakest regions in terms of job outlooks—the Northeast and California—finally saw strong economic improvements in the past year, although these areas as a whole saw no net job gains from 1991 to 1996. But over the long term, these still economically powerful areas are expected to further improve, particularly because of their relative strength in the areas of the economy that are still growing—business services, high technology, and media/communications.

In fact, Los Angeles, which saw the largest *decline* in jobs during the early 1990s, was a major growth city in 1997 in at least one vital indicator—the number of new corporate expansions in the downtown. Nevertheless, in terms of job growth, the two largest cities in America, LA and New York, will probably still lag behind other areas.

Most of the job growth throughout the United States was in service industries, and the one conclusion that can be derived from most of the above data is simple: Areas that embrace the new ways of doing business will continue to thrive, despite the periodic ups and downs of business cycles.

GENERAL BUSINESS PERIODICALS

Barron's	*BusinessWeek*
Dow Jones & Co.	McGraw-Hill, Inc.
200 Liberty St.	1221 Ave. of the Americas
New York, NY 10281	New York, NY 10020
212/416-2700; 800/544-0422	212/512-2000

Forbes
Forbes, Inc.
60 Fifth Ave.
New York, NY 10011
212/620--2200

Fortune
The Time, Inc., Magazine Company
Time & Life Bldg.
New York, NY 10020-1393
212/522-1212
800/541-1000

INC.
38 Commercial Wharf
Boston, MA 02110
617/248-8000
(Invaluable for targeting the fast-moving corporations that tend to do the most hiring.)

InternAmerica
Ford Careerworks
800/456-7335
(Bimonthly newsletter with many internships listed for liberal arts, technical, and vocational grads.)

Nation's Business
U.S. Chamber of Commerce
1615 H St., NW
Washington, DC 20062
202/463-5650

National Business Employment Weekly
P.O. Box 30
Princeton, NJ 08543-0300
800/323-6239
(Contains *Wall Street Journal* help-wanted ads, articles on job-hunting techniques, careers, etc.; special weekly sections, including "Engineering Weekly," "Computer," and "High Technology.")

Wall Street Journal
200 Liberty St.
New York, NY 10281
212/416-2000
800/568-7625

GENERAL BUSINESS DIRECTORIES

(Most of the following directories are extremely comprehensive, extremely useful—and extremely expensive. In most cases you may be better off using them at your local library.)

AMA's Executive Employment Guide
American Management Association
135 W. 50th St.
New York, NY 10020
212/536-8100
(Free to AMA members; lists search firms, job registries, etc.)

America's Corporate Families and International Affiliates
Dun's Marketing Services
3 Sylvan Way
Parsippany, NJ 07054
1-800-526-0651
201/455-0900

Business Organizations, Agencies, and Publications Directory
Gale Research, Inc.
835 Penobscot Bldg.
Detroit, MI 48226
800/877-4253

Business Publication Rates & Data
Standard Rate & Data Service, Inc.
1700 Higgins Rd.
Des Plaines, IL 60018
708/375-5000
(Lists business, trade, and technical publications in the United States and abroad.)

Directories in Print
Gale Research, Inc.
835 Penobscot Bldg.
Detroit, MI 48226
800/877-4253

Directory of Corporate Affiliations
Reed Reference Publishing
P.O. Box 31
New Providence, NJ 07974
800/323-6772

Dun & Bradstreet Million-Dollar Directory
Dun's Marketing Services
3 Sylvan Way
Parsippany, NJ 07054
800/526-0651
(Expensive, but extensive listings of leading U.S. corporations.)

Dun & Bradstreet Reference Book of Corporate Managements
Dun's Marketing Services
3 Sylvan Way
Parsippany, NJ 07054
800/526-0651

Dun's Business Rankings
Dun's Marketing Services
3 Sylvan Way
Parsippany, NJ 07054
800/526-0651

Dun's Career Guide
Dun's Marketing Services
3 Sylvan Way
Parsippany, NJ 07054
800/526-0651
(Lists employers, hiring areas, contact names, etc.)

Dun's Directory of Service Companies
Dun's Marketing Services
3 Sylvan Way
Parsippany, NJ 07054
800/526-0651
(Covers range of service industries, including management consulting, executive search services, public relations, engineering and architecture, accounting, auditing and bookkeeping, health services, legal and social services, research, hospitality, motion pictures, amusement, and recreational services.)

Dun's Regional Business Directory
Dun's Marketing Services
3 Sylvan Way
Parsippany, NJ 07054
800/526-0651
(Different volumes covering different regions of the United States.)

Encyclopedia of Associations
Gale Research, Inc.
835 Penobscot Bldg.
Detroit, MI 48226
800/877-4253

International Directory of Corporate Affiliations
Reed Reference Publishing
P.O. Box 31
New Providence, NJ 07974
800/323-6772

Job Hunter's Sourcebook
Gale Research, Inc.
835 Penobscot Bldg.
Detroit, MI 48226
800/877-4253

Moody's Industrial Manual
Moody's Investors Service, Inc.
99 Church St.
New York, NY 10007
212/533-0300
(Lists about three thousand publicly traded U.S. and international companies. Moody's also puts out manuals for bank and finance, public utilities, transportation, and municipals.)

Moody's Industry Review
Moody's Investors Service, Inc.
99 Church St.
New York, NY 10007
212/533-0300
(Rankings of about four thousand major firms.)

National Trade and Professional Associations
Columbia Books
1212 New York Ave., NW,
Suite 330
Washington, DC 20005
202/898-0662
(An inexpensive—$80 in 1996—
directory listing thousands of
associations.)

Peterson's Job Opportunities in Business
P.O. Box 2123
Princeton, NJ 08543-2123
609/243-9111
800/338-3282
(Inexpensive; lists hundreds of
corporations and organizations that
are hiring; includes detailed
information.)

Standard & Poor's Register of Corporations, Directors, and Executives
Standard & Poor's Corp.
25 Broadway
New York, NY 10004
212/208-8000
(Three volumes covering over fifty
thousand firms, brief financials,
names, addresses of major
executives, directors, new firms.)

Thomas Register
Thomas Publishing Co.
5 Pennsylvania Plaza
New York, NY 10001
212/695-0500
(Twelve-volume directory of U.S.
manufacturers.)

DATABASES

Career Network
Available through college placement
office.
(Online service that links college
placement offices with employees
nationwide. If it's been years since
you graduated, or if you never have,
check your nearest college or past
college attended; chances are you can
use the network, possibly for a fee.
Network lists jobs nationally.)

JobTRAK
310/474-3377
(The easiest way to use this database

is to go to a subscribing college
recruitment center. Corporations send
JobTRAK listings, and in turn sends
them to colleges of the corporation's
choice. Concentrated on the West
Coast, but expanding.)

Career Expo
513/721-3030
(Open-house recruitment; call for
locations and details.)

Job Bank USA
800/296-1USA
(Resume bank covering all business
levels.)

NORTHEAST AND MIDDLE ATLANTIC REGION

OUTLOOK: Diversifying—which should result in improvement over the long term.

The problems of the past—defense cutbacks, real estate woes, bank consolidations, telecommunications layoffs—have been offset by new regional strength as the Northeast diversifies. This region was hit harder by the recessions of the past, and even in the good economic climate prevailing in recent years, has taken longer to come out of the doldrums. But, for most of the area, good times returned in 1996 and 1997, should continue in the future although short-term bumps may offset good news somewhat, and net job gains in some areas may still be delayed.

Bright spots: high-tech businesses, mutual find operations, publishing, and, of course, finance in New York and outlying areas.

WHAT'S NEXT

▶ The New York metropolitan area: Getting better.

New York, which saw no net job gains in the period from 1991–1996, saw strong improvements economically in the past few years; in 1996, 44,500 *new* jobs were created. And despite the competitive job environment, it has many pluses for the motivated job seeker, since it is both a national and international business capital. The bottom line: Despite the possibilities of a renewed Wall Street downturn, New York will see long-term growth.

Key points: Point #1: New York remains the center of the financial services industry and, as such, remains a major employer. The problem, of course, is Wall Street's sensitivity to the national economy. When the economy falters, Wall Street cuts back—which, in turn, impacts on the rest of the New York area economy. However, Wall Street rebounds when the economy does—which spills over into the regional economy at large, as service industries, such as restaurants and retail, usually pick up in step with the financial industry.

Point #2: **An important growth area in New York**: Internet-related high-tech industries. Since 1996, industries in interactive software and on-line computer services have been booming—making New York the center of activity in this hot area. But be warned—this is also a very volatile area, with a high number of business failures as well. More specifically, the New York metro region has seen 4,000 new companies spring up, creating over 70,000 jobs. In New York City alone, 1,350 businesses have been created, with over 18,000 full-time staffers. Indicative of how important this industry is becoming: According to Coopers & Lybrand, television broadcasting employs 17,000 full-time employees in NYC; book publishing, another New York-based industry, 14,000. The good news: Employment is expected to double or triple over the next three years.

Point #3: Retailing has been heating up in New York City, in particular, as major retailers move into large spaces throughout the city. In addition, the revamp of the Times Square area, backed heavily by Disney, should result in an influx of merchants—and tourists . . . and jobs.

Point #4: The strong presence of the communications industry in this region also points to long-term opportunity. In the recent past the metropolitan area could well have been characterized as AT&T/IBM country. But now, with spin-offs, start-ups, and a high-tech talent resource pool, the area is attracting other high-tech companies. As demand for communications services rises nationwide, New York advertising and media companies similarly rise, creating employment opportunities.

A final strong point, and one of the most important, especially in the long term is the city's ties to the international community. New York still draws a large number of international real estate investors. While the rapid pace of acquisition has declined, Japanese and other foreign investors are still snapping up New York office buildings. International companies are more inclined to set up shop in New York than in lesser-known, less cosmopolitan areas. In addition, about half of the U.S. exports in service come from New York. Foreign tourists continue to flood in, and they spend about three times what American tourists do. With Europe's economy strengthening, expect an increased demand for New York's legal, consulting, and other services.

But one disturbing question remains: New York's position as an international business center depends on large U.S. businesses that have headquarters here. Will they stay in New York or will they opt for the lower taxes and better climates of the Sunbelt or other regions, as so many others have? To a great degree, the long-term health of New York rests on the answer to this question.

▶ New Jersey, Pennsylvania, Upstate New York, Long Island— mixed, as well.

New Jersey, like New York, was hard hit in recent years and is still lagging behind the rest of the country. Key problems: a sharp loss in manufacturing jobs. In addition, the once-strong pharmaceutical industry has been hurt by the rise in managed care and the erosion in profits. The result? Staff cutbacks. But over the long term, the pharmaceutical industry should remain a hiring force in the area—although some experts warn that cutbacks may continue over the short term. One trend to keep an eye on: start-up pharmaceutical companies have been hiring, even as the larger companies were laying off—in some cases, because they won contracts away from their larger competitors. These smaller companies, then, may continue to offer employment opportunities. In several other areas, New Jersey's outlook appears bright. In fact, in some cases, New York's loss has been New Jersey's gain—as financial services companies have been moving back-office operations across the Hudson into New Jersey to take advantage of lower taxes and lower costs in general. This trend should continue, and should offer increased employment opportunities. One final piece of good news: In recent months, New Jersey has been seeing a growth in small business and an increasing number of new business startups.

Pennsylvania: Upturns in both the foreign and domestic demand for steel, fabricated metals, machinery and chemicals, points to good prospects. Coming on particularly stong: Pittsburgh, with employment moving up higher than it was even before its previous pre-1990 high. All in all, the state is poised for stable growth and increasing job opportunities in the long term, especially as the national economy improves.

Upstate New York: Hopes are pinned on the newly created "Ceramics Corridor"—an area centering around Corning, NY, devoted to high-tech work in ceramics and electronics packaging, among other things. Formed through teamwork between Corning, IBM and three universities, the area is attracting attention and companies. Recently, 110 companies (including Corning, Westinghouse and Toshiba, as well as many small start-ups) have located here, bringing 31,500 jobs to the area. Also looking relatively promising: the Buffalo area, where an upsurge in manufacturing is expected to bring job gains of 3,000 to 5,000 over the next few years.

Long Island: The Long Island area is illustrative of some of the region's problems. The Northrop-Grumman merger of 1994 and the downturn of the aerospace industry resulted in the loss of 40,000 jobs, with ripple effects throughout the region. Less than 40% have been replaced, generally with low-wage service industry jobs. However, if local and regional government efforts to acquire such high-tech businesses as biotechnology, medical technology, communication, and computer software are successful, the economy may improve in the long run.

► **New England—some problem spots . . . but some bright spots as well.**

While one of the weaker regions in the nation overall, New England has a number of strengths. Among them: increasing numbers of software, communications and other high-tech companies, and growing biotechnology and environmental industries—lured by low office prices, a skilled workforce, venture capital ties, and the presence of top-notch universities.

More specifically: Vermont should benefit from tourism over the long term. A key factor: the Canadian economy. When the Canadian dollar is strong, there should be a resulting upsurge in Vermont's tourist industry. In addition, in a trend similar to that affecting western New York, several Canadian companies have moved to the state, lured by lower taxes and labor costs. *Eastern Massachusetts* is one of the region's stronger areas. Routes 128 and 495 are booming again. And, over the long term, the Boston/Lawrence/Salem/Lowell/Brockton area looks hot. It's one of the top 20 new job markets—with about 626,000 new jobs expected to be added over the next twenty years. Software employment has been particularly hot, adding about 40,000 new jobs over the past two years. Other areas that have been showing strength: banking, brokerage, and other financial services plus biotech and high-tech R & D. Repair of aging infrastructure is also creating jobs—for example, a Boston project to bury an elevated highway is bringing in 20,000 new jobs. *New Hampshire* will see growth in tourism as well. As for *Rhode Island,* efforts to shift its defense manufacturing to an R&D-oriented base may yield positive results in the long term. *Southern Maine* is feeling the positive impact of an influx of high-tech companies, while employment in *Northern Maine's* papers mills and logging facilities continues to decline. As for *Connecticut,* the defense industry decline and the resultant job losses may have bottomed out. Its insurance industry, which was hurt by troubles with real estate investments and health care reform, is restructuring. On one hand, Hartford's insurance prominence is in the past as the industry has moved to Des Moines, Minneapolis, and Tampa. However, Aetna's acquistion of US Healthcare and its new health care focus may help the area's poor employment situation. Plus the state is focusing on making itself business-friendly—by cutting corporate taxes, setting up a loan program for businesses, and establishing an agency to attract new businesses from other states and keep Connecticut companies in the state.

▶ **Washington, D.C., Maryland, and the Virginia suburbs: Long-term outlook is fairly bright.**

The area saw the negative effects of the trimmed payrolls of federal, state, and local agencies and nonprofit institutions. But with the influx of rapidly growing telecom and Internet companies, the overall prospects of the area are bright. This high-technology corridor is reported to be one of the country's top information-services job markets.

The region's economy has a high degree of stability because of the large number of government jobs. In addition, the six regional universities, and the large number of associations, lobbying organizations, and consulting groups in the area, promise further growth. Maryland's Prince George County is growing into a regional commercial center. Throughout, the large number of relatively high-paying white-collar jobs promises a strong service and retail sector in the long term. One key strength: a consistent influx of foreign tourists whose spending gives a boost to retail sales—and supports the hotel industry.

REGIONAL HOT SPOTS

PITTSBURGH, PA: Home to more than just big steel, Pittsburgh benefits from a number of large companies—including Bayer USA, Rockwell International, and Westinghouse—and a number of small, dynamic firms as well. This, plus strong cultural offerings and a pleasant life-style, make the area a good choice for the future.

SYRACUSE, NY: This was one of the few places in New York State to weather the recession with relatively little trouble. A key factor was its diversified economy. Another plus: Syracuse is well known for its excellent public school system.

BOSTON, MA: Looking particularly good for technical workers. High-tech jobs resurged here in early 1997, with very strong demand for software engineers leading the pack. Some experts predict employment growth in the double digits through 1999. And this high-tech boom is spilling over into service industries as well.

CONNECTICUT

LEADING CONNECTICUT EMPLOYERS

Aetna Life & Casualty Co.
1 Civic Center Plaza
Hartford, CT 06156-3224
203/273-0123
(Insurance: life, group, accident, and health, pensions, casualty and property.)

American Brands Inc.
1700 E. Putnam Ave.
Old Greenwich, CT 06870-0811
203/698-5000
(Tobacco.)

American Maize Products Co.
250 Harbor Dr.
Stamford, CT 06902
203/456-9000
(Corn products, tobacco.)

Ames Department Stores, Inc.
2418 Main St.
Rocky Hill, CT 06067-2598
203/257-2000
(Discount department stores.)

W. R. Berkley Corp.
P.O. Box 2518
165 Mason St.
Greenwich, CT 06830
203/629-2880
(Insurance.)

Boehringer Ingleheim Corp.
900 Ridgebury Rd.
Ridgefield, CT 06877
203/438-0311
(Pharmaceuticals.)

BTR, Inc.
333 Ludlow St.
Stamford, CT 06902
203/324-3600
(Machinery.)

Bowater, Inc.
1120 Post Rd.
Darien, CT 06820

203/656-7200
(Paper products.)

Caldor Corp.
20 Glover Ave.
Norwalk, CT 06850
203/849-2000
(Discount department stores.)

Champion International Corp.
1 Champion Plz.
Stamford, CT 06921
203/358-7000
Fax 203/358-2975
(Paper mills.)

Citizens Utilities Co.
3 High Ridge Rd.
Stamford, CT 06905
203/329-8800
(Telecommunications.)

Coca Cola Bottling Co. of New York
20 Horseneck Ln.
Greenwich, CT 06830
203/625-4000
(Beverages.)

Connecticut General Life Insurance Corp.
900 Cottage Grove Rd.
Bloomfield, CT 06002
203/726-6000
(Insurance: life, accident, and health.)

Connecticut Light & Power Co.
107 Sheldon St.
Hartford, CT 06105
203/665-5000
(Utility company.)

Connecticut Mutual Life Insurance Co.
140 Garden St.
Hartford, CT 06154
203/987-6500
(Life insurance.)

Crane Co.
100 First Stamford Pl.
Stamford, CT 06902
203/363-7300
(Industrial machinery.)

CVC International
707 Summer St.
Stamford, CT 06901
203/324-9261
(Home shopping.)

The Dexter Corporation
1 Elm St.
Windsor Locks, CT 06096
860/292-7675
(Chemicals.)

Dun & Bradstreet Corp.
187 Danbury Rd.
Wilton, CT 06897
203/834-4200
(Advertising and publishing.)

Duracell International
Berkshire Blvd.
Bethel, CT 06801
203/796-4000
(Personal products.)

Echlin Inc.
100 Double Beach Rd.
Branford, CT 06405
203/481-5751
(Automotive parts &
equipment.)

**ESPN (Entertainment & Sports
Programming Network)**
935 Middle St.
Bristol, CT 06010
203/585-2000
(Cable TV.)

First Fidelity Bank
Church & Elm Sts.
New Haven, CT 06510
203/929-5552
(Bank.)

GTE Corp
1 Stamford Forum
Stamford, CT 06901
203/965-2000

(Telephone operating;
telecommunications equipment and
services.)

**General Datacomm
Industries, Inc.**
1579 Straits Tpke.
Middlebury, CT 06762
203/574-1118
(Data communication network and
subsystems.)

General Electric Capital Corp.
260 Long Ridge Rd.
Stamford, CT 06927
203/357-4000
(Credit institution.)

General Electric Co.
3135 Easton Tpke.
Fairfield, CT 06432
203/373-2211
(Conglomerate—aircraft engines,
broadcasting, electronics, appliances,
communications, etc.)

General Re Corp.
695 E. Main St.
Stamford, CT 06901
203/328-5000
(Insurance.)

General Signal Corp.
1 High Ridge Pk.
Stamford, CT 06905
203/329-4100
(Machinery.)

Gerber Scientific, Inc.
83 Gerber Rd. W.
South Windsor, CT 06074
203/644-1551
(Computer services and
software.)

**Hamilton Standard
Company**
(subs. of United Technologies)
1 Hamilton Rd.
Windsor Locks, CT 06096
203/654-6000
(Aerospace products.)

ITT Hartford
(subs. of ITT Corp.)
Hartford Plz.
Hartford, CT 06115
203/547-5000
(Insurance.)

Hartford Life Insurance Co., Inc.
Hartford Plz.
Hartford, CT 06115
203/547-5000
(Insurance.)

Hubbell Incorporated
584 Derby-Milford Rd.
Orange, CT 06477
203/799-4100
(Electrical wiring devices, etc.)

Kaman Corp.
1332 Blue Hills Ave.
Bloomfield, CT 06002
203/242-4461
(Aircraft parts, bearings, drive shafts.)

Loctite Corp.
Ten Columbus Blvd.
Hartford, CT 06106
203/520-5000
(Chemicals.)

Norden Systems, Inc.
1 Norden Pl.
P.O. Box 5300
Norwalk, CT 06855
203/852-5000
(Aeronautical systems and instruments.)

Northeast Federal
50 State House Sq.
Hartford, CT 06103
203/280-1000
(Thrift institution.)

Northeast Utilities
400 Sheldon St.
Hartford, CT 06106
203/665-5000
(Utility.)

Olin Corp.
120 Long Ridge Rd.
Stamford, CT 06902
293/356-2000
(Chemicals.)

Otis Elevator Company
(subs. of United Technologies)
1 Farm Springs Rd.
Farmington, CT 06032
203/676-6000
(Elevators, escalators, etc.)

People's Bank
850 Main St.
Bridgeport, CT 06604-4913
203/338-7001
(Banking.)

Pepperidge Farm, Inc.
595 Westport Ave.
Norwalk, CT 06851
203/846-7000
(Food processing.)

Perkin-Elmer Corp.
761 Main Ave.
Norwalk, CT 06859
203/762-1000
(Scientific instruments.)

Phoenix Mutual Life Insurance Co.
1 American Row
Hartford, CT 06103
203/275-5000
(Insurance.)

Pitney Bowes, Inc.
1 Elmcroft Rd.
Stamford, CT 06926-0700
203/356-5000
(Office machines.)

The Pittston Co.
P.O. Box 120070
Stamford, CT 06912
203/978-5200
(Coal.)

Post Newsweek Stations, Inc.
3 Constitution Plz.
Hartford, CT 06103
860/493-6530
(Television.)

Pratt & Whitney Aircraft
(subs. of United Technologies)
400 Main St.
East Hartford, CT 06118
860/565-4321
(Aircraft, marine, and industrial
engines.)

Praxair, Inc.
39 Old Ridgebury Rd.
Danbury, CT 06810
203/837-8000
(Chemicals.)

Remington Products, Inc.
60 Main St.
Bridgeport, CT 06604
203/367-4400
(Personal electric products.)

Savin Corp.
333 Ludlow St.
Stamford, CT 06902
203/967-5000
(Copiers, fax machines.)

Shawmut National Corp.
777 Main St.
Hartford, CT 06115
203/728-2000
(Banking.)

SNET
227 Church St.
New Haven, CT 06506
203/771-5200
(Independent telephone company.)

Standard Fire Insurance Co.
151 Farmington Ave.
Hartford, CT 06156
203/273-0123
(Insurance.)

Stanley Works, Inc.
1000 Stanley Dr.
New Britain, CT 06053
203/225-5111
(Hand tools, home hardware, garden
products, etc.)

Thomson Newspapers
Metro Ctr.
1 Station Plz.

Stamford, CT 06902
203/425-2500
(Newspapers.)

Tosco Corp.
72 Cummings Pt. Rd.
Stamford, CT 06902
203/977-1000
(Petroleum products.)

Torrington Co.
59 Field St.
Torrington, CT 06790
203/482-9511
(Ball and roller bearings; machine
tool accessories.)

The Travelers Corp.
1 Tower Sq.
Hartford, CT 06183
203/277-0111
(Insurance.)
(subs. at the same address include:
Travelers Indemnity Co. and
Travelers Insurance Co.)

Ultramar Corp.
2 Pickwick Plz.
Greenwich, CT 06830
203/622-7000
Fax 203/622-7006
(Misc. energy.)

Union Carbide Corp.
39 Old Ridgebury Rd.
Danbury, CT 06817-0001
203/794-2000
(Chemicals, plastics, etc.)

**United States Surgical
Corp.**
150 Glover Ave.
Norwalk, CT 06850
203/866-5050
(Surgical and medical instruments
and apparatus.)

United Technologies Corp.
1 Financial Plz.
Hartford, CT 06103
203/728-7000
(Aircraft engines, electrical and
electronic parts, systems, etc.)

UST Corp.
100 W. Putnam Ave.
Greenwich, CT 06830
203/661-1100
(Tobacco.)

WaldenBooks, Inc.
201 High Ridge Rd.
Stamford, CT 06905
203/358-2000
(Chain bookstores.)

Witco Corp.
1 American Ln.
Greenwich, CT 06831-2559
203/552-2000
(Chemicals.)

Xerox Corp.
800 Long Ridge Rd.
Stamford, CT 06902
203/968-3000
(Office machinery, copiers,
computers, other electronic
equipment.)

CONNECTICUT DIRECTORIES

Connecticut Business Directory
American Business Directories
5711 S. 86th Cir.
P.O. Box 27347
Omaha, NE 68127
402/593-4600

*Connecticut, Rhode Island
Directory of Manufacturers*
Commerce Register Inc.
190 Godwin Ave.
Midland Park, NJ 07432
201/445-3000

*Harris State Industrial Directory—
Connecticut*
Harris Publishing Co.
2057 Aurora Rd.
Twinsburg, OH 44087
216/425-9000
800/888-5900

CONNECTICUT GOVERNMENT EMPLOYMENT OFFICES

Office of Personnel Management
(Federal job-information center.)
215/597-7440
912/757-3000

Job Service
Connecticut Labor Dept.
200 Folly Brook Blvd.
Wethersfield, CT 06109
203/566-5160
(State job-service center; lists local
state job offices.)

**State Recruitment and Testing
Center**
1 Hartford Sq. W.,
Suite 101A
Hartford, CT 06106
203/566-2501

DELAWARE

LEADING DELAWARE EMPLOYERS

Beneficial Corp.
301 N. Walnut St.
Wilmington, DE 19810
302/425-2500
(Lease & finance.)

Cigna Healthcare
1 Beaver Valley Rd.
Wilmington, DE 19803
302/477-3700
(Financial holding company, health care organization.)

Citicorp Banking Corp.
1 Penns Way
New Castle, DE 19720
302/323-3800
(Financial holding company.)

Columbia Gas System, Inc.
20 Montchanin Rd.
Wilmington, DE 19807-0020
302/429-5000
(Natural gas distribution.)

Delmarva Power & Light Co.
800 N. King St.
Wilmington, DE 19801
302/429-3376

E. I. du Pont de Nemours & Co.
1007 Market St.
Wilmington, DE 19898
302/774-1000
(Chemicals, environmental services, petroleum products, etc.)

Du Pont-Merck Pharmaceuticals Co.
P.O. Box 80722
Wilmington, DE 19880
301/992-5000
(Pharmaceuticals.)

W. L. Gore and Associates, Inc.
555 Paper Mill Rd.
Newark, DE 19711
302/738-4880

(Wire and cable, medical devices, fixtures, laminated fabric, etc.)

Hercules, Incorporated
Hercules Plz.
1313 N. Market St.
Wilmington, DE 19894
302/594-5000
(Electronic systems, propulsion systems, etc.)

Himont, Inc.
2801 Centerville Rd.
Wilmington, DE 19808
302/996-6000
(Resins, compounds, and alloys.)

ICI Americas, Inc.
3411 Silverside Rd.
Wilmington, DE 19810
302/887-3000
(Chemicals.)

MBNA Corp.
400 Christiana Rd.
Newark, DE 19713
302/453-9930
(Credit card services; collection; commercial banks.)

Matlack, Inc.
2200 Concork Pike
Wilmington, DE 19803
302/426-2700
(Trucking.)

Rollins Environmental Services
1 Rollins Plz.
Wilmington, DE 19803
302/426-2700
(Refuse systems, waste management.)

Rollins Truck Leasing Corp.
1 Rollins Plz.
Wilmington, DE 19899
302/426-2700
(Truck leasing.)

Star Building Services, Inc.
34 Blevins Dr.
Wilmington, DE 19720
302/324-1600
(Building cleaning and maintenance services.)

Star States Financial Services, Inc.
838 Market St.
Wilmington, DE 19801
302/573-3258
(Bank holding company.)

Townsend Farms, Inc.
Rte. 24
P.O. Box 468
Millsboro, DE 19966
302/934-9221
(Chickens.)

Wilmington Trust
1100 N. Market St.
Wilmington, DE 19801
302/651-1000
(Bank.)

DELAWARE DIRECTORIES

Delaware Business Directory
American Business Directories
5711 S. 86th Cir.
P.O. Box 27347
Omaha, NE 68127
402/593-4600

Harris State Industrial Directory—Delaware
Harris Publishing Co.
2057 Aurora Rd.
Twinsburg, OH 44087
216/425-9000
800/888-5900

DELAWARE GOVERNMENT EMPLOYMENT OFFICES

Office of Personnel Management
(Federal job-service center)
215/597-7440
912/757-3000

Employment and Training Division
Delaware Department of Labor
P.O. Box 616
Dover, DE 19903
302/739-5473
(State job-service center.)

WASHINGTON, DC

LEADING WASHINGTON, DC EMPLOYERS

Associated Press.
2021 K St., NW, Suite 600
Washington, DC 20006
202/828-6400
(Media company; newswire, broadcast services, etc.)

The Bureau of National Affairs, Inc.
1231 25th St., NW
Washington, DC 20037
202/452-4200
(Direct mail advertising services, software, periodicals, etc.)

Bell Atlantic/Washington, DC
1710 H St., NW
Washington, DC 20036
202/392-9900
(Telephone services.)

BET
(Black Entertainment TV)
1899 9 St., NE
Washington, DC 20018
202/608-2000
(Cable television.)

C-SPAN (Cable Public Affairs Network)
400 N. Capitol St., NW
Washington, DC 20001
202/737-3220
(Cable television.)

Danaher Corp.
1250 24th St., NW
Washington, DC 20037
202/828-0850
(Tools.)

The Donohoe Companies, Inc.
2101 Wisconsin Ave., NW
Washington, DC 20007
202/333-4977
(Real estate developer and contractor.)

Federal National Mortgage Association
3900 Wisconsin Ave., NW
Washington, DC 20016-2899
202/752-7000
(Secondary mortgage market.)

First American Bankshares, Inc.
1420 New York Ave., NW
Washington, DC 20005
202/626-1800
(Banking.)

GEICO Corp.
1 GEICO Plz.
Washington, DC 20076
301/986-3000
(Insurance.)

Giant Food
P.O. Box 1804
Washington, DC 20013
202/234-0215
(Supermarkets and restaurants.)

Harman International Industries, Inc.
1101 Pennsylvania Ave., NW, Suite 1010
Washington, DC 20036
202/393-1101
(Consumer electronics.)

Hay Group, Inc.
1500 K St., NW
Washington, DC 20005
202/637-6600
(Management services.)

INTELSAT—International Telecommunications Satellite Organization
3400 International Dr., NW
Washington, DC 20008
202/944-7800
(Communications services.)

International Monetary Fund
700 19th St., NW
Washington, DC 20431
202/623-7000
(Federal and federally sponsored credit agencies.)

The Kiplinger Washington Editors, Inc.
1729 H St., NW
Washington, DC 20006
202/887-6400
(Magazine and newsletter publishing.)

MCI Communications Corp.
1801 Pennsylvania Ave., NW
Washington, DC 20006
202/872-1600
(Telecommunications.)

Marriott International Corp.
1 Marriott Dr.
Washington, DC 20058
301/380-3000
(Hotels.)

NHP Inc.
1225 I St., NW
Washington, DC 20005
202/347-6247
(Real estate agents, managers,
developers, etc.)

National Geographic Society
1145 17th St., NW
Washington, DC 20036
202/857-7000
(Magazine, book publishing.)

National Public Radio
635 Massachusetts Ave., NW
Washington, DC 20001
202/414-2000
(Public radio broadcasting.)

National Railroad Passenger Corp.
(dba Amtrak)
400 N. Capitol St., NW
Washington, DC 20001
202/906-4700
(Railroads—terminals and
operation.)

Potomac Electric Power Co.
1900 Pennsylvania Ave., NW
Washington, DC 20068
202/872-2000
(Electric utility.)

Riggs National Bank
1503 Pennsylvania Ave., NW
Washington, DC 20005

202/835-6000
(Bank.)

**Sallie Mae (Student Loan
Marketing Association)**
1050 Thomas Jefferson St., NW
Washington, DC 20007
202/333-8000
(Guarantees student loans traded on
secondary market.)

United Press International
1400 I St., NW
Washington, DC 20005
202/898-8000
(Media company—newswire, radio
network, broadcast services.)

U.S. News & World Report
2400 N St., NW
Washington, DC 20037
202/955-2000
(Magazine publishing.)

Washington Gas Light Co.
1100 H St., NW
Washington, DC 20005
703/250-4440
(Natural gas utility.)

Washington Post Company
1150 15th St., NW
Washington, DC 20071
202/334-6000
(Newspaper and magazine
publishing, communications.)

WASHINGTON, DC DIRECTORIES

*Dalton's Baltimore-Washington
Metropolitan Directory*
Dalton's Directory
410 Lancaster Ave.
Haverford, PA 19041
800/221-1050
610/649-2680

*Harris State Industrial Directory—
Maryland/DC*
Harris Publishing Co.

2057 Aurora Rd.
Twinsburg, OH 44087
216/425-9000
800/888-5900

Washington, DC, Business Directory
American Business Directories
5711 S. 86th Cir.
P.O. Box 27347
Omaha, NE 68127
402/593-4600

WASHINGTON, DC GOVERNMENT EMPLOYMENT OFFICES

Office of Personnel Management
215/597-7440
912/757-3000
(Federal job-service center.)

Office of Job Service
Dept. of Employment Services
500 C St., NW, Room 317
Washington, DC 20001
202/724-7050

MAINE

LEADING MAINE EMPLOYERS

ABB Environmental Services
110 Free St.
Portland, ME 04101
207/775-5401
(Environmental services.)

Bath Iron Works Corp.
700 Washington St.
Bath, ME 04530
207/443-3311
(Ship building and repairing.)

L. L. Bean, Inc.
15 Casco St.
Freeport, ME 04033
207/865-4761
(Sporting goods/clothing retailer and mail order house.)

Central Maine Morning Sentinel
25 Silver St.
Waterville, ME 04901
207/873-3341
(Newspaper.)

Central Maine Power Co.
83 Edison Dr.
Augusta, ME 04330
207/623-3521
(Electric utility.)

Cianbro Corp.
1 Hunnewell Ave.
P.O. Box 1000
Pittsfield, ME 04967
207/487-3311
(Heavy construction.)

Dexter Shoe Co.
114 Railroad Ave.
Dexter, ME 04930
207/924-7341
(Shoes.)

Eastern Fine Paper, Inc.
517 S. Main St.
Brewer, ME 04412
207/989-7070
(Coated and printing paper.)

Emery-Waterhouse Co., Inc.
7 Rand Rd.
P.O. Box 659
Portland, ME 04102
207/775-2371
(Wholesale hardware.)

Forster Manufacturing Co., Inc.
Mill St.
E. Wilton, ME 04234
207/645-2574
(Wood products—clothespins, rolling pins, etc.)

Fraser Paper Ltd.
25 Bridge St.
Madawaska, ME 04756
207/728-3321
(Specialty papers.)

Hannaford Brothers
145 Pleasant Hill Rd.
Scarborough, ME 04074
207/883-2911
(Grocery stores.)

Key Bank of Maine, Inc.
286 Water St.
Augusta, ME 04330
207/623-5673
(Banking.)

Lincoln Pulp & Paper Co., Inc.
50 Katahdin Ave.
Lincoln, ME 04457
207/794-6721
(Tissue paper, pulp mills.)

Madison Paper Industries
Main St.
P.O. Box 129
Madison, ME 04950
207/696-3307
(Paper mills.)

McCain Foods, Inc.
Station Rd.
P.O. Box 159
Easton, ME 04740
207/488-2561
(Potato products, vegetables, etc.)

Prime Tanning Co.
Sullivan St.
Berwick, ME 03901
207/698-1100
(Leather tanneries.)

Shape, Inc.
26 Morin St.
Biddeford, ME 04005
207/282-6155
(Audio- and videotapes.)

UNUM Life Insurance Corp.
2211 Congress St.
Portland, ME 04122
207/770-2211
(Insurance.)

Webber Fuels
700 Main St.
Bangor, ME 04401
207/942-5505
(Fuel oil and petroleum product dealers.)

MAINE DIRECTORIES

Maine Business Directory
American Business Directories
5711 S. 86th Cir.
P.O. Box 27347
Omaha, NE 68127
402/593-4600

Harris State Industrial Directories—New England
Harris Publishing Co.
2057 Aurora Rd.

Twinsburg, OH 44087
216/425-9000
800/888-5900

Maine, Vermont, New Hampshire Directory of Manufacturers
Commerce Register, Inc.
190 Godwin Ave.
Midland Park, NJ 07432
201/445-3000

MAINE GOVERNMENT EMPLOYMENT OFFICES

Office of Personnel Management
215/597-7440
912/757-3000
(Federal job-service center.)

Job Service Division
Bureau of Employment Security
P.O. Box 309
Augusta, ME 04332
207/287-3431
(State job-service center.)

MARYLAND

LEADING MARYLAND EMPLOYERS

AAI Corp.
100 Industry Ln.
Hunt Valley, MD 21030
410/666-1400
(Aerospace systems and instruments.)

Allied Signal Technical Services Corp.
(div. of Allied-Signal
Aerospace Co.)
1 Bendix Rd.
Columbia, MD 21045
410/964-7000
(Integrated management and field
engineering services.)

Arinc Research Corp.
2551 Riva Rd.
Annapolis, MD 21401
410/266-4000
(Engineering and
telecommunications.)

Baltimore Gas & Electric Co.
Charles Ctr.
P.O. Box 1475
Baltimore, MD 21203-1475
410/234-5000
Fax 410/234-5367
(Electric and gas utility.)

Bell Atlantic Corp./Maryland
(subs. of Bell Atlantic)
1 E. Pratt St.
Baltimore, MD 21202
410/539-9900
(Regional telephone company.)

Black & Decker Corp.
701 E. Joppa Rd.
Baltimore, MD 21286
410/716-3900
(Power tools, accessories, outdoor
and household products.)

CSX Transportation, Inc.
100 N. Charles St.
Baltimore, MD 21201
410/237-2000
(Railroad—line haul operating.)

Choice Hotels, International
10770 Columbia Pike
Silver Spring, MD 20901
301/593-5600
(Hotels, motels.)

Citizens Bancorp
14401 Sweitzer Ln.
Laurel, MD 20707
301/206-6000
(Banking.)

Commercial Credit Co.
300 St. Paul Pl.
Baltimore, MD 21202
410/332-3000
(Consumer finance, financial
services, business insurance.)

COMSAT World Systems
6560 Rock Spring Dr.
Bethesda, MD 20817
301/214-3000
(Communications,
telecommunications.)

Computer Data Systems, Inc.
1 Curie Ct.
Rockville, MD 20850
301/921-7000
(Computer intergrated systems
design.)

Computer Sciences Corp.
130 Piccard Dr.
Rockville, MD 20850
301/670-2000
(Computer systems.)

The Discovery Channel
770 Wisconsin Ave.
Bethesda, MD 20814
301/986-1999
(Cable television.)

Crown Central Petroleum Corp.
1 N. Charles St.
Baltimore, MD 21201
410/539-7400
(Petroleum.)

Fairchild Space & Defense Corp.
20301 Century Blvd.
Germantown, MD 20874
301/428-6000
(Spacecraft and aerospace
electronics.)

Fidelity & Deposit Co. of Maryland
210 N. Charles St.
Baltimore, MD 21201
410/539-0800
(Banking.)

First Fidelity Bank
1 E. Baltimore St.
Baltimore, MD 21202
410/244-3360
(Banking.)

First Maryland Bancorp
25 South Charles St.
Baltimore, MD 21201
410/244-4000
(Banking—First National Bank of
Maryland.)

**General Electric Information
Services**
401 N. Washington St.
Rockville, MD 20850
301/340-4000
(Computer services.)

Hechinger Co.
3500 Pennsy Dr.
Landover, MD 20785-1691
301/341-1000
(Retail hardware and lumber stores.)

Host Marriott
10400 Fernwood Rd.
Bethesda, MD 20817
301/380-9000
(Hotels and gaming.)

Legg Mason, Inc.
111 S. Calvert St.
Baltimore, MD 21203
410/539-3400
(Brokerage, investment banking,
investment and real estate adviser.)

Legg Mason Wood Walker, Inc.
111 S. Calvert St.
Baltimore, MD 21202
410/539-3000
(Investment banking.)

Lockheed-Martin Corp.
6801 Rockledge Dr.
Bethesda, MD 20817
301/897-6000
(Aerospace; electronics; information
systems and materials.)

London Fog Industries
1332 Londontown Blvd.
Eldersburg, MD 21784
410/795-5900
(Rainwear.)

Manor Care, Inc.
10770 Columbia Pike
Silver Spring, MD 20901
301/681-9400
(Health care and lodging—retirement
communities.)

McCormick & Co., Inc.
P.O. Box 6000
Sparks, MD 21152-6000
410/771-7301
(Spices, flavorings, extracts, etc.)

Mercantile Bancshares Corp.
2 Hopkins Plz.
Baltimore, MD 21201
410/237-5900
(Banking.)

Miller & Long Co., Inc.
4824 Rugby Ave.
Bethesda, MD 20814
301/657-8000
(Construction—concrete work.)

Nations Bank
10 Light St.
Baltimore, MD 21202
410/605-5476
(Banking.)

Perdue Farms
Old Ocean City Rd.
Salisbury, MD 21802
410/543-3000
(Poultry processing.)

PHH Corp.
11333 McCormick Rd.
Hunt Valley, MD 21031
410/771-1900
(Integrated management services and
cost-control programs.)

Premier Management Group, Inc.
1505 Bloomfield Ave.
Baltimore, MD 21227
410/525-1800
(Real estate management.)

Preston Trucking Co., Inc.
151 Easton Blvd.
Preston, MD 21655
410/673-7151
(Motor carrier.)

**Procter & Gamble
Cosmetic and Fragrance Products**
11050 York Rd.
Hunt Valley, MD 21030
410/785-7800
(Cosmetics, personal and household
products, specialty foods.)

Rouse Co.
10275 Little Patuxent Pkwy.
Columbia, MD 21044
410/992-6000
(Real estate
developer/owner/operation.)

The Ryland Group, Inc.
1100 Broken Land Pkwy.
Columbia, MD 21044
410/715-7000
(Home construction, mortgages.)

SCM Chemicals Inc.
7 St. Paul St.,
Suite 1010
Baltimore, MD 21202
410/783-1120
(Chemicals.)

USF&G Corp.
100 Light St.
Baltimore, MD 21202
410/547-3000
(Insurance, financial services.)

Vitro Corp.
45 W. Gude Dr.
Rockville, MD 20850
301/231-1000
(Computer integrated system design.)

Westinghouse Electronic Systems
7323 Aviation Blvd.
Baltimore, MD 21240
410/765-1000
(Electronic systems; maintenance and
service.)

Whiting-Turner Contracting Co.
300 E. Joppa Rd.
Towson, MD 21286
410/821-1100
(General contracting, construction
management.)

MARYLAND BUSINESS PERIODICALS

Baltimore Business Journal
117 Water St.
Baltimore, MD 21202
410/576-1161

MARYLAND DIRECTORIES

Dalton's Baltimore-Washington
Metropolitan Directory
Dalton's Directory
410 Lancaster Ave.
Haverford, PA 19041
800/221-1050
610/649-2680

Directory of Central Atlantic States
Manufacturers
George D. Hall Company
50 Congress St.
Boston, MA 02109
617/523-3745
(Includes Maryland, Delaware,
Virginia, West Virginia, North
Carolina, and South Carolina.)

Harris Directory of Maryland
Manufacturers

Harris Publishing Company
2057 Aurora Rd.
Twinsburg, OH 44087
216/425-9000
800/888-5900

Harris State Directories—
Maryland/DC
Harris Publishing Co.
2057 Aurora Rd.
Twinsburg, OH 44087
216/425-9000
800/888-5900

Maryland Business Directory
American Business Directories
5711 S. 86th Cir.
P.O. Box 27347
Omaha, NE 68127
402/593-4600

MARYLAND GOVERNMENT EMPLOYMENT OFFICES

Office of Personnel Management
215/597-7440
912/757-3000
(Federal job-service center.)

Maryland Dept. of Employment
and Economic Development
1100 N. Eutaw St., Room 701
Baltimore, MD 21201
410/767-2000
(State job-service center.)

MASSACHUSETTS

LEADING MASSACHUSETTS COMPANIES

Addison-Wesley Publishing Co.
1 Jacob Way
Reading, MA 01867
617/944-3700
(Book publishing.)

Affiliated Publications, Inc.
135 Morrissey Blvd.
Boston, MA 02107
617/929-2000
(Newspaper publishing.)

Allmerica Property & Casualty
400 Lincoln St.
Worcester, MA 01653
508/855-7000
(Insurance.)

Americare Health Services, Inc.
264 Monsignor O'Brien Hwy.
Cambridge, MA 02141
617/628-5300
(Health services.)

Analog Devices, Inc.
1 Technology Way
Norwood, MA 02062
617/329-4700
(High-tech products.)

Avery-Dennison Mfg. Co.
1 Clarks Hill
Framingham, MA 01701
508/879-0511
(Office supplies.)

Bank of Boston Corp.
1 Financial Ctr.
Boston, MA 02111
617/434-3490
(Banking.)

**Blue Cross & Blue Shield
of Massachusetts**
100 Summer St.
Boston, MA 02110
617/832-5000
(Health insurance.)

Bolt, Beranek & Newman, Inc.
150 Cambridge Pk. Dr.
Cambridge, MA 02140
617/873-2000
(Private wide area networks,
software, etc.)

Bose Corp.
100 The Mountain Rd.
Framingham, MA 01701
508/879-7330
(Consumer audio equipment.)

The Boston Co., Inc.
1 Boston Pl.
Boston, MA 02108
617/722-7000
(Banking.)

Boston Edison Co.
800 Boylston St.
Boston, MA 02199
617/424-2000
(Electric utility.)

Boston Safe Deposit Trust Co.
1 Boston Pl.
Boston, MA 02108
617/722-7697
(Banking.)

Boston Scientific
1 Boston Scientific Pl.
Natick, MA 01760-1537
617/923-1720
(Medical supplies.)

**Bradlee's New England,
Inc.**
1 Bradlee Cir.
Braintree, MA 02184
617/380-8000
(Discount department stores.)

Bull Corp.
Technology Dr.
Billerica, MA 01821
508/294-6000
(Mainframes, personal
computers.)

Cabot Corp.
75 State St.
Boston, MA 02109
617/345-0100
(Chemicals.)

Cahners Publishing
275 Washington St.
Newton, MA 02185
617/964-3030
(Publishing.)

Commerce Group Inc.
211 Main St.
Webster, MA 01570
508/943-9000
(Insurance.)

**Commercial Union Insurance
Co.**
1 Beacon St.
Boston, MA 02108
617/725-6000
(Insurance.)

Thomas Cook Travel
100 Cambridge Pk. Dr.
Cambridge, MA 02138
(Travel agency.)

Data General Corp.
4400 Computer Dr.
Westboro, MA 01580
508/898-5000
(Minicomputers.)

Digital Equipment Corp.
111 Powdermill Rd.
Maynard, MA 01754
508/493-5111
(Computers.)

Dunkin Donuts, Inc.
P.O. Box 317
Randolph, MA 02368
617/961-4000
(Food convenience stores.)

Dynatech Corp.
3 New England Executive Pk.
Burlington, MA 01803
617/272-6100
(Computers.)

Eastern Enterprises
Nine Riverside Rd.
Weston, MA 07193
617/647-2300
(Natural gas.)

EG&G, Inc.
45 William St.
Wellesley, MA 02181
617/237-5100
(Engineering and construction
sources.)

EMC
171 South St.
Hopkinton, MA 01748-9103
508/435-1000
(Computer peripherals.)

Federal Reserve Bank of Boston
600 Atlantic Ave.
Boston, MA 02110
617/563-7000
(Federal Reserve bank.)

Fidelity Investments
82 Devonshire St.
Boston, MA 02109
617/570-7000
(Investments.)

Filene's
426 Washington St.
Boston, MA 02101
617/357-2100
(Department store.)

First National Bank of Boston
100 Federal St.
Boston, MA 02110
617/434-2200
(Banking.)

The Foxboro Company
33 Commercial St.
Foxboro, MA 02035
508/543-8750
(Indicating, controlling and
recording instruments, and control
systems.)

Friendly Ice Cream Corp.
1855 Boston Rd.
Wilbraham, MA 01095
413/543-2400
(Restaurants.)

GenRad, Inc.
300 Baker Ave.
Concord, MA 01742
508/287-7000
(Electrical measuring instruments,
electronics.)

Gillette Co.
800 Boylston St.
Boston, MA 02199
617/421-7000
(Personal electronic products.)

**GTE Government Systems
Corp.**
81 Hartwell Ave.
Lexington, MA 02173
617/861-1642
(Control, communication,
command, and intelligence
systems.)

Harcourt General Corp.
27 Boylston St.
Chestnut Hill, MA 02167
617/232-8200
(Retail stores, theaters.)

Hills Department Stores, Inc.
15 Dan Rd.
Canton, MA 02021
617/821-1000
(Department stores.)

H. P. Hood, Inc.
(subs. of Agway)
500 Rutherford Ave.
Charlestown, MA 02129
617/242-0600
(Food processing, dairy foods, citrus, etc.)

Houghton Mifflin Co.
2 Prudential Plz., Suite 1200
Boston, MA 02116
617/315-5000
(Book publishing.)

John Hancock Mutual Life Insurance Co.
P.O. Box 117
Boston, MA 02117
617/572-6000
(Life insurance.)

Jordan Marsh Stores Corp.
450 Washington St.
Boston, MA 02111
617/357-3000
(Department stores.)

LTX Corp.
LTX Park at University Ave.
Westwood, MA 02090
617/461-1000
(Measuring instruments.)

Lechmere, Inc.
300 Mishawum Rd.
Woburn, MA 01801
617/938-5959
(Consumer electronics store.)

Liberty Financial Companies
600 Atlantic Ave.
Boston, MA 02210
617/722-6000
(Insurance.)

Lotus Development Corp.
55 Cambridge Pkwy.
Cambridge, MA 02142
617/577-8500
(Computer software.)

Massachusetts Mutual Life Insurance Co.
1295 State St.

Springfield, MA 01111
413/788-8411
(Insurance.)

Millipore Corp.
80 Ashby Rd.
Bedford, MA 01730
617/275-9200
(Electronic instruments and measurement.)

Mitre Corp.
202 Burlington Rd.
Bedford, MA 01730
617/271-2000
(Commercial physical and biological research, systems engineering.)

NEC Technologies, Inc.
1414 Massachusetts Ave.
Foxboro, MA 01719
508/264-8000
(Computers, peripherals, etc.)

New England Electric System
25 Research Dr.
Westboro, MA 01582-0001
508/366-9011
(Utility.)

New England Power Service Co.
25 Research Dr.
Westboro, MA 01582
508/366-9011
(Utility.)

Norton Co.
1 New Bond St.
Worcester, MA 01606
508/795-5000
(Abrasive products.)

Nynex Information Resources Co.
35 Village Rd.
Middletown, MA 01949
508/762-1000
(Directory publishing.)

Nynex—New England
(Subs. of Nynex.)
125 High St.
Boston, MA 02110
617/743-6000
(Telecommunications.)

Ocean Spray Cranberries, Inc.
1 Ocean Spray Dr.
Middleboro, MA 02346
508/946-1000
(Cranberry beverages and foods.)

Parametric Technology
128 Technology Dr.
Waltham, MA 02154
617/894-7111
(Computer software.)

Polaroid Corp.
549 Technology Sq.
Cambridge, MA 02139
617/386-2000
(Photographic equipment and
supplies.)

Raytheon Co.
141 Spring St.
Lexington, MA 02173
617/862-6600
(Electronic components, equipment,
and systems.)

Reebok International Ltd.
100 Technology Center Dr.
Stoughton, MA 02072
617/341-5000
(Athletic and leisure shoe
manufacturer.)

Shawmut Corp.
1 Federal St.
Boston, MA 02210
617/292-2000
Fax 617/556-8004
(Banking.)

Smith & Wesson Corp.
2100 Roosevelt Ave.
Springfield, MA 01102
413/781-8300
(Weapons manufacturing.)

Stanhome Inc.
333 Western Ave.
Westfield, MA 01085
413/562-3631
(Direct sale of household
items, etc.)

Staples
100 Pennsylvania Ave.
Framingham, MA 01701-9328
508/370-8500
(Specialty stores.)

L. S. Starrett Co.
121 Crescent St.
Athol, MA 01331
508/249-3551
(Cutting tools.)

**State Mutual Life
Assurance Co.
of America**
440 Lincoln St.
Worcester, MA 01653
508/855-1000
(Life insurance.)

State St. Boston Corp.
225 Franklin St.
Boston, MA 02110
617/786-3000
(Banking.)

State St. Research
State St. Investment Trust
1 Financial Ctr.
Boston, MA 02111
617/357-1200
(Investments.)

**Stone & Webster Engineering
Corp.**
245 Summer St.
Boston, MA 02110
617/589-5111
(Engineering, power plant, chemical
plant, and refining construction.)

Stop & Shop Cos., Inc.
1385 Hancock St.
Quincy, MA 02169
617/380-8000
(Convenience stores.)

Stratus Computer, Inc.
55 Fairbanks Blvd.
Marlboro, MA 01752
508/460-2000
(Computers.)

TJX Cos.
7700 Cochituate Rd.
Framingham, MA 01701
508/390-1000
(Retail clothing stores, inc. T. J. Maxx.)

Talbot's Inc.
175 Beal St.
Hingham, MA 02043
617/749-7600
(Women's clothing stores/catalog sales.)

Teradyne, Inc.
321 Harrison Ave.
Boston, MA 02118
617/482-2700
(Electrical measuring instruments.)

Thermo Electron Corp.
81 Wyman St.
Waltham, MA 02154
617/622-1000
(Cogeneration systems, monitoring instruments, etc.)

Waban Inc.
1 Mercer Rd.
Natick, MA 01760
508/651-6500
(Home improvement stores.)

Wang Laboratories, Inc.
1 Industrial Ave.
Lowell, MA 01851
508/459-5000
(Computers and office machines.)

MASSACHUSETTS BUSINESS PERIODICAL

Boston Business Journal
200 High St., 4th Fl.
Boston, MA 02110
617/330-1000
(Weekly.)

MASSACHUSETTS DIRECTORIES

Harris Directory of New England Manufacturers
Harris Publishing Co.
2057 Aurora Rd.
Twinsburg, OH 44087
216/425-9000
800/888-5900

Harris State Directories—Massachusetts
Harris Publishing Co.
2057 Aurora Rd.
Twinsburg, OH 44087
216/425-9000
800/888-5900

Massachusetts Business Directory
American Business Directories
5711 S. 86th Cir.
P.O. Box 27347
Omaha, NE 68127
402/593-4600

Massachusetts Directory of Manufacturers
Commerce Register, Inc.
190 Godwin Ave.
Midland Park, NJ 07432
201/445-3000

MASSACHUSETTS GOVERNMENT EMPLOYMENT OFFICES

Office of Personnel Management
215/597-7440
912/757-3000
(Federal job-service center.)

Dept. of Employment Security and Training
Charles F. Hurley Bldg.
Government Ctr.
Boston, MA 02114
617/626-6010
(State job-service center.)

NEW HAMPSHIRE

LEADING NEW HAMPSHIRE EMPLOYERS

Abex
Liberty Ln.
Hampton, NH 03842
603/926-5911
(Aerospace and defense electronics.)

Bank of New Hampshire Corp.
300 Franklin St.
Box 600
Manchester, NH 03105
603/624-6600
(Banking.)

Brookstone, Inc.
17 Riverside Plz.
Nashua, NH 03062
603/880-9500
(Specialty stores.)

Cabletron Systems, Inc.
35 Industrial Way
Rochester, NH 03867
603/332-9400
(Local area network components.)

Chubb Life Insurance Co. of America
1 Granite Pl.
Concord, NH 03301
603/226-5000
(Life insurance.)

Ekco Group, Inc.
98 Spit Brook Rd.
Nashua, NH 03062
603/888-1212
(Housewares, kichenware, baking equipment, etc.)

First New Hampshire Bank
20 Fort Eddy Rd.
Manchester, NH 03101
603/229-3250
(Banking.)

Fleet Bank of New Hampshire
1155 Elm St.
Manchester, NH 03101
603/485-6500
(Banking.)

Grinnell Corp.
3 Tyco Pk.
Exeter, NH 03833
603/778-9200
(General industrial machinery and equipment.)

Guilford Transportation Industries, Inc.
7 Executive Pk. Dr.
Merrimack, NH 03054
603/429-1685
(Railroads, line haul operating.)

Hadco Corp.
12 Manor Pkwy.
Salem, NH 03079
603/898-8000
(Circuit boards.)

Harris-Heidelberr Corp.
121 Broadway
Dover, NH 03820
603/749-6600
(Printing machinery
/equipment.)

Kollsman Instrument Corp.
(div. of Sequa Corp.)
220 Daniel Webster Hwy.
Merrimack, NH 03054
603/889-2500
(Advanced electro-optical and
avionics systems.)

Lockheed Martin Corp.
95 Canal St.
Nashua, NH 03060
603/885-4321
(Advanced electronics systems,
etc.)

Lowell Shoe, Inc.
8 Hampshire Dr.
Hudson, NH 03051
603/880-8900
(Shoes.)

MPB Corp.
Precision Pk.
P.O. Box 547
Keene, NH 03431
603/352-0310
(Ball bearings.)

Markem Corp.
150 Congress St.
Keene, NH 03431
603/352-1130
(Printing machinery/equipment.)

Nashua Corp.
44 Franklin St.
Nashua, NH 03060
603/880-2323
(Photocopying supplies, paper,
labels, computer disks, etc.)

New Hampshire Ball Bearings
Rte. 202
Peterborough, NH 03458
603/924-3311
(Ball bearings.)

New Hampshire Oak
Liberty Lane
Hampton, NH 03842
603/926-1340
(Chemical and industrial products.)

Omni Hotels Corp.
500 Lafayette Rd.
Hampton, NH 03842
603/926-8911
(Hotels, restaurants.)

Standex International Corp.
6 Manor Pkwy.
Salem, NH 03079
603/893-9701
(Furniture, stationery, restaurant
equipment.)

The Timberland Co.
200 Domain Rd.
Stratham, NH 03885
603/772-9500
(Shoes.)

Tyco International, Ltd.
One Tyco Pk.
Exeter, NH 03833-1108
603/778-9700
(Metal products.)

Wheelabrator Technologies, Inc.
Liberty Ln.
Hampton, NH 03842
603/929-3000
(Heavy construction.)

NEW HAMPSHIRE BUSINESS PERIODICAL

Business New Hampshire Magazine
404 Chestnut St.,
Suite 201

Manchester, NH 03101-1803
603/626-6354
(Monthly.)

NEW HAMPSHIRE DIRECTORIES

Maine, Vermont, New Hampshire
Directory of Manufacturers
Commerce Register, Inc.
190 Godwin Ave.
Midland Park, NJ 07432
201/445-3000

Harris State Directories—
New England
Harris Publishing Co.
2057 Aurora Rd.
Twinsburg, OH 44087
216/425-9000
800/888-5900

New Hampshire Business
Directory
American Business Directories
5711 S. 86th Cir.
P.O. Box 27347
Omaha, NE 68127
402/593-4600

New Hampshire
Manufacturing Directory
Manufacturers' News, Inc.
1633 Central St.
Evanston, IL 60201
708/864-7000

NEW HAMPSHIRE GOVERNMENT EMPLOYMENT OFFICES

Office of Personnel Management
215/597-7440
912/757-3000
(Federal job-service center.)

Employment Service Bureau
Dept. of Employment Security
32 S. Main St.
Concord, NH 03301
603/224-3311
(State job-service center.)

NEW JERSEY

LEADING NEW JERSEY EMPLOYERS

AT&T Communications
of New Jersey
295 N. Maple Ave.
Basking Ridge, NJ 07920
908/221-2000
(Telephone communications.)

AT&T Network Systems
475 South St.
Morristown, NJ 07962
210/606-2000
(Telecommunication systems.)

AT&T Technologies, Inc.
1 Oak Way
Berkeley Heights, NJ 07922
908/771-2000
(Telecommunications and data
communications equipment.)

Allied-Signal, Inc.
101 Columbia Rd.
Morristown, NJ 07960
201/455-2000
(Conglomerate—inc. aerospace and
advanced electronics.)

American Cyanamid Co.
1 Cyanamid Plz.
Wayne, NJ 07470
201/831-2000
(Pharmaceuticals.)

American Home Products
5 Girlada Farms
Madison, NJ 07940
201/660-5000
(Drugs.)

American Re Corp.
555 College Road East
Princeton, NJ 08540
609/243-4200
(Insurance.)

**American Water Works
Company, Inc.**
1025 Laurel Oak Rd.
Box 1770
Kirkwood, NJ 08043
609/346-8200
(Water.)

Automatic Data Processing, Inc.
1 ADP Blvd.
Roseland, NJ 07068-1728
201/994-5000
(Data processing services.)

BASF Corp.
3000 Continental Dr. N.
Mt. Olive, NJ 07826
210/426-2600
(Chemicals.)

Becton Dickinson Co.
1 Becton Dr.

Franklin Lakes, NJ 07417
201/847-6800
(Medical supplies.)

Bell Atlantic/New Jersey
540 Broad St.
Newark, NJ 07102
201/649-2841
(Telephone services.)

Bell Communications Research
290 W. Mount Pleasant Ave.
Livingston, NJ 07039
201/740-3000
(Software.)

Block Drug Co., Inc.
257 Corneilson Ave.
Jersey City, NJ 07302
201/454-3000
(Health care products,
pharmaceuticals.)

**Bristol-Myers Squibb
Pharmaceuticals Corp.**
R. 206 & Province Line Rd.
Princeton, NJ 08540
609/252-4000
(Pharmaceuticals.)

Campbell Soup Co.
Campbell Pl.
Camden, NJ 08103-1799
609/342-4800
(Food processing.)

Church & Dwight Co., Inc.
469 N. Harnson St.
Princeton, NJ 08540
609/683-5900
(Soaps, detergents, baking soda,
etc.)

The Chubb Corp.
15 Mountainside Rd.
Warren, NJ 07059
908/903-2000
(Management services.)

Collective Bancorp
716 W. White Horse Pike
Cologne, NJ 08213
609/965-1234
(Bank.)

CPC International
700 Sylvan Ave.
Englewood Cliffs, NJ 07632-9976
201/894-4000
(Food processor.)

Days Inns of America
339 Jefferson Rd.
Parsippany, NJ 07054
201/428-9700
(Motels.)

Engelhard Corp.
101 Wood Ave.
Iselin, NJ 08830-0770
908/205-6000
(Industrial inorganic chemicals.)

GAF Chemicals Corp.
1361 Alps Rd.
Wayne, NJ 07470
201/628-3000
(Chemicals.)

General Public Utilities
100 Interpace Pkwy.
Parsippany, NJ 07054-1149
201/263-6500
(Utility.)

Grand Union Co.
201 Willowbrook Blvd.
Wayne, NJ 07470
201/890-6000
(Supermarkets.)

Great Atlantic & Pacific Tea
2 Paragon Dr.
Montvale, NJ 07645
201/573-9700
(Supermarkets & restaurants.)

Harve Bernard Ltd.
225 Meadowlands Pkwy.
Secaucus, NJ 07094
201/319-0909
(Women's apparel.)

Hoechst Celanese Corp.
Rte. 202—206
Somerville, NJ 08876
908/231-2000
(Chemicals, manmade fibers, etc.)

Hospitality Franchise Systems, Inc.
339 Jefferson Rd.
Parsippany, NJ 07054-0218
201/428-9700
(Hotels and motels; formerly Ramada
International Hotels & Resorts)

**Hoffman-LaRoche
Pharmaceutical, Inc.**
340 Kingsland St.
Nutley, NJ 07110
201/235-5000
(Pharmaceuticals.)

Ingersoll-Rand Company
200 Chestnut Ridge Rd.
Woodcliff Lake, NJ 07675
201/573-0123
(Compressors, pumps, etc.)

Johnson & Johnson
1 Johnson & Johnson Plz.
New Brunswick, NJ 08933
908/524-0400
(Pharmaceuticals, health care
products, etc.)

Lucent Technologies
600 Mountain Ave.
Murray Hill, NJ 07974
908/582-3000
(Scientific research, engineering,
development, and design.)

**Matsushita Electronics Corp. of
America**
1 Panasonic Way
Secaucus, NJ 07094
201/348-7000
(Appliances, television, radios, etc.)

Mennen Co.
51 Hanover Ave.
Morristown, NJ 07960
201/631-9000
(Personal care products.)

Merck & Co.
P.O. Box 100
Whitehouse Station, NJ 08889-0100
908/423-1000
(Pharmaceuticals.)

Nabisco Brands, Inc.
100 DeForest Ave.
Hanover, NJ 07936
201/503-2000
(Food processing.)

**Ortho McNeil
Pharmaceutical Corp.**
Rte. 202
P.O. Box 300
Raritan, NJ 08869
908/218-6000
(Pharmaceuticals.)

**Public Service Enterprise
Group, Inc.**
80 Park Plz.
Newark, NJ 07102
201/430-7000
(Utility.)

Sandoz Pharmaceuticals Corp.
(subs. Sandoz Corp.)
Rte. 10
East Hanover, NJ 07936
201/503-7500
(Pharmaceuticals.)

Sharp Electronics Corp.
P.O. Box 650
Mahwah, NJ 07430
201/529-8200
(Consumer electronics.)

Schering-Plough Corp.
1 Giralda Farms
Madison, NJ 07940-1000
201/882-7000
(Pharmaceuticals.)

Squibb Corp.
P.O. Box 4000
Princeton, NJ 08543
609/252-4000
(Pharmaceuticals, health care,
and personal care products.)

Sony Corp. of America
1 Sony Dr.
Park Ridge, NJ 07656
210/930-1000
(Electronic equipment.)

Summit Bancorporation
One Main St.
Chatham, NJ 07928
201/701-6200
(Bank.)

Supermarkets General Corp.
301 Blair Rd.
Woodbridge, NJ 07095
908/499-3000
(Supermarkets).

Toys "R" Us
461 From Rd.
Paramus, NJ 07652
201/262-7800
(Toy stores.)

Trump Taj Mahal Associates, Inc.
1000 Boardwalk
Atlantic City, NJ 08401
609/449-1000
(Casino/hotel.)

UJB Financial Corp.
301 Carnegie Ctr.
Princeton, NJ 08540
609/987-3200
(Bank.)

Union Camp Corp.
1600 Valley Rd.
Wayne, NJ 07470
201/628-2000
(Paper and lumber.)

Warner-Lambert Co.
201 Tabor Rd.
Morris Plains, NJ 07950
201/540-2000
(Pharmaceuticals.)

NEW JERSEY BUSINESS PERIODICAL

New Jersey Business
New Jersey Business & Industry
Assoc.

310 Passaic Ave.
Fairfield, NJ 07004
201/882-5004

NEW JERSEY DIRECTORIES

Harris State Industrial Directory—
New Jersey
Harris Publishing Co.
2057 Aurora Rd.
Twinsburg, OH 44087
216/425-9000
800/888-5900

New Jersey Business Directory
American Business Directories
5711 S. 86th Cir.

P.O. Box 27347
Omaha, NE 68127
402/593-4600

New Jersey Directory
of Manufacturers
Commerce Register, Inc.
190 Godwin Ave.
Midland Park, NJ 07432
201/445-3000

NEW JERSEY GOVERNMENT EMPLOYMENT OFFICES

Office of Personnel Management
215/597-7440
912/757-3000
(Federal job-service center.)

New Jersey Dept. of Labor
Labor Bldg. John Fitch Plaza
CN 058
Trenton, NJ 08625
609/292-2400
(State job-service center.)

NEW YORK

LEADING NEW YORK EMPLOYERS

ABC Inc.
77 W. 66th St.
New York, NY 10023-6298
212/456-7777
(Media communications.)

Alleghany Corp.
375 Park Ave.
New York, NY 10152
212/752-1356
(Property and casualty
insurance.)

Allegheny Power System
12 E. 49th St.
New York, NY 10017-1028
212/752-2121
(Electric utility.)

Ambac
One State Street Plz.
New York, NY 10004
212/668-0340
(Lease and finance.)

Amerada Hess
1185 Ave. of the Americas
New York, NY 10036
212/997-8500
(Energy.)

American Express Co.
American Express Tower
World Financial Ctr.
New York, NY 10285-4805
212/640-2000
(Diversified financial services.)

American International Group, Inc.
70 Pine St.
New York, NY 10270
212/770-7000
(Insurance.)

American Telephone & Telegraph Co. (AT&T)
32 Ave. of the Americas
New York, NY 10013-2412
212/387-5400
(Telecommunications.)

Arrow Electronics
25 Hub Dr.
Melville, NY 11747
516/391-1300
(Computer peripherals.)

Asarco
180 Maiden Lane
New York, NY 10038-4991
212/510-2000
(Nonferrous metals.)

Avnet Inc.
80 Cutter Mill Rd.
Great Neck, NY 11021
516/466-7000
(Computer peripherals.)

Avon Products
9 West 57th St.
New York, NY 10019-2683
212/546-6015
(Personal products.)

Backer Spielvogel Bates, Inc.
405 Lexington Ave.
New York, NY 10174
212/297-7000
(Advertising.)

The Bank of New York
48 Wall St.
New York, NY 10286
212/495-1784
(Banking.)

Bankers Trust Co.
280 Park Ave.
New York, NY 10017
212/250-2500
(Commercial banking.)

Bausch & Lomb, Inc.
One Bausch & Lomb Pl.
Rochester, NY 14604
716/338-6000
(Medical supplies.)

The Bear Stearns Companies, Inc.
245 Park Ave.
New York, NY 10167
212/272-2000
(Diversified financial services.)

Bell Aerospace Textron
(div. of Textron, Inc.)
2221 Niagra Falls Blvd.
Niagra Falls, NY 14304
716/297-1000
(Aerospace and electronic products and systems.)

Bell Atlantic/Nynex Mobile Co.
2000 Corporate Dr.
Pearl River, NY 10962
914/365-7200
(Cellular telephones.)

BHC Communications
767 Fifth Ave.
New York, NY 10153
212/421-0200
(Broadcasting and movies.)

Booz Allen & Hamilton Inc.
101 Park Ave.
New York, NY 10178
212/697-1900
(Management consulting.)

Bristol-Myers Squibb Co.
345 Park Ave.
New York, NY 10154-0037
212/546-4000
(Health care products, pharmaceuticals.)

Brown Brothers Harriman & Co.
59 Wall St.
New York, NY 10005
212/483-1818
(Commercial banking, brokerage, investment advisory services.)

Bulova Corp.
2615 Brooklyn-Queens Expwy.
Flushing, NY 11377
718/204-3399
(Watches.)

CBS, Inc.
51 W. 52nd St.
New York, NY 10019
212/975-4321
(Broadcasting.)

Cablevision Systems Corp.
1 Media Crossways
Woodbury, NY 11797
516/364-8450
(Cable television.)

Chase Manhattan Corp.
270 Park Ave.
New York, NY 10017
212/270-6000
(Banking.)

Ciba-Geigy Corp.
444 Saw Mill River Rd.
Ardsley, NY 10502
914/479-5000
(Pharmaceuticals.)

Citicorp
399 Park Ave.
New York, NY 10043
800/285-3000
(Holding company.)

Colgate-Palmolive
300 Park Ave.
New York, NY 10022-7499
212/310-2000
(Personal products.)

Computer Associates International
1 Computer Associates Plz.
Islandia, NY 11788-7000
516/342-5224
(Computer software.)

Computer Task Group Inc.
800 Delaware Ave.
Buffalo, NY 14209
716/882-8000

Consolidated Edison Company of New York, Inc.
4 Irving Pl.
New York, NY 10003
212/460-4600
(Electric utility.)

Corning Incorporated
1 Riverfront Plz.
Corning, NY 14831
607/974-9000
(Chemicals and chemical products, diagnostic substances, glassware, scientific instruments, telephone wire and cable, fiber optics systems and equipment, etc.)

C.S. First Boston
55 E. 52nd St.
New York, NY 10055
212/909-2000
(Underwriters, distributors, investment dealers.)

Dean Witter Reynolds Inc.
2 World Trade Ctr.
New York, NY 10048
212/392-2222
(Diversified financial services.)

Donaldson Lufkin & Jenrette
277 Park Ave.
New York, NY 10172
212/892-3000
(Investment brokers.)

Dover Inc.
280 Park Ave.
New York, NY 10017-1292
212/922-1640
(Misc. industrial equipment.)

Dow Jones & Co.
200 Liberty St.
New York, NY 10281
212/416-2000
(Newspaper publishing.)

Eastman Kodak Co.
343 State St.
Rochester, NY 14650
716/724-4000
(Photographic equipment and supplies, etc.)

Empire Blue Cross & Blue Shield
622 Third Ave.
New York, NY 10017
212/476-1000
(Health insurance.)

Equitable Life Assurance Society
787 Seventh Ave.
New York, NY 10019
212/554-1234
(Life insurance.)

Fidelity & Casualty Co. of New York
180 Maiden Ln.
New York, NY 10038
212/440-3000
(Insurance.)

First Empire State Corp.
One M&T Plz.
Buffalo, NY 14203
716/842-5445
(Bank.)

Forest Laboratories
909 Third Ave.
New York, NY 10022
212/421-7850
(Drugs.)

Frontier Communications Group
180 S. Clinton Ave.
Rochester, NY 14646-0700
716/777-1000
(Telecommunications.)

Gant Corp.
404 Fifth Ave.
New York, NY 10018
212/502-6400
(Apparel.)

Goldman Sachs & Co.
85 Broad St.
New York, NY 10004
212/902-1000
(Investment banking.)

GP Financial Corp.
41—60 Main St.
Flushing, NY 11355-3820
718/670-4356
(Thrift institution.)

Grey Advertising Inc.
777 Third Ave.
New York, NY 10017
212/546-2000
(Advertising.)

Guardian Life Insurance Co. of America
201 Park Ave. S.
New York, NY 10003
212/598-8000
(Insurance.)

Hearst Corporation
959 8th Ave.
New York, NY 10019
212/649-2000
(Communications media—book publishing, magazine publishing, etc.)

Hoechst Celanese Corp.
3 Park Ave.
New York, NY 10016
212/251-8000
(Textiles, etc.)

International Business Machines Corp. (IBM)
Old Orchard Rd.
Armonk, NY 10504
914/765-1900
(Computers, electronics systems, etc.)

International Flavors & Fragrances
521 W. 57th St.
New York, NY 10019
212/765-5500
(Specialty chemicals.)

International Paper Co.
2 Manhattanville Rd.
Purchase, NY 10577
914/397-1500
(Paper & lumber.)

Interpublic Group of Cos.
1271 Ave. of the Americas
New York, NY 10020
212/399-8000
(Advertising & publishing.)

ITT
1330 Ave. of the Americas
New York, NY 10019-5490
212/258-1000
(Property & casualty insurance.)

Jordache Enterprises, Inc.
226 W. 37th St.
New York, NY 10018
212/643-8400
(Clothing.)

Lehman Bros. Holdings
3 World Financial Ctr.
New York, NY 10285
212/526-7000
(Brokerage.)

Leucadia National
315 Park Ave. S.
New York, NY 10010
212/460-1900
(Insurance.)

Liz Claiborne
1441 Broadway
New York, NY 10018
212/354-4900
(Wearing apparel.)

Loew's
667 Madison Ave.
New York, NY 10021-8087
212/545-2000
(Tobacco.)

Long Island Lighting Co.
175 E. Old Country Rd.
Hicksville, NY 11801
516/755-6000
(Electric utility.)

Loral Corp.
600 Third Ave.
New York, NY 10016
212/697-1105
(Electronic systems and
components.)

R. H. Macy & Co.
151 W. 34th St.
New York, NY 10001
212/695-4400
(Department store.)

Macy's Northeast, Inc.
Herald Sq.
New York, NY 10001
212/695-4400
(Retailing.)

Marine Midland Bank, N.A.
1 Marine Midland Ctr.
Buffalo, NY 14203
716/841-2424
(Banking.)

Mark IV Industries, Inc.
501 John James Audubon Pkwy.
Buffalo, NY 14228
716/689-4972
(Conglomerate—auto parts, plastics,
pharmaceuticals.)

Marsh & McLennan Cos.
1166 Ave. of the Americas
New York, NY 10036-2774
212/345-5000
(Brokerage.)

MBIA, Inc.
113 King St.
Armonk, NY 10504
914/273-4545
(Lease & finance.)

McGraw-Hill, Inc.
1221 Ave. of the Americas
New York, NY 10020
212/512-2000
(Magazine and book publishing.)

Melville Corp.
1 Theall Rd.
Rye, NY 10580
914/925-4000
(Apparel stores.)

Merrill Lynch
World Financial Ctr.
North Tower
New York, NY 10281-1331
212/449-1000
(Diversified financial services.)

Metropolitan Life Insurance Co.
1 Madison Ave.
New York, NY 10010
212/578-2211
(Insurance.)

Moog, Inc.
Seneca & Jamison Rd.
East Aurora, NY 14052
716/652-2000
(Electrohydraulic servovalves, servocativators, etc.)

J. P. Morgan & Co., Inc.
60 Wall St.
New York, NY 10260-0060
212/483-2323
(Holding company.)

Morgan Guaranty International Finance Corp.
60 Wall St.
New York, NY 10260
212/483-2323
(Banking.)

Morgan Stanley & Co., Inc.
1221 Avenue of the Americas
New York, NY 10020
212/761-4000
(Diversified financial services.)

National Broadcasting Company, Inc.
30 Rockefeller Plz.
New York, NY 10112
212/664-4444
(Broadcasting.)

New York Life Insurance Co.
51 Madison Ave.
New York, NY 10010
212/576-7000
(Life insurance.)

New York State Electric & Gas
P.O. Box 3287
Ithaca, NY 14852-0001
607/347-4131
(Utility.)

Niagara Mohawk Power
300 Erie Blvd. W.
Syracuse, NY 13202
315/474-1511
(Utility.)

The New York Times Company, Inc.
229 W. 43rd St.

New York, NY 10036-3959
212/556-1234
(Newspaper publishing.)

Northrop-Grumman Corp.
1111 Stewart Ave.
Bethpage, NY 11714
516/575-2464
(Holding company. At same address: Grumman Aircraft Systems Division, Grumman Data Systems Division, Grumman Systems Group, Grumman Electronic Systems Division, Grumman Space Systems Division, Grumman International, Inc., etc.)

NYNEX Corp.
1095 Ave. of the Americas
New York, NY 10036
212/395-2121
(Telephone services.)

Ogden Corp.
2 Pennsylvania Plz.
New York, NY 10121
212/868-6100
(Industrial services.)

Ogilvy & Mather Worldwide
309 W. 49th St.
New York, NY 10019
212/237-4000
(Advertising.)

Olsten Corp.
175 Broad Hollow Rd.
Melville, NY 11747-8905
516/844-7800
(Business services.)

Omnicom Group
437 Madison Ave.
New York, NY 10022
212/415-3600
(Advertising & publishing.)

OnBancorp
101 S. Salinas St.
Syracuse, NY 13202
315/424-4400
Fax 315/424-5973
(Bank.)

Oneida Ltd.
134 Kenwood Ave.
Oneida, NY 13421
315/361-3000
(Silverware.)

Oppenheimer & Co., Inc.
Oppenheimer Tower
World Financial Ctr.
New York, NY 10281
212/667-7000
(Diversified financial services.)

PaineWebber Group Inc.
1285 Ave. of the Americas
New York, NY 10019
212/713-2000
(Diversified financial services.)

Pall Corp.
2200 Northern Blvd.
Greenvale, NY 11548
516/484-5400
(Air intake filters; internal
combustion engines, exc. auto.)

Penn Traffic
1200 State Fair Blvd.
Syracuse, NY 13209
315/453-7284
(Supermarkets & restaurants.)

PepsiCo, Inc.
700 Anderson Hill Rd.
Purchase, NY 10577
914/253-2000
(Beverage, food, etc.)

Pfizer, Inc.
235 E. 42nd St.
New York, NY 10017-5755
212/573-2323
(Pharmaceuticals.)

Philip Morris Companies, Inc.
120 Park Ave.
New York, NY 10017
212/880-5000
(Conglomerate—tobacco, food
processing, etc.)

Primerica Corp.
61 Broadway
New York, NY 10006

212/248-0600
(Consumer finance companies,
insurance brokerage, mutual funds,
etc.)

Prudential Securities, Inc.
1 Seaport Plz.
New York, NY 10292
212/214-1000
(Securities brokerage.)

Readers Digest Association, Inc.
1 Reader's Digest Rd.
Pleasantville, NY 10570-7000
914/238-1000
(Magazine publishing.)

Reliance Group Holdings
55 E. 52nd St.
New York, NY 10055
212/909-1100
(Insurance.)

**Republic New York Securities
Corp.**
452 Fifth Ave.
New York, NY 10018
212/525-6600
(Banking.)

RJR Nabisco
1301 Ave. of the Americas
New York, NY 10019-6013
212/258-5600
(Food.)

Rochester Community Savings Bank
40 Franklin St.
Rochester, NY 14604
716/258-3000
(Thrift institution.)

Saatchi & Saatchi Advertising
375 Hudson St.
New York, NY 10014
212/463-2000
(Advertising.)

Saks Fifth Avenue
611 Fifth Ave.
New York, NY 10017
212/753-4000
(Retailing.)

Salomon Brothers, Inc.
7 World Trade Center
New York, NY 10048
212/783-7000
(Diversified financial services.)

Smith Barney, Inc.
388 Greenwich St.
New York, NY 10013
212/816-6000
(Investment brokers.)

Teachers Insurance & Annuity Association of America
730 Third Ave.
New York, NY 10017
212/490-9000
(Pensions, insurance, and annuities for teachers and professors.)

Texaco, Inc.
2000 Westchester Ave.
White Plains, NY 10604
914/253-4000
(Petroleum exploration and refining, petrochemicals, etc.)

J. Walter Thompson Co.
466 Lexington Ave.
New York, NY 10017
212/210-7000
(Advertising.)

TIG Holdings
65 E. 55th St.
New York, NY 10022
212/446-2700
(Insurance.)

Time, Inc.
Time-Life Bldg.
Rockefeller Ctr.
New York, NY 10020-1393
212/522-1212
(Magazine and book publishing, cable TV, etc.)

Time Warner Inc.
75 Rockefeller Plz.
New York, NY 10019
212/484-8000
(Broadcasting, publishing.)

Travelers, Inc.
250 West St.
New York, NY 10013
212/723-3900
(Lease & finance.)

Turner Corp.
375 Hudson St.
New York, NY 10014
212/229-6000
(Builder.)

US Life Corp.
125 Maiden Ln.
New York, NY 10038
212/709-6000
(Insurance.)

U.S. Trust Co.
114 W. 47th St.
New York, NY 10036
212/852-1000
(Bank.)

Varity Corp.
672 Delaware Ave.
Buffalo, NY 14209
716/888-8000
(Auto parts.)

Viacom
1515 Broadway
New York, NY 10036
212/258-6000
(Broadcasting, movies, publishing.)

Westvaco Corp.
299 Park Ave.
New York, NY 10171
212/688-5000
(Paper & lumber.)

F. W. Woolworth Co.
233 Broadway
New York, NY 10279-0003
212/553-2000
(Discount stores.)

World Color Press, Inc.
360 Madison Ave., 3rd Flr.
New York, NY 10017
212/885-1200
(Commercial printing.)

Yonkers Contracting Co., Inc.
969 Midland Ave.
Yonkers, NY 10704
914/965-1500
(Highway and street construction.)

Young & Rubicam, Inc.
285 Madison Ave.
New York, NY 10017
212/210-3000
(Advertising.)

NEW YORK BUSINESS PERIODICALS

Crain's New York Business
220 E. 42nd St.
New York, NY 10017
212/210-0277
Fax 212/210-0799
(Weekly: annual directory issue lists
the top companies in New York.)

Long Island/Business
2150 Smithtown Ave.
Ronkonkoma, NY 11779
516/737-1700
(Weekly; puts out annual special
issue "Long Island Executive
Register," which lists area businesses
and includes contact names.)

NEW YORK DIRECTORIES

*Dalton's New York Metropolitan
Directory*
Dalton's Directory
410 Lancaster Ave.
Haverford, PA 19041
800/221-1050
610/649-2680
(also includes Northern New Jersey)

Greater Buffalo Business Directory
Greater Buffalo Chamber of
Commerce
300 Main Place Tower
Buffalo, NY 14202
716/852-7100

*Harris State Industrial Directory—
New York*
Harris Publishing Co.
2057 Aurora Rd.
Twinsburg, OH 44087

216/425-9000
800/888-5900

New York Business Directory
American Business Directories
5711 S. 86th Cir.
P.O. Box 27347
Omaha, NE 68127
402/593-4600

*New York Metropolitan Directory of
Manufacturers*
Commerce Register, Inc.
190 Godwin Ave.
Midland Park, NJ 07432
201/445-3000

*New York Upstate Directory of
Manufacturers*
Commerce Register, Inc.
190 Godwin Ave.
Midland Park, NJ 07432
201/445-3000

NEW YORK GOVERNMENT EMPLOYMENT OFFICES

Office of Personnel Management
215/597-7740
912/757-3000
(Federal job-service center.)

Job Service Division
New York State Dept. of Labor
State Campus
Bldg. 12
Albany, NY 12240
518/457-2612
(State job-service center.)

PENNSYLVANIA

LEADING PENNSYLVANIA EMPLOYERS

Acme Markets, Inc.
75 Valley Stream Pkwy.
Malvern, PA 19355
215/888-4000
(Food retailing.)

Advanta
200 Tournament Dr.
Horsham, PA 19044
215/657-4000
(Lease & finance.)

Air Products & Chemicals, Inc.
7201 Hamilton Blvd.
Allentown, PA 18195
610/481-7435
(Chemicals, industrial gases,
engineering services.)

Alco Standard
825 Duportail Rd.
Wayne, PA 19087
610/296-8000
(Business supplies.)

Allegheny Ludlum Corp.
1000 Six PPG Pl.
Pittsburgh, PA 15222
412/394-2800
(Steel.)

Aluminum Company of America
425 6th Ave.
Pittsburgh, PA 15219-1850

412/553-4545
(Aluminum mining and mills.)

AMP
P.O. Box 3608
Harrisburg, PA 17105-3608
717/564-0100
(Computer peripherals.)

ARA Services Inc.
ARA Tower
1101 Market St.
Philadelphia, PA 19107
215/238-3000
(Diversified services.)

Armco, Inc.
301 Grant St.
Pittsburgh, PA 15219
412/255-9800
(Steel production.)

Armstong World Industries, Inc.
313 W. Liberty St.
Lancaster, PA 17603
717/397-0611
(Floor coverings, building products,
furniture.)

Bell Atlantic Corp.
1717 Arch St.
Philadelphia, PA 19103
215/963-6000
(Telecommunications holding
company.)

Bell Atlantic Corp./Pennsylvania
1 Parkway
Philadelphia, PA 19102
215/466-9990
(Telephone service.)

Bethlehem Steel Corp.
1170 8th Ave.
Bethlehem, PA 18016-7699
610/694-2424
(Steel.)

Betz Laboratories, Inc.
4636 Somerton Rd.
Langhorne, PA 19053
215/355-3300
(Design, treatment, and control of
water systems, etc.)

Carpenter Technology Corp.
101 Bern St.
Reading, PA 19601
215/208-2000
(Specialty metals.)

CIGNA Corp.
1650 Market St.
Philadelphia, PA 19103
215/761-1000
(Insurance.)

Comcast
1500 Market St.
Philadelphia, PA 19102-2148
215/665-1700
(Broadcasting & movies.)

Consolidated Natural Gas
625 Liberty Ave.
Pittsburgh, PA 15222-3199
412/227-1000
(Utility.)

Conrail Corp.
1401 Walnut St.
Philadelphia, PA 19101
215/973-3827
(Railroad.)

Core States Financial
13 Chestnut St.
Philadelphia, PA 19103
215/973-3827
(Bank.)

Corporate and Professional Data Systems
200 James Pl.
Monroeville, PA 15746
412/372-2344
(Computer integrated systems
design.)

Crown Cork & Seal Co., Inc.
9300 Ashton Rd.
Philadelphia, PA 19136
215/698-5100
(Packaging machinery, corks, etc.)

Dauphin Deposit
213 Market St.
Harrisburg, PA 17101
717/255-2121
(Bank.)

Day & Zimmerman Inc.
1818 Market St.
Philadelphia, PA 19103
215/299-6600
(Engineering services, consulting, etc.)

Dick Corp.
P.O. Box 10896
Pittsburgh, PA 15236
412/384-1000
(Construction.)

DQE, Inc.
301 Grant St.
Pittsburgh, PA 15219
412/393-6000
(Electric utility.)

Equitable Resources, Inc.
420 Blvd. of the Allies
Pittsburgh, PA 15219
412/261-3000
(Natural gas and oil.)

Exide Corp.
645 Pennsylvania St.
Reading, PA 19601
215/378-0500
(Batteries.)

First Union Bank
Broad & Walnut Sts.
Philadelphia, PA 19109
215/985-6000
(Banking.)

**General Accident Insurance Co.
of America**
436 Walnut St.
Philadelphia, PA 19105
215/625-1000
(Insurance.)

Harsco Corp.
350 Poplar Church Rd.
Camp Hill, PA 17011
717/763-7064
(Plastics, metal products.)

H. J. Heinz Co.
606 Grant St.
Pittsburgh, PA 15219
412/456-5700
(Food processing.)

Hershey Foods Corp.
100 Crystal A Dr.
Hershey, PA 17033
717/534-4000
(Food processing.)

Integra Financial Corp.
4 PPG Pl.
Pittsburgh, PA 15222
412/644-7669
(Banking.)

Intelligent Electronics
411 Eagleview Blvd.
Exton, PA 19341
610/458-5500
(Electronics stores.)

Kaufman's
400 Fifth Ave.
Pittsburgh, PA 15219
412/232-2000
(Department store.)

Keystone Financial, Inc.
1 Keystone Plz.
Harrisburg, PA 17101
717/233-1555
(Bank.)

Lukens, Inc.
50 S. First Ave.
Coatesville, PA 19320
215/383-2000
(Plate steel, plate products, materials
handling equipment, etc.)

Mack Trucks, Inc.
2180 Mack Blvd.
Allentown, PA 18103
215/439-3011
(Trucks.)

Mellon Bank Corp.
Mellon Bank Ctr.
500 Grant St.
Pittsburgh, PA 15258-0001
412/234-5000
(Banking.)

Meridian Bancorp, Inc.
P.O. Box 1102
Reading, PA 19603
610/655-2000
(Banking.)

Metropolitan Edison Co.
2800 Pottsville Pike
Reading, PA 19605
215/929-3601
(Electric utility.)

Mylan Laboratories
130 7 St.
Pittsburgh, PA 15222
412/232-0100
(Drugs.)

Nustar
1332 Enterprise Dr.
West Chester, PA 19380
610/692-5900
(Cable TV.)

PECO Energy Co.
2301 Market St.
Philadelphia, PA 19103
215/841-4000
(Utility.)

PNC Bank
1 PNC Plz.
Pittsburgh, PA 15265
412/762-2666
(Banking.)

PPG Industries
1 PPG Pl.
Pittsburgh, PA 15222
412/434-3131
(Glass, construction materials.)

Pennsylvania Power Co.
1 E. Washington St.
Box 891
New Castle, PA 16101
412/652-5531
(Electric utility.)

Pennsylvania Power & Light Co.
2 N. Ninth St.
Allentown, PA 18101-1179
610/774-5151
(Utility.)

Pep Boys Manny Moe & Mack
3111 W. Allegheny Ave.
Philadelphia, PA 19132
215/229-9000
(Specialty stores.)

Philadelphia Newspapers, Inc.
3901 Market St.
Philadelphia, PA 19104
215/222-4000
(Newspaper publishing.)

Quaker State Corp.
255 Elm St.
Oil City, PA 16301
814/676-7676
(Lubricants, fuels, etc.)

Rhone-Poulenc Rorer, Inc.
500 Arcola Rd.
Box 1200
Collegeville, PA 19426
610/454-8000
(Pharmaceuticals.)

Rite Aid
P.O. Box 3165
Harrisburg, PA 17105-0042
717/761-2633
(Drug & discount stores.)

Rohm & Haas Co.
100 S. Independence Mall
Philadelphia, PA 19106-2399
215/592-3000
(Industrial and agricultural
chemicals, plastics, polymers, etc.)

Scott Paper Co., Inc.
1 Ind. Hwy. & Tinicum Is. Rd.
Philadelphia, PA 19113

610/522-5000
(Paper products, printing and
publishing paper, forest products,
etc.)

Sharon Specialty Steel, Inc.
Roemer Blvd.
Sharon, PA 16146
412/983-6000
(Steel.)

SmithKline Beecham Corp.
1 Franklin Plz.
Philadelphia, PA 19101
215/751-4000
(Pharmaceuticals, analytical products
for biomedical research.)

Sovereign Bancorp
P.O. Box 12646
Reading, PA 19612
610/320-8400
(Thrift institution.)

Strawbridge & Clothier
801 Market St.
Philadelphia, PA 19107
215/629-6000
(Department store.)

Sun Company, Inc.
10 Penn Center Plz.
Philadelphia, PA 19103-1699
215/977-3000
(Oil and gas.)

UGI Corp.
460 N. Gulph Rd.
Valley Forge, PA 19482
610/337-1000
(Natural gas.)

US Healthcare Inc.
980 Jolly Rd.
Blue Bell, PA 19422
215/628-4800
(Healthcare.)

USX Corp.-US Steel Group
600 Grant St.
Pittsburgh, PA 15219-4776
412/433-1121
(Steel, chemicals, petroleum, natural
gas, etc.)

Union Pacific
1170 8 Ave.
Bethlehelm, PA 18018
610/861-3200
(Railroad.)

Unisys Corp.
Township Line & Union Meeting
Blue Bell, PA 19422
215/986-4011
(Information systems, electronic
systems, and services.)

VF Corp.
1047 N. Park Rd.
Wyomissing, PA 19610
215/378-1151
(Wearing apparel.)

Westinghouse Electric Corp.
11 Stanwix St.
Pittsburgh, PA 15222-1384

412/244-2000
(Electronic systems and products.)

Woolrich, Inc.
1 Mill St.
Woolrich, PA 17779
717/769-6464
(Apparel.)

Wyeth-Ayerst Laboratories Div.
Lancaster Ave.
Radnor, PA 19101
215/688-4400
(Pharmaceuticals.)

York International Corp.
631 S. Richland Ave.
York, PA 17403
717/771-7890
(Air conditioning, heating,
refrigeration equipment.)

PENNSYLVANIA BUSINESS PERIODICALS

Philadelphia Business Journal
400 Market St., Suite 300
Philadelphia, PA 19106
215/238-1450
(Weekly.)

Pittsburgh Business Times
2313 E. Carson St., Suite 200
Pittsburgh, PA 15203
412/481-6397
FAX 412/481-9956
(Weekly.)

PENNSYLVANIA DIRECTORIES

*Dalton's Philadelphia Metropolitan
Directory*
Dalton's Directory
410 Lancaster Ave.
Haverford, PA 19041
800/221-1050
610/649-2680

*Harris Pennsylvania Industrial
Directory*
Harris Publishing Co.
2057 Aurora Rd.
Twinsburg, OH 44087
216/425-9000
800/888-5900

*Pennsylvania Business
Directory*
American Business Directories
5711 S. 86th Cir.
P.O. Box 27347
Omaha, NE 68127
402/593-4600

*Pennsylvania Directory of
Manufacturers*
Commerce Register, Inc.
190 Godwin Ave.
Midland Park, NJ 07432
201/445-3000

Pennsylvania Manufacturers
Register
Manufacturers' News, Inc.

1633 Central St.
Evanston, IL 60201
708/864-7000

PENNSYLVANIA GOVERNMENT EMPLOYMENT OFFICES

Office of Personnel Management
Career American Connection
U.S. Government Employment
Information Service
William J. Green, Jr. Federal Bldg.
600 Arch St., Room 1416
Philadelphia, PA 19106
215/597-7440
(Federal job-service center.)

Bureau of Job Service
Labor 7 Industry Bldg., Room 1115
Seventh and Forster Sts.
Harrisburg, PA 17121
717/787-3354
(State job-service center.)

RHODE ISLAND

LEADING RHODE ISLAND EMPLOYERS

American Insulated Wire Corp.
36 Freeman St.
Pawtucket, RI 02861
401/726-0700
(Insulated wire and cable.)

American Tourister, Inc.
91 Main St.
Warren, RI 02885
401/245-2100
(Luggage.)

Amica Mutual Insurance Co.
Lincoln Ctr. Blvd.
Providence, RI 02940
401/521-9100
(Insurance.)

Amtrol, Inc.
1400 Division Rd.
West Warwick, RI 02893
401/884-6300
(Fabricated platework.)

Brooks Drug, Inc.
242 Taunton Ave.
E. Providence, RI 02914
401/434-1400
(Drug stores.)

Brown & Sharpe Manufacturing
Co.
200 Frenchtown Rd.
North Kingston, RI 02852
401/886-2000
(Machine tool accessories.)

Carol Cable Co., Inc.
249 Roosevelt Ave.
Pawtucket, RI 02860
401/728-7000
(Wire and cable.)

Citizens Bank
1 Citizens Plz.
Providence, RI 02903
401/456-7098
(Savings bank.)

Cranston Print Works Co.
1381 Cranston St.
Cranston, RI 02920
401/942-3000
(Textile printing, finishing,
converting.)

A. T. Cross Co., Inc.
1 Albion Rd.
Lincoln, RI 02865
401/333-1200
(Pens, pencils, desk sets, etc.)

CVS
1 CVS Dr.
Woonsocket, RI 02895
401/765-1500
(Drug stores and supplies.)

Davol, Inc.
100 Sockanosset Crossrd.
Cranston, RI 02920
401/463-7000
(Orthopedic, prosthetic, and surgical
appliances and devices.)

Fleet Financial Group, Inc.
50 Kennedy Plz.
Providence, RI 02903
401/278-5800
(Banking.)

Gilbane Building Co.
7 Jackson Walkway
Providence, RI 02903
401/456-5800
(Commercial and industrial
construction.)

Hasbro, Inc.
1027 Newport Ave.
Pawtucket, RI 02861
401/431-8697
(Toys.)

Narragansett Electric Co., Inc.
280 Melrose St.

Providence, RI 02907
401/784-4000
(Utility.)

Nortek Inc.
50 Kennedy Plz.
Providence, RI 02903
401/751-1600
(Building materials.)

PlaySkool Inc.
1027 Newport Ave.
Box 1059
Pawtucket, RI 02861
401/431-8697
(Toys.)

Providence Energy Corporation
100 Weybosset St.
Providence, RI 02903
401/272-9191
(Natural gas distribution, real estate.)

Providence Journal Co.
75 Fountain St.
Providence, RI 02902
401/277-7000
(Newspaper publishing, television.)

Stanley Fastening Systems
Rte. 2
East Greenwich, RI 02818
401/884-2500
(Office equipment.)

Teknor Apex Co.
505 Central Ave.
Pawtucket, RI 02861
401/725-8000
(Plastics materials.)

Textron, Inc.
40 Westminster St.
Providence, RI 02903
401/421-2800
(Aerospace, helicopters, defense
systems, engines, etc.)

RHODE ISLAND BUSINESS PERIODICAL

Providence Business News
Herald Press, Inc.
300 Richmond St.

Providence, RI 02903
401/273-2201

RHODE ISLAND DIRECTORIES

Connecticut, Rhode Island
Directory of Manufacturers
Commerce Register, Inc.
190 Godwin Ave.
Midland Park, NJ 07432
201/445-3000

Harris State Industrial Directory—
Massachusetts/Rhode Island
Harris Publishing Co.
2057 Aurora Rd.
Twinsburg, OH 44087
216/425-9000; 800/888-5900

Rhode Island Business Directory
American Business Directories
5711 S. 86th Cir.
P.O. Box 27347
Omaha, NE 68127
402/593-4600

Rhode Island Directory of
Manufacturers
Dept. of Economic Development
1 W. Exchange St.
Providence, RI 02903
401/277-2601

RHODE ISLAND GOVERNMENT EMPLOYMENT OFFICES

Office of Personnel Management
215/597-7440
912/757-3000
(Federal job-service center.)

Job Service Division
Dept. of Employment Security
101 Friendship St.
Providence, RI 02903
401/277-3722
(State job-service center.)

VERMONT

LEADING VERMONT EMPLOYERS

BankNorth Group, Inc.
300 Financial Plz.
Burlington, VT 05401
802/658-9959

Ben & Jerry's Homemade, Inc.
Rte. 2 & 100
Waterbury, VT 05676
802/244-5641
(Ice cream.)

C & S Wholesale Grocers, Inc.
Old Ferry Rd.
Brattleboro, VT 05301
802/257-4371
(Wholesale grocery distributor.)

Cabot Creamery Co-op Corp.
Main St.
Cabot, VT 05647
802/563-2231
(Cheese and dairy products.)

Carris Reels, Inc.
Depot Ln.
Rutland, VT 05701
802/773-9111
(Plywood, pressboard, metal and
plastic reels for wire/cordage
industry.)

Champlain Cable Corp.
12 Hercules Dr.

Colchester, VT 05446
802/655-2121
(Wire and cable.)

Chittenden Bank
2 Burlington Sq.
Burlington, VT 05401
802/658-4000
(Banking.)

EHV-Weidmann Industries, Inc.
Memorial Dr.
P.O. Box 903
Industrial Pk.
St. Johnsbury, VT 05819
802/748-8106
(Electronic and electrical
equipment.)

Engelberth Construction, Inc.
2000 Mountain View Dr.
Colchester, VT 05446
802/655-0100
(Construction.)

Fonda Group, Inc.
15—21 Lower Newton St.
P.O. Box 329
St. Albans, VT 05478
802/524-5966
(Paper food containers, etc.)

Green Mountain Power Corp.
25 Green Mountain Dr.
South Burlington, VT 05403
802/864-5731
(Electric utility.)

IDX Corp.
1400 Shelburne Rd.
South Burlington, VT 05403
802/658-2664
(Medical software development.)

Key Bank of Vermont
149 Bank St.
Burlington, VT 05401
802/658-1810
(Banking.)

Killington Ltd.
Killington Rd.
Killington, VT 05751

802/422-3333
(Ski resort.)

Lane Press, Inc.
1000 Hinesburg Rd.
So. Burlington, VT 05403
802/863-5555
(Commercial printing.)

Mack Molding Co., Inc.
E. Arlington Rd.
Arlington, VT 05250
802/375-2511
(Molded plastics.)

Merchants Bancshares, Inc.
123 Church St.
Burlington, VT 05401
802/658-3400
(Banking.)

National Life Insurance Co.
1 National Life Dr.
Montpelier, VT 05604
802/229-3333
(Insurance.)

**National Life Investment
Management Co., Inc.**
1 National Life Dr.
Montpelier, VT 05604
802/229-9300
(Securities brokers and dealers,
investment advisors.)

Orvis, Inc.
10 River Rd.
Manchester, VT 05254
802/362-3750
(Mail order catalog house—sporting
goods, apparel, etc.)

Pizzagalli Construction Co.
772 Graniteville Rd.
Graniteville, VT 05654
802/658-4100
(General contractor.)

Rock of Ages Corp.
Box 482
Barre, VT 05641
802/476-3115
(Dimension stone mining/quarrying.)

Russell Corp.
117 Strongs Ave.
Rutland, VT 05701
802/775-3325
(Construction.)

Stratton Corp.
Stratton Mountain
RR1, P.O. Box 145
S. Londonderry, VT 05155-9406
802/297-2200
(Ski resort.)

Velan Valve Corp.
18 Ave. C
Griswold Industrial Park
Williston, VT 05495
802/863-2561
(Valves.)

Vermont Financial Services Corp.
100 Main St.
Brattleboro, VT 05301
802/257-7151
(Bank holding company.)

Vermont National Bank
100 Main St.
P.O. Box 804
Brattleboro, VT 05301
802/257-7151
(Banking.)

Vermont Yankee Nuclear Power Corp.
Ferry Rd.
Brattleboro, VT 05301
802/257-5271
(Electrical generator.)

VERMONT BUSINESS PERIODICAL

Vermont Business
2 Church St.
Burlington, VT 05401-4445

802/863-8038
(Monthly.)

VERMONT DIRECTORIES

Harris State Directory—New England
Harris Publishing Co.
2057 Aurora Rd.
Twinsburg, OH 44087
216/425-9000
800/888-5900

Maine, Vermont, New Hampshire Directory of Manufacturers
Commerce Register, Inc.

190 Godwin Ave.
Midland Park, NJ 07432
201/445-3000

Vermont Business Directory
American Business Directories
5711 S. 86th Cir.
P.O. Box 27347
Omaha, NE 68127
402/593-4600

VERMONT GOVERNMENT EMPLOYMENT OFFICES

Office of Personnel Management
215/597-7440
912/757-3000
(Federal job-service center.)

Employment Service
Dept. of Employment and Training
P.O. Box 488
Montpelier, VT 05602
802/229-0311
(State job-service center.)

THE SOUTHEAST, TEXAS, AND THE GULF STATES

OUTLOOK: Relatively good.

The South has been diversifying, expanding automotive assembly/parts manufacturing and moving into high-tech industries, services, and international trade, and away from old-line businesses like paper, pulp, and textiles. Expect weaker performance from the old-line manufacturing companies—such as textiles—but this should be offset by strength in the new industries.

WHAT'S NEXT

▶ Southeast: poised for long-term growth.

The key strength of the Southeast: low costs. Numerous companies have relocated to the Southeast to take advantage of these lower operating costs, and this trend should continue. In addition, there is a strong influx of new residents pouring into the area to seek job opportunities and a higher quality of life. As a result, *Florida, Georgia,* and *North Carolina* were among the top five states in population growth. Expect this sort of growth to continue.

Many of the industries in the Southeast perform well during economic good times. Among them: home furnishings, building products, textile manufacturers, appliance manufacturers, and auto-related companies—the area accounts for 127,000 automotive jobs, 13% of the nation's automotive workforce. While these industries are affected during economic slowdowns, whenever the economy rebounds and consumer confidence surges, these industries bounce back—which points to positive growth over the long term.

In addition, the increase of high-tech firms in the area will continue to spur growth and job creation, particularly in the *Research Triangle Park area in North Carolina.* Originally an R&D center for large companies, the Park area is now home to high-tech companies—software, semiconductors, drugs, biotech, and communications. The clustering of customers, competitors, and suppliers, plus a large labor pool, creates a base for further growth . . . and attractive job prospects. A sign of the strength of the Southeast in general: In one year alone, about 870,000 new jobs were created. Hot spot cities are: Austin, Orlando, Mobile, Dallas, and Raleigh.

▶ Some specifics for several Southeastern states.

Florida is one of the strongest states where employment is concerned. One key reason: its strong performance in tourism. Add to this a high number of retirees, a healthy amount of job growth—the job creation—and the long-term outlook is good. One area in particular that will continue to expand is health care. While health care is a hot industry throughout the country, it's especially strong in Florida, a key reason being the number of senior citizens who retire to Florida. Orlando continues strong, with tourism, television, conventions, movie production, and Walt Disney World adding jobs. Other strong industries: import/export, international banking (Miami is the number-two foreign banking center in the U.S.), and biomedical technology.

Tennessee will be steadily improving and growing. As home to the Saturn auto plant and growing in importance as an auto center, Tennessee will reap the benefits of continued stable car sales and expanding health care facilities. So too will *Kentucky,* with its Georgetown Toyota plant and its GE Appliance factory. The new auto plants have attracted networks of parts suppliers, with increased requirements for workers of all skills. Also benefiting will be *Mississippi* and *Alabama.* Mississippi is also benefiting from its thriving casino industry— which is generating hundreds of millions of dollars and offering a healthy number of employment opportunities. As for Alabama, it will be seeing growth in its forestry industry as well, due to environmental legislation limiting timber-cutting in the Pacific Northwest, and emerging high-tech industry. *West Virginia* is weaker, suffering from the downsizing of the coal industry. *Virginia* is going and growing strong. With its lower taxes, more amenable business environment and better quality of life, it has been attracting a number of companies away from Washington, D.C. Virginia may be on the way to becoming the East Coast's new technology center. Northern Virginia, the home of the Pentagon and where the Internet was created, is now home to many of the country's computer communications companies, including the fast growing on-line services industry— more than 1,100 businesses. This combination makes Virginia a bright spot for employment opportunities.

Georgia is adding jobs in a range of sectors. The greatest activity is in real estate, with more than 32,000 jobs slated to be added, according to Georgia State University data. One possible slowdown: Atlanta, which boomed due to the 1996 Olympics, is headed for flatter growth. While it added between 75,000 to 100,000 jobs each year since 1993, it's expected to add only about half that amount now. However, the long-term outlook is still fairly good, as the diversified economy remains strong, if not growing at the same pace as the last few years. One possible problem: overbuilding, both in the residential and commercial markets.

A regional best bet: *North Carolina* is growing in importance as a banking center. One reason: the NCNB-Sovran merger, which thrust the state into the spotlight. And the repercussions are very positive. In fact, some experts are pointing to Charlotte as the Atlanta of the future—that is, a focal point for new business and corporate relocations. Keep an eye on this area as it may really heat up.

And *South Carolina* is benefiting from the low cost of doing business in the state. An influx of new businesses, such as the $625 million BMW plant built in 1993, is translating into increased employment opportunities.

▶ **Texas and the oil-patch states: growing and going strong.**

Texas suffered a bit from the financial problems in Mexico. For example, retailers near the border suffered as fewer Mexicans crossed the border to shop. But overall Texas looks good for the long term. For the last few years, its economy has performed better than the rest of the country, and this trend should continue. Among the reasons—a diversified economy; an influx of new businesses, including such large companies as Exxon, GTE, and J.C. Penney; and world-class universities. Particularly hot: Austin (see below), Richardson, a Dallas suburb recently dubbed "Telecom Corridor" due to its growing telecommunications industry, and Houston, which has attracted a number of heavy-hitting companies and, as a port, continues to benefit from expanding world trade.

The outlook for the oil patch states is, as always, tied to a degree to the performance of the energy industry. More specifically:

Oklahoma is aggressively targeting California businesses that intend to relocate, focusing its efforts on the aviation and food industries. In addition, it has set up economic development offices in Pacific Rim countries, India, and Europe—all in an effort to draw new business. The outlook? Could be very interesting and very ripe for employment prospects.

Louisiana: Key to a bright long-term outlook: Louisiana's role as a gateway to the United States. More than one-third of domestic water-borne commerce and one-sixth of foreign sea trade moves through six deep-water ports in Louisiana. The bottom line, then, is simple: As U.S. trade exports continue to increase, so will port activity.

REGIONAL HOT SPOTS

AUSTIN, TX: Home of the University of Texas as well as four other colleges and two seminaries, Austin has a reputation for being a great place to live. It is also home to 500 software companies and 1,000 high-tech manufacturers. In 1997, hiring was very strong, and predictions were that 15,000 jobs would be added, particularly programmers and high-end managers. But entry-level hiring was also strong. As a cultural capital of Texas, Austin remained a dynamic city in more ways than one.

ORLANDO, FL: A job increase of 28% is predicted in the coming months and years, and even if the economy (still sizzling at the time of writing) turns down somewhat, most experts see this region as booming for many years to come. Key reasons: the wide diversity of jobs available—from software to leisure. More good news: Universal Studios plans to add almost 15,000 new jobs between now and 2001; Disney is building six new attractions—and planning to add 8,000 new jobs. Not for nothing is Orlando now one of the world's top tourist attractions.

ALABAMA

LEADING ALABAMA EMPLOYERS

Alabama Power Company
600 N. 18th St.
Birmingham, AL 35203
205/326-8002
(Utilities company.)

AmSouth Bancorp
20th St. and Fifth Ave. N.
P.O. Box 11007
Birmingham, AL 35203
205/320-7151
(Banking.)

American Cast Iron Pipe Co.
1501 31 Ave. N.
Birmingham, AL 35207
205/325-7701
(Iron foundries.)

Avex Electronics, Inc.
4807 Bradford Dr., NW
Huntsville, AL 35805
205/722-6000
(Semiconductors and related
devices.)

B E & K, Inc.
2000 International Pk. Dr.
Birmingham, AL 35243
205/969-3600
(Engineering services.)

BellSouth Services, Inc.
3196 Hwy. 280 S.
Birmingham, AL 35243
205/321-2524
(Telephone services.)

Blount, Inc.
4520 Executive Pk. Dr.
Montgomery, AL 36116
334/244-4000
(Industrial and commercial
construction; manufacturing. Also at
same address: Blount Construction
Division, Blount International Ltd.)

Boone Newspapers, Inc.
Tuscaloosa, AL 35403
205/752-3381
(Newspaper publishing.)

Brunos Inc.
800 Lake Shore Pkwy.
Birmingham, AL 35211-2486
205/940-9400
(Supermarkets.)

Buffalo Rock Co.
111 Oxmoor Rd.
Birmingham, AL 35209
205/940-9799
(Soft drinks.)

Coca-Cola Bottling Co.
4600 E. Lake Blvd.
Birmingham, AL 35217

205/841-2653
(Soft drink bottling.)

Compass Bank
15. S. 20th St.
Birmingham, AL 35233
205/933-3000
(Bank holding co.)

Courtaulds Fibers Inc.
Highway 43 N.
Axis, AL 36505
205/679-2200
(Manmade fibers.)

Diversified Products Corp.
309 Williamson Ave.
Opelika, AL 36801
205/749-9001
(Sporting goods and recreational
products.)

Drummond Co., Inc.
530 Beacon Pkwy.
Birmingham, AL 35209
205/945-6542
(Coal mining.)

Ebsco Industries, Inc.
5724 Hwy. 280 E.
Birmingham, AL 35242
205/991-6600
(Magazine subscription sales/service,
display fixtures, etc.)

Gulf States Paper Corp.
1400 River Rd., NE
Tuscaloosa, AL 35404
205/553-6200
(Paper and paper products, lumber
and other forest products.)

Gayfer's
3250 Airport Blvd.
Mobile, AL 36606
334/471-6000
(Department stores.)

Harbert Corporation
1 Riverchase Pkwy. S.
Birmingham, AL 35244
205/987-5500
(Construction and engineering,
cogeneration, real estate.)

Intergraph Corp.
8252 Hwy. 20 W.
Huntsville, AL 35894
205/730-2000
(Workstations and applications.)

Kinder-Care Learning Ctr., Inc.
2400 Presidents Dr.
Montgomery, AL 36116
334/277-5090
(Daycare centers, etc.)

Liberty National Life Insurance Co.
2001 Third Ave. S.
Birmingham, AL 35233
205/325-2722
(Life insurance.)

Morrison Inc.
9721 Morrison Dr.
Mobile, AL 36609
205/344-3000
(Cafeterias, restaurants, etc.)

Parisian, Inc.
750 Lakeshore Pkwy.
Birmingham, AL 35211
205/940-4000
(Apparel stores.)

Protective Life Corp.
2801 Hwy. 280 S.
Birmingham, AL 36223
205/879-9230
(Insurance.)

Regions Financial
417 20 St., N.
Birmingham, AL 35203
205/326-7060
(Bank.)

Russell Corporation
1 Lee St.
Alexander City, AL 35010
205/329-4000
(Apparel manufacturer.)

Rust International Inc.
100 Corporate Pkwy.
Box 101
Birmingham, AL 35242
205/995-7878

(Industrial design, engineering, construction.)

SCI Systems, Inc.
2101 Clinton Ave.
Huntsville, AL 35805
205/882-4800
(Computer and communications systems.)

Sonat, Inc.
1900 5
Birmingham, AL 35203
205/325-3800
(Utility.)

Sony Magnetic Products, Inc.
4275 W. Main St.
Dothan, AL 36301
334/793-7655
(Magnetic recording tapes.)

Southern Company Services, Inc.
42 Inverness Ctr. Pkwy.
Birmingham, AL 35242
205/870-6011
(Accounting, engineering, and technical services for Atlanta's Southern Co.)

Southern Natural Gas Co.
1900 Fifth Ave. N.
Birmingham, AL 35203
205/325-7410
(Utilities company.)

SouthTrust Bank of Alabama
420 20 St. N.
Birmingham, AL 35203
205/254-5000
(Banking.)

Torchmark Corp.
2001 Third Ave. S.
Birmingham, AL 35233
205/325-4200
(Insurance, financial planning services, management services.)

Vulcan Materials Co.
1 Metroplex Dr.
Birmingham, AL 35209
205/877-3000
(Chemicals, construction materials.)

Jim Wilson & Associates
4121 Carmichael Rd.
Montgomery, AL 36106
205/260-2500
(Real estate developers.)

Wolverine Tube, Inc.
125 Perimeter Pkwy., NW
Decatur, AL 35602
205/353-1310
(Metal tubing.)

ALABAMA BUSINESS PERIODICAL

Business Alabama Monthly
PMT Publishing
2465 Commercial Park Dr.
Mobile, AL 36606

334/473-6269
(Monthly magazine; puts out annual
"Top Public Companies," listing
leading area companies.)

ALABAMA DIRECTORIES

Alabama Business Directory
American Business Directories
5711 S. 86th Cir.
P.O. Box 27347
Omaha, NE 68127
402/593-4600

Alabama Directory
of Mining and Manufacturing
available from:
Harris Publishing Company
2057 Aurora Rd.
Twinsburg, OH 44087
216/425-9000
800/888-5900

Alabama Industrial Directory
Alabama Development Office
c/o State Capitol
Montgomery, AL 36130
334/242-0400

Alabama Manufacturers Register
Manufacturers' News, Inc.
1633 Central St.
Evanston, IL 60201
708/864-7000

Harris Southeastern Regional
Manufacturers Directory
Harris Publishing Co.
2057 Aurora Rd.
Twinsburg, OH 44087
216/425-9000; 800/888-5900

ALABAMA GOVERNMENT EMPLOYMENT OFFICES

Office of Personnel Management
520 Wynn Dr., NW
Huntsville, AL 35816
205/837-0894
(Federal job-service center.)

Employment Service
Dept. of Industrial Relations
649 Monroe St.
Montgomery, AL 36131
205/242-8055
(State job-service center.)

FLORIDA

LEADING FLORIDA EMPLOYERS

John Alden Financial Corp.
7300 Corporate Ctr. Dr.
Miami, FL 33126
305/715-2000
(Insurance.)

Allied Signal Aerospace Co.
2100 NW 62 St.
Fort Lauderdale, FL 33309
305/928-2100
(Avionics systems manufacturer.)

American Savings of Florida FSB
17801 NW Second Ave.
Miami, FL 33169
305/653-5353
(Thrift institution.)

AT&T Paradyne Corp.
8545 126th Ave.
Largo, FL 34643
813/530-2000
(Telecommunications equipment.)

Barnett Banks
50 N. Laura St.
Jacksonville, FL 32202
904/791-7720
(Banking.)

Barnett Bank of Tampa
101 E. Kennedy Blvd.
Tampa, FL 33602
813/227-2200
(Banking.)

Barnett Bank of Central Florida
390 N. Orange Ave.
Orlando, FL 32801
407/420-2700
(Banking.)

Barnett Bank of Pinellas County
200 Central Ave.
St. Petersburg, FL 33701
813/892-1703

Barnett Bank of South Florida, N.A.
701 Brickell Ave.
Miami, FL 33131
305/350-7100
(Banking.)

Burger King Corp.
17777 Old Cutler Rd.
Miami, FL 33157
305/378-7011
(Fast food restaurants.)

Carnival Corp.
3655 NW 87th Ave.
Miami, FL 33178
305/599-2600
(Cruise lines.)

CSF Holdings Inc.
1221 Brickell Ave.
Miami, FL 33131
305/577-0400
(Thrift.)

Darden Restaurants, Inc.
P.O. Box 593330
Orlando, FL 32859
407/245-4000
(Chain restaurants.)

Eckerd Corp.
P.O. Box 4689
Clearwater, FL 34618
813/399-6000
(Drug & discount stores.)

EG&G Florida, Inc.
412 High Point Dr.
Cocoa, FL 32926
407/631-7300
(Engineering services.)

Energizer Power Systems
U.S. Hwy. 441 N.
Box 147114
Alachua, FL 32615
904/462-3911
(Storage batteries.)

FPL Group, Inc.
700 Universal Blvd.
Juno Beach, FL 33408
407/694-6300
(Utility holding company.)

First Union National Bank of Florida
225 Water St.
Jacksonville, FL 32202
904/361-2265
(Banking.)

Florida Power & Light Co.
9250 W. Flagler St.
Miami, FL 33174
305/552-3552
(Utility.)

Florida Progress Corp.
1 Progress Plz.
St. Petersburg, FL 33733
813/824-6400
(Utility.)

GTE Florida Incorporated
1 Tampa City Ctr.
Tampa, FL 33602
813/224-4011
(Telecommunications.)

W. R. Grace
One Town Center Rd.
Boca Raton, FL 33486
407/362-2000
(Chemicals.)

Harcourt Brace and Co.
6277 Sea Harbor Dr.
Orlando, FL 32887
407/345-2000
(Book and periodical publishing.)

Harris Corp.
1025 W. NASA Blvd.
Melbourne, FL 32901
407/727-9100
(Electronic systems, semiconductors, communications, and office equipment.)

Home Shopping Network, Inc.
2501 118th Ave. N.

St. Petersburg, FL 33716
813/572-8585
(Cable television network.)

Independent Insurance Group
1 Independent Dr.
Jacksonville, FL 32202
904/358-5151
(Insurance.)

IVAX
8800 NW 36th St.
Miami, FL 33178-2404
305/590-2200
(Drugs.)

Kloster Cruise Ltd.
95 Merrick Way
Miami, FL 33134
305/447-9660
(Cruise line.)

Knight-Ridder, Inc.
1 Herald Plz.
Miami, FL 33132
305/376-3800
(Newspaper publishing.)

Martin Marietta Corp.
7700 Technology Dr.
Melbourne, FL 32904
407/984-2561
(Patriot missiles; other electronics and defense systems.)

Office Depot Inc.
2200 Old Germantown Rd.
Delray Beach, FL 33445
407/278-4800
(Specialty stores.)

Orlando Sentinel Communications Co.
633 N. Orange Ave.
Orlando, FL 32801
407/420-5000
(Newspaper publishing.)

Physicians Corp. Of America
5835 Blue Lagoon Dr.
Miami, FL 33126
305/267-6683
(Health care services.)

P-I-E Nationwide, Inc.
4814 Phillips Hwy.
Jacksonville, FL 32207
904/731-0580
(Motor freight carrier.)

**Pratt & Whitney Group—
Government Engine Business**
17900 Beeline Hwy.
Jupiter, FL 33478
407/796-2000
(Military aircraft and rocket
engines.)

Publix Super Markets, Inc.
1936 George Jenkins Blvd.
Lakeland, FL 33802
813/688-1188
(Supermarkets.)

Racal DataCom, Inc.
1601 N. Harrison Pkwy.
Sunrise, FL 33323
305/846-1061
(Telecommunications
equipment.)

Royal Caribbean Cruises, Ltd.
1050 Caribbean Way
Miami, FL 33132
305/539-6000
(Cruise line.)

Ryder System, Inc.
3600 NW 82nd Ave.
Miami, FL 33166
305/593-3726
Fax 305/593-4196
(Truck leasing, jet engine repair,
aircraft components sale and
leasing.)

St. Joe Paper Co.
1650 Prudential Dr.
Jacksonville, FL 32207
904/396-6600
(Packaging.)

Sensomatic Electronics
500 NW 12th Ave.
Deerfield Beach, FL 33442-1795
305/420-2000
(Business supplies.)

Sunbeam-Oster
2200 E. Las Olas Blvd.
Ft. Lauderdale, FL 33301
305/767-2100
(Appliances.)

TECO Energy Inc.
702 N. Franklin St.
Tampa, FL 33602
813/228-4111
(Electric utility.)

Tech Data
5350 Tech Data Dr.
Clearwater, FL 34620
813/539-7429
(Computer peripherals.)

Universal Studios—Florida
P.O. Box 10000
Lake Buena Vista, FL 32832
407/363-8000
(Entertainment company.)

Walt Disney World, Inc.
1375 Buena Vista Dr.
Lake Buena Vista, FL 32830
407/824-2222
(Amusement park, etc.)

Walter Industries
1500 N. Dale Mabry Hwy.
Tampa, FL 33607
813/871-4811
(Home building and financing,
etc.)

Jim Walter Corp.
4010 Boy Scout Blvd.
Tampa, FL 33607
813/873-4000
(Building materials.)

Winn-Dixie Stores Inc.
5050 Edgewood Ct.
Jacksonville, FL 32254
904/783-5000
(Supermarkets.)

FLORIDA BUSINESS PERIODICALS

Florida Trend
Box 611
St. Petersburg, FL 33731
813/821-5800
(Monthly.)

Miami Today
Box 1368
Miami, FL 33101
305/579-0211
(Weekly.)

Orlando Magazine
Box 2207
Orlando, FL 32802

407/539-3939
(Monthly.)

South Florida Business Journal
1050 Lee Wagner Blvd.
Ft. Lauderdale, FL 33315
305/359-2100
(Weekly.)

Tampa Bay Business
4350 W. Cyprus St.
Suite 400
Tampa, FL 33607
813/873-8225

FLORIDA DIRECTORIES

Florida Business Directory
American Business Directories
5711 S. 86th Cir.
P.O. Box 27347
Omaha, NE 68127
402/593-4600

Florida Manufacturers Register
Manufacturers' News, Inc.
1633 Central St.
Evanston, IL 60201
708/864-7000

Harris Directory of Florida Industries
Harris Publishing Co.
2057 Aurora Rd.
Twinsburg, OH 44087
216/425-9000
800/888-5900

FLORIDA GOVERNMENT EMPLOYMENT OFFICES

Office of Personnel Management
Commodore Bldg., Suite 125
3444 McCrory Pl.
Orlando, FL 32803-3701
407/648-6148
(Federal job-service center.)
215/597-7440
912/757-3000

Dept. of Labor and Employment Security
1320 Executive Ctr. Dr.
300 Atkins Bldg.
Tallahassee, FL 32399-0667
904/488-7228
(State job-service center.)

GEORGIA

LEADING GEORGIA EMPLOYERS

Aflac
1932 Wynton Rd.
Columbus, GA 31999
706/323-3431
(Life and health insurance.)

AGCO
4830 River Green Pkwy.
Duluth, GA 30136
404/813-9200
(Heavy equipment.)

Alumax
5655 Peachtree Pkwy.
Norcross, GA 30092-2812
404/246-6600
(Nonferrous metals.)

American Family Corp.
1932 Wynnton Rd.
Columbus, GA 31999
706/323-3431
(Insurance.)

Bank South, N.A.
55 Marietta St., NW
Atlanta, GA 30303
404/525-1859
(Banking.)

BellSouth Corporation
1155 Peachtree St., NE
Atlanta, GA 30309-3610
404/249-2000
(Bell regional holding company.)

Cable News Network, Inc.
(part of Turner Broadcasting System)
Box 105366
Atlanta, GA 30348
404/827-1500
(Cable television all-news network.)

Ciba Vision Care Corp.
2910 Amwiler Ct.
Atlanta, GA 30360
770/448-1200
(Optical care products.)

The Coca-Cola Company
1 Coca Cola Plz., NW
Atlanta, GA 30313
404/676-2121
(Beverages and food.)

Coca-Cola Enterprises Inc.
1 Coca Cola Plz., NW
Atlanta, GA 30313
404/676-2100
(Soft drinks, extracts and syrups.)

Coronet Industries, Inc.
1502 Coronet Dr.
Dalton, GA 30720
706/259-4511
(Carpeting.)

Cox Enterprises
1400 Lake Hearn Dr.
Atlanta, GA 30319
404/843-5000
(Communications media.)

Crawford & Co.
5620 Glenridge Dr., NE
Atlanta, GA 30342
404/256-0830
(Insurance agents; brokers and service.)

Delta Airlines, Inc.
Employment Office—Bldg. A2
Hartsfield-Atlanta International Airport
Atlanta, GA 30320
404/715-2501
(Airline.)

Digital Communications Associates
1000 Alderman Dr.
Alpharetta, GA 30202
770/442-4000
(Computer peripherals.)

Equifax, Inc.
1600 Peachtree St., NW

Atlanta, GA 30309
404/885-8000
(Credit information.)

Federal Reserve Bank of Atlanta
104 Marietta St.
Atlanta, GA 30303
404/521-8500
(Federal Reserve bank.)

First Financial Management
5660 New Northside Dr.
Atlanta, GA 30328
404/857-0001
(Financial data processing.)

First Union National Bank of Georgia
999 Peachtree St., NE
Atlanta, GA 30309
404/827-7100
(Banking.)

Flowers Industries, Inc.
200 U.S. Hwy. 19 S.
Thomasville, GA 31792
912/226-9110
(Food processing.)

Forstmann & Co., Inc.
161 Nathaniel Dr.
P.O. Box 1049
Dublin, GA 31027
912/275-5400
(Wool fabric mills.)

Genuine Parts
2999 Circle 75 Pkwy., NW
Atlanta, GA 30339
770/953-1700
(Auto parts.)

Georgia Gulf Corp.
400 Perimeter Ctr. Ter.
Atlanta, GA 30346
770/395-4500
(Chemicals.)

Georgia-Pacific Corp.
133 Peachtree St., NE
Atlanta, GA 30303
(Forest products.)

Georgia Power Co.
333 Piedmont Ave., NE

Atlanta, GA 30308
404/523-8023
(Utility.)

Gold Kist, Inc.
244 Perimeter Ctr. Pkwy., NE
Atlanta, GA 30346
404/393-5392
(Poultry processing.)

Gulfstream Aerospace Corp.
500 Gulfstream Rd.
Savannah International Airport
Savannah, GA 31407
912/965-3000
(Aircraft manufacturing, support, and services.)

HBO & Co.
301 Perimeter Ctr. N.
Atlanta, GA 30346
404/393-6000
(Computer software.)

Holiday Inns Worldwide
3 Ravinia Dr.
Atlanta, GA 30346-2149
770/604-2000
(Hotels, motels.)

Home Depot, Inc.
2727 Paces Ferry Rd.
Atlanta, GA 30339
404/433-8211
(Building supply retailer.)

Kemira, Inc.
President St. Ext.
Savannah, GA 31404
912/652-1000
(Inorganic pigments.)

Lanier Worldwide, Inc.
2300 Parklake Dr., NE
Atlanta, GA 30345
770/496-9500
(Dictating machines, fax machines, etc.)

Life Insurance Co. of Georgia
5780 Powers Ferry Rd., NW
Atlanta, GA 30327
770/980-5100
(Insurance.)

Macy's South, Inc.
180 Peachtree St., NW
Atlanta, GA 30303
404/221-7221
(Department stores.)

National Data Corp.
1 National Data Plz.
Atlanta, GA 30329
404/728-2000
(Electronic services.)

Nation's Bank
715 Peachtree St., NE
Atlanta, GA 30308
404/607-3400
(Banking.)

Primerica Financial Services
3120 Breckenridge Blvd.
Duluth, GA 30136
404/381-8444
(Insurance.)

Rollins, Inc.
2170 Piedmont Rd., NE
Atlanta, GA 30324
404/888-2000
(Pest control and lawn care.)

Roper Corp.
1507 Broomtown Rd.
La Fayette, GA 30728
706/638-5100
(Household cooking products.)

Scientific Atlanta, Inc.
1 Technology Pkwy. S.
Norcross, GA 30092
770/903-4000
(Equipment for telecommunications
and cable industries, etc.)

Shaw Industries
616 E. Walnut Ave.
Dalton, GA 30722-2128
706/278-3812
(Textiles.)

Southern Bell
675 W. Peachtree St., NE
Atlanta, GA 30375
404/529-8611
(Telephone services.)

The Southern Company
64 Perimeter Ctr. E.
Atlanta, GA 30346
404/393-0650
(Electric utility.)

Southwire Co.
1 Southwire Dr.
Carrolton, GA 30117
770/832-4242
(Extruded shapes and wire, copper
and copper alloy.)

SunTrust Banks
P.O. Box 4418
Atlanta, GA 30302
404/588-7711
(Banking.)

Swift Textiles, Inc.
1410 6 Ave.
Columbus, GA 31991
706/324-3623
(Textile mills.)

Synovus Financial Corp.
901 Front St.
Columbus, GA 31901
706/649-2387
(Bank.)

Trammel Crow Residential
2859 Paces Ferry Rd.
Suite 1400
Atlanta, GA 30339
770/801-1600
(Real estate developers.)

Turner Broadcasting System
190 Marietta St., NW
Atlanta, GA 30303
404/827-1700
(Broadcasting.)

Wachovia Bank of Georgia
191 Peachtree St., NW
Atlanta, GA 30303
404/332-5000
(Banking.)

West Point-Pepperell
507 W. 10th St.
West Point, GA 31833
706/645-4000
(Textiles, home furnishings.)

GEORGIA BUSINESS PERIODICALS

Atlanta Business Chronicle   404/249-1000
1801 Peachtree St., NE, Suite 150   (Weekly.)
Atlanta, GA 30309

GEORGIA DIRECTORIES

Georgia Business Directory
American Business Directories
5711 S. 86th Cir.
P.O. Box 27347
Omaha, NE 68127
402/593-4600

Georgia Manufacturers Register
Manufacturers' News, Inc.
1633 Central St.
Evanston, IL 60201
708/864-7000

Georgia Manufacturing Directory
Dept. of Industry, Trade and Tourism
Marquis II Tower
Ste. 1100
285 Peachtree Center Ave.
Box 56706

Atlanta, GA 30343
404/656-3607

Harris Georgia Manufacturers'
Directory
Harris Publishing Co.
2057 Aurora Rd.
Twinsburg, OH 44087
216/425-9000
800/888-5900

Harris Southeastern Regional
Manufacturers Directory
Harris Publishing Co.
2057 Aurora Rd.
Twinsburg, OH 44087
216/425-9000
800/888-5900

GEORGIA GOVERNMENT EMPLOYMENT OFFICES

Office of Personnel Management
Richard B. Russell Federal Bldg.
75 Spring St., SW, Room 960
Atlanta, GA 30303-3309
404/331-4315
912/757-3000
(Federal job-service center.)

Employment Service
148 International Blvd. N.,
Room 400
Atlanta, GA 30303
404/656-3017
(State job-service center.)

KENTUCKY

LEADING KENTUCKY EMPLOYERS

Accuride Corp.
(subs. Phelps Dodge Corp.)
2315 Adams Ln.

Henderson, KY 42420
502/826-5000
(Wheels.)

Arco Aluminum, Inc.
101 S. Fifth St.
Louisville, KY 40202
502/566-5700
(Aluminum bars, rods, ingots, etc.)

Ashland Oil, Inc.
P.O. Box 391
Ashland, KY 41114
606/329-3333
(Oil refining, transportation and marketing, chemicals, gasoline, etc.)

Bank One of Lexington
201 E. Main St.
Lexington, KY 40507
606/231-1000
(Banking.)

Blue Cross & Blue Shield of Kentucky
9901 Linn Station Rd.
Louisville, KY 40223
502/423-2011
(Health insurance.)

Brown & Williamson Tobacco Corp.
1500 Brown & Williamson Tower
Louisville, KY 40232
502/568-7000
(Tobacco products.)

Brown-Forman Corp.
850 Dixie Hwy.
Louisville, KY 49201
502/585-1100
(Liquors.)

Capital Holding Corp.
400 W. Market
Louisville, KY 40202
502/560-2000
(Holding company—insurance companies.)

Chi-Chi's, Inc.
10200 Linn Station Rd.
Louisville, KY 40223
502/426-3900
(Chain restaurants.)

Citizens Fidelity Corp.
500 W. Jefferson St.
Louisville, KY 40296

502/581-2100
(Banking.)

Commonwealth Life Insurance Co.
680 Fourth Ave.
Louisville, KY 40202
502/587-7371
(Life insurance.)

First Image Data Input
U.S. Hwy. 25 S.
London, KY 40741
606/878-7900
(Data processing/data entry services; computer peripherals; software.)

Humana, Inc.
500 W. Main St.
Louisville, KY 40202
502/580-1000
(Hospitals.)

I.C.H. Corp.
P.O. Box 7940
Louisville, KY 40257-0940
502/897-1861
(Insurance; holding company.)

Jefferson Pilot Life Insurance Co.
300 W. Vine St.
Lexington, KY 40507
606/253-5111
(Life insurance.)

KFC Corp.
1411 Gardiner Ln.
Louisville, KY 40213
502/456-8300
(Chain restaurants.)

Kentucky Utilities Co.
1 Quality St.
Lexington, KY 40507
606/255-1461
(Utility.)

Louisville Gas & Electric Co.
200 Main St.
Louisville, KY 40232-2030
502/627-2000
(Electric utility.)

Liberty National Bancorp, Inc.
416 W. Jefferson St.
Louisville, KY 40202
502/566-2000
(Banking.)

Link Belt Construction Equipment Co.
2651 Palumbo Dr.
Lexington, KY 40509
606/263-5200
(Construction machinery and equipment.)

Long John Silver
P.O. Box 11988
Lexington, KY 40579
606/388-6000
(Chain restaurant.)

Mazak Corp.
8025 Production Dr.
Florence, KY 41402
606/727-5700
(Wholesale industrial equipment and machinery.)

National City Bank
101 S. 5 St.
Louisville, KY 40202
502/581-4170
(Banking.)

National Processing Co.
1231 Durrett Ln.
Louisville, KY 40285
502/364-2000
(Data processing services.)

NSA—Div. of Southwire Co.
1627 State Rt. 271 N.
Hawesville, KY 42348
502/927-6921
(Secondary aluminum smelting/refining.)

Park Communications, Inc.
333 W. Vine St.
Lexington, KY 40507
606/252-7275
(Television.)

Peabody Coal Company
1951 Barrett Ct.
Box 1990
Henderson, KY 42420
520/827-0800
(Coal mining and handling.)

Providian
400 W. Market St.
Louisville, KY 40202
502/560-2000
(Insurance.)

Publishers Printing Co.
100 Frank E. Simon Ave.
Louisville, KY 40165
502/543-2251
(Commercial printing.)

Toyota Motor Manufacturing USA
1001 Cherry Blossom Way
Georgetown, KY 40324
502/868-2000
(Automobiles.)

Union Underwear Co., Inc.
700 Church St.
Bowling Green, KY 42101
502/781-9800
(Underwear manufacturing.)

Valvoline, Inc.
P.O. Box 14000
Lexington, KY 40512
606/357-7777
(Oils and greases.)

Henry Vogt Machine Co.
100 W. Ormsby Ave.
Louisville, KY 40210
502/634-1500
(Fabricated platework.)

KENTUCKY BUSINESS PERIODICAL

Business First
P.O. Box 249
Louisville, KY 40201

KENTUCKY DIRECTORIES

Harris Kentucky Industrial Directory
Harris Publishing Company
2057 Aurora Rd.
Twinsburg, OH 44087
216/425-9000
800/888-5900

Kentucky Business Directory
American Business Directories
5711 S. 86th Circle
P.O. Box 27347
Omaha, NE 68127
402/593-4600

Kentucky Directory of Manufacturers
Committee for Economic Development
Capital Plaza Tower
Frankfort, KY 40601
502/564-4886

Kentucky Manufacturers Register
Manufacturers' News, Inc.
1633 Central St.
Evanston, IL 60201
708/864-7000

KENTUCKY GOVERNMENT EMPLOYMENT OFFICES

Office of Personnel Management
(For federal job service centers see Ohio listing.)

Dept. for Employment Services
275 E. Main St., 2nd Fl.
Frankfort, KY 40621
502/564-5331
(State job-service center.)

LOUISIANA

LEADING LOUISIANA EMPLOYERS

Albemarle Corp.
451 Florida St.
Baton Rouge, LA 70801
504/388-8011
(Industrial organic chemicals.)

Arkla, Inc.
525 Milam St.
Shreveport, LA 71101

318/894-9165
(Gas transmission and distribution.)

Avondale Industries, Inc.
500 Edwards Ave.
New Orleans, LA 70123
504/733-4713
(Shipbuilding and repair.)

Century Telephone Ent., Inc.
100 Century Pk. Dr.
Monroe, LA 71203
318/388-9500
(Telecommunications.)

**Copolymer Rubber
& Chemical Corp.**
5955 Scenic Hwy.
Baton Rouge, LA 70805
504/355-5655
(Synthetic rubber.)

Entergy Group
639 Loyola Ave.
New Orleans, LA 79113
504/529-5262
(Electric services, natural gas
distribution.)

Ethyl Corp. Chemicals Group
451 Florida
Baton Rouge, LA 70801
504/388-8011
(Industrial organic chemicals.)

Exxon Chemical Americas
4999 Scenic Hwy.
Baton Rouge, LA 70805
504/359-7011
(Industrial inorganic chemicals.)

First Commerce Corp.
210 Barone St.
New Orleans, LA 70112
504/561-1371
(Banking.)

Freeport McMoran Agrico
1615 Poydras St.
New Orleans, LA 70112
504/582-4000
(Sulphur, phosphoric acid, etc.)

Freeport-McMoran Copper, Inc.
1615 Poydras St.
New Orleans, LA 70112
504/582-4000
(Agricultural mineral mining oil &
gas, etc.)

**Freeport-McMoran Resource
Partners**
1615 Poydras St.
New Orleans, LA 70112

504/582-4000
(Fertilizer chemicals, oil and natural
gas development, etc.)

Hibernia Corp.
313 Carondelet St.
New Orleans, LA 70166
504/533-3333
(Banking.)

**Lockheed Martin Manned Space
Systems**
P.O. Box 29304
New Orleans, LA 70189
504/257-3700
(Aerospace systems.)

Louisiana Power & Light Co.
142 DeLaronde St.
New Orleans, LA 70114
504/595-3100
(Electric utility.)

**Lykes Brothers Steamship Co.,
Inc.**
Lykes Ctr.
300 Poydras St.
New Orleans, LA 70130
504/523-5080
(Steamships.)

Maison Blanche, Inc.
1500 Main St.
Baton Rouge, LA 70802
504/389-7018
(Department store.)

Martin Mills, Inc.
6261 Main Hwy.
St. Martinville, LA 70582
318/394-6041
(Apparel—men's and boys' briefs
and T-shirts.)

McDermott International, Inc.
1450 Poydras St.
New Orleans, LA 70112
504/587-5700
(Power generation systems &
equipment engineering.)

**Murphy Exploration & Production
Co.**
P.O. Box 61780
New Orleans, LA 70161

505/561-2811
(Petroleum and natural gas
exploration and drilling.)

New Orleans Public Service
639 Loyola Ave.
New Orleans, LA 70113
504/595-3100
(Utility.)

Nicols Equipment Co.
2865 Mason Ave.
Baton Rouge, LA 70805
504/356-1301
(Industrial buildings/warehouses/
machinery, equipment repair, rental
and leasing.)

Pan American Life Insurance
601 Poydras St.
New Orleans, LA 70130
504/566-1300
(Life insurance.)

Picadilly Cafeterias, Inc.
3232 Sherwood Forest Blvd.
Baton Rouge, LA 70816

504/293-9440
(Restaurant food services.)

Premier Bancorp, Inc.
451 Florida St.
Baton Rouge, LA 70801
504/332-4020
(Banking—owns Premier Bank, N.A.)

Riverwood International Corp.
1000 Jonesboro Rd.
W. Monroe, LA 71292
318/362-2000
(Paperboard, paper bags, other paper
products.)

Shell Offshore, Inc.
P.O. Box 61933
New Orleans, LA 70161
504/588-6161
(Petroleum exploration and drilling.)

Tidewater, Inc.
1440 Canal St.
New Orleans, LA 70112
504/568-1010
(Oil field supplies.)

LOUISIANA BUSINESS PERIODICAL

Baton Rouge Business Report
Louisiana Business, Inc.
P.O. Box 1949

Baton Rouge, LA 70821
504/928-1700

LOUISIANA DIRECTORIES

Directory of Louisiana
Manufacturers
Department of Economic
Development
Box 94185
Capitol Station
Baton Rouge, LA 70804-9185
504/342-5383

Greater Baton Rouge
Manufacturers Directory
Greater Baton Rouge Chamber of
Commerce

564 Laurel St.
Box 3217
Baton Rouge, LA 70821
504/381-7125

Harris Directory of Louisiana
Manufacturers
Harris Publishing Co.
2057 Aurora Rd.
Twinsburg, OH 44087
216/425-9000
800/888-5900

*Louisiana Business
Directory*
American Business Directories
5711 S. 86th Cir.
P.O. Box 27347
Omaha, NE 68127
402/593-4600

*Louisiana Manufacturers
Register*
Manufacturers' News, Inc.
1633 Central St.
Evanston, IL 60201
708/864-7000

LOUISIANA GOVERNMENT EMPLOYMENT OFFICES

Employment Service
Office of Employment Security
P.O. Box 94094
Baton Rouge, LA 70804-9094
504/342-3016
(State job-service center.)

Office of Personnel Management
8610 Broadway,
Suite 305
San Antonio, TX 78217
210/805-2402
(Federal job-service center.)

MISSISSIPPI

LEADING MISSISSIPPI EMPLOYERS

Bancorp of Mississippi Inc.
1 Mississippi Plz.
Tupelo, MS 38801
601/680-2000
(Banking.)

Bill's Dollar, Inc.
P.O. Box 9407
Jackson, MS 39286
601/981-7171
(Discount stores.)

Bryan Foods, Inc.
100 Church Hill Rd.
West Point, MS 39773
601/494-3741
(Meat packing.)

CMC Industries, Inc.
1801 Fulton Dr.
Corinth, MS 38834
601/287-3771
(Telecommunications equipment.)

Croft Metals, Inc.
124 24 St.

McComb, MS 39648
601/684-6121
(Aluminum and plastic plumbing fixtures.)

Delta Pride Catfish, Inc.
Indianola Industrial Pk.
Hwy. 495
Indianola, MS 38751
601/887-5401
(Catfish processing.)

Deposit Guaranty
P.O. Box 1200
Jackson, MS 39215
601/354-8211
(Banking.)

Ergon, Inc.
2829 Lakeland Dr.
Jackson, MS 39208
601/933-3000
(Oil and gas, transportation, manufacturing.)

First Mississippi Corp.
700 North St.
Box 1249
Jackson, MS 39202
601/948-7550
(Organic crudes and intermediates,
dyes and pigments.)

Hancock Fabrics, Inc.
3406 W. Main St.
Tupelo, MS 38801
601/842-2834
(Sewing/needlework stores.)

Holiday Inns, Inc.
11200 E. Goodman Rd.,
Olive Branch, MS 38654
601/895-2941
(Motels/hotels.)

Ingall's Shipbuilding, Inc.
1000 W. River Rd.
Pascagoula, MS 39567
601/935-1122
(Shipbuilding.)

Stuart C. Irby Co.
815 E. State St.
Jackson, MS 39201
601/969-1811
(Construction electric power lines, etc.)

Jitney-Jungle Stores of America
453 N. Mill St.
Jackson, MS 39202
601/948-0361
(Food stores.)

KLLM Transport Services Inc.
3475 Lakeland Dr.
Box 6098
Jackson, MS 39208
601/939-2545
(Trucking.)

LDDS Communication
515 E. Amite St.
Jackson, MS 39201-2702
601/360-8600
(Telecommunications.)

McCarty Farms, Inc.
Industrial Park Dr.
Magee, MS 39111

601/849-3351
(Poultry processing, feed mills.)

McRae's, Inc.
3455 Hwy. 80 W.
P.O. Box 20080
Jackson, MS 39289
601/968-4400
(Department stores.)

Mississippi Chemical Corp.
P.O. Box 388
Yazoo City, MS 39194
601/746-4131
(Fertilizers.)

Mississippi Power Co.
2992 W. Beach Blvd.
Gulfport, MS 39501
601/864-1211
(Utility.)

Mississippi Power & Light Co.
711 Tombigbee St.
Jackson, MS 39201
601/969-2500
(Electric utility.)

Mississippi Valley Gas Co.
711 W. Capitol St.
Jackson, MS 39203
601/961-6900
(Natural gas distribution.)

Mobile Com
(subs. BellSouth)
1800 E. County Line Rd.
Jackson, MS 39157
601/957-7355
(Radio communications, holding
company.)

National American Corp.
2325 Hwy. 90
Gautier, MS 39553
601/497-3594
(Real estate developer.)

Peavey Electronics Corp.
711 A St.
P.O. Box 2898
Meridian, MS 39301
601/483-5365
(Commercial sound equipment.)

**South Mississippi Electric Power
Association**
7037 Hwy. 49 N.
Hattiesburg, MS 39402
601/268-2083
(Electric services.)

**Southern Farm Bureau Casualty
Insurance Co.**
1800 E. County Line Rd.
Ridgeland, MS 39157
601/957-7777
(Insurance.)

**Southern Farm Bureau Life
Insurance Co.**
140 Livingston Ln.
Jackson, MS 39213
601/981-7422
(Insurance.)

Trustmark National Bank
248 E. Capitol St.
Jackson, MS 39213
601/354-5111
(Banking.)

Tyson Foods
238 Wilmington
Jackson, MS 39204
601/372-7441
(Poultry processing.)

**United Technologies Motor
Systems**
401 S. McCrary Rd.
P.O. Box 2228
Columbus, MS 39702
601/328-4150
(Auto and aircraft motors.)

MISSISSIPPI BUSINESS PERIODICAL

Mississippi Business Journal
Venture Publications
P.O. Box 23607

Jackson, MS 39225
601/352-9035
(Monthly.)

MISSISSIPPI DIRECTORIES

Mississippi Business Directory
American Business Directories
5711 S. 86th Cir.
P.O. Box 27347
Omaha, NE 68127
402/593-4600

*Harris Directory of Mississippi
Manufacturers*
Harris Publishing Co.
2057 Aurora Rd.

Twinsburg, OH 44087
216/425-9000
800/888-5900

*Harris Southeastern Manufacturers
Directory*
Harris Punlishing Co.
2057 Aurora Rd.
Twinsburg, OH 44087
216/425-9000
800/888-5900

MISSISSIPPI GOVERNMENT EMPLOYMENT OFFICES

Office of Personnel Management
215/597-7440
912/757-3000
(Federal job-service center.)

Employment Service Division
Employment Service Commission
P.O. Box 1699
Jackson, MS 39215-1699
601/354-8711

NORTH CAROLINA

LEADING NORTH CAROLINA EMPLOYERS

Biggers Brothers, Inc.
920 Black Satchel Dr.
Charlotte, NC 28216
704/394-7121
(Wholesale institutional foods.)

Branch Banking & Trust Co.
223 W. Nash St.
Wilson, NC 27894
919/399-4111
(Banking.)

Broyhill Furniture Industries, Inc.
1 Broyhill Pk.
Lenoir, NC 28633
704/758-3111
(Furniture.)

Burlington Industries, Inc.
3330 W. Friendly Ave.
Greensboro, NC 27410
919/379-2000
(Textiles.)

Burroughs Wellcome Co.
3030 Cornwallis Rd.
Research Triangle Park, NC 27709
919/248-3000
(Pharmaceuticals.)

Carolina Freight Corp.
1201 E. Church St.
Cherryville, NC 28021
704/435-6811
(Motor carrier.)

Carolina Power & Light Co.
P.O. Box 1551
411 Fayetteville St. Mall
Raleigh, NC 27602
919/546-6111
(Utility.)

CCB Financial
111 S. Corcoran St.
Durham, NC 27701
919/683-7777
(Bank.)

Centura Banks
134 N. Church St.
Rocky Mount, NC 27802
919/977-440
(Bank.)

Century Furniture Ind.
401 11th St., NW
Hickory, NC 28601
704/328-1851
(Furniture.)

Cone Mills
1201 Maple St.
Greensboro, NC 27405
910/379-6220
(Textiles.)

Drexel Heritage Furnishings
201 N. Main St.
Drexel, NC 28619
704/433-3000
(Furniture.)

Duke Power Co.
422 S. Church St.
Charlotte, NC 28242-0001
704/373-4011
(Utility.)

Exide Electronics Group, Inc.
2708 Discovery Dr.
Raleigh, NC 27604
919/872-3020
(Electrical apparatus.)

Fieldcrest Cannon, Inc.
326 E. Stadium Dr.
Eden, NC 27288
910/627-3800
(Household furnishings—rugs,
sheets, etc.)

First Citizens Bancshares, Inc.
P.O. Box 27131
Raleigh, NC 27611
919/755-7000
(Banking.)

First Union Corp.
301 S. College St.
Charlotte, NC 28202
704/374-6565
(Banking.)

First Union Mortgage Corp.
2 First Union Ctr.
Charlotte, NC 28288
704/374-6161
(Mortgage banking, real estate,
etc.)

Food Lion, Inc.
2110 Executive Dr.
Salisbury, NC 28147
704/633-8250
(Supermarkets.)

Glaxo, Inc.
5 Moore Dr.
Research Triangle Park, NC 27709
919/990-5525
(Pharmaceuticals.)

GTE South Incorporated
4100 N. Roxboro Rd.
Durham, NC 27704
919/471-5000
(Telecommunications.)

Guilford Mills, Inc.
4925 W. Market St.
Greensboro, NC 27407
910/316-4000
(Textile mills, yarn, dyes.)

Hampton Industries, Inc.
2000 Greenville Hwy.
P.O. Box 614
Kinston, NC 28501
919/527-8011
(Apparel.)

Hardees Food Systems, Inc.
1233 Hardees Blvd.
Rocky Mount, NC 27804
919/977-2000
(Fast food restaurants.)

Harriet & Henderson Yarns, Inc.
1724 Graham Ave.
Henderson, NC 27536

919/430-5121
(Yarn spinning mill.)

Henredon Furniture Industries
400 Henredon Rd.
P.O. Box 70
Morganton, NC 28655
704/437-5261
(Furniture.)

Hoechst-Celanese Corp.
Fibers & Film Division
2300 Archdale Dr.
Charlotte, NC 28209
704/554-2000
(Manmade fibers, etc.)

Ingles Markets, Inc.
P.O. Box 6076, Hwy. 70
Ashville, NC 28816
704/669-2041
(Grocery stores, shopping centers.)

Integon Corp.
500 W. Fifth St.
Winston-Salem, NC 27101
910/770-2000
(Insurance.)

Interim Health Care
141 Providence Rd.
Charlotte, NC 28207
704/372-8230
(Medical employment agency.)

Jefferson-Pilot Corp.
P.O. Box 21008
Greensboro, NC 27410
910/691-3000
(Insurance.)

Lance, Inc.
P.O. Box 32368
8600 South Blvd.
Charlotte, NC 28273
704/554-1421
(Cookies, crackers, snack foods.)

L'Eggs Products, Inc.
P.O. Box 2495
Winston-Salem, NC 27102
910/768-9181
(Hosiery.)

Lowe's Companies, Inc.
P.O. Box 1111
N. Wilkesboro, NC 28656-0001
910/651-4000
(Home centers.)

Mitsubishi Semiconducter America
3 Diamond Ln.
Durham, NC 27704
919/479-3333
(Semiconductors.)

NationsBank
101 S. Tryon St.
Charlotte, NC 28255
704/386-5000
(Commercial banking.)

Nucor Corp.
2100 Rexford Rd.
Charlotte, NC 28211
704/366-7000
(Steel.)

Planters Lifesavers Co.
1100 Reynolds Blvd.
Winston-Salem, NC 27105
910/741-2000
(Nuts, candy, etc.)

Research Triangle Institute
3040 Cornwallis Rd.
Research Triangle Park, NC 27709
919/541-6000
(Commercial physical research, etc.)

R. J. Reynolds Tobacco Co.
401 N. Main St.
Winston-Salem, NC 27101
910/741-5000
(Tobacco.)

Rose's Stores, Inc.
218 S. Garnett St.
Henderson, NC 27536
919/430-2600
(Discount stores.)

Royal Insurance Co.
9300 Arrowpoint Blvd.
Charlotte, NC 28273
704/522-2000
(Insurance.)

Ruddick Corp.
2000 Two First Union Ctr.
Charlotte, NC 28282
704/372-5404
(Supermarkets.)

SAS Institute, Inc.
100 SAS Campus Dr.
Cary, NC 27513
919/677-8000
(Computer software development.)

Southern National Corp.
200 W. 2 St.
Winston-Salem, NC 27102-1250
910/671-2000
(Bank.)

Sprint MidAtlantic
720 Western Blvd.
Tarboro, NC 27886
919/823-9900
(Telephone services.)

Unifi, Inc.
7210 W. Friendly Ave.
Greensboro, NC 27410
910/294-4410
(Textiles.)

United Carolina Bancshares
127 W. Webster St.
Whiteville, NC 28472
910/642-5131
Fax 910/642-1276
(Bank.)

Volvo GM Heavy Truck Corp.
7825 National Service Rd.
Greensboro, NC 27409
910/279-2000
(Trucks.)

Wachovia Bank
100 N. Main St.
Winston-Salem, NC 27171
910/770-5000
(Banking.)

NORTH CAROLINA BUSINESS PERIODICAL

Business NC
5435-77 Center. Dr., Suite 50
Charlotte, NC 28217

704/523-6987
(Monthly.)

NORTH CAROLINA DIRECTORIES

Harris Industrial Directory—North Carolina
Harris Publishing Co.
2057 Aurora Rd.
Twinsburg, OH 44087
216/425-9000
800/888-5900

North Carolina Business Directory
American Business Directories
5711 S. 86th Cir.
P.O. Box 27347
Omaha, NE 68127
402/593-4600

NORTH CAROLINA GOVERNMENT EMPLOYMENT OFFICES

Office of Personnel Management
4407 Bland Rd.,
Suite 200
Raleigh, NC 27609
919/790-2822
(Federal job-service center.)

Employment Security Commission of North Carolina
P.O. Box 27625
Raleigh, NC 27611
919/733-7522
(State job-service center.)

OKLAHOMA

LEADING OKLAHOMA EMPLOYERS

C. R. Anthony & Co.
701 N. Broadway
Oklahoma City, OK 73125
405/278-7400
(Department stores.)

BOK Financial Corp.
1 Williams Ctr.
Tulsa, OK 74172
918/588-6000
Fax 918/588-6853
(Bank.)

Citgo Petroleum Corp.
6100 S. Yale Ave.
Tulsa, OK 74136
918/495-4000
(Petroleum refining, marketing, transportation.)

Fleming Companies, Inc.
6301 Waterford Blvd.
Box 26647
Oklahoma City, OK 73126
405/840-7200
(Food distribution.)

Flintco Companies, Inc.
1624 W. 21st St.
Tulsa, OK 74107
918/587-8451
(Construction.)

Hale-Halsell Co.
9111 E. Oine St.
Tulsa, OK 74115
918/835-4484
(Wholesale groceries.)

Helmerich & Payne, Inc.
1579 E. 21st St.
Tulsa, OK 74114
918/742-5531
(Oil/gas wells drilling, exploration,
chemicals manufacturing, real estate.)

Hilti, Inc.
5400 S. 122nd East Ave.
Tulsa, OK 74146
918/252-6000
(Power tools.)

Kerr-McGee Corp.
Kerr-McGee Ctr.
P.O. Box 25861
Oklahoma City, OK 73125
405/270-1313
(Petroleum/natural gas exploration,
processing, marketing petrochemicals.)

Macklanburg-Duncan Co.
4041 N. Santa Fe Ave.
Oklahoma City, OK 73118
405/528-4411
(Building specialty products.)

Mapco, Inc.
1800 S. Baltimore Ave.
Tulsa, OK 74119
918/581-1800
(Integrated natural resources.)

Noble Affiliates, Inc.
110 W. Broadway St.
Ardmore, OK 73401
405/223-4110
(Petroleum services.)

**Northrop Worldwide Aircraft
Services, Inc.**
P.O. Box 108

21 NW 44th St.
Lawton, OK 73505-0108
405/353-2733
(Aircraft maintenance and support
services.)

Northwest Energy Co.
7402 SW Blvd.
Tulsa, OK 74131
918/445-0521
(Pipeline transmission of natural
gas/petroleum products.)

Oklahoma Gas & Electric Co.
P.O. Box 321
101 N. Robinson Ave.
Oklahoma City, OK 73102
405/553-3000
(Utility.)

Oklahoma Publishing Co.
9000 N. Broadway Ext.
Oklahoma City, OK 73114
405/475-3311
(Newspaper publishing.)

Parker Drilling Co.
8 E. Third St.
Tulsa, OK 74103
918/585-8221
(Oil/gas wells drilling and
exploration.)

Phillips 66 Co.
411 S. Keeler Ave.
Bartlesville, OK 74003
918/661-4400
(Petroleum marketing; convenience
stores.)

Phillips Petroleum Co.
411 S. Keeler Ave.
Bartlesville, OK 74003
918/661-6600
(Petroleum exploration, production,
refining, marketing.)

Purolator Products Co.
2 Warren Pl.
6120 S. Yale
Tulsa, OK 74136
918/481-2500
(Motor vehicle parts and accessories.)

The Williams Companies, Inc.
1 Williams Ctr.
Tulsa, OK 74172

918/588-3900
(Pipeline transmission of natural gas, etc.; digital telecommunications.)

OKLAHOMA DIRECTORIES

Oklahoma Business Directory
American Business Directories
5711 S. 86th Cir.
P.O. Box 27347
Omaha, NE 68127
402/593-4600

Oklahoma Directory of Manufacturers and Processors
Oklahoma Dept. of Commerce
Box 26980
Oklahoma City, OK 73126
405/843-9770

OKLAHOMA GOVERNMENT EMPLOYMENT OFFICES

Office of Personnel Management
8610 Broadway, Suite 305
San Antonio, TX 78217
210/805-2402
(Federal job-service center.)

Employment Service Employment Security Commission
2401 N. Lincoln Blvd.
Oklahoma City, OK 73152
405/557-0200
(State job-service center.)

SOUTH CAROLINA

LEADING SOUTH CAROLINA EMPLOYERS

Bi-Lo, Inc.
207 W. Butler Rd.
Mauldin, SC 29662
803/297-3844
(Supermarkets.)

Clinton Mills, Inc.
600 Academy St.
Clinton, SC 29325
803/833-5500
(Textiles.)

Coats & Clark, Inc.
30 Patewood Dr.
Greenville, SC 29615
803/234-0331
(Thread, trim, etc.)

Delta Woodside Industries
233 N. Main St.
Greenville, SC 29601
803/232-8301
(Textiles.)

Figgie Beverage & Food, Inc.
300 Eagle Rd.
Goose Creek, SC 29445
803/572-6640
(Beverage processing products.)

First Citizens Bancorporation of South Carolina, Inc.
1230 Main St.
Columbia, SC 29201
803/771-8700
(Banking.)

Flagstar Cos.
203 E. Main St.
Spartanburg, SC 29319-0001
803/597-8000
(Supermarkets & restaurants.)

Graniteville Co.
133 Marshall St.
Graniteville, SC 29829
803/663-7231
(Textiles.)

Greenwood Mills, Inc.
104 Maxwell Ave.
Greenwood, SC 29646
803/229-2571
(Textiles.)

Hillrom Inc.
4349 Corporate Rd.
Charleston Heights, SC 29405
803/747-8002
(Medical equipment rental and
leasing.)

Insignia Financial Group, Inc.
1 Insignia Plz.
Greenville, SC 29601
803/239-1000
(Real estate managers.)

Klear Knit, Inc.
510 Sunset Dr.
Clover, SC 29710
803/222-3011
(Apparel.)

Liberty Corp.
2000 Wade Hampton Blvd.
Greenville, SC 29602
803/268-8111
(Insurance.)

Lockwood-Greene Engineers, Inc.
1500 International Dr.
Spartanburg, SC 29307
803/578-2000
(Engineering and architectural
services.)

Michelin Tire/North America
1 Pkwy. S.
Greenville, SC 29303
803/458-5000
(Tires, inner tubes.)

Milliken and Company
920 Milliken Rd.
Spartanburg, SC 29601
803/573-2020
(Textiles.)

Multimedia, Inc.
305 S. Main St.
Greenville, SC 29601
803/298-4373
(Newspaper publishing, television
production, and syndication.)

Oneita Industries, Inc.
Conifer St.
P.O. Box 24
Andrews, SC 29510
803/264-5225
(Knit outer- and underwear.)

**Policy Management
Systems Info.**
P.O. Box 10
Columbia, SC 29202
803/735-4000
(Computer software, support and
services.)

Post & Courier Publishing
134 Columbus St.
Charleston, SC 29403
803/577-7111
(Newspaper publishing, television
stations.)

SCANA Corp.
1426 Main St.
Columbia, SC 29201
803/748-3000
(Utility.)

Sonoco Products Co.
160 N. Second St.
Hartsville, SC 29550
803/383-7000
(Paper and plastic tubes, containers,
paperboard, etc.)

**South Carolina Electric
& Gas Co.**
1426 Main St.
Columbia, SC 29218
803/748-3000
(Utility.)

**South Carolina National
Bank**
101 Greystone Blvd.
Columbia, SC 29226
803/765-3000
(Banking.)

Springs Industries, Inc.
205 N. White St.
Fort Mill, SC 29715
803/547-1500
(Textiles.)

SOUTH CAROLINA BUSINESS PERIODICAL

Carolina Business
Box 12006
New Bern, SC 28561
919/633-5106

SOUTH CAROLINA DIRECTORIES

*Harris State Industrial Directory—
South Carolina*
Harris Publishing Co.
2057 Aurora Rd.
Twinsburg, OH 44087
216/425-9000
800/888-5900

South Carolina Business Directory
American Business Directories
5711 S. 86th Cir.
P.O. Box 27347
Omaha, NE 68127
402/593-4600

SOUTH CAROLINA GOVERNMENT EMPLOYMENT OFFICES

Office of Personnel Management
(Federal job-service center.)
(See North Carolina listing.)

Employment Service
P.O. Box 995
Columbia, SC 29202
803/737-2400
(State job-service center.)

TENNESSEE

LEADING TENNESSEE EMPLOYERS

Acme Boot Company, Inc.
1002 Stafford St.
Clarksville, TN 37040
615/552-2000
(Boots.)

Aladdin Industries, Inc.
703 Murfreesboro Rd.
Nashville, TN 37210
615/748-3000
(Thermalware.)

American General Life & Accident Insurance
310 8 Ave.
Nashville, TN 37250
615/749-1000
(Life, health, and accident insurance.)

American Uniform Co.
2180 Parker St., NE
Cleveland, TN 37311
615/476-6561
(Uniforms.)

Arcadian Corp.
6750 Poplar Ave., #600
Memphis, TN 38138
901/758-5200
(Fertilizers, etc.)

Astec Industries, Inc.
4101 Jerome Ave.
Chattanooga, TN 37407
615/867-4210
(Asphalt plants, construction equipment, etc.)

Autozone, Inc.
P.O. Box 2198
Memphis, TN 38101
901/495-6500
(Auto and home supply stores.)

Berkline Corp.
1 Berkline Dr.
P.O. Box 6003
Morristown, TN 37813
615/585-1500
(Furniture.)

Better-Bilt Aluminum Products Co.
704 12 St.
Smyrna, TN 37167
615/459-4161
(Metal doors, etc.)

Buster Brown Apparel, Inc.
2001 Wheeler Ave.
Chattanooga, TN 37406
615/629-2531
(Children's apparel/shoes.)

Columbia/HC Healthcare Corp.
1 Park Plz.
Nashville, TN 37203
615/327-9551
(Hospitals.)

Delta Beverage Group, Inc.
2221 Democrat Rd.
Memphis, TN 38132
901/344-7100
(Bottled and canned soft drinks.)

Dixie Yarns, Inc.
1100 S. Watkins St.
Chattanooga, TN 37404
615/698-2501
(Yarn spinning mills.)

Dollar General
104 Woodmont Blvd.
Nashville, TN 37205
615/783-2000
(Drug & discount stores.)

Dunavant Enterprises
3797 New Getwell Rd.
Memphis, TN 38118
901/369-1500
(Cotton merchant.)

Eastman Chemical Co.
100 N. Eastman Rd.
Kingsport, TN 37660
615/229-2000
(Specialty chemicals.)

Federal Express Corp.
2005 Corporate Ave.
Memphis, TN 38132
901/369-3600
(Air freight.)

First American Corp.
300 Union St.
Nashville, TN 37237-0708
615/748-2000
(Banking.)

First Tennessee National Corp.
165 Madison Ave.
Memphis, TN 38103
901/523-4444
(Banking.)

Fred's, Inc.
4300 New Getwell Rd.
Memphis, TN 38118
901/362-1000
(Department stores.)

Gaylord Entertainment
1 Gaylord Dr.
Nashville, TN 37214
615/885-1000
(Broadcasting & movies.)

**GKN/Parts Industries
Corp.**
601 S. Dudley St.
Memphis, TN 38104
901/523-7711
(Wholesale motor vehicle
supplies and parts.)

Genesco, Inc.
1415 Murfreesboro Pike
Nashville, TN 37217
615/367-7000
(Men's footwear.)

Guardsmark, Inc.
22 S. Second St.
Memphis, TN 38103
901/522-6000
(Security services, etc.)

Ingram Industries, Inc.
4400 Harding Rd.
Nashville, TN 37205
615/298-8200
(Inland marine transportation,
insurance, consumer products
distribution, etc.)

Johnstown Co.
2 Union Sq.
Chattanooga, TN 37402
615/756-1202
(Soft drinks.)

**Lockheed Martin Energy
Systems**
P.O. Box 2009
Oak Ridge, TN 37831
423/574-3764
(Radioactive isotopes, nuclear fuels,
etc.)

McKee Food Corp.
10000 McKee Rd.
Collegedale, TN 37315
423/238-7111
(Baked goods.)

**Nissan Motor Manufacturing
Corp. USA**
983 Nissan Dr.
Smyrna, TN 37167
615/459-1400
(Automobile manufacturing.)

Northern Telecom, Inc.
Northern Telecom Plz.
Nashville, TN 37228
615/734-4000
(Telephone equipment.)

Opryland U.S.A., Inc.
2802 Opryland Dr.
P.O. Box 2138
Nashville, TN 37214
615/889-6600
(Entertainment/amusement park.)

Philips Consumer Electronics
(subs. North American Philips)
1 Philips Dr.
Knoxville, TN 37914
615/521-4316
(Consumer electronics.)

Plasti-Line, Inc.
623 E. Emory Rd.
Powell, TN 37849
615/938-1511
(Sign and advertising specialists.)

Promus Cos., Inc.
850 Ridge Lake Rd.
Memphis, TN 38120
901/680-7200
(Hotels & gaming.)

**Provident Life and Accident
Insurance Co. of America**
1 Fountain Sq.
Provident Bldg.
Chattanooga, TN 37402
615/755-1011
(Life and accident insurance;
financial services.)

Reemay Inc.
70 Old Hickory Blvd.
Old Hickory, TN 37138
615/847-7000
(Yarn spinning mills.)

Service Merchandise Co., Inc.
7100 Service Merchandise Dr.
Brentwood, TN 37027
615/660-6000
(Discount department stores.)

Shoney's, Inc.
1727 Elm Hill Pike
Nashville, TN 37210
615/391-5201
(Restaurant chain.)

Horace Small Apparel Co.
350 28 Ave., N.
Nashville, TN 37209
615/320-1000
(Men's and boys' apparel.)

Smith & Nephew Richards, Inc.
1450 E. Brooks Rd.
Memphis, TN 38116
901/396-2121
(Medical supplies.)

State Industries, Inc.
500 Bypass Rd.
Ashland City, TN 37015-1299

615/792-9159
(Water heaters, pump tanks, etc.)

Sullivan Graphics Inc.
100 Winners Circle
Brentwood, TN 37027
615/377-0377
(Printing.)

SunTrust Bank of Nashville
P.O. Box 305110
Nashville, TN 37230
615/748-4096
(Banking.)

Textron Aerostructures
1431 Vultee Rd.
Nashville, TN 37217
615/361-2000
(Structures for aircraft and space vehicles.)

Union Planters Corp.
P.O. Box 387
Memphis, TN 38147
901/383-6000
(Banking.)

Varco Pruden Buildings
6000 Poplar Ave., Suite 400
Memphis, TN 38119
901/685-6000
(Construction.)

TENNESSEE BUSINESS PERIODICALS

Memphis Business Journal
Mid-South Communications, Inc.
88 Union Ave., Suite 102
Memphis, TN 38103
901/523-1000
(Weekly tabloid; covers business, agriculture, and industry issues in Memphis area—western Tennessee, northern Mississippi, eastern Arkansas.)

Nashville Business Journal
Mid-South Communications
Box 23229
Nashville, TN 37202
615/248-2222
(Weekly tabloid.)

TENNESSEE DIRECTORY

Tennessee Business Directory
American Business Directories
5711 S. 86th Cir.

P.O. Box 27347
Omaha, NE 68127
402/593-4600

TENNESSEE GOVERNMENT EMPLOYMENT OFFICES

Office of Personnel Management
200 Jefferson Ave.,
Suite 1312
Memphis, TN 38103-2335
901/544-3956
(Federal job-service center.)

Employment Service
Dept. of Employment Security
500 James Robertson Pkwy.
Nashville, TN 37245-0900
615/741-0922
(State job-service center.)

TEXAS

LEADING TEXAS EMPLOYERS

AMR Corp.
(parent company of American Airlines)
Box 619616
Dallas-Fort Worth Airport, TX
75261-9616
817/963-1234
(Airline.)

Anadarko Petroleum Corp.
17001 North Chase Dr.
Houston, TX 77060
713/875-1101
(Misc. Energy.)

American General Corp.
2929 Allen Parkway
Houston, TX 77253-3247
713/522-1111
(Insurance and financial services.)

**American National
Insurance Co.**
1 Moody Plz.
Galveston, TX 77550-7999
409/763-4661
(Insurance.)

Baker Hughes, Inc.
3900 Essex Ln.
Houston, TX 77227
713/439-8600
(Oil field production and services.)

Bank One, Texas, N.A.
1717 Main St.

Dallas, TX 75201
214/290-2000
(Holding company, financial
services.)

Bank One, Dallas
1717 Main St.
Dallas, TX 75265
214/290-2000
(Banking.)

Bank One, Houston
P.O. Box 2629
Houston, TX 77252
713/751-6100
(Banking.)

Bell Helicopter Textron, Inc.
(subs. of Textron)
600 E. Hurst Blvd.
Hurst, TX 76053
817/280-2011
(Rotary-wing aircraft.)

**Blue Cross & Blue Shield
of Texas**
901 S. Central Expwy.
Richardson, TX 75080
214/669-6900
(Health insurance.)

Brown & Root, Inc.
4100 Clinton Dr.
Houston, TX 77020
713/676-3011

(Construction, engineering, maintenance.)

Browning-Ferris Industries Inc.
P.O. Box 3151
Houston, TX 77253
713/870-8100
(Environmental & waste.)

Burlington Northern Inc.
777 Main St.
Ft. Worth, TX 76102-5384
817/333-2000
Fax 813/333-2314
(Railroad.)

Burlington Resources
5050 Westheimer Rd.
Houston, TX 77056
713/624-9500
(Misc. Energy.)

Cameron Industries
13013 NW Freeway
Houston, TX 77040
713/939-2211
(Petroleum services.)

Centex Corp.
3333 Lee Pkwy.
Dallas, TX 75219
214/559-6500
(Builder.)

Central & Southwest Group
1616 Woodall Rodgers Fwy.
Dallas, TX 75202
214/777-1000
(Electric utility.)

The Coastal Corporation
9 E. Greenway Plz.
Houston, TX 77046
713/877-1400
(Natural gas extraction, transportation and distribution, etc.)

Compaq Computer Corp.
20555 Hwy. 249
Houston, TX 77070
713/370-0670
(Computers.)

CompUSA
14951 N. Dallas Pkwy.
Dallas, TX 75240
214/383-4000
Fax 214/383-4276
(Electronic stores.)

Conoco Inc.
600 N. Dairy Ashford St.
Houston, TX 77079
713/293-1000
(Petroleum refining.)

Continental Airlines
2929 Allen Pkwy.
Houston, TX 77219
713/834-5000
(Airline.)

Convex Computer Corp.
3000 Waterview Pkwy.
Richardson, TX 75080
214/497-4000
(Computers.)

Cooper Industries
1001 Fannin St.
Houston, TX 77202
713/739-5400
(Misc. industrial equipment.)

Cullen/Frost Bankers
100 W. Houston
San Antonio, TX 78205
210/220-4011
(Bank.)

Daniel Industries, Inc.
9753 Pine Lake Dr.
Houston, TX 77055
713/467-6000
(Oil and gas field equipment.)

Dell Computer Corp.
2214 W. Braker Lane
Austin, TX 78758
512/338-4400
(Computers.)

Diamond Shamrock, Inc.
P.O. Box 696000
San Antonio, TX 78269-6000
210/641-6800
(Petroleum.)

Digicon, Inc.
3701 Kirby Dr.
Houston, TX 77098
713/526-5611
(Oil and gas field exploration
services.)

Dresser Industries, Inc.
P.O. Box 718
2001 Ross Ave.
Dallas, TX 75221-0718
214/740-6000
(Energy industry equipment and
services and chemicals.)

DSC Communications Corp.
1000 Coit Rd.
Plano, TX 75075-5813
214/519-3000
(Telecommunications.)

E-Systems Inc.
Greenville Division
10001 Jack Finney Blvd.
Greenville, TX 75403
903/455-3450
(Electronic systems and aircraft
servicing.)

E-Systems, Inc.
6250 LBJ Fwy.
Dallas, TX 75240
214/661-1000
(Electronic systems.)

El Paso Natural Gas Co. Inc.
100 N. Stanton St.
El Paso, TX 79901
915/541-2600
(Natural gas transmission.)

Electronic Data Systems Corp.
5400 Legacy Dr.
Plano, TX 75024
214/604-6000
(Data processing.)

Electrospace Systems, Inc.
1301 E. Collins Blvd.
Richardson, TX 75081
214/470-2000
(Electronic equipment.)

Enron Corp.
1400 Smith St.
Houston, TX 77002
713/853-6161
(Pipelines, energy exploration.)

Enserch Corp.
300 S. St. Paul St.
Dallas, TX 75201
214/651-8700
(Diversified energy operations.)

Epic Healthcare Group
P.O. Box 650398
Dallas, TX 75265
214/443-3333
(Hospitals.)

Exxon Corp.
225 E. Carpenter Fwy.
Irving, TX 75062-2298
214/444-1000
(Petroleum.)

Fairchild Aircraft
10823 NE Entrance Rd.
San Antonio, TX 78217
210/824-9421
(Aircraft manufacturing.)

Family Service Life Insurance Co.
9430 Old Katy Rd.
Houston, TX 77055
713/827-0459
(Life insurance.)

Farah Inc.
8889 Gateway Blvd. W.
El Paso, TX 79925
915/593-4444
(Men's trousers.)

Fina Oil & Chemical Co.
P.O. Box 2159
Dallas, TX 75221-2159
214/760-2399
(Misc. Energy.)

First Interstate Bank Texas, N.A.
1000 Louisiana St.
Houston, TX 77002
713/224-6611
(Banking.)

First USA
1601 Elm St.
Dallas, TX 75201
214/849-2000
(Lease & finance.)

Foley's
1110 Main St.
Houston, TX 77002
713/651-7038
(Department store.)

Fox Meyer Health
1220 Senlac Dr.
Carrollton, TX 75006
214/446-4800
(Drugs.)

Frito Lay, Inc.
7701 Legacy Dr.
Plano, TX 75024
214/334-7000
(Food processing.)

GSC Enterprises, Inc.
130 Hillcrest Dr. N.
Sulphur Springs, TX 75482
903/885-7621
(Wholesale groceries.)

GTE Southwest Inc.
2701 S. Johnson St.
San Angelo, TX 76904
915/944-5511
(Telephone services.)

Grocers Supply Co.
3131 E. Holcombe Blvd.
Houston, TX 77021
713/747-5000
(Wholesale groceries, drugs, hardware.)

Gulf State Utilities Co.
350 Pine St.
Beaumont, TX 77701
409/838-6631
(Electric utility.)

Halliburton Co.
500 N. Akard St.
Dallas, TX 75201-3391
214/978-2600
(Petroleum services.)

Halliburton Energy Services
2601 Belt Line Rd.
Carrollton, TX 75006
214/418-3000
(Oil and gas field machinery and equipment.)

Hoechst Celanese Chemical Co.
Chemicals Division
1601 LBJ Fwy.
Dallas, TX 75234
214/277-4000
(Chemicals.)

Houston Industries Incorporated
4400 Post Oak Pkwy.
Houston, TX 77027
713/629-3000
(Holding company—utilities; cable television; etc.)

Houston Lighting & Power Co.
611 Walker St.
Houston, TX 77002
713/228-7400
(Utility.)

Houston Pipe Line Co.
2900 North Loop W.
Houston, TX 77092
713/685-4200
(Natural gas transmission and sales.)

Houston Post Co.
4747 SW Fwy.
Houston, TX 77027
713/840-5600
(Newspaper publishing.)

Intermedics, Inc.
4000 Technology Dr.
Angleton, TX 77515
409/233-8611
(Electromagnetic and electrotherapeutic apparatuses.)

International Maintenance Corp.
2005 Industrial Pk. Rd.
Nederland, TX 77627
409/722-8031
(General contractors.)

Kaiser Aluminum Corp.
5847 San Felipe St.
Houston, TX 77057
713/267-3777
(Aluminum, etc.)

M. W. Kellogg Co.
601 Jefferson.
Houston, TX 77002
713/753-2000
(Chemical plant and refinery
construction; engineering
services.)

Kimberly-Clark Corp.
P.O. Box 619100
Dallas, TX 75261-9100
214/281-1200
(Personal products.)

Loral-Vought Systems
P.O. Box 650003
Dallas, TX 75265
214/603-1000
(Missiles and electronics subs. of The
LTV Corp.)

Lincoln Property Co.
500 N. Alkard, Suite 3300
Dallas, TX 75201
214/740-3300
(Real estate development and
management.)

Living Centers of America
15415 Katy Fwy.
Houston, TX 77094
713/578-4600
(Health care services.)

Lockheed-Martin Corp.
Fort Worth Division
1000 Lockheed Blvd.
Fort Worth, TX 76101
817/777-2000
(F-111 spares and support, F-16
airframe, radar, etc.)

Lockheed-Martin Corp.
2525 Bay Area Blvd.
Houston, TX 77058
713/333-5411
(Engineering services.)

Lufkin Industries, Inc.
601 S. Raquet
Lufkin, TX 75904
409/634-2211
(Oil and gas field machinery and
equipment.)

Lyondell Petrochemical Co.
1221 McKinney St.
Houston, TX 77010
713/652-7200
(Chemicals.)

**Manufacturing Auditing
Redemption Service**
4020 N. Mesa
El Paso, TX 79902
915/533-8893
(Coupon redemption services.)

Marathon Oil Co.
555 San Felipe St.
Houston, TX 77056
713/629-6600
(Oil and gas.)

Mary Kay Cosmetics, Inc.
8787 Stemmons Fwy.
Dallas, TX 75247
214/630-8787
(Cosmetics.)

Maxus Energy Corp.
717 N. Harwood St.
Dallas, TX 75201
214/953-2000
(Oil and gas exploration and
production.)

Maxxam Inc.
5847 San Felipe St.
Houston, TX 77057
713/975-7600
(Nonferrous metals.)

**Mitchell Energy &
Development Co.**
2001 Timberloch Pl.
The Woodlands, TX 77380
713/377-5500
(Crude petroleum and natural
gas.)

NCH Corp.
2727 Chemsearch Blvd.
Irving, TX 75062
214/438-0211
(Cleaning, sanitation and
maintenance chemicals, etc.)

Neiman-Marcus
1618 Main St.
Dallas, TX 75201
214/741-6911
(Department stores.)

NorAm Energy
P.O. Box 2628
Houston, TX 77252
713/654-7507
(Gas.)

Northrup-Grumman
Vought Ctr.
P.O. Box 655907
Dallas, TX 75265
214/266-2011
(Aircraft manufacturing subs. of The
LTV Corp.)

Panhandle Eastern Corp.
5400 Westheimer Ct.
Houston, 77056
713/627-5400
(Natural gas and pipeline holding
company.)

J.C. Penney Company, Inc.
6501 Legacy Dr.
Plano, TX 75024-3698
214/431-1000
(Department stores.)

Pennzoil Co.
1 Pennzoil Plc.
Houston, TX 77002
713/546-4000
(Petroleum refining.)

Rexene Corp.
5005 LBJ Fwy.
Occidental Tower
Dallas, TX 75244
214/450-9000
(Chemicals.)

S&B Engineers and
Constructors
7825 Park Pl. Blvd.
Houston, TX 77087
713/645-4141
(Heavy construction.)

Serv-Air, Inc.
9315 Jack Finney Blvd.
Greenville, TX 75402
903/454-2000
(Organizational and field
maintenance; repair of aircraft.)

Service Corp International
1929 Allen Pkwy.
Houston, TX 77219-0548
713/522-5141
(Personal products.)

Shell Oil Company
1600 Smith St.
Houston, TX 77002
713/241-6161
(Petroleum refining.)

Shell Pipe Line Corp.
1 Shell Plz.
P.O. Box 2463
Houston, TX 77252
713/241-6161
(Pipeline transportation, petroleum,
etc.)

Southland Corp.
2711 N. Haskell Ave.
Dallas, TX 75204
214/828-7011
(Supermarkets & restaurants.)

Southwest Airlines Co.
P.O. Box 3661
2702 Love Field Dr.
Dallas, TX 75235
214/904-4000
(Airline.)

Southwestern Bell Corp.
1752 E. Houston St.
San Antonio, TX 78299-2933
210/821-4105
(Telecommunications.)

Southwestern Life Corp.
500 N. Akard St.
Dallas, TX 75201
214/954-7111
(Insurance.)

Sysco Corp.
1390 Enclave Pkwy.
Houston, TX 77077-2099
713/584-1390
(Food wholesaler.)

Tandy Corp.
1800 One Tandy Ctr.
Fort Worth, TX 76102
817/390-3700
(Electronics.)

Temple Inland Inc.
303 S. Temple Dr.
Diboll, TX 75941
409/829-5511
(Packaging.)

Tenneco Inc.
1010 Milam St.
Houston, TX 77002
713/757-2131
(Petroleum, pipelines, land
management.)

Tesoro Petroleum Corp.
8700 Tesoro Dr.
San Antonio, TX 78217
210/828-8484
(Petroleum, natural gas.)

Texas Commerce Bancshares, Inc.
712 Main St.
Houston, TX 77002
713/216-7000
(Banking.)

Texas Instruments Inc.
13500 N. Central Expy.
Dallas, TX 75243
214/995-2011
(Computers and electronics.)

Texas Utilities Co.
1601 Bryan St.
Dallas, TX 75201-3411
214/812-4600
(Electric utility.)

Tracor, Inc.
6500 Tracor Ln.
Austin, TX 78725
512/926-2800
(Engineering services.)

Trammel Crow Co.
2001 Ross Ave.
Suite 3500
Dallas, TX 75201-2997
214/979-5100
(Real estate developer.)

Transco Energy Co.
2800 Post Oak Blvd.
Houston, TX 77056
713/439-2000
(Pipelines, oil, coal, etc.)

Trinity Industries Inc.
2525 Stemmons Fwy.
Dallas, TX 75207-2401
214/631-4420
(Heavy equipment.)

Union Pacific Resources Co.
P.O. Box 7
Fort Worth, TX 76101
817/877-6000
(Petroleum, natural gas.)

**Union Texas Petroleum Holdings,
Inc.**
P.O. Box 2120
1330 Post Oak Blvd.
Houston, TX 77056
713/623-6544
(Oil and gas exploration and
development, etc.)

Valhi Inc.
3 Lincoln Ctr.
5430 LBJ Fwy.
Suite 1700
Dallas, TX 75240
214/233-1700
(Chemicals.)

Varo Inc.
2800 W. Kingsley Rd.
Garland, TX 75061
214/840-5000

(Electronic systems and components, weapons delivery systems, etc.)

Western National
5555 San Felipe Rd.
Houston, TX 77056
713/888-7800
(Insurance.)

World Marketing Alliance
1705 Capital of Texas Hwy.
Austin, TX 7846
512/328-4220
(Financial securities.)

TEXAS BUSINESS PERIODICALS

Dallas Business Journal
4131 N. Central Expy.
Suite 310
Dallas, TX 75204
214/520-1010
(Weekly.)

Houston Business Journal
1 W. Loop S.
Suite 650
Houston, TX 77027
713/688-8811
(Weekly.)

TEXAS DIRECTORIES

Directory of Texas Manufacturers
University of Texas at Austin
Bureau of Business Research
Box 7459
Austin, TX 78713
512/471-1616

Harris Texas Manufacturers Directory
Harris Publishing Co.
2057 Aurora Rd.
Twinsburg, OH 44087
216/425-9000
800/888-5900

Texas Business Directory
American Business Directories
5711 S. 86th Cir.
P.O. Box 27347
Omaha, NE 68127
402/593-4600

Texas Manufacturers Register
Manufacturers' News, Inc.
1633 Central St.
Evanston, IL 60201
708/864-7000

TEXAS GOVERNMENT EMPLOYMENT OFFICES

Office of Personnel Management
8610 Broadway, Room 305
San Antonio, TX 78217
210/805-2402
(Federal job-service center—mail or phone only.)

Employment Service
Texas Employment Commission
101 E. 15th St.
Austin, TX 78778-0001
512/463-2222
(State job-service center.)

VIRGINIA

LEADING VIRGINIA EMPLOYERS

American Furniture Co., Inc.
Hairstan St. off Starling
Martinsville, VA 24112
703/632-2061
(Furniture.)

American Management Systems, Inc.
4050 Legato Rd.
Fairfax, VA 22033
703/841-6000
(Business data processing.)

Atlantic Research Corp.
(sub. of Sequa Corp.)
5945 Wellington Rd.
Gainesville, VA 22065
703/754-5000
(Aerospace.)

BDM International, Inc.
1501 BDM Way
McLean, VA 22102
703/848-5000
(Business services, government consulting.)

Bassett Furniture Industries, Inc.
245 Main St.
Bassett, VA 24055
703/629-6000
(Furniture, housewares.)

Bell Atlantic Corp. of Virginia
600 E. Main St.
Richmond, VA 23219
804/772-1591
(Telephone services.)

Bell Atlantic Network Services, Inc.
(subs. of Bell Atlantic)
1310 N. Court House Rd.
Arlington, VA 22201
703/974-3000
(Telecommunications network services.)

Blue Cross & Blue Shield of Virginia
2015 Staples Mill Rd.
Richmond, VA 23230
804/354-7000
(Health insurance.)

British Aerospace, Inc.
22070 Broderick Dr.
Sterling, VA 20166
703/406-2000
(Sale of aircraft, spare parts, and product support.)

Cable & Wireless Inc.
8219 Leesburg Pike
Vienna, VA 22182
703/790-5300
(Long distance telephone services.)

Canon Virginia Inc.
12000 Canon Blvd.
Newport News, VA 23606
804/881-6020
(Office machines.)

Central Fidelity Banks
1021 E. Cary St.
Richmond, VA 23219
804/697-6700
(Banking.)

Circuit City Stores Inc.
9950 Maryland Dr.
Richmond, VA 23233
804/527-4000
(Electronic stores.)

Colonial Williamsburg Foundation, Inc.
Goodwin Bldg.
P.O. Box 1776
Williamsburg, VA 23187
804/229-1000
(Hotel, gift shops, etc.)

Crestar Financial
919 E. Main St.
Richmond, VA 23219
804/782-5000
(Banking.)

CSX Corp.
901 E. Cary St.
Richmond, VA 23219
804/782-1400
(Railroad.)

Dan River, Inc.
2291 Memorial Dr.
Danville, VA 24541
804/799-7000
(Textiles.)

Dominion Resources Inc.
901 Byrd St.
Richmond, VA 23219
804/775-5700
(Electric utility.)

Dyn Corp.
2000 Edmund Halley Dr.
Reston, VA 22091
703/264-0330
(Technical and professional services.)

**Ericsson-GE Mobile
Communications**
1 Mountainview Rd.
Lynchburg, VA 24502
804/528-7000
(Cellular telephone equipment, etc.)

Ethyl Corp.
330 S. 4 St.
Richmond, VA 23219
804/788-5000
(Chemicals.)

The Fairchild Corporation
300 W. Service Rd.
Box 10803
Chantilly, VA 22021
703/478-5800
(Aerospace.)

**Federal Home Loan Mortgage
Corp.**
8200 Jones Branch Dr.

McLean, VA 22102
703/903-2000
(Secondary mortgages.)

First Colony
900 E. Byrd St.
Richmond, VA 23219
804/775-0300
(Insurance.)

First Union National Bank
30 Jefferson St.
Roanoke, VA 24011
703/563-7000
(Banking.)

First Virginia Banks, Inc.
6400 Arlington Blvd.
Falls Church, VA 22042-2336
703/241-4000
(Banking.)

Govt. Systems Corp.
15000 Conference Ctr. Dr.
Chantilly, VA 22021
703/818-4000
(Telephone communications.)

Gannett Co., Inc.
1100 Wilson Blvd.
Arlington, VA 22209
703/284-6000
(Newspaper publishing,
broadcasting.)

General Dynamics Corp.
3190 Fairview Park Dr.
Falls Church, VA 22042-4523
703/876-3000
(Tanks, submarines.)

Genicom Corp.
1 Genicom Dr.
Waynesboro, VA 22980
703/949-1000
(Business data processing.)

Honeywell Federal Systems, Inc.
7900 W. Pk. Dr.
McLean, VA 22102
703/734-7830
(Electrical power systems
contractors; computer installation.)

ITT Defense & Electronics, Inc.
(subs. ITT Corp.)
1000 Wilson Blvd.
Arlington, VA 22209
703/247-2942
(Defense electronics.)

Interbake Foods, Inc.
2821 Emerywood Pkwy., Suite 210
Richmond, VA 23294-3727
804/755-7107
(Cookies and crackers.)

James River Corp. of Virginia
120 Tredegar St.
P.O. Box 2218
Richmond, VA 23219
804/644-5411
(Paper and packaging.)

Landmark Communications, Inc.
150 W. Brambleton Ave.
Norfolk, VA 23510
804/446-2110
(Publishing, broadcasting.)

Lane Co., Inc.
E. Franklin St.
Altavista, VA 24517
804/369-5641
(Furniture.)

Life Insurance Company of Virginia
6610 W. Broad St.
Richmond, VA 23230
804/281-6000
(Life insurance.)

Mars Inc.
6885 Elm St.
McLean, VA 22101
703/821-4900
(Food processing.)

Media General Inc.
333 Grace St.
Richmond, VA 23293-0001
804/649-6000
(Publishing.)

Mobil Corporation
3225 Gallows Rd.
Fairfax, VA 22031

703/846-3000
(Holding company, oil and gas
exploration and refining. At same
address: Mobil Oil Corp.)

National Science Foundation
4201 Wilson Blvd.
Arlington, VA 22230
703/306-1234
(Foundation.)

Norfolk Southern Corp.
3 Commercial Pl.
Norfolk, VA 23510-2191
804/629-2600
(Railroad.)

O'Sullivan Corp.
1944 Valley Ave.
Winchester, VA 22601
703/667-6666
(Plastic, vinyl sheeting, molded
plastics.)

Overnite Transportation Co.
1000 Semmes Ave.
Richmond, VA 23224
804/231-8000
(Trucking.)

Owens & Minor Inc.
4800 Cox Rd.
Glen Allen, VA 23060
804/747-9794
(Medical supplies.)

PRC Inc.
1500 PRC Dr.
McLean, VA 22102
703/556-1000
(Computer services.)

Pulaski Furniture Corp.
301 N. Madison Ave.
Pulaski, VA 24301
703/980-7330
(Furniture.)

Reynolds Metals Co.
6601 Broad St.
Richmond, VA 23230
804/281-2000
(Aluminum.)

Richfood Holdings Inc.
2000 Richfood Dr.
Mechanicsville, VA 23111
804/746-6000
(Wholesale groceries.)

A. H. Robins Co., Inc.
1450 Cummings Dr.
Richmond, VA 23220
804/257-2253
(Pharmaceuticals, health and beauty aids.)

Sara Lee Knit Products
202 Cleveland Ave.
Martinesville, VA 24112
703/638-8841
(Textiles, apparel.)

Signet Banking Corp.
7 N. Eighth St.
Richmond, VA 23219
804/747-2000
(Banking.)

Smithfield Foods, Inc.
501 N. Church St.
Smithfield, VA 23430
804/357-4321
(Meat packing and processing.)

Sprint International Communications Corp.
12490 Sunrise Valley Dr.
Reston, VA 22091
703/689-6000
(Telecommunications.)

Stanley Furniture Co.
Hwy. 57 W.
Stanleytown, VA 24168
703/627-2000
(Furniture.)

Universal Leaf Tobacco Co.
P.O. Box 25099
Richmond, VA 23230
804/359-9311
(Tobacco.)

USAir, Inc.
2345 Crystal Dr.
Arlington, VA 22227
703/418-7000
(Airline.)

Virginia Electric & Power Co.
1 James River Plz.
Richmond, VA 23219
804/771-3000
(Utility.)

VIRGINIA BUSINESS PERIODICAL

Virginia Business
411 E. Franklin St.
Richmond, VA 23219

804/649-6000
(Monthly.)

VIRGINIA DIRECTORIES

Harris State Directory—Virginia
Harris Publishing Co.
2057 Aurora Rd.
Twinsburg, OH 44087
216/425-9000
800/888-5900

Virginia Business Directory
American Business Directories
5711 S. 86th Cir.
P.O. Box 27347
Omaha, NE 68127
402/593-4600

VIRGINIA GOVERNMENT EMPLOYMENT OFFICES

Office of Personnel Management
Federal Bldg., Room 220
200 Granby St.
Norfolk, VA 23510-1886
804/441-3355
(Federal job-service center.)

Employment Service
Virginia Employment Commission
P.O. Box 1358
Richmond, VA 23211
804/786-7097
(State job-service center.)

WEST VIRGINIA

LEADING WEST VIRGINIA EMPLOYERS

Ames Co.
3801 Camden Ave.
Parkersburg, WV 26101
304/424-3000
(Lawn and garden tools.)

Arch of West Virginia
P.O. Box 156
Yolyn, WV 25654
304/792-8246
(Coal mining.)

Ashland Coal Inc.
2205 5th Rd.
Box 6300
Huntington, WV 25701
304/526-3333
(Coal mining.)

Bell Atlantic Corp. of West Virginia
1500 MacCorkle Ave., S.E.
Charleston, WV 25314
304/343-9911
(Telephone services—subs. of Bell Atlantic.)

CNG Transmission Corp.
445 W. Main St.
Clarksburg, WV 26301
304/889-3141
(Natural gas transmission and production.)

Cannelton Coal
(Div. of Cyprus-Amax.)
101 Washington St. E.
Charleston, WV 25304
304/348-0500
(Coal mining.)

CSX Hotels Inc.
Rte. 60 W.
White Sulphur Springs, WV 24986
304/536-1110
(Resort hotel.)

Columbia Gas Transmission Corp.
1700 MacCorkle Ave., SE
Charleston, WV 25314
304/357-2000
(Natural gas transmission and distribution.)

Eastern Associated Coal Corp.
800 Laidley Tower
Box 1233
Charleston, WV 25301
304/344-0300
(Coal mining.)

Elk Run Coal Co., Inc.
State Rte. 3
P.O. Box 497
Sylvester, WV 25193
304/854-1890
(Coal mining.)

Gabriel Brothers Inc.
55 Scott Ave.
Morgantown, WV 26505
304/292-6965
(Family clothing stores.)

Huntington Bank
1 Huntington Sq.
Charleston, WV 25301
304/348-5000
(Banking; does business as
Commerce Bank.)

Intelligencer
1500 Main St.
Wheeling, WV 26003
304/233-0100
(Newspaper publishing.)

Marrowbone Development Co.
State Rte. 65
P.O. Box 119
Naugatuck, WV 25685
304/235-7650
(Coal mining.)

McJunkin Corp.
835 Hillcrest Dr. E.
Charleston, WV 25311
304/348-5211
(Industrial carbon.)

Monongahela Power Co.
1310 Fairmont Ave.
Fairmont, WV 26554
304/366-3000
(Electric utility.)

Mountaineer Gas Co.
414 Summers St.
Charleston, WV 25301
304/347-0500
(Natural gas transmission.)

Ogden Newspapers, Inc.
1500 Main St.
Wheeling, WV 26003
304/233-0100
(Newspaper publishing.)

**One Valley Bancorp of West
Virginia, Inc.**
Lee & Summit Sts.

Charleston, WV 25301
304/348-7294
(Banking.)

**Ravenswood Aluminum
Corp.**
Rt. 2 South
Ravenswood, WV 26164
304/273-6000; 800/258-6686
(Aluminum.)

Steel of West Virginia Inc.
P.O. Box 2547
Huntington, WV 25726
304/696-8200
(Steel products.)

**Stone & Thomas Dept.
Stores**
1030 Main St.
Wheeling, WV 26003
304/232-3344
(Department stores.)

Vecellio & Grogran, Inc.
2251 Robert E. Byrd Dr.
Beckley, WV 25801
304/252-6575
(Highway and street
construction.)

**Cecil I. Walker
Machinery Co.**
Rte. 60 E.
Belle, WV 25015
304/949-6400
(Construction and mining machinery
and equipment.)

Weirton Steel Corp.
400 Three Springs Dr.
Weirton, WV 26062
304/797-2000
(Steel.)

**Wheeling-Pittsburgh
Steel Corp.**
1134 Market St.
Wheeling, WV 26003
304/234-2400
(Steel.)

WEST VIRGINIA DIRECTORIES

Harris West Virginia Manufacturing Directory
Harris Publishing Company
2057 Aurora Rd.
Twinsburg, OH 44087
216/425-9000
800/888-5900

West Virginia Business Directory
American Business Directories
5711 S. 86th Circle

P.O. Box 27347
Omaha, NE 68127
402/593-4600

West Virginia Manufacturers Register
Manufacturers' News Inc.
1633 Central St.
Evanston, IL 60201
708/864-7000

WEST VIRGINIA GOVERNMENT EMPLOYMENT OFFICES

Office of Personnel Management
(Federal job-service center—
see Ohio listing; call
513/225-2720.)

Employment Service Division
Dept. of Employment Security
112 California Ave.
Charleton, WV 25305
304/558-1138
(State job-service center.)

THE MIDWEST

OUTLOOK: Strong over the long term, but possible short-term slowdowns.

Much of the Midwest did better than the rest of the country during the past few years—and the future looks bright. Key to the region's positive outlook? A strong manufacturing base that will be able to weather future downturns well. Another big plus: It's export oriented. Most Midwest states can trace one in six manufacturing jobs to export-related work; and Midwest exports are rising more rapidly than the rest of the country. One problem: With the dollar's recent rise, US exports are becoming more costly. This could put a crimp in the Midwest export boom—and affect employment.

WHAT'S NEXT

▶ **The Great Lakes region: long term, positive.**

The key reason? Good times for many of the major industries in the area—such Rust Belt standbys as machine tools, steel, and other heavy industries. With strong local economies and low unemployment, state development agencies in **Michigan** and **Ohio,** as well as several chambers of commerce, have had to resort to advertising campaigns to attract workers—even poaching to meet burgeoning production needs. The workers attracted include such skilled personnel as engineers and computer analysts, and also construction workers. Michigan's economy is no longer auto based. The state's total employment increased over 780,000 in the past ten years, while auto-related jobs fell by 50,000. The Big Three auto companies are faced with replacing the large numbers of retirements. Added bonus: Even when the Big Three are lagging, the influx of Japanese and European transplant companies into the area should somewhat stabilize employment in the auto industry. Another recent bonus: strong gains in real estate prices. Adding to the bright picture, a growing number of service companies is diversifying the regional economy—and increasing employment opportunities. Some hot job areas: sales/marketing, accounting, health care, and, of course, manufacturing.

▶ **Plains states: expect steady growth.**

Thanks to increasing global demand for crops and decreasing farm debt, the farm belt states are in for fairly smooth sailing.

Coming on strong: *Indiana,* which has an increasingly diversified economy—including healthy telecommunications and services companies.

Two other good bets: *Nebraska,* which has been seeing strong growth in telemarketing. Among the industries expanding there: credit-card operations, direct mail, education, construction, food processing. Nebraska's unemployment rate has been the lowest in the nation for the last three years to 1996. Hot jobs: systems analysts. *Iowa* is also home to a number of new industries as well—including plastics, and ethanol production. Bottom line: The entire Plains States region has recently had a consistently low jobless rate. As such, workers have been in high demand, with employment opportunities abounding. Best job areas: communications managers and engineers, and health care workers.

REGIONAL HOT SPOTS

TOLEDO, OH: Now a hub for the huge auto-parts industry, Toledo has in particular benefited from NAFTA (the North American Free Trade Agreement), which has enhanced its parts exports to Canada and Mexico—and resulted in a booming job market in 1997. The tight market even made wages at lower-level jobs rise as well, and experts predicted continuing job growth, helped also by the regional tourism and riverboat gambling. One problem on the horizon, however—a downturn in exports and car sales could impact employment negatively over the short term.

OMAHA, NEBRASKA: With a relatively low unemployment rate, Nebraska in recent years has had employers fighting over ways to *attract* workers. Help wanted ads increased 59% since 1993 at the largest local newspaper, the *Omaha World Herald.* Best news: half of all companies polled in the area recently planned to add jobs through 1997. For those relocating, consider also the following: lower living costs and crime rates. But on the downside: in 1995 the National Weather Service reported 46 snow days, and 8 days with subzero temperatures.

MINNEAPOLIS/ST. PAUL, MN: The Twin Cities consistently appear on best places to live and best places to locate a business surveys. Making them look good where employment is concerned: revived manufacturing, expansion of insurance, and a rise in medical, printing, high tech, and publishing companies. Unemployment has been exremely low—at only 2.8% in 1996. This, plus the fact that Minneapolis/St. Paul is home to industry giants in a range of industries—including 3M, Honeywell, General Mills, and Northwest Airlines—point to continued prospects.

ARKANSAS

LEADING ARKANSAS EMPLOYERS

ABF Freight System, Inc.
301 S. 11th St.
Fort Smith, AR 72901
501/785-6000
(Trucking.)

Acxiom Corp.
301 Industrial Blvd.
Conway, AR 72032
501/329-6836
(Information retrieval services.)

Alltel Corporation
One Allied Dr.
Little Rock, AR 72202
501/661-8000
(Independent telephone company.)

Alltel Information Services
4001 Rodney Parharm Rd.
Little Rock, AR 72212
501/220-5100
(Data processing services, software.)

American Freightways Corp.
2200 Forward Dr.
Harrison, AR 72601
501/741-9000
(Trucking.)

Arkansas Best Corp.
3801 Old Greenwood Rd.
Fort Smith, AR 72903
501/785-6000
(Trucking; computer services; real estate.)

Blue Cross & Blue Shield of Arkansas
50 Gaines St.
Little Rock, AR 72201
501/378-2000
(Group hospitalization and medical insurance plans.)

Arkansas Power & Light Co.
900 Louisana St.
Little Rock, AR 72202
501/377-4000
(Utilities.)

Baldor Electric Company
5711 R.S. Boreham Jr. St.
Fort Smith, AR 72901
501/646-4711
(Electric motors.)

Beverly Enterprises, Inc.
1200 S. Waldron Ave.
Fort Smith, AR 72903
501/452-6712
(Long-term health care, retirement facilities, etc.)

Dillard's Department Stores Inc.
1600 Cantrall Rd.
Little Rock, AR 72201
501/376-5200
(Department stores.)

Donrey Media Group
P.O. Box 17017
Fort Smith, AR 72917-7017
501/785-7015
(Media company—daily newspapers, cable tv, etc.)

Fairfield Communities, Inc.
2800 Cantrell Rd.
Little Rock, AR 72202
501/664-6000
(Residential and commercial construction and development.)

First Commercial Bank
400 W. Capitol Ave.
Little Rock, AR 72201
501/371-7000
(Bank.)

Harvest Foods
8109 I-30
Little Rock, AR 72209
501/562-3583
(Supermarkets.)

Hudson Foods Inc.
1125 Hudson Rd.
Rogers, AR 72756
501/636-1100
(Poultry processing.)

J.B. Hunt Transport Services Inc.
Highway 71 N.
P.O. Box 130
Lowell, AR 72745
501/820-0000
(Trucking.)

Millbrook Distribution Services
P.O. Box 790
Harrison, AR 72601
501/741-3425
(Service merchandising.)

Munro & Co. Inc.
190 Elmwood Dr.
Hot Springs, AR 71901
501/262-6000
(Men's shoes.)

Murphy Oil Corp.
200 Peach St.
El Dorado, AR 71730
501/862-6411
(Oil and gas exploration.)

Nucor-Yamato Steel Co.
5929 E. State Highway 18
Blytheville, AR 72310
501/762-5500
(Steel.)

Pace Industries Inc.
513 S. Highway 62—65 Bypass
Harrison, AR 72601
501/741-8255
(Aluminum die-castings.)

Peterson Farm, Inc.
250 S. Main St.
Decatur, AR 72722
501/752-3211
(Poultry hatcheries, feedlot cattle.)

Producers Rice Mill Inc.
518 E. Harrison St.
Stuttgart, AR 72160
501/673-4444
(Rice processing and marketing.)

Riceland Foods
2120 Park Ave.
Stuttgart, AR 72160
501/673-5500
(Rice milling, sales, soybean meal
and oil, etc.)

Southland Racing Corp.
1550 N. Ingram Blvd.

West Memphis, AR 72301
501/735-3670
(Greyhound racing.)

**Southwestern Bell Corporation—
Arkansas Division**
(operating subsidiary of
Southwestern Bell Corp.)
1111 W. Capitol
Little Rock, AR 72201
501/373-9800
(Telephone services.)

Stephens Inc.
111 Center St.
Little Rock, AR 72201
501/374-4361
(Underwriter, broker.)

TCBY Enterprises, Inc.
425 W. Capitol Ave.
Little Rock, AR 72201
501/688-8229
(Frozen yogurt manufacturing, retail
and franchise.)

Tyson Foods Inc.
2210 W. Oaklawn Dr.
Springdale, AR 72762
501/290-4000
Fax 501/290-4028
(Poultry processing.)

Wal-Mart Stores, Inc.
702 SW 8th St.
Bentonville, AR 72716-8007
501/273-4000
(Discount department stores.)

ARKANSAS BUSINESS PERIODICAL

Memphis Business Journal
Mid-South Communications, Inc.
88 Union; Suite 102
Memphis, TN 38103
901/523-1000

(Weekly tabloid, covers business,
agriculture and industry issues in
Memphis area—western Tennessee,
northern Mississippi, eastern
Arkansas.)

ARKANSAS DIRECTORIES

Arkansas Business Directory
American Business Directories
5711 S. 86th Cir.
P.O. Box 27347
Omaha, NE 68127
402/593-4600

Directory of Arkansas Manufacturers
Arkansas Industrial Development
Foundation
Box 1784

Little Rock, AR 72203
501/682-1121

Harris Arkansas Manufacturers Directory
Harris Publishing Co.
2057 Aurora Rd.
Twinsburg, OH 44087
216/425-9000
800/888-5900

ARKANSAS GOVERNMENT EMPLOYMENT OFFICES

Office of Personnel Management
(Federal job-service center—see
Texas listing.)

Employment Security Division
P.O. Box 2981
Little Rock, AR 72203
501/682-2127
(State job-service center.)

ILLINOIS

LEADING ILLINOIS EMPLOYERS

Abbott Laboratories
100 Abbott Park Rd.
Abbott Park, IL 60064-3500
708/937-6100
(Chemicals, food processing.)

Acme Steel Co.
13500 S. Perry Ave.
Riverdale, IL 60627
708/849-2500
(Steel works.)

Allied Van Lines Inc.
215 W. Diehl Rd.
Napierville, IL 60653
708/717-3000
(Motor carrier.)

Allstate Insurance Co.
Allstate Plz.

Northbrook, IL 60062
708/402-5000
(Insurance.)

American Manufacturers Mutual Insurance Co.
1 Kemper Dr.
Long Grove, IL 60047
708/320-2000
(Insurance.)

Ameritech
(Bell regional holding
company)
30 S. Wacker Dr.
Chicago, IL 60606
312/750-5000
(Telephone services.)

Amoco Corp.
P.O. Box 87703
Chicago, IL 60680-0703
312/856-6111
(Oil and natural gas exploration,
refining, marketing, distribution.)

Amoco Chemical Co.
200 E. Randolph Dr.
Chicago, IL 60680
312/856-3200
(Chemicals.)

Amoco Oil Co.
P.O. Box 87707
Chicago, IL 60680
312/856-6111
(Gasoline, motor oils, etc.)

Aon Corp.
123 N. Wacker Dr.
Chicago, IL 60606
312/701-3000
(Insurance, brokerage, financial
services holding co.)

Archer-Daniels-Midland Co.
4666 Fairs Pkwy.
Decatur, IL 62526
217/424-5200
(Flours, grains, soybean oil, etc.)

Bankers Life & Casualty Co.
222 Merchandise Mart Plz.
Chicago, IL 60654-2001
312/396-6000
(Insurance.)

Baxter International Inc.
One Baxter Pkwy.
Deerfield, IL 60015
708/948-3746
(Medical care products and
services.)

Borg-Warner
200 S. Michigan Ave.
Chicago, IL 60604
312/322-8500
(Automotive parts.)

Brunswick
One North Field Ct.
Lake Forest, IL 60045-4811

708/735-4700
(Home furnishings & recreation.)

CNA Financial Corp.
333 S. Wabash Ave.
Chicago, IL 60604
312/822-5000
(Insurance.)

Caremark International
2215 Sanders Rd.
Northbrook, IL 60062
708/559-4700
(Health care.)

Caterpillar Inc.
100 NE Adams St.
Peoria, IL 61629-1425
309/675-1000
(Construction, earth-moving and
materials handling equipment mfr.)

Centel Corp.
8725 W. Higgins Rd.
Chicago, IL 60631
312/399-2500
(Telephone services, products.)

Chicago Title & Trust Co.
171 N. Clark St.
Chicago, IL 60601
312/630-2000
(Title insurance, trust services.)

Chicago Tribune Co.
435 N. Michigan Ave.
Chicago, IL 60611
312/222-2222
(Newspaper publishing.)

**Citibank, Federal Savings Bank,
Illinois**
1 S. Dearborn St.
Chicago, IL 60603
312/263-6660
(Federal savings and loan
association.)

Comdisco
6111 N. River Rd.
Rosemont, IL 60018
708/698-3000
Fax 708/578-5540
(Business services.)

Commonwealth Edison Co.
400 Skokie Blvd.
Northbrook, IL 60002
708/559-1226
(Utility.)

Continental Bank Corp.
321 N. Clark St.
Chicago, IL 60610
312/321-1680
(Owns Continental Bank N.A.)

Continental Casualty Co.
CNA Plz.
Chicago, IL 60685
312/822-5000
(Insurance.)

Dean Foods
3600 N. River Rd.
Franklin Park, IL 60131
708/678-1680
(Food processor.)

Deere & Co.
John Deere Rd.
Moline, IL 61265-8090
309/765-8000
(Farm, industrial and grounds care
equipment, financing.)

Discover Card Services
2500 Lake Cook Rd.
Deerfield, IL 60015
708/405-0900
(credit card/credit plans.)

**Dominick's Finer Foods,
Inc.**
505 N. Railroad Ave.
Melrose Park, IL 60164
708/562-1000
(Retail food stores, food and drug
combo stores.)

R. R. Donnelly & Sons Co.
77 W. Wacker Dr.
Chicago, IL 60601-1696
312/326-8000
(Commercial printing.)

Eagle Food Centers, Inc.
Rte. 67 & Knoxville Rd.
Milan, IL 61264

309/787-7730
(Grocery stores.)

FMC Corp.
200 E. Randolph Dr.
Chicago, IL 60601
312/861-6000
(Machinery, chemicals.)

First Chicago Corp.
One First National Plz.
Chicago, IL 60670
312/732-4000
(Banking.)

Franklin Life Insurance Co.
1 Franklin Sq.
Springfield, IL 62703
217/528-2011
(Insurance.)

Fruit of the Loom
233 S. Wacker Dr.
Chicago, IL 60606
312/876-1724
(Wearing apparel.)

GATX Corp.
500 W. Monroe St.
Chicago, IL 60661
312/621-6200
(Lease & finance.)

General Instrument Corp.
181 W. Madison St.
Chicago, IL 60602
312/541-5000
(Electronics.)

W. W. Grainger Inc.
5500 W. Howard St.
Skokie, IL 60077-2699
708/982-9000
(Industrial services.)

Harris Trust & Savings Bank
111 W. Monroe St.
Chicago, IL 60603
312/461-2265
(Banking.)

Horace Mann Educators
1 Horace Mann Plz.
Springfield, IL 62701

217/789-2500
(Insurance.)

Household International Inc.
2700 Sanders Rd.
Prospect Heights, IL 60070-2799
708/564-5000
(Financial services.)

Illinois Bell
(subsidiary of Ameritech)
225 W. Randolph St.
Chicago, IL 60606
800/257-0902
(Telephone service.)

Illinois Central Railroad
455 N. Cityfront Plz. Dr.
Chicago, IL 60611-5504
312/755-7500
(Railroad.)

Illinois Tool Works
3600 W. Lake Ave.
Glenview, IL 60025-5811
708/724-7500
(Industrial equipment.)

Illinova
500 S. 27th St.
Decatur, IL 62521
217/424-6600
(Utility.)

IMC Fertilizer Group, Inc.
1 Nelson C. White Pkwy.
Mundelein, IL 60080
312/970-3000
(Chemicals.)

Inland Steel Industries Inc.
30 W. Monroe St.
Chicago, IL 60603
312/346-0300
(Steel.)

Itel Corp.
2 N. Riverside Plz.
Chicago, IL 60606
312/902-1515
(Computer systems.)

Kemper Corp.
1 Kemper Dr.
Long Grove, IL 60047

708/320-2000
(Investment, investment services,
insurance, etc.)

Kemper Financial Services
120 S. La Salle St.
Chicago, IL 60603
312/781-1121
(Investment services and products.)

Kraft Foods
Three Lakes Dr.
Northfield, IL 60093
847/646-2010
708/998-2000
(Food processing.)

Leo Burnett Co.
173 E. Delaware Pl.
Chicago, IL 60601
312/565-5959
(Advertising.)

**Lutheran General Health Care
System**
1775 Dempster St.
Park Ridge, IL 60068
708/696-2210
(Commercial and general building
operation.)

Marmon Group Inc.
225 W. Washington St.
Chicago, IL 60606
312/372-9500
(Industrial materials, etc.)

Marshall Field & Company
111 N. State St.
Chicago, IL 60602
312/781-1000
(Department stores.)

McDonald's Corporation
1 McDonald's Plz.
Oak Brook, IL 60521
708/575-3000
(Fast food restaurant chain.)

Mercury Finance
40 Skokie Blvd.
Northbrook, IL 60062
708/564-3720
(Lease & finance.)

Midway Airlines Inc.
5713 S. Central Ave.
Chicago, IL 60638
312/838-8100
(Regional airline.)

Molex Inc.
2222 Wellington Ct.
Lisle, IL 60532-1682
708/969-4550
(Computer peripherals.)

Montgomery Ward & Co., Inc.
535 W. Chicago Ave.
Chicago, IL 60671
312/467-2000
(Retail and catalog sales.)

Morton International Inc.
100 N. Riverside Plz.
Chicago, IL 60606-1596
312/807-2000
Fax 312/807-2881
(Specialty chemicals.)

Motorola, Inc.
1303 E. Algonquin Rd.
Schaumburg, IL 60196
708/576-5000
(Electronics.)

Nalco Chemical
1 Nalco Ctr.
Naperville, IL 60563-1198
708/305-1000
(Chemicals.)

Navistar International Corp.
455 N. Cityfront Plz. Dr.
Chicago, IL 60611
312/836-2000
(Autos & trucks.)

Newell Co.
29 E. Stephenson St.
Freeport, IL 61032
815/235-4171
(Home furnishings & recreation.)

Nicor Inc.
1844 W. Terry Rd.
Naperville, IL 60563
708/305-9500
(Gas.)

Northern Trust Co. Corp.
50 S. LaSalle St.
Chicago, IL 60603
312/630-6000
(Banking.)

Old Republic International
307 N. Michigan Ave.
Chicago, IL 60601
312/346-8100
(Insurance.)

Outboard Marine Corp.
100 Sea Horse Dr.
Waukegan, IL 60085
708/689-6200
(Marine products, lawn care products.)

Premark International Inc.
1717 Deerfield Rd.
Deerfield, IL 60015
708/405-6000
(Home furnishings & recreation.)

Quaker Oats Co.
321 N. Clark St.
Chicago, IL 60610
312/222-7111
(Food processing.)

Joseph T. Ryerson & Son
2558 W. 16th St.
Chicago, IL 60608
312/762-2121
(Carbon steel bars, plates, etc.)

Rykoff-Sexton, Inc.
1050 Warrenville Rd.
Lisle, IL 60532
708/964-1414
(Food wholesaling.)

St. Paul Bancorp Inc.
6700 W. North Ave.
Chicago, IL 60635
312/622-5000
(Thrift institution.)

Santa Fe Pacific Corp.
1700 E. Golf Rd.
Schaumburg, IL 60173-5860
708/995-6000
(Railroad.)

Sara Lee Corp.
700 W. Madison Ave.
Chicago, IL 60602-4260
312/726-2600
(Food.)

Sargent & Lundy
55 E. Monroe St.
Chicago, IL 60603
312/269-2000
(Engineering services.)

G. D. Searle & Co.
5200 Old Orchard Rd.
Skokie, IL 60077
708/982-7000
(Pharmaceuticals.)

Sears Consumer Financial Group.
2500 Lake Cook Rd.
Deerfield, IL 60015
708/405-0900
(Financial services, real estate.)

Sears, Roebuck & Co.
333 Beverly Rd.
Hoffman Estates, IL 60179
708/286-2500
(Retailing, financial services, insurance, real estate.)

Spiegel Inc.
3500 Lacey Rd.
Downers Grove, IL 60515
708/986-7500
(Mail-order retailer, chain stores.)

State Farm Mutual Automobile Insurance Co.
1 State Farm Plz.
Bloomington, IL 61710
309/766-2311
(Also at this address: State Farm Fire & Casualty Co.; State Farm Life Insurance Co.—insurance.)

Stone Container Corp.
150 N. Michigan Ave.
Chicago, IL 60601-7568
312/346-6600
(Packaging.)

Sun Times Co.
401 N. Wabash Ave.
Chicago, IL 60611
312/321-3000
(Newspaper publishing.)

Sundstrand Corp.
4949 Harrison Ave.
Rockford, IL 61108
815/226-6000
(Aerospace and defense parts.)

Sweetheart Cup Co. Inc.
7575 S. Kostner Ave.
Chicago, IL 60652
312/767-3300
(Paper cups, etc.)

Tang Industries Inc.
1699 Wall St.
Mt. Prospect, IL 60056
708/228-1860
(Metal fabricating and distribution.)

Tellabs Inc.
4951 Indiana Ave.
Lisle, IL 60532
708/969-8800
(Computer peripherals.)

Telephone & Data Systems Inc.
30 N. LaSalle St.
Chicago, IL 60602
312/630-1900
(Telecommunications.)

Tribune Company
435 N. Michigan Ave.
Chicago, IL 60611
312/222-3333
(Communications media.)

UAL Corp.
(parent of United Airlines)
1200 Algonquin Rd.
Elk Gove, IL 60666
842/952-4000
(Airline.)

Unicom Corp.
1 First National Plz.
Chicago, IL 60690
312/394-3110
(Electric utility.)

Unitrin Inc.
1 E. Wacker Dr.
Chicago, IL 60601
312/661-4600
(Insurance.)

USG Corp.
125 S. Franklin St.
Chicago, IL 60606
312/606-4000
(Building materials.)

Walgreen Co.
200 Wilmot Rd.
Deerfield, IL 60015
708/940-2500
(Drug stores.)

Westwood One Inc.—Chicago office
111 E. Wacker Dr.
Chicago, IL 60601
312/938-0222
(Radio network.)

Wheelabrator Technologies, Inc.
3003 Butterfield Rd.
Oak Brook, IL 60521
708/218-1700
(Heavy construction, etc.)

Whitman Corp.
3501 West Algonquin Rd.
Rolling Meadows, IL 60008
708/818-5000
(Beverages.)

WMX Technologies
3003 Butterfield Rd.
Oak Brook, IL 60521
708/572-8800
(Waste collection and disposal services.)

Wm. Wrigley Jr. Co.
410 N. Michigan Ave.
Chicago, IL 60611
312/644-2121
(Chewing gum.)

Zenith Electronics Corp.
1000 Milwaukee Ave.
Glenview, IL 60025-2423
708/391-7000
(Consumer electronics.)

Zurich Insurance Co.
1400 American Ln.
Schaumburg, IL 60173
708/605-6000
(Insurance.)

ILLINOIS BUSINESS PERIODICALS

Crain's Chicago Business
740 North Rush St.
Chicago, IL 60611
312/649-5370
(Weekly; publish yearly directory of leading companies.)

The Wall St. Journal (Midwest Edition)
Dow Jones & Co.
1 S. Wacker Dr.
Chicago, IL 60606
312/750-4000

ILLINOIS DIRECTORIES

Harris Illinois Industrial Directory
Harris Publishing Company
2057 Aurora Rd.
Twinsburg, OH 44087
216/425-9000
800/888-5900

Illinois Business Directory
American Business Directories
5711 S. 86th Cir.
P.O. Box 27347
Omaha, NE 68127
402/593-4600

Illinois Manufacturers Register
Manufacturers' News, Inc.
1633 Central St.
Evanston, IL 60201
708/864-7000

Illinois Services Directory
Manufacturers' News, Inc.
1633 Central St.
Evanston, IL 60201
708/864-7000

ILLINOIS GOVERNMENT EMPLOYMENT OFFICES

Office of Personnel Management
(Regional federal office)
175 W. Jackson Blvd.
Rm. 530
Chicago, IL 60604
312/353-2922
312/353-6192 (Job service line)
(Federal job-service center; for

Madison and St. Clair, see MO
listing.)
Employment Services
Employment Security Division
401 S. State St.
Chicago, IL 60605
312/793-5700
(State job-service center.)

INDIANA

LEADING INDIANA EMPLOYERS

American General Finance Inc.
601 NW 2nd St.
Evansville, IN 47701
812/424-8031
(Consumer loans, life and casualty
insurance.)

Ameritech Inc.
240 N. Meridan St.
Indianapolis, IN 46204
317/265-2266
(Telephone services.)

Anacomp, Inc.
1155 N. Meridian St.
Carmel, IN 46032
317/844-9666
(Computer systems and services.)

Arvin Industries, Inc.
1 Noblitt Plz.
Columbus, IN 47201

812/379-3000
(Automobile exhaust systems, metal
parts, etc.)
**Associated Insurance
Companies**
Monument Cir., Suite 200
Indianapolis, IN 46204
317/263-8000
(Insurance.)

Ball Corp.
345 S. High St.
Muncie, IN 47305
317/747-6100
(Packaging products.)

Banc One Indiana Corp.
111 Monument Cir.
Indianapolis, IN 46204
317/321-3000
(Banking.)

Bindley Western Industries
4212 W. 71st St.
Indianapolis, IN 46268
317/298-9890
(Drugs.)

Biomet Inc.
P.O. Box 587
Warsaw, IN 46581
219/267-6639
(Medical supplies.)

Boehringer Mannheim Corp.
9115 Hague Rd.
Indianapolis, IN 46256
817/849-9350
(Medical and surgical instruments,
equipment and supplies.)

CCP Insurance
1825 N. Pennsylvania St.
Carmel, IN 46032
317/573-6900
(Insurance.)

Central Newspapers, Inc.
135 N. Pennsylvania St., Suite 1200
Indianapolis, IN 46204
317/231-9201
(Newspaper publishing.)

Central Soya Co, Inc.
110 W. Berry St.
Fort Wayne, IN 46802
219/425-5100
(Soy proteins, lecithins, feed
manufacturing.)

Clark Equipment Co.
P.O. Box 7008
100 N. Michigan St.
South Bend, IN 46601
219/239-0100
(Heavy equipment.)

Conseco Inc.
11825 N. Pennsylvania St.
Carmel, IN 46032-4570
317/573-6100
(Life and health insurance.)

Cummins Engines Co., Inc.
500 Jackson St.
Box 3005

Columbus, IN 47201
812/377-5000
(Diesel engines and components.)

Delco Electronics Corp.
1 Corporate Ctr.
Kokomo, IN 46902
317/451-5011
(Avionics equipment.)

GTE North Incorporated
8001 W. Jefferson Blvd.
Fort Worth, IN 46804
219/461-2519
(Telecommunications.)

Great Lakes Chemical
1 Great Lakes Blvd.
Highway 52 NW
West Lafayette, IN 47906
317/497-6100
(Chemicals.)

Hillenbrand Industries, Inc.
700 State Rt. 46 E.
Batesville, IN 47006-8835
812/934-7000
(Hospital beds, medical equipment
rental, burial caskets, etc.)

Indiana Gas Company, Inc.
1630 N. Meridian St.
Indianapolis, IN 46202
317/926-3351
(Natural gas distribution.)

Indiana Michigan Power Co.
One Summit Sq.
Fort Wayne, IN 46802
219/425-2111
(Utility.)

Indiana National Bank (INB)
101 W. Washington St.
Indianapolis, IN 46204
317/267-7000
(Banking.)

Inland Container Corp.
4030 Vincennes Rd.
Indianapolis, IN 46268
317/879-4222
(Boxes.)

Kimball International, Inc.
1600 Royal St.
Jasper, IN 47549
812/482-1600
(Office and home furnishings, etc.)

Eli Lilly & Co.
Lilly Corporate Ctr.
Indianapolis, IN 46225
317/276-2000
(Pharmaceuticals.)

Lincoln National Corp.
200 E. Berry
Fort Wayne, IN 46802-2706
219/455-2000
(Insurance, pension investment
management.)

Magnavox Systems Co.
1313 Production Rd.
Fort Wayne, IN 46808
219/429-6000
(Aerospace and electronics
systems.)

Marsh Supermarkets, Inc.
9800 Crosspoint Blvd.
Indianapolis, IN 46256
317/594-2100
(Supermarkets.)

Mead Johnson & Co.
2400 W. Lloyd Exwy.
Evansville, IN 47712
812/429-5000
(Pharmaceuticals, etc.)

Miles Inc.
1127 Myrtle St.
Elkhart, IN 46514
219/264-8111
(Pharmaceuticals, diagnostics,
cleaning products.)

National City Bank of Indiana
100 W. Washington St.

Indianapolis, IN 46204
317/267-7000
(Banking.)

National Steel Co.
4100 Edison Lakes Pkwy.
Mishawaka, IN 46545
219/273-7000
(Steel.)

Nipsco Industries
5265 Hohman Ave.
Hammond, IN 46320
219/853-5200
(Utility.)

North American Van Lines, Inc.
5001 US Highway 30 W.
Fort Wayne, IN 46818
219/429-2511
(Motor carrier.)

Old National Bancorp
420 Main St.
Evansville, IN 47709
812/464-1200
(Bank.)

PSI Energy Inc.
1000 E. Main St.
Plainfield, IN 46168
317/839-9611
(Utility.)

Thompson Consumer Electronics
10330 N. Meridian St.
Indianapolis, IN 46201
317/267-5000
(Consumer electronics.)

Zimmer, Inc.
727 N. Detroit St.
Warsaw, IN 46580
219/267-6131
(Orthopedic, prosthetic and surgical
appliances and devices.)

INDIANA BUSINESS PERIODICAL

Indiana Business
1200 Waterway Blvd.
Indianapolis, IN 46202

317/692-1200
(Monthly.)

INDIANA DIRECTORIES

Harris Indiana Industrial Directory
Harris Publishing Company
2057 Aurora Rd.
Twinsburg, OH 44087
216/425-9000
800/888-5900

Indiana Business Directory
American Business Directories
5711 S. 86th Cir.

P.O. Box 27347
Omaha, NE 68127
402/593-4600

Indiana Manufacturers Directory
Manufacturers' News, Inc.
1633 Central St.
Evanston, IL 60201
708/864-7000

INDIANA GOVERNMENT EMPLOYMENT OFFICES

Office of Personnel Management
(Federal job-service center; see
Michigan listing,
  call 313/226-6950.)

Office of Personnel
402 W. Washington St.
Rm. W161
Indianapolis, IN 46204
317/232-3101

IOWA

LEADING IOWA EMPLOYERS

Allied Group
701 Fifth Ave.
Des Moines, IA 50391
515/280-4211
(Insurance.)

Amana Refrigeration, Inc.
2800 220th Trl.
Amana, IA 52203
319/622-5511
(Appliances.)

Amco Insurance Co.
701 Fifth Ave.
Des Moines, IA 50391
515/280-4211
(Insurance.)

Bandag, Inc.
2905 N. Highway 61
Muscatine, IA 52761
319/262-1400

(Tread rubber, other rubber
products.)

Bankers United Life Assurance Co.
4333 Edgewood Rd., NE
Cedar Rapids, IA 52402
319/398-8511
(Life Insurance.)

Casey's General Stores, Inc.
1 Convenience Blvd.
Ankeny, IA 50021
515/965-6102
(Food convenience stores.)

Collins General Aviation Division
(subs. of Rockwell)
400 Collins Rd., NE
Cedar Rapids, IA 52498
319/395-1000
(Communications, navigation and
flight control equipment.)

Delong Sportswear Inc.
Highway 6W
Grinnell, IA 50112-0189
515/236-3575
(Sportswear.)

EMC Insurance Group
717 Mulberry St.
Des Moines, IA 50309
515/280-2511
(Insurance.)

Equitable of Iowa Cos.
P.O. Box 1635
Des Moines, IA
50306-1635
515/245-6911
(Insurance.)

FDL Foods Inc.
701 East 16th St.
Dubuque, IA 52001
319/588-5400
(Pork products.)

Flexsteel Industries, Inc.
3400 Jackson St.
Dubuque, IA 52001
319/556-7730
(Furniture.)

Hon Industries, Inc.
414 E. 3rd St.
Muscatine, IA 52761
319/264-7400
(Office furniture.)

Hy-vee Food Stores Inc.
201 Court Ave.
Chariton, IA 50049
515/774-5151
(Food stores.)

IES Utilities, Inc.
300 Sheridan Ave.
Centerville, IA 52544
515/437-4400
(Utility.)

Interstate Power Co.
1000 Main St.
Dubuque, IA 52001
319/582-5421
(Utility.)

Life Investors Insurance Co.
4333 Edgewood Rd. NE
Cedar Rapids, IA 52499
319/398-8714
(Insurance.)

Lee Enterprises Inc.
215 N. Main St., Suite 400
Davenport, IA 52801
319/383-2100
(Newspaper publishing.)

MCI Consumer Markets
102 Sergeant Square Dr.
Sergeant Bluff, IA 51054
712/943-1000
(Telemarketing services.)

MCI Telecommunications Corp.
500 Second Ave., SE
Cedar Rapids, IA 52401
319/366-6600
(Telephone communications.)

Maytag Corp.
1 Dependability Sq.
Newton, IA 50208
515/792-7000
(Appliances.)

Meredith Corp.
1716 Locust St.
Des Moines, IA 50309
515/284-3000
(Magazine publishing.)

Mid American Energy Electric Co.
320 LeClaire St.
Davenport, IA 52801
319/326-7111
(Utility.)

Norwest Financial Services Inc.
206 8th St.
Des Moines, IA 50309
515/243-2131
(Consumer and commercial finance,
insurance and reinsurance, etc.)

Pioneer Hi-Bred International
400 Locust St.
Des Moines, IA 50309
515/248-4800
(Food processing.)

The Principal Financial Group
711 High St.
Des Moines, IA 50392
515/247-5111
(Insurance, financial services, etc. At same address: Principal National Life Insurance Co., Principal Casualty Insurance Co.)

Roquette America, Inc.
1417 Exchange St.
Keokuk, IA 52632
319/524-5757
(Corn starch and syrup.)

Statesman Group Inc.
405 6th Ave.
Des Moines, IA 50309
515/284-7500
(Insurance.)

Terra Industries, Inc.
600 Fourth St.
Sioux City, IA 51101
712/277-1340
(Holding company—chemicals, minerals, etc.)

United Fire Group and Casualty Co.
118 Second Ave., SE
Cedar Rapids, IA 52401
319/399-5700
(Insurance.)

Younker's Inc.
701 Walnut St.
Des Moines, IA 50309
515/244-1112
(Department stores.)

IOWA BUSINESS PERIODICAL

Business Record
100 Fourth St.
Des Moines, IA 50309

515/288-3336
(Weekly.)

IOWA DIRECTORIES

Directory of Iowa Manufacturers
Harris Publishing Company
2057 Aurora Rd.
Twinsburg, OH 44087
216/425-9000
800/888-5900

Iowa Business Directory
American Business Directories
5711 S. 86th Cir.

P.O. Box 27347
Omaha, NE 68127
402/593-4600

Iowa Manufacturers Register
Manufacturers' News, Inc.
1633 Central St.
Evanston, IL 60201
708/864-7000

IOWA GOVERNMENT EMPLOYMENT OFFICES

Office of Personnel Management
(Federal job-service center—see listing for MO; phone 816/426-7757.)

Job Service Program Bureau
Department of Job Service
818 5th Ave.
Des Moines, IA 50309
515/281-9607
(State job-service center.)

KANSAS

LEADING KANSAS EMPLOYERS

Air Midwest Inc.
2203 Air Cargo Rd.
Wichita, KS 67209
316/942-8137
(Regional air carrier.)

Allied Signal Inc.
400 N. Rogers Rd.
Olathe, KS 66062
913/782-0400
(Broadcasting.)

Associated Directory Services
7500 W. 110th St.
Shawnee Mission, KS 66210
913/451-6278
(Telephone directories.)

Associated Wholesale Grocers, Inc.
5000 Kansas Ave.
Kansas City, KS 66106
913/321-1313
(Wholesale groceries.)

BK Radio
2901 Lakeview Rd.
Ste. 100
Lawrence, KS 66049
913/842-0402
(Two-way mobile communications.)

**Boeing Commercial Airplanes—
Wichita Division**
P.O. Box 7730
3801 S. Oliver
Wichita, KS 67210
316/526-3153
(Aircraft manufacturer.)

Cessna Aircraft Co.
P.O. Box 7704
Wichita, KS 67277-7704
316/685-9111
(Aircraft.)

**Coca-Cola Bottling Co. of Mid-
America Inc.**
9000 Marshall Dr.

Shawnee Mission, KS 66215
913/492-8100
(Beverage bottler.)

Doskocil Companies, Inc.
321 N. Main St.
South Hutchison, KS 67505
316/663-1005
(Precooked meat, dry sausage
producer.)

Duckwall-Alco Stores Inc.
401 Cottage St.
Albilene, KS 67410
913/263-3350
(Discount stores.)

Fourth Financial Group
100 N. Broadway St.
Wichita, KS 67202
316/261-4444
(Multibank holding co.)

Kansas Gas & Electric Co.
120 E. 1st St. N
Wichita, KS 62701
316/261-6611
(Utility.)

Koch Industries Inc.
Rt. 2
Great Bend, KS 67530
316/793-3806
(Oil and gas exploration, chemicals,
minerals, etc.)

Learjet Inc.
1 Learjet Way
Wichita-Mid-Continent Airport
Wichita, KS 67209
316/946-2000
(Business jets.)

The Lee Apparel Company Inc.
9001 W. 67th St.
Shawnee Mission, KS 66202
913/384-4000
(Apparel.)

Marley Cooling Tower Co.
5800 Fox Ridge Dr.
Mission Woods, KS 66202
913/362-1818
(Cooling towers, boilers, etc.)

NCRA
2000 S. Main St.
McPherson, KS 67460
316/241-2340
(Gasoline blending plants, diesel fuels, oil.)

Pizza Hut Inc.
9111 E. Douglas
Wichita, KS 67207
316/681-9000
(Chain restaurants.)

Puritan-Bennett Corp.
9401 Indian Creek Pkwy.
Shawnee Mission, KS 66210
913/661-0444
(Medical and surgical instruments.)

Raytheon Aircraft Co.
Box 85
Wichita, KS 67201-0085

316/676-7111
(Aircraft, aerospace systems.)

Southwestern Bell—Kansas Division
220 East 6th St.
Topeka, KS 66603
913/276-1585
(Telephone company.)

US Sprint Communications Corp.
2330 Shawnee Mission Pkwy.
Shawnee Mission, KS 66205
913/624-3000
(Long-distance telecommunications.)

Western Resources
818 S. Kansas Ave.
Topeka, KS 66612
913/575-6300
(Utility.)

Yellow Freight System Inc.
10990 Roe Ave.
Box 7563
Overland Park, KS 66211
913/967-3000
(Trucking.)

KANSAS BUSINESS PERIODICAL

Wichita Business Journal
American City Business Journals, Inc.
110 S. Main St., Suite 202
Wichita, KS 67202
316/267-6406
(Weekly.)

KANSAS DIRECTORY

Kansas Business Directory
American Business Directories
5711 S. 86th Cir.
P.O. Box 27347
Omaha, NE 68127
402/593-4600

KANSAS GOVERNMENT EMPLOYMENT OFFICES

Office of Personnel Management
(Federal job-service center; see Kansas City MO listing.)

Division of Employment & Training
Dept. of Human Resources
401 SW Topeka Blvd.
Topeka, KS 66603-3182
913/296-5317
(State job-service center.)

MICHIGAN

LEADING MICHIGAN EMPLOYERS

ANR Pipeline Co.
500 Renaissance Ctr.
Detroit, MI 48243
313/496-0200
(Natural gas transmission.)

Allnet Communications Svc.
30300 Telegraph Rd.
Bingham Farms, MI 48025
313/647-4060
(Telephone services.)

Ameritech of Michigan
444 Michigan Ave.
Detroit, MI 48226
313/223-9900
(Telephone services.)

Amway Corp.
7575 East Fulton St.
Ada, MI 49301
616/676-6000
(Cleaning and other consumer products [direct sales].)

Auto Owners Insurance Co.
6101 Anacapri Blvd.
Lansing, MI 48917
517/323-1325
(Automobile insurance.)

Bissell Inc.
2345 Walker Rd., NW

Grand Rapids, MI 49544
616/453-4451
(Vacuum cleaners.)

Blue Cross & Blue Shield of Michigan
600 E. Lafayette Blvd.
Detroit, MI 48226
313/225-9000
(Insurance.)

Brunswick Divisa
525 West Laketon Ave.
Muskegon, MI 49441
616/725-3300
(Sporting and athletic goods.)

Chrysler Corp.
12000 Chrysler Dr.
Detroit, MI 48288-0001
313/956-5741
(Automobile manufacturer.)

Chrysler Financial Corp.
27777 Franklin Rd.
Southfield, MI 48034
810/948-3762
(Finance company.)

Citizens Banking Corp.
328 S. Saginaw St.
Flint, MI 48502
313/766-7500
(Banking.)

CMS Energy Corp.
330 Towncenter Dr.
Dearborn, MI 48126
313/436-9200
(Utility.)

Comerica Inc.
500 Woodward Ave.
Detroit, MI 48226
313/222-3300
(Banking.)

Consumers Power Co.
212 West Michigan Ave.
Jackson, MI 49201
517/788-0550
(Utility.)

Detroit Edison Co.
2000 2nd Ave.
Detroit, MI 48226
313/237-8000
(Electric utility.)

Donnelly Corp.
414 East 40th St.
Holland, MI 49423
616/786-7000
(Glass products.)

Dow Chemical Co. USA
2030 Willard H. Dow Ctr.
Midland, MI 48674
517/636-1000
(Diversified chemicals.)

Dow Corning Corp.
2200 Salzburg St.
Midland, MI 48640
517/496-4000
(Chemicals.)

Federal-Mogul Corp.
26555 Northwestern Pkwy.
Detroit, MI 48034
313/354-7700
(Motor vehicle parts and
accessories.)

**First of America Bank/
Michigan**
108 E. Michigan Ave.
Kalamazoo, MI 49007

616/376-9000
(Banking.)

First Federal of Michigan
1001 Woodward Ave.
Detroit, MI 48226-1967
313/965-1400
(Banking.)

Ford Motor Company
P.O. Box 1899
The American Rd.
Dearborn, MI 48121
313/322-3000
(Automobile manufacturer.)

Ford Motor Credit Co.
The American Rd.
P.O. Box 1732
Dearborn, MI 48126
313/322-3000
(Credit institution.)

**General Dynamics Land
Systems**
38500 Mound Rd.
Sterling Heights, MI 48310
313/825-4000
(Tanks and tank components.)

General Motors Acceptance Corp.
3044 West Grand Blvd.
Detroit, MI 48202
313/556-5000
(Credit institution.)

General Motors Corp.
3044 West Grand Blvd.
Detroit, MI 48202-3091
313/556-5000
(Automobile manufacturer.)

Gerber Products Co.
445 State St.
Fremont, MI 49412
616/928-2000
(Food processor.)

Haworth Inc.
One Haworth Ctr.
Holland, MI 49423
616/393-3000
(Office furniture.)

Herman Miller Inc.
855 E. Main Ave.
Zeeland, MI 49464
616/654-3000
(Office furniture.)

K Mart Corp.
3100 West Big Beaver Rd.
Troy, MI 48084-3163
810/643-1000
(Discount department stores.)

KH Corp.
38481 Huron River Dr.
Romulus, MI 48174
313/941-2000
(Motor vehicle parts and
accessories.)

Kellogg Co.
256 Porter St.
Battle Creek, MI 49107
616/961-2000
(Food processor.)

Kelly Services Inc.
999 West Big Beaver Rd.
Troy, MI 48084
810/362-4444
(Temporary employment
agencies.)

Lear Seating
21557 Telegraph Rd.
Southfield, MI 48034
810/746-1500
(Auto parts.)

MCN Corp.
500 Griswold St.
Detroit, MI 48226
313/256-5500
(Natural gas, data processing, etc.)

Meijer Inc.
2727 Walker Ave. NW
Grand Rapids, MI 49504
616/453-6711
(Department stores.)

Michigan Consolidated Gas Co.
500 Griswold St.
Detroit, MI 48226
313/965-2430
(Utility.)

Michigan National Corp.
Box 9065
27777 Inkster Rd.
Farmington Hills, MI 49334
810/473-4363
(Banking.)

NBD Bancorp, Inc.
611 Woodward Ave.
Detroit, MI 48226
313/225-1000
(Banking.)

National-Standard Co.
1618 Terminal Rd.
Niles, MI 49120
616/683-8100
(Steel wiredrawing, nails, etc.)

Old Kent Financial Corp.
111 Lyon St., NW
Grand Rapids, MI 49503
616/771-5000
(Bank holding co.)

Penske Corp.
13400 Outer Dr. W.
Detroit, MI 48239
313/592-5000
(Diesel manufacturing, truck leasing,
dealerships.)

Pulte
33 Bloomfield Hills Pkwy.
Bloomfield Hills, MI 48304-2946
810/647-2750
(Builder.)

Rouge Steel
3001 Miller Rd.
Dearborn, MI 48121-1699
313/390-6877
(Steel.)

**Source One Mortgages Service
Corp.**
27555 Farmington Rd.
Farmington Hill, MI 48334-3357
313/488-7000
(Mortgage bankers.)

Spartan Stores Inc.
850 76th St., SW
P.O. Box 8700
Grand Rapids, MI 49518
616/878-2000
(Grocery stores.)

Standard Federal Bancorporation
2600 West Big Beaver Rd.
Troy, MI 48084
810/643-9600
(Banking.)

Steelcase Inc.
901 41st St., SE
Grand Rapids, MI 49508
616/247-2710
(Office furniture.)

Stryker
2525 Fairfield Rd.
Kalamazoo, MI 49002
616/385-2600
(Medical supplies.)

Tecumseh Products Co.
100 East Patterson St.
Tecumseh, MI 49286
517/423-8411
(Auto & truck OEM.)

United Technologies Automotive
5200 Auto Club Dr.
Dearborn, MI 48126
313/593-9600
(Motor vehicle parts and
accessories.)

University Microfilms Inc.
300 N. Zee Rd.
Ann Arbor, MI 48103
313/761-4700
(Microfilms.)

Upjohn Co.
7000 Portage Rd.
Kalamazoo, MI 49001
616/323-4000
(Pharmaceuticals.)

Volkswagen of America Inc.
3800 Hamlin Rd.
Auburn Hills, MI 48326
313/340-5000
(Automobile manufacturer.)

Whirlpool Corp.
2000 NM63
Benton Harbor, MI 49022-2692
616/923-5000
(Appliance manufacturer.)

MICHIGAN BUSINESS PERIODICALS

Corporate Detroit
3031 W. Grand Blvd.
Southfield, MI 48202
313/872-6000
(Monthly.)

Crain's Detroit Business
1400 Woodbridge Ave.
Detroit, MI 48207-3187
313/446-6032
(Weekly.)

MICHIGAN DIRECTORIES

*Harris Michigan Industrial
Directory*
Harris Publishing Co.
2057 Aurora Rd.
Twinsburg, OH 44087
216/425-9000
800/888-5900

Michigan Business Directory
American Business Directories
5711 S. 86th Cir.
P.O. Box 27347
Omaha, NE 68127
402-593-4600

MICHIGAN GOVERNMENT EMPLOYMENT OFFICES

Office of Personnel Management
477 Michigan Ave.
Rm. 565
Detroit, MI 48226
313/226-6950
(Federal job-service center.)

Bureau of Employment Service
Employment Security Division
7310 Woodward Ave.
Detroit, MI 48202
313/876-5309
(State job-service center.)

MINNESOTA

LEADING MINNESOTA EMPLOYERS

AT&T Global Information Solutions
2700 Snelling Ave. N.
Roseville, MN 55113
612/638-8000
(Computers, prepackaged software.)

Bemis Company, Inc.
222 S. 9th St., Suite 2300
Minneapolis, MN 55402
612/376-3000
(Packaging, industrial products.)

Best Buy Co., Inc.
P.O. Box 9312
Minneapolis, MN 55440-9312
612/947-2000
(Electronics stores.)

CP Rail System
P.O. Box 530
Minneapolis, MN 55440
612/347-8000
(Railroad.)

Carlson Hospitality Group, Inc.
(subs. of Carlson Companies, Inc.)
700 Lakeshore Pkwy.
P.O. Box 59159
Minneapolis, MN 55305
612/540-5275
(Hotels and motels.)

Carlson Marketing Group Inc.
P.O. Box 59159

Minneapolis, MN 55459
612/540-5000
(Management consulting.)

Carlson/Wagonlit Travel
P.O. Box 59159
Minneapolis, MN 55459
612/540-5000
(Travel agencies.)

Data Card Corp.
11111 Bren Rd. W.
Minnetonka, MN 55343
612/933-1223
(Office machines.)

Dayton-Hudson Corp.
777 Nicollet Mall
Minneapolis, MN 55402
612/370-6948
(Department stores.)

Deluxe Data Systems Inc.
1080 County Rd. W.
St. Paul, MN 55126
612/483-7111
(Commercial printing, computer software.)

Donaldson Co., Inc.
1400 W. 94th St.
Minneapolis, MN 55431
612/887-3131
(Industrial and commercial equipment and machinery.)

Ecolab Inc.
Ecolab Ctr.
370 N. Wabasha St.
St. Paul, MN 55102
612/293-2233
(Specialty chemicals.)

Federal Cartridge Inc.
900 Ehlen Dr.
Anoka, MN 55303
612/421-7100
(Small arms ammunition.)

Fingerhut Corp.
4400 Baker Rd.
Minnetonka, MN 55343
612/932-3100
(Mail order.)

First Bank System
90 S. 6th St.
Minneapolis, MN 55402-4302
612/973-1111
(Banking.)

General Mills Inc.
1 General Mills Blvd.
Minneapolis, MN 55426
612/540-2311
(Food processor.)

Green Tree Financial Corp.
345 St. Peter St.
St. Paul, MN 55102-1639
612/293-3400
(Mobile manufactured housing
financing.)

Honeywell, Inc.
2701 4th Ave. S.
Minneapolis, MN 55408
612/951-1000
(Aerospace and electronics systems
and products.)

Hormel Foods Corp.
One Hormel Pl.
Austin, MN 55912-3680
507/437-5611
(Food processor.)

Hutchinson Technology Inc.
40 W. Highland Dr.
Hutchinson, MN 55350
612/587-3797
(Computer peripherals, electronics
and defense equipment.)

**Inter-Regional Financial Group,
Inc.**
Dean Bosworth Plz.
60 S. 6th St.
Minneapolis, MN 55402
612/371-7750
(Securities broker and dealer,
investment banking.)

**International Multifoods
Corp.**
Multifoods Tower
33 S. 6th St.
Minneapolis, MN 55402-0942
612/340-3300
(Food products.)

Jostens, Inc.
5501 Norman Ctr. Dr.
Minneapolis, MN 55437
612/830-3300
(Class rings, yearbooks, caps and
gowns, etc.)

Land O'Lakes Inc.
P.O. Box 116
Minneapolis, MN 55440
612/481-2222
(Dairy products.)

MTS Systems Corp.
14000 Technology Dr.
Eden Prairie, MN 55344
612/937-4000
(Measuring and controlling
devices.)

Medtronic Inc.
7000 Central Ave. NE
Minneapolis, MN 55432-3576
612/574-4000
(Medical equipment.)

**Minnesota Mining &
Manufacturing Co. (3M)**
3M Ctr.
St. Paul, MN 55144-1000
612/733-1110
(Diversified conglomerate.)

Minnesota Mutual Life Insurance Co.
400 N. Robert St.
St. Paul, MN 55101
612/298-3500
(Life insurance.)

Minnesota Power & Light Co.
30 W. Superior St.
Duluth, MN 55802
218/722-2641
(Utility.)

M.A. Mortenson Cos.
700 Meadow Ln. N.
Minneapolis, MN 55422
612/522-2100
(Construction.)

Nash Finch Co.
7600 France Ave. S.
Edina, MN 55435
612/832-0534
(Food wholesaler.)

National Car Rental System Inc.
7700 France Ave. S.
Edina, MN 55435
612/830-2121
(Car rentals.)

Northern States Power Co.
414 Nicollet Mall
Minneapolis, MN 55401
612/330-5500
(Utility.)

Northwest Airlines, Inc.
Minneapolis-St. Paul Airport
5101 Northwest Dr.
St. Paul, MN 55111-3034
612/726-2111
(Airline.)

Northwestern National Life Insurance Co.
20 Washington Ave. S.
Minneapolis, MN 55401
612/372-1800
(Insurance.)

Norwest Corporation
90 S. 7th St.
Minneapolis, MN 55402
612/667-1234
(Banking.)

Onan Corp.
1400 73rd Ave. NE
Fridley, MN 55432
612/574-5000
(Motors and generators.)

Patterson Dental Co.
1031 Menota Hts. Rd.
St. Paul, MN 55120
612/686-1600
(Dental equipment.)

Pillsbury Co.
Pillsbury Ctr.
200 S. 6th St.
Minneapolis, MN 55402
612/330-4966
(Food processing.)

Piper, Jaffrey, and Hopwood Inc.
222 S. Ninth St.
Minneapolis, MN 55402
612/342-6000
(Securities broker.)

Relia Star Financial
20 Washington Ave. S.
Minneapolis, MN 55401
612/372-5432
(Insurance.)

St. Jude Medical Inc.
1 Lillehei Plz.
St. Paul, MN 55117
612/483-2000
(Medical supplies.)

Sheldahl, Inc.
1150 Sheldahl Rd.
Northfield, MN 55057
507/663-8000
(Printed circuit boards, graphic displays, plastic processing.)

Smead Manufacturing Co.
600 East Smead Blvd.
Hastings, MN 55033
612/437-4111
(Filing folders, manila folders, index cards, etc.)

St. Paul Companies, Inc.
385 Washington St.
Minneapolis, MN 55102
612/221-7911
(Insurance, financial services.)

Starkey Laboratories Inc.
6700 Washington Ave. S.
Eden Prairie, MN 55344
612/941-6401
(Orthopedic, prosthetic and surgical appliances and devices.)

Super Valu Stores, Inc.
11840 Valley View Rd.
Eden Prairie, MN 55344
612/828-4000
(Food wholesaler.)

TCF Financial Corp.
801 Marquette Ave.
Minneapolis, MN 55402-3475
612/661-6500
(Banking, financial services.)

Tennant Co.
701 North Lilac Dr.
Minneapolis, MN 55422
612/540-1200
(Dirt sweepers, floor washing/polishing machines, wax, sealants and detergents.)

Thermo King Corp.
314 W. 90th St.
Bloomington, MN 55420
612/887-2200
(Air conditioning and refrigeration equipment.)

The Toro Company
8111 Lyndale Ave. S.
Bloomington, MN 55420
612/888-8801
(Lawn and garden equipment.)

United Health Care
9800 Bren Rd. E.
Minnetonka, MN 55343
612/945-8001
(Health care.)

Valspar Corp.
1101 South Third St.
Minneapolis, MN 55415
612/332-7371
(Paint, etc.)

Waldorf Corp.
2250 Wabash Ave.
St. Paul, MN 55114
612/641-4938
(Folding boxboard, corrugating medium.)

MINNESOTA DIRECTORIES

Minnesota Business Directory
American Business Directories
5711 S. 86th Cir.
P.O. Box 27347
Omaha, NE 68127
402/593-4600

Minnesota Manufacturers Register
Manufacturers' News, Inc.
1633 Central St.
Evanston, IL 60201
708/864-7000

MINNESOTA GOVERNMENT EMPLOYMENT OFFICES

Office of Personnel Management
Federal Bldg. Room 501
Ft. Snelling
Twin Cities, MN 55111
612/725-3430
(Federal job-service center.)

Dept. of Economic Security
690 American Ctr. Bldg.
150 E. Kellogg
St. Paul, MN 55101
612/296-3644
(State job-service center.)

MISSOURI

LEADING MISSOURI EMPLOYERS

Anheuser-Busch Companies, Inc.
1 Busch Place
St. Louis, MO 63118-1852
314/577-2000
(Brewery, food and beverage products.)

Black & Veatch Waste Service
8400 Ward Pkwy.
Kansas City, MO 64114
913/339-2000
(Engineering services.)

Boatmen's Bancshares Inc.
800 Market St.
St. Louis, MO 63101
314/466-6000
(Banking.)

Brown Group Inc.
8400 Maryland Ave.
St. Louis, MO 63105
314/854-4000
(Footwear, specialty retailing.)

Citicorp Mortgage Inc.
15851 Clayton Rd.
Ballwin, MO 63011
314/256-5000
(Mortgage banking.)

Commerce Bancshares Inc.
1000 Walnut St.
Kansas City, MO 64106
816/234-2000
(Banking.)

Datastorm Technologies Inc.
3212 Lemoine Ind. Blvd.
Columbia, MO 65215
314/443-3252
(Communications software.)

Edison Apparel Bros. Stores Inc.
501 N. Broadway
St. Louis, MO 63102
314/331-6000
(Stores [including Bakers, Chandlers (shoes), Jeans West, J. Riggings].)

A. G. Edwards & Sons, Inc.
1 N. Jefferson Ave.
St. Louis, MO 63103
314/289-3000
(Security brokers, dealers.)

Electronics & Space Corp.
(subs. of Emerson Electric Co.)
8000 W. Florissant Blvd.
St. Louis, MO 63136
314/553-3334
(Armament, communications, testing and other electronic systems.)

Emerson Electric Co.
P.O. Box 4100
8000 W. Florissant Blvd.
St. Louis, MO 63136
314/553-2000
(Electronic and consumer products, defense products and systems.)

Farmland Industries, Inc.
3315 N. Oak Trafficway
Kansas City, MO 64116
816/459-6000
(Petroleum refining.)

Graybar Electric Co.
34 N. Meramec Ave.
St. Louis, MO 63105
314/727-3900
(Electrical equipment wholesaling.)

H & R Block Inc.
4410 Main St.
Kansas City, MO 64111
816/753-6900
(Business services.)

Hallmark Cards Inc.
2501 McGee St.
Kansas City, MO 64108
816/274-5111
(Greeting cards.)

Harbour Group Ltd.
7701 Forsyth Blvd., Suite 600
Clayton, MO 63105
314/727-5550
(Medical products, cutting tools, etc.)

Hussmann Corp.
12999 St. Charles Rock Rd.
Bridgeton, MO 63044
314/291-2000
(Air conditioning, heating and
refrigeration equipment.)

Jefferson Smurfit
8182 Maryland, Ave.
St. Louis, MO 63105
314/746-1100
(Packaging.)

Kansas City Power & Light Co.
1201 Walnut St.
Kansas City, MO 64106
816/556-2200
(Utility.)

The Kansas City Star Co.
1729 Grand Ave.
Kansas City, MO 64108
816/234-4545
(Newspaper publishing—subs. of
Capital Cities/ABC, Inc.)

Leggett & Platt Inc.
No. 1 Leggett Rd.
Carthage, MO 64836
417/358-8141
(Home furnishings & recreation.)

Magna Group
1401 S. Brentwood Blvd.
St. Louis, MO 63144-1401
314/963-2500
(Bank.)

Mallinckrodt Group
7733 Forsyth Blvd.
St. Louis, MO 63105
314/854-5200
(Drugs.)

Marion Merrell Dow Inc.
P.O. Box 8480
9300 Ward Pkwy.
Kansas City, MO 64114-0480

816/966-4000
(Pharmaceuticals.)

Maritz, Inc.
1375 N. Hwy. Dr.
Fenton, MO 63099
314/827-4000
(Motivation, communication, market
research training, business travel.)

The May Department Stores Co.
611 Olive St.
St. Louis, MO 63101
314/342-6300
(Department stores.)

McDonnell Douglas Corp.
325 McDonnell Blvd.
St. Louis, MO 63042
314/232-0232
(Aircraft, aerospace products and
systems.)

McDonnell Douglas Aerospace
625 McDonnell Blvd.
St. Louis, MO 63042
314/232-0232
(Missiles and combat weapons.)

Memc Electronic Materials Inc.
501 Pearl Dr.
St Peter's, MO 63376
314/279-5000
(Semi-conductors and related
devices.)

Mercantile Bancorporation
721 Locust St.
St. Louis, MO 63101
314/425-2525
(Banking.)

Monsanto Chemical Co.
800 N. Lindbergh Blvd.
St. Louis, MO 63141
314/694-1000
(Chemical, agricultural products,
pharmaceuticals, plastics, etc.)

Payless Cashways Inc.
P.O. Box 419466
Kansas City, MO 64141-0466
816/234-6000
(Home improvement stores.)

Pulitzer Publishing Co.
515 N. 6th St.
St. Louis, MO 63101
314/231-5969
(Newspaper publisher, radio, and
television station owner.)

Ralston Purina Co.
Checkerboard Sq.
St. Louis, MO 63164
314/982-1000
(Food products.)

Roosevelt Financial Group
900 Roosevelt Pkwy.
Chesterfield, MO 63017
314/532-6200
(Bank.)

Sigma-Aldrich Corp.
3050 Spruce St.
St. Louis, MO 63103
314/771-5765
(Chemicals supplier.)

Southwestern Bell
100 N. Tucker
Rm. 1118
St. Louis, MO 63101
314/235-0299
(Telephone services.)

Sprint
Business Service Group
8140 Ward Pkwy.

Kansas City, MO 64114
913/624-3000
(Telecommunications.)

Sverdrup Corp.
13723 Riverport Dr.
Maryland Heights, MO 63043
314/436-7600
(Engineering, architectural services,
etc.)

UMB Financial
1010 Grand Ave.
Kansas City, MO 64106
816/860-7000
(Banking.)

Union Electric Co.
1901 Chouteau Ave.
St. Louis, MO 63112
314/621-3222
(Utility.)

UtilCorp United
911 Main St.
Kansas City, MO 64105
816/421-6600
(Energy.)

Venture Stores Inc.
2001 E. Terra Ln.
O'Fallon, MO 63366-0110
314/281-5500
Fax 314/281-7233
(Drug & discount stores.)

MISSOURI BUSINESS PERIODICALS

Kansas City Business Journal
1101 Walnut
Kansas City, MO 64106
816/421-5900
(Weekly.)

St. Louis Business Journal
Box 647
St. Louis, MO 63188
314/421-6200
(Weekly.)

MISSOURI DIRECTORIES

Harris Missouri Directory of
Manufacturers
IDC (div. of Harris Publishing Co.)
2057 Aurora Rd.

Twinsburg, OH 44087
216/425-9000
800/888-5900

Missouri Business Directory
American Business Directories
5711 S. 86th Cir.
P.O. Box 27347
Omaha, NE 68127
402/593-4600

Missouri Manufacturers Directory
Manufacturers' News Inc.
1633 Central St.
Evanston, IL 60201
708/864-7000

MISSOURI GOVERNMENT EMPLOYMENT OFFICES

Office of Personnel Management
Federal Bldg., Rm. 134
601 E. 12th St.
Kansas City, MO 64106
816/426-5702
(Federal job-service center)

Employment Service
Division of Employment Security
P.O. Box 59
Jefferson City, MO 65104
314/751-3790

NEBRASKA

LEADING NEBRASKA EMPLOYERS

Ag Processing Inc.
12700 W. Dodge Rd.
Omaha, NE 68154
402/496-7809
(Soybean oil.)

**American Signature
of Lincoln**
3700 NW 12th St.
Lincoln, NE 68521
402/474-5825
(Commercial printing.)

BeefAmerica Inc. Operating Co.
14748 W. Center Rd.
Omaha, NE 68144
402/896-2400
(Meat packing.)

Berkshire Hathaway Inc.
1440 Kiewit Plz.
Omaha, NE 68131
402/346-1400
(Fire, property, and casualty
insurance.)

**Commercial Federal
Corp.**
2120 S. 72nd St.
Omaha, NE 68124
402/554-9200
(Savings and loan.)

ConAgra Inc.
1 Con Agra Dr.
Omaha, NE 68102
402/595-4000
(Meat packing.)

Cushman Inc.
900 N. 21st St.
Lincoln, NE 68503
402/475-9581
(Transportation
equipment.)

Data Documents, Inc.
4205 S. 96th St.
Omaha, NE 68127
402/339-0900
(Computer paper.)

First Data Resources
(subs. American Express)
10825 Farnam Dr.
Omaha, NE 68154
402/222-7909
(Bank credit card processing, etc.)

First National of Nebraska Inc.
1620 Dodge St.
Omaha, NE 68102
402/341-0500
(Banking.)

FirstTier Bank
1700 Farnam St.
Omaha, NE 68102-2183
402/348-6000
(Bank.)

IBP Inc.
Highway 35
P.O. Box 515
Dakota City, NE 68731
402/494-2061
(Meat processing.)

Kawasaki Motor Manufacturing Corp. USA
6600 Northwest 27th St.
Lincoln, NE 68524
402/476-6600
(Motorcycles, all-terrain vehicles, etc.)

Kiewit Construction Group Inc.
3555 Farnam St.
Omaha, NE 68131
402/342-2052
(Hwy. and street construction, commercial and office building contractors, etc.)

Peter Kiewit and Sons' Inc.
3555 Farnam St.
Omaha, NE 68131
402/342-2052
(Metal cans, plastic bottles, construction.)

Lozier Corp.
3301 Dodge St.
Omaha, NE 68181
402/457-8000
(Store display fixtures.)

MFS Communications
3555 Farnam St.
Omaha, NE 68131
402/271-2890
(Telecommunications.)

Mutual of Omaha Insurance Co.
1334 Dodge St.
Omaha, NE 68175
402/342-7600
(Accident and health insurance.)

Omaha Public Power District
444 S. 16th Mall
Omaha, NE 68102
402/636-2000
(Utility.)

Omaha World-Herald Co.
World-Herald Sq.
Omaha, NE 68102
402/444-1000
(Newspaper publishing.)

Pamida Inc.
8800 F St.
Omaha, NE 68127
402/339-2400
(General merchandise store.)

Union Pacific Railroad Co.
1416 Dodge St.
Omaha, NE 68102
402/271-3530
(Railroad.)

Valmont Industries, Inc.
Hwy. 275
Valley, NE 68064
402/359-2201
(Irrigation systems, steel tubing, poles, etc.)

Werner Enterprises Inc.
14507 Frontier Rd.
Box 37308
Omaha, NE 68168
402/895-6640
(Trucking.)

West Telemarketing Corp.
3911 N. 93rd St.
Omaha, NE 68134

402/571-7700
(Telemarketing services.)

Woodmen Accident & Life Co.
1526 K St.
Lincoln, NE 68508
402/476-6500
(Insurance.)

**Woodmen of the World Life
Insurance Society**
1700 Farnam St.
Omaha, NE 68102
402/342-1890
(Insurance.)

NEBRASKA DIRECTORIES

Directory of Nebraska Manufacturers
Department of Economic Development
301 Centennial Mall
Box 94666
Lincoln, NE 68509
402/471-3111

Nebraska Business Directory
American Business Directories
5711 S. 86th Cir.
P.O. Box 27347
Omaha, NE 68127
402/593-4600

NEBRASKA GOVERNMENT EMPLOYMENT OFFICES

**Office of Personnel
Management**
(Federal job-service center—see
Missouri listing.)

Job Service
NE Dept. of Labor
550 S. 16th St.
Lincoln, NE 68509
402/471-9824
(State job-service center.)

NORTH DAKOTA

LEADING NORTH DAKOTA EMPLOYERS

Basin Electric
1717 E. Interstate Ave.
Bismarck, ND 58501
701/221-4400
(Utility.)

**Blue Cross & Blue Shield of North
Dakota**
4510 13th Ave., SW
Fargo, ND 58103
701/277-2227
(Group hospitalization plans.)

**Diagnostic Medical
Systems**
2101 N. University Dr.
Fargo, ND 58102701/237-9073
(Medical equipment and
supplies.)

Federal Beef Processors Inc.
750 9th St., NW
240 West Fargo, ND 58078
701/282-9570
(Meat packing.)

First Bank Fargo
505 2nd Ave. N.
Fargo, ND 58102
701/280-3500
(Savings bank.)

Forum Publishing Co.
101 5th St. N
Fargo, ND 58102
701/241-5432
(Newspaper publishing,
broadcasting.)

Hornbachers Food Inc.
2510 Broadway
Fargo, ND 58102
701/293-5444
(Grocery stores.)

Interstate Pipeline Co.
200 N. Third St., Suite 300
Bismarck, ND 58501
701/221-1200
(Crude petroleum and natural gas.)

MDU Resources Group Inc.
400 N. 4th St.
Bismarck, ND 58501
701/222-7900
(Utility.)

Minnkota Power Co-op Inc.
1822 Mill Rd.
Grand Forks, ND 58203
701/795-4000
(Utility.)

Sioux Manufacturing Corp.
Main St.
P.O. Box 400
Fort Totten, ND 58335
701/766-4211
(Plastic products, molding.)

Valley Markets Inc.
P.O. Box 13675
Grand Forks, ND 58208-3675
701/772-5531
(Grocery stores.)

Vanderhave USA Inc.
1215 Prairie Pkwy.
West Fargo, ND 58078
701/282-7338
(Farm supplies.)

Vanity Shop of Grand Forks
1001 25th St.
Fargo, ND 58102
701/237-3330
(Women's clothing stores.)

NORTH DAKOTA DIRECTORY

North Dakota Business Directory
American Business Directories
5711 S. 86th Cir.
P.O. Box 27347
Omaha, NE 68127
402/593-4600

NORTH DAKOTA GOVERNMENT EMPLOYMENT OFFICES

Office of Personnel Management
(Federal job-service center—see
Minnesota listing.)

**Employment & Job Training
Division**
Job Service North Dakota
1000 E. Divide Ave.
Bismarck, ND 58501
701/328-2825

OHIO

LEADING OHIO EMPLOYERS

ABX Air Inc.
145 Hunter Dr.
Airborne Air Park
Wilmington, OH 45177
513/382-5591
(Cargo express airline.)

AK Steel Holding
703 Curtis St.
Middletown, OH 45044-0001
513/425-5000
(Steel.)

AT&T Global Information Solutions
1700 S. Patterson Blvd.
Dayton, OH 45479
513/445-5000
(Computers, telecommunications services.)

American Electric Power Inc.
One Riverside Plz.
Columbus, OH 43215-2373
614/223-1000
(Electric utility.)

American Financial Corp.
1 E. Fourth St.
Cincinnati, OH 45202
513/579-6060
(Insurance.)

American Greetings Corp.
1 American Rd.
Cleveland, OH 44144
216/252-7300
(Greeting cards.)

Ameritech Ohio
45 Erieview Plz.
Cleveland, OH 44114
216/822-9700
(Telephone services.)

BP America Inc.
200 Public Sq.
Cleveland, OH 44114
216/586-4141
(Holding company.)

Bailey Controls Co.
29801 Euclid Ave.
Wickliffe, OH 44092
216/585-8500
(Industrial instruments.)

Banc One
100 East Broad St.
Columbus, OH 43215
614/248-5944
(Banking.)

Battelle Memorial Institute
505 King Ave.
Columbus, OH 43201
614/424-6424
(Non-profit scientific research and development.)

Bridgestone/Firestone Inc.
1200 Firestone Pkwy.
Akron, OH 44317
216/379-7000
(Tires, inner tubes, etc.)

Cardinal Health
655 Metro Place S.
Dublin, OH 43017
614/761-8700
(Drugs.)

Centerior Energy
6200 Oak Tree Blvd.
Cleveland, OH 44102
216/447-3100
(Electric utility.)

Charter One Financial
1215 Superior Ave.
Cleveland, OH 44114
216/589-8320
(Bank.)

Chiquita Brands International, Inc.
250 E. Fifth St.
Cincinnati, OH 45202
513/784-8000
(Food, food processing.)

Cincinnati Financial Corp.
6200 S. Gilmore Rd.
Cincinnati, OH 45014
513/870-2000
(Insurance holding company.)

CINergy Corp.
139 E. 4th St.
Cincinnati, OH 45202
513/381-2000
(Utility.)

Cincinnati Milacron Inc.
4701 Marburg Ave.
Cincinnati, OH 45209
513/841-8100
(Machine tools.)

Cincom Systems Inc.
2300 Montana Ave.
Cincinnati, OH 45211
513/662-2300
(Computer systems.)

Cintas Corp.
6800 Cintask Blvd.
Mason, OH 45040
513/459-1200
(Industrial services.)

The Cleveland Electric Illuminating Co.
55 Public Sq.
Cleveland, OH 44141
216/622-9800
(Utility.)

Comair Inc.
P.O. Box 75021
Cincinnati International Airport
Cincinnati, OH 45275
606/767-3500
(Regional air carrier.)

Cooper Tire & Rubber Co.
701 Lima Ave.
Findlay, OH 45840

419/423-1321
(Tires, inner tubes.)

Copeland Corp.
1675 Campbell Rd.
Sidney, OH 45365
513/498-3011
(Air conditioning, heating and refrigeration equipment.)

Crown Equipment Corp.
40 South Washington St.
New Bremen, OH 45869
419/629-2311
(Industrial trucks, trailers, etc.)

Dana Corp.
P.O. Box 1000
4500 Dorr St.
Toledo, OH 43615
419/535-4500
(Mobile fluid power products, etc.)

Diebold, Incorporated
5995 Mayfair Rd.
North Canton, OH 44707
216/489-4000
(Automated transaction systems [ATMs], security equipment.)

DPL Inc.
1065 Woodman Dr.
Dayton, OH 45432
513/224-6000
(Electric utility.)

Eaton Corp.
1111 Superior Ave.
Cleveland, OH 44114
216/523-5000
(Vehicle power train components, etc.)

The Elder-Beerman Stores Corp.
3155 El-Bee Rd.
Dayton, OH 45439
512/296-2700
(Department stores.)

Federated Department Stores
7 W. 7th St.
Cincinnati, OH 45202
513/579-7000
(Department stores.)

Ferro Corp.
1000 Lakeside Ave. E
Cleveland, OH 44114
216/641-8580
(Chemicals.)

Fifth Third Bankcorp
38 Fountain Sq. Plz.
Cincinnati, OH 45202
513/579-5300
(Banking.)

First Merit
106 S. Main St.
Akron, OH 44308-1444
216/384-8000
(Bank.)

GE Aircraft Engines
1 Neumann Way
Cincinnati, OH 45215-6301
513/243-2000
(Gas turbine engines.)

Gencorp Inc.
175 Ghent Rd.
Fairlawn, OH 44333
216/869-4200
(Industrial rubber products.)

Gibson Greetings Inc.
2100 Section Rd.
Cincinnati, OH 45237
513/841-6600
(Greeting cards.)

BF Goodrich Company
3925 Embassy Pkwy.
Akron, OH 44333-1799
216/374-2000
(Chemicals.)

The Goodyear Tire & Rubber Company
1144 East Market St.
Akron, OH 44316-0001
216/796-2121
(Tires, inner tubes.)

Hobart Corp.
701 S. Ridge Ave.
Troy, OH 45373
513/332-4000

(Arc welding equipment, metals, etc.)

Honda of America Manufacturing Inc.
24000 Honday Pkwy.
Marysville, OH 43030
513/642-5000
(Automobile manufacturer.)

Huntington Bancshares
41 S. High St.
Columbus, OH 43215
614/480-8300
(Bank.)

Kay Jewelers, Inc.
375 Ghent Rd.
Akron, OH 44333
216/668-5000
(Jewelry.)

KeyCorp
127 Public Sq.
Cleveland, OH 44114-1306
216/689-3000
(Bank.)

Kroger Co.
1014 Vine St.
Cincinnati, OH 45202-1100
513/762-4000
(Supermarkets.)

Lancaster Colony Corp.
37 W. Broad St.
Columbus, OH 43215
614/224-7141
(Giftware, glass products.)

LTV Aerospace and Defense Company
25 W. Prospect Ave.
Cleveland, OH 44115
216/622-5000
(Military aircraft, missiles, etc.)

The LTV Corp.
25 W. Prospect Ave.
Cleveland, OH 44115
216/622-5000
(Conglomerate)

LTV Steel Co.
(subs. of the LTV Corp.)
25 W. Prospect Ave.
Cleveland, OH 44115
216/622-5000
(Stainless steel, alloy steels, other
steels and steel products.)

Lazarus Stores
Federated Department Stores, Inc.
699 Race St.
Cincinnati, OH 45202
513/779-5980
(Department stores.)

Lexus-Nexus
9443 Springboro Pike
Dayton, OH 45342
513/865-6800
(Computerized legal, accounting and
research services.)

The Limited, Inc.
P.O. Box 16000
3 Limited Pkwy.
Columbus, OH 43230
614/479-7079
(Specialty stores [Limited, Express,
Victoria's Secret, etc.].)

Lincoln Electric Co.
22801 St. Clair Ave.
Cleveland, OH 44117
216/481-8100
(Welding equipment.)

Loral Systems Co.
1210 Massilion Rd.
Akron, OH 44315
216/796-2800
(Undersea and anti-submarine
defense systems.)

Lubrizol Corp.
29400 Lakeland Blvd.
Wickliffe, OH 44092-2298
216/943-4200
(Automotive lubricants.)

Marathon Oil Co.
539 South Main St.
Findlay, OH 45840

419/422-2121
(Oil and petroleum products.)

Mead Corp.
10 W. 2nd St.
Dayton, OH 45402
513/222-6323
(Paper.)

Mercantile Stores
9450 Seward Rd.
Fairfield, OH 45014-2230
513/881-8000
(Department stores.)

National City Bank
1900 East Ninth St.
Cleveland, OH 44114-3484
216/575-2222
(Banking.)

Nationwide Corp.
One Nationwide Plz.
Columbus, OH 43216
614/249-7111
(Insurance.)

Ohio Casualty Corp.
136 N. Third St.
Hamilton, OH 45011
513/867-3000
(Insurance.)

Ohio Edison Co.
1919 W. Market St.
Akron, OH 44313
216/384-5151
Fax 800/633-4766
(Utility.)

Owens-Corning Fiberglas Corp.
Fiberglas Tower
Toledo, OH 43659
419/248-8000
(Fiberglass, other industrial
products.)

Owens-Illinois, Inc.
1 Seagate
Toledo, OH 43666
419/247-5000
(Glass containers, etc.)

Parker Hannifin Corp.
17325 Euclid Ave.
Cleveland, OH 44112-1290
216/531-3000
(Fluid power systems.)

Premier Industrial
4500 Euclid Ave.
Cleveland, OH 44103
216/391-8300
(Electrical equipment.)

Procter & Gamble Co.
One Procter & Gamble Plz.
Cincinnati, OH 45202
513/983-1100
(Consumer products, foods, etc.)

Progressive Corp.
6300 Wilson Mills Rd.
Cleveland, OH 44143
216/461-5000
Fax 216/446-7699
(Insurance.)

Provident Bancorp
1 E. 4th St.
Cincinnati, OH 45202
513/579-2000
(Bank.)

Reliance Electric Co.
24701 Euclid Ave.
Cleveland, OH 44117
216/266-7000
(Telecommunications and industrial equipment.)

Revco DS Inc.
1925 Enterprise Pkwy.
Twinsburg, OH 44087
216/425-9811
(Drug & discount stores.)

Reynolds & Reynolds Co.
800 Germantown St.
Dayton, OH 45407
513/443-2000
(Computer systems and system supports, forms, etc.)

Riser Foods Inc.
5300 Richmond Rd.
Bedford Hts., OH 44146
216/292-7000
(Grocerices distribution.)

Roadway Express Inc.
1077 Gorge Blvd.
Akron, OH 48310
216/384-1717
(Shipping.)

Rubbermaid Inc.
1147 Akron Rd.
Wooster, OH 44691
216/264-6464
(Household products.)

Scripps Howard Newspapers Inc.
P.O. Box 5380
Cincinnati, OH 45202
513/977-3000
(Newspaper publishing, cable television, other media-related fields.)

Sealy Inc.
1228 Euclid Ave.
Cleveland, OH 44115
216/522-1310
(Mattresses.)

Sherwin-Williams Co.
101 Prospect Ave. NW
Cleveland, OH 44115-1075
216/566-2000
(Paints and coatings manufacturing and distribution.)

Society Bank
127 Public Sq.
Cleveland, OH 44114
216/689-8241
(Banking.)

Standard Register Co.
600 Albany St.
Dayton, OH 45408
513/443-1000
(Business forms.)

Star Banc
425 Walnut St.
Cincinnati, OH 45215
513/632-4000
(Bank.)

The Stouffer Corp.
3003 Bainbridge Rd.
Solon, OH 44139
216/248-3600
(Frozen foods, etc.)

Trinova Corp.
3000 Strayer
Maumee, OH 43537
419/867-2200
(Fluid conveying components and systems, etc.)

TRW Inc.
1900 Richmond Rd.
Cleveland, OH 44124-3760
216/291-7000
(High-tech products and services for electronics, auto, defense information systems.)

The Timken Co.
1835 Dueber Ave., SW
Canton, OH 44706
216/438-3000
(Ball bearings.)

United States Shoe Corp.
One Eastwood Dr.
Cincinnati, OH 45227-1197
513/527-7000
(Retail stores.)

Western & Southern Life Insurance
400 Broadway
Cincinnati, OH 45202
513/629-1800
(Insurance.)

Worthington Industries, Inc.
1205 Dearborn Dr.
Columbus, OH 43085
614/438-3210
614/438-3256
(Flat-rolled steel, etc.)

OHIO BUSINESS PERIODICAL

Crain's Cleveland Business
700 St. Clair Ave. West
Cleveland, OH 44113
216/522-1383
(Weekly.)

OHIO DIRECTORIES

Harris Ohio Industrial Directory
Harris Publishing Co.
21057 Aurora Rd.
Twinsburg, OH 44087
216/425-9000
800/888-5900

Ohio Business Directory
American Business Directories
5711 S. 86th Cir.
P.O. Box 27347
Omaha, NE 68127
402/593-4600

Ohio Directory of Manufacturers
Commerce Register, Inc.
190 Godwin Ave
Midland Park, NJ 07432
201/445-3000

Ohio Manufacturers Register
Manufacturers' News, Inc.
1633 Central St.
Evanston, IL 60201
708/864-7000

OHIO GOVERNMENT EMPLOYMENT OFFICES

Office of Personnel Management
200 W. Second St., Rm. 507
Dayton, OH 45402
513/225-2576
(Federal job-service center; but for counties north of and including: Van Wert, Auglaize, Hardin, Marion, Crawford, Richland, Ashland, Wayne, Stark, Carroll, and Columbiana, see Michigan listing.)

Employment Service Division
Bureau of Employment Services
145 S. Front St., Rm. 640
Columbus, OH 43215
614/466-2421
(State job-service center.)

SOUTH DAKOTA

LEADING SOUTH DAKOTA EMPLOYERS

Austad Co.
4500 East 10th St.
Sioux Falls, SD 57103
605/336-3135
(Mail-order golf equipment.)

Black Hills Corp.
625 9th St.
Rapid City, SD 57114
605/348-1700
(Utility.)

Citibank South Dakota N.A.
701 East 60th St. N.
Sioux Falls, SD 57104
605/331-2626
(Commercial banking, credit card operations.)

First Bank of South Dakota
141 N. Main Ave.
Sioux Falls, SD 57102
605/339-8600
(National trust companies.)

Gateway 2000
P.O. Box 2000
610 Gateway Dr.
North Sioux City, SD 57049-2000
605/232-2000
(Mail-order computers.)

Hospitality Services
506 S. Wilson St.
Aberdeen, SD 57402
605/229-5945
(Motel building and services.)

Hub City Inc.
2914 Industrial Ave.
Aberdeen, SD 57401
605/225-0360
(Mechanical power transmission equipment.)

Kesslers Inc.
615-621 6th Ave. SE
Aberdeen, SD 57401
605/225-1692
(Grocery stores.)

Norwest Bank South Dakota
101 N. Phillips Ave.
Sioux Falls, SD 57102
605/339-7300
(National trust companies.)

Northwestern Public Service Co.
88 Third St., SE
P.O. Box 1318
South Huron, SD 57350
605/352-8411
(Utility.)

Randalls Stores Inc.
1800 North Main St.
Mitchell, SD 57301
605/996-5593
(Grocery stores.)

Raven Industries Inc.
815 6th Ave.
Sioux Falls, SD 57104
605/336-2750
(Plastic, electronic, and apparel products.)

Sunshine Food Markets
P.O. Box 5108
Sioux Falls, SD 57117
605/336-2505
(Grocery stores.)

Super 8 Motels Inc.
1910 8th Ave., NE
Aberdeen, SD 57401
605/225-2272
(Motels.)

Simon Telelect Inc.
600 Oakwood Rd.
Watertown, SD 57201
605/882-4000
(Derricks, truck bodies, hydraulic cylinders.)

Trail King Industries Inc.
300 East Norway Ave.
Mitchell, SD 57301
605/996-6482
(Truck trailers.)

SOUTH DAKOTA DIRECTORIES

South Dakota Business Directory
American Business Directories
5711 S. 86th Cir.
P.O. Box 27347
Omaha, NE 68127
402/593-4600

South Dakota Manufacturers & Processors Directory
Governor's Office of Economic Development
711 E. Wells Ave.
Pierre, SD 57501-3369
605/773-5032

SOUTH DAKOTA GOVERNMENT EMPLOYMENT OFFICES

Office of Personnel Management
(Federal job-service center—see Minnesota listing.)

South Dakota Dept. of Labor
700 Governors Dr.
Pierre, SD 57501
605/773-3101
(State job-service center.)

WISCONSIN

LEADING WISCONSIN EMPLOYERS

Air Wisconsin, Inc.
WG390 Challenger Dr. #203
Appleton, WI 54915

414/739-5123
(Passenger and cargo air carrier.)

American Foods Group
520 Lawrence St.
Green Bay, WI 54302
414/437-6330
(Meat packing.)

Ameritech Wisconsin
722 N. Broadway
Milwaukee, WI 53202
414/678-3622
(Telephone services.)

Ashley Furniture Industries
1 Ashley Way
Arcadia, WI 54612
608/323-3155
(Furniture.)

Associated Banc-Corp
112 N. Adams St.
Green Bay, WI 54307-3307
414/433-3166
(Bank.)

Beloit Corp.
1 St. Lawrence Ave.
Beloit, WI 53511
608/365-3311
(Paper industries machinery.)

Briggs & Stratton Corp.
3300 N. 124th St.
Milwaukee, WI 53222
414/259-5333
(Internal combustion engines.)

Case
700 State St.
Racine, WI 53404
414/636-6011
(Heavy equipment.)

CUNA Mutual Insurance Group
5910 Mineral Point Rd.
Madison, WI 53705
608/238-5851
(Insurance.)

Consolidated Papers Inc.
P.O. Box 8050
231 1st Ave. N.
Wisconsin Rapids, WI 54495-8050
715/422-3111
(Paper mills.)

Employers Health Insurance Co.
1100 Employment Blvd.
Green Bay, WI 54344
414/336-1100
(Insurance.)

Employers Insurance of Wausau
2000 Westwood Dr.
Wausau, WI 54401
715/842-6479
(Insurance.)

First Financial Corp.
1305 Main St.
Stevens Point, WI 54481
715/341-0400
(Bank.)

Firststar Corp.
777 E. Wisconsin Ave
Milwaukee, WI 53202
414/765-4321
(Banking.)

Ft. Howard Corp.
1919 S. Broadway
Green Bay, WI 54304
414/435-8821
(Paper products [food containers,
etc.].)

Georgia Pacific Corp.
100 Wisconsin River Dr.
Port Edwards, WI 54469
715/887-5111
(Paper mills.)

Harley-Davidson Inc.
3700 W. Juneau Ave.
Milwaukee, WI 53208
414/342-4680
(Motorcycles.)

Johnson Controls Inc.
5757 N. Green Bay Ave.
Glendale, WI 53209
414/228-1200
(Electronic control systems,
automotive batteries, sealing,
containers, etc.)

S.C. Johnson & Son
1525 Howe St.
Racine, WI 53403

414/631-2000
(Household products.)

Journal Communications Inc.
333 W. State St.
Milwaukee, WI 53203
414/224-2000
(Newspaper publishing.)

Kohler Co.
444 Highland Dr.
Kohler, WI 53044
414/457-4441
(Plumbing products, engines, etc.)

Ladish Co., Inc.
5481 S. Packard Ave.
Cudahy, WI 53110
414/747-2611
(Iron and steel forgings.)

Land's End Inc.
Land's End Lane
Dodgeville, WI 53533
608/935-9341
(Catalog sales.)

MGIC
250 E. Kilburn Ave.
Milwaukee, WI 53202
414/347-6480
(Lease & finance.)

Manitowoc Co., Inc.
700 E. Magnolia Ave., Suite B
Manitowoc, WI 54220
414/684-4410
(Liftcranes, ice-making
equipment.)

Manpower International, Inc.
5301 N. Ironweed Ln.
Milwaukee, WI 53217
414/961-1000
(Business services.)

Marshall & Illsley
770 N. Water St.
Milwaukee, WI 53202
414/765-7801
(Banking.)

Menasha Corp.
1645 Bergstrom Rd.
Neenah, WI 54956

414/751-1000
(Packaging, forest products, plastics,
etc.)

Miller Brewing Co.
3939 W. Highland Blvd.
Milwaukee, WI 53208
414/931-2000
(Beer, ale brewing.)

Miller Group Ltd., Inc.
1635 W. Spencer St.
Appleton, WI 54914
414/734-9821
(Welding and soldering equipment.)

**Northwestern Mutual Life
Insurance Co.**
720 E. Wisconsin Ave.
Milwaukee, WI 53202
414/271-1444
(Life insurance.)

Oscar Mayer Foods Corp.
910 Mayer Ave.
Madison, WI 53704
608/241-3311
(Food processing.)

Oshkosh B'Gosh, Inc.
112 Otter Ave.
P.O. Box 300
Oshkosh, WI 54901
414/231-8800
(Clothing.)

Oshkosh Truck Corp.
2307 Oregon St.
Oshkosh, WI 54901
414/235-9150
(Heavy duty all-wheel drive
vehicles.)

Quad Graphics Inc.
W. 224 N. 3322 Duplainville Rd.
Pewaukee, WI 53072
414/691-9200
(Commercial printing.)

Schneider International
3101 Packerland Dr.
Green Bay, WI 54313
414/592-2000
(Trucking.)

Schreiber Foods Inc.
425 Pine St.
Green Bay, WI 54301
414/437-7601
(Cheese and meat processing.)

Snap-On Tools Corp.
2801 80th St.
Kenosha, WI 53131
414/656-5200
(Hand tools, automotive mechanic equipment.)

Time Insurance Co., Inc.
501 W. Michigan St.
P.O. Box 624
Milwaukee, WI 53201
414/271-3011
(Insurance.)

Universal Foods Corp.
433 E. Michigan St.
Milwaukee, WI 53202
414/271-6755
(Food processing.)

Wausau Insurance Cos.
2000 Westwood Dr.

Wausau, WI 54401
715/842-6479
(Insurance.)

Western Publishing Co.
1220 Mound Ave.
Racine, WI 53404
414/633-2431
(Book publishing.)

Wicof, Inc.
626 E. Wisconsin Ave.
Milwaukee, WI 53202
414/291-7000
(Natural gas.)

Wisconsin Electric Power Co.
231 W. Michigan St.
Milwaukee, WI 53201
414/221-3333
(Electric utility.)

Wisconsin Energy Corp.
231 W. Michigan St.
Milwaukee, WI 53291
414/221-2345
(Utility, investment holding company.)

WISCONSIN BUSINESS PERIODICALS

The Business Journal Serving Greater Milwaukee
American City Business Journals
600 W. Virginia St.
Suite 500
Milwaukee, WI 53204

414/278-7788
(Weekly.)

Corporate Report Wisconsin
Box 878
Memomonee Falls, WI 53052
414/255-9077

WISCONSIN DIRECTORIES

Classified Directory of Wisconsin Manufacturers
WMC Service Corporation
501 E. Washington Ave.
Box 352
Madison, WI 53701-0352
608/258-3400

Wisconsin Business Directory
American Business Directories

5711 S. 86th Cir.
P.O. Box 27347
Omaha, NE 68127
402/593-4600

Wisconsin Manufacturers Register
Manufacturers' News, Inc.
1633 Central St.
Evanston, IL 60201
708/864-7000

Wisconsin Services Directory
W M C Service Corporation
501 E. Washington Ave.
Box 352
Madison, WI 53701-0352
608/258-3400

WISCONSIN GOVERNMENT EMPLOYMENT OFFICES

Office of Personnel Management
(Federal job-service center—in
counties of Grant, Iowa, Lafayette,
Dane, Green, Rock, Jefferson,
Walworth, Waukesha, Racine,
Kenosha, and Milwaukee, see Illinois
listing and dial 312/353-6189; for all
other Wisconsin counties, see
Minnesota listing.)

Job Service
1819 Aberg Ave.
Suite C
Madison, WI 53704
608/242-4878
(State job-service center.)

THE WEST

OUTLOOK: Not as high flying as before, but still generally strong.

The California economy will moderate somewhat, but job prospects will remain strong as will the outlook in the Northwest. Some experts are predicting a high-tech slowdown in the Rocky Mountain states.

WHAT'S NEXT

▶ **California: boom will subside somewhat, but employment prospects will remain relatively strong.**

A few years back, it seemed as if the California job machine was in permanent stall. Then things began heating up. By 1997, the state recovered nearly all of the 500,000 jobs it lost in the early 1990s.

Paving the way: the entertainment industry and tourism. Film and TV production has jumped significantly and directly accounts for as many jobs as aerospace/defense. And when including related entertainment positions, the entire industry represents nearly twice the number of aerospace/defense jobs. The tourism industry continues to show significant increases; California has three of the United States's most popular theme parks.

And the state is fighting hard with certain new business-friendly regulations. Plus it has a number of factors on the plus side that make it one of the regions best poised for long-term strength. A key factor is its proximity to the Pacific Rim and its role as hub for Japan and other Pacific Rim countries; it is a participant in the economic growth of the booming Pacific Rim. In fact, Long Beach is now the nation's busiest container port. Other important strengths: the high percentage of high-technology industries and companies making California their home; the entertainment industry; a diverse manufacturing base; and the state's top-ranked university system. The state is entering the period with upward job creation momentum—in hot industries such as software, engineering, entertainment, and tourism. On the downside: the rising dollar will probably stall some of the export growth in entertainment and high tech, the two mainstays of the California economy. But experts predict that the job outlook will probably remain strong. One prediction: fewer Californians will leave the state, somewhat slowing growth in neighboring states. Even so, the UCLA forecasting group projects that California should add 880,000 new jobs by the end of 1998, including 470,000 jobs in the service sector. The service industries will be the driving force of California's expansion, according to the forecast.

▶ **The Pacific Northwest is seeing two trends at once: on one hand, weak industries are cutting jobs; on the other, stronger industries are adding.**

The good news: High tech is doing well in the area, making Oregon and Washington leading high-tech centers. On the downside, the timber industry, one of the traditional industries of the region, expects further job losses—totaling up to 45,000 more jobs in the area by 2000. In addition, the aerospace giant Boeing has been cutting some jobs as it restructures itself. But with the general improvement in aerospace (in particular, strong orders for Boeing) and a strong high-tech and computer industry, the region looks poised for strong long-term growth.

More specifically, in Oregon, Portland has been attracting high numbers of high-tech companies—one of the reasons its employment growth is among the strongest in the country. An added bonus: The influx of high-tech companies has resulted in a real estate/construction miniboom, with companies such as Intel, Fujitsu, and Sumitomo Titix expanding their plants to cope with increased business. Major worry for state residents: will the influx of job migrants hurt the state's much vaunted high quality of life?

Meanwhile, Washington, and in particular, Seattle, continues to add to its increasingly diversified economic base. The past two years saw strong hiring in biotechnology, computer software, and tourism in particular. Other strong points: the long-time presence of high-tech firms such as Microsoft, which still dominates the computer software industry, Japanese firms such as Matsushita and Fujitsu, and the area's growing presence in Far East trade, particularly through Seattle/Tacoma. Also adding to the strong outlook: the reemergence of aircraft giant Boeing as an industry factor, following substantial downsizing and restructuring, which received a healthy increase in orders and its merger with McDonnell Douglas. The company forecasts over $1 trillion may be spent by companies throughout the world to replace old aircraft as well as to meet new passenger growth through 2015. Although an optimistic scenario, it should be noted that Boeing is a world-class market player with over 70% of its sales coming from outside the U.S. The result? A positive effect on Seattle. One interesting note: With Seattle residents concerned about overdevelopment and city managers trying to steer away would-be relocators, Yakima, Spokane, Bellingham and Olympia may wind up the beneficiaries. The result? These four cities may offer increasing employment opportunities.

One possible problem for the Pacific Northwest region, however—a strong dollars will, of course, affect high-tech exportation. So short-term softening can be expected periodically.

▶ **Mountain and Southwestern states will also be riding the technology bandwagon.**

In addition to the high number of technology and software companies (and jobs), its status as one of the top vacation and retirement spots in the country, and rapid population growth has made this area a strong one in the past few years. But some experts are projecting a slowdown as the millennium nears.

Some specifics: **Arizona**—Phoenix has been a regional hot spot, as it shifts from a tourism-based economy to a major manufacturing economy—with semiconductor giant Motorola the city's second largest employer. Tucson continues to attract new software and other high-tech firms, as well as customer service operations and manufacturing companies. *Nevada* is coming on strong as well, reaping the benefits of both construction (which will be slowing down) and, most important, gambling. This makes Las Vegas in particular one of the best areas in the country where job growth is concerned.

Colorado will continue to benefit from a diversified economy, in particular from the high-tech and biotechnology firms that have moved here. The state is already home to about 5,000 high-tech companies. Denver in particular continues its transformation from an oil town of the 1980s into a diversified economy of the '90s with an inflow of financial, high-tech, and cable companies. Other areas that are in for a growth period are construction, business services, and, as the energy industry continues to improve, petroleum.

Another high tech high-flier, *Idaho,* with its active semiconductor industry. In addition, it has seen growth in business services, recreation, and government especially notable.

In *New Mexico,* Albuquerque has developed into a regional hot spot, attracting people disenchanted with California and big-city life. More to the point, in addition to its traditional public-sector health care and defense jobs, many new high-tech jobs are opening up as companies such as Intel, Motorola, and Philips Semiconductor increase their presence in the area. *Wyoming* is also slated for long-term improvement, especially as environmental legislation increases the use of low-sulfur coal.

▶ Alaska and Hawaii: fairly stable.

Hawaii's prospects are flat as tourism has declined in line with Japan's economic problems. As Japan's prospects improve, the state should experience an upturn in its economy, with positive spillover effects for other industries. Major problem: stifling government regulation has hurt business growth.

As for *Alaska,* improvement in the energy industry will fuel an improved outlook and eventual job growth. Tourism growth may offset any future declines in the state's oil business, and construction is going strong.

REGIONAL HOT SPOTS

SALT LAKE CITY, UT: Chosen as one of the best places for corporations by a *Forbes* magazine survey, Salt Lake City was a regional hot spot in 1997 with a strong 5.5% growth rate and an increasingly diversified economy. Best areas for jobs: biotechnology, high tech, and construction. Other pluses: a strong high-tech-oriented university system (3D computing was developed at the University of Utah) and pleasant surroundings with a good quality of life.

SEATTLE AREA, WA: Perennially on the lists as one of America's most livable cities, this city is also a haven for high-tech and engineering types, and home to giants like Boeing and Microsoft, as well as to a host of smaller high-tech firms. Growth last year was a strong 2.8%, as aviation bounded ahead and the computer industry boomed. Boeing found itself advertising online to attract employees, while Microsoft kept on expanding. In addition to software and computer-programming jobs, other strong job areas included construction-related jobs and food-service jobs. Add to this a high quality of life (as long as clouds and rainy winters don't bother you) and Seattle looks like a good long-term bet—particularly if you like technology.

ALASKA

LEADING ALASKA EMPLOYERS

Alaska Commercial Co.
550 W. 64th Ave.
Anchorage, AK 99518
907/276-2226
(General merchandise stores.)

Alaska Railroad Corp.
411 W. First Ave.
Anchorage, AK 99501
907/265-2494
(Railroads, line haul operating.)

Arco Alaska Inc.
700 G St.
Anchorage, AK 99501
907/276-1215
(Oil and gas exploration services, drilling, production.)

Arctic Slope Regional Construction Co.
1230 Agvik
Barrow, AK 99723
907/852-8633
(Pipeline construction.)

AT&T Alascom Inc.
210 East Bluff Dr.
Anchorage, AK 99501
907/264-7000
(Telephone communications.)

Carr-Gottstein Foods, Inc.
6411 A St.
Anchorage, AK 99518
907/561-1944
(Groceries, residential real estate developer.)

Era Aviation Inc.
6160 South Airpark Dr.
Anchorage, AK 99502
907/248-4422
(Air transportation.)

General Communication Inc.
2550 Denali St.
Anchorage, AK 99503
907/265-5600
(Telephone communications.)

Ketchikan Pulp Co.
7559 North Tongass Hwy.
Ketchikan, AK 99901
907/225-2151
(Pulp.)

Markair
6441 So. AirPark Dr.
Anchorage, AK 99502
907/245-5304
(Passenger and cargo air carrier.)

Martech USA Inc.
300 East 54th Ave.
Anchorage, AK 99518
907/561-1970
(Sanitary services—oil spill cleanup, etc.)

Natchiq Inc.
6700 Arctic St.
Anchorage, AK 99518
907/344-5757
(Oil and gas field services.)

Reeve Aleutian Airways Inc.
4700 West International
Airport Rd.
Anchorage, AK 99502-1091
907/243-4700
(Regional air carrier.)

Veco, Inc.
813 W. Northern Lights Blvd.
Anchorage, AK 99503
907/277-5309
(Construction and oil field
services.)

ALASKA BUSINESS PERIODICAL

Alaska Business
P.O. Box 241288
Anchorage, AK 99524
907/276-4373
(Monthly.)

ALASKA BUSINESS DIRECTORY

Alaska Business Directory
American Business Directories
5711 S. 86th Cir.
P.O. Box 27347

Omaha, NE 68127
402/593-4600
(Lists 26,000 businesses.)

ALASKA GOVERNMENT EMPLOYMENT OFFICES

**Office of Personnel
Management**
Phone service only
912/757-3000
(Federal job-service center.)

Employment Service
Employment Security Div.
P.O. Box 25509
Juneau, AK 99802
907/465-2712
(State job-service center.)

ARIZONA

LEADING ARIZONA EMPLOYERS

**AG Communications Systems
Corp.**
2500 W. Utopia Rd.
Phoenix, AZ 85027
602/582-7000
(Switchboards.)

Allied Signal Engines
111 S. 34th St.
Phoenix, AZ 85034
602/231-3434
(Aircraft and missile engine and
components manufacturers.)

America West Airlines Inc.
4000 E. Sky Harbor Blvd.
Phoenix, AZ 85034
601/693-0737
(Passenger and cargo
carrier.)

Arizona Public Service Co.
400 N. 5th St.
Phoenix, AZ 85004
602/250-1000
(Utilities.)

BankAmerica Arizona
101 N. First Ave.
Phoenix, AZ 85003
602/597-2371
(Banking.)

Bank One
201 N. Central Ave.
Phoenix, AZ 85004
602/261-2900
(Banking.)

**Best Western International,
Inc.**
6201 N. 24th Parkway
Phoenix, AZ 85016
602/957-4200
(Motels, restaurants.)

**Bryant/Universal Roofing
Inc.**
1245 S. 7th St.
Phoenix, AZ 85034
602/947-8323
(Roofing.)

Burr-Brown Corp.
6730 S. Tucson Blvd.
Tucson, AZ 85706
602/746-1111
(Microcomputer and electronics
systems and products.)

Circle K. Corp.
Phoenix Corporate Ctr.
3003 N. Central Ave.
Phoenix, AZ 85012
602/437-6000
(Convenience stores.)

Del Webb Corp.
6001 N. 24th St.
Phoenix, AZ 85016
602/805-8000
(Real estate, adult community
management and development.)

Dial Corp.
1850 Central Ave.
Phoenix, AZ 85077-2315
602/207-5600
(Personal care, food, household, and
laundry products.)

Finova Group Inc.
1850 N. Central Ave.
Phoenix, AZ 85004
602/207-6900 ·
(Lease & finance.)

First Interstate Bank of Arizona
100 W. Washington
Phoenix, AZ 85003
602/229-4690
(Banking.)

Jostens Learning Corp.
7878 North 16th St., Suite 100
Phoenix, AZ 85020
602/678-7272
(Computer integrated systems
design.)

Karsten Manufacturing Corp.
2201 W. Desert Cove
Phoenix, AZ 85029
602/870-5000
(Golf equipment, aluminum die-
castups, etc.)

Magma Metals Co.
7400 N. Oracle, No. 200
Tucson, AZ 85704
602/575-5600
(Copper mining.)

McCarthy Brothers Co.
802 N. First Ave., Suite 500
Phoenix, AZ 85003
602/262-8000
(Hotel/motel, commercial, and office
construction, etc.)

**McDonnell Douglas
Helicopter Co.**
5000 E. McDowell Rd.
Mesa, AZ 85205
602/891-3000
(Helicopter manufacturer.)

Micro Age, Inc.
P. O. Box 1920
2400 S. Micro Age Way
Tempe, AZ 85382
602/804-2000
(Electronics stores.)

Microchip Technologies, Inc.
2355 W. Chandler Blvd.
Chandler, AZ 85224
602/787-7200
(Computer chips.)

**Motorola Inc.—Government
Electronics Group**
Box 1417
8201 E. McDowell Rd.
Scottsdale, AZ 85257
602/441-3030
(R&D and production of advanced
electronic systems and equipment.)

Norwest Bank of Arizona
3300 N. Central Ave.
Phoenix, AZ 85012
602/248-2225
(Banking.)

Phelps Dodge Corp.
2600 N. Central Ave.
Phoenix, AZ 85004-3014
602/234-8100
(Metals.)

Phoenician Resorts Corp.
6000 E. Camelback
Scottsdale, AZ 85251
602/941-8200
(Hotels, resort, etc.)

Phoenix Newspapers, Inc.
120 E. Van Buren
Phoenix, AZ 85004
602/271-8000
(Newspaper publishing.)

Pinnacle West Capital Corp.
400 E. Van Buren St.
Phoenix, AZ 85004
602/379-2500
(Utility.)

Reinalt-Thomas Corp.
14631 N. Scottsdale Rd.
Scottsdale, AZ 85254
602/951-1938
(Retail tires and accessories.)

Rural/Metro Corp.
8401 E. Indian School Rd.
Scottsdale, AZ 85251
602/994-3886
(Fire protection, ambulance, security,
and other services.)

**Salt River Project
Agricultural Improvement
& Power District**
1521 N. Project Dr.
Tempe, AZ 85281
602/236-2205
(Electric utility.)

Shamrock Foods Co.
2228 N. Black Canyon Hwy.
Phoenix, AZ 85009
602/272-6721
(Food distributor.)

Sundt Corporation
4101 E. Irvington Rd.
Tucson, AZ 85714
602/748-7555
(Construction.)

Talley Industries Inc.
2702 N. 44th St., Suite 100A
Phoenix, AZ 85008
602/956-8530
(Defense electronics, agricultural
machinery, etc.)

United Metro Materials
701 N. 44th St.
Phoenix, AZ 85008
602/220-5060
(Concrete, highway and street
construction, etc.)

ARIZONA BUSINESS PERIODICALS

Arizona Business Gazette
Box 1950
Phoenix, AZ 85004
602/271-7300
(Weekly.)

The Business Journal
2910 N. Central Ave.
Phoenix, AZ 85012
602/230-8400
(Weekly; covers Phoenix and Valley
of the Sun.)

ARIZONA BUSINESS DIRECTORIES

Arizona Business Directory
American Business Directories
5711 S. 86th Cir.
P.O. Box 27347
Omaha, NE 68127
402/593-4600

Arizona Industrial Directory
Manufacturers' News, Inc.
1633 Central St.
Evanston, IL 60201
847/864-7000

ARIZONA GOVERNMENT EMPLOYMENT OFFICES

**Office of Personnel
Management**
Federal job-service center.
Phone Service Only:
912/757-3000

Department of Economic Security
P.O. Box 6123
Site Code 730A
Phoenix, AZ 85005
602/252-7771
(State job-service center.)

CALIFORNIA

TOP CALIFORNIA EMPLOYERS

ABC Radio Network
3321 S. La Cienega Blvd.
Century City, CA 90016
310/840-4912
(Broadcasting.)

AST Research Inc.
16215 Alton Pkwy.
Irvine, CA 92618
714/727-4141
(Computers.)

Acura Division
American Honda Motor Co.
1919 Torrance Blvd.
Torrance, CA 90501-2746
310/783-2000
(Car manufacturer.)

Adobe Systems
1585 Charleston Rd.
Mountain View, CA 94039-7900
415/961-4400
(Computer software.)

Advanced Micro Devices
1 AMD Place
Sunnyvale, CA 94086
408/732-2400
(Computer peripherals.)

H. F. Ahmanson & Co.
4900 Rivergrade Rd.
Irwindale, CA 91706
818/960-6311
(Savings and loan holding company.)

Air Touch Communications
One California St.
San Francisco, CA 94111
415/658-2000
(Telecommunications.)

Allergan Inc.
2525 Dolant, Dr.
Irvine, CA 92715
714/752-4500
(Optical health care products.)

Allied-Signal Aerospace Co.
2525 W. 190th St.
Torrance, CA 90504-6009
310/323-9500
(Aerospace manufacturer [avionics,
electronics, engines, etc.].)

ALZA Corp.
950 Page Mill Rd.
Palo Alto, CA 94304
415/494-5000
(Biotechnology.)

Amdahl Corp.
1250 E. Arques Ave.
Sunnyvale, CA 94086
408/746-6000
(Computers.)

American Honda Motor Co., Inc.
1919 Torrance Blvd.
Torrance, CA 90501-2746
310/783-2000
(Automotive manufacturer.)

American President Cos. Ltd.
1111 Broadway
Oakland, CA 95607
510/272-8000
Fax 810/272-8831
(Shipping.)

Amgen Inc.
1840 DeHavilland Dr.
Newbury Park, CA 91320-1789
805/447-1000
(Biotechnology.)

Ampex Corp.
401 Broadway
Redwood City, CA 94063
415/367-2011
(Recording tapes, video recording
systems, etc.)

Apple Computer
1 Infinite Loop
Cupertino, CA 95014
408/996-1010
(Computers.)

Applied Materials
3050 Bowers Ave.
Santa Clara, CA 95054
408/727-5555
(Computer peripherals.)

Atlantic Richfield Co.
515 S. Flower St.
Los Angeles, CA 90071-2256
213/486-3511
(Petroleum products.)

Autodesk, Inc.
111 McInnis Pkwy.
San Rafael, CA 94903
415/507-5000
(Computer peripherals.)

Avery Dennison Corp.
150 N. Ocean Grove Blvd.
Pasadena, CA 91103
818/304-2000
Fax 818/792-7312
(Business supplies.)

BankAmerica
555 California St.
San Francisco, CA 94104
415/622-3456
(Commercial banking.)

Bay View Capital
2121 S. El Camino Real
San Mateo, CA 94403-1897
415/573-7300
(Thrift institution.)

Bechtel Group Inc.
50 Beale St.
San Francisco, CA 94105
415/768-1234
(Construction engineering, advanced
systems, etc.—at same address:
Bechtel Power Corporation, Bechtel
National Inc., Bechtel Corporation,
Bechtel Enterprises, Bechtel Civil
Inc., and Bechtel, Inc.)

Beckman Instruments Inc.
2500 Harbor Blvd.
Fullerton,CA 92635
714/871-4848
(Automated systems and supplies for
life science research.)

Bergen Brunswig Corp.
4000 Metropolitan Dr.
Orange, CA 92668-3510
714/385-4000
(Medical products.)

Broadway Stores
3880 N. Mission Rd.
Los Angeles, CA 90031
213/227-2000
(Department stores.)

CBS Radio Division
7800 Beverly Blvd.
Los Angeles, CA 90036
213/852-2345
(Broadcasting.)

CalFed Inc.
5700 Wilshire Blvd.
Los Angeles, CA 90036
213/932-4200
(Thrift institution.)

Chevron Corp.
225 Bush St.
San Francisco, CA 94104-4289
415/894-7700
(Petroleum products.)

Chiron Corp.
4560 Horton St.
Emeryville, CA 94608-2916
510/655-8730
(Biotechnology.)

The Chronicle Publishing Co.
901 Mission St.
San Francisco, CA 94103
415/777-7444
(Newspaper publishing.)

City National Bank
400 N. Roxbury Dr.
Beverly Hills, CA 90210
310/888-6250
(Banking.)

Clorox
1221 Broadway
Oakland, CA 94612-1888
510/271-7000
(Personal products.)

Coast Savings Financial
1000 Wilshire Blvd.
Los Angeles, CA 90017-2457
213/326-2000
(Thrift institution.)

Computer Sciences Corp.
2100 E. Grand Ave.
El Segundo, CA 90245
310/615-0311
(Business services.)

Conner Peripherals
3081 Zanker Rd.
San Jose, CA 95134-2128
408/433-3340
(Computer peripherals.)

Consolidated Freightways
3240 Hillview Ave.
Palo Alto, CA 94304
415/494-2900
(Trucking.)

Countrywide Credit Ind.
155 N. Lake Ave.
Pasadena, CA 91101
818/304-8400
(Lease & finance.)

Del Monte Foods
1 Market St.
San Francisco, CA 94105
415/247-3000
(Food.)

Diamond Walnut Growers, Inc.
1050 Diamond St.
Stockton, CA 98205
209/467-6000
(Food.)

The Disney Channel
3800 W. Alameda Ave.
Burbank, CA 91505
818/569-7701
(Pay cable television services and
programming.)

Walt Disney Company
500 S. Buena Vista St.
Burbank, CA 91521
818/560-1000
(Entertainment.)

Dole Food
313555 Oak Crest Blvd.
Westlake Village, CA 91361
818/879-6600
(Food processor.)

Douglas Aircraft Co.
(div. of McDonnell Douglas Corp.)
3855 Lakewood Blvd.
Long Beach, CA 90846
213/593-5511
(Aircraft manufacturing.)

Downey Financial Corp.
3501 Jamboree Rd.
Newport Beach, CA 92660
714/854-3100
(Thrift institution.)

E! Entertainment Television, Inc.
5670 Wilshire Blvd.
Los Angeles, CA 90036
213/954-2400
(Cable TV.)

FHP International
9930 Talbert Ave.
Fountain Valley, CA 92708
714/964-6229
(Health care services.)

Firemans Fund Insurance Co.
777 San Marin Dr.
Novato, CA 94998
415/899-2000
(Insurance company.)

First Fed Financial
401 Wilshire Blvd.
Santa Monica, CA 90401-1490
310/319-6000
(Thrift institution.)

First Interstate Bancorp
633 W. 5th St.
Los Angeles, CA 90071
213/614-3001
(Bank.)

First Nationwide Corp.
88 Kearny St.
San Francisco, CA 94108
415/955-5800
(Thrift institution.)

Fleetwood Enterprises, Inc.
3125 Myers St.
Riverside, CA 92513-7638
909/351-3500
(Home furnishings & recreation.)

Fluor Corp.
3333 Michelson Dr.
Irvine, CA 92715
714/975-2000
(Engineering, construction.)

Foundation Health
3400 Data Dr.
Rancho Cordova, CA 95670
916/631-5040
(Health care services.)

Fox Broadcasting Company
10201 W. Pico Blvd.
Los Angeles, CA 90064
310/277-2211
(Broadcasting.)

Franklin Resources
777 Mariner's Island Blvd.
San Mateo, CA 94404
415/312-2000
(Lease & finance.)

Gap, Inc.
1 Harrison St.
San Francisco, CA 94105
415/952-4400
(Apparel retailer.)

Genentech Inc.
460 Point San Bruno Blvd.
S. San Francisco, CA 94080
415/225-1000
(Biotechnology.)

Glendale Federal Bank FSB
700 N. Brand Blvd.
Glendale, CA 91203
818/500-2000
(Thrift institution.)

Golden West Financial Corp.
1901 Harrison St.
Oakland, CA 94612
510/446-3420
(Savings and loan associations.)

GranCare, Inc.
300 Corporate Pointe
Culver City, CA 90230
310/645-1555
(Health care services.)

Great Western Financial Corp.
9200 Oakdale Ave.
Chatsworth, CA 91311-6519
818/775-3411
(Savings and loan associations.)

Group W Productions
10877 Wilshire Blvd.
Los Angeles, CA 90024
213/446-6000
(Film/video production)

Health Systems International
21600 Oxnard St.
Woodland Hills, CA 91367
818/719-6975
Fax 818/593-8591
(Health care services.)

Hewlett Packard Co.
3000 Hanover St.
Palo Alto, CA 94304
415/857-1501
(Computers.)

Hilton Hotels Corp.
9336 Civic Center Dr.
Beverly Hills, CA 90210
310/278-4321
(Hotels & gaming.)

Homestake Mining Co.
650 California St.
San Francisco, CA 94108-2788
415/981-8150
(Nonferrous metals.)

Hughes Aircraft Co.
(subs. of GM Hughes Electronics
Corp.)
P.O. Box 45066
7200 Hughes Terr.
Los Angeles, CA 90045
310/568-7200
(Aircraft manufacturer.)

Hunt-Wesson Foods
1645 W. Valencia Dr.
Fullerton, CA 92633
714/680-1000
(Food processing.)

Infiniti Division
Nissan Motor Co.
18501 S. Figueroa St.
Gardena, CA 90248
310/532-3111
(Car manufacturer.)

Informix
4100 Bohannon Dr.
Menlo Park, CA 94025
415/926-6300
(Computer software.)

Intel Corp.
P.O. Box 95054
2200 Mission College Blvd.
Santa Clara, CA 95052-8119
408/765-8080
(Semiconductors.)

**Kaiser Foundation
Health Plan**
1950 Franklin St.
Oakland, CA 94612
510/957-2686
(Health maintenance organization.)

Laboratory Corp. of America
4225 Executive Sq.
La Jolla, CA 92037
619/550-0600
(Health services.)

LSI Logic Corp.
1551 McCarthy Blvd.
Milpitas, CA 95035
408/433-8000
(Semiconductors.)

Levi Strauss & Co.
1155 Battery St.
San Francisco, CA 94111
415/544-6000
(Apparel.)

Lexus Division of Toyota
19001 S. Western Ave.
Torrance, CA 90501
310/618-4000
(Car manufacturer.)

Linear Technology
1630 McCarthy Blvd.
Milpitas, CA 95035
408/432-1900
(Electronic equipment.)

Litton Aero Products Division
21050 Burbank Blvd.
Woodland Hills, CA 91367
818/226-2000
(Electronic systems.)

Litton Industries
21240 Burbank Blvd.
Woodland Hills, CA
91367-6695
818/598-5000
(Electrical and electronics equipment.)

Lockheed Corp.
4500 Park Granada Blvd.
Calabasas, CA 91399
818/876-2000
(Aerospace manufacturer.)

Lockheed Martin Corp.
1111 Lockheed Way
Sunnyvale, CA 94089
408/742-4321
(Aerospace.)

Long Drug Stores
P.O. Box 5222
Walnut Creek, CA 94596
510/937-1170
(Drug & discount stores.)

MAI Systems Corp.
9600 Geronimo Rd.
Irvine, CA 92718
714/580-0700
(Software.)

Mattel Inc.
333 Continental Blvd.
El Segundo, CA 90245-5012
310/252-2000
(Toy manufacturer.)

Mazda Motors of America, Inc.
7755 Irvine Center Dr.
Irvine, CA 92718
714/727-1990
(Car manufacturer.)

MCA, Inc.
70 Universal City Plz.
Universal City, CA 91608
818/777-4000
(Entertainment company [film, records, etc.].)

McClatchy Newspapers
2100 Q St.
Sacramento, CA 95816
916/321-1000
(Newspaper publishing.)

McDonnell Douglas Space Systems
(div. of McDonnell Douglas Corp.)
5301 Balsa Ave.
Huntington Beach, CA 92647
714/896-3311
(Delta rocket, space station work package, strategic systems.)

McKesson Corp.
One Post St.
San Francisco,CA 94104
415/983-8300
(Drugs, chemicals, liquor.)

Merisel
200 Continental Blvd.
El Segundo, CA 90245-0984
310/615-3080
(Computer peripherals.)

Mervyn's
25001 Industrial Blvd.
Hayward, CA 94545
718/785-8800
(Speciality apparel stores.)

MGM/Pathe Communications Co.
2500 Broadway
Santa Monica, CA 90404
310/449-3040
(Film, etc.)

NBC
3000 W. Alameda Ave.
Burbank, CA 91523
818/840-4444
(Broadcasting.)

National Health Laboratories, Inc.
4225 Executive Sq.,
Suite 800
La Jolla, CA 92037
619/550-0600
(Health services.)

National Semiconductor Corp.
1090 Kifer Rd.
Sunnyvale, CA 94086
408/721-5000
(Semiconductors.)

Nestle Food Co.
800 N. Brand Blvd.
Glendale, CA 91203
818/549-6000
(Food products.)

Nissan Motor Corp.
18501 Figueroa St.
Gardena, CA 90248
310/532-3111
(Car manufacturer.)

Northrop Grumman
1840 Century Park East
Century City
Los Angeles, CA 90067-2199
310/553-6262
(Aerospace manufacturing.)

Occidental Petroleum Corp.
10889 Wilshire Blvd.
Los Angeles, CA 90024
310/208-8800
(Petroleum products.)

Oracle Systems Corp.
P.O. Box 659506
500 Oracle Pkwy.
Redwood Shores, CA 94065
415/506-7000
(Software.)

Pacific Bell
140 New Montgomery St.
San Francisco, CA 94105
415/542-9000
(Telephone services.)

PacifiCare Health Systems
5995 Plaza Dr.
Cypress, CA 90630-5028
714/952-1121
(Health care services.)

Pacific Enterprises
633 W. Fifth St.
Los Angeles, CA 90071
213/895-5000
(Diversified holding co.)

Pacific Gas & Electric Co.
525 Market St.
San Francisco, CA 94105
415/973-7000
(Utilities co.)

Pacific Mutual Life Insurance Co.
700 Newport Center Dr.
Newport Beach, CA 92660
714/640-3011
(Life insurance.)

Pacific Telesis Group
130 Kearny St.
San Francisco, CA 94108
415/394-3000
(Telecommunications.)

Paramount Pictures
555 Melrose Ave.
Hollywood, CA 90038
213/956-5000
(Film/video production)

Parsons Corp.
100 W. Walnut St.
Pasadena, CA 91103
310/440-2000
(Construction and engineering
services.)

Quantum Corp.
500 McCarthy Blvd.
Milpitas, CA 95035
408/894-4000
(Computer peripherals.)

Raychem Corp.
300 Constitution Dr.
Menlo Park, CA 94025
415/361-3333
(Electronics, automatic systems,
etc.)

**Rockwell Systems
Development**
2500 Seal Beach Blvd.
Seal Beach, CA 90740-8250
310/797-3311
(Aerospace, electronics systems,
etc.)

**Rockwell International Space
Systems Division**
12214 Lakewood Blvd.
Box 7009
Downey, CA 90242
310/922-2111
(Space shuttle contractors.)

Rohr Industries, Inc.
P.O. Box 850
Chula Vista, CA 92010
619/691-4111
(Major structural components for
aircraft.)

SCECorp.
2244 Walnut Grove Ave.
Rosemead, CA 91770
818/302-1212
(Electric and gas services.)

Safeway Stores Inc.
201 Fourth St.
Oakland, CA 94660
510/891-3000
(Supermarkets.)

San Diego Gas & Electric Co.
101 Ash St.
San Diego, CA 92101
619/239-7500
(Utility.)

Charles Schwab & Co., Inc.
101 Montgomery St.
San Francisco, CA 94104
415/627-7000
(Financial services.)

**Science Applications
International Corp.**
10260 Campus Point Dr.
San Diego, CA 92121
619/546-6000
(Scientific technical services and
products, defense systems.)

Seagate Technology Inc.
920 Disc Dr.
Scotts Valley, CA 95066
408/438-6550
(Disk drives, storage devices.)

Silicon Graphics
2011 N. Shoreline Blvd.
Mountain View, CA 94043-1389
415/960-1980
(Computer systems.)

Southern California Edison Co.
2244 Walnut Grove Ave.
Rosemead, CA 91770
818/302-6911
(Electric utility.)

Southern California Gas Co.
555 W. Fifth St.
Los Angeles, CA 90013
213/244-1234
(Gas company.)

Southern Pacific Lines
1 Market Plz.
San Francisco, CA 94105
415/541-1000
(Railroad transportation.)

Sumitomo Bank of California
320 California St.
San Francisco, CA 94104
415/445-8000
(Bank.)

Sun America
1999 Ave. of the Stars
Los Angeles, CA 90067-6022
310/772-6000
(Insurance.)

Sun Microsystems Corp.
2550 Garcia Ave.
Mountain View, CA 94043-1100
415/960-1300
(Computers—work stations, etc.)

Sybase
6475 Christie Ave.
Emeryville, CA 94608
510/658-3500
(Computer software.)

Syntex Corp.
3401 Hillview Ave.
Palo Alto, CA 94304
415/855-5050
(Biotechnology.)

Tandem Computers Inc.
19191 Vallco Pkwy.
Cupertino, CA 95014-2599
408/285-6000
(Computers.)

Teledyne Inc.
1901 Ave. of the Stars
Los Angeles, CA 90067-3201
310/277-3311
(Aerospace & defense.)

Tenet Healthcare Corp.
2700 Colorado Ave.
Santa Monica, CA 90404
310/998-8000
(Health care services.)

3Com Corp.
5400 Bayfront Plz.
P.O. Box 38145
Santa Clara, CA 95052-8145
408/764-5000
(Computer peripherals.)

The Times Mirror Company
220 W. 1st St.
Los Angeles, CA 90012
213/237-3700
(Communications media
[newspapers, etc.].)

Toyota Motor Sales U.S.A., Inc.
19001 S. Western Ave.
Torrance, CA 90509

310/618-4000
(Car manufacturer.)

Transamerica Corp.
600 Montgomery St.
San Francisco, CA 94111
415/983-4000
(Diversified financial
services.)

Transamerica Finance Inc.
1150 S. Olive St.
Los Angeles, CA 90015
213/742-4321
(Consumer lending, commercial
finance, etc.)

**Twentieth Century
Fox Film**
10201 W. Pico Blvd.
Los Angeles, CA 90064
310/277-2211
(Film/video production.)

Union Bank
350 California St.
San Francisco, CA 94104-1476
415/705-7000
(Bank.)

Universal City Studios Inc.
100 Universal City Plz.
Universal City, CA 91608
818/777-1000
(Film production.)

Unocal Corp.
1201 W. 5th St.
Los Angeles, CA 90017
213/977-7600
(Petroleum products.)

Varian Associates
3050 Hansen Way
Palo Alto, CA 94304
415/493-4000
(Electronic products.)

Vons Cos Inc.
P.O. Box 3338
Los Angeles, CA 90051-1338
818/821-7000
(Supermarkets & restaurants.)

Warner Brothers Inc.
4000 Warner Blvd.
Burbank, CA 91522
818/954-6000
(Entertainment company.)

WellPoint Health Networks
21555 Oxnard St.
Woodland Hills, CA 91367
818/703-4000
(Health care services.)

Wells Fargo Bank, N.A.
420 Montgomery St.
San Francisco, CA 94163
415/396-3814
(Banking.)

Western Atlas
360 N. Crescent Dr.
Beverly Hills, CA 90210-4867
310/888-2500
(Oilfield services.)

Western Digital Corp.
8105 Irvine Center Dr.
Irvine, CA 92718
714/932-5000
(Computer peripherals.)

Westwood One Inc.
9540 Washington Blvd.
Culver City, CA 90230
310/840-5000
(Broadcasting.)

CALIFORNIA BUSINESS PERIODICALS

Long Beach Business
2599 East 28th St.
Suite 212
Long Beach, CA 90806
310/988-1222
(Biweekly.)

Los Angeles Business Journal
5700 Wilshire Blvd., Suite 170
Los Angeles, CA 90036
213/549-5225
(Weekly.)

San Diego Business Journal
4909 Murphy Canyon Rd.
Suite 200
San Diego, CA 92123
619/277-6359
(Weekly.)

San Francisco Business Times
275 Battery St.
Suite 940
San Francisco, CA 94111
415/989-2522
(Weekly.)

CALIFORNIA DIRECTORIES

California Business Directory
American Business Directories
5711 S. 86th Cir.
P.O. Box 27347
Omaha, NE 68127
402/593-4600
(Two-volume set—North [includes San Francisco area] and South [includes Los Angeles area]. Each volume also available singly.)

California Manufacturers Register
Database Publishing Co.
1590 S. Lewis St.
Anaheim, CA 92805
800/888-8434

San Diego County Business Directory
Database Publishing Co.
1590 S. Lewis St.
Anaheim, CA 92805
800/888-8434

Southern California Business   1590 S. Lewis St.
Directory and Buyers Guide   Anaheim, CA 92805
Database Publishing Co.   800/888-8434

CALIFORNIA GOVERNMENT EMPLOYMENT OFFICES

Career America Connection
U.S. Government Employment
Information Services
Phone Service Only
912/757-3000

Job Service Division
Empl. Dev. Dept.
800 Capitol Mall
Sacramento, CA 95814
916/227-0300
(State job-service center.)

COLORADO

LEADING COLORADO EMPLOYERS

ANR Freight System Inc.
2585 31st St.
Denver, CO 80216
303/405-5588
(Holding company, trucking.)

Adolph Coors Co.
311 Tenth St.
Golden, CO 80401
303/279-6585
(Beer brewer.)

Amax Gold Inc.
9100 E. Mineral Cir.
Englewood, CO 80112
303/643-5000
(Mining.)

Anschutz Corp.
555 17th St., Suite 2400
Denver, CO 80202
303/298-1000
(Oil, mining, railroads, real estate.)

Bank One
1125 17th St.
Denver, Co 80202
303/296-7788
(Banking.)

C F & I Steel LP
1612 E. Abriendo Ave.
Pueblo, CO 81004
719/561-6000
(Steel production.)

COBE Laboratories Inc.
1185 Oak St.
Lakewood, CO 80215
303/232-6800
(Medical products.)

Coast to Coast Stores
501 S. Cherry St.
Denver, CO 80222
303/377-8400
(Housewares/giftwares retailer.)

Continental Express
Hangar 6
Stapleton International Airport
Denver, CO 80207
303/388-8585
(Regional air carrier [subs. of Continental].)

Current Inc.
8245 N. Union Blvd.
Colorado Springs, CO 80920

719/594-4100
(Greeting cards, stationery, etc.)

Cyprus AMAX Minerals Co.
9100 East Mineral Cir.
Englewood, CO 80112
303/643-5000
Fax 303/643-5269
(Mining.)

Gates Corp.
900 S. Broadway
Denver, CO 80209
303/744-1911
(Auto and industrial rubber products, batteries, other auto products.)

Gates Rubber Co.
999 S. Broadway
Denver, CO 80209
308/744-5640
(Belts, hoses, mechanical rubber goods.)

Hensel Phelps Construction
420 Sixth Ave.
Greeley, CO 80631
303/352-6565
(Commercial construction.)

ITT Federal Services Corp.
1330 Inverness Dr.
Colorado Springs, CO 80910
719/574-5850
(Ops & mtn. of communications, surveillance, radar detection sys.)

Keystone Resorts Management
P.O. Box 38
Keystone, CO 80435
970/468-2316
(Resort/hotel.)

KN Energy, Inc.
370 Van Gordon
Lakewood, CO 80228
302/989-1740
(Natural gas.)

Manville Corp.
717 7th St.
Denver, CO 80202
303/978-2000
(Building materials.)

Multi-Financial Securities
5350 S. Roslyn St.
Suite 310
Englewood, CO 80111
303/694-6710
(Insurance and securities brokers, etc.)

Newmont Mining Corp.
1700 Lincoln St.
Denver, CO 80203
303/863-7414
(Mining.)

Public Service Company of Colorado
225 7th St.
Denver, CO 80202
303/571-7511
(Utility.)

Rocky Mountain Hospital & Medical Services
700 Broadway
Denver, CO 80273
303/831-2131
(Group hospital plans.)

Samsonite Corp.
11200 East 45th Ave.
Denver, CO 80239
303/373-2000
(Luggage.)

Storage Technology
2270 S. 88th St.
Louisville, CO 80027
303/673-3832
(Information storage and retrieval.)

Tele-Communications Inc.
5619 DTC Pkwy.
Denver, CO 80211
303/843-8600
(Broadcasting & movies.)

Total Petroleum Ltd.—North America
900 19th St.
Denver, CO 80202
303/291-2000
(Oil and gas.)

US West Communications
7800 E. Orchard Rd.
Englewood, CO 80111
303/793-6500
(Bell regional holding company.)

US West Communications—
Mountain Bell
(subs. of US West)
1801 California St.

Denver, CO 80202
303/391-8300
(Telephone services.)

Vicorp Restaurants Inc.
400 W. 48th Ave.
Denver, CO 80216
303/296-2121
(Restaurant franchises.)

COLORADO BUSINESS PERIODICALS

Boulder County Business Report
4865 Sterling Drive, Suite 200
Boulder, CO 80301
303/440-4950
(Magazine covering Boulder County
business issues.)

Denver Business Journal
1700 Broadway, Suite 515
Denver, CO 80290
303/837-3500
(Weekly.)

COLORADO DIRECTORY

Colorado Business Directory
American Business Directories
5711 S. 86th Cir.

P.O. Box 27347
Omaha, NE 68127
402/593-4600

COLORADO GOVERNMENT EMPLOYMENT OFFICES

Office of Personnel Management
P.O. Box 25167
Denver, CO 89225
(Mail only.)
303/969-7050
(Federal job-service center.)

Employment Program
Div. of Employment & Training
1391 Spear Blvd., Suite 500
Denver, CO 80204
303/893-3382
(State job-service center.)

HAWAII

LEADING HAWAII EMPLOYERS

Alexander & Baldwin Inc.
822 Bishop St.
Honolulu, HI 96813

808/525-6611
(Water transportation.)

Aloha Airlines, Inc.
371 Aokea Pl.
Honolulu, HI 96819
808/244-9071
(Airline.)

Azabu USA Corp.
410 Atkinson Dr.
Honolulu, HI 96814
808/944-6855
(Hotel, shopping center
operation.)

Bancorp Hawaii Inc.
130 Merchant St.
Honolulu, HI 96813
808/537-8111
(Bank.)

Castle & Cooke Properties Inc.
650 Iwilei Rd.
Honolulu, HI 96817
808/548-4811
(Real estate sub-dividers,
developers, etc.)

Daiei USA Inc.
801 Kaheka St.
Honolulu, HI 96814
808/973-7248
(Department stores.)

Dillingham Construction Ltd.
614 Kapahulu Ave.
Honolulu, HI 96815
808/735-3211
(Construction—nonresidential
buildings.)

Dole Food Co.
650 Iliwei Rd.
Honolulu, HI 96817
808/548-6611
(Canned fruits.)

First Hawaiian Bank
1132 Bishop St.
Honolulu, HI 96813
808/525-6386
(Bank.)

GTE Hawaiian Telephone Inc.
161 Kinoole St.

Honolulu, HI 96720
808/933-6411
(Telephone company.)

Hawaii Electric Light Co.
1200 Kilauea Ave.
Hilo, HI 96720
808/935-1171
(Utility.)

Hawaiian Airlines Inc.
P.O. Box 30008
Honolulu, HI 96820
808/835-3700
(Airline.)

**Hawaiian Electric
Industries**
900 Richards St.
Honolulu, HI 96813
808/543-5662
(Utility.)

Hilton Hawaiian Village
2005 Kalia Rd.
Honolulu, HI 96815
808/949-4321
(Resort hotel.)

Kyo-Ya Co. Ltd.
2255 Kalakaua Ave.
Honolulu, HI 96815
808/931-8600
(Hotel, restaurants, etc.)

Liberty House, Inc.
1450 Ala Moana Blvd. #1300
Honolulu, HI 96814
808/945-5247
(Department stores.)

Maui Electric Co., Ltd.
210 W. Kamchmcha Ave.
Kahului, HI 96732
808/871-9777
(Utility.)

**Maui Land &
Pineapple Co.**
120 Kane St.
Kahului, HI 96732
808/877-3351
(Canned fruits.)

Outrigger Hotels Hawaii
2375 Kuhio Ave.
Honolulu, HI 96815

808/921-6600
(Resort hotel.)

HAWAII BUSINESS PERIODICALS

Hawaii Business
Box 913
Honolulu, HI 96808
808/946-3978
(Monthly.)

Pacific Business News
Box 833
Honolulu, HI 96808
808/596-2021
(Weekly.)

HAWAII DIRECTORIES

Hawaii Business Directory
American Business Directories
5711 S. 86th Cir.

P.O. Box 27347
Omaha, NE 68127
402/593-4600

HAWAII GOVERNMENT EMPLOYMENT OFFICES

Office of Personnel Management
Federal Bldg, Rm. 5316
300 Ala Moana Blvd.
Honolulu, HI 96850
808/541-2791
(Federal job-service center.)

Employment Service Division
Dept. of Labor & Ind. Rel.
830 Punchbowl St., Rm. 12
Honolulu, HI 96813
808/586-8711
(State job-service center.)

IDAHO

LEADING IDAHO EMPLOYERS

Albertson's Inc.
P.O. Box 20
Boise, ID 83726
208/385-6200
(Supermarkets.)

American Microsystems Inc.
2300 Buckskin Rd.
Pocotello, ID 83201

208/233-4690
(Semiconductors and related devices.)

Boise Cascade Corp.
1111 W. Jefferson St.
Boise, ID 83728-0001
208/384-6161
(Paper mills.)

Conda Mining Inc.
3010 Conda Rd.
Conda, ID 83230
208/547-4478
(Phosphate mining.)

First Interstate Bank of Idaho
877 Main
Boise, ID 83702
208/389-4011
(National trust companies with deposits.)

Hagadone Corporation
111 S. First St.
Coeur D'Alene, ID 83814
208/667-3431
(Newspaper publishing, hotels and motels.)

Idaho Power Co.
1221 W. Idaho St.
Boise, ID 83702
208/388-2200
(Utility.)

Lamb Weston Inc.
856 Russell St.
Twin Falls, ID 83301
208/733-5664
(Frozen foods.)

Micron Technology, Inc.
P.O. Box 6
2805 E. Columbia Rd.
Boise, ID 83706
208/368-4000
(Semiconductors and other equipment.)

Morrison-Knudsen Co., Inc.
Morrison-Knudsen Plz.
P.O. Box 73
Boise, ID 83729
208/386-5000
(Heavy construction, engineering, real estate development.)

Ore-Ida Foods, Inc.
220 W. Park Center Blvd.
Boise, ID 83706
208/383-6100
(Frozen foods.)

J.R. Simplot Co.
999 Main St., Suite 1300
Boise, ID 83702
208/336-2110
(Frozen and dehydrated potatoes, fertilizers, livestock.)

Waremart Inc.
8590 Fairview Ave.
Boise, ID 83704
208/377-0110
(Supermarkets.)

West One Bancorp
1015 Capitol Blvd.
Boise, ID 83702
208/383-7000
(Banking.)

IDAHO BUSINESS PERIODICAL

Idaho Business Review
P.O. Box 8866
Boise, ID 83707
208/336-3768
(Weekly.)

IDAHO DIRECTORIES

Idaho Business Directory
American Business Directories
5711 S. 86th Cir.
P.O. Box 27347
Omaha, NE 68127
402/593-4600

Inland Northwest Manufacturing
Directory
Spokane Area Economic
Development Council
N. 221 Wall
Ste. 310

Spokane, WA 99201
509/624-9285
(Covers western Montana, northern
Idaho and Oregon, and eastern
Washington.)

IDAHO GOVERNMENT EMPLOYMENT OFFICES

Office of Personnel
Management
(Federal job-service
center—see Washington
listing.)

Operations Div. Employment
Services
Department of Employment
219 Main St.
Boise, ID 83735
208/334-6200
(State job-service center.)

MONTANA

LEADING MONTANA EMPLOYERS

Coca-Cola Bottling Co. West, Inc.
4151 1st Ave. S.
Billings, MT 59101
406/245-6211
(Soft drink bottling.)

Columbia Falls Aluminum Co.
2000 Aluminum Dr.
Columbia Falls, MT 59912
406/892-3261
(Aluminum.)

Entech Inc.
16 E. Granite St.
Butte, MT 59701
406/782-4233
(Coal mining.)

First Bank Montana
303 N. Broadway
Billings, MT 59101
406/657-8000
(Banking.)

4Bs Restaurants Inc.
3495 W. Broadway
Missoula, MT 59802
406/543-8265
(Restaurant.)

Hennessey Co., Inc.
140 S. 24th St. W.
Billings, MT 59102
406/656-0100
(Department stores.)

Industrial Constructors Inc.
101 International Way
Missoula, MT 59802
406/523-1205
(Heavy construction.)

Montana Power Co., Inc.
40 E. Broadway
Butte, MT 59707
406/723-5421
(Utility.)

Montana Rail Link Inc.
101 International Way
Missoula, MT 59802
406/523-1500
(Railroads.)

Pacific Recycling
1404 3rd St., NW
Great Falls, MT 59404
406/727-6222
(Steel service center, farm
equipment, recycling.)

Stillwater Mining Co.
HC54 Box 365
Nye, MT 59061

406/328-6400
(Mining.)

Tractor & Equipment Co.
1835 Harnish Blvd.
Billings, MT 59101
406/656-0202
(Construction and mining machinery
and equipment.)

Washington Container Corp.
101 International Way
Missoula, MT 59802
406/523-1200
(Construction.)

MONTANA BUSINESS PERIODICAL

Montana Business Quarterly
University of Montana
Bureau of Business and Economic
Research
Missoula, MT 59812
406/243-5113

MONTANA DIRECTORIES

*Inland Northwest Manufacturing
Directory*
Spokane Area Economic
Development Council
N. 221 Wall
Suite 310
Spokane, WA 99201
509/624-9285
(Covers western Montana, northern

Idaho and Oregon, and eastern
Washington.)

Montana Business Directory
American Business Directories
5711 S. 86th Cir.
P.O. Box 27347
Omaha, NE 68127
402/593-4600

MONTANA GOVERNMENT EMPLOYMENT OFFICES

**Office of Personnel
Management**
(Federal job-service
center—see Colorado listing;
call 303/969-7050.)

**Job Service/Employment and
Training Division**
17715 Front St.
Helena, MT 59601
406/447-3200
(State job-service center.)

NEVADA

LEADING NEVADA EMPLOYERS

Aladdin Hotel
P.O. Box 98958
Las Vegas, NV 89193
702/736-0111
(Hotel/casino.)

Alliance Gaming Inc.
4380 Boulder Hwy.
Las Vegas, NV 89121
701/435-4200
(Slot machines, etc.)

Amerco Inc.
1325 Airmotive Way, Suite 100
Reno, NV 89502
702/688-6300
(U-Haul rentals.)

Bently Nevada Corp.
1617 Waters St.
Minden, NV 89423
702/782-3611
(Measuring and controlling
devices.)

Caesar's Palace, Inc.
3570 Las Vegas Blvd. S.
Las Vegas, NV 89109
702/731-7110
(Hotel/casino.)

California Hotel & Casino
12 Ogden Ave.
Las Vegas, NV 89101
702/385-1222
(Hotel/casino.)

Circus Circus Enterprises
2880 Las Vegas Blvd. S.
Las Vegas, NV 89109
702/734-0410
(Casino.)

Desert Palace Inc.
3570 Las Vegas Blvd. S.
Las Vegas, NV 89109
702/731-7110
(Casino.)

El Dorado Hotel Associates
345 N. Virginia St.
Reno, NV 89501
702/786-5700
(Hotel/casino.)

**First Interstate Bank of Nevada
N.A.**
1 E. First St.
Reno, NV 89501
702/784-3182
(Banking.)

Gold Coast Hotel & Casino
4000 W. Flamingo Rd.
Las Vegas, NV 89103
702/367-7111
(Casino.)

Golden Nugget Inc.
129 Fremont St.
Las Vegas, NV 89101
702/385-7111
(Casino.)

Harrah's
219 N. 2nd St.
Reno, NV 89501
702/786-3232
(Casino.)

Harvey's Casino Resort
Highway 508 Stateline Ave.
Stateline, NV 89449
702/588-2411
(Casino.)

Imperial Palace Inc. and Casino
3535 Las Vegas Blvd. S.
Las Vegas, NV 89109
702/731-3311
(Casino.)

International Game Technology
520 S. Rock Blvd.
Reno, NV 89502
702/688-0365
(Computer peripherals.)

Las Vegas Hilton Corp.
3000 Paradise Rd.
Las Vegas, NV 89109
702/732-5111
(Hotel/casino.)

Mirage Resorts
3400 Las Vegas Blvd. S.
Las Vegas, NV 89177-0777
702/791-7111
(Casino.)

Nevada Bell
(subs. of Pacific Telesis)
1450 Vassar St.
Reno, NV 89502
702/333-4939
(Telephone company.)

Nevada Power Co.
6226 W. Sahara Ave.
Las Vegas, NV 89151
702/367-5111
(Utility.)

Porsche Cars North America
100 W. Liberty St.
Reno, NV 89501
702/348-3000
(Automobiles, auto supplies and parts.)

Sahara Casino Partners LP
2535 Las Vegas Blvd. S.

Las Vegas, NV 89109
702/737-2111
(Casino.)

Sheraton Desert Inn, Inc.
3145 Las Vegas Blvd. S.
Las Vegas, NV 89109
702/733-444
(Hotel/casino.)

Showboat Inc.
2800 Fremont
Las Vegas, NV 89104
702/385-9123
(Casino.)

Sierra Construction Corp.
5255 S. Valley View
Las Vegas, NV 89118
702/739-1991
(Hotel/motel construction.)

Sierra Pacific Resources
6100 Neil Rd.
Reno, NV 89520
702/689-3600
(Utility.)

Southwest Gas Corp.
5241 Spring Mountain Rd.
Las Vegas, NV 89102
702/876-7011
(Utility.)

NEVADA BUSINESS PERIODICALS

Las Vegas Business Press
3335 Wynn Rd.
Las Vegas, NV 89102
702/871-6780
(Semi-monthly.)

Nevada Business Journal
2127 Paradise Rd.
Las Vegas, NV 89109
702/735-7003
(Bimonthly.)

NEVADA DIRECTORY

Nevada Business Directory
American Business Directories
5711 S. 86th Cir.
P.O. Box 27347
Omaha, NE 68127
402/593-4600

NEVADA GOVERNMENT EMPLOYMENT OFFICES

**Office of Personnel
Management**
912/757-3000
(Federal job-service center.)

Employment Service
Employment Security Dept.
500 E. Third St.
Carson City, NV 89713
702/687-4650
(State job-service center.)

NEW MEXICO

LEADING NEW MEXICO EMPLOYERS

Advanced Sciences Inc.
6739 Academy Rd., NE
Albuquerque, NM 87109
505/828-0959
(Commercial scientific research.)

Albuquerque Publishing Co.
7777 Jefferson St., NE
P.O. Drawer J-T
Albuquerque, NM 87109
505/823-7777
(Newspaper publishing.)

American Furniture Co., Inc.
1001 W. Broadway
Albuquerque, NM 87401
505/326-3393
(Furniture stores.)

Chino Mines Co.
210 Cortez
Hurley, NM 88043
505/537-3381
(Copper ores.)

Furr's Inc.
173 Montana Rd., N.W.
Albuquerque, NM 87107
505/344-6525
(Food retailing.)

Hondo Oil & Gas Co.
410 East College Blvd.
Roswell, NM 88201
505/625-8700
(Petroleum refining.)

**Honeywell Defense Avionics
Systems Division**
9201 San Mateo Blvd., NE
Albuquerque, NM 87113-2227
505/828-5000
(Electronic systems for military
aircraft.)

IBP Prepared Foods Inc.
5701 North McNutt Rd.
Santa Teresa, NM 88008
505/589-0100
(Prepared meat products.)

Mesa Airlines Inc.
2325 East 30th St.
Farmington, NM 87401
505/327-0271
(Regional air carrier.)

Navajo Refining Co.
501 East Main St.
Artesia, NM 88210
505/748-3311
(Petroleum refining.)

Plains Electric Generation
2401 Aztec Ave., NE
Albuquerque, NM 87107
505/884-1200
(Utility.)

Public Service Company of New Mexico
414 Silver Ave., SW
Albuquerque, NM 87102
505/848-2700
(Electric and water utility.)

Roadrunner Trucking Inc.
501 Industrial Ave., NE
Albuquerque, NM 87107
505/345-8856
(Motor carrier.)

Sandia Corp.
P.O. Box 5800
Albuquerque, NM 87185
505/844-5678
(Research laboratory.)

Sunwest Bank New Mexico
303 Roma, NW
Albuquerque, NM 87102
505/252-2211
(Banking.)

NEW MEXICO BUSINESS PERIODICALS

New Mexico Business Journal
2323 Aztec Rd., NE
Albuquerque, NM 87107
505/889-2911
(Monthly.)

Harris New Mexico Manufacturers Directory
Harris Publishing Co.
2057 Aurora Road
Twinsburg, OH 44087
216/425-9000
800/888-5900

NEW MEXICO DIRECTORIES

New Mexico Business Directory
American Business Directories
5711 S. 86th Cir.
P.O. Box 27347
Omaha, NE 68127
402/593-4600

New Mexico Manufacturing Directory
CEDRA-New Mexico State University
Box 30001, Dept. 3CR
Las Cruces, New Mexico 88003
505/646-6315

NEW MEXICO GOVERNMENT EMPLOYMENT OFFICES

Federal Building
See Colorado
303/969-7050
(Federal job-service center.)

Employment Service Employment Security Dept.
P.O. Box 1928
Albuquerque, NM 87103
505/841-8437
(State job-service center.)

OREGON

LEADING OREGON EMPLOYERS

Bank of America Oregon
121 SW Morrison
Portland, OR 97204
503/275-1234
(Savings and loan associations.)

Bear Creek Corp.
2518 S. Pacific Hwy.
Medord, OR 97501
503/770-2645
(Fruit orchard.)

Blue Cross & Blue Shield of Oregon
100 SW Market St.
Portland, OR 97201
503/225-5336
(Health insurance.)

CH2M Hill Companies Ltd.
2300 NW Walnut Blvd.
Corvallis, OR 97330
503/752-4271
(Engineering services.)

Evergreen International Airlines, Inc.
3850 Three Mile Ln.
McMinnville, OR 97128-9496
503/472-0011
(Cargo airline.)

Fred Meyer Inc.
3800 SE 22nd Ave.
Portland, OR 97202
503/232-8844
(Chain stores, drug & discount stores.)

Freightliner Corp.
4747 North Channel Ave.
Portland, OR 97217
503/735-8000
(Truck trailers.)

Graphic Arts Center Inc.
2000 NW Wilson St.
Portland, OR 97209
503/224-7777
(Commercial printing.)

Jantzen Inc.
411 N.E. 19th St.
Portland, OR 97237
503/238-5000
(Swimwear.)

Kaiser Foundation Health Plan of the Northwest
500 N.E. Multnomah St.
Portland, OR 97232
503/813-2500
(Hospital and medical service plans.)

Louisiana-Pacific Corp.
111 SW 5th Ave.
Portland, OR 97204
503/221-0800
(Paper & lumber.)

Mentor Graphics Corp.
8005 SW Beekman Rd.
Wilsonville, OR 97070
503/685-7000
(Computer software.)

Nike, Inc.
1 S.W. Bowerman Dr.
Beaverton, OR 97005-6453
503/671-6453
Fax 503/671-6300
(Athletic shoes, apparel.)

Oeco Corp.
4607 SE International Way
Milwaukie, OR 97222
503/659-5999
(Electronic components.)

PacifiCorp
700 NE Multnomah St.
Portland, OR 97232-4116
503/731-2000
(Electric utility.)

Portland General Corp.
121 SW Salmon St.
Portland, OR 97204
503/228-6332
(Electric utility.)

Precision Castparts Corp.
4600 SE Harney Dr.
Portland, OR 97206
503/777-3881
(Aerospace parts.)

RLC Industries Co.
P.O. Box 1088
Roseburg, OR 97470
503/679-3311
(Softwood veneer and plywood.)

Roseburg Forest Products
3443 S.W. Carnes Rd.
Roseburg, OR 97470
503/679-6767
(Forest products.)

Sequent Computer Systems Inc.
15450 SW Koll Pkwy.
Beaverton, OR 97006
503/626-5700
(Mainframe computers.)

Standard Insurance Co.
1100 SW Sixth Ave.
Portland, OR 97204
503/248-7000
(Insurance.)

Tektronix, Inc.
26600 S.W. Parkway Ave.
Wilsonville, OR 97070
503/627-7111

(Electronic control and display
systems.)

Thrifty Pay Less Inc.
9275 SW Peyton Ln.
Wilsonville, OR 97070
503/685-6127
(Drug stores.)

U.S. Bancorp
111 SW 5th Ave.
Portland, OR 97204
503/275-6111
(Banking.)

United Grocers Inc.
6433 SE Lake Rd.
Milwaukie, OR 97222
503/833-1000
(Wholesale groceries.)

Wacker Siltronic Corp.
7200 NW Front St.
Portland, OR 97210
503/243-2020
(Semiconductors and related devices.)

Willamette Industries Inc.
1300 SW 5th Ave.
Portland, OR 97201
503/227-5581
Fax 503/273-5603
(Paper & lumber.)

OREGON BUSINESS PERIODICALS

The Business Journal
American City Business Journals
P.O. Box 14490
Portland, OR 97214
503/274-8733
(Weekly.)

Oregon Business
610 SW Broadway
Suite 200
Portland, OR 97205
503/223-0304
(Monthly.)

OREGON DIRECTORIES

*Inland Northwest Manufacturing
Directory*
Spokane Area Economic
Development Council
N. 221 Wall St.
Ste. 310

Spokane, WA 99201
309/624-9285
(Covers western Montana, northern
Idaho and Oregon, and eastern
Washington.)

Oregon Business Directory
American Business Directories
5711 S. 86th Cir.

P.O. Box 27347
Omaha, NE 68127
402/593-4600

OREGON GOVERNMENT EMPLOYMENT OFFICES

Office of Personnel Management
Federal Bldg. Rm. 376
1220 S.W. Third Ave.
Portland, OR 97204
503/326-3141
(Federal job-service center.)

Employment Service
875 Union St., NE
Salem, OR 97311
503/378-3213
(State job-service center.)

UTAH

LEADING UTAH EMPLOYERS

Amalgamated Sugar Co.
2427 Lincoln Ave.
Ogden, UT 84401
801/399-3431
(Sugar.)

American Stores Co.
708 E. South Temple
Salt Lake City, UT 84102
801/539-0112
(Grocery stores.)

Associated Food Stores Inc.
1812 Empire Rd.
Salt Lake City, UT 84104
801/973-4400
(Grocery stores.)

Becton-Dickinson
9450 South State St.
Sandy, UT 84070
801/565-2300
(Surgical and medical instruments
and apparatus.)

Coca Cola Bottling Co.
875 South West Temple
Salt Lake City, UT 84110

801/530-5300
(Soft drinks.)

Corel-WordPerfect Corp.
1555 North Technology Way
Orem, UT 84057
801/222-4000
(Computer software.)

Dyno Noble Inc.
50 South Main St.
Salt Lake City, UT 84144
801/364-4800
(Explosives.)

**Evans and Sutherland Computer
Corp.**
600 Komas Dr.
Salt Lake City, UT 84108
801/582-5847
(Computer peripherals.)

First Health Strategies
2610 Decker Ln.
Salt Lake City, UT 84119
801/974-6550
(Insurance agents, brokers and
service.)

First Security Corp.
79 S. Main St.
Salt Lake City, UT 84111
801/246-6000
(Banking.)

Flying J Inc.
50 W. 990 S.
Brigham City, UT 84302
801/734-6400
(Petroleum products.)

Geneva Steel
10 S. Geneva Rd.
Orem, UT 84058
801/227-9000
(Steel.)

Huntsman Chemical Corp.
60 E. So. Temple, #2000
Salt Lake City, UT 84111
801/532-5200
(Plastics materials, synthetic resins.)

Iomega Corp.
1821 Iomega Way
Roy, UT 84067
801/778-1000
(Computer storage devices.)

JB's Specialty Restaurants, Inc.
1010 West 2610 South
Salt Lake City, UT 84119
801/974-4343
(Restaurants.)

Kennecott Corp.
10 East S. Temple St.
Salt Lake City, UT 84133
801/322-7000
(Copper mining.)

Ralph K. Little Co.
2681 Parleys Way
Salt Lake City, UT 84106
801/484-2200
(Business credit institution.)

Longyear Co.
2340 West 1700 South
Salt Lake City, UT 84104
801/972-1395
(Mining machinery.)

Mountain Fuel Supply Co.
180 East 1st South
Salt Lake City, UT 84111
801/534-5555
(Natural gas transmission and distribution.)

Northwest Pipeline Corp.
295 Chipeta Way
Salt Lake City, UT 84108
801/583-8800
(Gas transmission and distribution.)

Novell Inc.
122 E. 1700 S.
Provo, UT 84606
801/429-7000
(Computer software and services.)

Q Lube Inc.
1385 West 2200 South
Salt Lake City, UT 84119
801/972-6667
(Automotive services.)

Questar Corp.
180 East 1st South
Salt Lake City, UT 84111
801/534-5000
(Natural gas distribution.)

Questar Corp.
180 E. First South St.
Box 45433
Salt Lake City, UT 84145
801/534-5000
(Natural gas.)

Skywest Airlines
444 South River Rd.
St. George, UT 84790
801/634-3000
(Regional airline.)

Smith's Food & Drug Centers, Inc.
1550 South Redwood Rd.
Salt Lake City, UT 84104
801/974-1400
(Food and drug stores.)

Steiner Corp.
505 East South Temple
Salt Lake City, UT 84102
801/328-8831
(Linen supply.)

O. C. Tanner Manufacturing Inc.
1930 South State St.
Salt Lake City, UT 84115
801/486-2430
(Jewelry, precious metal.)

Thiokol Corp.
2475 Washington Blvd.
Ogden, UT 84401
801/629-2000

(Rocket motors for space shuttle, etc.)

Zion's Co-op Mercantile Institution
2200 South 900 West
Salt Lake City, UT 84119
801/579-6179
(Department stores.)

Zions Bancorp
1380 Kennecott Building
Salt Lake City, UT 84133
801/524-4787
(Banking.)

UTAH DIRECTORIES

Utah Business Directory
American Business Directories
5711 S. 86th Cir.
P.O. Box 27347
Omaha, NE 68127
402/593-4600

Utah Directory of Business and Industry
Department of Employment Security
Division of Economic Development
324 S. State St.
Suite 500
Salt Lake City, UT 84111
801/538-8700

UTAH GOVERNMENT EMPLOYMENT OFFICES

Office of Personnel Management
(Federal job-service center—see Colorado listing; call 303/969-7050.)

Employment Services/Field Oper.
Department of Employment Security
140 E. 300 So.
Salt Lake City, UT 84111
801/536-7400
(State job-service center.)

WASHINGTON

LEADING WASHINGTON COMPANIES

Ackerley Communications Inc.
800 Fifth Ave.
Seattle, WA 98104
206/624-2888
(Outdoor advertising services, etc.)

Adobe Systems Inc.
411 First Ave. S.
Seattle, WA 98104
206/470-7000
(Software.)

Advanced Technologies Laboratories, Inc.
P.O. Box 843
Kirkland, WA 98083
206/788-8602
(Surgical and medical instruments.)

Airborne Freight Corp.
3101 Western Ave.
Seattle, WA 98111
206/285-4600
(Express package delivery, freight forwarding.)

Alaska Airlines Inc.
19300 Pacific Hwy S.
Seattle, WA 98188
206/433-3200
(Airline.)

Allied Signal Aviation, Inc.
15001 NE 36th St.
Redmond, WA 98052
206/885-3711
(Avionic systems.)

Alpac Corp.
2300 26th Ave. S.
Seattle, WA 98144
206/323-2932
(Soft drinks.)

Associated Grocers Inc.
3301 S. Norfolk St.
Seattle, WA 98118
206/762-2100
(Wholesale groceries.)

AT&T Wireless Services Co.
5000 Carillon Pt.
Kirkland, WA 98083-9760
206/827-4500
(Cellular telephone service.)

Eddie Bauer Inc.
15010 NE 36th St.
Redmond, WA 98052
206/882-6100
(Retail stores.)

Boeing Co.
7755 E. Marginal Way S.
Seattle, WA 98124-2121
206/655-1131
(Aerospace.)

The Bon Marché
1601 Third Ave.
Seattle, WA 98101
206/506-7409
(Department store.)

Egghead Software Inc.
22011 SE 51st
Issaquah, WA 98029
206/391-0800
(Software stores.)

Eldec Corp.
16700 13th Ave. W.
Lynnwood, WA 98037
206/743-1313
(Electronic and electromechanical products for aerospace use.)

First Interstate Bank of Washington N.A.
999 Third Ave.
Seattle, WA 98104
206/292-3413
(Banking.)

Fluke Corp.
6920 Seaway Blvd.
Everett, WA 98203
206/347-6100
(Electronic test and measurement equipment.)

Food Services of America Inc.
18430 East Valley Hwy.
Kent, WA 98032
206/251-9100
(Wholesale groceries.)

General Insurance Co. of America
4330 Brooklyn Ave., N.E.
Seattle, WA 98185
206/545-5000
(Insurance.)

Group Health Cooperative of Puget Sound
521 Wall St.
Seattle, WA 98121
206/448-4141
(Health maintenance organization, hospital operator.)

GTE Northwest Inc.
1800 41st St.
Everett, WA 98201
206/261-5321
(Telephone service.)

Holland America Line
300 Elliot Ave. W.
Seattle, WA 98119
206/281-3535
(Cruise ships, travel services, etc.)

ICF Kaiser Hanford Co.
2430 Stevens Ctr.
Richland, WA 99352
509/376-7452
(Engineering and architectual services.)

Intalco Aluminum Corp.
4050 Mountain View Rd.
Ferndale, WA 98248
206/384-7061
(Aluminum.)

Intermec Corp.
6001 36th Ave. W.

Everett, WA 98203
206/348-2600
(Bar code printers and related products.)

Key Bank of Washington
1119 Pacific Way
Tacoma, WA 98402
206/593-3600
(Banking.)

Key Tronic Corp.
4424 N. Sullivan Rd.
Spokane, WA 99216
509/235-6100
(Computer keyboards.)

Lamb-Weston Inc.
8701 W. Gage Blvd.
Kennewick, WA 99336
509/735-4651
(Frozen fruits, juices, produce.)

LIN Broadcasting Corp.
5295 Carillon Pt.
Kirkland, WA 98033
206/828-1902
(Television production.)

Longview Fibre Co.
Fibre Way
Longview, WA 98632
206/425-1550
(Tree farming, logging, paper mill operator.)

Microsoft Corp.
One Microsoft Way
Redmond, WA 98052-6399
206/882-8080
(Computer software.)

Nintendo of America Inc.
4820 150th Avenue, NE
Redmond, WA 98052
206/882-2040
(Computer/video games.)

Nordstrom Inc.
1501 Fifth Ave.
Seattle, WA 98101-1603
206/628-2111
(Department stores.)

Olivetti North America
22425 Appleway Ave.
Liberty Lake, WA 99019
509/927-5600
(Microprocessor data terminal
systems and software.)

Paccar Inc.
777 106 Ave., N.E.
Bellevue, WA 98004
206/455-7400
(Heavy-duty truck manufacturing.)

Pacific Telecom Inc.
805 Broadway
Vancouver, WA 98660
206/696-0983
(Telephone communications.)

Price-Costco
10809 120th Ave., N.E.
Kirkland, WA 98033
206/803-8100
(Membership warehouse store.)

**Puget Sound Power &
Light Co.**
411 108 Ave., N.E.
Bellevue, WA 98004
206/454-6363
(Utility.)

Safeco Corp.
4333 Brooklyn Ave., N.E.
Seattle, WA 98185
206/545-5000
(Health and life insurance, financial
management.)

Safeco Properties Inc.
700 5th Ave.
Seattle, WA 9804
206/223-4500
(Building operation, developers, etc.)

Seafirst Corp.
701 5th Ave.
Seattle, WA 98104
206/358-3000
(Banking and financial services.)

Seattle Times Co.
1120 John St.
Seattle, WA 98109

206/464-2111
(Newspaper publishing.)

Todd Shipyards Corp.
1801 16th Ave., S.W.
Seattle, WA 98134
206/623-1635
(Shipbuilding, ship repair and
conversion.)

U R M Stores Inc.
7511 N. Freya St.
Spokane, WA 99207
509/467-2620
(Groceries.)

U.S. Bank of Washington
1420 5th Ave.
Seattle, WA 98101
206/344-3795
(Savings and loans.)

U.S. Marine Corp.
17825 59th Ave., N.E.
Arlington, WA 98223
206/435-5540
(Fiberglass pleasure boats.)

**US West Communications—Pacific
Northwest Bell**
(subs. of US West)
1600 Bell Plz.
Seattle, WA 98191
206/345-2211
(Telephone services.)

US West New Vector Group
3350 161 Ave., S.E.
Bellevue, WA 98008
206/788-6160
(Cellular telephone services.)

Washington Federal Inc.
425 Pike St.
Seattle, WA 98101
206/624-7930
(Thrift institution.)

**Washington Mutual Savings
Bank**
P.O. Box 834—SAS 1018
Seattle, WA 98111
206/461-2000
(Savings bank.)

Westin Hotel Co.
2001 Sixth Ave.
Seattle, WA 98121
206/443-5000
(Hotels.)

Weyerhaueser Co.
Weyerhaueser Bldg.
Tacoma, WA 98477
206/924-2345
(Forest products.)

WASHINGTON DIRECTORIES

Inland Northwest Manufacturing Directory
Spokane Area Economic
Development Council
N. 221 Wall St.
Ste. 310
Spokane, WA 99201
509/624-9285
(Covers western Montana, northern Idaho and Oregon, and eastern Washington.)

Washington Business Directory
American Business Directories
5711 S. 86th Cir.
P.O. Box 27347
Omaha, NE 68127
402/593-4600

Washington Manufacturers Register
Database Publishing Co.
1590 S. Lewis St.
Anaheim, CA 92805
800/888-8434

WASHINGTON GOVERNMENT EMPLOYMENT OFFICES

Office of Personnel Management
Federal Bldg. Rm 110
915 Second Ave.
Seattle, WA 98174
206/553-0888
(Federal job-service center.)

Employment Security Dept.
212 Maple Pk.
P.O. Box 9046
Olympia, WA 98507-9046
360/902-9585
(State job-service center.)

WYOMING

LEADING WYOMING EMPLOYERS

Bridger Coal Co.
P.O. Box 2068
Rock Springs, WY 82901
307/382-9741
(Coal mining.)

Cheyenne Newspapers, Inc.
702 W. Lincoln Way
Cheyenne, WY 82001
307/634-7964
(Newspaper publishing.)

Coastal Chemical Inc.
8305 Otto Rd.
Cheyenne, WY 82001
307/637-2700
(Fertilizers.)

Cordero Mining Co.
P.O. Box 1449
Gillette, WY 82717
307/682-8005
(Coal mining.)

FMC Wyoming Corp.
580 Westvaco Rd.
Green River, WY 82935
307/875-2580
(Chemicals: soda, phosphate, etc.)

Jackson Hole Ski Corp.
7658 Teewinot
Teton Village, WY 83025
307/733-2292
(Ski resort.)

Key Bank of Wyoming
1800 Carey Ave.
Cheyenne, WY 82001
307/771-3400
(Banking.)

Maverick Country Store, Inc.
1035 S. Washington St.
Afton, WY 83110
307/886-3861
(Convenience stores, filling stations.)

Mini Mart Inc.
907 N. Poplar St.
Casper, WY 82601
307/266-1230
(Filling stations, convenience stores.)

Norwest Bank, Wyoming N.A.
4441 E. 2nd St.
Casper, WY 82604
307/237-4000
(Banking.)

North Antelope Coal Co.
Caller Box 3032
Gillette, WY 82717
307/464-0012
(Coal mining.)

OCI Wyoming
LaBarge Rd.
P.O. Box 513
Green River, WY 82935
307/875-2600
(Mineral mining.)

SST Energy Corp.
8901 W. Yellowstone Hwy.
Casper, WY 82604
307/235-3529
(Oil and gas field exploration services.)

Sinclair Oil Corp.
100 E. Lincolnway
Cheyenne, WY 82334
307/324-3404
(Oil and gas, etc.)

T G Soda Ash Inc.
Mines Site
Granger, WY 82934
307/875-2700
(Soda, phosphate.)

Thunder Basin Coal Co.
5669 Clareton Hwy.
Gillette, WY 82718
307/939-1300
(Coal mining.)

University of Wyoming Research Corp.
P.O. Box 3355
Laramie, WY 82071
307/766-5353
(Research.)

WOTCO Inc.
415 1st St.
Mills, WY 82644
307/235-1591
(Fabricated structural metal.)

Wyoming Machinery Co.
5300 W. Old Yellowstone
Casper, WY 82604
307/472-1000
(Construction and mining equipment and machinery.)

WYOMING DIRECTORY

Wyoming Business Directory
American Business Directories
5711 S. 86th Cir.

P.O. Box 27347
Omaha, NE 68127
402/593-4600

WYOMING GOVERNMENT EMPLOYMENT OFFICES

Office of Personnel Management
(Federal job-service center—see Colorado listing, call 303/969-7050.)

Employment Service
Employment Security Commission
P.O. Box 2760
Casper, WY 82602
307/235-3611
(State job-service center.)